The Shadow of
a Dream

Economic Life and Death
in the South Carolina Low Country
1670-1920

Peter A. Coclanis

New York   Oxford
OXFORD UNIVERSITY PRESS

Oxford University Press

Oxford   New York   Toronto
Delhi   Bombay   Calcutta   Madras   Karachi
Petaling Jaya   Singapore   Hong Kong   Tokyo
Nairobi   Dar es Salaam   Cape Town
Melbourne   Auckland

and associated companies in
Berlin   Ibadan

Library of Congress Cataloging-in-Publication Data
Coclanis, Peter A., 1952-
The shadow of a dream : economic life and death in the South
Carolina low country, 1670-1920 / Peter A. Coclanis.
p.   cm.   Bibliography: p.   Includes index.
ISBN 0-19-504420-7
ISBN 0-19-507267-7 (pbk.)
1. Charleston Region (S.C.)—Economic conditions. I. Title.
HC108.C32C63   1988
330.9757'91—dc 19   88-4201

1 3 5 7 9 8 6 4 2

Printed in the United States of America

To My Parents,
Angelo and Kay Coclanis

Preface

This book examines the economic rise and fall of one small, but intriguing part of the American South, the low country of South Carolina. Though I focus on an area containing only about 13,000 square miles, I have tried to keep in mind the broader forces that affected the area's development. Indeed, it is in my view the manner in which so-called internal and external forces interacted that makes the history of this particular area so compelling.

The process by which such forces interacted to effect the low country's rise and fall was a protracted one and to treat of it adequately demands a considerable time frame. Thus, this study spans approximately two hundred fifty years. The study, moreover, seeks to span space as well, to bridge, as it were, the large, if somewhat artificial gap between town and country in the low country. It is especially important to do so in studying this area, I believe, because Charleston—the epicenter of the low country and the subject of much historical research—has never been integrated into the development of the region of which it was part. I do not purport to complete this task here; I hope only to make clear the point that the city was not independent of, but rather dependent upon developments far beyond its bounds. I hope, in other words, to rein in Charleston, something much of the citizenry of South Carolina has been urging for two hundred years. Thus, when I discuss Charleston's changing appearance—to cite but one example—I do so in order to gain greater insight into the history of the low country as a whole, for the evolution of both town and country is embodied and expressed in the city's face and form.

A word or two about matters of exposition and method. I view this study as an analytical essay rather than a work of narrative history, traditional or new. One will find few anecdotes or quotations in the text, relatively little description, and, at times, an intentional flattening of local detail. As a result, this study to some readers may seem closer to historical sociology than to history per se. I have tried in the footnotes, however, both to point interested readers toward suggestive

narrative sources and to provide full documentation for the positions taken in the essay.

Finally, the analytical framework employed in this study draws from many individual writers, traditions, and approaches: from various structuralists obviously and from both Marshall and Marx. From certain *Annalistes* and from several practitioners of *realismo magico*. It is fair to say, however, that the work rests ultimately on materialist premises and a belief in the power of materialist explanations both of the past and of the world in which we live today.

This study owes much to the generosity over the years of family, friends, teachers, colleagues, and institutions. I would like to take this opportunity to express my appreciation. First, I would like to thank my parents, Angelo and Kay Coclanis, without whose love and sacrifices this work would never have been begun, much less completed. My sisters, Jeanette Vogel and Mary Massé, throughout their lives have showered me with kindness. Would that I ever could thank them completely. To their husbands, Ron Vogel and Paul Massé, my heartfelt thanks as well.

Dr. and Mrs. Trent Busby have shown me uncommon generosity over the years. Their good will and hospitality will never be forgotten. George Terry, Lacy Ford, and David Carlton, three of our finest young southern historians, have for the past eight years shared their knowledge of their home region to an often perplexed outsider from Chicago. To them, I owe much. While I was a graduate student, Alan Gardner, Bernard Plum, and Barry Bienstock taught me much about American history; one could not ask for better classmates, critics, or friends. Dino Pappas, John Harding, and Jerry Palermo have proved loyal and supportive throughout the course of this project, indeed, for almost as long as I can remember. They know where they stand with me.

Many scholars, of course, have helped me over the years as well. Frederick Adams, Francis Wilhoit, Jackson Turner Main, Kenneth Jackson, Herbert Klein, John Garraty, Jack Greene, and Nathan Huggins made my undergraduate and graduate years memorable ones. George Rogers, Robert Weir, Tom Terrill, and Walter Edgar helped to make my four years in South Carolina equally worthwhile.

This study itself has benefited from the insightful criticism of numerous scholars. To Stanley Engerman, Lacy Ford, Elizabeth Fox-Genovese, Robert Gallman, Eugene Genovese, John Komlos, Roger Lotchin, and George Rogers—my humble thanks. Thanks, too, to Gavin Wright, Cathy McHugh, and Morton Rothstein for their helpful criticism of papers drawn from this study, and to Jan de Vries and James Riley, whose help proved indispensable in the sections of this study on the European rice trade.

Three research assistants—Marty Leary, Dave Marcotte, and Dale Steinhauer—helped to compile and analyze some of the data upon which this study is based. To each of them, my thanks.

While engaged in this project I had the opportunity to meet and work with Eileen McIlvaine and Allen Stokes, than whom there are no finer research librarians. To the entire staffs of the following libraries and archives, my sincere gratitude: The

Columbia University libraries, the South Caroliniana Library of the University of South Carolina, the South Carolina Department of Archives and History, the South Carolina Historical Society, the Charleston Library Society, the Robert Scott Small Library of the College of Charleston, the Southern Historical Collection of the University of North Carolina, the William R. Perkins Library of Duke University, the North Carolina State Archives, the Newberry Library, the Historical Society of Pennsylvania, the New York Public Library, the New-York Historical Society, the American Antiquarian Society, and the Harvard University libraries.

Sheldon Meyer and the entire staff at Oxford University Press treated me with kindness and solicitude; I hope that I have justified their faith in my work. As my study reached its final stages, I had the good fortune to work with Leona Capeless at Oxford, who proved both expert and sensitive in her editing. The fact that she had any copy at all to edit literally owes everything to a superb (and good-humored) typist, Peggy J. Clark.

The map and sketches in the book were done by Richard Gantt. His art historical knowledge and artistic talent proved vital in bringing this work to life.

This project, indeed, my entire education owes much to the financial support of numerous institutions. Scholarships and fellowships from Drake and Columbia universities financed my entire undergraduate and graduate educations and fellowships from the following institutions allowed me to embark upon—and complete—this project: the C.W. Cook Foundation, Mrs. Giles Whiting Foundation, Newberry Library, American Antiquarian Society, Newberry Library Summer Institute in Quantitative History, Richard D. Irwin Foundation, Lincoln Education Foundation, American Bar Foundation, Institute for Southern Studies of the University of South Carolina, the Kenan Foundation and the Society of Fellows of Columbia University, University of North Carolina, American Philosophical Society, Economic History Association, and the Charles Warren Center of Harvard University.

My intellectual and personal debt to my dissertation sponsor, Stuart W. Bruchey, is enormous. For he embodies everything that is noble about the academic tradition. I feel truly fortunate that I have had the benefit of his intelligence, integrity, and personal warmth for over a decade now.

My wife, Deborah, has given me the strength to finish this study. Her love and support transcend expression, at least by me. Then there is our son Angelo, whose arrival as this study neared completion was a wonderful reward indeed.

Chapel Hill   P.A.C.
December 1987

Contents

The Shadow of a Dream

Hamlet: "O God I could be bounded in a nutshell and count myself a king of infinite space, were it not that I have bad dreams."

Guildenstern: "Which dreams indeed are ambition, for the very substance of the ambitious is merely the shadow of a dream."

Hamlet

ACT II, SC. II

". . . Cities, like dreams, are made of desires and fears, even if the thread of their discourse is secret, their rules are absurd, their perspectives deceitful, and everything conceals something else."

I have neither desires nor fears," the Khan declared, "and my dreams are composed either by my mind or by chance."

"Cities also believe they are the work of the mind or of chance, but neither the one nor the other suffices to hold up their walls. You take delight not in a city's seven or seventy wonders, but in the answer it gives to a question of yours."

"Or the question it asks you, forcing you to answer, like Thebes through the mouth of the Sphinx."

Italo Calvino, Invisible Cities

Introduction:
The Sociology of Architecture
in Colonial Charleston

The Indian, considered an infidel by his Christian interrogators, was not sworn. His name, he said, was Diacan. Yes, he told interpreter Antonio Camuñas, he had seen the English settlement of San Jorge. According to the Indian, San Jorge consisted of about thirty small houses on one side of the river and four more on the other side. After adding a few details about his February visit to the settlement, Diacan ended his brief testimony. He did not sign the Spanish translation of his statement, prepared that same day by Juan Moreno y Segovia, because he could not write. Sergeant Major Don Manuel de Cendoya, Governor and Captain General of San Agustín, could write, however, and he signed the document on Diacan's behalf. It was notarized four days later, on March 26, 1672, and packed up for shipment to Spain. It reached Seville, with a number of other papers from San Agustín, on October 11. With this testimony, the city of Charleston slipped humbly into the historical record.[1] Neither Diacan nor Don Manuel de Cendoya could have foreseen, of course, what the four small houses "on the other side of the river" would later become. Both the leonine roar of the city at its apogee in 1820 and the wistful sighs that were heard there a century later were well beyond them.

This chapter deals neither with Charleston at its nineteenth-century peak nor with the town during its long twentieth-century decline. Instead, it examines Charleston's rise. It will be argued that patterns and processes associated with this rise contained, ironically or perhaps more properly dialectically, the conditions for both the city's and the South Carolina low country's brief period of pre-eminence and for their later demise. While the study as a whole focuses on economic questions, this chapter does not. Rather, it details a concomitant of Charleston's economic ascent, the city's changing face and form from about 1680 to the eve of the American Revolution. For through the silent language of architecture, the fundamental character of Charleston and, indeed, of colonial South Carolina in general is at least partially revealed.

3

To the inhabitants of early Charleston, life's limitations were clear. These limitations, imposed by their economy and reinforced by their God, were perhaps most vividly embodied by the walls surrounding the small settlement in which they lived. Scholars, it is true, have long maintained that Charleston, like Philadelphia, possessed a "modern" urban plan almost from the start.[2] While it would be a mistake to deny the influence of "modern" Renaissance plannning ideas on the layout of seventeenth-century Charleston, it is apparent that other traditions and factors were at work as well. Attempts to implement the principles of Alberti, Palladio, and Wren, that is to say, attempts to open up Charleston, to free it from the narrow confines of the medieval planning tradition, were tempered by both the enduring centripetal power of this older tradition and by the inhabitants' very real desires for adequate security and defense. Thus, Charleston's moat, its fortifications, and its walls. The town which emerged on the peninsula between the Ashley and the Cooper rivers after 1680 was, however, no gothic town, no medieval *bastide*. Nor was it "modern." It was, rather, a transitional entity, a hybrid containing elements of each.[3]

Across its moat and behind its walls, one found in Charleston, perhaps a bit incongruously, several broad and regular streets arranged in a "modern" grid-like pattern. Provisions for a central square, that characteristic feature of Renaissance urban planning, were also incorporated into the "Grand Modell" governing the town's development. These provisions, not surprisingly, proved premature at this time. Early Charlestonians, preferring protection to vista, valuing safety over sensibility, built a defensive fortification on the spot instead. Such compromises gave form to the little seaport, creating a town similar in many ways to both Vitry-le-François and to Londonderry, but one ultimately distinct from either.[4]

If the rectilineal nature of Charleston's streets can be considered a triumph of modernity, other characteristics of the town indicated that the victory was far from complete. Indeed, life within the walls had a most medieval feel and look. Goats, cows, sheep, and pigs roamed the unpaved streets of the little town, vying with humans for the right of way and contributing, alas, in their own inimitable way to the sounds and smells of early Charleston. Man, of course, did his part in this regard as well. The "privy question" and other problems related to waste disposal, serious matters in a place lacking even a rudimentary sewage system and cursed with a brackish water supply, commanded considerable attention and inspired a good deal of remedial legislation by the South Carolina Assembly. Many of these problems, as one can imagine, seemed more consequential, or at least more annoying, to those intrepid souls that braved Charleston's unlit streets at night. In these respects, then, medieval patterns endured unvanquished, the forces of modernity held at bay.[5]

Housing in Charleston in the late seventeenth century bore a similar medieval stamp. Early settlers in the town, apparently even those that came from the West Indies, looked back across the ocean for architectural inspiration. Vernacular architectural forms, especially those associated with the lower strata of English society, proved most influential. Thus, small frame structures, generally of oak or pine, soon dotted the Charleston landscape. These houses, like their English counterparts, were one or two stories in height and typically only one room deep.

With their steeply pitched roofs and tiny windows, their low ceilings and dark walls, they rather evoked the dour atmosphere of fifteenth-century northern Europe than the exuberance of a youthful colony in a strange new world. These simple and honest dwellings, which were perhaps fifteen feet by twenty-five feet in size, served Charleston well nonetheless. By providing both shelter and psychological comfort to the transplanted Europeans that dwelled within them, these brooding structures proved invaluable until the economic possibilities of the South Carolina low country could be successfully ferreted out.[6]

This simplicity and honesty were expressed elsewhere in the town's early architecture. Charleston's churches and taverns, the fonts of spiritual fulfillment, were unadorned little structures as were the town's only public buildings, the court of guard and the powder magazine.[7] The inhabitants of Charleston, at least the white inhabitants, did not suffer this honesty and simplicity gladly. Nor can one expect them to have done so. For it was a simplicity derived from scarcity, an honesty imposed. Seventeenth-century Charleston was in the last analysis a function of South Carolina's seventeenth-century economy. The limited surplus engendered by this economy before the successful commercial exploitation of naval stores and rice, that is, before the eighteenth century, informed and, indeed, determined Charleston's appearance, its size and growth. That only 1200 people lived in Charleston's eighty acres in 1700 was thus a result of South Carolina's economic weakness. So, too, was the town's medieval flavor and perhaps its honest feel.[8]

If the face of early Charleston expressed economic weakness, then the appearance of the town in the eighteenth century revealed South Carolina's increasing economic strength.[9] As this economy expanded, Renaissance planning principles gained greater currency in Charleston and by the end of the decade of the 1730s the town's architectural passage from medieval to modern was almost complete. No act so symbolized the impending triumph of the Renaissance aesthetic than the dismantling of the town's walls in 1718.[10] With this act, architectural perspective was brought to the Charleston landscape, the town's medieval fetters at last removed.

The imposition of Renaissance order was made manifest in other ways. Charleston's gridiron street plan, for example, was extended across the peninsula prior to 1740, bringing discipline to the unruly marshes, leaving broad paths and thoroughfares in their place. Furthermore, the town's long-awaited central square became a reality in the 1720s. This square was to fight a losing battle against various architectural encroachments throughout the eighteenth century. It was in the 1720s and 1730s, however, a man-made refuge from urban chaos, a serene departure from Charleston's increasingly kinetic economic pace. Thus, just as the steady tempo of plantation agriculture had replaced the economic arhythmia characteristic of South Carolina during its extractive stage, the order and proportion of Renaissance planning were now imposed on Charleston's once pinched and wrinkled face.[11]

The tone of street life also became more modern in this period. Work was begun, for example, on a sewage and drainage system for the town and various swamps, bogs, and low spots on the peninsula were filled. In addition, a number of

townsmen built fences and pens to prevent or at least impede their peripatetic livestock from wandering through the city's streets. Some of these barriers apparently
proved successful, though roaming animals, especially swine, plagued Charleston
still. Furthermore, Charlestonians began in the 1720s and 1730s to plant the gardens for which the city would later become famous. In so doing, they improved
both the appearance and the odor of the town. Thus, while Charleston's streets
remained unpaved and unlit, they had changed markedly by 1740 and had clearly
lost their medieval hue.[12]

Domestic architecture had changed by 1740 as well. Although it is true that
some Charlestonians continued to live in small frame structures similar to those discussed earlier, a growing number, benefiting from the expansion of the economy,
now dwelled in more substantial houses. Once again, the town's inhabitants had
looked to England for inspiration; this time, however, the Georgian forms associated with the gentry and bourgeoisie proved most influential. The new building
style in Charleston, derived from an architecture favored by England's rising middle class, expressed both the earnestness and confidence of this class. Houses built
in this style were almost square in shape and generally stood a full two and one-half
stories high, including the garret under their gently sloping shingled roofs. They
were usually two rooms deep and had a number of full-size sash windows. The
first floor was built at ground level and one entered the house without subterfuge,
directly through the front door which faced the street.

These houses were both larger and more open than their seventeenth-century
predecessors. Though some were used for dwelling purposes only, most served dual
functions, that of workplace as well as residence. A shop of some kind typically
dominated the first floor, with the owner or operator and his family generally living
on the floor above. In an interesting vertical twist given to residential housing
segregation in the town at this time, members of lower-class groups, such as slaves,
servants, and transients, resided in the garret "beneath the eaves." Most of these
houses were still built of wood, though brick was becoming more common. Small
wooden balconies, the forerunners of the piazzas common later, graced the fronts
of some of these structures. Various outbuildings—sheds, storehouses, privy, and
kitchen—stood near the main house, generally to its rear. With these, the domestic
complex was complete.[13]

The expansion of the South Carolina economy had altered Charleston in still
other ways. The town's population had, for example, increased by over 500
percent between 1700 and 1740 and its total area had nearly doubled. The number
of wharves serving the town rose from two in 1704 to eight in 1739. Several
distinct and specialized market areas had also developed in Charleston by 1740
and both the number of public buildings in town and the size of each had grown.
From Charles Shepheard's tavern to Saint Philip's Church, from the theatre which
catered to the town's rich to the workhouse which sheltered the poor, Charleston
had, thus, changed by 1740. Indeed, the methodical hammering of its black and
white carpenters had pounded away much of the coarseness and intimacy that had
characterized the town in the seventeenth century. Despite, or perhaps because of,
these changes, Charleston looked much like many other small English towns in

1740. Neither its climate nor its social system had yet forced the adjustments that would ultimately take Charleston far out of the mainstream.[14]

South Carolina's economy continued to expand through the rest of the colonial era. Indeed, on the eve of the American Revolution, the white population of the low country was by far the richest single group in British North America. With the area's wealth based largely on the expropriation by whites of the golden rice and blue dye produced by black slaves, the Carolina low country had by 1774 reached a level of aggregate wealth greater than that in many parts of the world even today. The evolution of Charleston, the center of low-country civilization, reflected not only the growing wealth of the area but also its spirit and soul.[15]

In some ways, of course, pre-Revolutionary Charleston had continued to develop along the lines drawn earlier in the eighteenth century. Periodic investment in social overhead capital, for example, had continued and was in large part responsible for the increasingly modern look of the town. Charleston's sewage and drainage system, begun in the 1730s, was extended in the late colonial period and a number of swamps and marshes in the town were reclaimed. While its streets remained unpaved, the construction of brick sidewalks on Charleston's main arteries made walking less burdensome, particularly when it rained. The addition of street lights in the 1760s also had a beneficial effect on Charleston, bringing order to the night, ending Nyx's frightful sway. Finally, private investment in fencing had by the late colonial period drastically reduced the problems caused by livestock ambling through town. The thoroughly modern problems produced by speeding carriages and coaches, however, quickly rose to take their place.[16]

The number of public buildings in Charleston continued to increase. The buildings constructed in the late colonial period, however, exhibited a splendor heretofore unknown. If the elegance of Saint Philip's Church reflected the capital accumulated by Charlestonians in the 1720s, then the grandeur of Saint Michael's, completed in 1761, expressed the rising surplus available to the same. Indeed, the latter building, with its imposing portico and mighty steeple, suggested the maturation of the city of Charleston, the consolidation of power in the town during its so-called golden age. The dignified appearance of other public buildings constructed in Charleston in this period—the State House and the Exchange among others—offers further evidence thereto.[17]

The economic expansion which underpinned both the improvements and the architecture mentioned above was at the same time responsible for subverting Charleston's Renaissance planning ideal. Though such expansion had earlier in the eighteenth century opened up Charleston, liberating the town from medieval constraints, the intensification of this expansion in the late colonial period reimposed some of the fetters it had previously taken away. Thus, Charleston's central square was lost to the builders and its long blocks and broad streets were increasingly partitioned into narrow alleys, rows, and lanes. Charleston's population, one must remember, exceeded 11,000 by 1770; Renaissance ideas about spatial organization, deemed appropriate in 1740 when the city was half that size, succumbed as growing numbers fought furiously over limited urban space.[18]

Domestic architecture in Charleston was also transformed in the period after 1740. Both the growing wealth of the white inhabitants and their successful adjustment to the climate of the area were evident in the new architectural styles. So, too, however, was their profound ambivalence about the nature of the society they helped create. Though other, simpler housing forms endured in the town, particularly among the poor, two building styles came to dominate the Charleston landscape, the double house and the famous single house.

The double house was thoroughly English in origin. Indeed, it is perhaps the quintessential expression of the formal Georgian classicism which so intoxicated upper bourgeois Englishmen of the day. Houses of this type, also known as four-over-fours, were large symmetrical structures with two floors of four rooms each. A central hallway ran the length of each floor, with two rooms and fireplaces on each side. These houses, which were generally made of brick, had low-pitched roofs and faced the street. One entered the well-appointed interior of the double house through an elaborate doorway. A portico, supported by columns, frequently enriched the entrance, adding decoration and perhaps some shade. To approach this entrance, one had to mount a flight of steps, for the first floor was set about ten feet above ground level over a brick basement. In both Charleston and the British West Indies, areas with hot, damp climates and asymmetrical caste-ridden social structures, it had become common by this time to elevate the first main floor in this way. This practice provided both the comfort and social distance deemed necessary by the dwellers therein. The forbidding wrought iron fences that so often stood between the double houses and the street added to this sense of distance, inspiring awe then and even today. The double house, with its complex of genuflecting outbuildings was, in essence, Charleston's "Big House," an expression of social power, the proud symbol of social rank.[19]

As the double house peered down at the streets of Charleston, the more reticent single house cast a furtive glance over its shoulder at the same. The single house, more common if less imposing than the double, perhaps best embodied the spirit of pre-Revolutionary Charleston; indeed, the town's inhabitants have maintained an almost totemic attachment to this style up until today. While some believe the single house originated in Charleston, others, pointing to English, African, and American prototypes, are not so sure. Available data indicate that both the house and the patterns of spatial organization associated with it represented adaptations made by Charlestonians to architectural forms and practices familiar elsewhere.[20]

The single house in many ways resembled a vernacular architectural form known today as the "I-house." This building type was common in both England and America during the seventeenth and eighteenth centuries. Though two stories tall, the I-house was only one room deep. Its length varied; generally, however, the dwelling contained two or more rooms per floor. A pitched roof covered the house, its slope and composition dependent on climate and terrain. One entered the I-house through a door on its side, not in its gable end. In both England and in most parts of America, including seventeenth-century Charleston, that door faced a road or street.[21]

Charleston Double House

The Charleston single house was, so to speak, a disoriented I-house; that is, one which had made a ninety-degree turn. Thus, the narrow gable end of the single house now faced the street; the entrance, about midway down one side of the building, faced the adjacent lot instead. This entrance opened into a hall, at the back of which was a staircase leading to the upper floor or floors of the house. There was one large room on each side of this hall and one on each side of the stairwell on all floors above. The single house, which was built close to the ground in the traditional manner, generally stood two or three stories tall. Builders used for its construction either brick in Flemish bond or wood.[22]

A colonnade often graced one side of the single house. This colonnade, called a piazza by Charlestonians, ran the length of the building. One entered the piazza through an ornate doorway that faced the street. Although this doorway appeared to lead directly into the house, it did not. Rather, it stood sentry for the inhabitants therein, adding another barrier between the street and the real entrance on the side of the house. This covered passageway, which was perhaps ten feet wide and one or two stories high, provided the inhabitants of the house with both additional living space and with relief from Charleston's summer heat. While such colonnades were

Charleston Single House

known in seventeenth-century England, the Charleston piazza seems to have come
from the West Indies and was probably of Afro-Caribbean origin.[23]

The concern for social distance and privacy suggested by the single house, its
hesitance if not retreat, revealed itself in other ways as well. Wooden shutters,
for example, covered all windows that faced the street. High brick walls or iron
spiked fences shielded the house and its various outbuildings from the turbulent
world beyond its gates. Indeed, the single house, shrouded by vines and gardens,
had become a compound for both its black slaves and the white elite.[24]

While the single house did exist in Charleston prior to 1740, it was not until the
late colonial period that this architectural form became common and not until then
that it became the central metaphor for both a people and an age.[25] Scholars have
traditionally argued that the single house resulted from and, indeed, demonstrated
the successful response of the town's white inhabitants to certain environmental
and developmental problems confronting them. To these scholars, the peculiarities
of the house were due either to the climate of the area or to the partitioning of
Charleston lots into long, narrow parcels as population had grown. More recently,
other scholars have pointed out that the single house drew heavily from West Indian

and African building styles. For them, the black diaspora is responsible not only for the single house but, as indicated earlier, for its piazza too.[26]

Though Charleston's hot summers and its narrow lots, and dwellings from Africa and perhaps other spots, were doubtless all necessary for the development of the single house, they offer, even when taken together, an insufficient explanation for that form's architectural and, indeed, mythopoeic status among the town's elite. For the single house becomes fully intelligible only when placed within the context of the class and caste structure of the society in which it stood. Charleston, one must always remember, was a city with a black majority. Most of these blacks, of course, were slaves. Furthermore, the distribution of wealth, status, and power even among the white minority was tremendously skewed. A small number of planters, merchants, and lawyers controlled the town, largely determining its look, feel, and general milieu. These men were aware of, and at times troubled by, the inequities of their society. They were equally aware that as time had passed both these inequities and the tensions arising from them had grown. All analyses of elite architecture, including the single house, must keep these basic points in view.[27]

As the double house loudly proclaimed the validity of Charleston's class structure, the single house turned away from the street, as if disturbed over what it had heard. Indeed, the sense of anxiety evoked by the single house was ominous. Louis Sullivan has written: ". . .what the people are within, the buildings express without; and inversely what the buildings are objectively is a sure index of what the people are subjectively."[28]

The single house spoke eloquently, if softly, for Charleston. The closed, repressive intellectual atmosphere that so pervaded the city in the late antebellum period was already evident in its architecture well before the Revolutionary War. In its recoil from the street and its retreat behind high walls, the single house suggested ambivalence, if not dissatisfaction, over the society to which it belonged.[29]

Though South Carolina's peripheral role in the world economy had made some Charlestonians wealthy and had transformed the city's face, the pathogenic nature of this role had sealed both Charleston's and South Carolina's fate.[30] The same logic responsible for Charleston's repressed architectural and intellectual development would ultimately stifle its economic development as well. It is with this logic that the remainder of this study will deal.

Even during its so-called golden age, then, shadows appeared in Charleston that did not bode well for the city and perhaps presaged its fall. While the popularity of the public reading of *Paradise Lost* in Charleston in 1768 had foreboding connotations, a 1776 inscription on a tombstone at St. Michael's was the darkest harbinger of all. For the apocalyptic prophecy on Charles Crosslett's stone, "Not lost, But Taken away From The Evil to come," did unfortunately prove true.[31]

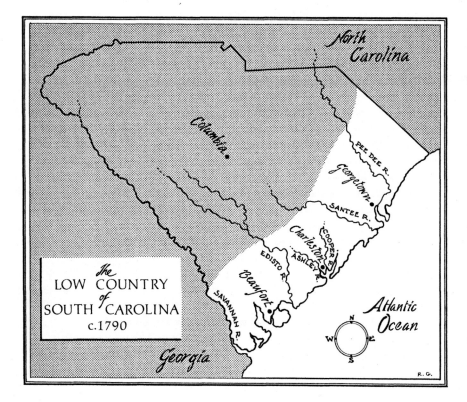

North Carolina

Columbia

PEE DEE R.

Georgetown

SANTEE R.

Charleston

COOPER R.

ASHLEY R.

EDISTO R.

Beaufort

SAVANNAH R.

The
LOW COUNTRY
of
SOUTH CAROLINA
c.1790

Georgia

Atlantic
Ocean

N
W E
S

R. G.

1

The Carolina Venture in Economic Context

In April 1670 an elderly Puritan led a small band of Englishmen down from the solid little frigate *Carolina* and onto the eerie lowland the Kiawah Indians called home. Though Europeans had moved through the history of the area for well over a century, their boot prints up to this time were faint. The lone and level sands of Kiawah, as in the antique land of Shelley's "Ozymandias," still stretched far away. The arrival of the *Carolina* changed the course of history at Kiawah, however, for with its coming, permanent European settlement—occupation if you will—had begun.[1]

The arrival of the frigate that spring day, indeed, the history of the colony founded by the adventurers that sprang from its hold, should be seen as characteristic, if relatively minor, episodes in the story of the commercial expansion of early modern Europe. This commercial expansion, moreover, was part of an even larger phenomenon which began in the twelfth century and stretched into the nineteenth century, the evolution of a market society. Though but an existential moment in the saga of this epochal development, South Carolina can only be understood within its context. And so, it is with the market that our narrative properly begins.

Scholars disagree both about the precise definition of a market society and about the exact time at which this type of society, however defined, became dominant in the West. Most would agree, however, that the evolution of a market society entailed a progressive loosening of traditional social and intellectual restraints on land, labor, and capital and a concomitant individuation, articulation, and commercialization of these factors of production. That the transformation of the various factors proceeded unevenly over space and time has led to much of the confusion concerning the dating of the "break" between traditional and market society in the West. It has, for example, led some scholars to argue that the market had become predominant as early as the twelfth or thirteenth century. It has led others to the position that the market's ascendance was coterminous with the Industrial Revolution, that is, with the 1750–1850 period. Recently, it has led still others to assert that the market did not predominate, at least among large

13

segments of the American population, until even later. One might assume that if this recent, somewhat disturbing, trend continues, the scholarly community will some day learn that a market society never existed at all. Until that time, however, it is perhaps fair to say that the process by which the West became a market society was an inexorable—if uneven—one, one which began in the twelfth or thirteenth century, was well along by the time South Carolina was founded in the seventeenth century, and was complete by the end of the nineteenth century. When viewed in this way, the precise timing of the "break" or "transition" becomes less important in any case than the irresistible force of the long-term process itself.[2]

Just as the evolution of a market society in the West proceeded at an uneven rate over the centuries, the pace and performance of the European economy varied as well. The founding of South Carolina in 1670 occurred during a relative slowdown in the European economy, that is, during the unspectacular, though extremely complex, period after the unparalleled commercial expansion of the "long sixteenth century" had ended. It is to this mystifying period that our attention will now turn.[3]

The European economy in the seventeenth century, in that interstice between the majestic sixteenth and eighteenth centuries, defies easy classification. Indeed, historians have long had trouble agreeing about even the most general character-istics of the period—one which lacked palpable developments such as the voy-ages of discovery or the Industrial Revolution upon which to anchor. During the past generation, however, two interpretations of the seventeenth-century European economy have dominated the historiography. Proponents of one argue that Europe and, indeed, many other parts of the world, experienced a severe economic crisis in the seventeenth century, a century which in the curious chronological sleight of hand practiced by historians of the early modern period, often runs to approxi-mately 1750.[4] Explanations of the crisis vary widely. Overpopulation, war, mon-etary instability, technological bottlenecks, outmoded economic institutions, and climatic change are, however, the most commonly cited independent variables, the ostensible reasons for the "century of depression." Whatever the reason or reasons, proponents of this interpretation agree that a general crisis occurred in the century, that economic stagnation, if not involution, pervaded the Western world in this age.[5]

A second important interpretive position developed in response to the thesis outlined above. This response rather modified than rejected outright the "general crisis" interpretation. While they, too, recognized symptoms of illness in the European economy, proponents of this second position performed the requisite dissection with a scalpel, not a cleaver. That the European economy decelerated in the seventeenth century they did not deny. Nor did they deny that parts of the continent such as Spain, Portugal, Italy, Germany, and the whole of eastern Europe experienced very severe economic shocks throughout the period. They argued instead that deceleration did not always mean stagnation, much less involution, that evidence for a number of particular economic crises does not lead *ipso facto* to the conclusion that a general crisis existed. Divergence, not crisis, these scholars contend, characterized the European economy in the seventeenth century. If Spain was the sick man of Europe, the Netherlands, northwestern France, England and,

according to recent research, England's American colonies, were apparently quite robust.[6]

The latter interpretation, that of European divergence in the seventeenth century, informs the argument presented in this study. Existing data on such variables as population, prices, trade, wages, and agricultural productivity indicate that economic deceleration meant different things in different places, that its impact on northwest Europe, for example, contrasted sharply with its devastating effect on the eastern half of the continent. And in no place in northwest Europe was this contrast so vivid as in England, progenitor of South Carolina, fulcrum of the modern world.[7]

However critical the seventeenth century may have been to England in a political sense, particularly during the Civil War era as important heads began to roll, the English economy expanded and, indeed, experienced some growth over the course of the century. Though marred by dislocations and serious, short-term setbacks such as that of the 1620s, the secular trend of the economy was upward. Even during the second half of the century, during Simiand's "B-Phase" of the world economy, this expansion did not end. On the contrary, steady, if modest, gains were made in population, income, and output from 1650 until the Industrial Revolution, as available economic statistics show.[8]

Thus, at the same time that Poland, to name but one example, was undergoing a process of economic involution, with both production for the market and total factor productivity plummeting at rapid rates, England, an economic backwater by European standards in the sixteenth century, had become the foremost power of the day. While there were many factors involved in both England's seventeenth-century economic expansion and in the divergence of England, the Netherlands, and parts of France from the rest of the continent which shared to a greater or lesser degree Poland's fate, only a few can be discussed here, namely, colonies, mercantilism, and foreign trade.[9]

The role of foreign trade in England's economic expansion during the early modern period is debatable. Many Marxists emphasize the "windfall" capital accumulated by England in this period from foreign trade, particularly trade with its colonies and eastern Europe, and argue that this windfall, along with expropriation from the peasantry at home, served as the engine for England's later economic growth.[10] Other writers, beginning with the physiocrats in the eighteenth century, have downplayed the impact of foreign trade on the European economy in this period, especially the trade with the American colonies. Instead, they contend that the extension and strengthening of domestic markets and the more efficient use of existing productive factors were far more important.[11]

Although some econometricians might presume otherwise, it appears impossible, given the sources with which historians must work, to state categorically which position is correct. It is possible to say, however, that those interested in economic matters in England and other parts of Europe in the seventeenth century were keenly interested in foreign trade and colonies and, indeed, operated on the assumption that what economists today call the "net export" component of national product was the key to economic expansion and growth. The title of perhaps the

most famous economic tract of this century, Mun's *England's Treasure by Forraign Trade* was not accidental, but illustrative of contemporary, that is to say, mercantilist, economic thought. It is to this body of thought, one which has fanned scholarly flames for two hundred years, that our discussion logically turns. [12]

To say almost anything about mercantilism is to invite controversy, for no question in economic history is so enduring, few problems more complex. Fierce battles have raged, for example, over the very existence of a coherent body of thought which can be labeled mercantilist. Moreover, even among those that have accepted the existence of such a body of thought, debate has continued over its definition, chronology, emphases, and alleged effects. Arcane problems relating to the reification of the concept have also troubled scholars in recent years, especially those of an epistemological bent. [13]

That a uniform pattern can be coaxed from the welter of programs and schemes, treatises and tracts, statutes, codes, edicts, and acts of an entire period in European history is a dubious proposition at best. Certain ideas and policies appear so frequently during the early modern era, however, that such recurrence can hardly be coincidence. Thus, while the points of those critical of the term "mercantilism" are well taken, there exists, this writer believes, sufficient coherence to the congeries of premises held by philosophers, policymakers, businessmen, propagandists, and others during the early modern era as to justify the use of the term to refer to mainstream economic thought between roughly 1500 and 1800, that is, from the eclipse of scholastic economics to the rise of the classical school. [14]

Though not a rigorous theory in the modern sense, mercantilism represented, nonetheless, a shared set of assumptions about economic and political power, about the emerging European nation-state and its need for such power, and about the ways in which this need could be met. In the broadest sense, mercantilists believed that national power best could be achieved through public and private policies which promoted political unification and economic expansion. They maintained that an active, even provocative, government was needed to oversee such policies and, thus, favored a considerable amount of official regulation and control over economic, political, and social life. These broad concerns are readily apparent in mercantilist formulations on economic matters, particularly in its embryonic growth strategy. Indeed, mercantilist growth strategy, like harmonic structure in Baroque music, informs an intricate, often complex, constellation of ideas and can help us to understand not only economic developments but political and social phenomena as well.

If distributive questions dominated scholastic economics, a concern for justice rather than more, this situation changed in the early modern period as production came to the fore. Showing relatively little interest in either per capita income or income distribution, mercantilists were preoccupied instead with increasing aggregate output. Cognizant of the correlation between economic and political might in the early modern world, mercantilists realized that an expansion of aggregate output would not only add to the long-term strength of the state but to its short-term revenue flow as well. They believed that this expansion would come about by both utilizing the various productive factors, particularly labor, more

efficiently and by increasing the stock of these factors. Governmental intervention in the economy was deemed necessary to accomplish these twin tasks. Mercantilists believed that such intervention should ideally encourage domestic production, particularly industrial production, discourage domestic consumption, particularly by the poor, and promote, by any means at all, external consumption of domestic commodities, goods, and services. If successfully implemented, this strategy would lead, according to mercantilists, to an increase in aggregate output, an expansion of exports, a favorable trade balance, and perhaps ultimately to export-led economic growth. In practice, the strategy led to the creation of a nationalistic, highly protectionistic economic landscape in the West, one marked by tariffs, bounties, monopolies, monetary restraints, internal economic controls, colonial ventures, and war.

The mercantilist growth scenario called for a build-up of state power and for the development of at least rudimentary social welfare programs as well. The political and military power of the nation-state must perforce be sufficient, mercantilists contended, to allow the effective imposition of the economic and social vision of those in control, that is, the vision of the coalescing aristocracy and bourgeoisie. As this vision often included policies intended to increase the level of extraction from the lower orders at home and policies designed to force entry into recalcitrant markets abroad, the development of strong nation-states, states with powerful enforcement mechanisms, is not surprising. Indeed, it is rather the relative moderation of the build-up of state might in certain places, such as England and the Netherlands, that is more difficult to explain. In these states and in others, one should note in any case, power was supplemented by paternalism, strictures enforced not only by leather but also by the dole. The mercantilists' concern with efficient utilization of the factors of production led them to believe that labor costs, that is, money wages and other forms of remuneration, should be at or near the subsistence level, a dangerous level which had aroused protest at various times in the past and might conceivably do so again. Various provisions were made, therefore, to ameliorate conditions in times of economic hardship, to alleviate the plight of some of those in constant need. These provisions, however modest, were not necessarily unsuccessful, for the spectre of peasant revolt, so haunting during subsistence crises in the medieval era, did, in fact, gradually recede.

Mercantilist growth strategy, then, was broad in conception, entailing economic, political, and social goals. Though the "strategy" is in some ways an ideal creation, an extrapolation from sundry observations, calculations, policies, and rationalizations, it accurately reflects the mercantilist impulse nonetheless. For the intellectual forces that animated phenomena so diverse as the English industrial codes, the poor laws, the Statute of Artificers, the Navigation Acts, the Anglo-Dutch naval wars, and the founding of South Carolina are comprehensible in this context alone.[15]

What, in conclusion, can one say about mercantilist economic thought? That such thought was deeply flawed is a commonplace. Indeed, scholars today generally agree that such growth that did occur in early modern Europe was due largely to increases in agricultural productivity and in domestic demand, developments

to which mercantilists were, in the first case, only casually committed and, in the second, actually opposed.[16] Moreover, few would deny that imprecise and ambiguous conceptualization and improper inversion of effect and causation often plagued mercantilist economic thought, thus limiting its explanatory power even further. This said, one hastens to add that contrary to traditional notions mercantilist economic thought was in some ways fairly sophisticated, as a review of the revisionist literature on the subject will make eminently clear.

So severely did Adam Smith damage "the mercantile system" in Book IV of *The Wealth of Nations* and so compelling were Smithian views among Western political economists in the nineteenth century that it was not until the end of that century that significant revisionist interpretations of the mercantile system began to appear. These were put forth by a number of German and English scholars who stated simply that governmental intervention in the economies of some of the nation-states of early modern Europe had proved beneficial rather than harmful to them as Smith and his followers had contended and, in addition, had hastened their political development.[17] While such conclusions drew immediate fire from scholars with rigid neoclassical orientations, others extended and elaborated upon them.[18] Lord Keynes, for example, defended mercantilist views in his *General Theory of Employment, Interest and Money*. In this work, he argued that mercantilists, unlike classical economists, recognized, if only intuitively, the complex relationship among such variables as the quantity of money available in an economy and that economy's price, investment, and employment levels. Not for nothing, according to Keynes, did mercantilists stress the need for a favorable trade balance, as the concomitant specie inflow resulting from this balance would lead to lower interest rates and ultimately to greater levels of investment and employment. Keynes was quite explicit about the fact that he championed the mercantilists' cause partly because their views seemed to offer venerable intellectual precedents not only for his own theoretical positions but for his unsettling policy recommendations as well.[19] Other revisionists have also seen modern elements in mercantilist economic thought. On the one hand, some have praised mercantilism because it bore a resemblance, at least in its later stages, to classical and neoclassical economics. These writers point in particular to the alleged mercantilist anticipation of key concepts such as specie flow and comparative advantage. Indeed, some even argue that there are similarities between mercantilist trade doctrines and the Heckscher-Ohlin-Samuelson model of comparative advantage, the basic market model of international trade today.[20]

The nature of the relationship between mercantilism and classical and neoclassical economics, however, apparently is in the eye of the beholder, for other revisionists have extolled mercantilist thought precisely because it bore in their opinion so little resemblance to these later doctrines. Working within the critical tradition of developmental economics, these writers have defended mercantilism not because of its alleged dalliance with certain classical and neoclassical notions but because mercantilism, with its emphasis on nationalism, protectionism, and governmental activism, was antithetical to liberal economics in so many fundamental ways. Moreover, they have gone on to argue that developing nations would

do well to emulate early modern Europe and adopt such neo-mercantilist measures as protective tariffs, industrial subsidies, and currency controls today.[21]

One final group of revisionists remains. While the writers discussed above have all contributed to our general understanding of mercantilism, they have told us more about the relationship between mercantilist thought and later economic doctrines than about either the era in which mercantilism flourished or the economic conditions mandating that it should.[22] Indeed, it is only by placing mercantilism in proper early modern context, as a small number of revisionists have, that the florescence of mercantilism can really be understood. One need not condone mercantilist policies to agree with these writers that certain characteristics of the European economy at this time—sticky markets, underdeveloped credit facilities, inadequate international flow mechanisms, structural dislocations, and chronic unemployment among others—help explain the existence of such policies and, furthermore, suggest that they were more serious, coherent, and economically rational than many previously have assumed.[23]

To the revisionists, then, the traditional depiction of mercantilism—as a specious theory supporting ineffectual policies designed to interfere unnaturally in economic life—is rather a caricature than an accurate representation of a complex and sophisticated body of thought. Despite their efforts, no new consensus about mercantilism has yet emerged. Debate has proved particularly intense in recent years over one specific aspect of mercantilism, colonies and colonization.[24] In the second half of this chapter, we shall discuss both the mercantilist position on colonies and colonization and Spanish, French, and English attempts to establish in Carolina settlements with firm foundations.

Mercantilists, one must remember, viewed colonies in the context of an overall growth strategy. While colonies were often considered useful, particularly to states with small or inaccessible domestic markets, they were not deemed indispensable. Thus, relatively few European nation-states made serious attempts during the early modern period to establish them. Even fewer succeeded. Among those states that did get involved in colonization, however, certain common beliefs about the role of colonies can in fact be discerned.[25]

That a colony should contribute in some way to the economic and political strength of the metropolis was to mercantilists an article of faith, in principle at least, *sine qua non*. To establish colonies that would complement the metropolitan economy was, after this, their primary goal. A colony would best complement the metropolitan economy, mercantilists believed, by supplying precious metals and raw materials to the metropolis in exchange for finished goods and commercial services. In order to ensure the continuation of this pattern of exchange, mercantilists argued that colonies should be kept completely dependent upon the metropolis. Indeed, to render a colony subservient was perhaps the fundamental imperative of metropolitan rule.[26]

Though in practice no relationship between colony and metropolis would meet all of these specifications, the differential worth of various colonies, according to mercantilists, could be measured in relation to this ideal. Mercantilists realized fairly quickly that colonies established in some areas tended to conform more

closely to their expectations than did those founded in others. In the Western Hemisphere, the colonies that conformed most closely to mercantilist postulations were located in an expansive area stretching from the Chesapeake southward to Brazil. That this was so is not surprising, for it was within this broad zone, which one imaginative scholar has labeled "the extended Caribbean," that the mineral wealth of the New World was centered and the most valuable agricultural commodities could be grown. While colonies existed beyond this band in less well-endowed areas both above and below, they generally competed against rather than complemented metropolitan economies and were thus deemed less valuable.[27]

The land along the southeast coast of North America was, of course, part of "the extended Caribbean" and captured the attention, as we shall see, of Europeans interested in colonization from the beginning of the sixteenth century. Though for well over a century colonizing efforts in the Southeast lagged, the evolution of the colonies ultimately established in this area makes clear the fact that if complementary and dependent development was the goal, then Europe, in retrospect, had not erred. It was to the English, however, that such development redounded, after earlier forays and probes into the area by the Spanish and French had foundered. That England succeeded where other nations had failed was due both to circumstance and to the triumph of will. Indeed, it is possible to argue that this success stemmed directly from the fact that the interest of Spain and France in the Southeast waned as that of England waxed.

Both Spain and France were involved in the Southeast long before England became interested in the area in the 1580s. Their involvement declined over time, however, as it became apparent that more attractive opportunities existed elsewhere. Both the Spanish and the French realized after their early incursions that though the Southeast had some economic potential, the prospects there were bleak in the short run. For despite a favorable climate and generally fertile soil, the Southeast lacked certain resources with which other areas were blessed. Neither spices nor precious metals, for example, were found in abundance, nor were the Southeastern Indians deemed readily exploitable in plantation agriculture. Other areas were even less promising, it is true, but investment opportunities in the Southeast were, nonetheless, considered unattractive in comparison to opportunities at home or in such places as the Moluccas, Mexico, or Peru. With resources limited and more pressing concerns, France thus pulled out of the Southeast altogether and Spain pulled back.

Though Spain continued to claim the entire Southeast, its presence in the area after 1587 was limited to a small fort and settlement at St. Augustine and a string of Indian missions. Furthermore, when England challenged Spain for control of the area in the seventeenth century, the Spanish response was muted and weak. Despite occasional attempts to force back the English tide, the Spanish seemed more concerned with retaining the foothold they had. Nevertheless, the significance of the Spanish presence in the Southeast cannot be denied. For with the *conquistadores*, the Jesuits, and the Franciscans, the Columbian exchange between Old World and New began. Many of the benefits of this exchange would accrue,

however, to England and not to Spain, for in this case at least the race went to the committed rather than to the swift.[28]

England's Elizabethan flirtation with the Southeast became serious under the first two Stuarts.[29] Indeed, the Southeast was perhaps the most alluring prize taken during that torrid period of English colonization, a period which also included English thrusts to the north and, more importantly, into the Caribbean. By the time of the Civil War, England had not only established dominion over the entire Chesapeake region but had tried, albeit unsuccessfully, to move into the area which later became North Carolina. Efforts to extend English authority into the area south of Virginia continued during the Interregnum. Not until the Restoration, however, did such efforts finally succeed. For not until then did everything that gave rise to Carolina finally converge.[30]

The passion with which Englishmen embraced American colonization in the first half of the seventeenth century burned even hotter during the Restoration. Enterprising Englishmen, taking advantage of Spanish weakness, grew ever more brazen in their challenges to Spain's territorial claims in the West, particularly on the mainland of North America and in the Caribbean. Since the sinews of Spanish power had long atrophied in the Southeast, this area not surprisingly commanded considerable attention. Attempts to settle the Carolina area were made, for example, from both Virginia and Massachusetts in the 1660s.[31] The real impetus came, however, from England and Barbados, where certain groups were keenly interested in the area, though, as we shall see, for different reasons.

In England, interest in the area south of Virginia centered, of course, on the eight men known to history as the Carolina proprietors.[32] While many of the details about the relationship among these men are unclear, a good deal is known about each. For present purposes, it is necessary to note only that each was wealthy, titled, and experienced in overseas investment and colonial affairs. Having secured charter rights from Charles II to the area between 29° and 36°30' north latitude, these men, in good mercantilist fashion, hoped to establish within this area colonies which would prove profitable both to themselves and the Crown. According to their design, all colonies established in the area would concentrate on the production of agricultural staples, from which the profits so desired would ultimately derive.[33]

In Barbados, on the other hand, interest in the Carolina region was more widespread. The recent sugar revolution on the island was largely responsible for this interest, as it had forced much of the Barbadian population at least to consider emigration. Those that promoted the settlement of Carolina hoped to take advantage of this widespread interest in emigration in order to establish a colony to which the Barbadian economy would be closely linked. Eager to reap the benefits of agricultural specialization and possibly even vertical integration, these promoters envisioned that the settlers of Carolina would specialize in provisions rather than staples, thereby allowing Barbadians to concentrate entirely on sugar. Carolina's development, so to speak, was to be mortgaged to this Barbadian sweet.[34]

That the proprietors and the Barbadian promoters of Carolina disagreed about the proper economic function of the colony they wished to establish in the Southeast is, in retrospect, quite clear. These differences were, in fact, soon clear to

each of these groups as well. Indeed, the early history of the colony ultimately established at "Ashley River" was informed by the struggle between them over the direction that the economy would take.[35] Potential differences were overlooked or perhaps glossed over in the 1660s, however, for neither group could then afford to do without that which the other was prepared to offer. Thus, when a group of Barbadian promoters offered in the mid-1660s to settle Carolina at its own expense in exchange for land, military stores, and certain political concessions, the proprietors, still hopeful of establishing the colony without loosening their own purse strings, were very willing to comply.[36]

Only after the Barbadians had twice failed in settlement attempts did it become apparent to the proprietors—or at least to one of the proprietors, Lord Ashley—that successful colonization would require greater initiative on the part of those who held the charter. For however enthusiastic Barbadians were about Carolina, they lacked sufficient resources, both human and financial, to proceed alone. Upon this realization, the proprietors, therefore, became more actively involved in the colonization effort. Under Ashley's leadership in the late 1660s, they formulated and adopted a constitution for Carolina, offered new settlement terms to prospective colonists, and stepped up their promotional efforts in England and Ireland. Perhaps most importantly, they began to inject capital into the project. Their efforts were soon rewarded.[37] For in the summer of 1669 the proprietors sponsored a colonizing expedition which, after eight months of travails, landed in Carolina and established at a place called Kiawah a European presence which the passage of time has not yet removed.[38]

The three vessels involved in the 1669 expedition from England to Carolina made several stops along the way. That the only scheduled stop in the New World was the one at Barbados at once underscores and symbolizes the dyadic nature of Carolina's early colonization. Indeed, though it is true that some "settlers" came to Carolina from other areas during the 1670–80 period, roughly 88 percent of those whose origins are known came from England or Barbados. Moreover, one should note that the tiny Caribbean island supplied almost as many "settlers" to Carolina as did England over the course of that decade.[39] Thus, Carolina—alone among the English colonies on the mainland of North America—felt the heat of the tropics from the start. Those that wish to understand the torridity of South Carolina's later history, its passion and its zeal, would do well to remember this point.

The early settlers at Kiawah came from disparate social backgrounds. While a number were of the "better sort"—mainly English gentry and large Barbadian planters and merchants—and more were middling artisans, yeomen, and planters, most were from groups at the bottom of the seventeenth-century social hierarchy. Those at the bottom seldom made it to Carolina without financial help or, in the case of some, coercion. As a result, Kiawah's early population consisted mainly of indentured servants and slaves.[40]

With the exception of those that had no choice in the matter, the early immigrants to Carolina had come in search of greater economic opportunity. Furthermore, the early immigrants were refreshingly clear about their economic intentions, seldom resorting to dissimulation, infrequently professing any ambiva-

lence about their goals. If Spaniards had come to the New World, as Bernal Diaz said, to serve God and also to get rich, and the English Puritans had come to build a city upon a hill, those that settled Carolina came for less ethereal reasons, that is, simply for cheap land to till.[41] While they doubtless chose to settle in Carolina mainly because of the area's soil and clime, economic opportunity there was to prove as much a function of proprietary policy as any resources they would find.

To have proposed that the true and absolute Lords Proprietors of Carolina were in any way responsible for that colony's economic success would have evoked paroxysms of disbelief in the scholarly community until fairly recently. Indeed, in the writings of the high priests of academe, the proprietors, like eight Levitical goats, were made to bear the blame for almost all of the colony's early problems. This is not to say that all scholars viewed proprietary policies toward Carolina in precisely the same manner. Whether their policies were perceived as pernicious or merely myopic, as reactionary or simply impractical, the proprietors were, however, subjected to considerable scholarly derision nonetheless.[42]

Scholarly views have finally begun to change in the last generation or so, as advances in research have brought to light certain implicit inconsistencies in the traditional interpretations. Recent research on the social and political history of seventeenth-century England has, for example, undermined the argument that there was something particularly pernicious about proprietary policy toward Carolina. When considered in the context of that violent and passionate century, one well-stuffed in the words of the poet Chapman with "undigested villainy," the policies of the proprietors appear quite moderate. Similarly, it has become increasingly difficult to sustain the thesis that the policies of the proprietors were either especially myopic or hopelessly impractical. That eight wealthy investors, experienced in various aspects of foreign trade, would expect to reap short-term gains by promoting the settlement of an argicultural colony is extremely unlikely. That these same men, veterans of the rough-and-tumble political world of the Interregnum and Restoration, able practitioners of *Realpolitik* themselves, would either finance Utopia or search for New Atlantis is impossible. Finally, the idea that the proprietors hoped to turn back the clock, to create a reactionary, even feudal, social system in Carolina no longer seems tenable. The fact that early proprietary policy was devised by Anthony Ashley Cooper, the most liberal politician in seventeenth-century England, in collaboration with John Locke, one of the chief architects of the Anglo-American political tradition, should have alerted historians to the possibility that the feudal variant of the traditional interpretation was dubious all along.[43]

Though traditional views about the proprietors have been called into question during the past generation, no historiographic revolution has yet occurred. For revisionist scholars have thus far chipped piecemeal at old assumptions, leaving systematic dismantlement for another day. One can, nevertheless, glean from the work of various revisionists the outlines of a new interpretive framework within which to view the role of the proprietors in Carolina's early history.[44]

Taken together, the revisionist works have shown that the proprietors were serious and competent promoters whose policies toward Carolina were both well-

planned and ably administered. Moreover, they have shown that the political and
constitutional ideas embodied in these policies were consistent with mainstream,
even progressive, positions in seventeenth-century England, that is to say, with
notions of limited, balanced government, government based, implicitly at least,
upon the consent of the ruled. The constitutional arrangement devised by the proprietors for Carolina, the infamous Fundamental Constitutions, is thus viewed in
the context of Restoration Whiggery. In this context, the arrangement is transformed from a reactionary constitutional schema into an enlightened and, yes,
liberal attempt to create a mixed polity similar in some ways to those of the Classical commonwealths, a polity, that is, in which power would be diffused broadly
enough among those with property to prevent tyranny, yet not so broadly as to
encourage "a numerous democracy," the development of which would threaten
elite control. In addition to their relative liberality on political and constitutional
matters, the proprietors, according to revisionists, also held advanced positions
on certain social questions, particularly on religious toleration, as both the Fundamental Constitutions and early proprietary instructions make clear.[45]

The revisionists have thus attempted to show that traditional views of early proprietary policies are unfounded. While their efforts have proved largely successful,
the fact that revisionists have paid little attention to the economic presuppositions
that underpinned these policies has retarded the completion of the interpretive
framework they have so admirably begun. For the lasting importance of the early
proprietors, the significance of their role, was due not so much to the fact that they
extended the notion of limited government to Carolina, but rather that they found
a way to do so without sacrificing their mercantilist goals.

That they were able to do this was no mean feat, for the need to attract settlers
to Carolina required concessions on the part of the proprietors, concessions which
could have rendered efficient economic exploitation along mercantilist lines difficult, if not impossible. Though it is with proprietary policy itself rather than with
the formulation of such policy that our interest mainly lies, it is worthwhile nonetheless to mention once again the two men that controlled proprietary policy toward
Carolina during the crucial period between 1669 and 1675. Indeed, it somehow
seems fitting that it was Lord Ashley and Locke, mercantilists instrumental in
the development of seventeenth-century political liberalism, who controlled proprietary policy over these years, who engineered the requisite concessions, who
were responsible, as it were, for the casting of the die.[46]

The concessions offered prospective settlers by the proprietors were liberal to
be sure. Seventeenth-century political liberalism differs considerably, however,
not only from the liberalism of our own day, of course, but from Smithian
liberalism, Manchester liberalism, and Millite liberalism as well. While it is true
that liberal thought of the seventeenth century had far-reaching, even revolutionary
implications, the immediate effects and, arguably, the intentions of those with
whom such thought is associated were much more limited. Indeed, for all their
talk of revolution, seventeenth-century liberals were rather more concerned with
reform.

When viewed in this way early liberalism becomes primarily a reform movement designed to support the alienation of property, bring greater protection to such

property once alienated, and better ensure the rights of the propertied against arbitrary actions on the part of the state. Anti-absolutism, constitutionalism, and the concomitant commitment to parliamentary supremacy become from this perspective means to ends rather than ends in themselves, strategies, so to speak, rather than goals. For the fundamental objective of seventeenth-century political liberalism, that is, the enhancement of the *effective* economic and political power of the nation-state and of a small, if growing elite, within this state, differed little from older, ostensibly more conservative doctrines. Moreover, whether reason, rationality, and natural law, or custom, the immemorial, and the ancient constitution were used to justify the reforms sought mattered little in the short run, for prior to the Financial Revolution, the political conclusions, programs, and enemies of both Lockean and Harringtonian liberals were essentially the same.[47]

Thus, despite certain theoretical assertions to the contrary, seventeenth-century liberal political thought was generally compatible with mercantilist economic principles. The basic compatibility between these bodies of thought perhaps best can be understood by considering the similarity of their positions on labor and on the power of the individual vis-à-vis the state. Though seventeenth-century liberals were often ambiguous, scholars now agree that their assertion of the right of the individual to his own labor—a right set forth in absolute terms by Locke in *Two Treatises*—was not meant to be taken literally. Indeed, scholars now concede that this right was severely qualified in liberal political theory as well as in mercantilist economic theory in the seventeenth century.[48] For according to both theories, the labor power of certain groups was to be controlled by governmental sanctions rather than by market forces, by institutions rather than price. Moreover, integral to both bodies of thought was the assumption that these groups must perforce sacrifice their labor and much of the fruit of their labor for the economic and political aggrandizement of the state and its ruling elites. The people, or at least most of the people, are envisioned, according to both then, not as masters of their economic fates but rather as servants, servants enthralled to both a powerful minority and a powerful state.[49]

By modernizing and streamlining the machinery of the state, seventeenth-century political liberalism served in the short run to reform rather than to subvert mercantilist growth strategy, to foster the implementation of mercantilist policies, and to rationalize elite control.[50] Furthermore, by encouraging the development of a "possessive" form of individualism among the propertied, it further diminished their notion of social corporatism, of obligation to others, especially to those in classes below.[51] The long-term effects of liberal political thought were, however, to prove far different. For the implications of such thought, particularly the implications of its pregnant, if inadvertent, assertion that *everyone* had the right to the "Property in his own Person," would later be used to justify vast economic and political transformations, transformations seventeenth-century liberals seldom contemplated and never sought.[52]

It is within the context outlined above that the concessions offered by the Carolina proprietors properly reside. The precise nature of these concessions, their exact liberal hue, was, however, tempered by the proprietors' recent memories of civil war, by their mercantilist conception of the role of colonies, and by the severe

labor shortage with which they were forced to deal.[53] Indeed, it is undeniable that these considerations stained the liberalism with which early proprietary policies were imbued. That the Fundamental Constitutions and the so-called Temporary Instructions, the Habeas Corpus Act and *Two Treatises of Government*, were the artistry of the same men working from the same palette is, nonetheless, quite clear.[54]

If the proprietors' concessions reflected their desire to yoke liberalism and mercantilism, the oxymoronic nature of these concessions suggests both the latent contradictions in this union and the sweet sorrow that it ultimately wrought. For in attempting to create an institutional environment which would at once prove coercive enough to allow rational exploitation of the economic resources of the Carolina low country and sufficiently accommodating to ensure the support of the propertied groups upon which the stability of the exploitation process would depend, the proprietors forged a peculiarly repressive liberalism, one which permitted some to be enslaved that others might be free. Skillful if problematic craftsmanship, this, as we shall see.

Thus, the cheap land the proprietors offered to white settlers, the generous headrights, the waiver of quitrents for twenty years. So, too, representative government, religious toleration, land registration, ease of naturalization, and a waiver of duties on imports and exports, a waiver with which not even the Crown could interfere. Hence, the £10,000 in five years the proprietors would spend on Carolina, the priceless time and energy to Ashley's "Darling" they would extend. And, alas, the labor system based on perpetual black bondage, a system which from the beginning the proprietors would encourage, promote, defend.[55]

That this curious coupling of lure and lash succeeded for a considerable period of time before things fell apart, before the center could no longer hold, reveals the genius of those seventeenth-century virtuosos, Ashley and Locke. However morally repugnant their policies appear today, one cannot gainsay the fact that they spurred the settlement of South Carolina, underpinned the colony's economic expansion and growth in the eighteenth century, and furnished the foundation upon which its famous political harmony was built. Furthermore, through the efforts of the proprietors among others, South Carolina became an exemplary mercantilist colony, that is, staple-producing, dependent, and complementary, and, in the last analysis, this was a colony's primary role.[56]

Such genius notwithstanding, severe problems would ultimately result from the policies of the early proprietors, policies which in the long run served like Othello's love, not wisely but too well. Indeed, Ashley and Locke's great seventeenth-century achievement would in the nineteenth century contribute to the low country's doom. For in hastening the creation of a society whose liberty derived from repression and whose fragile prosperity was based almost entirely on obsequence to the dictates of Europe and procrustean labor controls, the proprietors started the South Carolina low country down the path to stagnation from which it has not completely returned.[57]

2

Mise en Scène

To travel through South Carolina's early history is to endure, in Conrad's words, "a weary pilgrimage amidst hints for nightmares." In retrospect it is clear that the monstrous nature of that journey was related in no small way to the climate, the lands, and the waters of the area through which the red, white, and black actors passed. As Africa is said by Iberian historians to end at the Pyrenees, the tropics end only at the fall line. Moreover, if it is indeed true that Faulkner speaks for the South, his is not the only voice heard in South Carolina and he speaks *sotto voce* in the low country. Here, Fuentes, Roa Bastos, and García Márquez speak more forcefully. For the low country is less Yoknapatawpha than Macondo. Though it is true that the past is never dead there, it is rather death than time that lingers, a vague but oppressive gloom, timeless, encompassing all to come, all that has passed.

Let us begin with the ghosts. Of these, no place in North America has more than the South Carolina low country. Spirits, it is fair to say, literally possess the legends and lore of the area, adding a spectral dimension to this already haunting land. That hags and boo-hags, boo-daddies and drolls, cunjer-horses, spirit bears, and doctors to the dead teem in the low country is of considerable importance to the student of the area.[1] Indeed, the cultural persistence of the ghost lore of the low country and perhaps the continued existence as well of that form's attenuated analogue—the ancestor worship practiced by the remnants of the old low country elite—suggest something about the area and its history even today. For the prominence of the supernatural in the lore of the low country, the tenacity of its hold, is not fortuitous. It is rather a cultural response by the area's inhabitants, a response influenced by both the natural environment of the low country and by the inhabitants' backgrounds, traditions, and historical roles. Just as the appearance of Banquo's ghost helps unveil the murderer Macbeth, it is through the presence of the supernatural in the lore of the low country that some of the shadows shrouding the area can be lifted, that its history can be partially revealed.

As one looks into the low country's early history certain themes ring out: black majority, shocking mortality, a wealthy elite, mass misery, and always that inconsolable landscape, evoking loneliness, gloom, melancholy. It is, I submit, largely to these themes that the persistence of the spectral in legend and lore is due. For a people preserve in their folklore only the most memorable themes in their cultural past.[2] It is precisely because the low country's history is so dark, mortal, severe, and mournful that the dead have long dominated its folklore and that death and the ghostly have become such useful tropes.[3] All of these themes will receive attention in the course of this study; we shall focus in this chapter on only a few. We shall begin with a discussion of the physical characteristics of the low country and, with a somewhat ghostly touch, end with a discussion of the Southeastern Indians, the area's original occupants.

We shall never know what thoughts passed through the minds of sixteenth-century Europeans as they first encountered the puckered, wrinkled coastline of South Carolina. Perhaps these feral souls would have echoed the sentiments of Marlow, Conrad's narrator in *Heart of Darkness*, as the ship upon which he traveled oozed down the West African coast:

> Watching a coast as it slips by the ship is like thinking about an enigma. There it
> is before you—smiling, frowning, inviting, grand, mean, insipid, or savage, and
> always mute with an air of whispering, "come and find out."[4]

Though the applicability of Conrad to Carolina is, of course, a matter of taste and judgment, of two things we can be sure: it took many long years for Europeans to find out the South Carolina coastline and to find out what lay beyond. Indeed, before the coast would be charted and sounded, the interior mapped in an accurate way, well over two hundred years would pass, years of geographic misconceptions and cartographic disarray. Such geographic illusions as the Great Lake of the Piedmont and the Arenosa Desert to its east would regularly appear, for example, on maps of the Southeast until the eighteenth century. Whether due to honest error, gullibility, lie, or dream, it is in any case more important to note that such geographic chaff was slowly fanned away.[5]

Proceeding with our commentary to the kernel that remains, one finds that the state of South Carolina, like Caesar's Gaul, *est omnis divisa in partes tres*. While the borders of the modern state of South Carolina are certainly different from those of the colony that preceded it in the seventeenth and eighteenth centuries, the same Gaulish trifurcation of the area's physiography—coastal plain, piedmont, mountains—was recognized by early European observers as well. As early as 1672, for example, John Lederer, that perplexing and often perplexed German explorer, made note of these divisions, labeling them "the Flats, the Highlands, and the Mountains."[6] Most other writers have followed Lederer's lead and despite the ceaseless work of plate tectonics in the geologic moment since, his basic physiographic distinctions remain relevant today.[7]

While the banner of South Carolina's early history seemingly unfurled from east to west, it is impossible to see this banner clearly by focusing solely on the Atlantic rim. For the destiny of the intruders on the coastal plain was linked

from the beginning with both the peoples of the piedmont and with those of the mountains above. That Europeans preferred to live—and to die—with their African retainers on this plain does not change the fact that as these peoples hugged the shore, a red wind blew at their backs. We shall for this reason begin our discussion of the low country on higher ground.[8]

The weary, old Appalachian Mountains, nearing the end of their long journey southward, trudge through the extreme northwest corner of the modern state of South Carolina. Geologists refer to this corner, which includes portions of present-day Oconee, Pickens, and Greenville counties, as the Blue Ridge Province. Elevations in this area range from about 1000 feet to over 3500 feet above sea level. The undulating landscape characteristic of the province reveals the age of its geologic formations. Time has soothed the weathered bedrock of these mountains, removing all sense of youthful agitation from their visage, disclosing instead on their rounded faces of granite, gneiss, and schist the faults and folds of 500 million years. Thick, beard-like forests add further venerability thereto. The Blue Ridge Province, comprising only about 500 of the state's 31,055 square miles, nonetheless played an important part in South Carolina's early history. As the ancestral home of a portion of the mighty Cherokee Nation, the aboriginal group perhaps most influential in the evolution of colonial South Carolina, the mountains and valleys of the Blue Ridge Province served as settings for innumerable economic, social, and cultural encounters between Old World and New.[9]

The Piedmont Province lies to the southeast, stretching from the foothills of the mountains to the fall line. This province comprises an area of roughly 10,500 square miles and is characterized by gently rolling topography, with isolated monadnocks, occasional ridges, and, of course, those famous red hills. Elevations in this geologically dissected zone range from 1000 feet in the northwest to about 300 or 400 feet at the fall line in the southeast. Like the Blue Ridge Province, the Piedmont Province in general is underlain by Precambrian and early Paleozoic granite, gneiss, and schist, though high rank meta-sedimentary deposits are common near the fall line, which runs through the state more or less in a straight course from North Augusta through Columbia and Camden and on to Cheraw. South Carolina's three major river systems flow southeasterly through the piedmont and the area boasts rich, if easily eroded soils. Various Indian groups populated the piedmont both before and after Contact, including the Cherokee, the Catawba, and smaller Siouan tribes such as the Waxhaw. Though Europeans did not begin to settle the piedmont in large numbers until after 1750, the area was well known. Indeed, biologic, economic, and cultural exchange among red, white, and black had by 1750 occurred in the piedmont for over two hundred years.[10]

As the Blue Ridge and Piedmont provinces confess their age to geological divines, the Coastal Plain Province ingenuously avows its youth to the same. For all the seeming torpor of the area on a summer afternoon, the coastal plain is— to the geologist at least—impatient, if not impetuous, capricious, if not wanton; in a word, young. The callow sands, clays, and limestone that underlay the plain, ranging in age from a mere 90 million years to an almost embryonic 10,000, are not the only indicators of the area's geologic immaturity. Indeed, the incessant

tug of war between the plain and the continental shelf over the position of the shoreline—a struggle which has resulted in at least eleven major shifts since the Pleistocene—suggests both puerile indecision and adolescent pique.[11]

Girdled by the fall line on the west and the shoreline on the east, the coastal plain varies in breadth between about 120 and 150 miles, occupying a total area of more than 20,000 square miles or roughly two-thirds of the state. Geologists divide this broad plain into two reasonably distinct sections.[12] They quite logically refer to the upper third of the plain, which runs from the fall line to a line running roughly from Barnwell through Orangeburg and Bishopville and on to Bennettsville, as the upper coastal plain. This area as a whole is hilly, with elevations generally ranging from about 400 feet at the fall line to about 250 feet in the southeast. This said, one must add that at a few points along the fall line elevations are somewhat greater, at times approaching 600 feet. The various mounds, knolls, hillocks, and swells of the upper coastal plain are themselves divided into discrete groups, of which the Aiken Plateau, the Richland Red Hills, the High Hills of Santee, and the Congaree Sand Hills are the most important.[13]

As one moves toward the sea, however, hills become only memories. In that eighty- to one hundred-mile swath nearest the coast, elevation itself seems to have disappeared, as if lost in some forgotten savannah or drowned in some unknown swamp. To geologists this area is known both as the lower coastal plain and as the coastal terraces; to everyone else, it is simply the low country. From the Orangeburg Scarp—the eastern geological boundary of the upper coastal plain—to the sea, the land slopes perhaps two or three feet per mile, that is, almost imperceptibly. With slope mere intimation, a settler's 1671 remark that the country was "soe plaine & Levyll that it may be compared to a Bowling ally" even today rings true.[14]

Though the area is often described as featureless, it is in fact much more diverse ecologically than either the Blue Ridge or Piedmont Province. Indeed, to the natural scientist, the low country's marshes, forests, savannahs, and swamps are not only readily distinguishable from each other but together possess a composite flora that is almost criminal in its luxuriance.[15] Such luxuriance, however, does not extend to the mineral kingdom. To the consternation of sixteenth- and seventeenth-century Europeans, no rich veins of precious ores such as gold, silver, or copper were found in the low country. That these ores were wanting testifies rather to the immutability of nature's laws than to the inadequacy of their search. For such ores normally occur in igneous or metamorphic formations or in sedimentary deposits that are at least partially metamorphosed. In the unconsolidated sedimentary deposits of the low country, deposits which have undergone relatively little alteration over time, the occurrence of metallic ores in substantial quantities would thus be highly improbable. Non-metallic resources such as clay, sand, limestone, and calcereous marl, on the other hand, are well-nigh inexhaustible.[16]

The area's surface water resources are almost inexhaustible as well. The coastal plain is drained by four river systems, the Pee Dee, the Santee, the Edisto, and the Savannah. With the exception of the Edisto, each of these systems originates well above the fall line in a cascading mountain stream. As these streams slither

through the low country they become increasingly sluggish and their flood plains bloat. When they finally deposit their loads and reach the sea, harbors, bays, or coves form at their mouths. Amidst many of these harbors and bays lay isles and islands, particularly in the south. With these little bumps on the continent's shelf, the Carolina low country comes to a halt. Despite or perhaps because of certain factors discussed here and below, it was in the prostrate lands of the low country that the colony of South Carolina would center, that the tides of history would ebb and flow.[17]

No factor was so important as climate in shaping the early history of the low country. If it was the expansion of the market economy in the West that brought Europeans to South Carolina originally, it was the possibilities evoked by the incantatory song of that siren, climate, that seduced them into settling there for good. And it was, as we shall see, that same song that sent many of the early settlers to their dooms. Though others, perhaps properly, have summoned "climate" to explain why southerners and, thus, South Carolinians are allegedly so lazy, why they fight so much, and even why they talk the way they do, we shall limit our discussion to the relationships among climate, soil, and bio-ecology and climate, disease, and epidemiology, matters, in a literal sense, of life and of death.[18]

To speak of climate is not to speak of the Blizzard of '88 or even of the Summer of '83. For climate is not the same as weather. Climate, it is true, subsumes weather, but it is at once broader and more profound. It penetrates far beneath the surface world of daily highs and lows, seasonal conditions, or even yearly trends. Climate is, to paraphrase Langston Hughes, deep like the rivers, a summation, as it were, of an area's weather through the fathoms of time.[19]

However difficult it is to reduce an area's present-day climate to meaningful generalization, problems become even greater as one sinks further and further into the abysmal depths of the past. The inherent deficiencies in modern statistical portraits of climate seem minor indeed in comparison with the impressionistic limnings available for periods of history long elapsed. By combining the discoveries of geologists and biologists with the findings they themselves have made through both traditional methods and techniques drawn from dendroclimatology, phenology, and palynology, historians and historical climatologists have, however, overcome some of the problems occasioned by the dearth of statistics before the mid-eighteenth century and have traced the outlines of climate history much further back.[20] In so doing, it has become clear to such scholars that climate, if not exactly protean, does nonetheless change, even over relatively brief periods of time. Most climatologists now agree, for example, that the earth's climate was generally somewhat cooler and wetter during the early modern period—the period with which we are most concerned—than it is today. Furthermore, many argue that this coolness and wetness had important implications for humans in some parts of the world.[21] I mention this here not because South Carolina was one of the areas in which climatic change during this period had great biological and social effects. Indeed, scattered data from the seventeenth and eighteenth centuries indicate that South Carolina's climate was about the same then as it is today.[22] Moreover, even assuming changes of the magnitudes posited by proponents of the "little ice age"

thesis, it is doubtful, given South Carolina's geographical position on the earth, that humans living in the area would have been affected much in any case. Rather than because of its direct effects on South Carolina then, I have mentioned early modern climatic change in order to make the point that climate, like history, is both pattern and process. Though readily apprehensible, this crucial point is all too often either overlooked altogether or completely misunderstood.

Various interpretive frameworks are available to those that would classify the climate of the South Carolina low country. If one wishes, one can, for example, use a scheme originally developed by Walter Raleigh. According to this scheme, part of the low country is included in Paradise, though it should be noted that most of the region merely bordered on the Edenic.[23] Another framework, this one developed by the German climatologist Wladimir Köppen early in the twentieth century, is, however, probably more appropriate. For this classification system, modified slightly over the years, is still considered standard among most climatologists today.[24]

Based upon monthly, seasonal, and yearly temperature and precipitation figures and upon the characteristic vegetation of given areas, the Köppen system recognizes five basic climatic categories on the earth, namely, tropical-rainy; dry; humid, mild-winter temperate; humid, severe-winter temperate; and polar. Each of these categories is broken down into a number of subcategories, with each of the subcategories entailing a greater level of climatic specificity. In the Köppen system, the South Carolina low country falls into the humid, mild-winter temperate category and the humid subtropical climatic subcategory. Within this subcategory, the low country fits into an even smaller division reserved for humid subtropical areas without distinct dry and rainy seasons. Climates of this type generally are found on the eastern sides of continents and are concentrated between latitudes of 25°and 40°. They are characterized by abundant precipitation, usually between thirty and sixty-five inches annually. Though precipitation is spread throughout the year, most is concentrated in the warmer months and during the summer, thunderstorms are common. Mean temperatures range between 75° and 80°F. in summer and 40° and 50°F. in winter. Temperatures typically fluctuate widely between day and night in humid subtropical areas, however, and these areas are often the scenes of violent weather, particularly typhoons, hurricanes, and earthquakes.[25]

Despite such violence, climates of this type are very conducive to agriculture and, hence, to human habitation. Blessed with long growing seasons of two hundred days or more, plentiful rainfall during the growing season, and winters cool enough to control, if not end, the proliferation of certain biotic pests, humid subtropical areas have, in fact, proved historically to be among the most productive agricultural regions in the world. In addition to the South Carolina low country, most of the southeastern quadrant of the United States falls into this climatic subcategory as do such areas as central and southern China, the southern parts of Korea and Japan, eastern Australia, the southeastern coast of South Africa, most of France and Greece, parts of Italy and Turkey, and southern Brazil, Uruguay, and the pampas of Argentina. Though a wide variety of agricultural and pastoral activities take place in these areas, the most important commodities produced are

rice, cotton, and tobacco.[26] That these three commodities have—at one time or another—informed the agricultural histories of so many seemingly disparate parts of the world raises serious questions about the alleged uniqueness of South Carolina and, in so doing, raises the intriguing possibility of some type of *histoire structurale* instead.[27]

Available climatic data reveal just how closely the South Carolina low country conforms to the Köppen subcategory described above. The following measurements, for example, illustrate this point: annual precipitation, about 50 inches; mean summer temperature, about 80°F; mean winter temperature, between about 47° and 50°F. That the growing season in the low country varies between about 240 and 295 days and that the area's average relative humidity is about 75 percent offer evidence of this essential conformity too. Indeed, in a climatic subcategory renowned for range, volatility, and violence, the South Carolina low country— hotter in July than Barbados, damp and chilling in January, and cursed by tropical storms and occasional hurricanes in the months in between—seems almost an embodiment of Köppen's humid subtropical ideal.[28]

Climate, to be sure, manifests itself in many ways. If, on the one hand, its subtle psychological effects on humans are often discernible—one thinks of Aschenbach in *Death in Venice* and Tomasi di Lampedusa's Sicilians—climate also presents itself in bolder display. And nowhere is it more clearly expressed than in the soil, flora, and fauna characteristic of a given region or place.

A word of caution must be voiced before we go any farther, however, for soil, flora, and fauna are neither independent of nor immune to the activities of man. Indeed, as both cultural ecologists and ecological historians have repeatedly— and rightfully—pointed out in recent years, the character of human settlement areas is determined through a dialectical relationship between natural and cultural forces rather than by natural forces alone.[29] The precise role that man plays in this relationship varies considerably, of course, over space and time. In certain areas—New England, for example—European settlement in the early modern period dramatically transformed the environment. In other areas, such as the South Carolina low country, the effect of European settlement on the environment was more modest, perhaps because the natural landscape was less malleable and less remitting. In the swamps and bogs of the low country, early-modern Europeans, like the Amerindians that preceded them, were forced to make most of the concessions and accommodations, which illustrates a point often overlooked in the recent ecological literature: while the relationship between man and nature is, indeed, dialectical, it is not—even in the Promethean West—necessarily reflexive or reciprocal. With this in mind, let us move on to the soils of the low country.[30]

There are two main approaches to the study of soils, the pedological and the edaphological. In the former, one is concerned with the soil alone, that is, with the origin, classification, and description of that biochemically weathered product of nature, composed of organic and inorganic matter, air, and water, that blankets the uppermost layer of the earth. In the latter, one is concerned not only with the above properties of this product of nature but also with the soil's capacity to support life, particularly plant life. In the brief discussion that follows below, we

shall examine the low country's soils in such a way as to incorporate elements from each of these points of view.[31]

The soils of the low country are generally inorganic in nature, though there exist in some of the area's swamps and bogs soils containing enough organic matter to be classified as organic. There are, in addition, scattered occurrences of so-called half-bog soils which partake of some of the characteristics of both inorganic and true organic soils.[32] The inorganic or mineral soils vary widely in color, ranging from white, yellow, and red to gray, brown, and black. The organic and half-bog soils, thick with decayed vegetation, are generally dark brown or black. Color, in and of itself, is of minor importance to soil scientists. It can, however, tell us something about both the formation and composition of a particular soil. Darker soils, for example, generally contain larger amounts of humus, a decomposed organic material, colloidal in nature, that is crucial to plant growth. Red and yellow colors, on the other hand, often reflect the presence of iron compounds in the soil, especially sesquioxide of iron or hydrated iron oxide, while grayish soils in the same general area typically reflect the presence of reduced iron compounds such as ferrous oxide and indicate that these soils are poorly drained and suffer from a relative lack of oxygen.[33]

Colonial South Carolinians were quite conscious of soil color and considered color—and its frequent correlate, vegetation—to be good predictors of a soil's promise. They believed, for example, that the dark-colored hardwood bottom lands and the cypress and tupelo swamps of the low country were more fertile than those lands with light-colored sandy soils where gymnosperms of various kinds and scrubby vegetation grew. Time and millions of dollars in agricultural research have proved that the prognostications of early Carolinians were essentially correct.[34]

The low country's mineral soils vary in both texture and structure as well. Texture refers to the size of the mineral particulates of which a given soil is composed; structure, to the arrangement of these particulates into aggregates. Though the specific biochemical principles involved lie beyond the scope of this essay, one should note that the texture and structure of any given soil largely determine the amounts of water and organic matter retained in that soil and, hence, its capacity to sustain life.[35]

Soils from each of the main textural classes—sand, silt, and clay—are found in the low country. Most of the area's mineral soils do not fit precisely into one of these classes but are rather some type of loam, that is, a roughly balanced mixture of sand, silt, and clay. In theory, a true loam soil must be 7 to 27 percent clay, 28 to 50 percent silt, and less than 52 percent sand; in practice, however, the designation is used more loosely to refer to mineral soils that approach this mix.[36] The best agricultural soils of the low country are generally classified as loams, sandy loams, or clay loams. These soils typically occur on the sea islands and on or near the flood plains of the low country's many streams. Like most good agricultural soils, these soils and, indeed, the low country's soils generally, have compound structures, with structure varying from horizon to horizon. The surface horizon is typically granular in structure; the subsoil, blocky or blocky angular.[37]

We have thus far focused our attention rather narrowly on the characteristics of the soils of the South Carolina low country. None of these soils, however, is unique to this area; each, in fact, occurs in many other places as well. In order to understand better the soils of the low country, it is therefore necessary to place such soils within a broader context, one which encompasses not just the Southeast nor even North America, but rather the entire world.

Pedologists, like all scientists and some historians, are concerned with system, method, and classification. Indeed, science itself is inconceivable without the same. It is therefore not surprising that soil scientists have expended a great deal of time and effort attempting to classify the world's soils in systematic ways. Two major systems of soil classification have resulted from these efforts and are in general use today. One is based upon soil genesis, that is, the process of soil formation; the other, on morphological differentiation.[38]

That the soils of the low country are classified in one system as Red and Yellow Podzols, Wiesenböden, and Humic-Gleys and in the other classified instead as Ultisols in the main is necessary to our argument but insufficient just the same.[39] For our concerns are not onamastic; nor for that matter are they taxonomic in any formal way. Rather, our chief concern at this time is with the worldwide distribution of such soils and, concomitantly, with the close correlation between this distribution and the distribution of humid subtropical climatic regimes. Indeed, to those that recall our earlier discussion of climate, the list of places with such soils—the southeastern quadrant of the United States, central and southern China, the southern parts of Korea and Japan, eastern Australia, the southeastern coast of South Africa, southern Brazil, Uruguay, and the pampas of Argentina—is by now a familiar litany.[40] Though the relationship among climate, soil, and crop mix is not perfect nor the intervening variables completely clear, the degree of fit in this relationship is striking, the implications vast it would appear. For all the importance of human will in history—and the role of volition is in no way mean—one must nonetheless acknowledge the unsettling fact that it was nature, particularly in pre-industrial times, that often ruled and reigned. The fact that the flora and to a lesser extent the fauna of the low country were expressions of climate supports this point as well. And it is with this fact that our section on climate and matters of life will conclude.

Biogeographers generally divide the earth into a small number of plant zones, each based upon the appearance, characteristics, and process of formation of a type of vegetation. The particular type of vegetation upon which a given zone is based will under natural conditions dominate that zone. Most of the earth's land and by far the greatest part of the land's vegetation is included in three of these zones, namely, the forest, grassland, and desert zones. Each of these three zones, one should note, also contains a number of subdivisions based upon more specific criteria.[41]

The South Carolina low country fits into a subdivision of the forest zone known as the warm temperate rain forest. This subdivision comprises areas whose vegetation reflects an unusual admixture of associations normally found in temperate

deciduous forests and tropical rain forests. Warm temperate rain forests generally contain, for example, not only broad-leaved evergreens but also broad-leaved deciduous trees and various types of conifers. These forests tend to be denser than temperate deciduous forests though not so dense as tropical rain forests. The difference in density between the warm temperate rain forest and the latter is much more pronounced, however, at the canopy level than at lower levels. For epiphytes, lianas, and thick underbrush, characteristic features of the tropical rain forest, frequently occur in warm temperate rain forests as well. Such epiphytes as the Spanish "moss" and mistletoe of the South Carolina low country are two cases in point.[42]

Warm temperate rain forests stand or at least would stand if "natural" conditions prevailed not only in the South Carolina low country, of course, but also in other parts of the world.[43] That the most important warm temperate rain forests occur along the coastal plain of the southeastern quadrant of the United States, in southern China and Japan, in southeast Australia and southeastern South Africa, and in southern Brazil and neighboring portions of Uruguay and Paraguay is not surprising in light of our earlier discussions of climate and soil. The importance of these areas notwithstanding, we must perforce limit our comments in the section below to the warm temperate rain forest that begins along the coast of South Carolina and extends inland for upwards of one hundred miles.[44]

Though vast forests of pines, including such species as loblolly, slash, pitch and particularly longleaf cover the South Carolina low country today, the true climax community of the area is rather that comprising the numerically inferior broadleafs. Indeed, broadleafs—whether evergreens such as live oak and magnolia or deciduous species of tupelo, cypress, hickory, and gum—probably dominated the area in numerical terms originally and would in time likely become dominant again if human activity in the low country ceased for a prolonged period. For broadleafs, which grow on the richest lands of the low country, have felt the farmer's sharp axe and his hot flames for hundreds of years. Pines, on the other hand, grow almost anywhere and except during the first year of growth and during the period between their sixth and eighth years, are highly resistant to fire and, hence, to both nature's and man's combustive ways. These factors have interacted over time to keep the forests of the low country, indeed, the entire vegetable system of the area, in a pine sub-climactic or pyric climactic state.[45]

That pines have long dominated the low country's vegetation system has not necessarily proved unfavorable to the area's economy, however, for to these trees the livelihood of many a Carolinian over the years was owed. Indeed, the pine forests that yielded the tar and pitch that allowed the infant colony of South Carolina in the early eighteenth century to gain an economic foothold are vital even today to two of the low country's major employers, the giant lumber companies Georgia-Pacific and Westvaco. It is, as we shall see later, not solely to "barren" pine lands that the low country's relative underdevelopment is due.[46]

The correlation between climate and animals is, as indicated earlier, less precise than the correlation among climate, soils, crops, and natural vegetation. For animals, particularly higher animals, are both intelligent enough and sufficiently

mobile to render survival possible over a wide range of environmental conditions. As a result of the dispersive ability of animals, zoogeographers have found classification to be a serious, though by no means insoluble problem. Their solution, which is based upon the zoogeographical concept "animal regions," differs from schemes of classification discussed elsewhere in this essay, however, and thus demands a brief explanation.[47]

An animal region is perhaps best defined as a broad area possessing a particular combination of fauna which distinguishes this area in a fundamental way from all others. Moreover, this combination must include families, particularly mammalian families, that are found only in this area. Thus, while faunal classification, like climatic, pedological and vegetational classification, is based upon distinction and differentiation, it alone goes so far as to require that each of its categories entail a certain degree of exclusivity and not just variation.[48]

The particular faunal combination in any animal region today is based broadly upon the interaction of geographic, climatic, and historical factors in that area's past, factors which led over time to differential regional patterns of faunal evolution and radiation.[49] Though birds, fish, and invertebrates appear, of course, in all parts of the world, we shall follow zoogeographical convention and concentrate in the discussion below on other animal forms instead.[50] The fauna of the region to which South Carolina belongs, one which essentially comprises the entire Northern Temperate Zone, is dominated by placental mammals, particularly by advanced and highly specialized rodents, insectivores, carnivores, and ungulates. These mammals dominate this vast region because they have proved most adaptable to the climatic, geographic, and historical conditions which have prevailed in the Northern Temperate Zone since the end of the Pleistocene Ice Age. Furthermore, as time has passed, they have both extended and strengthened their regional control.[51]

There are presently at least thirty-nine native species of land mammals in the low country of South Carolina. With the exception of bison, elk, and wolves which no longer occur in the area, the native mammalian fauna of the low country has apparently undergone little change since the early modern era. Among the native placental mammals found in the area are shrews, moles, squirrels, gray foxes, otters, minks, the legendary white-tailed deer, and occasionally even mountain lions and black bears.[52]

The fauna of South Carolina is dominated by placental mammals then, but there still exists in the area and, indeed, in the rest of the southern half of the United States a number of lower animal forms as well, including various reptiles, a marsupial, and an edentate. Such forms distinguish this region to a certain extent from other parts of the Northern Temperate Zone, where these lower animal forms have essentially given way. There are, it is true, alligators in eastern China as well as in the southeastern part of the United States, but marsupials and edentates are found neither in Europe nor anywhere in Asia north of the Himalayan mountain range.[53]

The existence in the southern half of the United States of these lower forms—forms generally associated with South and Central America—has led some scholars to believe that the part of North America south of the Ohio River system constitutes

a separate animal region, one combining, as it were, temperate and "neotropical" characteristics and traits.[54] Most scholars, however, still consider the area to be part of the Northern Temperate or Holarctic faunal region. For these scholars believe that despite the occurrence there of opossums, armadillos, peccaries, and certain tropical snakes, temperate faunal forms, that is to say, placental mammals, occur in such numbers as to absorb these lower forms into the region without changing it in any fundamental way.[55]

Thus, if a certain degree of ambiguity exists in the South between temperate and tropical faunal regimes, such ambiguity also exists in the area's climate, soil, and vegetation as we have already seen. Moreover, this sense of ambiguity will not disappear after the discussion to follow below, for in terms of disease, epidemiology, and death, temperate South Carolina during the early modern period seemed, alas, quite tropical.

Climate and disease, disease and climate. For thousands of years man has sensed a close relationship between the two. Indeed, until the discovery of the germ theory in the nineteenth century, climate was perceived among the scientifically minded at least to be a primary cause of human illness. Moreover, the bond between climate and disease was felt to be indissoluble. Though we now believe that germs and not climate per se cause disease, the bond mentioned above has not been severed but merely loosened, the relationship made less direct perhaps but no less real. For disease or rather what any given society chooses to label disease does not result from the work of infectious organisms alone but from the astonishingly complex interaction among such infectious agents, the environment—which, of course, includes climate—and human hosts. In early modern South Carolina the interaction among these variables made of both town and country a "great charnel-house" and, in so doing, exacted from white, red, and black alike a terrifying toll.[56]

Even by the standards of the day, standards which were nothing if not appalling, life in early modern South Carolina was a peculiarly fragile, some would say doubtful proposition. This fragility, this doubt was due in large part to the great commingling of peoples in South Carolina, a commingling which grew out of the imperatives of early modern Europe's economic expansion. For from this commingling came epidemiological disequilibrium, from which disequilibrium in turn came demographic disaster.[57] Indeed, Conrad's "merry dance of death and trade" began early in the sixteenth century in the land which later became South Carolina and continued without interruption for several centuries thereafter. The choreography of this ferocious dance will be discussed below, its baneful patterns drafted.

Disease patterns, scholars have found, vary widely over space and time. Sleeping sickness, that is, African trypanosomiasis, is no problem in Tokyo, for example, and cancer has long since replaced bubonic plague as the scourge of the West. Though these are admittedly extreme examples, they do illustrate the fact that diseases do not occur stochastically but within particular spatial and temporal contexts. On the surface this fact appears obvious but it is worth careful consideration nonetheless, for as the integration of the world becomes more complete, the

tremendous regional variations in disease patterns that previously existed at once lessen and become increasingly difficult to grasp. In the early sixteenth century, however, when such integration had only begun, these regional variations were striking indeed.[58]

The concept of disease environments or epidemiological regionalism, simply stated, means that different geographical areas are characterized by disease patterns that are distinguishable from each other. The degree of susceptibility of an individual or group to the endemic diseases of a given region depends largely upon that individual's or group's inherited and acquired immunities to these diseases. Such immunities are believed to develop from exposure to the same. Generally speaking, the longer the exposure, the greater the immunity. In practical terms this means that natives will possess a greater degree of immunity to the endemic diseases of a given region than will migrants. Moreover, the susceptibility of any migrant to the endemic diseases of the area entered will depend largely upon the degree of epidemiological variation between this area and the area from which that migrant arrived.[59]

So far, so good. From our discussion up to this point, it would appear that the implications of epidemiological regionalism are relatively clear, that is, that natives of a given region will experience lower rates of morbidity and mortality than will migrants and that the rates for migrants themselves will vary as well. Unfortunately, this is not necessarily the case, for though migrants leave behind many things, they cannot escape their own epidemiological pasts. By bringing along the diseases—and the immunities—of the areas from which they left, migrants at once complicate the disease patterns of the regions that they enter and threaten the lives of the native population in their new homelands. The degree of danger posed to the native is, as one would expect, largely dependent upon the degree of interregional epidemiological variation between the area into which migrants have entered and the areas that they have left. Migration, thus, always changes and often completely transforms the disease pattern of the receiving region. Transformation is, as we shall see, most profound when variation among the disease environments involved is greatest and, thus, when drastically different diseases interact. In areas of greatest transformation mortality for natives and migrants alike generally jumps tremendously for a given period of time until a new equilibrium is reached, until a stand-off, as it were, between hosts and agents is attained again.[60]

The migration of peoples from Europe and Africa to the New World during the early modern period was the most massive intercontinental transfer of population the world had known up to that time. Although this migration brought together peoples from innumerable disease environments—such environments often comprise acres rather than continents, nation-states, or even miles—we can for purposes of analysis divide all of these environments into three great regional groupings: Europe-North Africa, sub-Saharan Africa, and the Americas.[61] Certain broad generalizations can be made about the disease pattern characteristic of each of these groupings. A word of caution, however, must be raised from the start. The diseases and immunities said to be endemic in a regional grouping such as Europe-North Africa are not necessarily endemic in every single disease environment within the

same. Moreover, levels of endemicity vary as well. The precise assortment of diseases and immunities in any given disease environment is, thus, a function of local factors, that is to say, to the degree of isolation of the area in question, to climate, and to terrain.[62]

Europe and North Africa, which had long been involved in a vast trade network that stretched from the Atlantic Ocean to China, had by the sixteenth century experienced, as a concomitant of this involvement, most of the diseases found in the temperate portions of the Afro-Eurasian land mass. Smallpox, influenza, measles, chicken pox, whooping cough and other so-called childhood maladies, tuberculosis, diphtheria, and even a mild form of malaria (*P. vivax*) were, for example, all endemic in Europe and North Africa by the sixteenth century and most humans living in this area had, thus, acquired a certain degree of immunity to each of these diseases.[63]

Most of these maladies were found in sub-Saharan Africa as well. In this area, however, a number of tropical diseases—yellow fever, yaws, dengue fever, sleeping sickness, and *falciparum* malaria among others—were also endemic. The native population of sub-Saharan Africa, thus, had a wider range of diseases with which to contend than did the peoples directly to the north of them. Conversely, they also had a wider range of immunological defenses than did either Europeans or North Africans.[64]

Across the Atlantic, in the Americas, a third pattern can be discerned, one which in comparison to the Old World patterns outlined above, appears strikingly different. Though all statements about epidemiological conditions in pre-Columbian America must be considered tentative at best, both North and South America were, from all indications, relatively free of infectious diseases, with the possible exception of venereal syphilis. The reasons for the relative freedom of pre-Columbian populations from infectious diseases, at least from those with epidemic potential, are still unclear. The explanations advanced thus far, which are based upon variables ranging from the infrequency of human communication to the relative unimportance of animal domestication, must perforce be treated merely as hypothetical possibilities, for no scholar has yet marshalled the evidence necessary to establish his case irrefutably. Despite such explanatory problems, it is fair to say nonetheless that on the eve of colonization America had not yet experienced the wide range of diseases by which the Old World had long been wracked.[65]

Such, then, were the epidemiological patterns in Old World and New before the Atlantic Ocean was spanned. With the turn of the fifteenth century, however, a new epidemiological era began. Even as Europeans and Africans were crossing the ocean sea, the former in search of lucre, the latter involuntarily, they passed along to each other unwittingly to be sure, both completely new diseases and old ones in new strains. This exchange continued, indeed, intensified when Africans and Europeans landed on American shores. For there they met with peoples that up until this time knew not the deadliest diseases on the ocean's other side. Though the precise effects of the ensuing epidemiological cacophony differed over time and space, of the basic pattern that emerged there can be no doubt. That death rates increased for white, red, and black alike is apparent and it is equally clear as

well that for certain groups in certain places the Columbian exchange had proved a cruel one indeed, transforming the New World into a kind of earthly hell.[66]

Death, we have argued thus far, faithfully attended the Old World's expansion into America. If its grim ministrations were evident in all parts of the New World, its attendance proved particularly constant under certain conditions, that is, when black and white migrants settled tropical or subtropical areas with substantial Indian populations. For in such areas under such conditions both migrants and natives faced the widest array of infectious diseases. Measles, smallpox, influenza, whooping cough, yellow fever, and various strains of *falciparum* malaria, for example, each performed its deadly work in such areas, while some of these diseases—yellow fever and *falciparum* malaria in particular—attended man less faithfully or at least less frequently in more temperate climes.[67] Thus, in certain tropical and subtropical areas—the Greater Antilles, northeast Brazil, the lowlands of the Spanish Main, and, alas, the South Carolina low country—early white and black migration led to epidemiological devastation.

For Native Americans, peoples that lacked familiarity with these diseases, the Old World's epidemiological intrusion meant social breakdown and ultimately virtual annihilation. Whites and blacks fell in great numbers as well but because of their immunities to some of these diseases, such groups managed to survive if not to prevail. Given the extent of Indian depopulation, it is no surprise, of course, that when Europeans found that these areas were suitable for plantation staples, they were compelled to rely upon another labor force. With immunities to certain Old World diseases and acknowledged agricultural skills, readily exploitable Sudanese and Bantu peoples from Africa were thus soon to replace among others the vanishing Arawaks, Tupinambas, and Caribs, and the so-called Cusabos. Let us now turn directly to the South Carolina low country and its dark epidemiological past, that to the generalizations above we might add data more exact.[68]

Old World diseases probably arrived in the low country prior to Europeans and Africans themselves. Just as smallpox had reached the Incas before Pizarro, European and African microparasites had in all likelihood reached the low country from *la Florida* before either Gordillo or Ayllón. We are in any case sure that Old World diseases arrived with the first European and African settlers. For a severe sickness—certain evidence from Oviedo suggests that it was malaria—was reported at San Miguel de Gualdape, the first Old World settlement in the low country, shortly after it was planted in August 1526. In light of South Carolina's later history, it is interesting to note that the collapse of this first settlement was hastened by this sickness as well as by some type of Negro slave revolt.[69]

Microparasites from the Old World survived the collapse of the settlement at San Miguel de Gualdape and those of other early settlements too. These microparasites, present from the beginning and given early vent, were to plague the inhabitants of the low country throughout the early modern period, though their furtive attacks were, to reverse the phrase, more real than apparent. Indeed, the Old World's deadliest killers, temperate and tropical, were soon plying their trades in the area, in the employ of that grim ferryman, artisans of hell.

Merely to enumerate the diseases that visited the low country in this period is a ponderous task.[70] Such was the banality of pathogenic evil that to chronicle completely such visitations would be, in the words of the Great Bard, "weary, stale, flat, and unprofitable." The imprecision of disease diagnosis in the early modern period would in any case render such a chronicle unreliable. Thus, instead of misleading accounts of individual diseases, the area as a whole in capsule. Wave after wave of epidemic, with malaria, filariasis and, to a lesser degree, yellow fever, endemic. All of the temperate and tropical diseases mentioned heretofore and dysentery, typhus, and typhoid fever, to which almost no immunities could be secured. Through the interaction of hosts, environment, and agents of infection, what can only be described as a disease explosion.[71]

In a climate that could "break even the strongest constitution," mortality was great in every season.[72] For whites, such mortality would center on the cruel months from June through October. Though less is known about seasonal patterns for black and red, data indicate that mortality for these groups was spread more evenly through the year. These differences in seasonality notwithstanding, the consequences of high mortality among white, black, and red alike were glaring. Such consequences will be discussed below, that we might appreciate the havoc reaped from diseases sown.[73]

The demographic history of the white population of the low country suggests that however great its offenses against black and red, this population is more to be pitied than reviled, treated compassionately rather than condemned. For if whites garnered most of South Carolina's riches, they did not do so cheaply, but only at great personal expense. Indeed, from the current reconstruction, perhaps we should say reconstitution, of this population's demographic past, it is becoming increasingly clear that nowhere in North America was life for whites more fleeting than in Carolina's funereal lowlands. That this population had difficulty sustaining itself naturally until the 1770s is startling, it is true, but certain demographic details from the three low-country parishes studied most completely are at once more ghastly and more incredible.[74]

Ghastly and incredible. How else can one describe the situation that existed during the colonial period in Christ Church Parish, one of South Carolina's most important parishes and one of its oldest? For of the whites whose births and deaths are recorded in the Christ Church Parish Register, 86 of every 100 were dead before the age of twenty! And of those lucky males born before 1760 that managed to survive past the age of twenty, over 80 percent had succumbed before reaching fifty.[75]

Let us move on to St. John's Parish, where chances of survival were a little better. Even here, however, almost one-third of the males and females that somehow survived to their twentieth year, never reached the age of forty.[76] Nor does the situation change much as we move between town and country. In St. Philip's Parish, that is, Charleston and its environs, we find that the crude death rate among the white population was terrifically high: between 52 and 60 per thousand, for example, in the period from 1722 through 1732.[77] Burial to baptism ratios in the parish also support the argument that mortality levels were great in the eighteenth

century. Between 1720 and 1750, 2883 burials were recorded in the parish register. During this same period, 863 baptisms were reported.[78] Imbalances between burials and baptisms, one hastens to add, were not uncommon in early modern cities. Moreover, as Allan Sharlin has pointed out, such imbalances were not only due to high rates of urban mortality, but also to peculiarities in the sex ratios and age-structures of urban populations, peculiarities due to heavy in-migration. One cannot, therefore, merely cite St. Philip's dreary ratio between burials and baptisms to "prove" that a demographic disaster had occurred.[79] A comparison of the burial/baptism ratio in St. Philip's with that in Bridgetown, Barbados—a port with a similar pattern of in-migration—lends credence, however, to the thesis of West Indian-like demographic devastation.[80]

Though our data for Charleston and Bridgetown are neither perfect nor perfectly compatible, these data are, indeed, sufficient to indicate broad trends and to render informed generalization possible. Statistical data pertaining to life and death are available for St. Michael's Parish, Barbados—Bridgetown and areas adjacent—between 1648 and 1694. This was a period of rapid growth in Bridgetown, just as the period between 1720 and 1750 was in Charleston. The ratio between burials and baptisms in Charleston between 1720 and 1750 was 3.34 to one, slightly less than the four to one ratio in Bridgetown over the course of the period designated above.[81]

While differences exist between the ratios for the parishes embracing Bridgetown and Charleston, these differences are much smaller than those between either of these parishes and, let us say, the port of Boston. Using a slightly different ratio, that of burials to births, we find that in Boston this ratio was 1.47 to one between 1704 and 1733, while that in Charleston, for example, was much higher, 2.99 to one between 1720 and 1750.[82] One can, it is true, explain part of this difference in terms of Boston's more equal sex ratio, but it would be inconsistent with the findings made by demographic historians over the past fifteen years if differential rates of mortality in New England and the lower South did not explain the residual.[83]

In any case it is clear that demographic conditions in Bridgetown and Charleston were roughly comparable. If, as scholars have long told us, white mortality in the West Indies was truly terrible, then a similar conclusion regarding Charleston and the low country in general seems unavoidable. Let us end our discussion of the white population of the low country on a provocative note by mentioning the fact that Anglican missionaries in colonial South Carolina frequently asked to be transferred to stations in the Americas that they considered less sickly, stations that they felt had better, healthier climes, stations that, if their requests were granted, would allow them to preach to the faithful under bright Caribbean skies![84]

For the black population that such missionaries would leave behind—a population, one should note, that Anglican clergymen in the colonial period would never Christianize—the demographic damage wrought was also severe, though perhaps not quite so grave as that for whites.[85] For blacks, like whites, had difficulty achieving a sustained natural increase in their numbers during the colonial period. Indeed, after experiencing such natural increase until the 1720s, the black popula-

tion failed to do so again until the 1760s. Moreover, even then the rate of natural increase achieved was weak; in the 1760s and 1770s, for example, this rate was only about half of that achieved by similar populations in the Chesapeake. That this particular pattern existed in the low country in the eighteenth century requires an explanation, especially given the fact that the distinguishing feature of North American slavery in general during the eighteenth and nineteenth centuries was precisely the opposite, that is, sustained natural increase among enslaved blacks.[86]

It is, however, a far simpler task to call for such explanation than actually to explain natural increase and decrease in the black population. For the decrease between 1730 and 1760 was the result of no one factor alone. That deaths were more numerous than births we know, but did this situation exist because mortality was high or fertility low? Or perhaps fertility was high but mortality higher still, and what of the adult sex ratio? More specifically, was it the African-born segment of this population, its age-structure, or even its patterns of lactation? Was it overwork and diet deficiency or merely the expansion of the rice industry? Was this natural decrease due to amenorrhea, sterility, and widespread abortion? Or was it simply in the end the diseases that constantly wracked this population? There are, it seems, many possible scenarios.[87]

That natural decrease was brought about through the interaction of many of these factors is highly probable, yet two in particular—the spread of rice cultivation and the increased importation of African labor—seem most responsible. For these two factors set in motion the complex process that led inexorably to natural decrease in the low country's slave population. With the rapid increase in rice production in South Carolina during the 1720s—which increase I have described in considerable detail elsewhere—African laborers began to pour into the province.[88] The influx of these laborers profoundly affected both the fertility and mortality schedules for the province's black population as a whole. Stated simply, the increase in African slave importations lowered the aggregate fertility rate and raised the aggregate mortality rate for South Carolina's slave population. Such changes led to natural decrease in this population between roughly 1730 and 1760.

Fertility declined chiefly because the sex ratio among African imports was so unbalanced. Even assuming that female slaves from Africa were as fertile as those born in South Carolina—a conservative assumption which discounts the strong possibility that fertility among African-born women was lower than that for creoles because of certain differences in the age-structures and lactation practices of these two groups—the fact that roughly two-thirds of all imports were males would lead *ipso facto* to a decline in aggregate fertility, for the percentage of the total slave population "at risk" to bear children would decrease.[89]

Aggregate mortality, on the other hand, increased primarily because these African immigrants lacked immunities to at least some of the disease strains found in the low country. Available data from the Chesapeake and the West Indies—areas with quite similar disease environments—indicate, for example, that one-third of the Africans imported would die within their first three years in the New World.[90] And a strange new world it was indeed, one in which the euphemism "seasoning" would be used to describe this grim process that would quickly take

the life of one in three! Nor would the completion of this three-year sentence mark the end of the African immigrants' tribulations, for mortality rates among the African-born would remain considerably higher than rates for those slaves suckled on American shores.[91]

Mortality may also have increased in the low country, one should note, simply because rice cultivation entailed more arduous labor in unhealthier areas than did earlier economic activities such as cattle-raising and naval-stores production. Differential occupational mortality rates existed for slaves in the West Indies as Barry Higman and Michael Craton have shown, and such differentials probably existed in South Carolina as well. That natural decrease among the black slave population in South Carolina occurred precisely during the decades when the African-born percentage of the total slave population was greatest and when rice was cultivated primarily in mosquito-infested inland swamps certainly lends credence to our scenario.[92]

The black population of the low country, caught between the blades of the demographic scissors described above, failed then to sustain itself naturally for much of the eighteenth century. Though such natural decrease was unusual in North America during the eighteenth and nineteenth centuries, it was characteristic of areas experiencing heavy African in-migration, areas such as northeastern Brazil, the Greater Antilles, and, indeed, the seventeenth-century Chesapeake.[93] Amidst these black demographic ruins, we must, however, be careful to note nonetheless that the damage done to the Negro population of the low country was less devastating than that done to white and red. Once this is understood, one can make sense of the fact that despite the ravages discussed above, the population of the low country was for most of the eighteenth century over two-thirds black.[94]

Even after our disheartening discussions of white and black mortality, it is difficult to comprehend the profound agony suffered by the Indians of the low country during the early modern period. For how does one measure the obliteration of societies and the extirpation of entire peoples? How does one gauge desolation or quantify despair? Though we can produce some numbers, we can never fully appreciate the burden that these forlorn peoples were forced to bear.[95]

That these numbers themselves inspire little confidence limits comprehension even more. For the population history of pre-Columbian America—history upon which all estimates of aboriginal population decline after 1492 necessarily rest— is currently in a state of flux, with the chasm between rival positions almost impossibly wide.[96] Scholars, it is true, agree that Indian population dropped precipitously after Old World and New were linked, but whether 8 million or 113 million Indians—to cite the most extreme estimates—lived in the Americas on the eve of the Conquest is still a matter of debate. Moreover, estimates of pre-Columbian population in the area north of Mexico, the area with which we are most concerned, vary as widely, that is to say, from about 900,000 to over 18 million.[97] It is, of course, of great importance whether high or low estimates ultimately prevail, for the higher the estimate of pre-Columbian population, the greater the demographic disaster incurred, the greater the Indians' travails. Whatever the final result of these scholarly disputations—it appears at this time, for example, that

about 2.2 million Indians lived in the area north of Mexico on the eve of the Conquest—one point is already quite clear, that is, that the nineteen indigenous chiefdoms and tribes of the South Carolina low country had by 1770 virtually disappeared.[98]

The disappearance of the Indians of the low country, indeed, the disappearance of aboriginal groups further inland as well did not escape the notice of eighteenth-century Carolinians. Writing in 1770, Lieutenant Governor William Bull, Jr., perhaps best captured the spirit of bemused detachment with which whites at the end of the colonial era viewed the passing of the Native Americans from the historical stage:

> I cannot quit the Indians without mentioning an observation that has often raised my wonder. That in this Province, settled in 1670 (since the birth of many a man now alive) then swarming with Tribes of Indians, there remains now, except the few Catawba's, nothing of them but their names, within three hundred miles of our sea coast; no traces of their emigrating or incorporating into other nations, nor any accounting for their extinction by war or pestilence equal to the effect.[99]

Though Bull's analysis was somewhat overstated—Cherokees and Creeks were to play important roles in South Carolina during the American Revolution—his argument is essentially correct. For the Indians of South Carolina succumbed slowly to many forces rather than to one spectacular epidemic or one military event. Old World diseases, particularly smallpox, measles, and malaria were the chief reasons behind the decline in Indian population, but other factors—chronic warfare, enslavement, forced and voluntary expatriation, and demoralization brought about by the collapse of native social organization in the face of ever expanding European power and ever increasing European domination—also contributed to the downfall of the low-country Indians' civilization. But the end came only gradually as we shall see.[100]

We do not know how many Indians were living in the low country at the turn of the sixteenth century; our first estimates date only from the period between 1562 and 1576. During this fifteen-year period, there were, according to these estimates, approximately 1750 Indians in the area. Given the demographic experience of Native Americans in other parts of the hemisphere, it is, however, quite likely that a major decline in the aboriginal population of the low country and, indeed, the rest of the Southeast had already occurred by 1562. For drastic reductions in Indian population had resulted from European and African penetration into other areas in the first half of the sixteenth century, areas such as the Greater Antilles, the central highlands of Mexico, and the highlands of Peru. In these places, population dropped most dramatically immediately after such penetration, that is, within a generation or two. Although the Southeast was less densely settled than these other areas and despite the fact that the Old World's penetration in the first half of the sixteenth century was incomplete to say the least, European and African diseases had certainly gained a foothold in the area and scattered evidence—large, but deserted villages, abandoned temple mounds, and reports of great pestilences and collapsing empires—suggest that Indian population throughout the Southeast had by the 1560s significantly decreased.[101]

In any case, we are sure that the Indian population of the low country declined after the 1562–76 period. Data can in fact be marshalled to illustrate the rate at which this population decreased: 1750 Indians between 1562 and 1576; 1350 by 1579; 1000 during the 1672–82 period; 800 by 1715; 500 by the end of 1716; 250 or less by 1756. In other words, for every seven Indians that dwelled in the low country in 1576, less than two centuries later, only one remained. Moreover, their numbers continued to decline in the nineteenth century until stasis and slow growth were in the twentieth century finally attained. By then, however, the Indian of the low country had become a vestige of an earlier era, a faint trace, as it were, of another day.[102]

That the Indians of the low country would ever appear vestigial would have amazed the Europeans and Africans who entered the area during the sixteenth and seventeenth centuries, in fact, even until the Yamassee War ended or at least abated in 1716. For until that time the Indians of the low country were a formidable force indeed. Not only had they contributed in important ways to the cultural development of the area but they had also shaped to a considerable degree its early history.[103]

Unlike the more advanced aboriginal groups to the west that survived the acculturation process and remained economically and politically powerful until the nineteenth century, the Indians of the low country were unable to withstand the onslaught of the Old World's biological and cultural invasion. Forced to bear the brunt of this onslaught, the low-country Indians, Indians who did not partake fully of the so-called Mississippian cultural tradition, were thus eliminated as major factors in the Southeast after the early eighteenth century.[104] Whether their elimination could have been avoided is, of course, one of those historical imponderables; I suspect, however, that they were inevitable victims—not abject wretches to be sure but inevitable victims nonetheless—of the expansion of the world economy. To say this is not to sentimentalize the plight of the low-country Indians, for few peoples could have survived the cruel coupling that marked such expansion, the coupling of biological fury and human immorality. It is perhaps fitting that we conclude our discussion of the historical theatre in which our drama took place with the Indians of the low country silently leaving the stage. And so we end, as we began, with the ghosts that remain.

3

The Economic Rise of the
South Carolina Low Country

"Ici plus particulierement l'amour des Richesses a peuplé le pays d'individus de toutes les Nations, de sectes d'opinions et de issueurs opposeés. La richesse aura donc eté le point de départ du trait caracteristique des Caroliniens."

Mons. Chateaufort,
*Mémoire sur la Caroline et le
commerce de la France . . .(1786)*

It was a long, hard ride for the Huguenot Samuel Peyre from his home in French Santee to the city of Charleston. Down the private path carved out of the wilderness to the Craven County Highway. Down that highway for a number of miles, through Mattasee, Flowery Cane, and Fountain Run swamps. Then, into Berkeley County. Down the Berkeley County Highway past Biggan Church, then, after crossing Fair Forest Swamp, down the highway further until it became the Congaree Road. Down the Congaree Road for a good piece, then across the stream where the Mepkin Bridge later stood. Down the road further still, until, reaching Strawberry, he would spend the night at an inn. After rising early the next day, he would continue down the Congaree Road to Bonneau's Ferry over the eastern branch of the Cooper River. Upon crossing that stream, he would pick up the Congaree Road again and continue on until he crossed three small creeks, French Quarter, Gibson's, and Clouter's by name. Continuing on a little further, he would ride up on his tired mount to the east bank of the Cooper River. After crossing that wide, wide river, he would catch the King's Highway, the highway to Charleston. With luck, by nightfall he would ride into the city. Clearly, the trip from the French Santee area to Charleston in, let us say, 1740 was not easy. For French Santee was for all practical purposes the "outback" of the colony of South Carolina at that time.[1]

To our good fortune, a few of Samuel Peyre's papers somehow have survived, from which we can glean some information about life in remote parts of the low country during the first half of the eighteenth century. Perhaps the most illuminating information is to be found in Peyre's "Daybook," in which book the Huguenot apparently kept the information that he considered of vital importance to his life. In this book, we find, for example, data on births, deaths, and marriages in the

Peyre family, various remedies and cures, notes on religious matters, and a number of aphorisms and adages. None of this is surprising, for such is the expected stuff of "frontier" life in America during the colonial period. We find something else, however, that does not quite square with the conventional wisdom about life in the eighteenth-century outback, for along with the scribblings mentioned above, we find—inevitably, I believe—"An Interest Table at 10 Pr. Ct."[2]

That interest table suggests much about the early history of the South Carolina low country. I do not focus on the table, however, because I believe, with the neoclassicists, that the interest rate per se represents the summation of economic life, but because I believe that this table symbolizes in a broad, if somewhat elusive sense the key role of the market and the power of the market ethos in early South Carolina. For beneath the veneer of paternalism and the sheen of patriarchy in the low country were always the talons of the market, their hold sure, their mark deep.

This is not to imply that the market pervaded life in the seventeenth century to the extent that it does today. The market economy in the West did not emerge like Athena, fully grown and fully armed, but gradually, unevenly, after hundreds of years of endogenous changes in the productive mode or, better yet, modes that preceded it. Despite this qualification, it was the social ethos of the market, which ethos is readily distinguishable even today, that animated South Carolina from the start.

My emphasis on the market distinguishes to a degree my interpretation of South Carolina's early economic history from the standard interpretation. According to the latter, South Carolina's early economic history is divided into two distinct "stages," with the colony progressing linearly from a rather aimless "pioneer" stage of economic life to a much more heavily commercialized stage dominated by plantation agriculture.[3] This interpretation is not wrong but somewhat opaque, for it cloaks the early proceedings in South Carolina in unjustified innocence, investing the early white settlers in unwarranted disinterest, if not the homespun garb of retreat. South Carolina's economic history, as we shall see, best can be understood when viewed within the context of the market from the start. And while it is true that the elaboration of the market economy encompassed many qualities, only the market's earliest propagandists would see innocence among them. To say this is not to deny nor to denigrate the courage and enterprise commonly associated with the pioneer experience, but merely to point out that courage and enterprise rest comfortably in a market context. Indeed, in some ways, to cast one's fate to the market, to commercialize self was a singularly courageous and enterprising act.[4]

Risking reification for the sake of elegance of exposition, I shall argue that it was "the market" that led to the founding of South Carolina, that brought white and black settlers there, that created the conditions under which the whites of the low country could achieve in the eighteenth century a degree of economic success that the world had seldom seen before, and that ultimately unleashed the forces that would this success devour. In this chapter I shall delineate the low country's rise, its economic will to power. The problems inherent in its rise and their eventual manifestation will be discussed in the chapter that follows.

While I shall try to treat the economic history of the South Carolina low country analytically and, in so doing, shall try to marshal evidence to "prove" my

case whenever possible, I suffer no delusion that any evidence—even that which Lenin sardonically labeled "irrefutable bourgeois statistics"—is epistemologically conclusive.[5] Moreover, I know full well that historians create history as they write about it. The patriarch's point in García Márquez's *Autumn of the Patriarch*, that "it [doesn't] matter whether something . . . was true or not, God damn it, it will be with time," is well taken.[6] What follows then is an interpretation, an impression if you will, of a dismal little corner of the world in a brutish period long past.

Several key questions inform this chapter and the next. How did the low country get so rich in the eighteenth century? What accounts for the area's later stagnation and decline? Why is it so poor today? Why do present development efforts in the low country center upon extractive industries, military installations, and the tourist trade, that is, on low-skill, low-wage, "third world-like" economic activities?

To answer these questions is no simple task, for each is related to the exceedingly complex metahistorical process of economic growth. We shall try first to isolate the most important forces involved in determining the evolution of the low-country economy and, then, to show how the particular conjuncture of these forces was for a time permissive, even libertine with respect to growth, but how subsequent permutations in the relationship among these forces severely chastened the low-country economy, condemning the inhabitants of the area to one hundred years of hardship and pain, something a majority of the inhabitants had known all along.

What, then, were these powerful forces, the relative position of which largely determined the low country's economic course? Abstracting from innumerable possibilities, from countless social facts, we find four. First, the natural environment, of course. Secondly, the particular *mentalité* of the hegemonic actors in South Carolina, that is, of the whites of the low country and their British sources of capital.[7] The *mentalité* of these actors, as stated previously, was informed from the start by a fierce adherence to the social ethos of the market. One can, if one so desires, broaden this characterization and, following the leads of Weber, Tönnies, Parsons, Redfield, Hoselitz, and others, go on to say that, in psychological and behavioral terms, the hegemonic actors in the low country were recognizably modern rather than traditional.[8] I have certain problems with the concepts "traditional" and "modern," however, and therefore prefer to stick to the narrower formulation, to the marketplace, so to speak.[9] Whether we call this *mentalité* modern or rational, market-oriented or capitalist, we find in any case a basic willingness among the hegemonic groups to respond to the stimuli and signals of the market in an economically rational way. Given this *mentalité*, the market itself looms large as a determinant. Thus, our third set of forces are those relating to supply and demand possibilities at any particular time. Such possibilities, as we shall see, can be either cruel or kind. Finally, institutional forces, for the institutional environment created by low-country whites, their British creditors, and the Crown determined the degree to which the same groups were allowed to channel their desires into a successful response to the market possibilities with which they were confronted. Let us now look more closely at each of these sets of forces.

We already have discussed the natural environment of the South Carolina low country in considerable detail; little more need be said here. One should

note, though, that the limits within which an economy functions at any given time essentially are set by two variables, available technology and the natural environment. In the early modern period, the state of technology in the West was such that, of these two variables, the delimitative power of the natural environment was truly dominant.

Of the role of the market ethos among whites of the low country we also previously have spoken, but, here, much more need be said. For this ethos did not penetrate all populations in seventeenth- and eighteenth-century America to the same extent. In the low country, however, it was manifest from the start: manifest in the economically rational manner in which productive factors in the area were utilized and in the white population's response to price, manifest, too, in the degree to which exports and long-distance trade pervaded economic life. Indeed, when Thomas Nairne in his famous *Letter from South Carolina*, written in 1710, defined planters—which occupational classification was synonymous with farmers in America at that time—as "those who live by their own and their Servants Industry, improve their Estates, follow Tillage or Grasing, and make those Commodities which are transported from hence to *Great Britain*, and other Places," he knew whereof he spoke.[10] By making the ability to export an integral part of his definition of a South Carolina planter, Nairne captured very well the external orientation of the early low-country economy.

The dominance of the market ethos was apparent in other ways as well: in the harmony and unity for which low-country whites—at least those outside of Charleston—were justifiably famous by the mid-eighteenth century, for example.[11] While some have suggested that this harmony illustrates the persistence of a "traditional" social order based on ascription and kinship in the low country, I submit that social harmony was rather *prima facie* evidence of precisely the opposite, that is, of the dominance of a recognizably "modern," or better yet, market-oriented society. For in the low country, the degree of discipline imposed by the market—"Interest" in the language of early modern moral philosophers—was such as to successfully countervail the darker, unrulier, socially disruptive "Passions" of power and corruption, thereby allowing the area's white inhabitants to embark, in essential harmony, on the path to growth. Later in the low country's history, however, when the area's economic fortunes had begun to ebb, the aforementioned passions, alas, would be heard from again.[12]

After issuing a brief caveat some pages back, we have gone on at some length about the dominance of the market ethos in early South Carolina. That we not be accused of slighting contradictory evidence, however, let us note again that the triumph of the market ethos was not yet complete. There were, for example, still some controls on the factors of production, of which the most obvious, of course, were those on the low country's labor force. Moreover, there were in comparison to later centuries more pronounced backward-bends in all supply curves, for the "double-entry" mind-set had not developed fully and profit-maximizing behavior was less widespread. Furthermore, there were isolated pockets in the low country where the populace was if not disinterested, then relatively uninvolved in the marketplace. That such pockets were atypical of the low country and probably atypical of South Carolina as a whole, a brief aside at this time will make clear.[13]

It has become fashionable in recent years to argue that certain sections of British America in the eighteenth century, the South Carolina backcountry included, were inhabited by European populations relatively indifferent, if not actively opposed to market exchange. Moreover, among these populations, it is often alleged, lived certain "alienated" groups of "outcastes" and "banditti" whose resistance to the market manifested itself in acts of violence and terrorism against targets closely associated in the public mind with market exchange. If not quite "social bandits" or "primitive rebels," these resisters nonetheless are seen as self-conscious opponents of the spread of the market economy.[14]

That the "banditti" of the South Carolina backcountry were as often as not registered landowners, that some were known land speculators, that many filed lawsuits against so-called Regulators, and that none seemed to show any disinclination to go after money in its various forms cast considerable doubt on any interpretation which views these lawbreakers in this way.[15] For cash, whatever some historians would tell us, is not really good to eat. It is much more likely, I believe, that these men and women were simply part of the small, lawless element present on many American frontiers during the last two hundred years: in South Carolina, Virginia, and Minas Gerais in Brazil in the eighteenth century, in Texas or Arizona in the nineteenth century, and in the Canadian Klondike in the early twentieth century. In each of these locales, such elements opportunistically attempted to take advantage of the underdeveloped state of social and institutional sanctions against certain behaviors and acted in a manner that society—or at least those that ordered society—saw as contrary to community norms. Ironically, such "criminal" behavior may have reflected an exaggerated economic rationality. One can, if one so desires, advance a much more far-reaching critique of the market ethos by viewing such behavior in this way, that is to say, by focusing attention on the amorality implicit in this ethos rather than by advancing the fanciful notion that the lawless were actually honorable resisters against the tawdriness of the human spirit in the market age. Romantics on the left demand a culture myth, it seems; theirs pertains to the nobility of man in some primeval or at least pre-market day.

In any case, in the South Carolina backcountry, the "banditti" quickly passed from the scene. One should note, too, that from early on the area's white inhabitants had been sending wagon after wagon of corn, hemp, and indigo down the famous King's Highway to Charleston, to be sold both in that city and in markets far away.[16] For in neither the low country nor the backcountry of eighteenth-century South Carolina was production for the market ever seriously questioned, much less the object of general disdain. Indeed, South Carolina was in many ways a product—a victim, if you will—of its markets. And it is to these markets that we now shall turn.

South Carolina owed its existence to the economic transformation of Europe during the early modern period. While in its complexity this transformation may be likened to a Baroque fugue, with related economic, political, and social episodes, we shall focus here on what is for our purposes the subject of the fugue: the rise in aggregate demand in parts of Europe. Without this development South Carolina would not, could not have been conceived.

This rise in aggregate demand was itself a very complex phenomenon, particularly in the 1650–1750 period, for that period was one of very slow population growth in contrast to the 1450–1650 period, that is, to the so-called long sixteenth century. Moreover, as we saw in Chapter 1, European economies diverged in the 1650–1750 period, with most stagnating or retrogressing, with only the northwest experiencing significant economic gains. In the discussion below, we shall be referring mainly to the most dynamic parts of northwest Europe—England and the Dutch Republic—though our comments apply to a lesser extent as well to parts of France and Germany. Furthermore, one should note that only certain regions of England and the Dutch Republic were dynamic, while other parts of these rising nation-states shared the plight of Europe as a whole.[17]

The increase in aggregate demand in northwest Europe was largely a function of economic growth. The sources of such growth are the subject of considerable controversy and need not concern us here. Suffice it to say that as a result of the growth that apparently occurred—scholars disagree among themselves whether such growth was due primarily to increasing agricultural productivity, proto-industrialization, the secular decline in transaction costs, the rise of the "rational" spirit, or the so-called primitive accumulation—each component of aggregate demand, that is, consumption, investment, government expenditures, and exports grew more rapidly than population.[18] Moreover, as aggregate demand grew, the structure of demand changed as well. This change is of vital importance to us, for it was precisely this change in structure that makes South Carolina's economic history intelligible. The application of a bit of basic price theory will show us why this is so.

Economists have found over the years that in market economies demand changes with changes in consumers' incomes. Indeed, they have developed a number of analytical tools that have allowed them to gain some insight into the manner in which income and demand interact. One such tool is of particular use to us: the concept known as "income elasticity of demand."

Income elasticity of demand refers to the degree to which the quantity demanded of any given commodity changes with changes in a buyer's income. If the quantity demanded moves sharply as income changes, income elasticity of demand for a given commodity is said to be high. If, on the other hand, the quantity demanded does not change much with changes in income, income elasticity is said to be low.[19]

Income and demand, one should note, can vary positively or negatively. The income elasticity of demand for most goods is either positive—in which case, an increase in income will lead to an increase in demand—or zero—in which case, an increase in income will not change demand. The income elasticity for some goods is negative, however; thus, an increase in income will lead, under certain conditions, to a decrease in demand for these so-called inferior goods.[20] According to economists, income elasticity of demand for basic foodstuffs is low or even negative, once income has risen much beyond subsistence levels. Moreover, they have found that as per capita income rises further, one can expect to see a relative shift in the structure of demand away from basic foodstuffs and towards agricultural

commodities with higher, positive income elasticities such as meats, dairy products, fruits, vegetables, and non-essential dietary condiments and supplements, and, as Engel's law posits, towards non-agricultural goods, commodities, and services.[21]

The concept "income elasticity of demand" can be used to help explain the changing structure of demand in northwest Europe in the seventeenth and eighteenth centuries, particularly in the period between roughly 1650 and 1750. As both aggregate demand and real per capita income or purchasing power rose in this area, the structure of demand shifted in relative terms towards commodities, goods, and services with higher, positive income elasticities. This shift is not surprising in light of the fact that much of the population in this area by now had advanced well beyond the level of subsistence.[22]

In response to this shift in the structure of demand, supply began to shift in a similar fashion. The proportion of the area's resources used to meet the demand for basic foodstuffs, thus, declined—a decline aided by rising agricultural productivity—and resources were increasingly "freed" for reallocation to other uses.[23] This process of reallocation, one should note, was supported throughout— often unwittingly—by the policies of the mercantilist state. The phrase "reallocation of resources," of course, is in some ways a euphemism behind which misery, expropriation, and exploitation seek shelter, but whatever term or phrase we prefer to use to describe this process, what we are describing is essentially a relative shift in supply in response to increased demand for commodities, goods, and services of higher income elasticities.

The reallocation of northwest Europe's economic resources resulted in a relative shift of labor and capital toward large cities and, somewhat paradoxically, into new types of agriculture and into rural industries. It resulted, too, in the transatlantic reallocation of displaced, redundant, or expectant labor and of surplus capital.[24] Thus, the rise in per capita income in northwest Europe and the concomitant change in the level and structure of demand led to a complex, convoluted intercontinental reallocation of land, labor, and capital—a reallocation which led, on the one hand, to the increased production of manufactured goods at home and, on the other, to the production of so-called staples in the colonies established across the Ocean Sea. And, as one relatively minor result of this vast reallocation, the English colony of South Carolina was founded in the year 1670.

The returns accruing to the venturers involved in the founding of the colony, indeed, to the white settlers of South Carolina in general, ultimately would depend upon their ability, given the limitations of both early-modern technology and early-modern political organization, to arrange their society in such a way as to permit the transformation of available—better yet, attainable—productive factors into articles for which the effective demand in Europe itself or in areas within Europe's commercial orbit was great. More specifically, they had to find ways to convert the area's natural resources—land, in the language of the classicists—into articles of sufficient market value to provide rates of return equal to or greater than those possible in other investment arenas.

Though the South Carolina low country was blessed, as we saw in Chapter 2, with a good, if narrow resource base, one well-suited to both early-modern

technology and early-modern demand, the European venturers had to solve difficult problems before efficient economic exploitation could begin. Like most New
World colonies, South Carolina at the outset was plagued by a severe, almost
expressionistic distortion in its factor endowment, that is to say, the colony had
an incredible abundance of land, with acute shortages of both capital and readily
exploitable labor. Moreover, to compound the problems related to factor distortions, the South Carolina low country, with the meeting of Old World and New,
was quickly transformed into a very dangerous disease environment and, thus,
into a peculiarly mortal place in which to seat economic production and market
exchange. The men who controlled the European venture in South Carolina, men
whose freedom was narrowly circumscribed by both mercantilist strictures and
biological sanctions, hoped, therefore, to erect a social order that would permit,
indeed, promote efficient economic exploitation by somehow attracting and retaining sufficient stocks of capital and labor to allow European managerial talent,
utilizing such stocks, to produce articles whose exchange value was high enough
to ensure the viability of the colony, the well-being of the European settlers, and
the pleasure of the Crown.

The degree of success of the social order envisioned would depend largely, of
course, upon the creation of institutions that would facilitate the rendering of hopes
into reality. The institutional framework within which South Carolina evolved, one
can fairly say, proved conducive to efficient economic exploitation along mercantilist lines for a considerable period of time. This framework, as we have already
seen, was informed from the very beginning by strong institutional commitments
both to political liberalism and racial slavery.[25] However much this institutional
framework assaults modern sensibilities, its creation represented an economically
rational, indeed, rather ingenious response by the European hegemonists to the
economic possibilities and problems with which they were confronted. For through
the seemingly unnatural institutional liaison between freedom and order, between
liberty and restraint, the European venturers in South Carolina were able over time
to procure the labor and capital necessary to attain that which both they and the
Crown most sought: stable production within a mercantilist context and, of course,
profitable market exchange. Perhaps in another setting, certainly in another age,
the institutional framework created in South Carolina—a framework which allowed
some a considerable degree of economic and political freedom, while keeping most
of the population enslaved—would have retarded economic expansion, thereby
limiting the prospects for material gain. But in that early-modern setting, on that
historical stage, the particular relationship among resources, markets, institutions,
and *mentalité* was such as to send South Carolina on its way.

That South Carolina was able to continue so far down the road originally taken
owes much, of course, to the indulgence of other institutions as well.[26] Indeed, the
overall configuration of a number of key normative complexes in the low country—
those relating to kinship, education, religion, and governmental organization—
proved most accommodating to early-modern economic expansion. Few scholars,
it should be noted, have viewed the evolution of these institutions in the low
country in favorable terms. When concerned at all with such normative complexes,

they generally have argued or rather asserted that the low country's economic rise occurred despite limitations imposed by what might be called institutional inarticulation.[27]

Though it is true that the casual, seemingly incidental kinship patterns in the low country, the narrowness of the educational system, the straitened realm of God, indeed a certain lack of elaboration in Caesar's realm, too, appear at first glance to testify to the arrested state of institutional development in the area in comparison, let us say, to New England, I submit that such patterns testify rather less to institutional arrestment than to the institutional embodiment of the white hegemonists' world view.[28] For under closer examination there emerges a coherent pattern to these institutions, a method if you will, a method consistent with and supportive of the political-economic framework with which we have already dealt. Most of the low country's normative complexes were marked by a certain exiguity to be sure. Let us not, however, lose sight of the fact that to those who raced through the low country in pursuit of the main chance, excessive institutional weight—at least in the short run—would not have proved beneficial, but a ponderous handicap. Full-bodied, fleshy institutions, that is to say, were neither necessary nor desired. For to those who ran that primal race, to those who would be swift, less in the way of institutional elaboration was incontrovertibly more.

We are now in position to interpret South Carolina's economic history in an analytical manner. Previous treatments of the colony's economic history have suffered, I believe, from both an excessive concern with description and an unfortunate tendency to focus almost exclusively on surface events. Two approaches have dominated the historiography up until now. In one, the economic evolution of the colony is treated anecdotally as a mélange of incidents which led through either transubstantiation or at best fortuitous accident from one economic "stage" to the next.[29] In this approach, individuals are emphasized. Moreover, they are associated with, and deemed personally responsible for the key developments in South Carolina's economic history: Sir John Yeamans and Negro slavery, Captain Thurber and the beginnings of the rice industry, Eliza Pinckney and the production of indigo in the 1740s. *Dei ex machina!*

In the other leading approach, a more important approach which we already have touched upon earlier in this chapter, the economic history of colonial South Carolina is seen as a two-stage process, as a progression, that is, from a "pioneer" to a "plantation" economy.[30] This approach represents an improvement over the other; it has some descriptive power and a good deal of alliterative merit. Nonetheless, it has little analytical acuity. For the pioneer to plantation framework focuses too much attention on linear stages and superficial changes in South Carolina's economic history and not enough on its structural continuities. In so doing, it regularly confuses effects and cause.

Indeed, this schemà, which seems to entail a transition from one mode of production to another, is actually an artificial one in many ways, for the market informed both the value-orientation and the behavior of the white hegemonists from the start. Among the Europeans in the colony, a strong desire for wealth and a ready disposition to exploit others to attain it were constants. Over time, means,

not ends changed. For did the sturdy "pioneers" of early South Carolina, those intrepid graziers and farmers that scholars love to praise, have any trouble at all about "harvesting" Indian slaves?[31]

The transition from "pioneer" to "plantation" South Carolina did not signal moral declension, then, as is sometimes implied, or a shift in *mentalité*. It represented rather an economically rational, indeed, quite predictable response by market-oriented whites to changing factor proportions and changing market possibilities. Though differences in production functions of various activities would eventually have great ramifications in South Carolina, the very fact that whites were disposed to shift resources in a manner which we today deem to be economically rational is the most crucial explanatory variable of all.

This being the case, we can employ theory based upon classical conceptions of comparative advantage and international trade to help us understand the evolution of the South Carolina low country's economy.[32] To be sure, such theory has a number of problems, among them a certain simplicity which, though formally elegant, is highly abstract, a disregard of the role of power in the determination of patterns of economic specialization, and, perhaps, as Arghiri Emmanuel has suggested, a failure to appreciate the extent to which tendencies toward conditions of international equilibrium are distorted because labor is relatively immobile in comparison to capital.[33] These problems notwithstanding, such theory—hinted at by Smith, elaborated upon by Ricardo, and further refined in the Heckscher-Ohlin-Samuelson model which, with certain qualifications, is considered the standard reformulation of the classical position today—can provide that which interpretations based upon transubstantiation, accident, or alliteration lack: a reasonably coherent structure to South Carolina's economic history, history which up until now has been studied as *l'histoire événementielle*, that is, the mere history of events.[34]

According to the theory of comparative advantage, of course, an area will tend to specialize, *ceteris paribus*, in the production of those articles for which it is in terms of its relative endowment of land, labor, and capital best suited. Generally speaking, suitability is considered synonymous with abundance. International output and income will thus be maximized if each area specializes in the production of articles fashioned from relatively abundant factors and trades for, rather than produces, those articles for which it is, because of its relative factor endowment once again, ill-suited. As Ricardo pithily put it in his famous example of two-nation, two-commodity trade, both Portugal and England would be relatively better off if the former produced nothing but wine and the latter nothing but cloth.[35]

Whites in South Carolina responded to the economic problems with which they were confronted in a manner consistent with the principle of comparative advantage. Given the factor endowment of the area in the late seventeenth century—an abundance of land and scarcities of both labor and capital—they therefore attempted at first to maximize the use of land in their economic activities, for while the other factors were at a premium, this one alone they could easily command. Over time, however, the production of land-intensive commodities in the low country allowed white South Carolinians to attract or accumulate enough capital and to mobilize—either through inducement or compulsion—sufficient stocks of

labor to effect certain changes in the area's relative factor endowment. These changes led, as the modern theory of comparative advantage postulates, to both transformations in existing production functions and to an expansion in the range of economic possibilities available to the white inhabitants of the low country. The range of such economic activities, one should note, was not fixed by God or nature alone, but was, as we have seen, a function at any given time of a complex of variables, including those related to the environment, technology, markets, institutions, and of course *mentalité*.

In any case, early land-intensive activities, activities which included not only mixed agriculture but rudimentary extraction and plunder—the stuff of Marxian primitive accumulation—as well, gradually gave way to economic activities requiring relatively greater inputs of labor and capital. The rise of plantation agriculture in the low country, a development which dates from the early eighteenth century, should be seen in this light, as should other developments such as the beginnings of both elementary agricultural processing and of low value-added manufacturing in the low country and the expansion in the area of the commercial and service sectors of the economy. Though none of these activities was characterized by what we would today consider a modern production function, each involved relatively greater inputs of labor and capital than did such activities as lumbering, ranching, hunting, and enslaving, activities that were characteristic of the low-country economy in the seventeenth century. South Carolina's famous pioneer to plantation sequence is more accurately described, then, not simply as a transition from drift to mastery, but as an economically rational response to changing economic possibilities, a response overseen from the start by economically rational white men. That the early economic growth of the low country, indeed, the later stagnation and decline of the area, too, all grew out of this famous sequence attests to both the limitations of economic rationality in a world of contradictions and to the efficacy of the dialectical world view.[36]

Before discussing this sequence in greater detail, let us make a few further comments about the nature of the factors of production relating directly thereto. The evolution of the market economy in the West entailed among other things, as we have already seen, a progressive loosening of traditional social and intellectual constraints on land, labor, and capital and a concomitant individuation, articulation, and commercialization of these factors of production. The degree to which such constraints had been loosened by about 1700 and, thus, the relative extent to which the market economy in the West had progressed by that time can be ascertained or at least approximated by both acquainting ourselves with the state of land, labor, and capital in the South Carolina low country at that time and by examining the relationship among the same.

On the one hand, the market's progress by the turn of the seventeenth century was impressive indeed. Market-responsiveness was widespread enough and factor mobility great enough by that time, for example, to allow a vast intercontinental transfer of labor and capital from Africa and Europe to America, where such factors, when recombined with New World land, were transformed into articles for which the effective demand among European consumers was great. This was,

to put it mildly, no mean entrepreneurial feat. Yet one must also remember that despite the relative degree of individuation, articulation, and commercialization of the productive factors involved therein, economic activity in eighteenth-century America—even Plantation America—was not unambiguously modern. Though the market and the market ethos predominated in economic life, certain outmoded, even archaic social and intellectual encumbrances on land, capital, and, alas, labor still remained.

To the economist, of course, land is not merely that part of the earth's surface not covered by water but rather all natural resources, all "free gifts" of nature, as it were. In the South Carolina low country, "land," broadly defined, was viewed through the prism of the market from the start. Despite a farrago of formal, often academic encumbrances on land—tenure by free and common socage with quitrents attending thereto, a system of property inheritance informed by conditional fee, and restrictive access to certain natural resources, for example—this productive factor was in practical terms relatively unembarrassed, heavily commercialized, and readily alienable, as the aboriginal inhabitants of the area, among others, quickly learned. Indeed, the white inhabitants of colonial South Carolina over time were to prove far more concerned with increasing safeguards on landed property than with any residual encumbrances on land from an earlier age.[37]

Encumbrances on capital—physical, financial, and human—were somewhat greater; moreover, they were more complex. Such encumbrances as existed, however, failed to hold back the irrepressible tide of the market nonetheless. There were, to be sure, mercantilist restrictions on avenues of investment and political and moral injunctions against usurious lending and sumptuous display.[38] So, too, were there sanctions imposed upon a majority of the population which limited its acquisition of certain income-creating skills and laws interdicting specific forms of capital utilization, including those time-honored prohibitions, derived from the Judeo-Christian tradition, against engrossing, forestalling, and regrating.[39] But however much these fetters combined to delay the process by which capital became individuated, articulated, and commercialized in the South Carolina low country, they never succeeded in stopping the process completely nor, for that matter, in impeding it in any fundamental way. For despite the encumbrances mentioned above, market forces, particularly those relating to comparative costs and comparative advantage, were the most important determinants of investment patterns in the low country and, more broadly, of capital's fate. Thus, to capital as to land, the weight of premodern millstones was slight.

Such millstones proved more burdensome to labor though, and their weight has sunk historians, sociologists, and economists into a grave, even ponderous interpretive fight. Moreover, since the issue over which this battle roars concerns the instauration in the New World of archaic modes of labor control, all of which involved to some degree the capitalization of labor, our comments above about the pennyweight of the past upon capital are, by implication at least, in some jeopardy. Briefly put, the fact that the labor force in Plantation America during the early modern period was dominated by bondsmen rather than free men, that is to say, by men and women coerced to toil ingenuously by dint of power rather

than insidiously by wage and price, has led some scholars—orthodox Marxists in particular—to describe the mode of production in such areas as pre-capitalist or, to paraphrase Yeats, as some rough economic beast slouching toward capitalism.[40] Though Marx himself, like most great thinkers, equivocated on many important interpretive issues, I believe that the wage relationship was indeed, as orthodox Marxists contend, central to his definition of the capitalist mode of production.[41] To accept Marx canonically, then, is to accept this fact. To do so, however, is also to subject capitalism—the crucial development of the past quincentennium—to analytical evisceration. For capitalism does not turn solely on the wage relation but on an intricate axis involving variables such as the degree of commercialization of other factors, commodity production, certain qualitative dimensions of exchange, rationality of spirit, and accumulation.

Thus, though servants and slaves dominated the labor force of Plantation America during the early modern period, one should not infer that the moment of capitalism had not yet occurred, for such means of labor control must not be considered in isolation but in the context of the elaboration of the Atlantic economy as a whole. Indeed, the creation of a free labor force in England and other parts of northwest Europe was part and parcel of the same process which in the New World allowed human beings themselves and not merely their labor power to be bought and sold.[42] That the "archaism" of bound labor prevailed in parts of the New World during the early modern period is attributable, then, less to economic retrogression than to market forces, technological considerations, and the man/land ratio.[43] One should note, however, that the bondsman's precise legal status, the bondsman's origins and hue, was a function not only of these considerations but also, as a number of scholars recently have pointed out, of other factors such as timing, racism, epidemiological concerns, and perhaps considerations relating to human capital.[44]

To say that the labor force in the South Carolina low country was severely encumbered during the early modern period is obviously a truism.[45] Nevertheless, one still should not infer *ipso facto* that the productive mode in the area was something other than capitalism. For the overall levels of factoral individuation, articulation, and commercialization, encumbrances notwithstanding, were recognizably modern, contrasting sharply with levels associated with either a vague period of "transition" or alternative modes. For Marxists to deny either the efficacy of the market or the existence of capitalism in South Carolina after reviewing the relevant social facts of the case would require, as we shall see, either contortive logic or, ironically, an act of blind faith.

Beneath the level of the market, of course—in the cellar of the countinghouse, so to speak—dwells the human need to provide for subsistence. Indeed, unless minimal subsistence requirements are met, more complex processes such as trade— a process which involves as Dudley North tersely observed "a commutation of superfluities"—cannot exist at all.[46] In South Carolina the problem of subsistence was solved quickly, at least in comparison to time frames common in many other early modern colonies in the New World. Though the first years were lean ones even in South Carolina, with men and women alike actually existing for a time

on a scant pint of peas each per day, the colonists there experienced no true "starving time" and before long were more concerned with filling their coffers than their bellies.[47] The problems of "material life," to use Braudellian terminology, thus, were soon superseded by those born of surplus, that is to say, by those of accumulation and exchange.[48]

The specific articles which the white hegemonists in fact accumulated, those that they in fact exchanged, can be properly explained only in relation to the factor endowment of the low country, as we have already seen. Early efforts to produce staples in the area not surprisingly crashed on the shoals of labor and capital limitations. Despite much experimentation, staples were to prove of little economic significance in the low country for well over a generation. For though cotton and tobacco, sugar and rice, indigo, silk, ginger, and wine all from the start were tested and tried, each demanded more in the way of labor and capital inputs than the fledgling colony could readily provide.[49] Indeed, even the small grains so beloved by Europeans soon gave way to the staff of southeastern aboriginal life, the remarkable cereal maize. That so intimate an attachment could be loosened so easily was due in part to necessity—maize grew better in the low country—but also to the fact that the American crop could be grown with less labor intensity.[50]

If the free white settlers in early South Carolina saw visions of sugar, dreamt dreams of gold, they occupied themselves for the most part in less fanciful activities once their stomachs were full. Instead of large-scale staple production, then, what we see is a gradual adjustment to factoral realities. This adjustment received support, not at all fortuitously, from certain Barbadian interests that hoped to make of Carolina the colony of a colony.[51] In any case, with capital—broadly defined to include knowledge about the area—scarce in the low country, labor scarcer still, the white hegemonists were soon attempting to maximize the use of land in their economic activities, which course of action was nothing if not rational. Experimenting with staples when they could, they were more concerned to plant some corn, raise some stock, kill some deer, cut some wood. And to trade with pirates and Indians too, to enslave the latter and from them steal. For they hoped that such activities, however primitive, however questionable in moral terms, would, if successful, impel the economy of the low country and, in so doing, increase local stocks of labor and capital.[52]

The actual economic history of the low country conformed quite closely to the envisioned scenario. Between 1670 and 1700 or so, such land-intensive activities not only dominated the South Carolina economy but in absolute terms continued to grow. Sometime around the turn of the eighteenth century, though, relative factoral proportions in the low country had shifted sufficiently to allow those that organized production there a greater degree of flexibility in economic matters and, thus, a greater degree of choice in their economic roles. That the economic space within which the white hegemonists in the low country operated had expanded somewhat by 1700 is to imply not in the least, however, that these men and women had assumed real control of their economic fates. To be sure, the role of volition had increased and some economic choices there were, but such involved not wanton displays of free will but choices, let us say, among raising cattle, enslaving Indians,

producing naval stores, and—this, for the first time—engaging in staple agriculture in a serious way.[53]

The latter two activities—each of which involved relatively greater inputs of labor and capital than did either raising cattle or "harvesting" Indian slaves—and, to a lesser extent, the deerskin trade, informed the economic history of the low country during the first twenty or twenty-five years of the eighteenth century. For just as supply constraints on these activities were easing, European demand for forest products, rice, and leather increased. White Carolinians, lured by the mistress profit, charmed or, better yet, enthralled by bounties and credit chains, therefore committed themselves and their resources to the production of articles for which the effective demand in Europe was great and growing—or so it seemed.

As the process of accumulation and exchange proceeded in the low country, economic life in the area became more complex. Though the economy of the low country would be wedded to primary production for centuries to come, the secondary and tertiary sectors of the economy had become sufficiently distinguishable by the early eighteenth century to bear brief notice. The factor endowment of the low country at this time precluded, of course, the development of either large-scale manufacturing activities or elaborate commercial facilities. Moreover, such secondary and tertiary activities as did develop there were mean and inefficient in comparison to those characteristic of economically advanced areas such as southeast England and the Dutch Republic. By accommodating certain simple needs of the area's population—rudimentary processing, crude manufacturing, basic provisioning, and short-term financing in particular—the secondary and tertiary sectors of the South Carolina economy, faithful indices of labor and capital inflows, played limited, but important economic roles nonetheless.[54]

That such activities failed to develop further was due to the increasingly powerful role in the low-country economy of rice and, later, indigo. Indeed, these hungry crops, with their voracious appetites for low-country land, labor, and capital, were to leave all other market activities in the area with only morsels over which to fight.[55]

The relative shift in the utilization of productive factors in the low country— a shift away from the skin trade, the forest products industries, and the other land-intensive activities mentioned previously—can be explained in a number of ways. One can point with some justification, for example, to the depletion of the deer population in the Southeast, the changes in British laws concerning bounties for naval stores, and even to the founding of the colony of Georgia, another "pioneer" economy, as it were, to help explain this shift. There were doubtless other explanatory variables at work here as well; one, related to the reestablishment after the close of the Great Northern War of Scandinavian and Baltic sources of supply for the British naval-stores market, immediately comes to mind. Sometimes, however, as the fourteenth-century scholastic philosopher William of Ockham first observed, a more elaborate explanation is adduced than the given problem being explained demands. Such, I think, is true in this particular case. For the relative shift away from each of the economic activities mentioned above was a function of precisely the same economically rational process that made staple production on

a large scale in the low country possible, indeed, ineluctable in the first place.[56] The process of which I speak, of course, is informed once again by principles of comparative advantage and comparative costs, whereby production possibilities are determined largely by potential profit and potential loss. Given the levels of effective demand for the various articles that the white hegemonists in the low country could supply between roughly 1725 and 1775, it should come as no surprise to see a shift from economic endeavors for which profit possibilities were relatively low to staple agriculture for which profit possibilities, under prevailing relationships among land, labor, and capital, were relatively high. And so, agricultural staples— rice and, after the mid-1740s, indigo as well—were primarily responsible for shaping the contours of the low country's economy from the beginning of the second quarter of the eighteenth century to the time of the American Revolution.

These were heady days for the low country, or at least for the area's white population. Writing in 1809, the renowned historian David Ramsay concluded that: "Few countries have at any time exhibited so striking an instance of public and private prosperity as appeared in South Carolina between the years 1725 and 1775."[57] Ramsay's conclusion has been confirmed by a spate of recent historical studies as well. In the next section we shall examine more closely the contours of this economy that we might position ourselves better to understand whence this prosperity came and how it was ultimately lost.

Prosperity is, of course, the great desideratum of economic man. It is a condition made possible by economic growth, by which we mean a sustained rise in per capita income or output and not merely aggregate economic expansion. Though the South Carolina low country did indeed experience a remarkable period of economic growth in the eighteenth century and though such growth did lead— as Ramsay observed—to flush times for the area's white inhabitants, the rate of economic growth that actually occurred, lest we forget, was much smaller than the rate of aggregate economic expansion. To say this is not to disparage the low country's eighteenth-century economic achievement. The area's economic performance in that period stands up quite well, in fact, even to recent historical comparisons. For unlike many developing areas today which fall victim to a "population trap" once growth occurs, whereby any increase in per capita income is soon wiped away by a concomitant rise in population, the economy of the low country continued to grow over the course of the eighteenth century, never succumbing to such entrapment.[58] Given early modern economic possibilities, this was, to say the least, an impressive accomplishment. Let us focus our attention for the moment, however, not upon the rate at which per capita income grew but rather upon the rates at which total population and aggregate output expanded.

The rate at which the population of the British colonies in North America increased has struck the imagination of the demographically inclined for over two hundred years. Malthus's famous observation that British North America had experienced "a rapidity of increase, probably without parallel in history," generally has held up well over the years, as in a broad way have similar observations made by eighteenth-century writers on demographic matters such as Franklin and Wig-

glesworth and the observations made by the *philosophes* Count Buffon and Abbé Raynal as well.[59] If modern historical demographers have shown that the population of the area as a whole did not grow in the precise manner that Malthus had suggested, they have also demonstrated that rates of population growth—growth due, one should note, both to natural increase and immigration—approached and at times surpassed the levels which Malthus and other early writers believed to obtain.[60]

The population history of colonial South Carolina is at once straightforward and difficult to explain. For is it not a bit paradoxical that this colony—site of terrifying epidemiological devastation to red, white, and black alike—was among the fastest-growing areas of British North America during the seventeenth and eighteenth centuries?[61] Yet, demographic data readily can be marshalled to demonstrate that the colony's population did indeed rapidly increase. Decennial estimates of both the total population of South Carolina between 1670 and 1780 and the white and black components of the same appear in Table 3-1. Population growth rates, compounded

Table 3-1. South Carolina Population Estimates

Year	Total	White	Black	%Black
1670	200	170	30	15.00
1680	1,200	800*	400*	33.33
1690	3,900	2,400	1,500	38.46
1700	5,704	3,260	2,444	42.85
1710	10,883	5,115*	5,768*	53.00
1720	18,393*	6,525*	11,868*	64.52
1730	30,000	10,000	20,000	66.67
1740	59,155*	20,000*	39,155*	66.19
1750	65,000*	25,000	40,000*	61.54
1760	89,740*	36,740	53,000*	59.06
1770	124,244	49,066	75,178	60.51
1780	180,000	83,000	97,000	53.89

Sources: All estimates without asterisks are from *Historical Statistics of the United States: Colonial Times to 1970*, Department of Commerce, Bureau of the Census, 2 vols. (Washington: U.S. Government Printing Office, 1975), 2: 1168. Estimates with asterisks are either my own or are from other sources. Estimates for:

1680: Based on Peter Wood's statement that even in the earliest years between one-third and one-fourth of South Carolina's population was black and on the fact that in *Historical Statistics* the black percentage of the total population of South Carolina in 1690 is 38.46. See Wood, *Black Majority*, pp. 25-26; *Historical Statistics*, 2: 1168.

1710: Based on the fact that in 1708 South Carolina's population was 50.12 percent black and by 1720, 64.52 percent black. My estimate for 1710 is a rough interpolation. For white and black population figures in 1708, see Governor Johnson and Council to the Board of Trade, September 17, 1708, Records in the British Public Record Office Relating to South Carolina, 1663-1782, 36 volumes in facsimile, South Carolina Department of Archives and History, 5: 203-210.

1720: Based on "An Exact Account of the Number of Inhabitants who pay Tax in the Settlement of South Carolina for the yeare 1720 with the Number of Slaves in each parish," Records in the British Public Record Office Relating to South Carolina, 9: 22-23. This source lists 1305 taxpayers and 11,868 slaves. I multiplied the number of taxpayers by 5 to reach an estimate of total white population.

1740: Based on Wood, *Black Majority*, pp. 152-153. For the black population estimate, also see James H. Easterby et al., eds., *The Colonial Records of South Carolina, 1st series: The Journal of the Commons House of Assembly, 1736-*, 13 vols. to date (Columbia: Printed for the South Carolina Department of Archives and History, 1951-), vol.: *1741-1742*, March 2, 1742, p. 460.

1750: Based on Philip D. Morgan, "The Development of Slave Culture in Eighteenth Century Plantation America" (Ph.D. dissertation, University College London, 1977), pp. 284-286.

1760: Based on Morgan, "The Development of Slave Culture in Eighteenth Century Plantation America," pp. 284-286.

Table 3–2. South Carolina Population: Annual Compound Growth Rates

Year	Total	Growth Rate	White	Growth Rate	Black	Growth Rate
1670	200		170		30	
		19.6%		16.8%		29.6%
1680	1,200		800		400	
		12.5		11.6		14.1
1690	3,900		2,400		1,500	
		3.9		3.1		5.0
1700	5,704		3,260		2,444	
		6.7		4.6		9.0
1710	10,883		5,115		5,768	
		5.4		2.5		7.5
1720	18,393		6,525		11,868	
		5.0		4.4		5.4
1730	30,000		10,000		20,000	
		7.0		7.2		6.9
1740	59,155		20,000		39,155	
		0.9		2.3		0.2
1750	65,000		25,000		40,000	
		3.3		3.9		2.9
1760	89,740		36,740		53,000	
		3.3		2.9		3.6
1770	124,244		49,066		75,178	
		3.8		5.4		2.6
1780	180,000		83,000		97,000	
1670–1770		6.6		5.8		8.1
1670–1780		6.4		5.8		7.6

Sources: See Table 3-1.

annually for both decennial periods and for the 1670–1780 period as a whole, appear in Table 3-2.[62] The population of South Carolina, these tables indicate, grew rapidly, more rapidly, in fact, during most of the decennial periods and over the 110-year period as a whole than did the total population of British North America, a fact borne out in Table 3-3.

Upon closer inspection, the paradox mentioned above, like most others, reveals itself, yielding to a degree of logical coherence if not complete linearity. Indeed, we can, I believe, identify both a proximate cause and another higher level, perhaps ultimate cause for the seemingly paradoxical relationship between life and death, between demographic affirmation and negation, so to speak, in the South Carolina colony. We shall begin our inspection by disaggregating our demographic data on the colony as a whole to see whether differences existed between patterns obtaining in the low country and those that held in the backcountry. The latter area, upwards of 80 or 100 miles from the sea, was little inhabited by Europeans or Africans prior to the 1730s and was still sparsely settled by such groups as late as 1750. After that date, however, settlement of the area—particularly by

Table 3-3. Estimated Population of American Colonies*, 1670-1780, and South
Carolina's Share of Total American Population

	White	Black	Total
1670	107,400	4,535	111,935
SC	170	30	200
SC%	0.16	0.66	0.18
1680	144,536	6,971	151,507
SC	800	400	1,200
SC%	0.55	5.74	0.79
1690	193,643	16,729	210,372
SC	2,400	1,500	3,900
SC%	1.24	8.97	1.85
1700	223,071	27,817	250,888
SC	3,260	2,444	5,704
SC%	1.46	8.79	2.27
1710	286,845	44,866	331,711
SC	5,115	5,768	10,883
SC%	1.78	12.86	3.28
1720	397,346	68,839	466,185
SC	6,525	11,868	18,393
SC%	1.64	17.24	3.94
1730	538,424	91,021	629,445
SC	10,000	20,000	30,000
SC%	1.86	21.97	4.77
1740	755,539	150,024	905,563
SC	20,000	39,155	59,155
SC%	2.65	26.10	6.53
1750	934,340	236,420	1,170,760
SC	25,000	40,000	65,000
SC%	2.68	16.92	5.55
1760	1,267,819	325,806	1,593,625
SC	36,740	53,000	89,740
SC%	2.90	16.27	5.63
1770	1,688,254	459,822	2,148,076
SC	49,066	75,178	124,244
SC%	2.91	16.35	5.78
1780	2,204,949	575,420	2,780,369
SC	83,000	97,000	180,000
SC%	3.76	16.86	6.47

Sources: Historical Statistics of the United States, 2: 1168; Table 3-1.

*American Colonies: Maine, New Hampshire, Vermont, Plymouth, Mass., Rhode Island, Connecticut, New York,
New Jersey, Pennsylvania, Delaware, Maryland, Virginia, North Carolina, South Carolina, Georgia, Kentucky, and
Tennessee

emigrants from the low country and by Scotch-Irish and German immigrants
of limited means—began in earnest and continued on through the remainder of
the eighteenth century.[63] Although extant data are sketchy at best, the population
of the backcountry apparently had grown to about 36,000 by 1770. This number included about 30,000 whites and 6,000 Negro slaves. [64] The racial composition
of the backcountry, thus, was strikingly different from that of the colony as a

whole. Indeed, when disaggregated, the population figures presented in Table 3-1 seem to suggest the existence of two discrete demographic regimes in South Carolina: one, governing the overwhelmingly black population in the lowlands nearest the coast, the other, the overwhelmingly white population of the backcountry.

Disaggregated population statistics for South Carolina in the year 1770—the only year for which even rough estimates of the relative population breakdown between low country and backcountry are possible—appear in Table 3-4. These statistics and those in Table 3-1 indicate among other things that while the backcountry was filling up and the black population of the low country growing in a continuous, if somewhat uneven manner, the white population of the low country was about the same in 1770 as it had been thirty years earlier, that is to say, in 1740.[65]

The last point, one should note, is not unimportant, for once we understand why the white population of the low country failed to grow between 1740 and 1770 we are in a position for the first time to truly understand the demographic history of colonial South Carolina, to gain an *aperçu*, as it were, into its internal dynamics. The South Carolina low country, we argued in Chapter 2, was for a variety of reasons a very mortal environment for white, red, and black alike in the early modern period, particularly until the middle of the eighteenth century. High mortality levels, in fact, led over time, as we have seen, to the virtual disappearance of an entire people, the American Indian, from the low country. That the area's white and black populations were able not only to avoid the redman's fate but to sustain themselves and even to grow was due not to natural increase but to heavy European and African immigration flows. Indeed, given prevailing levels of mortality in the low country, the rates at which white and black immigrants poured into the area prior to 1740 or so says much about the degree of economic opportunity there and, alas, even more about *mentalité*.[66]

As time passed, however, economic opportunity for white immigrants in the low country—an area increasingly dominated by large-scale plantation agriculture—declined and fewer white immigrants arrived in the area. Few that did arrive, moreover, came to stay. Though the native white population of the low country probably began to increase naturally sometime during the second half of the eighteenth century, the fact that a considerable number of native whites—displaced by the plantation regime—lit out during the same period for Georgia, Florida, and the Carolina backcountry negated the possible significance of white population growth by natural means.[67] White population, largely a function of the degree of economic opportunity available, thus began to stagnate in the low country, while black population growth, deemed necessary for the area's continued economic viability, was sustained.[68] At the same time, groups of whites with similar aspirations as those that lived in the low country but with more limited means began to flood into the backcountry, which area was not only healthier but seemed to them to offer far greater opportunity than the increasingly rigid economy of the low country. Thus, the paradox which allowed South Carolina to grow rapidly in population despite high mortality rates in the most populous part of the colony can be explained in a

Table 3–4. Estimated Population, South Carolina Low Country and Backcountry, 1770

	White	Black	Total
South Carolina	49,066	75,178	124,244
Low Country	19,066	69,178	88,244
Backcountry	30,000	6,000	36,000

proximate way by pointing to heavy, if divergent streams of immigration and on a higher, almost eschatological plane by tracing the trail of opportunity. For it is quite clear that in colonial South Carolina whites sought salvation and redemption through the pursuit of material gain.

Available data on landholding patterns in colonial South Carolina are consistent with the population trends outlined above. Here, too, then, we find complexity and contradiction within a broad pattern of expansion. The pace of landed expansion in the colony of South Carolina is illustrated in Table 3-5 below, wherein appear estimates of the total number of acres granted in South Carolina, or at least the acres upon which quitrents were due. Such expansion, these data suggest,

Table 3–5. The Expansion of Landholdings in South Carolina

Year	Acres Granted (Cumulative Totals)
1720	1,163,319
1725	1,186,503
1731	1,453,875
1734	1,752,271
1735	2,045,796
1736	2,404,800
1737	2,565,528
1738	2,696,353
1739	2,762,425
1740	2,789,713
1741	2,817,187
1760	3,464,373
1761	3,508,480
1762	3,522,680
1763	3,536,530
1764	3,614,683
1765	3,676,975
1766	3,761,924
1767	3,935,380
1768	4,000,526
1769	4,127,078
1770	4,264,371
1771	4,461,286
1772	4,750,602

Sources: Clowse, *Economic Beginnings in Colonial South Carolina 1670-1730* (Columbia: University of South Carolina Press, 1971), p. 255; Alan D. Watson, "The Quitrent System in Royal South Carolina," *William and Mary Quarterly*, 3d series, 33 (April 1976): 183-211, especially pp. 198, 201, 209. Note that the figures for 1720, 1725, and 1731 are for the number of acres upon which taxes were paid. These figures, thus, should be considered minimum figures for acres granted as of each of these dates. See Watson, pp. 198, 209.

was noteworthy more for its steadiness than its velocity, but beyond that what can we say? Not much, we must admit, and, that, only with difficulty. For the statistical data currently available, like those for population, are fraught with ambiguity. The problem, always the problem in South Carolina history, it seems, is the difference—in this particular case in landholding patterns—between the low country and the backcountry. By focusing solely upon aggregate data, however, this difference cannot be seen. A brief statistical exercise will illustrate this point.

Data presented in Table 3-6 reveal that the man/land ratio or, more precisely, the white man/granted land ratio in South Carolina changed dramatically over time. There were, for example, almost 760 acres of legally granted land for every white wealth-holder in 1720, but only 370 acres per white wealth-holder a half-century later in 1770. Though this drop in and of itself cannot be construed to signify for South Carolina a radical transformation in the structure of economic opportunity such as that purportedly occurring in parts of rural New England in the second half of the eighteenth century—370 acres is, after all, a far cry from the figure of 43 acres per adult male found in Suffolk County, Massachusetts in 1786—could it perhaps denote nonetheless a secular trend toward deconcentration of land ownership in the colony as a whole, a trend which for the grandees of the low country could have marked the beginning of the end?[69]

The tentative answer to this question, extant data indicate, is no. Indeed, in St. John's Berkeley Parish, the only low-country parish thus far studied in depth, George Terry has found that land concentration actually increased a bit during the second half of the eighteenth century, with the great estates remaining largely intact. In 1763, for example, 39 percent of the landholders in the parish owned estates of 500 acres or less and 38 percent of the landholders owned over 1000 acres of land. By 1793, however, only about 23 percent of the landholders owned

Table 3-6. Granted Acreage per White Inhabitant and per White Wealth-holder in South Carolina

Year	Acres Granted	White Inhabitants	White Wealth-holders
1720	1,163,319	6,525	1,532
Acres Granted Per		178.29	759.35
1731	1,453,875	10,000 (1730)	2,347
Acres Granted Per		145.39	619.46
1740	2,789,713	20,000	4,695
Acres Granted Per		139.49	594.19
1760	3,464,373	36,740	8,624
Acres Granted Per		94.29	401.71
1770	4,264,371	49,066	11,518
Acres Granted Per		86.91	370.23

Sources: See Table 3-1 and Table 3-4. Figures for white wealth-holders were derived by dividing figures for white population by 4.26. The divisor is that used by Alice Hanson Jones to derive "free wealth-holders" in the South from figures on "free population." Though there were a small number of free blacks in colonial South Carolina, the free population, for statistical purposes, is essentially the white population. See Jones, *Wealth of a Nation To Be: The American Colonies on the Eve of the Revolution* (New York: Columbia University Press, 1980), p. 42.

less than 500 acres, with almost 49 percent now owning over 1000 acres. In the latter year, in fact, nearly 21 percent of the landholders in the parish owned at least 4000 acres of land! Moreover, since the mean size of landholdings in the low country in the early nineteenth century, according to Mark D. Kaplanoff, was 871 acres—a staggering figure dwarfing those for other parts of the United States at the time—it is difficult realistically or even probabilistically to argue that significant deconcentration had yet occurred in this part of the state.[70] That this situation existed should not much surprise students of South Carolina's early history, for the low country's rice-indigo cycle—halcyon days for the area's elite— was during this period at its apogee. Lands in the low country were bought and sold, of course, in response to changing fortunes, in response to changing needs, but, pending extensive land-record linkage for the state as a whole, it seems fair to suggest that those that would understand the decline over time in acreage per white wealth-holder in eighteenth-century South Carolina should seek their answer further west. For it was in all likelihood the influx into the backcountry of white immigrants of relatively limited means—an influx hastened, one should note, by the colony's liberal headrights policy and the so-called Township scheme—that was primarily responsible for the decline that we have just seen.[71] To be sure, landed expansion proceeded into certain pockets of the low country, into the area's previously-ungranted interstices, but the aggregate trends discernible in Table 3-6 are due for the most part to the settlement of the backcountry by thousands of small farmers and not to any trend toward land deconcentration in the eighteenth-century low country. Thus, to consider either land or population in early South Carolina is to beckon, as it were, both Heraclitus and Parmenides, for amidst aggregate change and flux, we find also a degree of constancy.

There was, however, nothing constant about total output in the colony. Indeed, so far as we are able to determine, output in South Carolina expanded at relatively high rates during most decades of the seventeenth and eighteenth centuries and at a high rate for the colonial period as a whole. All statements about colonial output, of course, must be regarded warily, for they all are based upon extrapolations of one sort or another, most commonly upon extrapolations from presumed export/output or capital/output ratios. Moreover, because such ratios change over time in the real world, if not always in the academy, and because such changes are, in fact, often unfaithful to the economist's beloved assumption of linearity, the tentative nature of all statements based upon extrapolation is further accentuated, the measure of uncertainty increased.[72] In this respect, the statements that follow about output in colonial South Carolina are in no way exceptional.

Data on output in seventeenth-century South Carolina are particularly slight. Those with which we must work, exasperatingly curt remarks on exports, for example, do suggest, however, that output did indeed grow. To determine the rate of economic expansion solely from scattered snippets on exports—we know, among other things, that four tons of beef and pork were exported to Barbados in 1679, that the total value of exports from the colony was about £2000 sterling in 1687, and that six or seven shiploads of beef and pork were exported from South Carolina in 1690—is clearly impossible, but because we also know the approximate rate at which population grew during the period we can hazard a

guess that the rate of expansion of total output was roughly comparable.[73] In fact, if South Carolina's experience was anything like the experience of British colonies in other parts of seventeenth-century America, the colonies in New England, the Chesapeake region, and the West Indies in particular, it is not inconceivable that output may even have expanded by a slightly greater amount than that which can be attributed to population growth alone.[74] The South Carolina economy, in other words, not only expanded in the seventeenth century, but also may have grown. Though much more work obviously is needed, enough data can be adduced—slaves in increasing numbers, greater stocks of capital, greater personal wealth in general among inventoried decedents, and increasingly close scrutiny by the Crown—to suggest that the supposition that growth occurred in seventeenth-century South Carolina may well be true.[75]

The imprecision which has plagued our discussion of aggregate output in South Carolina thus far becomes less troublesome as we approach the turn of the seventeenth century. From 1697 to the eve of the American Revolution, economic data are sufficient to allow us to estimate output with greater confidence and with far greater accuracy. That data become both more abundant and more reliable over time is due largely to the fact that once factoral proportions in South Carolina and, indeed, other parts of America changed enough to allow efficient production of articles of value to the metropolis, the Crown became quite interested in trade statistics and, *mirabile dictu*, the political arithmeticians charged with compiling such statistics became in their computations more exact. There exist today for this reason a number of excellent eighteenth-century trade series for both the colonies and Great Britain. Such series are not without problems, it is true, but to those that wish to understand the expansion of aggregate output in the colonies, they are nonetheless extremely helpful.[76] For few colonies are such series so helpful, though, as for South Carolina, a colony which not only was closely tied to the metropolis in terms of trade, but one which during the eighteenth century apparently had a very high export/output ratio. Thus, for South Carolina, statistics on bilateral trade with England necessarily weigh heavily in any estimation of the rate at which aggregate output grew.[77]

Estimates of the mean "official" value and the mean "official" value per capita of South Carolina's trade with England at various points in the eighteenth century, therefore, are presented in tables 3-7 and 3-8.[78] Compound growth rates for South Carolina's export and import trades with England appear in Table 3-9. The calculation of these rates and estimates entailed first of all the estimation of the proportionate share held by South Carolina of the total trade of North Carolina and South Carolina with England, for in the British trade statistics used in the construction of these tables, no further anatomization than "Carolina" is to be found. Fortunately, sufficient data exist elsewhere for us to gauge in a rough way the North Carolina–South Carolina breakdown.[79]

As tables 3-7 through 3-9 show clearly, the aggregate value of South Carolina's export and import trades with England grew substantially over the course of the eighteenth century. South Carolina's exports to England expanded especially rapidly in the period between 1700 and 1740 and during the decade of the 1760s, with the colony's exports to the metropolis stagnating, indeed, even declining

Table 3–7. "Official" Value of "Carolina" and South Carolina Exports to England (£ sterling)

Period	"Carolina" Mean Annual Exports	SC % of Total Exports	SC Mean Annual Exports	SC Total Pop.	SC White Pop.
1698–1702	£ 12,898.6	90	£ 11,608.74	5,704 (1700)	3,260 (1700)
P.C. Exports				£2.035	£3.561
1708–1712	18,765.8	90	16,889.22	10,883 (1710)	5,115 (1710)
P.C. Exports				£1.552	£3.302
1718–1722	60,200.4	90	54,180.36	18,393 (1720)	6,525 (1720)
P.C. Exports				£2.946	£8.303
1728–1732	128,444.2	90	115,599.78	30,000 (1730)	10,000 (1730)
P.C. Exports				£3.853	£11.560
1738–1742	207,061.6	90	186,355.44	59,155 (1740)	20,000 (1740)
P.C. Exports				£3.150	£9.318
1748–1752	208,633.2	90	187,769.88	65,000 (1750)	25,000 (1750)
P.C. Exports				£2.889	£7.511
1758–1762	190,902.2	90	171,811.98	89,740 (1760)	36,740 (1760)
P.C. Exports				£1.914	£4.676
1768–1772	404,072.6	85	343,461.71	124,244 (1770)	49,066 (1770)
P.C. Exports				£2.764	£7.00

Sources: Historical Statistics of the United States, 2: 1168, 1176–77; Table 3–1 . Aso see footnotes 78 and 79 of this chapter.

during the war-torn decades of the 1740s and 1750s. Imports from England rose more steadily in value over time, with rates of expansion relatively robust in most decades of the 1700–1770 period and for this seventy-year period as a whole. Only during the 1710s and 1740s, these data indicate, could the rates at which imports expanded in value be characterized as slow.

Certain problems emerge, however, when we attempt to measure and explain changes over time in the per capita rather than aggregate value of South Carolina's trade with England. This situation exists not so much because the task of measurement in this case is one of unusual difficulty, but because the term "per capita" is ambiguous and thus can be used in several different ways. Whether we conclude that the per capita value of South Carolina's trade with England was

Table 3–8. "Official" Value of "Carolina" and South Carolina Imports from England (£ sterling)

Period	"Carolina" Mean Annual Imports	SC % of Total Imports	SC Mean Annual Imports	SC Total Pop.	SC White Pop.
1698–1702	£ 13,046.8	90	£ 11,742.12	5,704 (1700)	3,260 (1700)
P.C. Imports				£2.059	£3.602
1708–1712	20,110.2	90	18,099.18	10,883 (1710)	5,115 (1710)
P.C. Imports				£1.663	£3.538
1718–1722	21,167.6	90	19,050.84	18,393 (1720)	6,525 (1720)
P.C. Imports				£1.036	£2.920
1728–1732	57,132.2	90	51,418.98	30,000 (1730)	10,000 (1730)
P.C. Imports				£1.714	£5.142
1738–1742	139,178.4	90	125,260.56	59,155 (1740)	20,000 (1740)
P.C. Imports				£2.117	£6.263
1748–1752	149,263	90	134,336.7	65,000 (1750)	25,000 (1750)
P.C. Imports				£2.067	£5.373
1758–1762	212,629	90	191,366.1	89,740 (1760)	36,740 (1760)
P.C. Imports				£2.132	£5.209
1768–1772	320,304	85	272,258.4	124,244 (1770)	49,066 (1770)
P.C. Imports				£2.191	£5.549

Sources: Historical Statistics of the United States, 2: 1168, 1176–77; Table 3–1. Also see footnotes 78 and 79 of this chapter.

growing slowly, moderately, or rapidly over the course of the eighteenth century depends largely upon whether we use "per capita" to denote the total population of South Carolina, the white population of the colony, or only the white population of the low country. If we use the total population of South Carolina in our calculations, data in tables 3-7 and 3-8 show that the per capita value of both exports and imports fluctuated between individual decades, but grew slowly over the 1700–1770 period as a whole. If, however, we include only the white population of the colony in our calculations—colonial economic historians have probably used this definition of per capita more commonly than they have the others when dealing with South Carolina—we find, of course, both higher per capita values for each ten-year bench mark and a faster growth rate for the entire 1700–1770 period than

Table 3–9. Annual Compound Growth Rates of South Carolina's Exports to and Imports from England (£ sterling, "Official" Values)

Period	SC Exports Annual Mean	Growth Rate Compounded Annually	SC Imports Annual Mean	Growth Rate Compounded Annually
1698–1702	£ 11,608.74		£ 11,742.12	
		3.8		4.4
1708–1712	16,889.22		18,099.18	
		12.4		0.5
1718–1722	54,180.36		19,050.84	
		7.9		10.4
1728–1732	115,599.78		51,418.98	
		4.9		9.3
1738–1742	186,355.44		125,260.56	
		0.1		0.7
1748–1752	187,769.88		134,336.70	
		−0.9		5.6
1758–1762	171,811.98		191,366.10	
		7.2		3.6
1768–1772	343,461.71		272,258.40	
1700–1770		5.0		4.6

Sources: See Tables 3–7 and 3–8.

we did when using per capita to denote the total population of South Carolina, both white and black, free and chattel.[80] Once again, let us refer back to tables 3-7 and 3-8. When utilizing the second definition of the term "per capita," it is important to note, a curious statistical pattern comes into view. Per capita values for both exports and imports peak not at the end of the colonial period but much earlier, the former in 1730, the latter in 1740. Does this contravene the traditional notion that the golden age of the South Carolina economy was the period just prior to the Revolution? Well, yes and no.

While it is true that the value of exports and imports per white inhabitant in South Carolina did indeed peak in 1730 and 1740 respectively, such a summary statement masks regional variation in trade patterns within the colony. In so doing, it conceals vast differences between the low country and the backcountry. As we have argued at some length earlier in this chapter, aggregate data for the colony of South Carolina must be used carefully once backcountry settlement gained momentum, that is to say, after the middle of the eighteenth century. For the task of "breaking" the frontier in the backcountry claimed for a considerable period of time economic resources that were being utilized in the low country in contrast to produce rice and indigo for the metropolis to exchange, as it were, for spices and silver serving sets, for broadcloth, fustian and felt hats, for metalware of all types and kinds, and an occasional mahogany highboy perhaps. The low country, in other words, was integrated far more completely into the Atlantic economy during the late colonial period than was the Carolina backcountry, a point the following exercise in statistical disaggregation will bear out.

South Carolina's total white population in 1770, we have seen, was 49,066; of this total, about 30,000 lived in the backcountry. South Carolina's leading

exports to England in the late colonial period—rice, indigo, deerskins, and forest products—were, with the exception of perhaps 10 percent of the indigo, controlled almost entirely, however, by low-country whites.[81] Indeed, the low country's proportionate share of the total value of South Carolina's exports to England in the late colonial period was probably somewhere around 95 percent. Let us assume, *faute de mieux*, that 95 percent of the colony's imports from England, measured by value, were controlled by low-country whites as well. We can now recalculate the data for 1768–72 in tables 3-7 and 3-8, so that we can evaluate the relative importance for the low country and the backcountry respectively of bilateral trade with the metropolis. This recalculation follows in Table 3-10 below. The differential importance of trade with England for each area is striking. Moreover, by disaggregating our statistical data on foreign trade we can make better sense of South Carolina's economic history. For we are now able to link trends in white per capita exports and imports prior to 1750—which trends refer essentially to whites in the low country—with disaggregated figures for low-country whites in 1770. Thus, whereas the mean value of white per capita exports to England in 1730 was about £11.5 sterling, we now can see that the per capita figure for whites living in the same general area did not decline in the late colonial period, but rather grew to over £17 sterling by 1770. Each of these figures by the way dwarfs estimates for 1768–72 of the value of overseas exports—total overseas exports and not just those to England—per white inhabitant in any of the other mainland colonies.[82] Disaggregation, thus, has enabled us, I believe, not only to establish more clearly the long-term continuities in the low country's economic history but also to focus more closely upon the extraordinarily high value of white per capita exports and imports in the area, a key factor in the low country's eighteenth-century prosperity, one with which we shall deal later in the chapter.

Before going any further in our discussion of South Carolina's early-modern economic expansion, it should be mentioned that, as time passed, the colony

Table 3–10. Per Capita Exports to and Imports from England—South Carolina Low Country and Backcountry, 1768–1772 (£ sterling, "Official" values)

	Mean Annual Exports 1768–1772	Total Population (1770)	White Population (1770)
Low Country	£326,288.62	88,244	19,066
per capita		£3.70	£17.11
Backcountry	£ 17,173.08	36,000	30,000
per capita		£0.48	£ 0.57
	Mean Annual Imports 1768–1772		
Low Country	£258,645.48	88,244	19,066
per capita		£2.93	£13.57
Backcountry	£ 13,612.92	36,000	30,000
per capita		£0.38	£ 0.45

grew more important to the Crown in relative terms as well. The growing relative importance of South Carolina to the Crown can be seen readily in Table 3-11, wherein are presented data on the relative shares of "Carolina"—both North Carolina and South Carolina—and South Carolina individually in the overall export and import trades between England and the continental colonies from Georgia to Maine. That South Carolina's share of the total value of exports from the mainland colonies to England grew from less than 4 percent at the turn of the seventeenth century to just under 29 percent in 1770 is important to note, as is the fact that the colony's relative share of total continental imports from England over this seventy-year period grew far less dramatically. This statistical oddity, though in itself of limited causal significance, reflected, as we shall see, both South

Table 3-11. "Carolina's," South Carolina's, and the South Carolina Low Country's Shares of American Colonies'* Exports to and Imports from England (Annual Mean) (£ sterling, "Official" values)

Period	Exports	%	Imports	%
1698–1702	£ 304,279		£ 347,337.4	
Carolina	12,898.6	4.24	13,046.8	3.76
SC (85%)	11,608.74	3.81	11,742.12	3.38
1708–1712	310,290.4		282,151	
Carolina	18,765.8	6.05	20,110.2	7.13
SC (90%)	16,889.22	5.44	18,099.18	6.41
1718–1722	464,056		378,933	
Carolina	60,200.4	12.97	21,167.6	5.59
SC (90%)	54,180.36	11.67	19,050.84	5.03
1728–1732	584,618		509,039.6	
Carolina	128,444.2	21.97	57,132.2	11.22
SC (90%)	115,599.78	19.77	51,418.98	10.10
1738–1742	732,884.4		789,213	
Carolina	207,061.6	28.25	139,178.4	17.63
SC (90%)	186,355.44	25.43	125,260.56	15.87
1748–1752	806,950.2		1,151,039.4	
Carolina	208,633.2	25.85	149,263	12.97
SC (90%)	187,769.88	23.27	134,336.7	11.67
1758–1762	732,450.4		1,939,868.4	
Carolina	190,902.2	26.06	212,629	10.96
SC (90%)	171,811.98	23.46	191,366.1	9.86
1768–1772	1,185,110		2,526,803.6	
Carolina	404,072.6	34.10	320,304	12.68
SC (85%)	343,461.71	28.98	272,258.4	10.77
1768–1772 SC Low Country (95% of SC)	326,288.62	27.53	258,645.48	10.24

Source: *Historical Statistics of the United States*, 2: 1176. Also see footnote 79 of this chapter.

*New England, New York, Pennsylvania, Virginia and Maryland, Carolina, Georgia are the overall designations used.

Carolina's growing economic strength and the colony's increasing socioeconomic asymmetry.[83]

We have concentrated thus far, quite properly I believe, on South Carolina's bilateral trade with England. Indeed, available data suggest that this trade alone accounted for most of South Carolina's total foreign trade by the late colonial period. Closely bound to England by ties of trade, South Carolina, it seems, conformed almost perfectly to the mercantilist conception of the ideal colony, that is, one which complemented rather than competed with the metropolis, one dependent upon rather than subversive of metropolitan political and economic power. Yet even in this prototypical dependency, roughly a quarter of total overseas trade was carried on, not directly with the metropolis, but with other nations or other overseas colonies.[84] Furthermore, coastal trade, which we shall define as trade conducted with the British colonies on the North American mainland, was not unimportant, reaching a level of magnitude equal to perhaps 10 percent of the colony's total overseas trade by the end of the colonial period.[85] South Carolina's total export trade, measured in official value, thus, probably exceeded £500,000 yearly by the late colonial period or at least between 1768 and 1772.[86] Despite certain differences in the composition of South Carolina's export trade to various geographical areas—differences that might have given the backcountry a slightly greater share of South Carolina's total export trade than it had of the colony's trade to England alone—it seems fair to say nonetheless that if the official value of low-country exports to England alone came to over £17 sterling per white inhabitant in 1770 and if exports to England constituted less than 70 percent of South Carolina's total export trade, then the value per white inhabitant of the low country's total export trade must have exceeded £20. That the value of exports per white inhabitant of the low country was over £20 sterling annually in the late colonial period is remarkable, for this figure, so far as we know, exceeded white per capita income in most other parts of British North America at that time.[87] Even after allowing for the fact that the export/output ratio in the low country probably was higher than in other parts of North America—perhaps .25 to .30 in the low country rather than .15 to .20 for the colonies as a whole—and for the fact that much of the output was the result of the labor of Negro slaves, we are left with the impression that the whites of the low country had a very large output indeed under their control. As we shall see later in the chapter, data on wealth in the low country—data drawn from probate inventories of estates, that is, from completely different sources—confirm that the impression about output alluded to above is highly accurate.[88]

Exports, then, constituted a major component of total output in colonial South Carolina. Moreover, in terms of the categories used in national income accounting, we know far more about this component of output than we do about private consumption and investment or governmental expenditures. That the composition of South Carolina's exports changed over time, increasingly moving away from extractive products and toward one or two plantation staples, we have already seen. We shall attempt in the section below, however, to analyze more closely South Carolina's export sector in order to focus attention upon the commodities

associated with the low country's eighteenth-century economic rise and, alas, with the area's later economic undoing.

Through the labors of many fine economic historians over the years, we now have a reasonably good picture of South Carolina's export trade in the eighteenth century.[89] If certain details still are unclear and if gaps remain for a number of years, about overall export patterns in eighteenth-century South Carolina we nonetheless know a great deal. South Carolina, available data show, exported a wide range of commodities—almost all of which would be considered primary in nature—during the colonial period. Such data also reveal a contrary trend; a few commodities—rice, deerskins, tar, pitch, and, by the middle of the eighteenth century, indigo—totally dominated the colony's export trade, generally constituting 80 to 90 percent or even more of its total value. Indeed, during the late colonial period, rice and indigo alone, the keys to the kingdom, as it were, constituted about 75 percent of South Carolina's export trade in terms of value. Both of these trends—the varied nature of South Carolina's exports and the rise of rice and, later, indigo—are apparent in tables 3-12 through 3-15. Utilizing export data originally compiled by South Carolina Lieutenant-Governor James Glen, in Table 3-12 we have broken down in elaborate detail the Charleston export trade for one year, the period from November 1, 1747 to November 1, 1748. [90] In tables 3-13 through 3-15 we provide statistical data delineating the increase in the exportation of rice and indigo from South Carolina over the course of the eighteenth century. Note that alternative figures for 1768–72 are provided in tables 3-13 and 3-15. These figures represent estimations of per capita exports of rice and indigo from the South Carolina low country alone. Note, too, the degree to which the data in tables 3-13 through 3-15 on the expansion of the rice and indigo export industries correspond with the data presented earlier on the aggregate expansion of the South Carolina economy. It was, it seems, to the tune played by rice and indigo that the South Carolina economy danced, and, as we shall see below, because of this tune that the whites of the low country—a people renowned for their love of music—saw their wealth in the eighteenth century greatly enhanced.[91]

To the economist, exports and output, topics with which we have just dealt, are considered flow concepts, denoting flows of commodities or money over a given period of time. Wealth, however, generally is not considered a flow or stream, but rather a stock, that is, an accumulated supply of resources, tangible and intangible, that have market value. Though wealth is not itself a flow, it is, ironically, a reflection of past output flows and is largely responsible for determining the size of future output flows. Wealth and output, stock and flow, are thus separate in theory, but in practice are inextricably bound.

South Carolina was born of European wealth. Youth was an economically awkward and painful time for the colony, however, and from the colony's initial stock, further wealth did not rapidly accrue. So long as South Carolina's output was dominated by primitive extraction, plunder, and windfalls rather than by more intensive activities, the output stream would remain weak and intermittent and thus incapable of generating the continuous power necessary for sustained wealth accumulation to take place. Not until the 1690s or even the first decade of the eighteenth century did this stream discharge with sufficient strength and regularity

to sustain such accumulation, for the production of rice and naval stores had by this time both swelled and routinized the flow. As the eighteenth century progressed, of course, the stream began to surge, particularly after mid-century when the economic activities mentioned above were supplemented by the production of indigo. As per capita output in the South Carolina low country advanced, white per capita wealth followed suit. Indeed, by the eve of the American Revolution, this stream had left to the white inhabitants of the low country, speaking figuratively of course, sediments of gold. Though the stream would later become a maelstrom, in the eighteenth century it flowed strong and true.

That the sequence described above actually occurred can be demonstrated in a variety of ways. One can, for example, analyze—as we did in the introduction to this study—change over time in the representative architecture of the low country.[92] Surely, eighteenth-century forms, particularly those of the so-called golden age, suggest that the white inhabitants of the low country had greater wealth at their disposal in, let us say, 1765 than they had in 1680. One need not rely, however, on the gentle voice of architecture alone. For changes over time in other artifact patterns offer more insistent evidence thereto. Indeed, it is well known that goods associated with rising wealth levels in the early modern period—imported ceramics, paintings, books, clocks, and glassware, to name but a few—were increasingly common in the low country as time passed. Such "impressionistic" evidence notwithstanding, economic historians, perhaps exhibiting undue caution, have generally desired more. We shall therefore relegate such evidence to corroborative status in the discussion of wealth that follows below and bring "harder" data—data culled from probate inventories of estates—to the fore.[93]

Quantitative data on wealth, like those on output, are scarce for South Carolina's early history. The best sources of such data for the colonial period, probate inventories of estates, do not appear with any regularity before 1722.[94] One can, however, get some idea about wealth-holding patterns in early South Carolina by extracting data from the sixty-two scattered inventories that still exist for the period from 1670 to 1721. Though the representativeness of these early inventories cannot be ascertained, the data contained within them are consistent, one should note, with both data on exports and output from the same period and with data on wealth drawn from inventories from the 1722–76 period, a period in which inventories are in great supply.

Data drawn from these early inventories indicate that some accumulation probably did take place during the first half-century of South Carolina's history. The figure for mean personal wealth, for example, for the thirty-four decedents from the 1670–94 period for whom inventories still exist is £229.71 sterling. The mean figure for the twenty-eight decedents from the 1695–1721 period for whom we have inventories is, however, somewhat higher, £297.61 sterling.[95] Obviously, one should not exaggerate the importance of these findings; they are significative rather than determinative, indeed, intentionally so. With a data base so small and scattered, further analysis, I believe, simply would not do. The mean wealth of the white inhabitants of South Carolina, sixty-two surviving inventories suggest, probably increased somewhat during the first fifty years of the colony's history. That is what we know.

Table 3–12. Charleston, S.C. Exports November 1, 1747–November 1, 1748

Commodity Exported	Amount of Value in S.C. Currency (nearest £)	Percentage of Total Export Value
Rice	£618,750	54.78
Indian Corn	19,654	1.74
Barley	75	
Oranges	1,776	
Peas	3,053	
Potatoes	175	
Onions	75	
Bullocks	308	
Hogs	450	
Sundries	500	
Beef	11,466	1.01
Pork	31,140	2.76
Bacon	275	
Butter	1,040	
Pitch	12,422	1.10
Common Tar	4,872	
Green Tar	727	
Turpentine	5,992	
Rosin	242	
Masts	135	
Bolt-Sprits	48	
Booms	60	
Oars	50	
Indigo	117,353	10.39
Potash	60	
Turpentine Oil	195	
Cotton-wool	175	
Sassafras	330	
Boards	2,458	
Cedar Boards	491	
Cedar Plank	665	
Cedar Posts	26	
Cypress Boards	840	
Cypress Boards	612	
Pine Boards	558	
Pine Boards	3,830	
Pine Boards	5,929	
Pine Boards	388	
Pine Planks	16	
Baywood Planks	294	
Scantling	70	
Shingles	2,547	
Staves	3,977	
Timber	218	
Walnut	154	
Casks	347	
Hoops	36	

Table 3–12. Charleston, S.C. Exports November 1, 1747–November 1, 1748 (cont.)

Commodity Exported	Amount of Value in S.C. Currency (nearest £)	Percentage of Total Export Value
Canes	16	
Pumps	18	
Beaver Skins	300	
Calf Skins	282	
Deer Skins	252,000	22.31
Tallow	810	
Hogs Lard	514	
Silk–raw	1,600	
Bees Wax	250	
Myrtle Wax	175	
Leather–tanned	18,123	1.60
Soap	70	
Candles	510	
Bricks	35	

£1,129,557*
or £161,365 sterling (at 7 to 1)

Top Ten Exports

Commodity Exported	Amount of Value in S.C. Currency (nearest £)	Percentage of Total Export Value
Rice	£ 618,750	54.78
Deer Skins	252,000	22.31
Indigo	117,353	10.39
Pork	31,140	2.76
Naval Stores**	24,548	2.17
Lumber Products***	23,490	2.08
Indian Corn	19,654	1.74
Leather–tanned	18,123	1.60
Beef	11,466	1.01
Peas	3,053	0.27
	£1,119,577	99.12%

*Actual total is £1,129,561–6s. in Glen's *Description*; the total above differs slightly because the value of each commodity has been rounded to the nearest pound.
**Naval Stores
  –Pitch, Common Tar, Green Tar, Turpentine, Rosin = £24,255 or 2.15%
  –Masts, Bolt-Sprits, Booms, Oars = £293 more or £24,258 or 2.17%
***Lumber Products
  –Planks, Boards, Scantling, Shingles, Staves, Hoops, Casks, Posts, etc. = £23,490 or 2.08%

Source: "An Account of the Several Species and Quantities of Commodities of the Produce of South-Carolina, which were exported from thence at the Port of Charles-Town, in One Year, from 1st November 1747 to 1st November 1748; together with the Rate and Amount of the Value of each, in Sterling Money and in South Carolina Currency," in James Glen, *A Description of South Carolina. . .* (London: R. and J. Dodsley, 1761), pp. 50–55.

Note: Table 3–12 refers *only* to produce of South Carolina exported, for Glen lists re-exports of non-South Carolina produce on pp. 56–58.

Table 3–13. Pounds of Rice Exported per Capita, South Carolina, 1698-1772

Period	Annual Average Exports (Pounds)	Total S.C. Population	Est. White Population	Est. Black Population
1698–1702	268,602	5,704 (1700)	3,260 (1700)	2,444 (1700)
	Lbs. Per Capita	47.09	82.39	109.90
1708–1713 (1712 missing)	1,763,790	10,883 (1710)	5,115 (1710)	5,768 (1710)
	Lbs. Per Capita	162.07	344.83	305.79
1718–1722	6,227,918	18,393 (1720)	6,525 (1720)	11,868 (1720)
	Lbs. Per Capita	338.60	954.47	524.77
1728–1732	16,905,652	30,000 (1730)	10,000 (1730)	20,000 (1730)
	Lbs. Per Capita	563.52	1690.56	845.28
1738–1742	30,547,455	59,155 (1740)	20,000 (1740)	39,155 (1740)
	Lbs. Per Capita	516.40	1527.37	780.17
1748–1752	30,285,618	65,000 (1750)	25,000 (1750)	40,000 (1750)
	Lbs. Per Capita	465.93	1211.42	757.14
1758–1762	39,903,255	89,740 (1760)	36,740 (1760)	53,000 (1760)
	Lbs. Per Capita	444.65	1086.10	752.89
1768–1772	66,327,975	124,244 (1770)	49,066 (1770)	75,178 (1770)
	Lbs. Per Capita	533.85	1351.81	882.28

Alternative 1768–1772 figures using low-country population only

Period	Annual Average Exports (Pounds)	Total Low-Country Population	Est. White Population	Est. Black Population
1768–1772	66,327,975	88,244	19,066	69,178
	Lbs. Per Capita	751.64	3,478.86	958.80

Sources: Table 3-1; *Historical Statistics of the United States,* 2: 1192.

We can, however, say much more about wealth-holding patterns in South Carolina from 1722 until the Revolution. Probate inventories of estates for this period are abundant, reliable, and apparently fairly representative, at least with a qualification or two. The great majority of the inventories, even after 1750, are for low-country decedents.[96] This being the case, generalizations drawn from such sources must be carefully delimited; in no way, for example, do they apply to the white population that lived beyond the fall line. Moreover, wealth data drawn

Table 3–14. South Carolina Rice Exports, Annual Compound Growth Rates, 1700–1770

Period	Annual Average Exports (Pounds)	Annual Compound Growth Rate (%)
1698–1702	268,602	
		20.7%
1708–1713 (1712 missing)	1,763,790	
		13.4
1718–1722	6,227,918	
		10.5
1728–1732	16,905,652	
		6.1
1738–1742	30,547,455	
		− 0.1
1748–1752	30,285,618	
		2.8
1758–1762	30,903,255	
		5.2
1768–1772	66,327,975	
1700–1770		8.2

Source: Historical Statistics of the United States, 2: 1192.

from probate records do not faithfully depict wealth patterns among all decedents, much less wealth patterns for the living population as a whole. Numerous studies have shown that such data overstate the actual wealth levels of any given society, because "probate-type" decedents tend to be somewhat wealthier than those who died without inventories being taken, and both older and wealthier than a society's average wealth-holder. Though others have attempted to correct for such inherent biases in probate records by calculating ratios and weights with which to adjust downward wealth data taken from inventories so that they better approximate wealth levels of the living population at any given time—in her wealth estimates for the pre-Revolutionary South, for example, Alice Hanson Jones has used a weight (multiplier) of 0.76 to convert figures on wealth for "probate-types" to figures for "all wealth-holders"—no "corrections" have been made in the wealth data presented below. So little is known as yet about the age-structure of the white population of the low country and about changes in the age-structure of this population over time that to attach precise weights to our data on the wealth of inventoried decedents would be to obfuscate rather than to clarify. Better at this time, I believe, merely to say that the wealth figures presented here are probably a little high in relation to the white living population of the low country at any given time.[97]

It is, of course, no longer unusual, even for historians of the lower South, to use probate records to shed light on matters social and economic. Indeed, a number of scholars already have used probate records in a systematic manner to assemble series on wealth levels and wealth distribution in eighteenth-century South Carolina. In addition to the pioneering studies by established scholars such as Jackson Turner

Table 3–15. Pounds of Indigo Exported per Capita, South Carolina, 1748–1775

Period	Annual Average Exports (Pounds)	Total S.C. Population	Est. White Population	Est. Black Population
1748–52	57,460	65,000 (1750)	25,000 (1750)	40,000 (1750)
	Lbs. Per Capita	0.88	2.30	1.44
1758–62	481,140	89,740 (1760)	36,740 (1760)	53,000 (1760)
	Lbs. Per Capita	5.36	13.10	9.08
1768–72	561,340[1]	124,244 (1770)	49,066 (1770)	75,178 (1770)
	Lbs. Per Capita	4.52	11.44	7.47
1775	1,122,200[2]	152,122[3]	66,033[3]	86,089[3]
	Lbs. Per Capita	7.38	16.99	13.03

Alternative 1768–72 figures using low-country estimated exports and population

1768–72	Annual Average Exports (Pounds)[4]	Total Low-Country Population		
	505,206	88,244	19,066	69,178
	Lbs. per Capita	5.72	26.50	7.30

Sources: Table 3-1; *Historical Statistics of the United States*, 2: 1189.

[1]Includes 196 casks not tallied in *Historical Statistics of the United States* for 1768 and 302 casks not tallied for 1772. I assumed casks contained 350 pounds of indigo. Five untallied "boxes" for 1772 are not included.

[2]For 6½ months ending February 24, 1775.

[3]1775 population estimates were made by linear interpolation from population estimates for 1770 and 1780 in Table 3-1. No attempt has been made to compute logarithmically because of disruptions/dislocations in trend occasioned by the American Revolution.

[4]Note that in this estimate of low-country indigo exports in the 1768–72 period, I have assumed that 10 percent of the indigo exported from South Carolina in that period was grown in the backcountry.

Main and Alice Hanson Jones, the work of younger scholars in recent years—Richard Waterhouse, William Bentley, and George Terry in particular—has greatly enhanced our understanding of wealth-holding patterns in the colony.[98] In the discussion of wealth that follows below I shall utilize data collected by these scholars in combination with data of my own in order to enhance our understanding not only of wealth-holding patterns in the low country but also of the rate at which wealth was being accumulated in the area and of the relationship among wealth, output, and economic growth.

Let us begin with some basic figures on mean and median personal wealth in the low country. William Bentley has compiled such data for the forty-one year period from 1722 to 1762; his findings, which are based upon 2209 inventories of estates, are presented in Table 3-16. By utilizing John J. McCusker's findings on international exchange rates in the eighteenth century, we can convert Bentley's figures on mean personal wealth, which are given in South Carolina currency, into more readily comparable sterling figures. Such conversions are made in Table 3-17.[99]

Table 3–16. Mean and Median Personal Wealth of White Inventoried Decedents, South Carolina, 1722–1762 (£ S.C. currency)

Period	Observations	Mean	Median
1722–26	183	£2730	£1070
1727–31	167	2632	1610
1732–36	196	3090	1425
1737–41	197	3238	1450
1742–46	401	4060	2010
1747–51	177	5155	2080
1752–56	407	5405	2230
1757–62	481	6039	2160

Source: Bentley, "Wealth Distribution in Colonial South Carolina," pp. 34, 40, 48, 53, 59, 64, 69, 74.

Personal wealth, Bentley's data indicate, grew at a rapid rate in South Carolina during the eighteenth century, increasing from a mean figure of about £417 sterling between 1722 and 1726 to about £863 sterling between 1757 and 1762. Despite lackluster returns for two quinquennia, the annual compound rate at which mean personal wealth grew during this period as a whole was 2.2 percent when calculated in terms of local currency and 2.0 when calculated in sterling.[100] Such rates, by early modern standards, were phenomenal. Moreover, the gains in wealth were for the most part real and not merely nominal; prices both in South Carolina and England, so far as we can tell, rose much more slowly during this period than Bentley's figures for mean personal wealth.[101]

Though Bentley's wealth data are not broken down at the local level, other data suggest that white personal wealth was rising both in town and country. This can be seen in tables 3-18 and 3-19, wherein appear data illustrating changes over time in a rural parish, St. John's Berkeley, and in Charleston, South Carolina's primate city. If the data in these tables are at all reliable, it seems likely that personal wealth levels were rising during the eighteenth century for the white population of the low country in general.

Table 3–17. Mean Personal Wealth of White Inventoried Decedents, South Carolina, 1722–1762 (£ S.C. currency and £ sterling)

Period	Mean S.C. Currency	McCusker's Currency/Sterling Ratio	Mean £ Sterling
1722–26	£2730	6.55	£416.79
1727–31	2632	6.89	382.00
1732–36	3090	7.09	435.82
1737–41	3238	7.61	425.49
1742–46	4060	7.00	580.00
1747–51	5155	7.30	706.16
1752–56	5405	7.03	768.85
1757–62	6039	7.00	862.71

Sources: Table 3–16; McCusker, *Money and Exchange*, pp. 222–24.

Table 3–18. Distribution of Personal Wealth, St. John's Berkeley Parish, 1720-1779

Estate Value	Percentage of Estates in Each Category		
(£ S.C. Currency)	1720–1739	1740–1759	1760–1779
0–100	2.6	3.1	0.0
101–250	10.2	7.3	0.0
251–500	10.2	4.2	7.7
501–1,000	12.8	9.3	5.8
1,001–2,500	28.2	14.6	17.3
2,501–5,000	25.6	12.5	15.4
5,001–10,000	7.7	24.9	25.0
Over 10,000	2.6	25.0	28.0

Sources: Terry, " 'Champaign Country,' " p. 283. Note the Terry's data refer to the personal wealth of white inventoried decedents. One can get a rough idea of the value of these estates in sterling by dividing the currency figures above by seven. For more precise estimates of sterling values, however, see McCusker, *Money and Exchange*, pp. 222–24.

Before going any further in our discussion of white wealth-holding patterns in the South Carolina low country, we must come to grips with a problem relating to one particular component of personal wealth, that being the component made up of human property. Although property in slaves certainly was recognized and arguably was indispensable in the low country in the eighteenth century, many economists today believe that estimates of real wealth in early modern societies suffer when the value of human property is included in the calculations. Such economists, following Mill, often argue that since the real wealth of a given society, *ceteris paribus*, remains the same regardless of the legal status of the labor force, it is illogical to include the value of slaves in wealth estimates when the value of free labor routinely is omitted.[102]

There is, I believe, considerable merit and, indeed, logic to this position, especially if one is interested in addressing comparative questions about regional or national wealth in free and slave societies respectively. For other questions,

Table 3–19. Distribution of Personal Wealth, Charleston, 1722–1732 and 1763–1788

Estate Value	Percentage of Estates in Each Category	
(£ sterling)	1722–1732	1763–1788
0–100	51.59	26
100–199	8.73	13
200–499	19.05	23
500–999	14.29	10
1000–2000	3.97	9
Over 2000	2.38	19

Sources: Books A–I and Charleston County Inventories 1732–1736, Records of the Secretary of State, Miscellaneous Records, Main Series, South Carolina Department of Archives and History; Jackson Turner Main, *The Social Structure of Revolutionary America* (Princeton: Princeton University Press, 1965), p. 59 fn. 13. Note that these data refer to the personal wealth of white inventoried decedents. Note, too, that Main's data for the late eighteenth century are actually from 1763 to 1768 and 1783 to 1788.

particularly to those relating to the economic dynamics of a single slave society or to the relative power of a class or caste within such a society, the rationale for omitting slave wealth from calculations of total wealth is less compelling. Indeed, one cannot sever slave wealth from other forms of wealth in a slave society without paying a severe interpretive price. For such a society was what it was in large part because its labor force was bound. There was a certain economic logic at work in slave societies which informed production, consumption, and investment decisions. This logic was founded first and foremost upon the capitalization of labor, however alien and distasteful this may seem to the modern mind. Efforts to analyze wealth in slave societies by using classical and neoclassical economic criteria are often illuminating to be sure, but they must be supplemented by analyses that respect the criteria of a world we long have left behind. Thus, in the discussion that follows data on both total wealth and total nonhuman wealth will be presented.

First, however, a few points on method. The figures on mean personal wealth presented in the tables above incorporate the value of wealth in slaves. Fortunately for our purposes, William Bentley compiled data on the percentage of mean personal wealth that slave wealth constituted between 1722 and 1762. Such percentage figures appear in Table 3-20.

With these percentages, we can, if we so choose, calculate figures for mean nonhuman wealth between 1722 and 1762. While we shall forgo these calculations here, data assembled through such calculations will prove important later in the chapter when we construct estimates of total wealth and total nonhuman wealth for the low country.

To construct such estimates, however, other problems must also be solved. Despite their many virtues, probate inventories of estates in South Carolina do not give us a complete picture of white wealth-holding patterns in the colony. With few exceptions, such sources omit real property from evaluation. In order to estimate total wealth, we, thus, need to know something about the relationship between personalty and realty; more specifically, we must attempt to estimate the share of total wealth that appeared in inventories of estates.[103]

This problem is more difficult than it seems at first glance. To link land records—deeds of transfer, bills of sale, even newspaper advertisements containing

Table 3–20. Slave Wealth as a Percentage of Total Wealth, South Carolina, 1722–1762

Period	Percentage
1722–26	45%
1727–31	48
1732–36	40
1737–41	48
1742–46	48
1747–51	50
1752–56	51
1757–62	51

Source: Bentley, "Wealth Distribution in Colonial South Carolina," Table 55, p. 82.

price data—to probate records for even one individual is, in the southern colonies, a painstaking task. To do so for enough individuals to make possible an informed estimate of the relationship between real and personal wealth in an entire region is obviously more difficult still. Nevertheless, some data on this relationship are available. Estimates made from these data do not conform completely, however, as we shall see.

The best available estimates are those of Alice Hanson Jones and William Bentley; those made by Jones refer to one particular part of the low country, those by Bentley to the low country as a whole. In her 1980 work *Wealth of a Nation To Be*, Jones estimated that land constituted about 31.4 percent of the overall wealth of wealth-holders in the Charleston District—the low country was divided into three districts, of which this was one—in 1774.[104] In a study completed two years earlier, Bentley, basing his conclusions on quite limited data, found that the ratio of "non-land" wealth to "land-wealth" in South Carolina—actually the low country—was 3.63 to 1.0 in the eighteenth century.[105] By converting Bentley's ratio into percentages, we find that "land-wealth" constituted 21.6 percent of total wealth. The estimates of Jones and Bentley, thus, differ somewhat, though not egregiously.

In our effort to convert figures on personal wealth into more meaningful figures on total wealth, how, then, shall we proceed? By pretty much accepting the estimates of Jones, I believe. Indeed, it is my impression after working with the public records of colonial South Carolina for a decade—an impression shared, one should note, by George Terry, whose knowledge of South Carolina's probate records is unparalleled—that wealth in land constituted, as Jones suggests, approximately a third of the total wealth of low-country wealth-holders. In Table 3-21, therefore, I have provided estimates of mean *total* wealth of low-country wealth-holders between 1722 and 1762 which reflect the assumption that the personalty/realty ratio in the area was two to one. Under such an assumption, figures for mean personal wealth alone are raised by about 50 percent.

The data in this table, which have been calculated both in currency and sterling, indicate immediately that the mean total wealth per inventoried wealth-holder was

Table 3–21. Estimates of Mean Total Wealth of White Inventoried Decedents, South Carolina, 1722–1762[1]

	Mean Personal Wealth		Mean Total Wealth	
Period	£ S.C. Currency	£ sterling	£ S.C. Currency	£ sterling
1722–26	2730	416.79	4092.95	624.88
1727–31	2632	382.00	3946.03	572.72
1732–36	3090	435.82	4632.68	653.41
1737–41	3238	425.49	4854.57	637.92
1742–46	4060	580.00	6086.96	869.57
1747–51	5155	706.16	7728.64	1058.72
1752–56	5405	768.85	8103.45	1152.69
1757–62	6039	862.71	9053.97	1293.42

Sources: Tables 3–16 and 3–17; Jones, *Wealth of a Nation To Be*, p. 380. Also see footnote 104 of this chapter.
[1]Note that these data refer almost exclusively to low-country decedents.

Table 3–22. Estimates of Mean Total Wealth per White Inhabitant, South Carolina, 1722–1762[1]

Period	S.C. Currency	£ Sterling	1978 Dollars
1722–26	£ 960.79	£146.68	$ 7,958.86
1727–31	926.30	134.44	7,294.71
1732–36	1087.48	153.38	8,322.40
1737–41	1139.57	149.75	8,125.43
1742–46	1428.86	204.12	11,075.55
1747–51	1814.23	248.52	13,484.69
1752–56	1902.22	270.59	14,682.21
1757–62	2125.34	303.62	16,474.42

Sources: Table 3–21; Jones, *Wealth of a Nation To Be*, pp. 10, 42.

[1]Note that these data refer almost exclusively to low-country whites.

very high indeed. To get a better sense of the heights attained, one need only point out that a pound sterling during this period was equal to about $54.26 in 1978 dollars.[106] Through simple conversion we find that the figure for mean total wealth per inventoried wealth-holder in the low country was thus about $70,181 between 1757 and 1762. Similarly, if we assume that there were 4.26 free inhabitants in the low country per wealth-holder—Alice Hanson Jones's estimate for the South as a whole in 1774—we find through simple division that white per capita wealth in the low country in the 1757–62 period, for example, was £303.62 sterling, that is to say, about $16,474 in 1978 dollars.[107] Indeed! Estimates of white per capita wealth in the low country not only for the 1757–62 period but for seven other periods between 1722 and 1762 as well are presented in Table 3-22. Finally, those that prefer, for whatever reason, to exclude human wealth from consideration, will find mean figures for total nonhuman wealth per wealth-holder and total nonhuman wealth per white capita in tables 3-23 and 3-24 respectively.

These data, taken together, reveal that the South Carolina low country, for all its climatic rigor and its epidemiological agony, nonetheless offered some of

Table 3–23. Estimates of Total Nonhuman Wealth of Probated Wealth-holders, South Carolina, 1722–1762[1]

Period	Mean Nonhuman Personal Wealth		Mean Nonhuman Wealth	
	£ S.C. Currency	£ sterling	£ S.C. Currency	£ sterling
1722–26	1501.50	229.24	2864.45	437.32
1727–31	1368.64	198.64	2682.67	389.36
1732–36	1854.00	261.49	3396.68	479.08
1737–41	1683.76	221.26	3300.33	433.68
1742–46	2111.20	301.60	4138.16	591.17
1747–51	2577.50	353.08	5151.14	705.64
1752–56	2648.45	376.73	5346.90	760.58
1757–62	2959.11	422.73	5974.08	853.44

Sources: Table 3–21; Bentley, "Wealth Distribution in Colonial South Carolina," Table 55, p. 82.

[1]Note that these data refer almost exclusively to low-country decedents.

Table 3–24. Estimates of Mean Total Nonhuman Wealth per White Inhabitant,
South Carolina, 1722–1762[1]

Period	S.C. Currency	Pounds Sterling	1978 Dollars
1722–26	£ 672.41	£102.66	$ 5,570.33
1727–31	629.73	91.40	4,959.36
1732–36	797.34	112.46	6,102.08
1737–41	774.72	101.80	5,523.67
1742–46	971.40	138.77	7,529.66
1747–51	1209.19	165.64	8,987.63
1752–56	1255.14	178.54	9,867.58
1757–62	1402.37	200.34	10,870.45

Sources: Table 3–22; Bentley, "Wealth Distribution in Colonial South Carolina," Table 55, p . 82.
[1]Note that these data refer almost exclusively to low-country whites .

its inhabitants the possibility of rapid wealth accumulation during the eighteenth
century. I use the pronoun "some" advisedly. While we shall deal in the next
chapter with the distribution of wealth in the low country, it should be noted here
that it was not only the area's bondsmen that lived impecuniously. The figures on
white wealth presented above are impressive to be sure. They are, however, mean
figures, a point about which we must be clear. Indeed, despite such figures, many
whites apparently lived at approximately the same level as bondsmen, passing
through the same Ricardian straits.

Lieutenant-Governor James Glen, that most perceptive observer, estimated in
1751, for example, that 5000 to 6000 of the white inhabitants of the colony—
roughly 20 percent of the white population—had only "a bare subsistence."[108]
Certain data suggest that Glen's estimate was correct. That the bottom fifth of
Charleston's inventoried wealth-holders between 1722 and 1732 possessed personalty worth on average only £11.27 sterling surely supports this point. Moreover,
the fact that almost 15 percent of the inventoried wealth-holders in St. John's
Berkeley Parish between 1740 and 1759 possessed personalty worth less than £71
sterling and the fact that over 24 percent of all inventoried wealth-holders in South
Carolina between 1736 and 1775 held personalty worth less than £100 sterling are
also consistent with Glen's observation.[109] But, of this, more later. We came here
to praise South Carolina's eighteenth-century economic performance, not to disparage it. And surely there was much about this performance that was worthy of
praise.

Whether judged in terms of the total wealth of its white population or in terms of
the rate—2 to 2.2 percent annually—at which such wealth grew, the performance
of the low country's economy, data from the 1722–62 period suggest, was truly
remarkable. For nowhere else in British North America or perhaps in the world for
that matter did so sizable a population live so well. Furthermore, this population,
if Jones's estimates are correct, did even better in the years that followed. By
1774, according to Jones, the figure for mean total wealth per "probate" wealth-
holder in the Charleston District had grown to £2,337.7 sterling, that is to say, to
$126,844 in 1978 dollars! The true significance of this finding does not register

completely until one considers that the next highest regional figure found by Jones was that for Anne Arundel County, Maryland—£660.4 sterling per inventoried wealth-holder, which figure is less than 30 percent of the figure mentioned above for the Charleston District. One can safely conclude from the foregoing, I believe, that in relative terms at least, most of the white inhabitants of the eighteenth-century low country had done extraordinarily well.[110]

Of course, it is true that our evaluation of the low country's eighteenth-century economic performance would change considerably were we to include the area's total population and not just its white inhabitants in our analysis of regional wealth. This is more or less true of many other parts of the colonial South as well. It is important to remember, however, as Edwin Perkins has recently pointed out, that though mean wealth figures in such areas drop substantially when blacks are taken into account, mean per capita wealth and, indeed, income are still higher in 1774 in the southern colonies than in colonies further north.[111] Moreover, since it is quite likely that the living standards of the South's black population—black "income," as it were—remained fairly constant over the course of the eighteenth century while those of whites improved considerably, we still must explain the accumulation of wealth by whites in the South in general and in the low country specifically. And it is to the causes of such accumulation in the latter area that we now shall turn.

To explain the sources of economic growth and its presumed concomitant, wealth accumulation, is at once remarkably simple and impossibly complex. Growth occurs, of course, when changes in factor inputs and/or changes in the productivity with which new or existing factors are used lead to an increase in per capita output. This much is elementary. To go beyond this, however, is to enter extremely uncertain intellectual territory. With more courage perhaps than judgment, we shall enter these unruly intellectual marchlands nonetheless.

Given the commercial nature of South Carolina, it is fitting and perhaps not surprising that we shall take the market route. For just as the market was responsible for South Carolina's birth, it was the market that conditioned the colony's economic growth. More specifically, it was, I believe, the size of factor and product markets and the relative ability of the white inhabitants of the South Carolina low country, given the physical and technological constraints of the day, to respond to such markets that largely determined levels both of output and wealth. Whether one feels that this was so because market size and the degree of market responsiveness determined the extent of specialization and the division of labor or the amount of surplus value extracted and the degree of labor exploitation is immaterial. For the market is the protagonist both in *The Wealth of Nations* and *Das Kapital*.

In the case of the South Carolina low country, it was in particular the area's integration into the Atlantic economy, that is, into a network of factor and product markets of intercontinental scope, that mattered most. The size of markets in this economy enabled the economic actors of the low country to take advantage of gains issuing from international specialization, greater division of labor, surplus extraction, and exploitation in order to overcome the rude sufficiency imposed upon

them by internal factoral constraints. Once freed from the prison of self-sufficiency, the white inhabitants of the low country were able to shift resources into economic activities for which the area, because of its factoral endowment, seemed best-suited. Though for some this shift would mean a greater degree of exploitation and for others greater risk and uncertainty, there is no doubt that international trade, by bringing into play economic forces associated with comparative advantage and comparative cost, occasioned shifts to the right in the production-possibility curves both of the South Carolina low country and of the entire Atlantic world. [112]

The low country's integration into the Atlantic economy was made possible in a practical sense by the successful commercial production in the area of articles for which the effective demand in the Atlantic world was sufficient enough to induce Atlantic trading nations and their colonies to regularize and routinize commercial relations with the low country, thereby enabling the area to share to some degree at least in the economic benefits arising from wider markets. Such benefits, triggered initially by the success of the low country's export sector, would prove crucial for sustaining the area's economic growth.

The key role of the export sector in the process by which the low country and, indeed, certain other colonies were integrated into the Atlantic economy and thus set on the path to economic growth has led some scholars to argue that classical and neoclassical theories of comparative advantage inadequately explain the growth scenario in such "newly settled" areas and, therefore, must be supplemented by corollaries or even distinct theories that allow for greater specificity. Such concerns have resulted in numerous models of "export-led" growth and development, the most prominent—and fashionable—of which is that labeled the staples theory of economic growth. [113] This "theory," despite the claims of some of its more enthusiastic proponents, represents less a discrete theory than a corollary of the conventional theory of comparative advantage. Whereas true theory is able to explain or predict a broad class of phenomena by linking such phenomena logically to a few basic principles, staples "theory" rather attempts to explain the growth process in a small number of "newly settled" areas on the basis of slight, albeit useful modifications of, or perhaps better, elaborations upon, an existing theory, that of comparative advantage. [114]

In describing how unemployed or underemployed resources, particularly those falling under the rubric "land," were rendered productive in some "newly settled" areas because of the existence of foreign markets for articles of high raw-material content—articles for which demand in the "newly settled" areas themselves was minimal—the staples "theory" contributes to our understanding of the historical growth process in such areas. Yet is not the exportation of such articles, indeed the economic employment in any way of "bundles" and "deposits" of relatively abundant natural resources precisely what we should expect of a "newly settled" area if comparative advantage is, in fact, good theory? I believe so. Nevertheless, to the extent that the employment of staples theory has focused attention on the role of the export sector in determining the pace of economic growth in parts of British North America during the early modern period, it has had a salutary effect on the study of American economic history. The fact, however, that both staples

theorists and those that have employed such theory have often, in Shakespeare's words, "o'reached themselves," extending their argument about the importance of the export sector to areas and time periods for which it is inappropriate has proved less salutary.[115] Moreover, the fact that a number of these scholars have gone on to explain differential patterns of social development in terms of the production functions of various staples—which explanations assume, as it were, preordained production functions at any given time for tobacco, rice, wheat, sugar, and so on—has proved similarly disappointing.[116] It is one thing to emphasize the social concomitants—for a given area—of the production function of a particular commodity produced there. It is quite another to suggest that either the production function for that staple or the social concomitants arising therefrom is somehow fixed.

Consider wheat, for example. It is commonly believed that widespread production of this crop in "newly settled" areas led to the development in such areas of social orders characterized by small units of production, a free labor force, a relatively even wealth distribution, and many forward and backward economic linkages. The Middle Colonies and parts of the Chesapeake region in the eighteenth century are frequently cited as representative "wheat" areas.[117] In another "newly settled" area, Mexico, however, wheat was associated during the colonial period, with great estates, a bound labor force, a relatively uneven wealth distribution, and with relatively few linkages.[118] This leads one to believe that there is more to social development than that which can be attributed to the "technical requirements" of a particular staple alone. Some staples theorists, it is true, qualify their "theory" to include only areas "newly settled" by English-speaking peoples, but does this not imply both a certain tentativeness about the "technical requirements" of wheat production and a cultural dimension to patterns of economic growth? The production function of a crop in a given area at a particular time, like the export sector of the economy of a given area at a particular time, can tell us much about patterns of economic growth and social development in that area. It tells us far less, however, about economic growth or social development per se. It is here, I believe, that many ardent proponents of staples "theory" are prone to err.

While exports, particularly staple exports, did indeed inform the economic history of the South Carolina low country during the early modern period, their precise role is often misunderstood. That exports were in some way responsible for the growth cycle in the low country is not doubted, for without wider markets it is impossible that output and wealth could have reached the levels that they did. But economic gains issuing from wider markets were often indirect and cannot always be linked easily to export growth. These considerations notwithstanding, scholars in recent years generally have argued that there were a few key sources of growth in the low country and other parts of British North America during the early modern period. Several sources—productivity gains in the shipping industry and maritime trade, the extraction of surplus value from bound labor, increases in agricultural productivity, and a rise in the real value of exports from the American colonies—are mentioned most frequently, with individual scholars generally stressing only one or two.[119] Moreover, in their quest for analytical precision, recent scholars, like the

political arithmeticians of the seventeenth century, generally have sought to express themselves as much as possible in terms of "Number, Weight, or Measure," as Sir William Petty had exhorted long ago.[120] In so doing, however, such scholars often have neglected other nonquantifiable sources of growth. In the discussion that follows we shall break with the recent traditions mentioned above by arguing that there were many quiet, almost insidious sources of growth at work in the low country, that early-modern growth is far too complex to reduce to statistical precision, and that there is therefore no one key to growth to be found.

Once we disabuse ourselves of the notion that we ever can unlock completely the mysteries of economic growth and wealth accumulation, we can begin to apprehend the complexity of such processes and begin to appreciate the profound beauty of their intricacy. Some of the intricacies of growth and accumulation in the South Carolina low country will be highlighted below as we discuss changes in factor inputs and changes in factor productivity. We shall focus upon such changes because it is, as we have seen, conventional among economists interested in the sources of growth to frame their analyses in this way.

Combined inputs of land, labor, and capital in the South Carolina low country apparently grew faster than population—at least faster than the white population—during the colonial period. This is much easier to assert, however, than to prove conclusively. All statements about land and labor inputs in particular must be regarded cautiously, for we lack good statistical data on such matters as the amount of land *in production* in the low country over time, on the length of the work day in the area, on labor participation rates, and on relative labor intensity. With these points in mind, let us begin by considering inputs of land.

We know precious little about change over time in the size of landholdings in the low country as a whole. Data from one parish, St. John's Berkeley, suggest that mean acreage per landholder may have grown a bit during the second half of the eighteenth century, but obviously no conclusions about land inputs can be based upon such meager evidence.[121] Increases in the mean size of landholdings would not tell us much in any case about the amount of land in production at any given time. One might think, however, that because the expansion of the low-country rice industry was much more rapid than the growth of population in the area and because much of this expansion occurred on land previously unemployed, the increase in the total amount of land in production in the low country also must have outstripped population growth. Such expansion notwithstanding, this would not necessarily be true, for the acreage employed in the rice industry constituted only a small fraction of the total landholdings in the low country.[122] Moreover, because some low-country land fell into disuse as labor and capital were shifted into rice and because rice was far less land-intensive than "pioneer" activities such as herding and hunting, by no means can we be certain that inputs of land per capita did not actually fall over time. Thus, concerning land inputs we must acknowledge that in analytical terms we know scarcely anything at all.

About labor inputs we at least can infer something more. Indeed, from the fact that the black proportion of the total low-country population grew during the colonial period and the fact that rice and indigo, which increasingly dominated the

area's economy, were much more labor-intensive than earlier economic activities, certain inferences can be made and some provisional conclusions drawn. Available data indicate, for example, that almost all blacks in the low country were slaves.[123] The low country's labor force, of course, also consisted mainly of slaves. Most of this slave labor force was involved in some way in the production of rice or indigo. If these crops required much more sweat and toil than did hunting, fishing, or tending cows, it seems likely that per capita labor inputs among the slave population—whether through higher participation rates or greater intensity—must have risen as well. Precisely how much is impossible to tell, however, because productivity was also increasing not only in rice production but in the economy as a whole. That per capita labor inputs increased over time in the low country is supported, one should also note, by the findings of a number of other historians.[124] Though one need not necessarily go so far as Forrest McDonald did when he stated that "[t]he South Carolina planters' callous disregard for human life and suffering was probably unmatched anywhere west of the Dnieper," it seems reasonable to say that with the coming of rice and indigo to the area, the labor force of the low country worked both harder and longer.[125]

We can speak much more confidently about capital accumulation in the low country and hence about the increasing importance over time of capital inputs in the area's hypothetical aggregate production function.[126] Indeed, enough data are available on capital in the low country to allow us to discuss this factor in terms of Petty's beloved number, weight, and measure. William Bentley has assembled data from probate inventories of estates on the amount of capital held by inventoried wealth-holders in the low country between 1722 and 1762 and on changes in the relative proportion of total personal wealth constituted by capital over the same period. Defining capital as that portion of personal wealth "clearly used for business purposes and not for household consumption," that is, using the term "capital" to denote inventories of goods and crops, livestock, and reproducible, man-made goods used in the fabrication or improvement of other goods, Bentley has found that the amount of capital held by inventoried wealth-holders in the low country grew from a mean figure of £ 325 current money between 1722 and 1726 to £ 720 current money between 1757 and 1762.[127] Moreover, the long-term increase in the amount of capital held per inventoried wealth-holder stands up, indeed, perhaps even grows larger, according to Bentley, when figures are adjusted to account for changes in the price level over the period, that is to say, when figures are calculated in real terms.[128]

More significant perhaps is the fact that the proportion of total personal wealth constituted by capital also grew. Capital constituted about 14 percent of total personal wealth between 1722 and 1726 and about 16 percent between 1757 and 1762.[129] Though this percentage increase in itself is quite modest, it becomes more impressive when we remember how quickly total personal wealth was growing during this period. Indeed, that the rate of capital accumulation in the low country outstripped that of personal wealth accumulation as a whole between 1722 and 1762 is in some ways remarkable. For if Alice Hanson Jones's data for the Charleston District in 1774 are correct, producers' capital constituted by that time only about

11 percent of the total personal wealth of "probate-type" decedents, despite the fact that the mean figure for producers' capital per decedent had risen in monetary terms to over £1211 current money—an absolute gain of almost £500 current money per decedent since the period from 1757 to 1762.[130]

In any case, whether producers' capital constituted 16 percent, 14 percent, or even 11 percent of the total personal wealth of inventoried decedents in the low country during the eighteenth century, of one thing we can be sure: such capital, considered in absolute terms, was being accumulated at a rapid rate of speed. And economic historians have found that in the early modern period, that is, before the great productivity gains of the industrial age, the accumulation of producers' capital—whether circulating or fixed—was responsible for much of the dynamism that a given economy displayed. Furthermore, though data are limited and imprecise, it is probable that the relative stock of financial capital also increased over time in the low country. If so, this would have contributed to the area's economic dynamism as well.[131]

So far as we know, then, capital and labor inputs grew faster than the white population of the low country during the eighteenth century, while details about inputs of land remain very sketchy. If we assume, however, that land, labor, and capital inputs combined still outpaced white population, then we have a plausible explanation—a relative increase in factor inputs—for some part of the rise in output per white inhabitant and, thus, of the increase in white per capita income and wealth.

Output, income, and wealth in the low country also grew, of course, because of gains in the productivity with which land, labor, and capital were used. Indeed, if we define productivity gains broadly to include all changes that "improved" the relationship between inputs and output, we must include not only gains due to technical changes but those due to "improving" market conditions and to changes in economic organization as well.[132] To discuss productivity is, thus, to discuss change, both revolutionary transformations and quotidian permutations alike. In early modern South Carolina, as in the rest of the early modern world, it was due mainly to changes of the latter sort that the production possibilities frontier shifted to the right. It is to such changes that we now shall turn.

Few of the productivity gains realized in early-modern South Carolina resulted from technical improvements. Though many South Carolinians in this period were interested both in the methods and findings of "modern" science and in the possible technological implications of the same, the lag between scientific discoveries and the economic application and subsequent diffusion of such discoveries was in general very long indeed.[133] Thus, most productivity gains resulted rather from changing market conditions and from innovations in economic organization.

There is, however, one major exception in the low country to this generalization. Technical improvements in rice cultivation were important sources of aggregate productivity gains. Such improvements were occasioned mainly by the shift of rice cultivation from higher grounds to inland swamps and then gradually to tidal swamps nearer the sea. They resulted in greater yield per acre and greater yields per worker; in short, they increased productivity. One should note, however,

that the connection between the geographical shift in rice production in the low country and increased productivity was indirect. For this shift allowed the area's "improving" farmers to employ irrigation in the cultivation of rice and it was irrigation rather than geography per se that led to productivity gains. Irrigation increased productivity in the cultivation of rice not only by assuring the plant of sufficient moisture at each stage of growth but also by protecting it from birds and insects and from competing weeds. With the task of weeding less onerous, some labor, of course, also was saved. With the passage of time, irrigation works became more elaborate in the low country and with further elaboration came further productivity gains. Certain data exist to bear out this point.[134]

Contemporary estimates of rice yields in the low country in the early eighteenth century, that is, before the employment of irrigation, generally run up to about 1000 pounds of clean rice per acre. By the time of the American Revolution, however, when almost all low-country rice was produced in irrigated inland- or tidal swamps, yields were much greater. Though estimates vary, about 1500 pounds of clean rice per acre seems to have been the norm.[135] Data on yield per worker support these findings. Indeed, we see a similar increase in this index over the course of the eighteenth century. Whereas James Glen, writing in 1748, stated that it was a "common computation throughout the Province" that a good working hand on a rice plantation produced about 2250 pounds of clean rice per year, the figure for an *average* hand apparently had grown to about 3000–3600 pounds yearly during the second half of the eighteenth century, with good hands capable of even more.[136]

Thus, technical improvements—irrigation and, to a much lesser extent, certain refinements in the processing of the rice grain—did, in fact, play some part in increasing the aggregate productivity of the low-country economy.[137] Even in rice production, however, where technical change was most striking, it is difficult to separate those gains due strictly to technology from those accruing from a complex amalgam of increasing factor inputs, technological improvements, and changes in economic organization. For the shift to irrigated rice cultivation in the low country was coextensive with shifts toward greater labor intensity, more capital inputs—dams, gates, ditches, and so on—and toward organizational forms themselves conducive to greater economic productivity. Such changes in economic organization, that is to say, the advent of the task system and the increasing relative importance over time of plantations with more than thirty slaves, arguably had as much to do with gains in productivity as technological change.

As Philip Morgan recently has shown, the task system rather than the gang system gradually emerged as the dominant method of labor organization on low-country rice plantations.[138] Under the task system a slave was responsible for completing a specified amount of work, a certain number of standardized "tasks" as it were, after which tasks had been completed each slave was "free" to do what he or she so chose. It was under this system that productivity on rice plantations grew. By injecting the incentive of free time into the labor equation, low-country planters were able at once to increase the productivity of the work force—task requirements grew over time—and to lessen the possibility of serious labor unrest by making the peculiar institution seem somewhat more bearable.

The fact that low-country plantations increased in size over time also may have contributed to the productivity gains accrued. Though questions relating to the existence of economies of scale in the Cotton South still burn hot, most observers today believe that such economies did in fact exist in sugar and rice production because relatively greater amounts of fixed capital generally were associated with these crops.[139] In an econometric analysis of the American rice industry in the nineteenth century, Dale Swan has found that economies of scale in the production of this crop probably began when plantations reached considerable size, that is, when such units had about $25,000 worth of nonhuman capital and about thirty slaves.[140] Swan's data, based on census returns, are much more complete than data presently available for the colonial period. We still do not know much, for example, about changes in the capitalization of low-country plantations in that period. We do know something, however, about changes over time in slaveholding patterns on such plantations.

Data from St. John's Berkeley Parish indicate that the proportion of plantations with more than thirty slaves grew substantially during the colonial period.[141] Moreover, we also know that the proportion of slaves in South Carolina who lived on plantations with more than thirty slaves went from 29 percent in the 1720s to 64 percent in the 1770s.[142] It thus seems highly probable, if these data are correct, that a greater proportion of low-country planters captured economies of scale in rice production as time passed. With the capture of such economies, average costs per unit of production would fall, the relationship between inputs and output would improve, and productivity would thus increase. We shall never know for sure, of course, whether economies of scale played a major role in bringing about the productivity gains in the low-country rice industry in the eighteenth century. The possibility that they did is real, however, which illustrates the fact that it is difficult indeed to separate the contribution of technology to increased productivity in the rice industry from contributions due to changes in factor inputs and in economic organization, for in this case at least, technology, factor inputs, and economic organization are closely, perhaps even inextricably bound.

Such difficulties seem less severe when we attempt to explain other sources of productivity gains in the low-country economy. For outside of the rice industry, the contribution of technological innovation to increased productivity in the low country was indirect, manifest mainly in the relative decline in prices of British manufactured goods imported into the area.[143] Those that would explain other sources of productivity gains, therefore, must look for the most part to changes in economic organization. Let us begin by looking at organizational changes in the lubricants of the market mechanism, that is to say, in transportation, distribution, and communications.

The transportation, distribution, and communications systems of the West were marked by a number of changes during the early-modern period. Indeed, several scholars have argued that gains resulting from such changes—the increased productivity of transoceanic shipping in particular—were primarily responsible for the economic growth that occurred in British North America during that period.[144] Whether or not gains of this type did, in fact, bear primary responsibility for the

economic growth of the colonies in British North America need not concern us here. Whether or not such gains contributed to growth and accumulation in the South Carolina low country does concern us, however, and, as we shall see, to this question the answer is clear.

Available data indicate that both the efficiency with which goods were transported and distributed and the efficiency with which economic information was disseminated improved slowly in the low country over time. The rates at which such improvement occurred, however, suggest that productivity gains in these areas were not crucial or indispensable to growth and accumulation in the low country, but instead part of a broad, multifaceted growth process. This can be seen through a brief analysis of productivity gains in the shipping industry.

Despite the fact that productivity gains in shipping are of especial importance to the interpretations of early American economic growth espoused by a number of scholars, none of them argues that such gains were due much to technical improvements in the ships themselves or in the art of navigation. Rather, they argue that gains in shipping were due mainly to organizational changes, particularly those due to economies of scale. Such changes—the fall over time in the number of guns per vessel and the rise in the ton/crew ratio, secular declines as well in freight rates, mean port-times, and the F.O.B./C.I.F. price differential—are considered key sources of economic growth.[145] Though it is true that when measured by these indices the productivity of shipping involved in the low country's trade did improve over time, the degree of improvement was modest, particularly until the Seven Years' War had ended and the Treaty of Paris been signed. For until the eighteenth-century struggle for empire between France and Great Britain was settled in favor of the latter, productivity gains in shipping were severely limited and at times even reversed because both the number of guns and crewmen per vessel and wage- and insurance rates during these years of intermittent warfare were often artificially high. Certain data from the Charleston Naval Lists can be used to illustrate some of these points. Data illustrating changes over time in the crew size and armaments of the Charleston fleet are presented in tables 3-25 and 3-26.[146]

As these tables show, both the decline in armaments per vessel and the improvements in the ton/crew ratio for the most part postdate the French defeat in 1763. Similarly, other scholars have shown that much of the decline in shipping insurance rates also awaited the outbreak of peace.[147] Though the decline in transoceanic freight rates was secular in nature and though it is probable that mean port-times also gradually decreased, it is unlikely that these factors alone explain the sharp rise in wealth in the low country between 1722 and 1762.[148] Indeed, even if we broaden our definition of "shipping" to include distribution and inland transportation, we still cannot adequately explain the low country's economic rise.

The advent of central warehousing, the improvement of port facilities, and gains made in packaging—the mean size of the barrels in which rice was shipped, for example, grew from 350 pounds in 1720 to 525 pounds by 1755—certainly played roles in this rise, however.[149] So, too, did numerous improvements in the low country's inland transportation network. South Carolinians, one must remember, invested heavily in social overhead capital during the colonial period.[150]

Table 3–25. Number, Mean Size, and Mean Crew Size of Vessels Clearing Charleston, 1717–1766

Year	Number	Mean Size (tons)	Mean Crew Size
1717	126	54	
1718	129	59	
1719	122	54	
1720	109	52	
1724	111	65	9
1731	181	65	8
1732	154	58	8
1734	180	65	8
1735	195	67	8
1736	178	70	8
1737	158	70	8
1738	155	69	8
1758	197	79	12
1759	201[1]	78	12
1760	217	75	10
1762	234	68	9
1763	337	71	9
1766	313	82	8

Source: Clowse, *Measuring Charleston's Overseas Commerce,* 1717–1767, pp. 112–14. Also see footnote 146 of this chapter.

[1]By my count, 203.

Table 3–26. Number of Vessels and Number of Armed Vessels Clearing Charleston, 1724–1766

Year	Vessels Clearing	Armed Vessels Clearing
1724	111	50
1731	181	88
1732	154	62
1734	180	89
1735	195	98
1736	178	77
1737	158	77
1738	155	68
1758	197	97
1759	201[1]	100
1760	217	112
1762	234	111
1763	337	69
1766	313	2

Source: Clowse, *Measuring Charleston's Overseas Commerce,* 1717–1767, pp. 112–14. Also see footnote 146 of this chapter.

[1]By my count, 203.

Such investment resulted in a good, if narrowly conceived internal transportation network, one which facilitated the flow of goods and commodities in and out of the province rather than the flow of people within it. This type of transportation network, of course, is found commonly in export-oriented plantation and mining areas even today. The linear character of such transportation networks, that is to say, the fact that their proper analogue is the conveyor belt rather than the grid often has had certain deleterious effects in the long run on the economies of plantation and mining regions, the South Carolina low country included. The creation of such a network in the low country during the colonial period, indeed, the creation of *any* network at all, initially proved beneficial to the area's economy nonetheless.[151]

Moreover, qualitative improvements in transport facilities over time may have boosted productivity as well. Though data are sketchy, the fact that bridges replaced ferries in many places as time passed and the fact that extant engineering specifications suggest qualitative improvements in roads over time—main public highways, if statutes can be trusted, were generally 16 to 20 feet wide early in the eighteenth century, but 20, 30, or even 40 feet wide after 1720—are most instructive.[152] These gains, too, however, like those made in transoceanic shipping and in distribution and from the spread itself of the inland transportation network, were but part of the finely textured shift to the right in the low country's production-possibility frontier.

Improvements in communications, particularly in business communications, helped bring about this shift as well. Writing from America in 1674, Carolina proprietor Peter Colleton observed in a letter bound for the metropolis:

> . . . I confesse I am amazed at the variety of newes I have Rec'd from England & am like a man who sees people dancing at a distance & not hearing the Musick, wonders what they are doing . . .[153]

Though such feelings of amazement would never disappear completely during the colonial period, the "distance" between Old World and New lessened considerably in the eighteenth century, and economic "musick" emanating from the Old World became increasingly audible in the New.

Paralleling the improvements in shipping and distribution mentioned above were improvements that increased the efficiency with which market information was gathered, disseminated, and used. This is not to say that business communications during the colonial period were ever truly efficient in a modern sense. For no business environment in which it was necessary to send four to six or even more copies of a letter across the ocean to ensure that at least one would reach the desired destination safely could ever be so constituted. But communications did improve gradually in a number of ways.[154]

Transatlantic communications between South Carolina and England, for example, became more structured and systematic over time, to which both the establishment of the Carolina Coffee House in London in the late seventeenth century—coffee houses in this period were great centers of business activity—and the organization of regular postal and packet service between colony and metropolis in the eighteenth century attest. Moreover, business communications were further improved by the establishment, somewhat later, of coffee houses and regular postal

service in South Carolina as well. Finally, one should not overlook newspapers: their emergence in South Carolina in the eighteenth century greatly facilitated the flow of commerce, both by providing relatively up-to-date information on local and international markets and by providing a medium for local advertising.[155]

It may even be possible to gauge in a rough way the increasing elaboration of the low country's communications system by noting that Charleston, which did not even have a permanent newspaper until 1732, by 1765 had three.[156] Though we do not have accurate circulation figures for these papers, we do know that in 1764 one of them, the *South-Carolina Gazette*, regularly was available at more than fifty places in the lower South, from Brunswick, North Carolina, to Pensacola and Mobile in West Florida.[157] It is inconceivable that the spread of Charleston newspapers throughout the lower South did not improve the working of the market in the area, for by linking remote regions more completely to the centers of economic activity, the effect of improved lines of communications is to increase the knowledge available to actors in the market. Increased knowledge, of course, presumably leads to more rational economic decisions and more rational economic decisions to increased economic efficiency. Thus, coffee houses, postal service, newspapers: communications improvements that increased the productivity of the low-country economy, little by little, but inexorably.

Productivity gains, however, did not end here. For the political-economic framework within which the low country evolved became increasingly conducive to growth and accumulation as time passed, enabling the white inhabitants of the area better to utilize the information improved communications had brought to hand. Indeed, creative institutional adjustments in both the public and private sectors contributed in no small way to the low country's eighteenth-century economic rise. Let us look first at the role of government; the contribution of the private sector will be examined by and by.

We have already discussed the essentials of political economy in the low country: the market first of all, mercantilism, liberalism, slavery. We shall not concern ourselves here with reconstructing the moral and philosophical bases of political economy in the area nor shall we attempt to assess the contribution of the political-economic "framework" per se to increased productivity. What we shall concern ourselves with, however, are certain ways in which specific governmental actions and policies contributed over time to increased productivity in the low country and, hence, to the area's increased output, income, and wealth.

Though historians rightfully consider the advent of political stability in South Carolina to be the most important legacy of the royal takeover of the colony in 1730, a piece of legislation passed in the immediate aftermath of the takeover, the so-called Land Act of 1731, may have had a more profound impact on the colony's economic growth.[158] For among this act's many provisions was one mandating the systematic registration of land, and with systematic land registration, that is to say, with secure titles to land, an incipient capital market based on land mortgages began. Land and slaves, of course, always had proved useful as collateral in the colony but only after 1731—as both the Mortgage Books and the Deed Books in the South Carolina Department of Archives and History illustrate—did a full-scale,

reliable mortgage capital market emerge in the low country.[159] Long-term debt of this sort was instrumental in the seventeenth-century economic ascents of England and the Dutch Republic, a point not lost upon Messieurs Ashley and Locke, who had tried unsuccessfully to establish a system of governmental land registration in their "darling" Carolina from the start.[160] The prescience of these two men was considerable, for the economic explosion in the low country in the eighteenth century was financed by mortgage debt at least in part.

Governmental monetary and fiscal policies in South Carolina on balance also contributed to increased productivity and economic growth. Attempts to increase the capital stock in the colony by expanding the money supply, whether through the issuance of bills of credit, public orders, or tax certificates, often paid returns to the colony as a whole, not so much because of any inherent inability of the colony to attract capital but because international specie flow mechanisms during the early modern period were marked by certain structural rigidities which limited the speed with which capital flowed.[161] Thus, the most rational response to military exigencies or immediate economic opportunities, that is, to Indian wars or increases in demand for rice or other commodities, was often for the government to issue paper currency. To the extent that the expansion of the colony's capital stock increased the efficacy of its military or economic response, governmental monetary policy aided productivity. This conclusion seems particularly valid in light of the fact that a recent econometric study has shown that there was little correlation in South Carolina between inflation and the expansion of the paper money stock.[162] In South Carolina, then, as in other colonies and developing nations both historically and today, a reasonable public debt is more beneficial than at first glance it might seem.

The main contours of fiscal policy in South Carolina also were conducive to productivity gains. Indeed, such contours—low, moderately regressive taxes by the standards of the day and substantial expenditures on the maintenance of order and on social overhead capital—seem in retrospect almost ideally suited to foster growth and productivity in an export-oriented, slave-labor staple colony. By keeping capital in the hands of those that used it most productively and by spending money in a manner that supported the economic efforts of the same, the fiscal policies of the government of South Carolina were responsible, during the eighteenth century at least, for part of the low country's productivity gains.[163]

A number of productivity gains also resulted from the increased degree of articulation in the private sector as time passed, particularly from the increased degree of articulation in the mercantile and financial realms. Articulation, of course, implies specialization and specialization, economic growth. Increased economic specialization in the low country is nowhere more apparent than in the rise over time in the number of rungs on the mercantile ladder. Thus, the undifferentiated "merchant" of the turn of the seventeenth century was replaced as time passed by a whole cast of characters, including hucksters, retailers, wholesalers, country factors, Charleston factors, and masters of vendue.[164]

With occupational specialization on the rise, business practices in the low country not surprisingly became more sophisticated over time. By the late colo-

nial period, for example, we begin to see more advanced accounting practices—rudimentary double-entry, increasingly—the discounting of bills of exchange, and the beginnings of elaborate bill-collecting and advertising campaigns.[165] Though we still know little about the tempo of business life in the low country, there is also some evidence to suggest that as time passed business was transacted at a quicker pace. The surviving business correspondence of two prominent Charleston merchants, Robert Pringle and Henry Laurens, can be used to illustrate this point. Whereas Pringle wrote an average of about 126 business letters a year in the early 1740s, Laurens averaged about 310 yearly in the late 1750s. To be sure, no firm conclusions can be drawn from two sets of records, but the trend is nonetheless in the direction we should expect if the pace of business did indeed quicken.[166]

Even more important perhaps were the allied changes in financial life. The early spread of the system of "book debt" or bookkeeping barter throughout the colony and the strengthening of transatlantic credit chains indicate, for example, that the processes of capital-broadening and capital-deepening were both taking place. Indeed, so tensile did these transatlantic credit chains become that on the eve of the Revolution the per capita debt of South Carolina's white inhabitants to British creditors was higher than that in any other mainland colony.[167] Moreover, the processes of capital-broadening and capital-deepening in the low country were further enhanced over time by the creation through discounting of a secondary market in commercial paper and, more importantly, by the development of the market for long-term debt.

We already have mentioned the development of a mortgage market in land and slaves, but repayment schedules on other types of debt instruments such as promissory notes and bonds apparently also lengthened as time passed. Data are available in the Judgment Rolls of the South Carolina Court of Common Pleas to support this point.[168] There exist in these court records complete data on 168 promissory notes and 282 bonds made between 1703 and 1737. If we divide this thirty-five-year period roughly in half and then analyze the repayment terms on debt instruments contracted in each subperiod, we find that the length of time allowed for repayment was somewhat greater between 1720 and 1737 than between 1703 and 1719. The precise repayment schedules for promissory notes and bonds appear in tables 3-27 and 3-28 respectively. Borrowers, these tables suggest, were increasingly able over time to invest borrowed funds in longer-term projects. This trend in all likelihood not only continued through the rest of the eighteenth century but also probably intensified. Furthermore, the fact that it became increasingly common in South Carolina for loans to be carried beyond their due dates so long as the interest was paid turned many of the debts contracted into virtual annuities.[169] This, too, hastened capital formation and accumulation in the low country.

As time passed, some embryonic financial intermediaries developed as well. By the 1750s, South Carolina churches, lodges, educational institutions, and charitable societies had become important internal sources of long-term capital. Indeed, South Carolina newspapers in the late colonial period are replete with advertisements from such institutions, announcing the availability of considerable sums—the South Carolina Society, for example, offered up to £6,000 current money in 1752—to

Table 3–27. Repayment Terms on Promissory Notes in South Carolina, 1703–1737

Repayment Terms	1703–1719		1720–1737		1703–1737	
	No.	%	No.	%	No.	%
On demand	39	66.10	52	47.71	91	54.17
3 months or less	17	28.81	37	33.94	54	32.14
3 to 6 months	2	3.39	14	12.84	16	9.52
6 to 12 months	1	1.69	6	5.50	7	4.17
More than 12 months	0	0.00	0	0.00	0	0.00
	59	99.99	109	99.99	168	100.00

Source: South Carolina Court of Common Pleas, Judgment Rolls, 1703–1790, Boxes 1–22, South Carolina Department of Archives and History. Note that these data were taken from debt instruments enclosed with materials in "debt" and "trespass on the case" suits brought before the South Carolina Court of Common Pleas.

individuals seeking funds for long-term investment. Given the course of the South Carolina economy in the eighteenth century we find ourselves confronted with the strong and powerfully symbolic possibility that the colony's social and cultural institutions helped *directly* as well as indirectly to create an economy based on rice and slaves. Thus, it is likely that such institutions as the Vestry of St. Thomas and St. Dennis, Solomon's Lodge of Free Masons, the Free School of Childsbury, and the Society for the Relief of the Widows and Children of the Church of England at once facilitated capital mobilization and formation in the colony and helped to bring misery and pain to a considerable number of people from Guinea, Angola, and the Senegambia.[170]

Finally, interest rates in South Carolina, despite short-term fluctuations, fell slowly over the course of the eighteenth century. Though actual rates varied a bit in practice, the legal interest rate in South Carolina was 10 percent until 1748 when it dropped to 8 percent. There it remained until 1777 when it fell another point to 7 percent.[171] That interest rates in South Carolina were falling reflected both the increasing stability of the economic environment there and the

Table 3–28. Repayment Terms on Bonds, South Carolina, 1703–1737

Repayment Terms	1703–1719		1720–1737		1703–1737	
	No.	%	No.	%	No.	%
On demand	6	4.22	6	4.29	12	4.25
3 months or less	44	30.99	37	26.43	81	28.72
3 to 6 months	35	24.65	35	25.00	70	24.82
6 to 12 months	55	38.73	55	39.29	110	39.01
More than 12 months	2	1.41	7	5.00	9	3.19
	142[1]	100.00	140[2]	100.01	282	99.99

Source: South Carolina Court of Common Pleas, Judgment Rolls, 1703–1790, Boxes 1–22, South Carolina Department of Archives and History. Note that these data were taken from debt instruments enclosed with materials in "debt" and "trespass on the case" suits brought before the South Carolina Court of Common Pleas.

[1]One additional incomplete bond not included.
[2]Two additional incomplete bonds not included.

increasing availability of financial capital. Yet because rates were still higher in South Carolina than rates prevailing in northwest Europe, European savings continued to flow to the colony, particularly so long as profits remained high in rice and indigo. Thus, through the processes of capital-broadening and capital-deepening, and through long-term debt, declining interest rates, and the rise of financial intermediaries—in addition to those mentioned above, several short-lived private banks had been established—developments in the financial realm contributed to increased productivity in South Carolina too.[172]

In addition to increases in factor inputs and in factor productivity, the conditions of the market itself, supply and demand that is to say, also played a part in the low country's economic rise over the course of the eighteenth century. Simply put, it appears that the prices of South Carolina's principal eighteenth-century exports, rice and indigo (see tables 3-29 and 3-30), increased more over time than the prices of

Table 3–29. South Carolina Rice Prices, 1722-1775 (shillings sterling per hundredweight)

Year	Price	Year	Price
1722	5.17	1750	8.98
1723	6.01	1751	6.53
1724	6.16	1752	7.93
1725	5.62	1753	9.55
1726	6.57	1754	6.20
1727	8.03	1755	5.82
1728	6.62	1756	4.83
1729	6.38	1757	4.82
		1758	6.16
1730	6.29	1759	9.40
1731	5.32		
1732	6.02	1760	7.35
1733	5.72	1761	5.51
1734	8.64	1762	4.76
1735	8.26	1763	6.31
1736	6.85	1764	6.01
1737	8.89	1765	6.35
1738	9.60	1766	8.13
1739	5.47	1767	8.01
		1768	9.26
1740	4.71	1769	8.62
1741	7.45		
1742	6.29	1770	6.76
1743	4.91	1771	7.28
1744	4.23	1772	12.03
1745	2.29	1773	9.04
1746	2.24	1774	7.37
1747	4.43	1775	6.59
1748	6.44		
1749	8.28		

Sources: Coclanis, "Rice Prices in the 1720s and the Evolution of the South Carolina Economy," p. 538; Cole, *Wholesale Commodity Prices in the United States 1700-1861*, 2: 15-69; McCusker, *Money and Exchange*, pp. 222-24. Note that prices from 1722 to 1731 should be considered South Carolina farm prices, while prices from 1732 to 1775 are Charleston wholesale prices.

Table 3–30. South Carolina Indigo Prices, 1747–1775 (shillings sterling per pound)

Year	Price
1747	2.43
1748	2.62
1749	2.53
1750	2.74
1751	2.81
1752	3.45
1753	4.30
1754	3.98
1755	4.33
1756	3.50
1757	3.75
1758	3.57
1759	3.55
1760	2.96
1761	3.22
1762	3.84
1763	4.03
1764	3.43
1765	3.28
1766	3.10
1767	2.98
1768	3.13
1769	3.76
1770	3.65
1771	4.46
1772	5.52
1773	4.14
1774	4.71
1775	4.32

Sources: Cole, *Wholesale Commodity Prices in the United States 1700–1861*, 2: 28–70; McCusker, *Money and Exchange*, pp. 223–24. All prices are Charleston wholesale prices.

the goods imported into South Carolina from England, the colony's leading trading partner by far.[173] South Carolina's principal exports, in other words, apparently rose in real value over time. Though this conclusion, as we shall see, is most tenable, it should not be considered irrefutable. For we lack good quantitative data on the precise breakdown of English imports into the colony.[174] From all indications, however, South Carolina's imports from England mainly consisted of a variety of finished and semi-finished goods, particularly cloth, articles of clothing, and goods fashioned of various metals and sundry woods. On this point, available primary sources—newspapers, account books, and mercantile papers— are clear.[175]

It thus seems reasonable to assume, *faute de mieux*, that the aggregate price level of all goods imported into South Carolina at any given time was consistent with the general price level in England at that time. This assumption seems

particularly reasonable given the fact that we know that movements in the prices of those goods most frequently involved in the English export trade—broadcloth, hats and stockings, linens, and ironware among others—indeed were consistent for the most part with movements in the general price level in England.[176] Moreover, tariffs would not affect this assumption either, for import duties on English goods sent to the American colonies were prohibited under the Navigation Acts.

We can therefore use John J. McCusker's English wholesale commodity price index to represent movements in the prices of English goods imported into South Carolina during the eighteenth century.[177] If we compare this index with the prices of South Carolina's principal exports, rice and indigo, we find, just as we asserted above, that these exports did indeed increase in real value over time. Such comparisons are in fact made in figures 3-1 and 3-2. Market conditions, more specifically, the increase in the real value of South Carolina's leading exports over time, thus, seem to have contributed to the low country's eighteenth-century economic rise. Regardless of one's views on questions concerning the relative burden upon South Carolina of formal colonial status, it is clear that the low

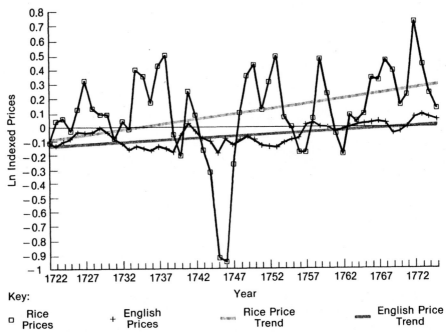

Key:

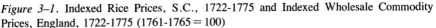

| □ Rice Prices | + English Prices | ⸱⸱⸱⸱⸱ Rice Price Trend | ▬ English Price Trend |

Figure 3–1. Indexed Rice Prices, S.C., 1722-1775 and Indexed Wholesale Commodity Prices, England, 1722-1775 (1761-1765 = 100)

Sources: Coclanis, "Rice Prices in the 1720s and the Evolution of the South Carolina Economy," p . 538; Cole, *Wholesale Commodity Prices in the United States 1700-1861*, 2: 15-69; McCusker, "The Current Value of English Exports, 1697 to 1800," p. 619. Note that I have re-indexed McCusker's series on wholesale commodity prices in England, changing the base from 1700-1702 to 1761-65 in order to make the rice series more directly comparable . The trend lines above are based upon semi-averages. On the semi-average method, see Ya-lun Chou, *Statistical Analysis with Business and Economic Applications* (New York: Holt, Rinehart and Winston, 1969), pp . 540-42. Note, too, that for the sake of accuracy, the graph employs a semilogarithmic projection .

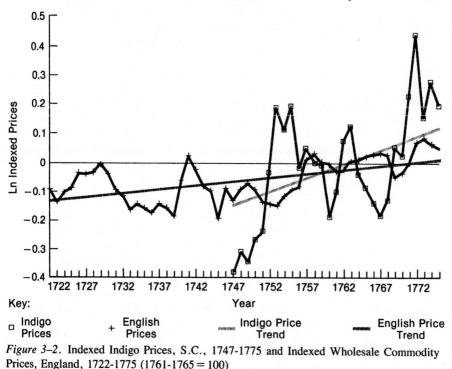

Key:

| □ Indigo Prices | + English Prices | ▬ Indigo Price Trend | ▬ English Price Trend |

Figure 3–2. Indexed Indigo Prices, S.C., 1747-1775 and Indexed Wholesale Commodity Prices, England, 1722-1775 (1761-1765 = 100)

Sources: Cole, *Wholesale Commodity Prices in the United States 1700-1861*, 2: 28-70; McCusker, "The Current Value of English Exports, 1697 to 1800," p. 619. Note that I have re-indexed McCusker's series on wholesale commodity prices in England, changing the base from 1700-1702 to 1761-65 in order to make the indigo series more directly comparable. The trend lines above are based upon semi-averages. On the semi-average method, see Chou, *Statistical Analysis with Business and Economic Applications*, pp. 540-42. Note, too, that for the sake of accuracy, the graph employs a semilogarithmic projection.

country's position in the international market generally was favorable in the eighteenth century, much more favorable, as we shall see in the next chapter, than it would be ever again.

A final point remains. Before closing our discussion we must mention once again that some part of the growth we have seen in the eighteenth-century low country resulted from the exploitation of the black majority by white women and men. Exploitation, of course, has become a catch-word in the twentieth century, a slogan as it were, used in reference to almost any kind of unfairness, injustice, inequity to man. We shall use the term more narrowly here, however, to denote that part of the marginal product of slave labor in the low country that was not returned to the slave labor force but was instead expropriated by slave owners, thus contributing to wealth accumulation among the free population.[178]

Estimates of the "rate" of such exploitation in the American South under slavery vary widely, that is to say, from about 10 percent to as much as 50 percent.[179] Data are still far too incomplete, however, to attach a precise percentage figure to the rate of exploitation in the low country specifically. Though they were not measuring exploitation directly, it is instructive to note nonetheless that Ralph Gray

a..d Betty Wood recently have found that the annual upkeep cost for a male slave in Georgia in the 1740s was estimated to be £3.46 sterling, while that for a white male servant was estimated to be £9 sterling or roughly two-and-a-half times as much![180] Until further research is conducted, though, let it suffice to say that the economic rise of the low country in the eighteenth century owed something to the labor exploitation permitted under the institution of slavery.

Thus, increases in both factor inputs and total factor productivity as well as changes in market conditions and the exploitation permitted by the institution of Negro slavery all contributed to the low country's remarkable economic record in the eighteenth century. On a deeper level, of course, the economic possibilities of the low country were given form by the particular relationship at that time among natural- and market forces, man's institutions, and his mind. As we have seen, the relationship among such forces in the low country during the eighteenth century was such as to lead to aggregate expansion and intensive growth, increasing social stability, and the accumulation of vast wealth. To a society, in other words, that, despite tremendous mortality, had entered into its so-called golden age.

For all its luster and its early accomplishments, however, the low country was not able to sustain its economic and social success and the area fell into stagnation and decline during the nineteenth and twentieth centuries. In the next chapter we shall attempt to explain the reasons for the low country's subsequent demise. In so doing, we shall argue that some of the reasons were closely related to, in fact, grew out of conditions associated with the area's eighteenth-century economic rise. Despite its many impressive achievements the economy of the low country during the eighteenth century was not an unalloyed success. No economy ever is, of course, for, as one would-be poet in eighteenth-century South Carolina noted with wry wit, even "the Nicest Gingerbread is spotted with Flyshits."[181]

4

"Lay dis body down": The Economic Demise of the Low Country

On January 22, 1737, a "very Melancholy accident" was reported in the *South-Carolina Gazette*. A planter's son and a Negro slave, according to the newspaper, disappeared while traveling by canoe down the Ashley River for Charleston, where the former—apparently a young boy—was to attend school. Being missed, a search was launched after them. This effort notwithstanding, neither the white boy nor the Negro slave ever was seen alive again. Their bodies ultimately were found, however, ". . . sticking in the Mud in the said River, their Arms clasping one another."[1] Their deathly embrace seems, in retrospect, a fitting metaphor for the economic history of the area they both called home. *Requiescant in pace.*

The economy of the South Carolina low country collapsed in the nineteenth century. Collapse did not come suddenly—many feel, for example, that the area's "golden age" lasted until about 1820—but come it did nonetheless.[2] By the late nineteenth century it was clear that the forces responsible for the area's earlier dynamism had been routed, the dark victory of economic stagnation virtually complete. Indeed, so complete was this victory that much of the low country remains languid even today. In this chapter we shall attempt to explain some of the reasons for the low country's demise. In so doing, it is hoped that we shall also gain greater insight into the nature of the area's eighteenth-century rise.

That the economy of the South Carolina low country was in ruins by the end of the nineteenth century there is general scholarly agreement. The particular road to ruination, however, is still a matter of scholarly debate. While it is true that the low country's dismal economic position has been explained in a variety of ways over the years, most explanations, nevertheless, fall within one or the other of two broad interpretive schemes. In one, economic collapse is attributed to the direct impact of civil war and the concomitant dislocations occasioned by emancipation. The combined effects of these phenomena, it is claimed, were both necessary and sufficient to bring down an economic order the health of which essentially was sound as late as 1861. In the other, the plantation economy of the low country

is seen as a tenuous one from the start, moreover, one whose severe limitations and structural problems clearly were evident by 1861. According to proponents of this interpretive scheme, the problems associated with civil war and emancipation exacerbated rather than initiated the low country's economic downfall. Which of these two interpretive schemes—each of which, one should note, has an analogue that purportedly explains the evolution of the southern economy as a whole—is correct? We shall argue below that the latter position is closer to the truth, that is to say, that the low country's economic problems were structural in nature and that its economic demise did not begin with Fort Sumter but many years before.[3]

This said, one hastens to add that the economy of the low country was not moribund in the antebellum period. Maudlin depictions of the low country in deep decay, melancholy reports of grass growing "uninterrupted" in some of Charleston's main business districts, however familiar, exaggerate the area's economic plight by half.[4] For the low country's antebellum economic decline was relative rather than absolute—at least until the eve of the Civil War. A brief look at certain data on population, output, trade, and wealth in the low country will bear out this point.

After growing rapidly in the colonial period, the population of the South Carolina low country increased at a much slower rate in the period from the American Revolution through the Civil War.[5] This can be seen in Table 4-1 below, wherein appear decennial—in one case, vicennial—figures on the low country's

Table 4-1. Population of the South Carolina Low Country, 1770–1870

Year	Total	White	Black Slave	Free Black	Total Black	Percentage Black
1770	88,244	19,066	69,178[1]	— —	69,178	78.39%
1790	107,860	28,644	78,000	1,216	79,216	73.44
1800	132,673	33,873[2]	97,170	1,630	98,800	74.47
1810	151,208	38,061	110,711	2,436	113,147	74.83
1820	181,731[3]	44,612	132,637	4,482	137,119	75.45
1830	196,040	47,433	143,748	4,859	148,607	75.80
1840	192,291	50,612	137,253	4,426	141,679	73.68
1850	209,262	59,328	144,782	5,152	149,934	71.65
1860	218,015	69,928	142,805	5,282	148,087	67.92
1870	213,098[4]	69,455		143,643	143,643	67.41

Sources: See Chapter 3 above for estimate of low-country population in 1770; United States Department of Commerce and Labor, Bureau of the Census, *Heads of Families at the First Census of the United States Taken in the Year 1790. South Carolina* (Washington, D.C.: United States Government Printing Office, 1908), p. 9; *Second Census of the United States, 1800* (Washington, D.C.: Duane, 1801), p. 2M; *Third Census of the United States, 1810, Book 1: Aggregate Amount of Persons Within the United States in the Year 1810,* (Washington, D.C.: n.p., 1811), p. 79; *Fourth Census of the United States, 1820,* Book 1 (Washington, D.C.: Gale and Seaton, 1821), pp. 26-27; *Fifth Census of the United States, 1830* (Washington, D.C.: Duff Green, 1832), pp. 94-95; *Sixth Census of the United States, 1840* (Washington, D.C.: Thomas Allen, 1841), pp. 44-46; *Seventh Census of the United States, 1850* (Washington, D.C.: Robert Armstrong, 1853), pp. 338-339; *Eighth Census of the United States, 1860: Population* (Washington, D.C.: United States Government Printing Office, 1864), p. 452; *Ninth Census of the United States, 1870: Statistics of Population* (Washington D.C.: United States Government Printing Office, 1872), pp. 60-61.

[1]Includes free blacks
[2]*Census* reads 33,863, but subtotals add to 33,873
[3]*Census* addition is slightly off in all categories; *Census* total is 180,360, but subtotals add to 181,731
[4]Plus sixty-five Indians. Low-country Indians, of whom there were always a small number, were not included in census enumerations between 1790 and 1860.

total population and the various components of the same between 1770 and 1870. Annual compound growth rates for each subperiod and for the 1770–1870 period as a whole appear in Table 4-2. Population growth, these tables reveal, was particularly slow in the low country in the half-century after 1820. Moreover, we find that there were more Negro slaves in this quintessential plantation area in 1830 than in 1860, a finding the significance of which should not be minimized.

The population history of Charleston, the marrowy center of the low country, conforms closely to the population history of the body of which it was part. During the colonial period, the port town grew in a continuous, if somewhat uneven manner, increasing in size from about 800 inhabitants in 1690 to approximately 12,800 in 1776. The annual compound growth rate for this 86-year period was 3.3 percent and Charleston on the eve of the Revolution was the fourth largest city in British North America, exceeded in size only by Philadelphia, New York, and Boston. Population estimates for the town at various bench marks during this period are presented in Table 4-3, as are growth rates for the intervals between bench marks and for the 1690–1776 period as a whole.

Charleston maintained its pattern of brisk growth in the period from 1776 to 1800. Although the South Carolina port had dropped to fifth in size among North American cities behind Philadelphia, New York, Baltimore, and Boston by the

Table 4–2. Low-Country Population: Annual Compound Growth Rates, 1770–1780 (percentage)

Year	Total	White	Black Slave	Free Black	Total Black
1770					
	1.0	2.1	0.6		0.7
1790					
	2.1	1.7	2.2	3.0	2.2
1800					
	1.3	1.2	1.3	4.1	1.4
1810					
	1.9	1.6	1.8	6.3	1.9
1820					
	0.8	0.6	0.8	0.8	0.8
1830					
	−0.2	0.7	−0.5	−0.9	−0.5
1840					
	0.8	1.6	0.5	1.5	0.6
1850					
	0.4	1.7	−0.1	0.2	−0.1
1860					
	−0.2	−0.1			−0.3
1870					
1770–1860	1.0	1.5	0.8		0.8
1770–1870	0.9	1.3			0.7

Sources: See Table 4–1. On compound growth rates, see Chapter 3, footnote 62.

Table 4–3. Estimated Population of Charleston and Annual Compound Growth Rates of Population, 1690–1776.

Year	Population	Growth Rate
1690	800	
		4.1%
1700	1,200	
		6.2
1710	2,200	
		3.0
1720	2,950	
		2.1
1730	3,650	
		5.6
1740	6,300	
		2.7
1750	8,200	
		1.9
1755	9,000	
		1.5
1760	9,700	
		1.4
1765	10,400	
		2.0
1770	11,500	
		1.8
1776	12,800	
1690–1776		3.3

Sources: See extracts of John Stewart's Letters, Mss. Locke, C. 30, Bodleian Library, Oxford University, Oxford, England (microfilm available at South Carolina Historical Society, Charleston, S.C., in collection entitled "John Locke, Correspondence, 1673–1704"); Francis Le Jau to the Secretary, April 15, 1707, in Frank J. Klingberg, ed., *The Carolina Chronicle of Dr. Francis Le Jau 1706–1717*, University of California Publications in History, vol. 53 (Berkeley: University of California Press, 1956), pp. 22–23, especially p. 22; "Mr. Neves List of Watch Men 8[ber] the 2th 1710," The American Papers of the Society for the Propagation of the Gospel, 16, Correspondence—South Carolina, 1702–1710, p. 271, Lambeth Palace Library, London, England (microfilm version, by World Microfilm Publications in association with the Lambeth Palace Library, is available at the South Caroliniana Library of the University of South Carolina, Columbia S.C.); Appendix 1–D; Peter A. Coclanis, "Death in Early Charleston: An Estimate of the Crude Death Rate for the White Population of Charleston 1722–1732," *South Carolina Historical Magazine* 85 (October 1984): 280–291; James Glen, An Attempt towards an Estimate of the Value of South Carolina, For the Right Honourable the Lords Commissioners for Trade and Plantations, March 1750/1, Records in the British Public Record Office Relating to South Carolina, 1663–1782, 36 vols. in facsimile, 24: 303–330, esp. p. 310, South Carolina Department of Archives and History, Columbia, S.C.; *South-Carolina Gazette,* June 19, 1755; _____, "A Curious New Description of Charles-Town in South-Carolina...," *The Universal Museum* 1 (August 1762): 435–37 and (September 1762): 477–79, especially p. 435; George Milligen-Johnston, *A Short Description of the Province of South-Carolina...*, (London: Printed for John Hinton, 1770), pp. 31–32; Alexander Hewatt, *An Historical Account of the Rise and Progress of the Colonies of South Carolina and Georgia*, 2 vols. (London: Printed for Alexander Donaldson, 1779), 2: 290–91; T.P. Harrison, ed., *Journal of a Voyage to Charlestown in So. Carolina by Pelatiah Webster in 1765*, Publications of the South Carolina Historical Society (Charleston: Published by the Society, 1898), pp. 4,10; John Bartram, "Diary of the Journey through the Carolinas, Georgia, and Florida, from July 1, 1765, to April 10, 1766," annotated by Francis Harper, in *Transactions of the American Philosophical Society*, new series, 33 (1942–44): 1–120, especially p. 15; William Bull to the Earl of Hillsborough, November 30, 1770, Records in the British Public Record Office Relating to South Carolina, 32: 365–406, especially p. 388; William Gerard de Brahm, *De Brahm's Report of the General Survey of the Southern District of North America*, ed. Louis de Vorsey, Jr. (Columbia: University of South Carolina Press, 1971), p. 90; *Wells's Register: Together With an Almanack... For the Year of our Lord 1774*, Twelfth ed. (Charleston: Robert Wells, 1774), p. 83; Chapman Milling, ed., *Colonial South Carolina: Two Contemporary Descriptions* (Columbia: University of South Carolina Press, 1951), p. 109. For alternative estimates of the population of early Charleston, see Carl Bridenbaugh, *Cities in the Wilderness: The First Century of Urban Life in America 1625–1742* (New York: Oxford University Press, 1971; originally published 1938), pp. 6, 143, 303.

latter year, Charleston was by that time a city with well over 20,000 inhabitants, over half of whom were black. The town, then, marched into the nineteenth century without apparent strain, much less enervation or exhaustion. Or so it seemed.

For Charleston's growth slowed considerably in the period between 1800 and 1860, a fact borne out in tables 4-4 and 4-5. Though it is true that the town's population nearly doubled during this sixty-year period, such an increase paled in comparison to increases experienced by other large cities on the Atlantic coast. During the same period, for example, Philadelphia and Boston experienced seven-fold increases in population, while Baltimore enjoyed an eight-fold increase. New York did better still, experiencing a thirteen-fold increase in numbers between 1800 and 1860.

Charleston, the fourth largest city in the United States in 1790 and the fifth largest in 1800, fell to twenty-second in population by 1860. Nor did the Carolina port hold its position in the second half of the nineteenth century; indeed, by 1900 Charleston, with a population of only 55,807, had fallen to sixty-eighth in size among cities in the United States. The degree to which the town had been left behind during the nineteenth century by its main eighteenth-century rivals—Philadelphia, New York, and Boston—is illustrated in Table 4-6. Clearly, Charleston, a major international port in 1800 and an important southern port in 1860, by 1900 harbored only memories. But we are getting ahead of ourselves, for lest we forget, both Charleston and the low country in general grew in numbers during the 1800–1860 period, though both were declining relatively.[6]

Aggregate output in the low country, so far as we can tell, also grew in the 1800–1860 period. Like population growth in the area, however, the rise in aggregate output apparently was irregular and, in comparison to other regions in the United States, relatively slow. Nowhere can this be seen more clearly than in the rice industry, the low country's *raison d'être* and, alas, a principal reason for its demise as well.

Table 4-4. Charleston Population, 1770–1870

Year	Total	White	Black Slave	Free Black	Total Black	Percentage Black
1770	11,500	5,200	6,275	25	6,300	54.78%
1790	16,359	8,089	7,684	586	8,270	50.55
1800	20,473	9,630	9,819	1,024	10,843	52.96
1810	24,711	11,568	11,671	1,472	13,143	53.19
1820	25,356[1]	11,229	12,652	1,475	14,127	55.71
1830	30,289	12,828	15,354	2,107	17,461	57.65
1840	29,261	13,030	14,673	1,558	16,231	55.47
1850	42,985	20,012	19,532	3,441	22,973	53.44
1860	40,522	23,376	13,909	3,237	17,146	42.31
1870	48,922[2]	22,749		26,173	26,173	53.50

Sources: See tables 4–1 and 4–3. For 1870, also see *Ninth Census of the United States, 1870: Statistics of Population,* pp. 258, 380.

[1]*Census* reads 24,780, but subtotals add to 25,356

[2] Plus 34 Indians for a total population of 48,956. There were probably a few Indians living in Charleston during the 1770-1860 period as well, though they were excluded in census enumerations. Note that when Indians are included in 1870 totals, the black component of Charleston's total population falls to 53.46 percent.

Table 4–5. Charleston Population: Annual Compound Growth Rates, 1770–1870 (percentage)

Year	Total	White	Black Slave	Free Black	Total Black
1770					
	1.8	2.2	1.0	17.1	1.4
1790					
	2.3	1.8	2.5	5.7	2.7
1800					
	1.9	1.9	1.7	3.7	1.9
1810					
	0.3	−0.3	0.8	0.0	0.7
1820					
	1.8	1.3	2.0	3.6	2.1
1830					
	−0.3	0.2	−0.5	− 3.0	−0.7
1840					
	3.9	4.4	2.8	8.2	3.5
1850					
	−0.6	1.6	−3.3	− 0.6	−2.9
1860					
	1.9	−0.3			4.3
1870					
1770–1860	1.4	1.7	0.9	5.6	1.1
1770–1870	1.5	1.5			1.4

Sources: See Table 4–4.

Table 4–6. Population of Philadelphia, New York, Boston, and Charleston and the Rank of Each in U.S. Urban Hierarchy, 1775–6 to 1900

	Philadelphia		New York		Boston		Charleston	
Year	Pop.	Rank	Pop.	Rank	Pop.	Rank	Pop.	Rank
1775-6	32,073	1	25,000	2	16,000	3	12,800	4
1790	42,520	1	33,131	2	18,038	3	16,359	4
1800	69,403	1	60,489	2	24,937	4	20,473	5
1810	91,874	2	96,373	1	33,250	4	24,711	5
1820	112,772	2	123,706	1	43,298	4	25,356	6
1830	161,410	2	202,589	1	61,392	4	30,289	6
1840	220,423	2	312,710	1	93,383	5	29,261	9
1850	340,045	2	515,547	1	136,881	4	42,985	12
1860	565,529	2	805,658	1	177,840	5	40,522	22
1870	674,022	2	942,292	1	250,526	7	48,956	26
1880	847,170	2	1,206,299	1	362,839	4	49,984	35
1890	1,046,964	3	1,515,301	1	448,477	5	54,955	52
1900	1,293,697	3	3,437,202[1]	1	560,892	5	55,807	68

Sources: Carl Bridenbaugh, *Cities in Revolt: Urban Life in America, 1743–1776* (New York: Capricorn Books, 1964; originally published, 1955), p. 216; Billy G. Smith, "Death and Life in a Colonial Immigrant City: A Demographic Analysis of Philadelphia," *Journal of Economic History* 37 (December 1977): 863–89, especially p . 871; Table 3; *Seventh Census of the United States, 1850*, p . lii; *Eighth Census of the United States, 1860: Population*, pp. 225, 337, 431–32, 452, and passim; *Ninth Census of the United States, 1870: Statistics of Population*, p . 380; *Twelfth Census of the United States, 1900: Population*, pt . I (Washington, D.C.: United States Government Printing Office, 1901), p. lxix.

[1]Brooklyn included.

Figures for rice exports from the low country on the eve of the American Revolution and on rice production in the area at various points in the antebellum period are presented in Table 4-7 below. It seems fair to conclude from data presented in this table and from data available elsewhere that in aggregate terms rice output in the low country grew between the Revolution and the Civil War, with most of the growth coming in the decades immediately preceding the clash between the Blue and the Gray.[7] Figures on rice exports per capita and rice production per capita, which are also included in the table, reveal, however, that despite a significant rise in aggregate output between the Revolution and the Civil War, in per capita terms, the inhabitants of the low country were exporting more rice annually between 1768 and 1772 than they were even producing, much less exporting, during the antebellum era. The extent to which these "disappointing" figures on

Table 4-7. Total and per Capita Exports of Clean Rice, 1768–1772, and Total and per Capita Production of Clean Rice, 1820–1859, South Carolina Low Country

Period	Pounds Exported (Annual Average)	Pounds Produced	Total Low-Country Population
1768–72	66,327,975		88,244 (1770)
	Pounds per Capita		751.64
1820[1]		43,951,800	181,731 (1820)
	Pounds per Capita		241.85
1830[2]		74,010,600	196,040 (1830)
	Pounds per Capita		377.53
1839		59,654,911	192,291 (1840)
	Pounds per Capita		310.23
1849		104,759,672	209,262 (1850)
	Pounds per Capita		500.62
1859		117,125,073	218,015 (1860)
	Pounds per Capita		537.23

Sources: See Table 3-13; J.L. Dawson and H.W. DeSaussure, *Census of the City of Charleston, South Carolina, for the Year 1848* . . . (Charleston: J.B. Nixon, 1849), pp. 118–19; *Sixth Census of the United States, 1840*, p. 192; *Seventh Census of the United States, 1850*, p. 346; *Eighth Census of the United States, 1860: Agriculture*, (Washington, D.C.: United States Government Printing Office, 1864), pp. 128–129. Note that the figure for rice production for 1849 differs from the figure given in the *Seventh Census of the United States, 1850* because the figure given for clean rice in the census is actually for rough rice. See J.D.B. De Bow, *Statistical View of the United States . . . Being a Compendium of the Seventh Census* . . . (Washington, D.C.: 1854), pp. 170, 173–174. I am indebted to Robert E. Gallman for pointing out this fact. Note, too, that in estimating clean rice production for 1849, I assumed that 45 pounds of rough rice were equal to 30 pounds of clean rice.

[1]Year ending September 30 (Oct. 1, 1819–Sept. 30, 1820)
[2]Year ending September 30 (Oct. 1, 1829–Sept. 30, 1830)

rice production per capita during the antebellum period were due to structural changes in the economy of the low country rather than to structural limitations and weaknesses in the same is, of course, debatable. Unfortunately, it is also probably unanswerable. That rice prices were fairly stable during the period—in general, at higher levels than they had been during the colonial era—adds kindling to this already combustible interpretive issue.[8]

Though rice dominated the low-country economy, other agricultural and nonagricultural activities also were important. Here, too, we find gains in output during the 1800–1860 period. In the agricultural sector, for example, cotton, which emerged as the second staple of the low country after the collapse of the indigo industry late in the eighteenth century, grew to substantial proportions by the late antebellum period. With long-staple or Sea Island varieties in the low country severely constrained by geography and short-staple varieties in competition with low cost, high quality cotton from the West, cotton production in the area grew in the face of formidable obstacles, however, and thus, within narrowly circumscribed limits.[9]

The lumber and naval-stores industries—extractive activities that had played prominent roles in the low country early in the eighteenth century—re-emerged in the nineteenth century as well and, after the late 1840s, became fairly important in parts of the region, particularly in the districts of Georgetown and Horry. These activities, which were sometimes classified as agricultural and at other times as industrial, in no way rivaled rice or cotton but nonetheless served to render allegedly barren land productive, if not spectacularly profitable.[10]

Aggregate output in the low country also grew as a result of the expansion of manufacturing activity in the area during the antebellum period. Indeed, though both small and rudimentary by northeastern standards, the low country's manufacturing sector, which was dominated by agricultural- and raw-material processing, had attained some significance by the eve of the Civil War.[11] In 1849, for example, the value of the annual product of manufacturing activity in the low country exceeded $3 million; a decade later the value of the same approached—if Ernest Lander is correct, may even have exceeded—$5 million. Moreover, during the late antebellum period, Charleston was the third largest manufacturing center in the entire South, trailing only Richmond and New Orleans.[12] Manuscript census data on manufacturing activity in both Charleston and each of the districts of the low country in 1849 and 1859 are presented in Table 4-8. It is clear from the data in this table that if the low-country economy remained wedded to plantation staples in the antebellum period, this bond did not foreclose the possibility of dalliances with certain processing and fabricating industries.[13]

The rise in aggregate output, not only in the low country but in its hinterland as well, was reflected in the growth of both internal and external trade and commerce during the antebellum era. Indeed, since aggregate output includes the value of services as well as goods, increased trade not only reflected but also contributed in its own right to the area's economic expansion. Intrastate trade in South Carolina grew substantially in the first sixty years of the nineteenth century. Transportation improvements—roads, canals, and particularly railroads—and the development of

Table 4–8. Value of Manufactures and Value Added in Manufacturing, South Carolina Low Country, 1849 and 1859

| District | 1849 | | 1859 | |
	Value	Value Added	Value	Value Added
Beaufort	$ 50,530	$ 39,850	$ 74,445	$ 47,779
Charleston	2,743,505	1,260,666	2,262,436	1,378,811
Colleton	17,150	15,650	missing	missing
Georgetown	66,519	31,208	1,558,300	507,590
Horry	137,231.50	58,656	467,043	141,876
Marion	— —	— —	131,658	73,702
Williamsburg	— —	— —	188,596	78,274
Total	$3,014,935.50	$1,406,030	$4,682,478	$2,228,032

Sources: Manuscript returns, Seventh Census of the United States, 1850, Manufactures, South Carolina; Manuscript returns, Eighth Census of the United States, 1860, Manufactures, South Carolina, South Carolina Department of Archives and History. Missing information and deficiencies in reporting suggest that the data above best can be used to illustrate broad trends.

a number of fall-line and upcountry towns and "trading places" facilitated the efforts of market-oriented Carolinians to traffic and trade, buy and sell.[14] Despite the jump in intrastate trade in South Carolina during the antebellum period, one would do well to note that in comparison to states in other regions—states in the Midwest especially—the size of the internal market in South Carolina was very modest even in 1860.[15] That the internal market was still so limited was due, as we shall see, primarily to the fact that by 1860 the economy of South Carolina had been shaped and in some ways distorted by its external markets for well over a century and a half.

Whether measured in terms of shipping statistics, the value of foreign exports, or even the volume of bills and receipts from the West, it is clear that South Carolina's commercial intercourse with both other countries and other states increased between 1800 and the advent of the Civil War. This can be seen in tables 4-9 through 4-11 below, wherein appear serial data on vessel entries and clearances at Charleston, tonnage entering Charleston from foreign countries and clearing Charleston for foreign countries, and the value of exports from the Palmetto State. Moreover, one roughly can gauge the scope of trade between South Carolina and the West from the export figures in Table 4-11. Between 1850 and 1860, for example, the value of foreign exports from South Carolina nearly doubled. Cotton and rice, so far as we can tell, accounted for over 95 percent of the value of foreign exports from South Carolina during this period. Over the course of the decade, one in which both cotton and rice prices generally were stable, cotton production in South Carolina—and presumably exports of cotton produced in the Palmetto State as well—rose by about 17.5 percent, while exports of South Carolina rice remained about the same.[16] Given these data on production, exports, and prices and the importance of cotton and rice in the composition of South Carolina's export mix, it is extremely unlikely that one can explain the increase in the total value of South Carolina's foreign exports between 1850 and 1860 by focusing upon goods

Table 4–9. Vessels Entering and Clearing Charleston, 1768–1772 and 1828–1848

Year	Entries	Clearances
1768	448	429
1769	433	434
1770	455	451
1771	489	487
1772	452	485
1828	786*	643*
1829	1276	1108
1830	1239	1290
1831	1264	1304
1832	1359	1274
1833	1274	1287
1834	1402	1360
1835	1320	1330
1836	1409	1368
1837	1618	1579
1838	1866	1818
1839	1969	1994
1840	1740	1772
1841	1673	1610
1842	1718	1713
1843	1742	1733
1844	1820	1853
1845	2008	1973
1846	1905	1892
1847	1914	1882
1848	1879	1847

*Nine months only

Sources: Converse D. Clowse, *Measuring Charleston's Overseas Commerce, 1717–1767: Statistics from the Port's Naval Lists* (Washington, D.C.: University Press of America, 1981), p. 108; Dawson and DeSaussure, *Census of the City of Charleston, South Carolina, for the Year 1848*, pp. 60-71.

and commodities produced in the Palmetto State alone. Indeed, with the development during the decade of good rail connections between South Carolina and the West, it is in all likelihood to the latter area—to that area's cotton in particular—that we should look to explain the residual.[17]

Though the data on trade presented thus far show plainly that South Carolina was not commercially stagnant during the antebellum period as is sometimes alleged, other evidence can be marshalled in support of the proposition that in relative terms both Charleston and South Carolina were losing considerable ground. Charleston, for example, lost much of its ability to import directly from Europe during the antebellum period, having become in many ways a satellite of ports further north. Nor did the town retain its earlier status as the South's leading port: by 1860, Charleston ranked well behind New Orleans and Mobile, and Savannah was gaining fast.[18] The relative decline of South Carolina in general and Charleston especially in terms of external trade and commerce is starkly expressed in tables 4-12 and 4-13, wherein are presented some data on trade for a number of states

Table 4–10. Tonnage Entering Charleston From Foreign Countries and Tonnage Clearing Charleston for Foreign Countries 1821–1860 (thousands of tons)

Year	Tonnage Entering	Tonnage Clearing	Year	Tonnage Entering	Tonnage Clearing
1821[1]	49	64	1841	54	87
1822[1]	46	63	1842	63	95
1823[1]	53	78	1843[2]	79	112
1824[1]	57	79	1844	74	93
1825[1]	45	74	1845	71	117
1826	56	82	1846	56	75
1827	64	93	1847	74	91
1828	50	73	1848	61	89
1829	51	90	1849	98	143
1830	72	72	1850	96	121
1831	53	77	1851	92	138
1832	52	89	1852	101	140
1833	49	86	1853	94	131
1834	54	100	1854	89	123
1835	53	82	1855	88	140
1836	56	96	1856	121	161
1837	58	88	1857	126	143
1838	64	106	1858	126	145
1839	54	81	1859	129	161
1840	60	105	1860	126	179

Source: Robert G. Albion, *The Rise of New York Port, 1815–1860* (Newton Abbot, Devon, England: David & Charles, 1970; originally published 1939), pp. 392–93. One should note that Albion used a rounding method which occasionally results in discrepancies between figures given above and the closest thousand .

[1]Figures for 1821–25 are for South Carolina rather than Charleston alone . Totals for Charleston alone, however, would be almost the same as those for South Carolina as a whole .

[2]Nine months only

during the antebellum period. In trade as in output, manufacturing, and population, then, South Carolina—especially the low country—despite absolute gains, was continually falling back.

What, one might ask, did the low country's "relative decline" actually mean to the inhabitants of the area? That is to say, how did the area compare over time to other regions in the United States in terms of per capita income and wealth?[19] Available data from two bench marks, eighty-five years apart, indicate, as logic would suggest, that the contagion diagnosed above was manifest by 1860 in these indices as well. Here, too, then, we find evidence of a relative deterioration in the low country's well-being, its economic health, between the time of the American Revolution and the eve of the Civil War. One cannot stress too strongly, however, that deterioration—until the late 1850s at least—still was relative, that there was yet no need to sound the knell. Indeed, though its economic condition was weakening, the low country did not succumb at once; rather, it clung to life for decades yet to come.

In 1774 the South Carolina low country was by many standards of measurement the wealthiest area in British North America, if not the entire world. This, Alice Hanson Jones's fine studies on wealth and wealth-holding patterns in the eighteenth

Table 4–11. Value of Exports from South Carolina, 1815–1860 (millions of dollars)

Year	Value of Exports	Year	Value of Exports
1815	$ 6	1839	$10
1816	10	1840	10
1817	10	1841	8
1818	11	1842	7
1819	8	1843[1]	7
1820	8	1844	7
1821	7	1845	8
1822	7	1846	6
1823	6	1847	10
1824	8	1848	8
1825	11	1849	9
1826	7	1850	11
1827	8	1851	15
1828	6	1852	11
1829	8	1853	15
1830	7	1854	11
1831	6	1855	12
1832	7	1856	17
1833	8	1857	16
1834	11	1858	16
1835	11	1859	17
1836	13	1860	21
1837	11		
1838	11		

Source: Albion, *The Rise of New York Port*, p. 390. One should note that Albion used a rounding method which occasionally results in discrepancies between figures given above and the closest million. For figures on exports from South Carolina between 1791 and 1815, see *De Bow's Review* 2 (December 1846): 402.

[1] Nine months only

century have made clear.[20] The difference in mean per capita wealth between the free population of the Charleston District—the most populous of the low country's three districts in the late eighteenth century—and similar populations in other parts of British North America can be seen in Table 4-14 below. The data presented in the table reveal that when both human and nonhuman wealth are included in calculations of mean per capita wealth, the difference between the low country and the other areas is tremendous; when human wealth is excluded, the gap, of course, narrows but is quite substantial nonetheless.

Though these data obviously tell us much about differential wealth-holding patterns in British North America, they do not tell us everything. In omitting servants and slaves—potential wealth-holders and, early-modern causuistry notwithstanding, certainly human beings—from consideration, they leave out almost 23 percent of the population of the colonies in general, alas, over 78 percent of the population of the low country. By combining Jones's basic wealth data for 1774 with my own estimate of the population of the Charleston District in the same year, we can derive estimates of mean per capita wealth for the total population of the low country, not just for that portion of the population that was free.[21] Such estimates

Table 4–12. Value of Exports from Selected Coastal States, 1815–1860 (millions of dollars)

Year	NY	MA[1]	PA	MD	LA	SC	GA	AL	VA
					States				
1815	10	5	4	5	5	6	4		6
1816	19	10	7	7	5	10	7		8
1817	18	11	8	8	9	10	8		5
1818	17	11	8	7	12	11	11	– –	7
1819	13	11	6	5	9	8	6	– –	4
1820	13	11	5	6	7	8	6	– –	4
1821	13	12	7	3	7	7	6	– –	3
1822	17	12	9	4	7	7	5	– –	3
1823	19	13	9	6	7	6	4	– –	4
1824	22	10	9	4	7	8	4	– –	3
1825	35	11	11	4	12	11	4	– –	4
1826	21	10	8	4	10	7	4	1	4
1827	23	10	7	4	11	8	4	1	4
1828	22	9	6	4	11	6	3	1	3
1829	20	8	4	4	12	8	4	1	3
1830	19	7	4	3	15	7	5	2	4
1831	25	7	5	4	16	6	3	2	4
1832	26	11	3	4	16	7	5	2	4
1833	25	9	4	4	18	8	6	4	4
1834	25	10	3	4	26	11	7	5	5
1835	30	10	3	3	36	11	8	7	6
1836	28	10	3	3	37	13	10	11	6
1837	27	9	3	3	35	11	8	9	3
1838	23	9	3	4	31	11	8	9	3
1839	33	9	5	4	33	10	5	10	5
1840	34	10	6	5	34	10	6	12	4
1841	33	11	5	4	34	8	3	10	5
1842	27	9	3	4	28	7	4	9	3
1843[2]	16	6	2	2	27	7	4	11	1
1844	32	9	3	5	30	7	4	9	2
1845	36	10	3	5	27	8	4	10	2
1846	36	10	4	6	31	6	2	5	3
1847	49	11	8	9	42	10	5	9	5
1848	53	13	5	7	40	8	3	11	3
1849	45	10	5	8	37	9	6	12	3
1850	52	10	4	6	38	11	7	10	3
1851	86	12	5	5	54	15	9	18	3
1852	87	16	5	6	49	11	4	17	2
1853	78	19	6	7	68	15	7	16	3
1854	122	21	10	11	60	11	4	13	4
1855	113	28	6	10	55	12	7	14	4
1856	119	29	7	11	80	17	8	23	5
1857	134	30	7	13	91	16	10	20	7
1858	108	22	6	10	88	16	9	21	7
1859	117	18	5	9	101	17	15	28	6
1860	145	17	5	9	107	21	18	38	5

Key: New York, Massachusetts, Pennsylvania, Maryland, Louisiana, South Carolina, Georgia, Alabama, Virginia
(– –) indicates less than $1 million.
[1]MA figures include Maine until 1820.
[2]Nine months only.

Source: Robert G. Albion, *The Rise of New York Port*, p. 390. One should note that Albion used a rounding method which occasionally results in discrepancies between figures given above and the closest million. One should also note that the export figures cited by Albion for the U.S. – to which his figures on the exports of individual states presumably are related – differ from export figures for the U.S. compiled by Douglass C. North, particularly during the 1850s. See North, *The Economic Growth of the United States, 1790–1860* (Englewood Cliffs, N.J.: Prentice-Hall, 1961), p. 233.

Table 4–13. Value of Imports into Selected Coastal States, 1821–1860 (millions of dollars)

Year	NY	MA	PA	MD	LA	SC	GA	AL
				States				
1821	23	14	8	4	3	3	1	– –
1822	35	18	11	4	3	2	– –	– –
1823	29	17	13	4	4	2	– –	– –
1824	36	15	11	4	4	2	– –	– –
1825	49	15	15	4	4	1	– –	– –
1826	38	17	13	4	4	1	– –	– –
1827	38	13	11	4	4	1	– –	– –
1828	41	15	12	5	6	1	– –	– –
1829	34	12	10	4	6	1	– –	– –
1830	35	10	8	4	7	1	– –	– –
1831	57	14	12	4	9	1	– –	– –
1832	53	18	10	4	8	1	– –	– –
1833	55	19	10	5	9	1	– –	– –
1834	73	17	10	4	13	1	– –	– –
1835	88	19	12	5	17	1	– –	– –
1836	118	25	15	7	15	2	– –	– –
1837	79	19	11	7	14	2	– –	– –
1838	68	13	9	5	9	2	– –	– –
1839	99	19	15	6	12	3	– –	– –
1840	60	16	8	4	10	2	– –	– –
1841	75	20	10	6	10	1	– –	– –
1842	57	17	7	4	8	1	– –	– –
1843[1]	31	16	2	2	8	1	– –	– –
1844	65	20	7	3	7	1	– –	– –
1845	70	22	8	3	7	1	– –	– –
1846	74	24	7	4	7	– –	– –	– –
1847	84	34	9	4	9	1	– –	– –
1848	94	28	12	5	9	1	– –	– –
1849	92	24	10	4	10	1	– –	– –
1850	111	30	12	6	10	1	– –	– –
1851	111	32	14	6	12	2	– –	– –
1852	132	33	14	6	12	2	– –	– –
1853	178	41	18	6	13	1	– –	– –
1854	195	48	21	6	14	1	– –	– –
1855	164	45	15	7	12	1	– –	– –
1856	210	43	16	9	16	1	– –	– –
1857	236	47	17	10	24	2	– –	– –
1858	178	42	12	8	19	2	– –	– –
1859	229	43	14	9	18	1	– –	– –
1860	248	41	14	9	22	1	– –	1

Key: New York, Massachusetts, Pennsylvania, Maryland, Louisiana, South Carolina, Georgia, Alabama

(– –) indicates less than $1 million.

[1]Nine months only.

Source: Albion, *The Rise of New York Port,* p. 391. One should note that Albion used a rounding method which occasionally results in discrepancies between figures given above and the closest million.

Table 4-14. Wealth per Free Capita in New England, the Middle Colonies, and the Charleston District, 1774 (£ sterling)

Area	Total Wealth	Nonhuman Wealth
New England	38.2	38.0
Middle Colonies	45.8	44.1
Charleston District	416.0	179.6

Source: Alice Hanson Jones, *Wealth of a Nation To Be: The American Colonies on the Eve of the Revolution* (New York: Columbia University Press, 1980), pp. 58, 380. Note that the figures above are for physical wealth. Note, too, that per capita figures for the Charleston District were derived by dividing figures on wealth per free wealthholder in the district by 4.26. The divisor is that used by Jones for the South as a whole in 1774. See Jones, p. 42.

for both the Charleston District—our proxy for the low country—and other parts of British North America appear in Table 4-15. As we can see, mean total wealth per capita still is far higher in the low country than in these other areas, while mean nonhuman wealth per capita was 1.4 percent lower in the low country than in New England and about 12 percent lower than in the Middle Colonies. According to most, but not all, standards of measurement, then, the low country—or the Charleston District at least—was far wealthier than either New England or the Middle Colonies in 1774.

By the eve of the Civil War, however, this situation had changed in several important ways, each of which suggested a relative decline in the economic fortunes of the inhabitants of the low country. Though it is true that by most standards of measurement, mean per capita wealth still was higher in the low country than in New England or the Middle Atlantic states, the gap between these areas and the low country had narrowed considerably. Moreover, while according to one standard of measurement—mean nonhuman wealth per capita—the low country had trailed both New England and the Middle Colonies even in 1774, the distance separating the low country and these other areas, which in 1774 had been short, by 1860 had greatly increased. Let us now look more closely at these changes in regional wealth and wealth-holding.

One can calculate mean per capita wealth for the population of specified areas in the United States in 1860 by using aggregate data on wealth and population available in the federal census for that year. Indeed, one can do so in a number of ways. Figures on mean total wealth per free capita and mean total wealth per capita for each district in the low country and for the area as a whole in 1860 are presented, for example, in tables 4-16 and 4-17 respectively.[22] For most purposes, one or the other of these standards of measurement will do; for some, however,

Table 4-15. Wealth per Capita in New England, the Middle Colonies, and the Charleston District, 1774 (£ sterling)

Area	Total Wealth	Nonhuman Wealth
New England	36.6	36.4
Middle Colonies	41.9	40.2
Charleston District	83.2	35.9

Source: Jones, *Wealth of a Nation To Be*, pp. 54, 380. For an explanation of the method used to derive the total population of the Charleston District in 1774, see footnote 21 in this chapter.

Table 4–16. Wealth per Free Capita in the South Carolina Low Country in 1860

District	Population			Wealth	
	White	Free Black	Total Free	Aggregate	Per Capita
Beaufort	6,714	809	7,523	$ 29,970,071	$3,983.79
Charleston	29,188	3,622	32,810	63,646,736	1,939.86
Colleton	9,255	354	9,609	33,453,472	3,481.47
Georgetown	3,013	183	3,196	12,905,879	4,038.13
Horry	5,564	39	5,603	1,873,152	334.31
Marion	11,007	232	11,239	16,486,510	1,456.90
Williamsburg	5,187	43	5,230	11,157,107	2,133.29
Low Country	69,928	5,282	75,210	$169,492,927	$2,253.60

Sources: *Eighth Census of the United States, 1860: Population*, p. 452; *Eighth Census of the United States, 1860: Statistics* (Washington, D.C.: United States Government Printing Office, 1866), p. 312.

one might wish also to calculate figures for nonhuman wealth. Indeed, if one wishes—as we do—to compare the per capita wealth of an area where slavery was important with others where free rather than bound labor was the rule, it is particularly important to produce per capita figures not only for total wealth in the slave society but for its nonhuman wealth too.

In order to calculate the value of nonhuman wealth in a given area, one must know both the size of the slave population in the area and that population's approximate value. Census data, of course, are available on the size of the slave population in the low country, but we ourselves must construct estimates of this population's value. This is more difficult than one might suspect, for, so far as we can tell, the prices of low-country slaves did not conform very well to slave prices in the South in general. Most scholars estimate that the average value of a slave in the South on the eve of the Civil War was between about $900 and $1200, with prime hands worth about $1800 apiece, the aged and infirm virtually worthless, and most other slaves somewhere in between.[23] The best data on slave prices in the low country, those compiled by U.B. Phillips, suggest, however, that prices were

Table 4–17. Wealth per Capita in the South Carolina Low Country in 1860

District	Population			Wealth	
	Free	Slave	Total	Aggregate	Per Capita
Beaufort	7,523	32,530	40,053	$ 29,970,071	$748.26
Charleston	32,810	37,290	70,100	63,646,736	907.94
Colleton	9,609	32,307	41,916	33,453,472	798.11
Georgetown	3,196	18,109	21,305	12,905,879	605.77
Horry	5,603	2,359	7,962	1,873,152	235.26
Marion	11,239	9,951	21,190	16,486,510	778.03
Williamsburg	5,230	10,259	15,489	11,157,107	720.32
Low Country	75,210	142,805	218,015	$169,492,927	$777.44

Sources: *Eighth Census of the United States, 1860: Population*, p. 452; *Eighth Census of the United States, 1860: Statistics*, p. 312.

considerably lower in this area, with prime hands valued at about $1200–$1250 and the "average" slave worth $600–$625 or roughly half as much.[24] Though it is not completely clear why this should be so, it appears that Phillips was indeed correct. For even at $900 per slave, the value of human property alone in the low country in 1860 would have been far greater than the value of *all* of the personal property that—according to the census-takers at least—the inhabitants of the low country owned.[25]

Faute de mieux, let us assume, then, that the average value for each of the low country's 142,805 slaves in 1860 was about $600 or $625. With this information we can, through simple multiplication and division, estimate mean nonhuman wealth per free capita and mean nonhuman wealth per capita in the low country in 1860.[26] Such estimates appear below.

Mean Nonhuman Wealth, South Carolina Low Country, 1860

Per Free Capita	$1,066.88–$1,114.34
Per Capita	$ 368.05–$ 384.42

Thus, we have calculated the "per capita" wealth of the "inhabitants" of the low country in 1860 in four different ways, a necessary task given the existence and importance in the area of Negro slavery. In comparing per capita wealth in the low country in 1860 with figures for Massachusetts, New York, and Pennsylvania, that is, with figures for New England and the Middle Atlantic states, our task is somewhat easier to complete, for by that time there no longer were any slaves in these three northeastern states, the concept "human property" having become obsolete in each. To calculate mean per capita wealth for these states in 1860, therefore, one need merely turn to the 1860 census for aggregate figures on wealth and population and do some simple division. Gone are the ambiguities over matters of definition. The results of such calculations appear in Table 4-18. In Table 4-19, these results are juxtaposed with those on mean per capita wealth in the low country. If we then compare the patterns discernible in Table 4-19 with those in tables 4-14 and 4-15, we find that by 1860 Massachusetts, New York, and Pennsylvania—proxies for New England and the Middle Colonies, so to speak— have all improved their positions *vis-à-vis* the South Carolina low country. The degree to which this was so can be seen more clearly in Table 4-20, wherein the data for New England and the Middle Colonies in 1774 and for Massachusetts, New York, and Pennsylvania in 1860 are expressed as percentages of mean per capita wealth in the Charleston District and the low country respectively.

Table 4–18. Wealth per Capita in Massachusetts, New York, and Pennsylvania in 1860

State	Population	Aggregate Wealth	Per Capita Wealth
Massachusetts	1,231,066	$ 769,651,672	$625.19
New York	3,880,735	2,316,743,547	596.99
Pennsylvania	2,906,215	1,659,208,924	570.92

Sources: Eighth Census of the United States, 1860: Population, pp. 218-19, 326-27, 410-11; *Eighth Census of the United States, 1860: Statistics,* pp. 304, 308, 311.

Table 4-19. Wealth per Free Capita and Wealth per Capita in Massachusetts, New York, and Pennsylvania, and the South Carolina Low Country in 1860

Area	Total Wealth	Nonhuman Wealth
Wealth per Free Capita		
Massachusetts	$ 625.19	$ 625.19
New York	596.99	596.99
Pennsylvania	570.92	570.92
S.C. Low Country	2253.60	1066.88–1114.34
Wealth per Capita		
Massachusetts	$ 625.19	$625.19
New York	596.99	596.99
Pennsylvania	570.92	570.92
S.C. Low Country	777.44	368.05–384.42

Sources: See tables 4–16, 4–17, and 4–18 and text above.

That the low country had declined relative to these other areas in terms of per capita wealth—measured in any way—is, thus, plain to see. Moreover, given the fact that the cost-of-living apparently was much higher during the antebellum period in the Southeast than in either New England or the Middle Atlantic states, the relative position of the low country by the eve of the Civil War probably was worse than the above data indicate.[27]

After the war, of course, the bottom fell out of the low-country economy and the area declined not only relatively but, for a time at least, absolutely as well. The relative decline of the area between 1865 and 1900 in terms of mean per capita income and wealth is well known and need not concern us much here. Suffice it to say that at the turn of the nineteenth century the low country was perhaps the poorest part of the poorest census region in the United States. That mean per capita income in this region in 1900 was but 45 percent of the national average and only 32.8 percent of the average for New England and the Middle Atlantic states will give us some idea of the depths to which the region had fallen.[28]

The possibility of a secular absolute decline in the economic fortunes of the inhabitants of the area deserves greater attention, for it is a staggering possibility,

Table 4-20a. Wealth of New England and the Middle Colonies as Percentages of Wealth in the Charleston District, 1774

Area	Total Wealth	Nonhuman Wealth
Wealth per Free Capita		
New England	9.18%	21.16%
Middle Colonies	11.01	24.55
Wealth per Capita		
New England	43.99	101.39
Middle Colonies	50.36	111.98

Sources: See tables 4–14 and 4–15.

Table 4–20b. Wealth of Massachusetts, New York, and Pennsylvania as Percentages of Wealth of the South Carolina Low Country, 1860

State	Total Wealth	Nonhuman Wealth
Wealth per Free Capita		
Massachusetts	27.74%	58.60%–56.10%
New York	26.49	55.96–53.57
Pennsylvania	25.33	53.51–51.23
Wealth per Capita		
Massachusetts	80.42%	169.87–162.63
New York	76.79	162.20–155.30
Pennsylvania	73.44	155.12–148.51

Sources: See tables 4–16 through 4–19.

indeed, in a North American context. Some data exist, however, that suggest that such a decline may, in fact, have occurred. In 1870, the last year in the nineteenth century for which quantitative data on individual wealth were assembled for the census, mean per capita wealth in the low country was $347.96.[29] This figure was between 5.46 percent and 9.48 percent lower than the estimated figure for mean nonhuman wealth per capita in the low country in 1860.[30] Moreover, if Richard Easterlin's estimates of regional income in the South Atlantic states are correct and if capital/output or wealth/income ratios in the area remained relatively stable between 1860 and 1880, it seems likely that per capita wealth in the low country still was lower in the latter year than it had been twenty years before.[31] Furthermore, it is not impossible, given the degree of stagnation and decline in the rice and Sea Island cotton industries in the late nineteenth century, that per capita income and wealth levels in the low country even in 1900 may not have exceeded levels reached before the war. To be sure, the economic effects of stagnation and decline in these industries must be weighed against other, positive developments: the advent of the phosphate industry, the growth of the manufacturing sector, and the spread of short-staple cotton cultivation in parts of the low country. At times, however, even silver linings have clouds and in the low country in the late nineteenth century, even positive economic developments were laden with contradictions. Thus, we find that the phosphate industry rose and fell in a generation, that the manufacturing sector was limited increasingly to raw-material processing and low value-added operations, and that the impressive increase of short-staple cotton production in such counties as Marion, Williamsburg, and Hampton occurred during a period of extremely unfavorable market conditions.[32]

Not to belabor the point much further, but the fact that population grew substantially in the low country in the decades after the Civil War also helps to explain the relatively limited effect of even positive economic developments in the area. Figures on population and the rate of population growth in the low country between 1870 and 1920 appear in Table 4-21. For a varied and complex set of reasons, many of which are still unclear today, both white and black population in the low country rose significantly after and at least partially as a result of

Table 4–21. Population of the South Carolina Low Country and Rates of Population Growth, Compounded Annually, 1870–1920

	Low Country Population			Rates of Growth (%)		
Year	White	Black	Total[1]	White	Black	Total
1870	69,455	143,643	213,163			
				2.58	2.94	2.82
1880	89,571	191,900	281,507			
				0.87	0.92	0.91
1890	97,638	210,405	308,153			
				1.59	0.72	1.00
1900	114,290	226,132	340,515			
				0.58	−0.87	−0.36
1910	121,056	207,238	328,330			
				1.57	−0.03	0.59
1920	141,406	206,561	348,104			
1870–1920				1.43	0.73	0.99

Sources: Ninth Census of the United States, 1870: Statistics of Population, pp. 60–61; *Tenth Census of the United States, 1880: Population* (Washington, D.C.: United States Government Printing Office, 1883), p. 407; *Eleventh Census of the United States, 1890: Population, Part I* (Washington, D.C.: United States Government Printing Office, 1895), pp. 427, 440, 443, 448; *Twelfth Census of the United States, 1900: Population, Part I,* pp. 555, 569, 572; *Thirteenth Census of the United States, 1910: Population, Vol. III* (Washington, D.C.: United States Government Printing Office, 1913), pp. 658, 660, 662, 664; *Fourteenth Census of the United States, 1920: Population, Vol. III* (Washington, D.C.: United States Government Printing Office, 1922), pp. 927, 929–933. Note that some scholars view the southern population figures in the 1870 census to be seriously flawed. See Roger L. Ransom and Richard Sutch, *One Kind of Freedom: The Economic Consequences of Emancipation* (New York: Cambridge University Press, 1977), pp. 53–54, 329. Note, too, that the negative growth rates for the black population of the low country between 1900 and 1920 were due to net out-migration. See George A. Devlin, "South Carolina and Black Migration 1865–1940: In Search of the Promised Land" (Ph.D. dissertation, University of South Carolina, 1984).

[1] Includes a small number of American Indians and Asians.

the Civil War and emancipation. Rising numbers put additional pressure on the area's economy, which already was severely strained. Though sustained economic growth theoretically may be possible even under such conditions, as Ester Boserup among others has maintained, in the low country real economic improvement would not come until well into the twentieth century and in some ways the area never has recovered completely from its fall from economic grace. In the remainder of this book we shall attempt to explain the dialectical nature of the relationship between the low country's eighteenth-century rise and its subsequent and prolonged travails.[33]

The low country's eighteenth-century economic rise, its economic will to power, was based upon its specialization in the production of plantation staples with bound labor. Such specialization, under prevailing market conditions, generally proved highly profitable to those individuals in both the low country and in Europe with capital directly involved in the production or distribution of such staples, particularly rice and indigo. Moreover, linkages engendered by the production of these staples benefited others both in the low country and the metropolis, primarily those whose skin color was such as to allow them control over the use and fruit of their own labor and capital.

Also associated with the low country's economic rise, though partially hidden by the rapidity of its ascent, was the economy's tendency, however, toward structural disarticulation, factoral distortions, and asymmetrical development. To be sure, the long-term effects of such tendencies are not necessarily pernicious. At times, structural disarticulation, distortion, and asymmetry can lead ultimately to sustained economic growth and development; one thinks immediately of Albert Hirschman's famous "unbalanced" path to growth.[34] In the case of the South Carolina low country, such tendencies, for a variety of reasons, ultimately led elsewhere. It is precisely this fact that we wish to explain.

As we argued in the last chapter, the particular relationship among certain key classes of independent variables largely determine the structure, pace, and performance of an economy at any given time. We have identified four such classes, under which are subsumed variables relating to the environment, markets, institutions, and *mentalité*. The relationship among these classes of variables was such in the low country during the early modern period that the area's specialization in plantation agriculture and its fierce commitment to bound labor were both predictable and, given existing production possibilities, economically rational. Indeed, in an economistic sense the white hegemonists' response to the production possibilities with which they were confronted commands a certain grudging respect even today. For despite short-term cyclical fluctuations, the economic order which emerged in the low country proved a very powerful "growth engine" over the course of the eighteenth century. And in an early modern context, lest we forget, intensive economic growth was no mean feat. All things considered, however, neither economic rationality nor one hundred years of material improvement is enough for us to proclaim the eighteenth-century economy of the low country a categorical success. Though its achievements certainly were considerable, this economy's inherent structural limitations later were to prove largely responsible for the area's relative underdevelopment.

For the emergence in the low country of a pattern of economic specialization informed by staple crops and bound labor led concomitantly to the emergence of an economic order whose internal structure and external orientation hindered both ready adaptation and further elaboration. The indurate nature of the low-country economy would prove to be no particular problem so long as the relationship among the sets of variables mentioned above held true. In the nineteenth century, however, this relationship changed, indeed, changed in such a way as to threaten not only accumulated stocks of wealth in the area but also future income flows.

In retrospect, the economic demise of the low country in the nineteenth century seems almost inevitable, for the changes alluded to above had left the area, if not totally defenseless, then, at the very least, extremely vulnerable. Whereas the particular forces operating in and upon the low country in the eighteenth century had proved unusually conducive to economic growth, the new circumstances proved almost uniformly unfavorable. Indeed, if in spirit the conjuncture of forces during the Age of Reason can be likened to a lively English ayre, the new conjuncture resembled nothing so much as a dirge. This can be seen in any number of ways. Let us turn first to the changes attending the progress of the market economy.

   That the low country's demise would issue largely from such progress would
have surprised, perhaps even shocked, most of the area's white inhabitants in the
first part of the nineteenth century. While it is doubtless true that the market and
its implications were intellectually and morally discomfiting to some Americans at
this time, low-country whites were far less concerned with the profundities of the
market than with its results. And certainly the market, up until then, had proven
itself consoling in such consequentialist terms. But as it progressed further—and
progress, ironically, signifies not only evolution, improvement, and amelioration
but also deterioration, as in a progressive disease—it helped to bring about far-
reaching changes with far different consequences for the low country. Some of
these changes did not affect the economy very much. Thus, the democratization of
politics, the romanticization of the arts, the appeal, among some, of a new materialist ontology, the recrudescence, among others, of the evangelical heart.[35] Other
changes mattered more, however, and when conjoined with certain institutional
and environmental forces—impedimenta, if you will—led to the deterioration and
ultimate death of the low-country rice industry, the area's *raison d'être* and the
main source of its earlier prosperity.
   The market's progress in the nineteenth century was developmental as well as
spatial, of course, and the economy of the low country, judged solely in terms of
functional viability, lost on both counts. To put it another way, changes in the
realms of both production and circulation worked against the low country. First,
the realm of production.
   As the market developed, the alienability of labor—increasingly made manifest
in the wage relationship—gained prominence in the West, taking on over time
all the accoutrements of ideology. With historical necessity and human agency
combining to bring new life to the old Lockean idea that everyone had the right
to his own labor power, this idea began to be taken more literally. The idea, in
fact, became an obsession in some places, though certainly not in South Carolina,
which resisted it with like passion.
   Despite a good showing rhetorically—Carolinians often got the better of free
labor advocates in both formal and substantive terms during the antebellum period—and on the battlefield during the Civil War, the citizenry of the Palmetto State
was forced, as a result of the South's defeat, to abandon slavery, a system of labor
which had been of monumental importance to its economy for over one hundred
fifty years.[36] As is well known, the system that replaced slavery—a bewildering
complex based on scratch freeholdings, manifold tenancy and cropping arrangements, and reconstituted plantations—transformed agriculture not just in the low
country or in South Carolina but throughout the South.[37] In recent years it has
become clear that for a variety of reasons, not the least of which was the devastation
wrought by the war itself, the efficiency of staple crop production often declined
sharply under the new system. It is equally clear, moreover, that neither the war
nor the transition to free labor helped the competitive position of the low-country
rice industry. But these developments did not kill it in and of themselves. For
there were other factors at work as well, factors that had less to do with Lincoln,
swamp angels, and Sherman's General Order No. 15, than with the development
of alternative sources of supply.

It is impossible to appreciate fully the importance of such alternative sources without recourse to the first principles of the low-country rice industry. From the start and, alas, to the finish, rice production in the low country meant production geared for external markets. To be sure, some rice always was consumed within the region itself, but local consumption was only of limited importance, consisting, as it did, mainly of inferior "nonmerchantable" grades of whole grain, small and broken rice, and such by-products as straw and offal.[38] Rather, the ultimate consumers of Carolina rice, by and large, did not reside or, for that matter, graze in the low country but far outside the region: in Europe, the West Indies, and in parts of North and South America hundreds, even thousands of miles away. Thus, the peculiar force and power of any serious competitive threats to the low country's market position. Lest we get ahead of ourselves, however, let us look more closely at the market for rice in the West, for we scarcely can understand the magnitude of the low country's loss unless we know something of what it had once possessed.

Of the great tropical and semitropical staples in the Americas, rice was by far the least significant. Despite the pretensions of low country planters and the puffery of later apologists for the industry, rice was never vital to the West. In comparison with sugar, cotton, and tobacco, which have been described with some accuracy in the literature as mighty, kingly, and holy commodities respectively, rice was but a humble footman or sexton, lacking even a hint of sovereignty in the marketplace.[39] Unlike the situation in parts of the East, where the cereal's power was virtually complete, in the West rice was nothing more or less than a versatile and cheap dietary substitute, supplement, or complement, particularly useful for feeding *lumpen* groups—slaves, orphans, soldiers, the poor–in the absence of, or instead of more desirable small grains. Rice, of course, also had other uses, but its contributions as an animal feed and in the distilling industry, for example, were modest as well.[40] Even when rice rose to significance in the U.S. brewing industry late in the nineteenth century, its employment therein was less a function of choice than one of price.[41] In sum, rice could hardly be deemed indispensable; its versatility and cost made it vendible, however, over a vast area stretching from Peru and Argentina to the shores of the Black Sea.

Such geographic reach notwithstanding, one area, Europe, constituted by far the greatest single market for rice in the West. This was true throughout the history of commercial rice production in South Carolina. Demand emanating from the West Indies and other areas was significant as well, but, as Table 4-22 clearly indicates, Europe was always the center of foreign demand.

Moreover, this table reveals that within Europe itself, demand for U.S. rice was considerable in the south—particularly in Spain and Portugal—but much greater in the north. Though it is impossible to chart precisely the course of northern European commodity flows in the eighteenth and nineteenth centuries, extant data, scattered widely in customs records, toll registers, and commercial manuals and journals, indicate that Germany was the center of consumption on this part of the Continent, with large quantities of rice entering the various German states and principalities from ports such as Amsterdam, Rotterdam, Hamburg, Bremen, and Danzig.[42] Significant amounts of rice were consumed elsewhere in northern

Table 4–22. U.S. Rice Exports by Destination, 1730–1739, 1790–1799, and 1850–1859

	1730–39	1790–99	1850–59
Total Exports (tons)	104,696	324,115	311,975
Destination (percentage of total)			
Northern Europe	77.4%	64.2%	48.6%
Southern Europe	17.6	8.2	0.9
North America	5.0	0.7	1.9
West Indies and Central America		25.6	36.3
South America	0.0	0.0	11.3
Africa	0.0	0.9	0.5
Asia	0.0	0.1	0.4
Uncertain	0.0	0.3	0.0
Total	100.0	100.0	99.9

Sources: United States Department of Commerce, Bureau of the Census, *Historical Statistics of the United States: Colonial Times to 1970*, 2 vols. (Washington, D.C.: United States Government Printing Office, 1975), 2:1192; James Glen, *A Description of South Carolina* . . . (London: R. and J. Dodsley, 1761), p. 93; Clowse, *Measuring Charleston's Overseas Commerce, 1717–1767*, pp. 59–64; *American State Papers* . . ., Class IV: Commerce and Navigation, Vol. VII (Washington, D.C.: Gales and Seaton, 1832), pp. 32, 122, 235, 284, 308, 339, 359, 381, 414, 428; *U.S. House of Representatives Executive Documents, Second Session, 31st Congress, No. 604, Vol. 8; U.S. Senate Executive Documents, First Session, 32d Congress, No. 628, Vol. 16; U.S. Senate Executive Documents, Second Session, 32d Congress, No 662, Vol. 5; U.S. Senate Executive Documents, First Session, 33d Congress, No. 703, Vol. 12, Part 2; U.S. Senate Executive Documents, Second Session, 33d Congress, No. 750, Vol. 5; U.S. House of Representatives Executive Documents, First Session, 34th Congress, No. 865, Vol. 16; U.S. Senate Executive Documents, Third Session, 34th Congress, No. 886, Vol. 13; U.S. Senate Executive Documents, First Session, 35th Congress, No. 931, Vol. 14; U.S. Senate Executive Documents, Second Session, 35th Congress, No. 989, Vol. 15; U.S. Senate Executive Documents, First Session, 36th Congress, No. 1034, Vol. 2.*

Note that the broad geographic units listed in the table should be considered final rather than intermediate destinations for the most part. The figures for the 1730s required some manipulation. According to Glen, 6 percent of total rice exports was consumed in Great Britain, Ireland, and the British Plantations. Data in Clowse and Coclanis indicate that very little was consumed in Great Britain or Ireland during this period. Thus, I estimated that 5 percent of total exports went to the British Plantations and 1 percent to Great Britain and Ireland. See Clowse, *Measuring Charleston's Overseas Commerce, 1717–1767*, pp. 59–64; Peter A. Coclanis, "Bitter Harvest: The South Carolina Low Country in Historical Perspective," *Journal of Economic History* 45 (June 1985): 251–59, especially p. 254.

Europe, however: with regularity in France, Belgium, and the Netherlands, for example, and, as the Sound tolls reveal, at least intermittently in Scandinavia and the eastern Baltic as well.[43] Furthermore, internal consumption in Great Britain, which generally had been quite limited in the eighteenth and early nineteenth century, increased after that time, especially after the repeal of the Corn Laws in 1846.[44] As alluded to earlier, some shipments of rice, having worked their way down the Danube, made it all the way to the Romanian ports of Ibraila and Galatz but shipments to that region paled in comparison with shipments to the west and north.[45]

South Carolina was the West's leading supplier of rice in the eighteenth century, dominating not only the European trade but also that of the Americas. Its domination, of course, was never complete. Rice was grown in Spain and Portugal, and rice grown in Piedmont and Lombardy supplied the Italian peninsula. Moreover, considerable quantities of Spanish and Italian rice also were shipped to France.[46] After about 1760, South Carolina's neighbor, Georgia, became a significant exporter in its own right, and by the end of the century Brazil had as well, with the latter enjoying particular market success, not surprisingly, in Portugal. Finally, some Indian rice found its way to Europe throughout the century.[47]

As the nineteenth century began, however, neither Italy, Georgia, Brazil, or India seemed to pose a serious threat to South Carolina's market position. In retrospect, neither Italy nor Brazil did. Georgia posed some problems, it is true, but the erosion of South Carolina's rice markets in the nineteenth century did not result primarily from direct competition with its immediate neighbor, but from the West's seemingly inexorable commercial expansion into Bengal, Java, and Lower Burma in the East Indies and Louisiana, Arkansas, and Texas in the Old Southwest.[48] Over time it was these areas that knocked low-country rice out of Europe, out of the American market, and, eventually, out altogether. Of these, Bengal proved the first major threat.

Bengali rice, of course, had long been arriving in Europe, both from the Levant and via transoceanic routes, but shipments increased dramatically once England's economic and political penetration of the Subcontinent intensified in the early nineteenth century. The story of England's penetration into India is well known and need not concern us here. For our purposes it is sufficient to note that such penetration, which was spurred in part by supply disruptions occasioned by the American Revolution, proceeded rapidly in the case of rice: even before the 1820s rice produced by Bengali peasants was cutting significantly into South Carolina's markets in northern Europe.[49] Moreover, a second East Indian supply source, the Dutch-controlled island of Java, rose to prominence in these same markets shortly thereafter.

This island, the pearl of the Malay archipelago, had been trading directly with the West since it fell under Portuguese control in the sixteenth century, but its effective integration into the Western economy did not come about for several centuries. Indeed, it was not until the establishment in 1830 of the so-called *Cultuurstelsel* or Culture System by the Dutch that such integration really began in earnest. With the establishment of this system, which essentially forced the indigenous population to produce cash crops for the state, tropical commodities from the island such as coffee, sugar, and indigo began streaming into Amsterdam and, later, Rotterdam, thence to be distributed throughout Europe.[50]

Rice originally was not included in the system—it was added in 1843—but the general intensification of production and Western control that the *Cultuurstelsel* at once reflected and represented led to massive exports of this commodity to Europe as well. In fact, as early as the late 1830s, so far as we can tell, Java rice surpassed U.S. rice in the main northern European entrepôts.[51] For a variety of internal reasons, including a series of export-induced rice famines on the island, Java did not last long as a major rice exporter to Europe, but by the 1850s nearby Lower Burma was being transformed by the British from a closed, underpopulated "natural" economy into what would soon become the greatest rice exporter in the world.[52] Before we proceed any further, it seems appropriate to ask what it was about Bengal, Java, and Lower Burma in particular and about the Western economy as a whole that led both to the rise of the East Indies as a supply source and to the stagnation of U.S. rice exports from roughly 1790 to the time of the Civil War.[53]

Such questions are difficult to answer categorically, though we certainly can offer some suggestive possibilities. As Marx pointed out long ago, "windfalls"

often resulted from the effective linkage of pre-capitalist, non-capitalist, or "nat-ural" economies to that of the West and such a linkage did, in fact, occur in Bengal, Java, and Lower Burma in the nineteenth century. With labor in these areas amazingly cheap by Western standards and the land perfectly suited for rice production—the Burma Delta is often seen as the buckle of the world's rice belt—it is understandable that Westerners looked favorably upon the East Indies as a source of supply.[54] Such favor seems even more understandable in light of the fact that the indigenous populations already were experienced and relatively efficient rice producers and the fact that by this time European power could be projected effectively in the fetid paddies of Backergunge, on the green terraces of Kedjawèn, and along the muddy banks of the Irrawaddy.[55]

Other factors, however, were at work as well. Technological and organiza-tional improvements in transoceanic shipping along with the *Pax Britannica* low-ered the cost of carriage and insurance and the coincident development of Aus-tralia and California—development spurred by the discovery of gold in both areas between 1849 and 1851—assured that numerous vessels returning to Europe from the Pacific would be interested in a bulky back-haul like rice.[56] The customs pref-erences accorded colonial produce added further encouragement, if any was need-ed, but with or without such preferences East Indian rice could undersell higher-quality rice anywhere in Europe. Indeed, given the uses made of rice at this time and the groups for whom the cereal was intended, it is in no way surprising that the European market responded less to Carolina quality than to East Indian price.[57]

So intense was this pressure from the East, in fact, that as early as 1838 rice from this area was being sold even in Charleston for less than South Carolina rice.[58] U.S. tariff barriers—rice, interestingly enough, was specifically enumerated for the first time in 1846—proved sufficiently high, however, to stem the Eastern tide during the rest of the antebellum period. Though such tariffs may well say something about the putative rigidity of the South's commitment to free trade, they are perhaps even more important as *ipso facto* evidence that southerners would not give up their rice markets without a fight.[59]

The various attempts during the antebellum period to increase domestic rice consumption—South Carolinians tried, for example, to get rice included on an equal footing with wheat in the daily ration of the U.S. Army—and to expand markets in the West Indies and South America offer further evidence thereto. These efforts, by the way, were not totally unsuccessful. Domestic rice consumption did increase as did demand in other parts of the Americas, particularly in Cuba, a late-blooming plantation colony with thousands of hungry slaves to feed.[60]

But the penetration of East Indian rice into Europe was not turned back. Rather, it accelerated sharply as time passed. As a result of both the dislocations in the U.S. industry occasioned by the Civil War and, perhaps more importantly, the decline in transportation costs occasioned by the advent of the steamship and the opening of the Suez Canal, East Indian rice poured into Europe in the late nineteenth century. Exports to Europe from Lower Burma alone, for example, averaged over 682,000 tons of clean rice equivalents *annually* between 1881 and 1890, which figure exceeded total rice production in the United States for the entire decade of the 1880s, or the decade of the 1850s for that matter![61]

Nor was Europe the only area swamped by East Indian rice in the late nineteenth century, a period in which commodity markets were being rapidly integrated throughout the world.[62] Thus, the United States, once the world's great rice-exporter, became a major importer in this period and remained one until well into the twentieth century, as Table 4-23 illustrates. This was so despite the aforementioned duties imposed on imported rice. In other parts of the world, we find a similar pattern of rising imports from the East as well.[63]

The economic effects of integration, moreover, did not end once foreign rice passed through the customs gates. In the United States, the reality of international competition underpinned and reinforced the geographic shift of domestic rice production from the South Atlantic region to the Old Southwest, to Louisiana, Arkansas, and Texas specifically.[64] Rice cultivation in South Carolina and Georgia, one recalls, was intensive in nature and numerous problems militated against the successful continuation of this type of cultivation in the postbellum period. Indeed, given such problems—a list of which would include damage done to production facilities during the war, the reduction in the labor participation rate after Appomattox and the concomitant breakdown in labor discipline, the severe shortage of capital in the area, and the long-term declines in both soil fertility and total factor productivity along the coastal plain—it is apparent why production shifted in relative terms toward the southwestern states, where many of these problems bore less urgency.[65]

Not only was cheap, fertile, readily irrigable land available in Louisiana, Arkansas, and Texas but, after the so-called rice revolution of the mid-1880s, more rational, extensive cultivation techniques were successfully implemented in this region. Such techniques, which were based upon the employment of midwestern small-grain technology, rationalized production and allowed for the achievement, once again, of economies of scale in the rice industry. At the same time, the relative importance of scarce, unruly labor in the production process was reduced. Though these techniques, alas, proved unworkable in South Carolina and Georgia, they clearly enabled producers in the Southwest to persevere, at times, even to thrive despite competition from the Far East.[66]

Thus, we find the low-country rice industry increasingly pressured in the second half of the nineteenth century, not only by foreign rice but by rice grown in other parts of the United States. As a result of the market's progress, the low country was being squeezed, and it was this squeeze, which began before the Civil War but intensified afterward, that marked the beginning of the end. Just as rice had made the low country, it was rice that would do it in. But not immediately.

For the low country's agricultural capitalists and its urban bourgeoisie tried hard to save their economy. Though a number of scholars in recent years have alleged that these groups displayed little entrepreneurial initiative in the nineteenth century, alleging, in fact, that they rejected values commonly associated with a bourgeois *mentalité*, I believe that the historical record clearly shows that low-country planters and merchants responded to the area's economic problems with considerable vigor, albeit within the limits imposed by the environment, the low country's economic structure, and by the area's position in the international economic hierarchy.[67]

Table 4–23. Rice Imports to and Exports from the United States, 1872–1911 (millions of pounds)

Year (ending June 30)	Imports		Exports	
	Rice	Rice Flour, Rice Meal, and Broken Rice[a]	Rice	Rice Bran, Meal, and Polish[b]
1872	74.6		0.4	
1873	83.8		0.3	
1874	73.3		0.6	
1875	59.4		0.3	
1876	71.6		0.4	
1877	64.0		1.3	
1878	47.5		0.6	
1879	75.8		0.7	
1880	57.0		0.2	
1881	68.7		0.2	
1882	79.4		0.1	
1883	96.7		0.1	
1884	106.6		0.2	
1885	81.1	38.0	0.2	
1886	60.1	37.5	0.3	
1887	56.0	47.9	0.6	
1888	100.8	54.8	0.4	
1889	132.2	54.1	0.4	
1890	68.4	55.7	0.4	
1891	133.1	81.3	0.3	
1892	85.1	63.0	c	10.3
1893	81.1	66.5	0.8	13.0
1894	86.8	55.4	0.8	10.0
1895	141.3	78.3	0.1	1.5
1896	78.2	68.5	1.3[d]	13.7
1897	133.9	63.9	0.4	3.5
1898	129.8	60.5	0.6	5.6
1899	153.8	50.3	0.9	14.5
1900	93.6	23.0	12.9	28.1
1901	74.6	42.6	1.1	24.4
1902	75.7	82.0	0.6	29.0
1903	78.3	91.3	0.5	19.2
1904	75.3	78.9	2.4	26.7
1905	43.4	63.1	74.9	38.4
1906	58.5	108.1	4.0	34.2
1907	71.3	138.3	2.4	27.7
1908	87.6	125.2	2.2	26.2
1909	88.8	134.1	1.6	18.9
1910	82.7	142.7	7.0	19.7
1911	76.7	132.1	15.6	14.5

Sources: U.S. Department of the Treasury, *Statistical Abstract of the United States, 1881. Fourth Number* (New York, 1964), pp. 74–75, 97; U.S. Department of the Treasury, *Statistical Abstract of the United States, 1891. Fourteenth Number* (New York, 1964), pp. 131, 136, 158; U.S. Department of the Treasury, *Statistical Abstract of the United States, 1901. Twenty-fourth Number* (Washington, D.C., 1902), pp. 192, 220; U.S. Department of Commerce, *Statistical Abstract of the United States, 1911. Thirty-fourth Number* (Washington, D.C., 1912), pp. 421, 455. Note that after June 30, 1900 commerce with Puerto Rico and Hawaii is not included in the foreign commerce of the United States. George K. Holmes, however, includes these areas in his calculations of U.S. rice imports and exports between 1901 and 1911. See U.S. Department of Agriculture, Bureau of Statistics, *Rice Crop of the United States, 1712–1911*, by George K. Holmes, Circular 34 (Washington, D.C., 1912). Note, too, that the U.S. first becomes a net importer in 1861.

[a]first stated 1885
[b]first stated 1892
[c]included in "Rice Bran, Meal and Polish"
[d]896,000 pounds damaged

It is true, of course, that the hegemonic groups in the area did not transform the low country into another Massachusetts or New York after the advent of the area's economic difficulties, but can we really castigate such groups for this "failure," given the low country's historical role and its available production possibilities? I think not. Indeed, upon appreciating the limitations within which these groups operated, it is fair to say that their efforts to increase productivity, redirect the western trade, and to diversify the low-country economy to a degree are indicative of considerable enterprise rather than entrepreneurial lethargy.[68] That these efforts were not terribly successful underscores the low country's longstanding structural problems: disarticulation, factoral distortions, and economic asymmetry. Thus, if the indigenous bourgeoisie failed to play a most revolutionary part in the nineteenth century, it was not for lack of effort but because of the obstacles that it faced.[69]

How much more could low-country planters and merchants have done in any case in an area in which over 50 percent of total wealth at the time of the Civil War was comprised of human beings? Not much, I am afraid. Is it really a sign of entrepreneurial weakness that much of the available capital—indigenous as well as national and international—was invested in western cotton lands or in extraregional manufacturing activities rather than in the low country? Moreover, are we to believe that such investment was somehow less rational? Can diversification have proceeded much further than it did in a sickly, swampy region in which markets and urban settlement were thin? In a region lacking readily accessible power sources can we realistically expect local capitalists, given nineteenth-century technological constraints, successfully to have emulated Lowell or Manchester or even Graniteville? Or can we expect Charleston suddenly to have transformed itself into a major entrepôt? Finally, could Charleston, which was sadly lacking in educational facilities, immediately have established itself as a citadel of learning such as Heidelberg or Edinburgh? The answer to each of these questions, current scholarly fashions notwithstanding, is no.[70]

That the low country's position was as compromised as such serial denial suggests, admittedly, seems implausible at first glance. The plantation complex of the area, after all, was both rationally conceived and rationally ordered; moreover, it included some of the largest and most heavily capitalized units of production in the United States at the time of the Civil War.[71] The marketing structure which supported this complex, furthermore, was more efficient than similar structures elsewhere in the U.S.—certainly it was more efficient than that of the agricultural North—at least until 1840 and probably considerably longer.[72] Indeed, if we define marketing as the American Marketing Association has often urged, as "the performance of business activities directed toward and incident to the flow of goods and services from producer to consumer or user," a more efficient marketing structure than that which existed in the low country and other parts of the Plantation South in, let us say, 1860 is difficult realistically to conceive, as even Harold D. Woodman—a Marxist who views the antebellum South as essentially pre-capitalist—has pointed out.[73]

In light of the well-known efficiency of the factorage system, the size and scope

of the low country's transportation and warehousing facilities, the resources and repute of the area's banks, and the business climate created by the state—low taxes, a modern, "developmentalist" code of commercial law, and a stable and basically consensual political order—why, then, was the low country so disempowered when demand for rice began to wilt?[74] To answer this question we must distinguish between marketing structure and economic structure, the latter of which is both broader and ultimately more powerful and delimiting. As we soon shall see, by the mid-nineteenth century, the low country's economic structure and, thus, its economic fate, was linked more closely to rice and one or two other staples than many in our voluntaristic age would have us believe.

In its power to tyrannize an area, rice, as Braudel has suggested, is perhaps unmatched among the world's major cereals.[75] In the low country, its tyrannical reign lasted for almost two hundred years. During this period rice, *il riso amaro*, "the bitter rice," as the cereal was known in Italy, made great fortunes and brought great pain, made the low country wealthy and was largely responsible for its decay. The extent of its informative powers in the area perhaps best can be seen through a brief examination of profits and output in the industry.

Though data on potential profits in the rice industry are sketchy, those that do exist indicate that rates of return were quite substantial in the eighteenth century, but in the nineteenth century steadily decreased. Indeed, if Dale E. Swan's revised estimates are correct, the average rate of return for South Carolina and Georgia rice farms and plantations in 1859 was no longer positive at all, but an astounding −28.3 percent. To be sure, large rice plantations may still have enjoyed positive rates of return on the eve of the Civil War, but it appears that in comparison with the eighteenth century, rates of return in the rice industry had dropped drastically nonetheless.[76] Moreover, it is unlikely that this trend ever was reversed. In the postbellum period, the mean size of agricultural units declined sharply in the low country and with this decline, the relative importance of scale economies diminished as well. Similarly, the costs of labor and capital rose in this period as yields per acre and the real price of rice fell.[77] Given such conditions, it is hardly surprising that the records of the great rice-planting families of the area—the Sparkmans, Grimballs, Manigaults, and Vander Horsts to cite but a few—strongly support the notion that the profit picture remained dismal in the low-country rice industry in the decades after the war. The data brought together in Table 4-24 illustrate the argument made above.

Profits obviously are not unrelated to output, though the nature of their relationship is quite complex. The precise manner in which profits were determined, however, need not concern us here, for we are primarily interested in another question, that being, why did output remain so high for so long when profits likely were negative or very low at best?

That rice output in the low country, though declining, remained very substantial until the turn of the nineteenth century can be seen in Table 4-25 wherein appear census data on rice production in the United States and South Carolina between 1839 and 1919. If the economic behavior of the black labor force in the low country in the decades after the Civil War is completely encapsulated in the slogan "no

Table 4–24. Estimated Annual Net Rates of Return on Investment, South Carolina and Georgia Rice Plantations and Farms, 1710–1860 (percentage)

Year or Period	Net Rate of Return
1710	12.5%
1740–1770	13.5 to 33.5
1768	25.0
1768	26.7
1828–1840	−6.2 to 4.9
1832	1.44
1830's–1840's	0.33 to 1.0
1841–1852	−6.57 to 0.1
1850	−3.05
1850–1860	−4.73 to −3.52
1859	−28.3

Sources: Thomas Nairne, *A Letter from South Carolina* . . ., 2d ed. (London: Printed for R. Smith, 1718), pp. 48–49; Ralph Gray and Betty Wood, "The Transition from Indentured to Involuntary Servitude in Colonial Georgia," *Explorations in Economic History*, 2d ser., 13 (October 1976): 353–70; Henry Laurens to Richard Oswald, April 27, 1768, in Philip M. Hamer, George C. Rogers, Jr., *et al.*, eds., *The Papers of Henry Laurens*, 10 vols. thus far (Columbia: University of South Carolina Press, 1968–), 5: 663–69, especially p. 668; Henry Laurens to James Grant, December 22, 1768, in Hamer, Rogers, *et al.*, eds., *The Papers of Henry Laurens*, 6: 231–34, especially p. 233; James M. Clifton, "Hopeton, Model Plantation of the Antebellum South," *Georgia Historical Quarterly* 66 (Winter 1982): 429–49; Entry, June 3, 1832, John Berkley Grimball Diary, 1: 20–22, Southern Historical Collection, University of North Carolina, Chapel Hill, N.C.; *De Bow's Review* 6 (October–November 1848): 285–304; especially p. 287; Herbert A. Kellar, ed., *Solon Robinson, Pioneer and Agriculturalist: Selected Writings*, 2 vols . (Indianapolis: Indiana Historical Bureau, 1936), 2: 364–68; John R. Hetrick, "Treatise on the Economics of Rice Production in Georgetown County, South Carolina: The Middle Period, 1786 to 1860" (M.A. thesis, University of South Carolina, 1979), pp. 138–220, especially pp. 188, 214; Dale E. Swan, *The Structure and Profitability of the Antebellum Rice Industry 1859* (New York: Arno Press, 1975), Preface, pp. 75–84 especially. Note that in the estimates for 1710, 1828–40, 1830s–40s, 1841–52, 1850, and 1850–60, it is clear that imputed interest has not been subtracted . I have therefore adjusted original estimates by subtracting 10 percent from that of 1710 and 7 percent from the others .

Some idea of the profit picture in the low-country rice industry during the postbellum period can be gained from extant estimates of returns by individual planters. See Manuscript Plantation Book, Dirleton Plantation, 1868–1869, p. 77, James Ritchie Sparkman Collection, South Caroliniana Library, University of South Carolina, Columbia, S.C.; Entry, August 26, 1873, John Berkley Grimball Diary, 17:127, Southern Historical Collection; "A Knotty Problem for Rice Millers," unsigned [in Arnoldus Vander Horst's hand], c . 1874, Arnoldus Vander Horst V Family Papers, South Carolina Historical Society, Charleston, S.C.; Records of Gowrie Plantation, 1876–1881 [under J.B. Heyward], Louis Manigault Papers, Manuscript Department, William R. Perkins Library, Duke University, Durham, N.C. The most detailed of these estimates, that of J.R. Sparkman for Dirleton Plantation in 1868, indicates a net return of roughly −21.0 percent. In utilizing this estimate, indeed, any of the estimates in Table 4–24, one should keep in mind both the rather rudimentary nature of agricultural accounting in eighteenth- and nineteenth-century America and the data limitations upon which modern scholarly estimates are based .

more mudwork," as one scholar recently has proclaimed, how are we to explain the 47.4 million pounds of clean rice produced in the state in 1899, over 90 percent of which came from the low country? The power of rice, it seems, transcended both colorful slogans and—if certain scholars are to be believed—the heart-felt desire of blacks in the area to withdraw from the market and move toward a "moral economy."[78] Indeed, such was the hold of rice upon black and white alike in the low country that it inhibited to a considerable degree the equilibrating power of supply and demand and that, certainly, was no mean feat.

For rice, particularly paddy rice, is an intransigent crop, as venerable civilizations in the East long have known. One need not subscribe to Wittfogel's notion of "oriental despotism" to realize that a hydraulic agricultural regime in which labor

Table 4–25. Rice Production in the United States, 1839–1919
(millions of pounds of clean rice)

	1839	1849	1859	1869	1879	1889	1899	1909	1919
Total Production	80.8	143.6	187.2	73.6	110.1	128.6	250.3	658.4	1,065.2
Primary Production States									
South Carolina	75.0%	74.3%	63.6%	43.9%	47.3%	23.6%	18.9%	2.5%	0.4%
Georgia	15.3	18.1	28.0	30.2	23.0	11.3	4.5	0.7	0.2
North Carolina	3.5	2.5	4.1	2.8	5.1	4.6	3.2	0.0	0.0
Louisiana	4.5	2.0	3.4	21.5	21.1	58.8	69.0	49.6	45.3
Texas	0.0	0.0	0.0	0.1	0.1	0.1	2.9	41.2	15.0
Arkansas	0.0	0.0	0.0	0.1	0.0	0.0	0.0	5.9	19.2
California	0.0	0.0	0.0	0.0	0.0	0.0	0.0	0.0	19.6

Source: Coclanis, "Economy and Society in the Early Modern South," pp. 387–97. The figure for clean rice in 1849 differs from the figure given in the *Seventh Census of the United States, 1850* because the figure given for clean rice in the census is actually for rough rice. See De Bow, *Statistical View of the United States . . . Being a Compendium of the Seventh Census*, pp. 170, 173–74. In estimating clean rice production for 1849, I assumed that 45 pounds of rough rice were equal to 30 pounds of clean rice.

and capital intensity are high—the South Carolina low country included—is likely to be characterized by asymmetrical and, thus, coercive power relationships and by relatively slow responses to seemingly unambiguous market signals and signs.[79] Moreover, the inertial tendencies inherent in a hydraulic regime are reinforced in this case by the fact that marginal labor productivity in the production of paddy rice declines very slowly rather than very fast. That is to say, paddy rice can respond to added increments of labor with relatively equal increments in output for so long that seemingly rational shifts to other techniques, other crops, other economic sectors, or even to other geographic regions often are held back.[80] Thus, it should not surprise us that in the low country, an area whose options were few, the cultivation of paddy rice remained very important until the early twentieth century, despite the fact that it apparently was produced far less efficiently and certainly less profitably there than in either the Southwest or the Far East.[81]

By 1920, however, the era of commercial rice production in the low country was over, the area's lifeblood drained to the last. Without rice the low country became what it was before rice: a desolate wasteland. For such were the environmental possibilities and constraints in the low country that rice, despite its drawbacks, constituted the best hope for sustained economic progress that the area ever had. Though it is true that other primary activities—lumbering, naval-stores production, indigo and cotton cultivation, and phosphate-mining—all were tried with varying degrees of market success in the low country, none ever proved so significant to the area as the rice industry. Whether because of lack of remuneration or surfeit of competition, the quality of product or restrictions in geographic range, such activities were often short-lived and/or of local importance only, never informative, always complementary.

That market specialization in rice and, to a lesser extent, in a few other staples probably maximized the long-term growth of the low country testifies not only to

the limitations of the area itself but also to the limitations of economic rationality. For the low country's economic collapse did not result from illogic but from an economically rational growth strategy.

History has proven that the problems inherent in a plantation economy—disarticulation, factoral distortions, and economic asymmetry—are acceptable in an economistic, if not a moral sense so long as net proceeds from staples are sufficient to generate sustained gains in per capita income or output. It is only when net proceeds are insufficient to do this that such problems become unacceptable. When insufficiency becomes chronic, an economy enthralled to plantation staples pays a terrible price indeed. Such insufficiency, alas, came to characterize the low-country economy during the second half of the nineteenth century. The low country's collapse came, however, because net proceeds from the staples produced in the area were insufficient rather than because of market specialization in plantation staples per se. If one chooses to criticize the hegemonists of the low country, let him do so, then, on the grounds that they underestimated the risks involved in staple specialization rather than because of their putative pre-bourgeois *mentalité*.

As a number of economists and economic historians in recent years have reminded us, the degree of risk involved in any economic activity should be studied carefully, for this variable can shed considerable light on the economic decision-making process and, in addition, can help scholars better to evaluate micro and macroeconomic strategies.[82] When risk is introduced into the low-country equation, it is, in fact, quite easy to criticize the hegemonists of the area for committing themselves so heavily to one or two staples as to compromise their economic security. Indeed, one wonders why the hegemonic groups did not willingly reduce this commitment, especially given the fact that at various times in the low country's history—the 1740s, the 1780s, the 1820s, and the entire period between 1865 and 1900, for example—this commitment had led to serious economic setbacks. Furthermore, did they not know that the price elasticity of demand for rice was greater than that for staples such as tobacco or wheat and that numerous substitutes were—or would soon be—available not only for their rice but for their indigo, cotton, and phosphates as well?[83]

Though it is easy to castigate these men and women for their economic and moral behavior both *sub specie aeternitatis* and from the standpoint of today, no one in the late twentieth century, given our own record, should moralize excessively. That the social order of the low country was economically and morally flawed is certainly true, but let us acknowledge the fact that once the commitment to staples was made, the options available to the hegemonists were few. And as we have argued at some length previously, this commitment was made late in the seventeenth century.

Staple production in the low country, we have also argued, led to a regional economic structure characterized by disarticulation, factoral distortions, and asymmetry. The low-country economy, that is to say, was structurally disjointed, lacking organic linkage between the pattern of domestic production and local developmental needs.[84] Oriented toward production for national- and international- rather than local markets, the low-country economy, thus, was able, on the one hand, to

capture productivity gains made possible by international specialization but, on the other, was rendered dependent upon the vagaries of this wider economy. When net proceeds from its staples were high, as in the eighteenth century, the low country did very well indeed; when proceeds dropped precipitously in the late nineteenth century, however, the area was brought to its knees. Let us look more closely at the economic structure which emerged in the low country in the eighteenth century that we might better understand how it impeded growth in the area once demand for low-country staples waned.

In its structure, the low-country economy affords evidence that South Carolina was once an exemplary mercantilist colony. For disarticulation, factoral distortions, and economic asymmetry are stigmata, so to speak, wounds left by staple production, dependence, and subservience, which, as we saw in Chapter 1, were key mercantilist desiderata. Thus, what we shall refer to in the section below as problems and weaknesses of the low-country economy are from an alternative viewpoint indices of England's eighteenth-century mercantilist success.

The structural weaknesses and problems of the low-country economy were related dialectically to the dominance in the area of plantation staples, the location of the markets for which these staples were destined, and the production functions associated in the low country with such commodities. Moreover, as we have seen, these weaknesses and problems resulted largely from economic decisions that at one time seemed economically rational. Indeed, given the hegemonists' *mentalité*, it is clear that a small number of economic and demographic considerations—the low country's factor endowment, the technical requirements of rice production, relative labor costs, and the differential epidemiological patterns among whites, Indians, and blacks—seemed logically to mandate both the deployment of African laborers in the low country and the creation of a set of institutional sanctions coercive enough to ensure that the labor force would be adequate to serve the hegemonists' economic needs. And what, one might ask, were these needs? In an eighteenth-century context, that is to say, in a context in which international demand for low country staples was rising, the answer is fairly obvious: to produce staples, export staples, and, through the importation of luxury goods and other commodities alike, to reap the benefits of the same.

Though these needs—which admit of a certain mechanistic simplicity characteristic of the eighteenth century—were, in fact, met for a considerable period of time, the economic structure required for their fulfillment contributed mightily to the low country's later undoing. For this structure was to prove a pathogenic one, too rigid and unbalanced to support the low country when the market conditions prevailing in the eighteenth century changed. In the remainder of this chapter we shall explain more precisely what we mean.

Let us begin by saying that the low country, even at its nadir, was far wealthier than much of the developing world today.[85] Despite this fact, it is nonetheless true that in terms of structure the low-country economy during the period with which we are concerned shares many characteristics with plantation societies in certain parts of the so-called periphery. Such characteristics, scholars have found, have prevented plantation areas from attaining developmental levels commensurate with their economic potential, however limited such potential may in fact be.[86]

In structure, if not in income or output, then, the low country resembled other plantation societies, indeed, almost to a parodic degree.

In such societies, the economic structure generally is characterized by an inordinate primary sector and small secondary and tertiary sectors, a thin, disarticulate internal market, a linear "conveyor belt" transport system, and an urban system tending toward primate form rather than lognormalcy. As a concomitant of the "hydrocephalic" urban hierarchy in many plantation societies, both capital markets and financial services of all types are typically highly centralized as well. Investment in human capital—by which we mean investment in education, health care, etc., rather than in capitalized labor—is slighted in such areas and the distributions of income and wealth are highly skewed. Nonhuman capital accumulation in plantation societies historically has proved to be relatively low, and the bourgeoisie is often of the *comprador* variety, preferring to buy and sell and/or to innovate along established lines rather than to try something completely new.[87]

Obviously the South Carolina low country was an overwhelmingly agricultural region in the eighteenth and nineteenth centuries. The extent to which this was so in 1840, for example, is illustrated in Table 4-26 below, wherein appear figures

Table 4–26. Occupational Structure of the South Carolina Low Country, 1840

District	Mining	Agric.	Commerce	Manu. & Trades	Nav. of Ocean	Navig. Inland	Professions & Engineers
Beaufort	0	16,845	38	837	6	7	96
Charleston	0	9,787	779	1,317	300	37	359
Colleton	0	14,631	12	63	0	3	61
Georgetown	0	8,345	31	640	36	5	37
Horry	0	1,992	0	4	0	0	6
Marion	0	5,489	18	105	0	1	32
Williamsburg	0	3,815	12	218	0	22	10
Low Country	0	60,904	890	3,184	342	75	601
South Carolina	51	198,363	1,958	10,325	381	348	1,481

Number of Persons Employed in

Low-Country Occupational Structure by Percentages

Occupational Group	Percentage of Labor Force
Mining	0.00%
Agriculture	92.28
Commerce	1.35
Manufacturing and Trades	4.82
Navigation–Ocean	0.52
Navigation–Inland	0.11
Professions & Engineers	0.91
	99.99%

Source: *Sixth Census of the United States, 1840*, pp. 46–47. Note that elsewhere in the 1840 census seven inhabitants of the low country were classified as miners of salt. See p. 191. For data on the occupational structure of the free population of South Carolina in 1860, see *Eighth Census of the United States, 1860: Population*, pp. 454–55.

on employment by sector for each district in the low country and for the area as a whole. In that year, we find that over 92 percent of the labor force in the area was engaged in agricultural activities, with the remainder divided among manufacturing, commerce, the professions, and the shipping industry. Although the proportion of the low country's labor force that was engaged in agriculture and other primary activities declined slowly in the second half of the nineteenth century, it is relatively simple to show that primary activities were still dominant in both the low country and the state in general as that century closed.[88]

It is much more difficult, however, to "prove" that the internal market in the low country was both disarticulate and thin. No longer is it sufficient merely to assert that the internal market in the South was held back by the maldistribution of income and wealth in the area and by the existence of a bound labor force. This, Stanley L. Engerman among others has made clear.[89] If the proposition can never be proved beyond all doubt, the weight of the evidence indicates nonetheless that even during the low country's "golden age" the internal market in the area was indeed both disarticulate and thin.

Thinness and disarticulation are implied, for example, by the fact that a considerable proportion of the vessels entering Charleston to "trade" in South Carolina carried nothing but ballast.[90] The chronic complaints of eighteenth- and nineteenth-century merchants about the dullness of markets in the low country, particularly the stickiness of demand in the area, affords more explicit evidence thereto.[91] Moreover, the degree of seasonal variation in mercantile life in the low country—the torpor of summer affected commerce no less than other activities—suggests market thinness and disarticulation as well.[92]

Perhaps the strongest evidence that the internal market in the low country was both disarticulate and thin, however, is of a negative nature: the sheer lack of interior towns and trading places in the area. On the eve of the Civil War, for example, no interior town with so many as 500 inhabitants even existed in the low country. There were, one should note, three coastal towns with populations greater than 1000 in the low country at this time—Charleston, Georgetown, and Beaufort—and between six and eight towns with more than 1000 inhabitants in the state of South Carolina as a whole.[93] It is clear, nonetheless, that the economy of the low country functioned, however well, without developing the interior towns that in the North served as crucial market nodes.[94] Indeed, in the low country, interior market towns were not necessary, if the truth be known. In this area as in other parts of the Plantation South, the institution of slavery worked in a circuitous manner to obviate the need of them.

As Robert E. Gallman and Ralph V. Anderson have shown, southern planters, recognizing that—or at least behaving as though—their bondsmen were fixed rather than variable capital, sought to utilize their labor power in an efficient manner. Among other things, this meant taking advantage of the fact that in the off-season and at slack times during the growing season the marginal cost of labor supplied by slaves was either negative or zero. Therefore, planters generally sought to diversify their operations, keeping their laborers busy at a wide range of activities in addition to cultivation of one or two market staples. Ironically, what we see developing in the Plantation South, then, is considerable

microeconomic diversification within a context of regional staple specialization. Such diversification, which often allowed individual plantations a high degree of self-sufficiency in foodstuffs, clothing, furniture, farm equipment, and tools, rendered superfluous the local market town, the economic purpose of which largely had been usurped by slaves working at home.[95]

Though low-country plantations apparently were not so self-sufficient in foodstuffs as plantations in other parts of the South, the pattern outlined above generally holds true for the area.[96] Thus, the small-scale, prosaic market interaction that united town and country in the North—a union which proved crucial to that region's economic growth—was missing not only in the low country but throughout the Plantation South. In this way, then, the economic imperatives of staple production with slave labor for national and international markets inhibited both the development of interior towns in the low country and the elaboration and integration of local markets as well.[97]

Not surprisingly, the transportation and urban systems that emerged in the low country also reflected these imperatives. In so doing, these systems reinforced the inherent tendency of the low-country economy toward market disarticulation. Though the transport needs of the early white inhabitants of the low country were, of course, varied, one—the need to get low-country commodities to market— clearly stood out. Since the market for these commodities was across the sea for the most part, the transportation system of the low country was designed primarily to facilitate connections between seats of production in the interior and coastal ports. A linear system of roads and water passages connecting sundry points in the interior to Charleston and, to a much lesser extent, to Georgetown and Beaufort resulted from this design. The basic configuration of this system did not change much in the antebellum period despite the addition of turnpikes, canals, and railroads. Indeed, substantial change did not come until after the Civil War and even then such change as did occur essentially involved reorienting the transport system so as to facilitate the movement of goods from the interior to the Northeast rather than to South Carolina ports. Connections between points in the interior remained contingent upon the position of these points in relation to extraregional markets, especially markets to the north. Thus, by 1900 South Carolina had yet to develop a well-integrated transport grid. Linearity still informed the transport system of the low country, indeed, of the state in general; the terminus of the system had merely shifted from Charleston to New York.[98]

As urban patterns are closely associated with transport patterns, let us shift our attention at this time to the urban system that emerged in the low country of South Carolina. Throughout the eighteenth century and for much of the nineteenth as well, the urban population of the low country was concentrated, of course, almost entirely in Charleston. The extent to which this was so in the second half of the eighteenth century can be seen through an analysis of South Carolina provincial tax receipts, which exist for the period between 1761 and 1769. During this period urban lots in the colony were taxed at a flat rate which varied from year to year. Over the course of the decade, 95.99 percent of the tax receipts from urban lots not just in the low country but in the colony as a whole came from the city of

Charleston alone.[99] Moreover, Charleston's dominance in the low country had not much declined by the eve of the Civil War. Census data from 1860 reveal that at that time the city's population was 40,522, while the total population of all other "urban" places in the low country with more than 200 inhabitants probably did not exceed 4000.[100]

That the low country developed—and retained—a primate rather than lognormal hierarchy for so long was due, once again, mainly to the fact that the area's economy was based upon the production of plantation staples with slave labor for extraregional rather than local or regional markets.[101] Indeed, both the size of Charleston and the overall configuration of the area's urban hierarchy were delimited by the position of the low country in the international economy. The institution of slavery, as we have seen, inhibited the development of interior market towns in the low country; furthermore, none of the staples produced in the area, neither rice nor cotton nor indigo, engendered forward, backward, fiscal, or consumption linkages sufficient enough to transform any of the coastal ports necessary for the export trade—not Charleston and certainly not Georgetown or Beaufort—into either a leading manufacturing center or a true commercial entrepôt.[102] Charleston, of course, developed some manufacturing and served some of the functions of an entrepôt, but the city remained essentially a shipping point and what Sombart would have called a "center of consumption" for the low country's hegemonic groups.[103] Thus, the imperatives that informed the economic structure of the low country left Charleston far behind its main eighteenth-century rivals in the North and led to the emergence and long retention in the area of the type of urban hierarchy economists and economic geographers today generally associate with simple, export-oriented, dependent economies.[104]

The low country, we asserted earlier, shared certain other characteristics with plantation societies of the periphery as well. Given what we already know about the area's economic, transportation, and urban structures, it is hardly surprising that capital markets and financial services in the low country—as in many plantation societies—were highly centralized. One can illustrate this point in a number of ways. Extant records of the South Carolina Court of Common Pleas reveal, for example, that of the 1309 debt actions between 1703 and 1737 which provide information on the place in South Carolina where the debt in question was contracted, Charleston was the site named in 1265 or almost 97 percent of the cases. The precise geographical breakdown appears in Table 4-27. Since the Court of Common Pleas met in Charleston, however, it is likely that Charleston creditors took greater advantage of the legal system than creditors elsewhere in the province and likely, therefore, that the figures for the city in Table 4-27 are somewhat inflated. Still, an examination of South Carolina provincial tax receipts for the period from 1761 through 1769 reveals that 77.9 percent of the money-at-interest in the colony as a whole during the period was owed to Charlestonians.[105]

The city's domination of financial life not only in the low country but in South Carolina in general persisted in the nineteenth century. As of January 1860, Charleston banks controlled 98.23 percent of the banking capital in the low country and 74.32 percent of the banking capital in the entire state.[106] The "hydrocephalic" nature of financial life in South Carolina is, thus, difficult to deny.

Table 4–27. Site in South Carolina Where Debt in Question Was Contracted in Debt Actions and Trespass on the Case Actions Before the South Carolina Court of Common Pleas, 1703–1737

Site Named	Debt Actions	Trespass on the Case Actions	Total
Charleston	649	616	1265
Berkeley County	8	12	20
South Carolina	17	1	18
Childsbury	1	0	1
Goose Creek	1	0	1
James Island	0	1	1
Combahee	1	0	1
Colleton County	0	1	1
Pee Dee River	1	0	1
	678	631	1309

Source: South Carolina Court of Common Pleas, Judgment Rolls, 1703–1790, Boxes 1–22, South Carolina Department of Archives and History. Note that in nineteen other actions foreign states were named.

So, too, is the fact that the low country, indeed, the South in general, developed formal educational institutions very slowly, lagging far behind New England in the eighteenth century and the North as a whole in the nineteenth century.[107] Data on school enrollment rates, literacy, libraries, and per capita public expenditures on education can be marshalled to bear out this point. In 1849, for example, the number of whites in the low country who attended school was equal to 58.05 percent of the white population between the ages of 5 and 14. In contrast, the number of whites in Illinois who attended school in 1849 was equal to 74.96 percent of the white population between the ages of 5 and 14 in that state, while in Massachusetts the number of whites who attended school in 1849 exceeded the white population between 5 and 14 by a full 10.94 percent![108]

If we include blacks—the great majority of whom were juridically prohibited from participating in the low country's educational system—in our calculations, the relative performance of the low country drops precipitously. Moreover, the figures for the area begin to resemble the figures in many peripheral areas today. For the number of students in the low country attending school in 1849 was equal to only 18.18 percent of the *total* population between the ages of 5 and 14 in the area, while the percentages given above for Illinois and Massachusetts are virtually unchanged when blacks are included.[109] Similar gaps separated the low country from these states in other educational indices during the antebellum period. Though the relationship between education and economic development is a complex one and the causal lines between the two often are unclear, the fact that educational opportunity historically was so limited for the majority population in the low country and other plantation areas cannot but have hindered economic and social progress in these areas at least to some degree.[110]

Inequality did not end with education in the low country. Indeed, from early on, the distributions of wealth and, presumably, income in the area also were highly skewed. In the most complete study thus far undertaken on the distribution

of wealth in the low country during the colonial period, William G. Bentley, utilizing data drawn from probate inventories of estates, has found that personal wealth among white inventoried decedents was already quite unevenly distributed by the 1720s, but that inequality increased rather slowly over the next forty years or so. This can be seen clearly in Table 4-28, wherein appear Bentley's key findings on the degree of inequality among white inventoried decedents—Gini coefficients of concentration and wealth shares held by the top 10 percent of wealth-holders—for each of eight subperiods between 1722 and 1762. Whereas the Gini coefficient was .63 for the cohort inventoried in the period 1722–26, this coefficient had risen to .67 for the cohort inventoried between 1757 and 1762. Similarly, while the top 10 percent of wealth-holders in the 1722–26 cohort controlled 48 percent of the wealth of their cohort as a whole, the share controlled by the top 10 percent of wealth-holders in the 1757–62 cohort had risen to 57.9 percent. The trend toward greater wealth concentration apparently continued through the remainder of the colonial period. In another similar study, Bentley has found, for example, that by 1775–76 the Gini coefficient had increased to .70.[111] Moreover, concentration apparently increased over time in rural and urban areas alike. In St. John's Berkeley Parish, a wealthy rice-producing area northwest of Charleston, George D. Terry has found, for example, that the distribution of wealth among white inventoried decedents became increasingly concentrated between 1720 and 1779, while my own data and those of Jackson Turner Main suggest that a similar phenomenon occurred in the city of Charleston over the course of the eighteenth century.[112]

Given the fact that the low country was experiencing rapid economic growth during that century, the trend toward greater inequality in wealth-holding is not surprising. As Simon Kuznets demonstrated long ago, a trend toward greater inequality historically has proved to be characteristic of societies during the earlier phases of economic growth.[113] It is my belief, furthermore, that the increase in inequality enhanced the performance of the low-country economy during the eighteenth century by acting in Schumpeterian fashion to concentrate capital in the

Table 4–28. The Distribution of Personal Wealth Among White Inventoried Decedents in the South Carolina Low Country, 1722–1762

Period	Gini Coefficient	Percentage of Wealth Held by Top 10% of Wealth-holders
1722–26	0.63	48.0%
1727–31	0.54	38.1
1732–36	0.63	48.9
1737–41	0.61	46.0
1742–46	0.61	47.8
1747–51	0.64	53.1
1752–56	0.63	48.0
1757–62	0.67	57.9

Source: William G. Bentley, "Wealth Distribution in Colonial South Carolina" (Ph.D. dissertation, Georgia State University, 1977), pp. 34, 40, 48, 53, 64, 69, 74.

hands of large planters and merchants during a period of rising world demand for relatively capital-intensive agricultural staples such as rice and indigo. It is important to note in any case that though wealth inequality among the white inhabitants of the low country apparently was increasing during the eighteenth century, mean and median wealth levels for the white population were rising as well. This point is often lost on those that choose to focus upon distributional questions alone.[114]

However beneficial the trend toward concentration may have proved in the eighteenth century as world demand for low-country staples rapidly grew, it does not necessarily follow that the continuance of this trend would prove beneficial to the low-country economy in the nineteenth century when, from all indications, economic growth in the area slowed. So far as we can tell at this time, however, the trend toward concentration did, in fact, continue. Although many questions remain unanswered, detailed studies of wealth distribution in Charleston, the rural parishes and districts of the low country, and the South as a whole support this point. Let us consider Charleston first.

In Table 4-29 below, I have presented some data, drawn from probate records, on the distribution of personal wealth among white inventoried decedents in Charleston during the eleven-year period from 1722 through 1732. In Table 4-30 these data are compared with census data compiled by Michael P. Johnson on the distribution of real and personal wealth among the free population in the city in 1860. To be sure, such a comparison is problematic: admittedly, we are comparing somewhat different populations by drawing from somewhat different types of sources, which sources, in fact, define wealth somewhat differently. Despite obvious problems, scholars have found comparisons such as those in Table 4-30

Table 4–29. The Distribution of Personal Wealth Among White Inventoried Decedents from Charleston, 1722–1732

Lower Limit Percentile of Wealth Group	Wealth Share of Group	Cumulative Share of Total Wealth
10%	51.37%	51.37%
20%	20.26	71.63
30%	10.86	82.49
40%	7.22	89.71
50%	4.27	93.98
60%	2.66	96.64
70%	1.69	98.33
80%	0.95	99.28
90%	0.55	99.83
100%	0.17	100.00

Gini coefficient = 0.6623; N = 126; Schutz coefficient = 0.52

Sources: Books A–I and Charleston County Inventories 1732-1736, Records of the Secretary of State, Miscellaneous Records, Main Series, 1671–1973, 153 vols., South Carolina Department of Archives and History. For data on the distribution of wealth among these decedents by pound sterling groups, see Table 3–19. On the use of inventories in analyses of wealth distribution in colonial America, see, for example, Daniel Scott Smith, "Underregistration and Bias in Probate Records: An Analysis of Data from Eighteenth-Century Hingham, Massachusetts," *William and Mary Quarterly*, 3d ser., 32 (January 1975): 100–110.

Table 4–30. The Distribution of Personal Wealth Among White Inventoried Decedents from Charleston, 1722–1732 and the Distribution of Personal and Real Wealth Among the Free Population of Charleston, 1860

Lower Limit Percentile in Wealth Group	1722–1732		1860	
	Wealth Share of Group	Cumulative Share of Wealth	Wealth Share of Group	Cumulative Share of Wealth
10%	51.37%	51.37%	76.9%	76.9%
20%	20.26	71.63	16.2	93.1
30%	10.86	82.49	5.3	98.4
100%	17.51	100.00	1.6	100.0

Gini coefficient: 1722–1732 = 0.6623; 1860 = 0.887

Sources: See Table 4–29; Michael P. Johnson, "Wealth and Class in Charleston in 1860," in Walter J. Fraser, Jr., and Winfred B. Moore, Jr., eds., *From the Old South to the New: Essays on the Transitional South* (Westport, Connecticut: Greenwood Press, 1981), pp. 65–80, especially p. 67.

both useful and relatively accurate.[115] Thus, we can assume from the fact that the Gini coefficient of concentration was .66 among white inventoried decedents in Charleston between 1722 and 1732 and the fact that the Gini coefficient was .89 for the free population in the city in 1860 that the distribution of wealth among the free population in Charleston did indeed become more unequal over time.[116]

Trends are less clearcut for predominantly rural sections of the low country. Data on wealth concentration in these areas in 1824 and 1860 are presented in tables 4-31 and 4-32 respectively. Here, again, there are certain problems of comparison: the findings for 1824 are based on the tax returns of individuals, while

Table 4–31. Wealth Concentration Among Taxpayers, South Carolina Low Country, 1824

Parish/District	Number	Gini Coefficient	Schutz Coefficient
All Saints	159	.79	.68
Prince William	309	.73	.59
St. Bartholomew	340	.72	.59
St. James Santee	77	.72	.58
Horry	372	.71	.58
St. Peter	387	.71	.56
Marion	220	.70	.57
St. Stephen	110	.70	.56
Prince George	374	.69	.56
St. James Goose Creek	193	.68	.54
St. George Dorchester	164	.66	.52
Williamsburg	316	.65	.50
Christ Church	110	.61	.48
St. Paul	163	.60	.48
St. Helena	305	.59	.46
St. Thomas & St. Dennis	65	.57	.43
St. John Colleton	164	.53	.39

Source: 1824 Lower Division Tax Returns, South Carolina Department of Archives and History.

Table 4–32. Wealth Concentration Among Free Households, South Carolina Low Country, 1860

Parish/District	Number	Gini Coefficient	Schutz Coefficient
Prince George	705	.84	.73
All Saints	57	.83	.72
St. James Santee	101	.83	.72
St. Stephen	204	.83	.72
St. Peter	585	.78	.66
Prince William	400	.78	.65
St. Bartholomew	999	.78	.65
St. John Berkeley	280	.76	.66
St. Luke	374	.76	.63
St. Paul	213	.74	.61
Christ Church	230	.73	.58
St. James Goose Creek	358	.72	.58
St. George Dorchester	451	.70	.56
St. Thomas & St. Dennis	52	.67	.54
St. Andrew	71	.66	.52
Charleston Neck-St. Philip	83	.64	.49
St. John Colleton	149	.60	.45
St. Helena	240	.52	.49

Source: Manuscript returns, Eighth Census of the United States, 1860, Population, South Carolina, South Carolina Department of Archives and History.

those for 1860 are based on census data relating to the real and personal property of households, some of which contained a number of potential taxpayers.[117] Because most individuals included within such households held little or no wealth in 1860, the main conclusion to be drawn from the tables—rising rural wealth concentration during the antebellum period—seems safe despite differences in the units of comparison.

Attempts to compare rural wealth distribution in the colonial and antebellum periods are more troublesome, particularly if one tries to do so by comparing the data for 1824 with the aggregate data in Table 4-28. It is not at all obvious from such a comparison, for example, that rural wealth was more concentrated in 1824 than in the 1757–62 period. Bentley's figures for 1757–62—and his figures for 1775–76 for that matter—are based upon data for the low country as a whole, which is to say they include Charleston, while the figures for 1824 are for largely rural areas. This problem in and of itself renders all interpretation somewhat conjectural.

Numerous studies, including our own, have found, of course, that concentration levels in urban centers were greater than levels in rural areas in the eighteenth and nineteenth centuries.[118] This being the case, it is quite conceivable that by factoring out Charleston from Bentley's colonial data, the resultant concentration levels for the rest of the low country would be lower than levels reached by 1824. On the other hand, it is also conceivable that the introduction in the late eighteenth century of cotton—a more "democratic" staple than rice—actually may have reduced wealth

concentration slightly in rural parts of the low country between the Revolution and 1824. Given the present state of knowledge, either scenario is plausible.

Whatever the trend between the late colonial period and 1824, we can conclude with some confidence that levels of rural wealth concentration were significant throughout the period in question. Moreover, it is clear from Table 4-32 that by 1860 concentration had risen markedly not only in comparison with 1824 levels but in comparison with any reasonable estimate of levels reached prior to the Revolutionary War. This last point receives further support, one should note, from recent studies that put the Gini coefficient of concentration at .67 among free wealth-holders in the South as a whole in 1774 and at .845 among free white men in the region in 1860.[119]

Furthermore, as wealth concentration increased in the low country, wealth-holdings in the area—as in most plantation societies—became increasingly concentrated in the form of human beings. Whereas William G. Bentley found that capitalized labor constituted between 45 and 51 percent of the personal wealth of inventoried white decedents in the low country in each of eight subperiods between 1722 and 1762, slave wealth, estimated conservatively, constituted between 77 and 80 percent of the total personal wealth of the white population of the area in 1860.[120] Thus, while capital in the form of producers' durables—which form is generally associated with greater productivity—became increasingly important to the economies of New England and the Middle Atlantic states between the middle of the eighteenth century and the middle of the nineteenth, the white inhabitants of the low country over the course of this period shifted their personal assets rather more toward investment in Negro slaves.[121]

Though this shift seems almost inevitable in light of what we have said about the low country's environment and economic structure and about its subordinate role in the international economy, no satisfactory explanation is possible without mentioning the active participation of the area's planters and merchants themselves. To be sure, these men and women, like similar groups in other plantation economies, operated under severe limitations. And, clearly, when "encouraged" by their creditors and by European tariff policies to invest in rice and slaves, they generally did so.[122] But they did so—and this is crucial—not because they were powerless or ineffectual or because they were apathetic about their economic fate but because this path also seemed to them the most rational one to take.[123] Despite the sharp decline in the profit structure of the rice industry in the antebellum period, they were right: it was, alas, with rice more than with anything else that the area's comparative advantage, such as it was, still remained. For by then, the low country's economic options were very few indeed.

By the time of the Civil War, a century and a half of staple production with bound labor for extraregional markets had warped the low-country economy. Moreover, the economic structure which had emerged—a structure oriented toward and conducive to rice production and exportation—rendered difficult alternative economic activities. In a land of swamps, bogs, and half-bogs, that is to say, in a land with limited possibilities from the start, this structure proved a ponderous

handicap. Thus, when the rice market completely collapsed at the turn of the nineteenth century, the low country collapsed too.[124] Though the inhabitants of the area, white and black alike, have certainly tried to jog the low-country economy ever since, their efforts have proved largely unsuccessful.

Attempts to rebuild the agricultural economy by emulating the Dutch and particularly the Danes—peoples that had enjoyed considerable success practicing intensive, diversified, locally oriented agriculture on soils similar to those of the low country—foundered for a variety of reasons: inadequate knowledge, the limited size of urban markets, the general lack of economic integration in the area, and, perhaps most importantly, the shortage of capital.[125] The retention of capital, it is true, had always been problematic in the low country. Behind traditional stereotypes about the existence and operation of transatlantic and transregional credit chains in the Plantation South, we do, indeed, find transatlantic and transregional credit chains operating in the low country—and taut ones at that. Further hemorrhaging also occurred whenever low-country merchants, bankers, or planters utilized either indigenous capital or funds that had escaped repatriation to pursue investment opportunities outside the region.[126] But such longstanding problems, however serious, reached new, nightmarish proportions after the Civil War. After 1865, though, the main problem was not so much the hemorrhaging of capital but the inability of an economically pallid area to secure desperately needed transfusions.

With income levels in the low country falling, with much of the area's wealth destroyed or forcibly redefined into oblivion, with social instability now the norm, and with the formerly rock-solid State of South Carolina itself in a position of virtual default by 1873, capital became extremely scarce in the area and remained so for a long time. This was particularly true, one should note, for those interested in agricultural innovation or diversification.[127] Conjoined with all the other burdens borne by the low country, the persistent insufficiency of capital, thus, rendered hopeless most efforts at agricultural change. In light of such conditions, it is not surprising to find that with the exception of the tobacco areas of the Pee Dee, the agricultural sector of the low country has never really recovered from the shocks sustained in the late nineteenth and early twentieth century.[128]

In the absence of a strong agricultural base, developmental efforts in the low country in the twentieth century have relied mostly upon extractive industries— forest products primarily—low value-added manufacturing, military installations, and, increasingly, tourism and the resort industry.[129] In its developmental strategy the low country shares much with other former plantation economies, not the least of which similarities are a low regional wage-scale and an emphasis— overemphasis, I believe—on tourism and the creation of what has become known derisively in the Caribbean as a "pimps and bellhops" economy. And so, the low country, but for certain enclaves, remains one of the poorest parts of one of the poorest states even today.[130]

The last phenomenon mentioned above—the rise of the tourist industry— merits a brief word or two before we close because of its economic and symbolic importance to the low country. As a developmental strategy, tourism has venerable roots in the area, stretching back at least to the late nineteenth century when a few

promoters lit upon the area as a convenient way station between the Northeast and Florida.[131] These early efforts to promote tourism dovetailed nicely with other, broader efforts at commercial promotion of the low country, most notably, of course, that culminating in the disastrous South Carolina Interstate and West Indian Exposition, held in Charleston between December 1, 1901, and May 31, 1902. Promotional efforts continued even after this fiasco, however, and the tourism/resort/spa idea took on a new twist early in the twentieth century as rich northerners began to buy up huge parcels of idle rice and cotton lands for use as personal hunting and fishing preserves. Thus, by the 1930s we find—particularly if we choose to look in the autumn or winter—a new register of low-country elites, a register comprised of many of the "usual suspects" from the Northeast: Cranes, Doubledays, du Ponts, Guggenheims, Huttons, Kidders, Luces, Roosevelts, Vanderbilts, Wideners, and Yawkeys to name but a few.[132]

Two other developments were less dramatic but ultimately more important to the low-country tourist industry: the rise, primarily in the period after World War II, of coastal resorts such as Myrtle Beach, catering to "middle-class" whites from the upcountry and from out-of-state, and the gradual "creation" of Historic Charleston as a second web for the tourist trade.[133] Thanks largely to these developments, if and when outsiders think of the low country today, they generally think of boardwalks and beaches, high-toned golf and tennis facilities, luxuriant formal gardens, and Historic Charleston's beauty, charm, and grace. Local claims notwithstanding, the low country is, thus, presented in disemboweled form, cut off, alienated, and estranged from its earlier economic history. But the past is still there, beneath what Marx would have called the integuments of the late twentieth century.[134]

That this is so can be seen in a number of ways. There is, for example, an island near Charleston known as Kiawah, which is today the site of a famous luxury resort. The island signifies more than cabanas and cocoa butter, however; indeed, it is at once testament to, and logical culmination of three hundred years of history. For one hundred eighty of those years the entire island was owned by one family—the Vander Horsts—which operated a large Sea Island cotton plantation there in the nineteenth century. By the early twentieth century this plantation had been reduced to a collection site for the leaves and cuttings used once a year in low-country churches during Palm Sunday services, a profound and, perhaps, profoundly symbolic reduction to say the least. After decades of continued stagnation, the island finally was sold by the Vander Horst family in 1952 to an Aiken, South Carolina, lumber company, and Kiawah was sold again, this time to foreign interests, in 1974. In recent years the island has witnessed an economic resurrection of sorts, having been transformed by a Kuwaiti investment group into the luxury resort mentioned above. Even in this rarified, five-star atmosphere, the essence of the area's history can still be gleaned, for while a few feast, many serve, as has been true in the low country almost from the time William Sayle's boot first struck sand in April 1670.[135]

Let us in conclusion attempt to place the historical experience of the low country within a broader frame. The low country, it is clear, did not progress linearly toward development after the instauration of the capitalist mode of production

in the area. In this, the experience of the area differs from the experience postulated in both neoclassical and classical Marxist formulations on economic development.[136] Neither, however, did the capitalist mode of production lead to the progressive deterioration of the low-country economy, to the development of underdevelopment, so to speak. In this, the history of the low country fails to conform to *dependencia* or neo-Marxist models either.[137] Nor, for that matter, was the experience of the low-country economy an example of what Jagdish N. Bhagwhati has called "immiserizing growth," wherein a developing economy experiencing rapid expansion, under certain specified conditions, can actually lose ground because of the sectoral dislocations such expansion occasions.[138]

Where, then, does that leave the low country? Within an alternative developmental framework, I believe, that of *noncumulative development*. According to this frame, which had some adherents in the early 1950s and has been revived more recently by Albert O. Hirschman, staple specialization need not lead only to development, underdevelopment, or growth *cum* immiserization, but also at times and in certain places to "once-over" growth, followed by sporadic downturns and relative stagnation.[139] Such a framework helps one make sense of the economic history of the South Carolina low country—an area built by and for rice—which grew very rapidly in the eighteenth century but which has lacked real dynamism since the second quarter of the nineteenth century and has never really done well again after rice began to decline. Though not truly underdeveloped, the area nonetheless is today uncommonly poor by the standards of the West. For rice, as produced in this particular market setting, left behind an unfortunate legacy: an economic structure characterized by disarticulation, distortion, and asymmetry, a poor, uneducated black majority, a desolate landscape, and a forlorn and miserable history.

This legacy testifies not only to the informative power of rice but to the strengths and weaknesses of the capitalist productive mode. Just as the market was largely responsible for the low country's rise, it was largely responsible for the area's later decline as well. For its siren song lured the area into a pattern of economic and social development which was conducive to economic growth under one limited set of conditions—great external demand for plantation staples produced in the low country—but which would thwart progressive economic adjustments if these conditions ever changed, that is to say, if external demand for low-country staples ever faltered. And, as we have seen, external demand did indeed falter. It is possible, of course, that in the low country, a fragile ecological area with limited economic possibilities, development was doomed from the start. But by establishing an economy whose health was dependent almost entirely upon the vagaries of international demand for commodities, the hegemonists, in effect, sealed the low country's fate.

I know moon-rise I know star-rise
Lay dis body down

I walk in de moonlight I walk in de starlight
Lay dis body down

I'll walk in de graveyard I'll walk through de graveyard
Lay dis body down

I'll lie in de grave and stretch out my arms
Lay dis body down

I'll lie in de grave and stretch out my arms
Lay dis body down

I go to de judgment in de evenin' of de day
Lay dis body down

And my soul and your soul will meet in de day
Lay dis body down

Lay Dis Body Down[140]
As sung in the
First South Carolina
Volunteers

Epilogue

In 1970, three hundred years after the establishment of the first permanent English settlement in the area known today as South Carolina, Charles Towne Landing opened for business. Situated more or less on the original site of the city of Charleston, Charles Towne Landing is said to reflect "the same tranquility found by the early settlers." Thus, one finds at the popular tourist attraction "eighty acres of landscaped gardens" and an "Animal Forest," a replica seventeenth-century trading vessel, and a "colonial village." One finds concession stands and a large, well-stocked gift and toy store at Charles Towne Landing as well. A visitor can "walk, bicycle, or take a tram tour" of the facility and, in addition, can participate in "special events" such as the "Arts and Crafts Festival" and the "Founder's Day Celebration." Charles Towne Landing is open daily from 9 a.m. to 5 p.m. and admission charges as of December 1987 were as follows: Adults $4.00; Senior Citizens $2.00; Students (ages six through fourteen) $2.00. There is no admission charge for children under six years of age. According to advertising copy provided by the current proprietors of Charles Towne Landing, "from first settlement to plantation to park, not much has changed."[1]

Writing of Charleston after a brief visit to the city in 1905, Henry James, the proconsul of sensibility at the dawn of the modern age, described the South Carolina port town as a "flower-crowned waste."[2] James's description, alas, remains true to the mark even today. That the city of Charleston, both its fundaments and soul, is captured by this oxymoron reflects the contradictions that have shaped the history not only of Charleston itself but of the low country as a whole. For both Charleston's crown of flowers and the desolate vesture in which much of the city is wrapped testify to the informative power of the forces discussed hitherto. We would all do well to remember this simple, painful fact.

However beautiful is Restoration Charleston—and it is indeed beautiful in a delicate, vaguely effeminate way—it constitutes but part of a metropolitan area characterized rather more by tattered ghettos, honky-tonk squalor, and faceless

suburbs that have sprouted since World War II in response to the flight of the white bourgeoisie.[3] Charleston, that is to say, is part "Quaint Old Charleston" to be sure, but it is in the main chicken shacks, trailer parks, and motels of quick release, gin mills, collapsing walls, and dowdy subdivisions with lush romantic names. And, in truth, it is this shadow world, neither restored nor "mellowed by time," that strikes a more responsive chord with me.[4] Here, amidst the broken bottles, the suburban carports, and the sleaze, there are signs of life and energy at least. Indeed, despite the beauty of the lower peninsula and despite Restoration Charleston's "insidious charm," the area somehow seems spiritless and lifeless—"inanimate" in James's words—devoid of social richness, at times, it seems, of any humanity at all, More like a museum than a field of human interaction, Restoration Charleston suggests atrophy rather than affirmation. Neither transplanted Italian arts festivals nor candlelight house tours nor Sanforized versions of history, however, can completely conceal Charleston's true essence, in Aristotelian terms, its entelechy. And so, "Quaint Old Charleston," which strives always to appear tragic in order to beguile, will never evoke true tragedy but a pitiable *tragedy manqué*.[5]

Urban form, like history, always tells a story and, thus, always involves questions of narrativity and narration. Narration, moreover, implies a linear structure and the employment of selected "facts" to sustain it. Because the selection of facts for any particular narrative is not completely foreordained but is in part a matter of volition, those ultimately chosen reveal much about the individual narrator and about social relations in the society in which he lives and writes.[6] That "Charleston," with few exceptions, signifies Quaint Old Charleston, Historic Charleston, proud, preserved temple of veneration, perhaps reveals less about the city itself than about the shortcomings of both our own society and our historical imaginations.[7] For St. Michael's Church and Church's Fried Chicken, Meeting Street manse and burnt-out shell, all grew out of the same historical process that, beginning in the seventeenth century, brought white and black settlers to the land the Kiawah Indians called home. In a famous essay, completed in 1940, the critic Walter Benjamin wrote: "There is no document of civilization which is not at the same time a document of barbarism."[8] Until such time that all of us who love Charleston and the South Carolina low country understand this point and begin to act upon this understanding, the city—"America's Best-Kept Secret" according to advertisements—will unfortunately a secret remain.

APPENDIX

Demographic Perspectives on Eighteenth-Century Charleston

Appendix I-A

*Seasonal Mortality in Charleston and Boston
During the First Half of the Eighteenth Century*

Sufficient data are available to allow the reconstruction of seasonal mortality patterns for whites in Charleston and for whites, blacks, and Indians in Boston during the first half of the eighteenth century. The data presented in the tables and graph below illustrate both regional and racial differences in mortality patterns during this period. The particular procedure used to construct the tables and graph below—a procedure which at first glance seems needlessly complex—was designed to take into account variation in the length of months and, indeed, years and to standardize our data so that they may more easily be compared to data compiled for other areas. The procedure is fully explained in Darrett B. Rutman, Charles Wetherell, and Anita H. Rutman, "Rhythms of Life: Black and White Seasonality in the Early Chesapeake," *Journal of Interdisciplinary History* 11 (Summer 1980): 29–53, especially pp. 30–32.

Appendix

Table A–1. White Seasonal Mortality in Charleston

Month	St.Philip's Charleston Recorded Burials, 1720–1750	Daily Average by Month 1720–1750 as Percentage of Daily Average, 1720–1750
January	175	71.54%
February	140	62.81
March	154	62.96
April	143	60.41
May	212	86.67
June	265	111.95
July	328	134.09
August	331	135.32
September	420	177.43
October	355	145.13
November	193	81.53
December	166	67.86
	2882[a]	

[a]There were, after correcting for double-counting, actually 2883 burials recorded between 1720 and 1750 . It was impossible, however, to establish the month of burial for one person .

Source: Salley, ed., *Register of St. Philip's Parish . . . 1720–1758.*

Table A–2. White Seasonal Mortality in Boston

Month	Deaths— 1708, 1711–1740[a]	Daily Average by Month 1708,1711–1740 as Percentage of Daily Average 1708, 1711–1740
January	870	85.18%
February	717	77.03
March	751	73.53
April	769	77.80
May	813	79.60
June	866	87.61
July	894	87.53
August	1,159	113.47
September	1,506	152.36
October	1,497	146.57
November	1,185	119.89
December	1,007	98.59
	12,034	

[a]No 1720 data.

Source: Boston News-Letter, 1709–1740/1 .

Table A–3. Black and Indian Seasonal Mortality in Boston

Month	Deaths — 1708, 1711–1740[a]	Daily Average by Month 1708,1711–1740 as Percentage of Daily Average 1708, 1711–1740
January	243	115.82%
February	186	97.28
March	192	91.51
April	221	108.85
May	237[b]	112.96
June	176	86.68
July	171	81.50
August	159	75.78
September	204	100.47
October	237	112.96
November	220	108.35
December	226[b]	107.72
	2,472	

[a]No 1720 data.

[b]No figures were available for December 1716 and May 1721. I have therefore used the monthly means for December and May from the other twenty-nine years as proxies for burials in December 1716 and May 1721.

Source: Boston News-Letter, 1709–1740/1.

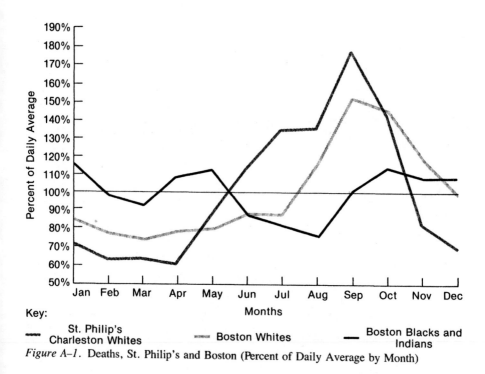

Key:

— St. Philip's Charleston Whites   ▬ Boston Whites   ━ Boston Blacks and Indians

Figure A-1. Deaths, St. Philip's and Boston (Percent of Daily Average by Month)

Appendix I-B

Table B–1. Recorded Burials, Baptisms, and Births, Parish of St. Philip's Charleston, 1720–1750

Year	Burials	Baptisms	Births
1720	40	12	25
1721	39	13	10
1722	40	17	28
1723	34	35	28
1724	26	28	25
1725	40	25	24
1726	30	33	29
1727	53	30	22
1728	68	33	24
1729	56	19	27
1730	40	29	34
1731	69	25	27
1732	149	29	32
1733	61	29	30
1734	60	27	30
1735	105	19	31
1736	93	25	37
1737	135	36	51
1738	213	33	34
1739	198	30	28
1740	136	29	33
1741	91	23	21
1742	106	41	45
1743	96	40	34
1744	92	35	42
1745	186	26	35
1746	101	38	43
1747	136	47	65
1748	138	33	29
1749	137	8	19
1750	115	16	23
Total	2883	863	965

Source: Salley, ed., Register of St. Philip's Parish . . . 1720–1758.

Appendix I-C

White Family Structure in Charleston, Bridgetown, and Bristol

In the absence of population censuses and tax lists it is difficult indeed to comment with confidence about white family structure in early Charleston. Some idea of family structure can be gained, however, by extracting certain data from the wills of early Charlestonians. Accordingly, I have extracted such data from wills made by Charlestonians between 1720 and 1732. These data are presented in tables C-1 and C-2.

In analyzing the data extracted from these wills, the following assumptions have been made:

(1) if the writer of a will is married, his or her spouse will be mentioned in the will;
(2) if children are mentioned in a will but no spouse is mentioned, then the will is that of a widow or widower;
(3) if the writer of a will has children, he or she will mention all of them in the document;
(4) if neither children nor spouse is mentioned, or, conversely, if spouse or both spouse and children are mentioned but are said to be living outside of South Carolina, then the writer of the will is deemed a single householder.

That such assumptions are perilous is doubtless true. Moreover, as one might expect, other problems arise from using wills rather than censuses or tax lists to ascertain family structure, problems related to biases inherent in wills themselves. We can, however, still learn something about the family structure of the white population—particularly that part of the population which is overlooked when reconstitution techniques are employed—through the use of wills. Let us therefore accept these perils and problems and proceed.

So that we can place our data on white family structure in Charleston in broader context, I have also included in the tables available data on white family structure in two other areas, namely, Bridgetown, Barbados and Bristol, Plymouth. As the data from these places are from censuses rather than wills, they should be accorded greater significance than the data from Charleston. Despite the crudeness of the Charleston data it is apparent that in terms of white family structure the South Carolina port had much more in common with Bridgetown than with the little agricultural village far to its north.

Table C–1. White Family Structure in Charleston, Bridgetown, and Bristol

	Bridgetown 1680 Census		Charleston Wills 1720–1732		Bristol 1689 Census	
Households	351[a]		152		70	
	N	%	N	%	N	%
Married couples	231	65.8	83	54.6	68	97.1
Widows/Widowers	31	8.8	23	15.1	2	2.9
Single Householders	89	25.4	46[b]	30.3	0[d]	0.0
	351	100.0	152	100.0	70	100.0
Children mentioned	330		206[c]		226	

[a]English households
[b]Includes seven with spouses not living in S.C.; five in England, one in Ireland, one in North Britain.
[c]Includes ten children apparently living outside of S.C.; does not include unspecified number of "children" in two wills.
[d]Demos points out, however, that one or perhaps even three singles (men) may have lived in Bristol, but probably not as fully constituted households.

Sources: Records of the Secretary of State of South Carolina, Miscellaneous Records, Main Series, 1671–1973, 153 vols. (vols. covering 1720–1740 period), South Carolina Department of Archives and History; Lothrop Withington, contrib., "South Carolina Gleanings in England," *South Carolina Historical Magazine* 5 (July 1904): 161–67, and 9 (July 1908): 122–26, especially p. 124; Richard S. Dunn, "The Barbados Census of 1680: Profile of the Richest Colony in English America," *William and Mary Quarterly*, 3d series, 26 (January 1969): 3–30; Dunn, *Sugar and Slaves*, p. 107; John Demos, *A Little Commonwealth: Family Life in Plymouth Colony* (New York: Oxford University Press, 1970), pp. 62–81, especially pp. 67, 78–79; Demos, "Families in Colonial Bristol, Rhode Island: An Exercise in Historical Demography," *William and Mary Quarterly*, 3d series, 25 (January 1968): 40–57, especially pp. 43–44.

Table C–2. Children Per Family in Charleston (1720–1732), Bridgetown (1680), and Bristol (1689)

	Number of Children in Family												
	0	1	2	3	4	5	6	7	8	9	10		
Number of Families:													
Charleston[a]	78	21	19	10	7	5	7	2	1	0	0	=	150
Bridgetown	198	58	52	22	7	11	2	1	0	0	0	=	351
Bristol[b]	7	10	11	12	9	8	6	4	1	0	1	=	69

[a]Two other families that mention unspecified number of "children" have not been included.
[b]Demos includes only 69 families.

Sources: Records of the Secretary of State of South Carolina, Miscellaneous Records, Main Series, 1671–1973, 153 vols. (vols. covering 1720–1740 period), South Carolina Department of Archives and History; Withington, contrib., "South Carolina Gleanings in England," *South Carolina Historical Magazine* 5 (July 1904): 161–67, especially pp. 163–64, and 9 (July 1908): 122–26, especially p. 124; Dunn, *Sugar and Slaves*, p. 109; Demos, *A Little Commonwealth*, p. 194.

Appendix I-D

An Estimate of the Crude Death Rate for the White Population of Charleston, 1722–1732

Estimates of crude death rates for populations in the colonial South are rare, particularly estimates of such rates for the region's urban populations. The reason for this is clear: the data necessary for the calculation of crude death rates—base population figures and accurate mortality counts—have proved extremely limited over time and space. Such limitations have proved especially serious for students of early South Carolina, for vital records are far scantier for this colony than for those further north.[1] The estimate presented below, that of the crude death rate for the white population of Charleston, should thus be seen as a crude one indeed, as the first word on a complex and important subject rather than the last.

Let us begin with an estimate of Charleston's white population between 1722 and 1732, the period covered in our study. This period was chosen, one should note, both because some data on population and mortality are available for these years and because this period, within which one major epidemic occurred, seemed to typify mortality conditions in Charleston during the first half of the eighteenth century. At the start of this period in 1722, the Parish of St. Philip's, that is, Charleston and areas immediately adjacent, had a permanent white adult male population of about 300 according to available population counts. Since a small number of these men lived outside of town—17 according to a militia list in 1722—I have used the figure 283 to represent Charleston's permanent white adult male population in that year. This figure, I might add, is identical to that for taxpayers in St. Philip's Parish in 1720.[2]

By 1732 Charleston's permanent white adult male population had apparently grown by almost 25 percent to approximately 350. Various sources were used to derive this figure, including contemporary estimates of Charleston's total white and black population, estimates of the number of houses in the town, jury lists, and contemporary estimates of the size of particular segments of the town's population.[3]

In order to derive the total permanent white population of Charleston in 1722 and 1732, I multiplied the figures for the permanent white adult male population mentioned above by 4.5. This multiplier is slightly smaller than the one generally used to derive estimates of

permanent white population from figures for white heads of household alone. The multiplier seemed reasonable nonetheless, given the population structure of Charleston and, indeed, those of many other early modern cities as well. Moreover, it is consistent with multipliers used by George Terry and Philip Morgan, perhaps the foremost students of South Carolina's early demographic history. Using this multiplier, then, we arrive at a figure of 1273 for Charleston's permanent white population in 1722 and 1575 for the town's permanent white population in 1732. To establish estimates of Charleston's permanent white population for the years between 1722 and 1732, I have assumed that the total increase of 302 for the period as a whole occurred as a result of equal annual increments of 30.2.[4]

Charleston's total white population did not consist, however, of permanent inhabitants alone, but of both permanent inhabitants and temporary residents. Charleston, one must remember, was for practical purposes the only urban center in South Carolina at this time and perhaps more importantly the colony's only port. A large number of transients, particularly transient sailors, were thus living in the town at any given time. Since these temporary residents were "at risk" to die and, indeed, were included in the town's mortality statistics, we must find a way to adjust our population estimates to allow for their presence. Fortunately, enough data are available to allow us to make a rough estimate of the number of such transients in Charleston during this period.

Utilizing sources dating from 1720 we learn that at the peak of the Charleston shipping season, that is, in February and March, there were typically 400–500 sailors in town, most of whom were transients. From these same sources we also learn, however, that during the summer months the number of sailors in town typically fell drastically, for far fewer ships arrived at the port of Charleston during the hot season.[5]

Available data in the British Public Record Office on ship entries and clearances at Charleston between 1722 and 1732 tend to support these generalizations. Shipping activity in the port of Charleston, we find, was far greater in the quarter from December 25 to March 25 than in the quarter from June 25 to September 29, while shipping activity in the spring and fall quarters fell somewhere between the winter peak and summer lull.[6] The difference between the winter and summer levels of shipping activity in Charleston, one should note, was even greater than these data on entries and clearances indicate, for the largest vessels—those involved in the rice trade—seldom entered Charleston before October and seldom cleared after the month of June.[7]

If roughly 400–500 sailors were in Charleston at the peak of the shipping season as early as 1720, it seems fair to assume that between 1722 and 1732 the number of sailors *and* transients in town during the peak season averaged at least 500. If an average of 500 sailors and transients resided in Charleston from, shall we say, December 25 to March 25 in each year from 1722 to 1732, perhaps 200 resided in town during the slack summer months and 350 during the spring and fall quarters of this eleven-year period. Thus, in the period from 1722 to 1732, an average of about 350 whites would temporarily be living in Charleston at any given time. These temporary residents must perforce be considered in any analysis of Charleston's total white population.

To say that our estimate of Charleston's transient population is rudimentary is to belabor the obvious. No allowance has been made, for example, for the British naval squadrons that occasionally visited Charleston in this period nor have I seen fit, given the purpose of this exercise, to analyze Charleston's shipping patterns in greater detail. Despite such shortcomings, it seems fair to say nonetheless that by adding 350 per year to our earlier estimates of Charleston's white population between 1722 and 1732 we can more faithfully reconstruct Charleston's demographic past.[8] With such adjustments—corrections if you will—we arrive at our final estimates of the town's white population. Let us now turn to the subject of white mortality in this eighteenth-century southern city.

Our basic data on mortality in Charleston during the 1722–1732 period come from the St. Philip's Parish Register.[9] Though this parish included a small area immediately adjacent to Charleston as well as the town itself, all burials at St. Philip's are treated as Charleston burials in this study. Deaths in Charleston so outnumbered those in that part of the parish beyond the town's limits in any case that no appreciable difference in our estimate of Charleston's crude death rate would ensue even if we did choose to distinguish between town and parish.

While the problem mentioned above is a minor one, two others—both related to the under-registration of burials in our basic source—are more serious and therefore will be discussed in some detail. Problems relating to the under-registration of events in available vital record series have long plagued scholars working on the demographic history of early America. Such under-registration of events typically occurs for one of two reasons: either because events relating to individuals who theoretically should have been included in the records of a particular church or town have been omitted from these records because of lax or careless recording practices or policy considerations, or because the vital records of entire groups—nonconformists in Anglican parish registers, for example—have been systematically excluded.[10]

Under-registration in the mortality records with which we are dealing occurred, alas, for both of these reasons. Some burials were "lost" in St. Philip's Parish because of laxness or carelessness; others because dying infants often did not the records make. Still other persons were omitted, however, not because they died as infants nor because of some weary sexton's frailties, but because they once had chosen to worship God in other ways. That such problems make the task of calculating Charleston's crude death rate more difficult is undeniable. Certain adjustments can be made, however, to help overcome the problems posed by under-registration, making a rough calculation of Charleston's crude death rate possible.

In his noted study of mortality rates in Massachusetts before 1860, Maris Vinovskis pointed out that even in the vital records of colonial New England—the part of British America in which such records were most complete—deaths were typically under-registered by between 40 and 80 percent.[11] That rates of under-registration were so high in the relatively homogeneous towns of colonial New England is striking, for presumably little of the under-registration in this area occurred because large groups whose religious beliefs deviated from community norms were being systematically excluded from the records. Rather, such under-registration as occurred in New England was apparently due to laxness, carelessness, and perhaps most importantly to customary recording practices regarding the deaths of infants.[12] With such under-registration rates in mind, let us consider under-registration in the burial records of St. Philip's Charleston.

If laxness, carelessness, and customary recording practices essentially explain why deaths were under-registered in the burial records of New England by between 40 and 80 percent, it seems reasonable to assume that deaths were also under-recorded in the St. Philip's Parish Register by approximately the same percentage for these same reasons. I have therefore made some upward adjustments in the recorded burial figures for St. Philip's. I have given the records-keepers of St. Philip's Parish the benefit of the doubt, however, and have assumed that their records were more complete than those of their New England brethren. Rather than adjusting burials upward by, shall we say, 60 percent—midway between 40 and 80 percent—I have recalculated burials under three different assumptions, each of which represents an upward adjustment of less than 60 percent. These adjustments, which are shown in column 3 of tables D1–3, attempt to compensate for the omission of individuals—Anglicans, visitors and transients, and a few Huguenots—whose names should have been listed in the St. Philip's Parish burial records, but were not.

Since members of certain religious groups in Charleston—Presbyterians, Congregationalists, Baptists, Quakers, and most Huguenots—were systematically excluded from the burial records in the St. Philip's Parish Register, we must also adjust for their exclusion if we are to estimate the crude death rate for the town's white population.[13] Fortunately, data are available from 1732 and 1756 that can give us some idea of the percentage of the white population that died in Charleston in these years that would be systematically excluded from the records in the St. Philip's Parish Register. About 26 percent of the white population that died during the two-month period in 1732 for which data exist belonged to religious groups whose members were normally excluded from the burial records of St. Philip's Parish; this percentage was even higher at 31.4 percent in 1756.[14] If these data are at all representative—and I believe that they are—one can get a rough estimate of the total number of whites dying in Charleston in a given year by adjusting upward our corrected figures from the St. Philip's Register alone by about 30 percent. I have made this final adjustment in column 4 of tables D1–3. With our estimates of white population and white mortality now complete, we can at long last calculate the crude death rate for the white population of Charleston during the 1722–32 period.

As we see in column 5 of tables D1–3, the crude death rate in Charleston was between about 52 and 60 per thousand during the eleven-year period as a whole, the precise rate depending upon the preferred adjustment in column 3. Whether the crude death rate in Charleston during this period was actually 52, 56, or 60 per thousand is less important, however, than the overall conclusion one must draw from these data, namely, that mortality levels in the city of Charleston were, even by preindustrial standards, very high indeed. One can perhaps get a better sense of the level of mortality in Charleston at this time by comparing the crude death rate in the town with available estimates of crude death rates for populations in other parts of the early modern world. A number of estimates are therefore presented in Table D-4 below. As these data indicate, Charleston's unenviable reputation as a "great charnel-house" was—at least for the first part of the eighteenth century—well deserved. That mortality levels apparently dropped substantially in Charleston in the second half of the eighteenth century is significant, but still does not negate the fact that for several generations the town's inhabitants had found it difficult indeed to elude death's dreadful grasp.[15]

Table D–1.

Year	(1) Adjusted Population	(2) St. Philip's Recorded Burials	(3) Adjusted St. Philip's Burials (+30%)	(4) Plus 30% For Other Congregations	(5) Crude Death Rate Per 1000
1722	1,623	40	52	67.60	41.65
1723	1,653.2	34	44.2	57.46	34.76
1724	1,683.4	26	33.8	43.94	26.10
1725	1,713.6	40	52	67.60	39.45
1726	1,743.8	30	39	50.70	29.07
1727	1,774	53	68.9	89.57	50.49
1728	1,804.2	68	88.4	114.92	63.70
1729	1,834.4	56	72.8	94.64	51.59
1730	1,864.6	40	52	67.60	36.25
1731	1,894.8	69	89.7	116.61	61.54
1732	1,925	149	193.7	251.81	130.81
	19,514	605	786.5	1,022.45	52.40

Appendix

I have attempted in this essay to estimate the crude death rate for the white population of Charleston during the 1722–32 period from available data on population and mortality for these years. Limitations of these data made certain extrapolations necessary, extrapolations that I have tried to explain as clearly as possible on the pages above. Through the use of such extrapolations we have been able to calculate the crude death rate for Charleston's white population for this period and have found the rate to be very high even by preindustrial standards. That we have found such mortality rates in Charleston confirms eighteenth-century beliefs about the unhealthiness of the town. Though our estimates are admittedly rough ones, they are at present all that we have.

Table D–2.

Year	(1) Adjusted Population	(2) St. Philip's Recorded Burials	(3) Adjusted St. Philip's Burials (+ 40%)	(4) Plus 30% For Other Congregations	(5) Crude Death Rate Per 1000
1722	1,623	40	56	72.80	44.85
1723	1,653.2	34	47.6	61.88	37.43
1724	1,683.4	26	36.4	47.32	28.11
1725	1,713.6	40	56	72.80	42.48
1726	1,743.8	30	42	54.60	31.31
1727	1,774	53	74.2	96.46	54.37
1728	1,804.2	68	95.2	123.76	68.59
1729	1,834.4	56	78.4	101.92	55.56
1730	1,864.6	40	56	72.80	39.04
1731	1,894.8	69	96.6	125.58	66.28
1732	1,925	149	208.6	271.18	140.87
	19,514	605	847	1,101.10	56.43

Table D–3.

Year	(1) Adjusted Population	(2) St. Philip's Recorded Burials	(3) Adjusted St. Philip's Burials (+ 50%)	(4) Plus 30% for Other Congregations	(5) Crude Death Rate per 1000
1722	1,623	40	60	78.00	48.06
1723	1,653.2	34	51	66.30	40.10
1724	1,683.4	26	39	50.70	30.12
1725	1,713.6	40	60	78.00	45.52
1726	1,743.8	30	45	58.50	33.55
1727	1,774	53	79.5	103.35	58.26
1728	1,804.2	68	102	132.60	73.49
1729	1,834.4	56	84	109.20	59.53
1730	1,864.6	40	60	78.00	41.83
1731	1,894.8	69	103.5	134.55	71.01
1732	1,925	149	223.5	290.55	150.93
	19,514	605	907.5	1,179.75	60.46

Table D–4.   Crude Death Rates: Comparative Data

Place	Period	Crude Death Rate per 1000
St. Botolph's without Bishopsgate Parish, London	1591–1603	29.3
Cogenhoe, England	1618–1628	13.4–17.9
Dedham, Mass.	1648–1700	24–27
Clayworth, England	1676–1688	41.25
England and Wales	1701–1750	28–36
Philadelphia	1722	32.9
	1730	32.1
	1731	62.5
	1732	31.5
Finland	1722–1800	27.4
Denmark	1735–1800	28.1
Norway	1735–1800	26.2
Iceland	1735–1800	28.2
Sweden	1736–1800	28.1
England	1541–1871	25.9 (median)

Sources: Mary F. Hollingsworth and T.H. Hollingsworth, "Plague Mortality Rates by Age and Sex in the Parish of St. Botolph's without Bishopsgate, London, 1603," *Population Studies* 25 (March 1971): 131–46, p. 143 especially; Peter Laslett and John Harrison, "Clayworth and Cogenhoe," in H.E. Bell and R.L. Ollard, eds., *Historical Essays 1600–1750 Presented to David Ogg* (London: Adam & Charles Black, 1963), pp. 157–84, pp. 173, 176 especially; Lockridge, "The Population of Dedham, Massachusetts, 1636–1736," pp. 332–33; A.M. Carr–Saunders, *World Population: Past Growth and Present Trends* (Oxford: The Clarendon Press, 1936), pp. 60–63; Smith, "Death and Life in a Colonial Immigrant City: A Demographic Analysis of Philadelphia," p. 871; H. Gille, "The Demographic History of the Northern European Countries in the Eighteenth Century,' *Population Studies* 3 (June 1949): 3–65, pp. 33, 65 especially; E.A. Wrigley and R.S. Schofield, *The Population History of England 1541–1871: A Reconstruction* (Cambridge: Harvard University Press, 1981), p. 311. One should also note that E.A. Wrigley has alleged that many preindustrial cities experienced high mortality, with crude death rates "frequently running up to 50 per 1,000 or more." Allan Sharlin, however, has recently challenged Wrigley's contention that mortality levels in preindustrial European cities were extraordinarily high. See Wrigley, *Population and History*, World University Series (New York: McGraw-Hill, 1969), p. 97; Sharlin, "Natural Decrease in Early Modern Cities: A Reconsideration." Note, too, that in certain marshy areas in England, where problems with malaria were great, death rates were, at times, comparable to those in the South Carolina low country. See Mary Dobson, " 'Marsh Fever'—The Geography of Malaria in England," *Journal of Historical Geography* 6 (October 1980): 357–89.

Notes for Appendix I-D

1. For good discussions of the types of sources with which those interested in the demographic history of colonial South Carolina must work, see Philip D. Morgan, ed., "Profile of a Mid-eighteenth Century South Carolina Parish: The Tax Return of St. James' Goose Creek," *South Carolina Historical Magazine* 81 (January 1980): 51–65; George D. Terry, "'Champaign Country': A Social History of an Eighteenth Century Lowcountry Parish in South Carolina, St. Johns Berkeley County" (Ph.D. dissertation, University of South Carolina, 1981), pp. 90–142, 361–64.

2. On mortality conditions in Charleston in the first half of the eighteenth century, see Chapter 2.

My estimate of Charleston's permanent white male population in 1722 is derived from the following sources: Governor James Moore, Jr., to the Board of Trade, March 21, 1720/1, Records in the British Public Record Office Relating to South Carolina, 1663–1782, 36 vols. in facsimile, 9: 23, South Carolina Department of Archives and History, Columbia, S.C.; Attorney General Richard West to the Board of Trade, April 11, 1723, Records in the British Public Record Office Relating to South Carolina, 10: 74–76, South Carolina Department of Archives and History; Richard Shelton to the Board of Trade, Received and Read May 24, 1723, in W. Noel Sainsbury *et al.*, eds., *Calendar of State Papers, Colonial Series, America and West Indies*, 44 vols. thus far (London: 1860–), vol.: 1722–1723, pp. 265–66; "A List of Mens Names under the Command of Capt. Garratt Vanvelsin . . . ,"

August 5, 1722, and "A List of the Company Under the Command of Capt. Lucas Stotenburgh . . . ," August 4, 1722, in Great Britain, Public Record Office, Colonial Office, America & West Indies, CO 5/358, ff. 254–55v, ff. 256–57v. One should note that I used microfilm copies of the militia lists in CO 5/358. See British Manuscripts Project, D-420, CO5/358, Original Correspondence—Board of Trade A (1–121), August 1720–December 1722, A79, A80, South Carolina Department of Archives and History.

3. My estimate of Charleston's permanent white adult male population in 1732 is derived from the following sources: "A Short Memorial on the Present State of the Church & Clergy in his Majesty's Province of So Carolina in America, by Wm Tredwell Bull," August 10, 1723, The Fulham Papers in the Lambeth Palace Library, American Colonial Section, 40 ms. vols, 9: 118–21, especially p. 118, Lambeth Palace Library, London, England; Alexander Garden's "Answers to Queries addressed to Clergy," April 15, 1724, The Fulham Papers in the Lambeth Palace Library, American Colonial Section, 9: 160, Lambeth Palace Library; Engrossed Act No. 530, August 20, 1731, Acts, Bills, and Joint Resolutions, 1691–, Records of the General Assembly, South Carolina Department of Archives and History; Thomas Cooper and David J. McCord, eds., *The Statutes at Large of South Carolina*, 10 vols. (Columbia: A.S. Johnston, 1836–1841), 3: 274–87; Jean Pierre Purry, *Proposals . . . Drawn Up at Charles-Town, In September, 1731* (1732), reprinted in B.R. Carroll, comp., *Historical Collections of South Carolina*, 2 vols. (New York: Harper & Brothers, 1836), 2: 121–40, especially p. 129; Alexander Hewatt, *An Historical Account of the Rise and Progress of the Colonies of South Carolina and Georgia*, 2 vols. (London: Printed for Alexander Donaldson, 1779), 2: 15; Governor Robert Johnson to the Board of Trade, September 18, 1732, Records in the British Public Record Office Relating to South Carolina, 15: 229–34, especially p. 229, South Carolina Department of Archives and History. One should note that I used microfilm copies of the records from the Lambeth Palace Library cited above. The microfilm version of these records, produced by World Microfilms of London in 1970, is available at the South Caroliniana Library, University of South Carolina, Columbia, S.C.

4. Early modern cities with high rates of in-migration such as Charleston generally contained populations with fewer children per adult than did cities with low rates of in-migration or rural areas. On this point, see, for example, Allan Sharlin, "Natural Decrease in Early Modern Cities: A Reconsideration," *Past and Present* 79 (May 1978): 126–38. For some rough data on family structure in Charleston in the 1720s, see Appendix I-C.

Having found that the average family size in the parish was 4.5 in the first part of the eighteenth century, George Terry uses a multiplier of 4.5 to convert figures for white heads of household into estimates of total white population in St. John's Berkeley Parish. Though Philip Morgan uses a multiplier of 5 to make a similar conversion in his analysis of the 1745 tax list for St. James' Goose Creek Parish, he states that his multiplier "might be thought to be generous." See Terry, "'Champaign Country,'" p. 71; Morgan, "A Profile of a Mid-eighteenth Century South Carolina Parish," p. 53, footnote 8.

Our population estimates, one should note, are consistent with certain other data as well. South Carolina's permanent white population between 1730 and 1732 was roughly 10,000. According to the South Carolina tax bill for 1731, the taxpayers of Charleston were required to pay one-sixth of the total levy. Given the nature of the colony's tax system at this time, this would mean that about one-sixth of South Carolina's permanent white population lived in Charleston. Our estimate of Charleston's permanent white population in 1731 was about 1545, that is, 15.45 percent of the colony's total permanent white population. This figure, of course, is quite close to the blunt "one-sixth" figure in the tax bill. See United States Department of Commerce, Bureau of the Census, *Historical Statistics of the United States: Colonial Times to 1970*, 2 vols. (Washington, D.C.: United States Government Printing Office, 1975), 2: 1168; Cooper and McCord, eds., *Statutes*, 3: 308–17.

Moreover, according to both Purry and Hewatt, Charleston had between 500 and 600 houses in 1731. Our estimate of Charleston's permanent white population in that year was 1545. The black population in Charleston was roughly equal to the permanent white population of the town through much of the eighteenth century. In the absence of precise figures, let us assume that there were also 1545 blacks in Charleston in 1731. By adding the above figures for white and black populations together and then adding another 350—our estimate of the average number of white transients in

Charleston at any given time during the 1722–32 period—we get a figure of 3440 for Charleston's total population in 1731. If we divide this number by 550—the approximate number of houses in town if Purry and Hewatt are correct—we get a figure of about 6.25 persons per house. In his important study of mortality in eighteenth-century Philadelphia, Billy G. Smith estimates that there were in that town about 6.27 persons per house, an estimate with which our data on Charleston are consistent. See Purry, *Proposals*, reprinted in Carroll, *Historical Collections*, 2: 129; Hewatt, *An Historical Account*, 2: 15; Billy G. Smith, "Death and Life in a Colonial Immigrant City: A Demographic Analysis of Philadelphia," *Journal of Economic History* 37 (December 1977): 863–89, especially p. 864.

One should also note, however, that our estimate of Charleston's total population at this time is considerably smaller than that of Carl Bridenbaugh. See *Cities in the Wilderness: The First Century of Urban Life in America 1625–1742* (New York: Oxford University Press, 1971; originally published 1938), p. 303, footnote 1.

5. See Robert Johnson to the Board of Trade, January 12, 1719/20, Records in the British Public Record Office Relating to South Carolina, 7: 233–50, especially pp. 249–50; Daniel Bell to Samuel Wragg, March 4, 1719/20, Records in the British Public Record Office Relating to South Carolina, 7: 315–16; Queries Relating to South Carolina answered by Joseph Boone and John Barnwell, August 23, 1720, Records in the British Public Record Office Relating to South Carolina, 8: 59–77, especially pp. 61–62, South Carolina Department of Archives and History.

6. Great Britain, Public Record Office, Colonial Office, America and West Indies, CO 5/509, South Carolina, Shipping Returns, December 1721 to December 1735. One should note that I used these records in microfilm form (British Manuscripts Project, PRO Reel #52/3 & 4) at the South Carolina Department of Archives and History. Quarterly ship entries and clearances at the port of Charleston between December 25, 1721 and December 25, 1732 were as follows:

Entries

	Number	Quarters for Which Data Exist	Average
Dec. 25–Mar. 25	293	6	48.83
Mar. 25–June 24	133	4	33.25
June 25–Sept. 29	117	4	29.25
Sept. 29–Dec. 25	184	4	46.00

Clearances

	Number	Quarters for Which Data Exist	Average
Dec. 25–Mar. 25	343	6	57.17
Mar. 25–June 24	178	4	44.50
June 25–Sept. 29	96	4	24.00
Sept. 29–Dec. 25	133	4	33.25

7. See, for example, Leila Sellers, *Charleston Business on the Eve of the American Revolution* (Chapel Hill: University of North Carolina Press, 1934), pp. 63–64, 154–55.

8. It should be noted at this time that no allowance will be made for possible differences in seasonal mortality patterns for transient and permanent populations. So little is known about the backgrounds of transients, particularly of transient sailors, that to attempt to adjust our data to correct for possible differences of this sort would only bring a false precision to our estimates of crude death rates for whites in Charleston. For an analysis of white seasonal mortality patterns in eighteenth-century Charleston, see Appendix I-A.

9. A.S. Salley, Jr., ed., *Register of St. Philip's Parish, Charles Town, South Carolina, 1720–1758* (Charleston: Walker, Evans & Cogswell, 1904).

10. On these two sources of under-registration, see, for example, D.E.C. Eversley, "Exploitation of Anglican Parish Registers by Aggregative Analysis," in E.A. Wrigley, ed., *An Introduction to English Historical Demography: From the Sixteenth to the Nineteenth Century* (New York: Basic Books, 1966), pp. 44–95.

11. Maris A. Vinovskis, "Mortality Rates and Trends in Massachusetts Before 1860," *Journal of Economic History* 32 (March 1972): 184–213, especially p. 196. For under-registration rates in particular villages and towns in New England, see, for example, Kenneth A. Lockridge, "The Population of Dedham, Massachusetts, 1636–1736," *Economic History Review*, 2d series, 19 (1966): 318–44, pp. 332–33 especially; Susan L. Norton, "Population Growth in Colonial America: A Study of Ipswich, Massachusetts," *Population Studies* 25 (November 1971): 433–52, p. 439 especially; Daniel Scott Smith, "The Demographic History of Colonial New England," *Journal of Economic History* 32 (March 1972): 165–83, especially p. 171.

12. See, for example, the works cited in footnote 11 above. One should also note that Lorena S. Walsh and Russell R. Menard point out in their pioneering study of mortality in seventeenth-century Maryland that "the deaths of children are rarely noted in the records" of that colony. See Walsh and Menard, "Death in the Chesapeake: Two Life Tables for Men in Early Colonial Maryland," *Maryland Historical Magazine* 69 (Summer 1974): 211–27, especially p. 219.

13. Vital records covering certain years in the first half of the eighteenth century still exist for two congregations in Charleston other than that of St. Philip's, namely, the Circular Church and the Quaker Meeting. By comparing the burial records in the registers for these congregations with the burial records in the St. Philip's Parish Register, we find that each of the listings is different from the others. Moreover, there is no overlap among them. See Mabel L. Webber, ed., "Register of the Independent or Congregational (Circular) Church, 1732–1738," *South Carolina Historical Magazine* 12 (1911): 27–37, 53–59, 135–40; Transactions of the Society of Friends in Charleston, South Carolina, 1719–1769, Society of Friends Collection, South Carolina Historical Society, Charleston, S.C.; Salley, ed., *Register of St. Philip's Parish . . . 1720–1758.*

14. One hundred twenty-four whites died and were buried in Charleston between July 1 and August 28, 1732. Of these, 92 or 74.2 percent were buried at St. Philip's, while the remaining 32 were buried at the Presbyterian, French, and Quaker cemeteries. Similarly, there were 153 white burials recorded in the Charleston Bill of Mortality for 1756. Of these, 105 or 68.6 percent were buried at St. Philip's, while the remaining 48 were buried in the Congregational, Presbyterian, French, and Baptist cemeteries. See *South-Carolina Gazette*, September 2, 1732; George Sheed, *Births and Burials in the Parish of St. Philip, Charles-Town, from Dec. 25th, 1755, to Dec. 25th, 1756*, undated handbill, reprinted in Joseph I. Waring, *A History of Medicine in South Carolina 1670–1825* (Columbia: South Carolina Medical Association, 1964), p. 64.

15. The quote is from the English translation of the 1686 pamphlet *Remarques sur la "Nouvelle Relation de la Caroline," par un Gentilhomme François—MDCLXXXVI*, which appeared in *The Magnolia; or Southern Apalachian*, new series, 1 (October 1842): 226–30, especially p. 228. The original pamphlet apparently no longer exists.

For a general discussion of mortality conditions in the South Carolina low country during the first half of the eighteenth century, see Chapter 2.

My ongoing work on eighteenth-century Charleston as well as that of Scott Wilds of the University of Pennsylvania support the argument that mortality levels were substantially lower in the town during the second half of the eighteenth century than they had been during the first half. Data in several sources dating from the second half of the eighteenth century support this argument as well. See, for example, *South-Carolina Gazette*, June 19, 1755; Lionel Chalmers, *An Account of the Weather and Diseases of South-Carolina*, 2 vols. (London: E. and C. Dilly, 1776), 1: 36–37; Hewatt, *An Historical Account*, 2: 292.

There were many reasons for the drop in mortality levels in Charleston in the second half of the eighteenth century. These include: the acquisition by the town's inhabitants of immunities to certain diseases endemic in the low country; improvements in sanitation and drainage in the town; certain changes in the behavioral patterns and living arrangements of Charlestonians that rendered them less susceptible to disease during the most sickly seasons; the absence of severe outbreaks of certain epidemic diseases, particularly yellow fever and smallpox, between about 1760 and 1790. Such epidemic diseases had ravaged Charleston during the first half of the century.

NOTES

Introduction

1. Deposition of Diacan, March 22, 1672, in José Miguel Gallardo, trans., "The Spaniards and the English Settlement in Charles Town," *South Carolina Historical Magazine* 37 (April 1936): 49–64 and (July 1936): 91–99. Diacan's deposition appears on pages 54–56.

2. See, for example, Frederic R. Stevenson and Carl Feiss, "Charleston and Savannah," *Journal of the Society of Architectural Historians* 10 (December 1951): 3–9; Christopher Tunnard and Henry Hope Reed, *American Skyline: The Growth and Form of our Cities and Towns* (New York: The New American Library, 1956; originally published in 1955), pp. 45–46; Samuel G. Stoney, *This Is Charleston: A Survey of the Architectural Heritage of a Unique American City*, 3d revised edition (Charleston: The Carolina Art Association, 1976; originally published in 1944), pp. 9, 11. On the original gridiron plans of Charleston and Philadelphia, see Carl Bridenbaugh, *Cities in the Wilderness: The First Century of Urban Life in America 1625–1742* (New York: Oxford University Press, 1971; originally published in 1938), pp. 12–13; John W. Reps, *The Making of Urban America: A History of City Planning in the United States* (Princeton: Princeton University Press, 1965), pp. 157–79.

3. On Charleston's early layout and its defensive fortifications, see *A Plan of Charles Town from a Survey by Edward Crisp in 1704*, Map Collection, South Caroliniana Library, University of South Carolina, Columbia, S. C.; Howard J. Nelson, "Walled Cities of the United States," *Annals of the Association of American Geographers* 51 (March 1961): 1–22, esp. pp. 4–6; Larry E. Ivers, *Colonial Forts of South Carolina 1670–1775* (Columbia: Published for the South Carolina Tricentennial Commission by the University of South Carolina Press, 1970), pp. 40–42; Samuel Lapham, *Our Walled City: Charles Town, Province of South Carolina 1678–1718* (n.p.: Published by Society of Colonial Wars in the State of South Carolina, 1970), pp. 1–11.

On medieval city planning, see Lewis Mumford, *The Culture of Cities* (New York: Harcourt, Brace, 1938), pp. 13–72; Paul D. Spreiregen, *Urban Design: The Architecture of Towns and Cities* (New York: McGraw-Hill, 1965), pp. 8–12: Howard Saalman, *Medieval Cities* (New York: George Braziller, 1968), pp. 11–45; Arthur B. Gallion and Simon Eisner, *The Urban Pattern: City Planning and Design*, 3d edition (New York: D. Van Nostrand, 1975), pp. 35–42; Edmund N. Bacon, *Design of Cities*, revised edition (New York: Penguin Books, 1976), pp. 92–105.

On the "modern" Renaissance urban planning tradition, see Mumford, *The Culture of Cities*, pp. 73–142; Spreiregen, *Urban Design*, pp. 12–28; Giulio C. Argan, *The Renaissance City* (New York: George Braziller, 1969), passim; Gallion and Eisner, *The Urban Pattern*, pp. 43–64; Bacon, *Design of Cities*, pp. 106–61.

4. On Charleston's "Grand Modell" and its relationship to the actual development of the town, see Henry A. M. Smith, "Charleston—The Original Plan and the Earliest Settlers," *South Carolina Historical Magazine* 9 (January 1908): 12–27; *A Plan of Charles Town from a Survey by Edward Crisp in 1704*; George Hunter, *The Ichnography of Charles-Town at High Water* (London: Published by B. Roberts and W. H. Toms, 1739); Reps, *The Making of Urban America*, pp. 175–79. The data on Charleston's earliest settlers in Smith's article must be supplemented by Surveys of Charles Town Lots, 1679–1757, 1 ms. vol., Office of the Surveyor General, South Carolina Department of Archives and History, Columbia, S.C.

On the earliest plans of Vitry-le-François, France and Londonderry, Northern Ireland, see Reps, *The Making of Urban America*, pp. 6–7, 13–15, 177; E. A. Gutkind, *International History of City Development*, 8 vols. (New York: The Free Press, 1964–72), 5: 103–104; Gilbert Camblin, *The Town in Ulster; An Account of the Origin and Building of the Towns of the Province and the Development of Their Rural Setting* (Belfast: W. Mullan, 1951); Reps, "$C^2 + L^2 = S^2$? Another Look at the Origins of Savannah's Town Plan," in Harvey H. Jackson and Phinizy Spalding, eds., *Forty Years of Diversity: Essays on Colonial Georgia* (Athens: University of Georgia Press, 1984), pp. 101–51.

5. On the problem of roaming livestock in early Charleston, see Thomas Cooper and David J. McCord, eds., *The Statutes at Large of South Carolina*, 10 vols. (Columbia: A.S. Johnston, 1836–41), 7: 5–6, 7–12, 36–37, 47–49.

On the "privy question," see Cooper and McCord, *Statutes*, 7: 5–6, 7–12. The privy or "house of ease" or "house of offices" as it was sometimes called was the source of many of the sanitation problems that arose in early modern cities. One of these problems was satirized and, indeed, immortalized in Swift's poem "Strephon and Chloe." See Harold Williams, ed., *The Poems of Jonathan Swift*, 3 vols. (Oxford: Clarendon Press, 1937), 2: 584–93. For later discussions of the "privy question" in Charleston, see Charleston *South Carolina Gazette*, May 9, 1768; Ordinance, August 29, 1836, *A Digest of the Ordinances of The City Council of Charleston From the Year 1783 to Oct. 1844 . . .*, Prepared under Resolution of the City Council by George B. Eckhard (Charleston: Walker & Burke, 1844), p. 43.

On the lack of a drainage system in early Charleston, see Alexander S. Salley, ed., *Journal of the Commons House of Assembly of South Carolina*, 22 vols. (Columbia: Printed for the Historical Commission of South Carolina by the State Company, 1907–1947), 14: 5; Bridenbaugh, *Cities in the Wilderness*, pp. 160–61.

On efforts to clear Charleston's streets of weeds and underbrush, see Cooper and McCord, *Statutes*, 7: 1–3; 2: 76, 77.

On Charleston's brackish water, a problem which plagued the town through the eighteenth century, see Gideon Johnston to the Secretary, July 5, 1710, in Frank J. Klingberg, ed., *Carolina Chronicle: The Papers of Commissary Gideon Johnston 1707–1716*, University of California Publications in History, vol. 35 (Berkeley: University of California Press, 1946), p. 62; George Fenwick Jones, trans., "John Martin Boltzius' Trip to Charleston, October 1742," *South Carolina Historical Magazine* 82 (April 1981): 87–110, esp. p. 95; T. P. Harrison, ed., *Journal of a Voyage to Charlestown in So. Carolina by Pelatiah Webster in 1765*, Publications of the South Carolina Historical Society (Charleston: Published by the Society, 1898), p. 16; Capt. Martin, A Description of Charles Town in 1769, ms., South Caroliniana Library; H. Roy Merrens, "A View of Coastal South Carolina in 1778: The

Journal of Ebenezer Hazard," *South Carolina Historical Magazine* 73 (October 1972): 177–93; esp. p. 185; Alexander Hewatt, *An Historical Account of the Rise and Progress of the Colonies of South Carolina and Georgia*, 2 vols. (London: Printed for Alexander Donaldson, 1779), 2: 290; Roger Lamb, *An Original and Authentic Journal of Occurrences during the late American War, from its Commencement to the Year 1783* . . . (Dublin: Printed by Wilkinson & Courtney, 1809), p. 294.

The fact that various bottled waters and elixirs were commonly sold in Charleston throughout the colonial period is perhaps another indication that the town's water supply left something to be desired. See, for example, *South Carolina Gazette*, March 2, 1734; November 16, 1734; November 13, 1736.

Carl Bridenbaugh, on the other hand, asserts that Charleston had excellent water. See Bridenbaugh, *Cities in the Wilderness*, p. 62.

6. On English vernacular architectural forms in the seventeenth century, see, for example, Henry Glassie, *Pattern in the Material Folk Culture of the Eastern United States* (Philadelphia: University of Pennsylvania Press, 1968), pp. 64–67; M. W. Barley, *The English Farmhouse and Cottage* (London: Routledge and Kegan Paul, 1961); Barley, *The House and Home: A Review of 900 Years of House Planning and Furnishing in Britain* (Greenwich, Conn.: New York Graphic Society, 1963), pp. 25–26, 40–47; Raymond B. Wood-Jones, *Traditional Domestic Architecture in the Banbury Region* (Manchester: Manchester University Press, 1963); J. T. Smith, "The Evolution of the English Peasant House to the Late Seventeenth Century: The Evidence of Buildings," *Journal of the British Archeological Society*, 3d ser., 33 (1970): 122–47; Eric Mercer, *English Vernacular Houses: A Study of Traditional Farmhouses and Cottages* (London: H. M. Stationery Office, 1975), pp. 23–33 and passim.

On American domestic architecture in the seventeenth century, see Fiske Kimball, *American Architecture* (Indianapolis: Bobbs-Merrill, 1928), pp. 17–31; Louis B. Wright *The Cultural Life of the American Colonies 1607–1763* (New York: Harper & Row, 1957), pp. 196–99; William H. Pierson, Jr., *American Buildings and Their Architects*, 2 vols. (Garden City, N. Y. : Doubleday, 1970), 1: 22–60; John Demos, *A Little Commonwealth: Family Life in Plymouth Colony* (New York: Oxford University Press, 1970), pp. 24–35; Leland M. Roth, *A Concise History of American Architecture* (New York: Harper & Row, 1979), pp. 13–27.

On architectural forms in the seventeenth-century South in general and in Charleston in particular, see Henry Chandlee Forman, *The Architecture of the Old South: The Medieval Style, 1585–1850* (Cambridge: Harvard University Press, 1948), pp. 3–5, 98–104, 177–82; Thomas T. Waterman, *The Dwellings of Colonial America* (Chapel Hill: University of North Carolina Press, 1950), pp. 11–113; Fred Kniffen, "Folk Housing: Key to Diffusion," *Annals of the Association of American Geographers* 55 (December 1965): 549–77; Glassie, *Pattern in the Material Folk Culture of the Eastern United States*, pp. 64–124; Peirce F. Lewis, "Common Houses, Cultural Spoor," *Landscape* 19 (January 1975): 1–22; Cary Carson, "Homestead Architecture in the Chesapeake Colonies," unpublished paper, 1981; Cary Carson, Norman F. Barka, William M. Kelso, Garry Wheeler Stone, and Dell Upton, "Impermanent Architecture in the Southern American Colonies," *Winterthur Portfolio* 16 (Summer/Autumn 1981): 135–96; Upton, "The Origins of Chesapeake Architecture," in *Three Centuries of Maryland Architecture* (Annapolis: Maryland Historical Trust, 1982), pp. 44–57; Mills Lane, *Architecture of the Old South: South Carolina* (Savannah: The Beehive Press, 1984), pp. 9–32; Alice R. Huger Smith and D. E. Huger Smith, *The Dwelling Houses of Charleston, South Carolina* (Philadelphia: J. B. Lippincott, 1917), pp. 339–58; Bridenbaugh, *Cities in the Wilderness*, pp. 8–11.

The best contemporary descriptions of Charleston in the seventeenth century are found in Maurice Mathews' "A Contemporary View of Carolina in 1680," *South Carolina Historical Magazine* 55 (July 1954): 153–59; T. A. , *Carolina; or a Description of the Present State of that Country and the Natural Excellencies thereof* . . . (London: Printed for W. C. , 1682); Samuel Wilson, *An Account of the Province of Carolina* . . . (London: Printed by G. Larkin for Francis Smith, 1682); A. S. Salley, ed., "Letters of Thomas Newe, 1682," in A. S. Salley, ed., *Narratives of Early Carolina 1650–1708* (New York: Barnes & Noble, 1967; originally published in 1911), pp. 181–87; Louis Thibou Letter, September 20, 1683, South Caroliniana Library. Note that the accounts by T. A. and Wilson are also reprinted in Salley's *Narratives*.

Several early estate inventories contain data on domestic architecture in seventeenth-century South Carolina and, thus, proved useful in developing the argument above. See Inventory, Alexander Pepin, March 18, 1689, Records of the Secretary of the Province 1675–1695, pp. 342–44; Inventory, Nicholas Townsend, April 16, 1694, Records of the Secretary of the Province 1692–1700, pp. 130–32; Inventory, James Beamor, May 11, 1694, Records of the Secretary of the Province 1692–1700, pp. 165–66. These manuscript records are part of the series, Records of the Secretary of State, Miscellaneous Records, Main Series, 1671–1973, 153 vols., at the South Carolina Department of Archives and History. For additional data on domestic architecture in early Charleston, see Lease Between Richard Tradd . . . and Gabriel Ribouleau . . . , February 12, 1694, Grant Book C, Register of the Province 1694–1707; Secretary of the Province 1722–1740, p. 13, in the same record series.

One should note that cypress and cedar were also used in the construction of wooden dwelling houses in seventeenth-century Charleston; pine and oak, however, probably predominated in the early years. See Smith and Smith, *Dwelling Houses*, pp. 339–58.

While most houses in seventeenth-century Charleston were built of wood as indicated above, brick dwellings were not unknown. See, for example, Inventory, Joseph Pendervas, July 13, 1695, Records of the Secretary of the Province 1692–1700, pp. 222–23; Will, Joseph Croskeys, December 2, 1700, Records of the Secretary of the Province, Will Book 1687–1710, p. 72, South Carolina Department of Archives and History.

7. On the location of Charleston's early churches and public buildings, see *A Plan of Charles Town from a Survey by Edward Crisp in 1704*. The powder magazine, which is not shown in Crisp's map, was provided for by a legislative act in 1703 and built shortly thereafter. See Cooper and McCord, *Statutes*, 7: 28–33.

For descriptions of Charleston's earliest church buildings, see Frederick Dalcho, *An Historical Account of the Protestant Episcopal Church in South Carolina* . . . (Charleston: E. Thayer, 1820), pp. 26–27; Edward McCrady, *A Sketch of St. Philip's Church, Charleston, S. C.* (Charleston: The Walker, Evans & Cogswell Co., 1901), pp. 7–9; George Howe, *History of the Presbyterian Church of South Carolina* (Columbia: Duffie & Chapman, 1870), pp. 72–73, 132–47; David Ramsay, *The History of the Independent or Congregational Church in Charleston, South Carolina, From its Origin Till the Year 1814* . . . (Philadelphia: Printed for the Author by J. Maxwell, 1815), pp. 3–7; George N. Edwards, *A History of the Independent or Congregational Church of Charleston South Carolina* (Boston: The Pilgrim Press, 1947), pp. 1–8; Arthur H. Hirsch, *The Huguenots of Colonial South Carolina* (Durham: Duke University Press, 1928), pp. 50–60; Leah Townsend, *South Carolina Baptists, 1670–1805* (Florence, S.C.: Florence Printing Co., 1935), pp. 5–11; Stephen B. Weeks, *Southern Quakers and Slavery: A Study in Institutional History*, Johns Hopkins University Studies in Historical and Political Science, Extra Volume, XV (Baltimore: Johns Hopkins Press, 1896), pp. 93–94.

On inns and taverns in colonial Charleston, see Bridenbaugh, *Cities in the Wilderness*, pp. 107–15, 270–77; Bridenbaugh, *Cities in Revolt: Urban Life in America 1743–1776* (New York: Capricorn Books, 1964; originally published in 1955), pp. 156–62, 358–61. Data on the town's earliest taverns can also be gleaned from Cooper and McCord, *Statutes*, 2: v, 77, 85–86, 113–15, 198–99; Records of the South Carolina Court of Common Pleas, Judgment Rolls, 1703–1790, Boxes 1–2, passim, South Carolina Department of Archives and History.

8. On the South Carolina economy in the seventeenth century, see Lewis C. Gray, *History of Agriculture in the Southern United States to 1860*, 2 vols. (Gloucester, Mass.: Peter Smith, 1958; originally published in 1933), 1: 50–59; Converse D. Clowse, *Economic Beginnings in Colonial South Carolina 1670–1730* (Columbia: University of South Carolina Press, 1971), pp. 1–138; David L. Coon, "The Development of Market Agriculture in South Carolina, 1670–1785" (Ph. D. dissertation, University of Illinois, 1972), pp. 73–163. My own interpretation of South Carolina's seventeenth-century economy appears in Chapter 3 of this study.

For the derivation of the estimate of Charleston's population in 1700, see Chapter 4. My estimate, one should note, is considerably smaller than that of Bridenbaugh. See *Cities in the Wilderness*, pp. 143–44.

The area within Charleston's walls was actually 81.4 acres. I calculated this figure by measuring on a map the area within the bounds of Water, Meeting, Market, and East Bay streets in modern Charleston, that is, the area surrounded by the town's walls in the early colonial period. The area measured (with a polar planimeter) was 2.64 square inches. The Department of Planning and Urban Development of the City of Charleston kindly provided me with a measurement of the number of feet from the southeast corner of Meeting and South Market streets to the northeast corner of Meeting and Water (2,680 feet). By dividing that number by the distance in inches between these two points on the map utilized in all calculations (City of Charleston, Visitor's Map, 1979), I was able to derive the scale of this map (1 inch = 1158.92 feet). By squaring the scale of the map (1158.92), multiplying the derived figure by 2.64, and dividing the total by 43,560 (number of square feet per acre), one can calculate the number of acres within the bounds mentioned above. That figure, once again, is 81.4 acres. I would like to thank Chris Fales of the Charleston Department of Planning and Urban Development for helping me with these calculations.

9. On the contours of South Carolina's economy in the eighteenth century, see Gray, *History of Agriculture*, 1, passim, Leila Sellers, *Charleston Business on the Eve of the American Revolution* (Chapel Hill: University of North Carolina Press, 1934); Clowse, *Economic Beginnings*, pp. 139–250; Coon, "The Development of Market Agriculture," pp. 164–347; Marc Egnal, "The Economic Development of the Thirteen Continental Colonies, 1720 to 1775," *William and Mary Quarterly*, 3d series, 32 (April 1975): 191–222; Peter A. Coclanis, "Rice Prices in the 1720s and the Evolution of the South Carolina Economy," *Journal of Southern History* 48 (November 1982): 531–44; Robert M. Weir, *Colonial South Carolina: A History* (Millwood, N.Y.: KTO Press, 1983), pp. 141–72; Coclanis, "Bitter Harvest: The South Carolina Low Country in Historical Perspective," *Journal of Economic History* 45 (June 1985): 251–59; Coclanis, "The Rise and Fall of the South Carolina Low Country: An Essay in Economic Interpretation," *Southern Studies* 24 (Summer 1985): 143–66. Also see chapters 3 and 4 of this study.

10. On the dismantling of the walls, see Hunter, *The Ichnography of Charles-Town at High Water*; Nelson, "Walled Cities of the United States," pp. 4–6; Lapham, *Our Walled City*, pp. 1–11. These walls, one should note, were partially destroyed already as a result

of the hurricanes of 1713 and 1714. See Thomas Hasell to the Secretary, October 11, 1718, Records of the Society for the Propagation of the Gospel, Letter Books, Series A, 1702–1737, 26 ms. vols., 13: 189–92, Archives of the Society for the Propagation of the Gospel, London, England. I used the microfilm version of the S.P.G. records issued by Micro Methods, Ltd., of East Ardsley, Wakefield, Yorkshire, England in 1964.

11. See Hunter, *The Ichnography of Charles-Town at High Water*; Stevenson and Feiss, "Charleston and Savannah," pp. 3–9; Reps, *The Making of Urban America*, pp. 175–79; Cooper and McCord, *Statutes*, 3: 461; 7: 74–75. Note that other road extensions and improvements in Charleston were carried out under the provisions of the Highway Act of 1721 and, thus, do not appear in the South Carolina statutes. See Cooper and McCord, *Statutes*, 9: 49–57.

12. On the beginnings of Charleston's sewage and drainage system, see Cooper and McCord, *Statutes*, 3: 405; *South Carolina Gazette*, March 30, 1734; Bridenbaugh, *Cities in the Wilderness*, pp. 318–19.

On early efforts to reclaim low spots in Charleston, see Ramsay, *The History of South Carolina from Its First Settlement in 1670, to the Year 1808*, 2 vols. (Charleston: Published by David Longworth for the author, 1809), 2: 70–75; J.L.E.W. Shecut, *Shecut's Medical and Philosophical Essays* (Charleston: Printed for the author by A.E. Miller, 1819), pp. 1–14; Robert Mills, *Statistics of South Carolina* . . . (Charleston: Hurlbut and Lloyd, 1826), pp. 391–93.

On wandering livestock in Charleston, see *South Carolina Gazette*, December 12, 1741; Cooper and McCord, *Statutes*, 7: 75–79, esp. p. 76; Bridenbaugh, *Cities in the Wilderness*, pp. 167–68, 323. For evidence on the construction of fencing in Charleston, see *South Carolina Gazette*, September 9, 1732; December 21, 1734; April 3, 1736; July 17, 1736.

Gardens had apparently become quite common in Charleston by the mid–1730s. See *South Carolina Gazette*, October 14, 1732; January 6, 1733; March 10, 1733; April 14, 1733; June 16, 1733; March 30, 1734; September 14, 1734; December 7, 1734; December 14, 1734; February 22, 1735; March 8, 1735; April 12, 1735; July 19, 1735; November 29, 1735; January 31, 1736; February 7, 1736; February 28, 1736; April 3, 1736; June 26, 1736; August 14, 1736; November 6, 1736; November 13, 1736; Robert Pringle to Andrew Pringle, June 14, 1740, and Robert Pringle to James Henderson, October 10, 1740, in Walter B. Edgar, ed., *The Letterbook of Robert Pringle*, 2 vols. (Columbia: University of South Carolina Press, 1972), 1: 222–25, 253–54. Additional data on gardening in South Carolina can be found in [Deas], Commonplace Book, 1749, South Carolina Historical Society, Charleston, S.C. Also see E.T.H. Shaffer, *Carolina Gardens* (Chapel Hill: University of North Carolina Press, 1939), pp. 120–32; Loutrel W. Briggs, *Charleston Gardens* (Columbia: University of South Carolina Press, 1951), pp. 1–59; George C. Rogers, Jr. , *Charleston in the Age of the Pinckneys* (Norman: University of Oklahoma Press, 1969), pp. 83–86.

Charleston's streets were unpaved throughout the whole colonial period. For corroboration of this point, see the works mentioned in footnote 16 below. On Charleston's lack of street lights in the first half of the eighteenth century, see Bridenbaugh, *Cities in the Wilderness*, p. 169, and *Cities in Revolt*, p. 242.

13. On Charleston's domestic architecture in the first half of the eighteenth century, see Albert Simons and Samuel Lapham, Jr., *Charleston, South Carolina*, The Octagon Library of Early American Architecture (New York: Press of the American Institute of Architects, Inc., 1927), pp. 19–23; Kimball, *American Architecture*, pp. 35–37; Albert Simons, "Architectural Trends in Charleston," *Antiques* 97 (April 1970): 545–55; Marie Ferrara Hollings, "Brickwork of Charlestown to 1780" (M.A. thesis, University of South

Carolina, 1978), pp. 46–52; Robert P. Stockton, "The Evolution of Rainbow Row" (M.A. thesis, University of South Carolina, 1979), pp. 1–2, 143–44.

Excellent data on both Charleston architecture and on building techniques, materials, costs, etc., in the first half of the eighteenth century appear in Elizabeth Sindrey, Estate Account Book, 1705–1721, South Carolina Historical Society; Charles Pinckney Manuscripts, 1737–1751, South Caroliniana Library. There is, in addition, some useful information on vernacular architecture in eighteenth-century South Carolina in Stanley South's *Method and Theory in Historical Archeology* (New York: Academic Press, 1977), pp. 83–139, 141–64 and in Martha A. Zierden's "Urban Archaeology in Charleston: A Museum Interpretation," *South Carolina Antiquities* 16 (1984): 29–40.

On the concept of vertical residential segregation, see, for example, James E. Vance, Jr., "Land Assignment in the Precapitalist, Capitalist, and Postcapitalist City," *Economic Geography* 47 (April 1971): 101–20; John Langton, "Residential Patterns in Pre-Industrial Cities: Some Case Studies from Seventeenth-Century Britain," *The Transactions of the Institute of British Geographers* 65 (July 1975): 1–27; Cary Carson, "Segregation in Vernacular Buildings," *Vernacular Architecture* 7 (1976): 24–29. For suggestions of this type of residential segregation in eighteenth-century Charleston, see *South Carolina Gazette*, September 2, 1732; June 29, 1734; December 14, 1734; January 31, 1736. This kind of housing arrangement would, of course, be most appropriate in households with small numbers of servants or slaves. In households with larger numbers of slaves, outbuildings were used to shelter them.

For good descriptions of typical Charleston houses of the 1730s, see *South Carolina Gazette*, June 29, 1734; December 14, 1734; March 8, 1735; January 31, 1736; February 5, 1737. A number of similar houses are still standing, including those at 106 Broad Street, 59 Church Street, 79 Church Street, 101 East Bay, 5–7 Tradd Street, 44–40–38 Tradd Street, and 10–8 Tradd Street. Pictures of these buildings appear in Stoney, *This Is Charleston*, pp. 16, 28, 30, 43, 100–102. The engraving entitled "Prospect of Charles Town," published in London by B. Robert and W. H. Toms in 1739, also provides excellent data on Charleston architecture in the 1730s. Note especially the small balconies on the fronts of many of the buildings shown in the engraving.

Finally, for an interesting description of Charleston in the 1720s, see Brian J. Enright, contrib., "An Account of Charles Town in 1725," *South Carolina Historical Magazine* 61 (January 1960): 13–18.

14. Charleston's total population in 1740 was about 6,300. For the derivation of this estimate, see Chapter 4. Bridenbaugh's estimate for 1742, one should note, is slightly higher. See *Cities in the Wilderness*, p. 303.

Charleston's settled area had grown to 153.24 acres by 1739. I calculated this acreage figure by plotting the settled areas shown in *The Ichnography of Charles-Town at High Water* onto a modern map of the town (City of Charleston, Visitor's Map, 1979), measuring this area with a polar planimeter (4.97 square inches), and then converting the figure measured to acres through the same procedure discussed in detail in footnote 8.

On the increase in the number of wharves in Charleston, see *A Plan of Charles Town from a Survey by Edward Crisp in 1704*; Hunter, *The Ichnography of Charles-Town at High Water*. For comparative purposes, one should note that Boston had over forty wharves as early as 1722. See John Bonner, *The Town of Boston in New England* (Boston: printed by Fra. Dewing, 1722). The original Bonner plan is in the Stokes Collection, New York Public Library, New York, N. Y. Also see Walter M. Whitehill, *Boston: A Topographical History*, Second edition, enlarged (Cambridge: The Belknap Press of Harvard University, 1968), pp. 22–46.

On the development of differentiated market areas in Charleston, see Hunter, *The Ichnography of Charles-Town at High Water;* Salley, *Journal of the Commons House of Assembly of South Carolina*, 18: 55, 57, 80–83. The "New Market" existed by 1734; it is mentioned in an advertisement in the *South Carolina Gazette*, September 21, 1734. Also see Sellers, *Charleston Business*, pp. 79–96; Stevenson and Feiss, "Charleston and Savannah," pp. 3–9; Rogers, *Charleston in the Age of the Pinckneys*, pp. 86–87. Similar differentiation occurred in Boston at the same time. See Karen J. Friedmann, "Victualling Colonial Boston," *Agricultural History* 47 (July 1973): 189–205.

On the opening of Charles Shepheard's tavern, see *South Carolina Gazette*, March 2, 1734.

On the second St. Philip's Church building, see Cooper and McCord, *Statutes*, 2: 352; 3: 111, 179; Clergy of South Carolina to the Secretary, July 12, 1722, Records of the Society for the Propagation of the Gospel, Letter Books, Series A, 16: 76–78; Richard J. Hooker, ed., *The Carolina Backcountry on the Eve of the Revolution: The Journal and Other Writings of Charles Woodmason, Anglican Itinerant* (Chapel Hill: University of North Carolina Press, 1953), p. 70; Dalcho, *An Historical Account of the Protestant Episcopal Church in South Carolina*, pp. 120–26; McCrady, *A Sketch of St. Philip's Church*, pp. 15–18. A picture of the church appears in *The Gentleman's Magazine* 23 (June 1753): plate opposite p. 260.

On Charleston's new theatre, which opened on February 12, 1736, see *South Carolina Gazette*, January 31, 1736; Eola Willis, *The Charleston Stage in the XVIII Century* (Columbia: The State Co., 1924), pp. 21–25; Frederick P. Bowes, *The Culture of Early Charleston* (Chapel Hill: University of North Carolina Press, 1942), pp. 101–3; Mary Julia Curtis, "The Early Charleston Stage: 1703–1798" (Ph.D. dissertation, Indiana University, 1968), pp. 19–20.

Tickets to the theatre were expensive, generally costing from 15–20 to 40s. current money each in the 1730s. See *South Carolina Gazette*, January 18, 1735; March 22, 1735; January 31, 1736; March 6, 1736; March 13, 1736; March 20, 1736; November 6, 1736. The highest paid artisans in Charleston made approximately 40s. current money per day in this period; most made roughly half as much. Laborers, sailors, and soldiers made between about £8 and £12 current money per month plus rations. For fragmentary data on wage levels in the 1700–1740 period, see James Glen, *A Description of South Carolina* . . . (London: Printed for R. and J. Dodsley, 1761), p. 80; James H. Easterby *et al.*, eds., *The Colonial Records of South Carolina*, 1st series: *The Journal of the Commons House of Assembly, 1736–*, 13 vols. to date (Columbia: Printed for the South Carolina Department of Archives and History, 1951–), *vol.: September 12, 1739–March 26, 1741*, pp. 428–29; Records of the South Carolina Court of Common Pleas, Judgment Rolls, Box 1, C, 668 (Hollybush v. Hurlock); Box 1, C, 693 (Reynolds v. Wright); Box 4, B, 213 (Jones v. Skinner); Box 4, B, 214 (Quelch v. Stephens); Box 4, B, 218 (Skinner v. Pight); Box 4, B, 245 (Brand v. Buridge); Box 4, B, 254 (Goble v. Hayes); Box 10, A, 139A (Stevenson v. Fenn); Box 16, A, 162A (Sauseau v. Flavell); Box 21, A, 48A (Salton v. Hale); Box 22, A, 57A (Roche v. Gascoyne); Box 22, A, 58A (Panton v. Freeman), South Carolina Department of Archives and History; Elizabeth Sindrey, Estate Account Book, leaves 57, 67, 73, South Carolina Historical Society. Wage rates for men serving on the scout boats in 1732 and as soldiers at the Port Royal garrison in 1737 appear in the *South Carolina Gazette*, April 22, 1732; March 26, 1737. Also see Richard Walsh, *Charleston's Sons of Liberty: A Study of the Artisans 1763–1789* (Columbia: University of South Carolina Press, 1959), pp. 143–45; *Historical Statistics of the United States: Colonial Times to 1970*, Department of Commerce, Bureau of the Census, 2 vols. (Washington: U.S. Government Printing Office, 1975), 2: 1196. For illuminating looks at wage levels in Boston and Philadelphia, see Gary

B. Nash, *The Urban Crucible: Social Change, Political Consciousness, and the Origins of the American Revolution* (Cambridge: Harvard University Press, 1979), pp. 392–94 and passim; Billy G. Smith, "The Material Lives of Laboring Philadelphians, 1750 to 1800," *William and Mary Quarterly*, 3d series, 38 (April 1981): 163–202. Finally, to convert South Carolina wages—which are given in proclamation money or current money—to sterling, see John J. McCusker, *Money and Exchange in Europe and America, 1600–1775: A Handbook* (Chapel Hill: University of North Carolina Press, 1978), pp. 121n, 222–23.

On the Charleston Work House, see Hunter, *The Ichnography of Charles-Town at High Water*; *South Carolina Gazette*, March 30, 1734; Cooper and McCord, *Statutes*, 3: 430; Minutes of the Vestry, St. Philip's Parish, 1732–1755, W. P. A. typescript, pp. 13–14, 39, South Caroliniana Library; Bridenbaugh, *Cities in the Wilderness*, pp. 385, 396.

Black slave carpenters were quite common in colonial South Carolina. Moreover, they were considered the most valuable slaves in the province. See Philip D. Morgan, "The Development of Slave Culture in Eighteenth Century Plantation America" (Ph.D. dissertation, University College London, 1977), pp. 100–42, esp. pp. 110, 119–20. For general background on skilled slaves in colonial South Carolina in general and in Charleston in particular, see Peter H. Wood, *Black Majority: Negroes in Colonial South Carolina From 1670 through the Stono Rebellion* (New York: Knopf, 1974), passim; Philip D. Morgan, "Black Life in Eighteenth-Century Charleston," *Perspectives in American History*, New Series, I (1984): 187–232.

On the constant hammering which informed the "soundscape" of the pre-industrial city, see R. Murray Schafer, *The Tuning of the World* (New York: Knopf, 1977), pp. 53–67.

15. On the aggregate level of wealth in colonial South Carolina, see Alice Hanson Jones, *Wealth of a Nation To Be: The American Colonies on the Eve of the Revolution* (New York: Columbia University Press, 1980), pp. 258–341, 343–74 especially; Richard Waterhouse, "South Carolina's Colonial Elite: A Study in the Social Structure and the Political Culture of a Southern Colony, 1670–1760" (Ph.D. dissertation, Johns Hopkins University, 1973), pp. 161–77. On the sources of this wealth and the evolution of the South Carolina economy in the eighteenth century, see the works cited in footnote 9. On South Carolina's "golden" rice, see Duncan Clinch Heyward, *Seed from Madagascar* (Chapel Hill: University of North Carolina Press, 1937), pp. 3–10. Also see chapters 3 and 4 of this study.

16. On improvements in Charleston's sewage and drainage system in the late colonial period, see Cooper and McCord, *Statutes*, 3: 694; 4: 112; 9: 697–705; Hewatt, *An Historical Account of the Rise and Progress of the Colonies of South Carolina and Georgia*, 2: 289; Bridenbaugh, *Cities in Revolt*, pp. 28–29, 237–38.

On land reclamation in Charleston during the same period, see Cooper and McCord, *Statutes*, 3: 643; 7: 85–87, 87–90; Ramsay, *The History of South Carolina*, 2: 70–75; Shecut, *Shecut's Medical and Philosophical Essays*, pp. 15–28; Mills, *Statistics of South Carolina*, pp. 391–93.

On Charleston's unpaved streets and its brick sidewalks, see, for example, Harrison, *Journal of a Voyage to Charlestown in So. Carolina by Pelatiah Webster in 1765*, p. 5; —————, "Charleston, S.C., in 1774 as Described by an English Traveller," *Historical Magazine* 9 (November 1865): 341–47, esp. p. 343; Bernhard A. Uhlendorf, trans. and ed., *The Siege of Charleston With an Account of the Province of South Carolina: Diaries and Letters of Hessian Officers from the von Jungkenn Papers in the William L. Clements Library* (Ann Arbor: University of Michigan Press, 1938), p. 327; Joseph W. Barnwell, ed., "Diary of Timothy Ford 1785–1786," *South Carolina Historical Magazine* 13 (July 1912): 132–47 and (October 1912): 181–204. Ford's comments on Charleston's streets appear on page 141. Also see Bridenbaugh, *Cities in Revolt*, pp. 29, 238–39.

On the introduction of street lights in Charleston, see Bridenbaugh, *Cities in Revolt*, p.

262; Cooper and McCord, *Statutes*, 9: 705–8. In a 1764 letter to a Carolina merchant then in Philadelphia, Henry Laurens asks for information on urban improvements in the Quaker City, including details on the town's regulations on the lighting of streets. Henry Laurens to William Hopton, May 29, 1764, in Philip M. Hamer, George C. Rogers, Jr., *et al.*, eds., *The Papers of Henry Laurens*, 10 vols. thus far (Columbia: University of South Carolina Press, 1968–), 4: 292–93.

On the declining number of wandering livestock on Charleston's streets, see Cooper and McCord, *Statutes*, 7: 75–79; Bridenbaugh, *Cities in Revolt*, p. 32. Though declining in significance, this problem was not solved completely until much later. See, for example, *South Carolina Gazette*, November 5, 1744; Proceedings, August 22, 1837, Charleston City Council Papers, Box 1, Special Collections, Robert Scott Small Library, The College of Charleston, Charleston, S. C.; Ordinance, August 29, 1837, *A Digest of the Ordinances of the City Council of Charleston*, p. 43.

On the traffic problems caused by speeding carriages and wagons, etc., see Cooper and McCord, *Statutes*, 9: 697–705; Bridenbaugh, *Cities in Revolt*, pp. 34–35, 243–44; Yi-fu Tuan, *Landscapes of Fear* (New York: Pantheon Books, 1979), pp. 152–53.

17. For details on St. Michael's Church, see Cooper and McCord, *Statutes*, 7: 79–85; Hooker, *The Carolina Backcountry on the Eve of the Revolution*, pp. 70–71; Dalcho, *An Historical Account of the Protestant Episcopal Church in South Carolina*, pp. 184–89; John Kershaw, *History of the Parish and Church of Saint Michael Charleston* (n.p.: privately printed, 1915), pp. 7–9; Beatrice St. Julien Ravenel, *Architects of Charleston* (Charleston: Carolina Art Association, 1945), pp. 27–33; George W. Williams, *St. Michael's, Charleston, 1751–1951* (Columbia: University of South Carolina Press, 1951), pp. 129–308, esp. pp. 129–51; Pierson, *American Buildings and Their Architects*, 1: 136–37.

On the State House, see Cooper and McCord, *Statutes*, 3: 753; Harrison, *Journal of a Voyage to Charlestown in So. Carolina by Pelatiah Webster in 1765*, pp. 4–5.

On the Exchange, which has recently been renovated, see Cooper and McCord, *Statutes*, 4: 257–61; Ravenel, *Architects of Charleston*, pp. 39–43; Rogers, *Charleston in the Age of the Pinckneys*, pp. 61–62; Videau L. B. Kirk, "Charleston Exchange," in the National Society of the Colonial Dames of America publication, *Three Centuries of Custom Houses* (Hartford, Conn.: Published by the Colonial Dames of America, 1972), pp. 161–65.

On the status of Charleston's square in the pre–revolutionary era, see A.S. Salley, ed., "Diary of William Dillwyn During a Visit to Charles Town in 1772," *South Carolina Historical Magazine* 36 (1935): 1–6, 29–35, 73–78, 107–10, esp. p. 6; _____, "Charleston, S.C., in 1774, as Described by an English Traveller," p. 342; William Gerard De Brahm, *De Brahm's Report of the General Survey of the Southern District of North America*, ed. Louis De Vorsey, Jr. (Columbia: University of South Carolina Press, 1971), p. 90; Stevenson and Feiss, "Charleston and Savannah," pp. 3–9; Rogers, *Charleston in the Age of the Pinckneys*, p. 58.

18. On the encroachments on Charleston's square, see Stevenson and Feiss, "Charleston and Savannah," pp. 3–9; Reps, *The Making of Urban America*, p. 177. Also see the other works cited in the last paragraph of footnote 17 above.

For discussions of Charleston's changing street pattern, see Stoney, *This Is Charleston*, pp. 9, 11; Stevenson and Feiss, "Charleston and Savannah," pp. 3–9. The changes are best illustrated, however, by comparing plans of the town for 1704, 1739, and 1788. See *A Plan of Charles Town from a Survey by Edward Crisp in 1704*; Hunter, *The Ichnography of Charles-Town at High Water*; E. Petrie, *Plan of the City of Charleston, South Carolina, from a Survey Taken by E. Petrie, 1788*. Petrie's *Plan* appears in Jacob C. Milligan's *Charleston Directory and Revenue System, 1790* (Charleston: T.R. Bowen, 1790).

For a detailed examination of Charleston's population in the late colonial period, see Chapter 4 of this study. One should note that the total area included in Charleston's "Grand Modell" — a little over three hundred acres — was settled by the time of the American Revolution. Several suburbs had begun to develop as well. See Stoney, *This Is Charleston*, pp. 11, 13; Rogers, *Charleston in the Age of the Pinckneys*, pp. 55–63.

19. On the double house in eighteenth-century America in general and in Charleston in particular, see Kimball, *American Architecture*, pp. 46–52; Wright, *The Cultural Life of the American Colonies 1607–1763*, pp. 199–206; Pierson, *American Buildings and Their Architects*, 1: 61–94, 111–30; Lewis, "Common Houses, Cultural Spoor"; Smith and Smith, *The Dwelling Houses of Charleston, South Carolina*, pp. 50–53, 359–75; Simons and Lapham, *Charleston, South Carolina*, pp. 19–23; Ravenel, *Architects of Charleston*, pp. 1–5; Simons, "Architectural Trends in Charleston"; Henry F. Cauthen, Jr., *Charleston Interiors* (Charleston: Published by the Preservation Society of Charleston, 1979), pp. 9–10; Lane, *Architecture of the Old South: South Carolina*, pp. 33–85; Allen G. Noble, *Wood, Brick, and Stone: The North American Settlement Landscape*, 2 vols. (Amherst: The University of Massachusetts Press, 1984), 1:62–64. A number of outstanding examples of the double house are still standing in Charleston. These include the dwellings at 39 Church Street, 27 King Street, 64 South Battery, 6 Glebe Street, and 15 Meeting. For pictures of these buildings, see Stoney, *This Is Charleston*, pp. 28, 54, 61, 71, 96. The dwelling at 27 King Street is, of course, the famous Miles Brewton House, one of the greatest Palladian buildings in America. On this house and its builder, Ezra Waite, see Caroline Wyche Dixon, "The Miles Brewton House: Ezra Waite's Architectural Books and Other Possible Design Sources," *South Carolina Historical Magazine* 82 (April 1981): 118–42. For an example of a double house plan drawn in the eighteenth century, see Double house plan, c. 1760 (?), Ball Family Papers, South Carolina Historical Society.

On the wrought iron fences and gates that often protected the double house, see Alston Deas, *The Early Ironwork of Charleston* (Columbia: Bostick & Thornley, 1941), pp. 11–23 especially; John Michael Vlach, *The Afro-American Tradition in Decorative Arts* (Cleveland: The Cleveland Museum of Art, 1978), pp. 111–21. Vlach, one should note, also has written an interesting study about an ornamental ironworker in modern Charleston. See *Charleston Blacksmith: The Work of Philip Simmons* (Athens: The University of Georgia Press, 1981).

20. George Rogers, for example, emphasizes the Charleston origin of the single house, while Fred Kniffen, Henry Glassie, and Peirce Lewis refer to similar housing forms in other parts of England and America. One should note that Thomas Fuller, commenting in 1662 on the houses of Exeter, England, wrote that they ". . .stand sideways backwards into their yards, and only endways with their gables towards the street." Karl Heider, drawing from and, indeed, going beyond the theme sketched out by John Vlach, suggests that the single house may have been of West African origin. See Rogers, *Charleston in the Age of the Pinckneys*, p. 66; Kniffen, "Folk Housing: Key of Diffusion"; Glassie, *Pattern in the Material Folk Culture of the Eastern United States*, pp. 49–124 and especially pp. 218, 220; Lewis, "Common Houses, Cultural Spoor"; Thomas Fuller, *The Worthies of England*, ed. John Freeman (London: Allen & Unwin, Ltd., 1952; originally published in 1662), p. 141; Vlach, *The Afro-American Tradition in Decorative Arts*, pp. 122–38; Karl G. Heider, "The Charleston Single House: Negotiating Good Form between Africa and Britain," paper delivered at the Fourth Annual Symposium on Language and Culture in South Carolina, University of South Carolina, Columbia, S.C., March 14, 1980.

21. On the "I-house," see Barley, *The English Farmhouse and Cottage*; Wood-Jones, *Traditional Domestic Architecture in the Banbury Region*; Kniffen, "Folk Housing: Key to

Diffusion"; Glassie, *Pattern in the Material Folk Culture of the Eastern United States*, pp. 49–124, 216–20; Demos, *A Little Commonwealth*, pp. 24–35; Lewis, "Common Houses, Cultural Spoor"; Abbott Lowell Cummings, *The Framed Houses of Massachusetts Bay, 1625–1725* (Cambridge: The Belknap Press of Harvard University, 1979), pp. 22–39; Dell Upton, "The Power of Things: Recent Studies in American Vernacular Architecture," *American Quarterly* 35 (Bibliography 1983): 262–79, especially pages 272–74.

22. For discussions of the Charleston single house, see Smith and Smith, *The Dwelling Houses of Charleston, South Carolina*, pp. 43–45; Simons and Lapham, *Charleston, South Carolina*, pp. 77–81; Glassie, *Pattern in the Material Folk Culture of the Eastern United States*, pp. 218, 220; Simons, "Architectural Trends in Charleston"; Lewis, "Common Houses, Cultural Spoor"; Kenneth Severens, *Southern Architecture: 350 Years of Distinctive American Buildings* (New York: E.P. Dutton, 1981), pp. 13–14; Noble, *Wood, Brick, and Stone*, 1: 60–62.

On the style of brickwork used in the construction of the single house and, indeed, of the double house as well, see Simons, "Architectural Trends in Charleston," pp. 551, 554; Hollings, "Brickwork of Charlestown to 1780," pp. 46–83.

Numerous single houses still stand in Charleston, including the dwellings at 90, 92, and 94 Church Street, 61 Tradd Street, and 75 King Street. For pictures of these buildings, see Stoney, *This Is Charleston*, pp. 32, 62, 104; Simons, "Architectural Trends in Charleston," p. 548.

23. On the Charleston piazza, see George Milligen-Johnston, *A Short Description of the Province of South Carolina: With an Account of the Air, Weather, and Diseases, at Charlestown, Written in the Year 1763* (London: Printed for John Hilton, 1770), pp. 31–32; Hewatt, *An Historical Account of the Rise and Progress of the Colonies of South Carolina and Georgia*, 2: 290; John Bartram, "Diary of a Journey through the Carolinas, Georgia, and Florida, from July 1, 1765, to April 10, 1766," annotated by Francis Harper, in *Transactions of the American Philosophical Society*, new series, 33 (1942–44): 1–120, especially p. 30. Also see Waterman, *The Dwellings of Colonial America*, pp. 79–80; Simons, "Architectural Trends in Charleston." On piazzas in the West Indies, see the article by Albert Simons cited above; Colin G. Clarke, *Kingston, Jamaica: Urban Development and Social Change, 1692–1962* (Berkeley: University of California Press, 1975), pp. 3–4; Vlach, *The Afro-American Tradition in Decorative Arts*, pp. 122–38, esp. p. 137.

Note that "piazzas" are mentioned in a South Carolina statute in 1700. The lawmakers appear to have used the word at that time, however, to refer to the small balconies that were added to the fronts of many Charleston buildings in the colonial period. See Cooper and McCord, *Statutes*, 7: 16–17; "Prospect of Charles Town"; *South Carolina Gazette*, November 15, 1760; _____, "A Curious New Description of Charles-Town in South-Carolina . . .," *The Universal Museum* 1 (August 1762): 435–37 and (September 1762): 477–79, esp. p. 435; Deas, *The Early Ironwork of Charleston*, pp. 12–13.

24. On the walls and fences shielding the single house, see Shaffer, *Carolina Gardens*, p. 129; Deas, *The Early Ironwork of Charleston*, pp. 11–23; Simons, "Architectural Trends in Charleston"; Vlach, *The Afro-American Tradition in Decorative Arts*, pp. 111–21. For an insightful discussion of the single house in a later period, see William W. Freehling, *Prelude to Civil War: The Nullification Controversy in South Carolina, 1816–1836* (New York: Harper & Row, 1965), pp. 16–17.

25. The famous Robert Brewton House at 71 Church Street, for example, was built sometime prior to 1733. Moreover, Robert Stockton suggests that the single house may have existed in Charleston even before 1700. The single house became much more prevalent in any case during the long rebuilding period in Charleston after the devastating fire of 1740.

See Smith and Smith, *The Dwelling Houses of Charleston, South Carolina*, pp. 43–47; Stoney, *This Is Charleston*, p. 30; Stockton, "The Evolution of Rainbow Row," pp. 143–44.

26. On the single house as an architectural accommodation by the white population to either the South Carolina climate or to the partitioning of Charleston lots, see Hewatt, *An Historical Account of the Rise and Progress of the Colonies of South Carolina and Georgia*, 2: 290; Duc de la Rochefoucauld-Liancourt, *Travels through the United States of North America . . .* , trans. H. Neuman (London: R. Phillips, 1799), p. 556; Smith and Smith, *The Dwelling Houses of Charleston, South Carolina*, p. 26; Bowes, *The Culture of Early Charleston*, pp. 112–13; Samuel Chamberlain and Narcissa Chamberlain, *Southern Interiors of Charleston, South Carolina* (New York: Hastings House, 1956), p. 9; Simons, "Architectural Trends in Charleston"; Lewis, "Common Houses, Cultural Spoor"; Stoney, *This Is Charleston*, pp. 23, 25; G. E. Kidder Smith, *A Pictorial History of Architecture in America*, 2 vols. (New York: American Heritage Publishing Co., 1976), 1: 278; Cauthen, *Charleston Interiors*, pp. 8–9; Severens, *Southern Architecture*, pp. 13–14; Noble, *Wood, Brick, and Stone*, 1: 60.

Karl Heider, on the other hand, emphasizes the African influence on the development of the single house. See Heider, "The Charleston Single House." Also see Vlach, *The Afro-American Tradition in Decorative Arts*, pp. 122–38.

27. Blacks outnumbered whites by a small margin in Charleston through most of the eighteenth century. The black/white population ratio and other aspects of Charleston's eighteenth-century demographic history are discussed in considerable detail in Chapter 4.

On the distribution of wealth in colonial South Carolina, see Jones, *Wealth of a Nation To Be*, pp. 258–341, 343–74 especially; Waterhouse, "South Carolina's Colonial Elite," pp. 161–77; William George Bentley, "Wealth Distribution in Colonial South Carolina" (Ph.D. dissertation, Georgia State University, 1977), pp. 25–77, 103–14; George D. Terry, "'Champaign Country': A Social History of an Eighteenth Century Lowcountry Parish in South Carolina, St. Johns Berkeley County" (Ph.D. dissertation, University of South Carolina, 1981), pp. 243–97. Also see Chapter 4 of this study.

My own data on the distribution of wealth in Charleston between 1722 and 1732 reveal that even after excluding blacks—a group comprising a majority of the town's population but one which in effect held no part of the community's total wealth—Charleston's wealth distribution was more skewed than the distributions in New York and Philadelphia at the same time. Indeed, the degree of concentration which existed in Charleston by the 1720s would not be reached in these northern ports until the 1760s and 1770s. Charleston's wealth distribution and the assumptions and problems involved therein are examined at length in Chapter 4 of this study. For comparative purposes only, it should be noted here that the Schutz and Gini inequality coefficients for the distribution of personal wealth in Charleston—among white decedents with inventories between 1722 and 1732—were .52 and .66 respectively. See Gary Nash, "Up from the Bottom in Franklin's Philadelphia," *Past and Present* 77 (November 1977): 57–83; Bruce M. Wilkenfeld, "The Social and Economic Structure of the City of New York, 1695–1796" (Ph.D. dissertation, Columbia University, 1973), pp. 22, 58–59, 80, 122, 158, 192. For a summary of the literature on wealth distribution in colonial America, see Gloria L. Main, "Inequality in Early America: The Evidence from Probate Records of Massachusetts and Maryland," *Journal of Interdisciplinary History* 7 (Spring 1977): 559–81. Note that I excluded the city of Boston from the discussion above because I was unable to find any inequality coefficients for the wealth distribution of the town for any time after 1687 and before 1771. Gary Nash has, however, compiled some data on wealth in Boston between these years. See *The Urban Crucible*, pp. 396–400. Also see Nash,

"Urban Wealth and Poverty in Pre-Revolutionary America," *Journal of Interdisciplinary History* 6 (Spring 1976): 545–84; G. B. Warden, "Inequality and Instability in Eighteenth-Century Boston: A Reappraisal," *Journal of Interdisciplinary History* 6 (Spring 1976): 585–620. For data on Boston's wealth distributions in 1687, 1771, and 1790, see James A. Henretta, "Economic Development and Social Structure in Colonial Boston," *William and Mary Quarterly*, 3d series, 22 (January 1965): 75–92; Allan Kulikoff, "The Progress of Inequality in Revolutionary Boston," *William and Mary Quarterly*, 3d series, 28 (July 1971): 375–412.

On the political and social power of a relatively small group of white men in colonial South Carolina in general and in Charleston in particular, see Josiah Quincy, *Memoir of the Life of Josiah Quincy, Junior, of Massachusetts Bay: 1744–1775*, ed. Eliza Susan Quincy (Boston: Little, Brown, 1875; originally published in 1825), pp. 86–89 especially; Robert M. Weir, " 'LIBERTY AND PROPERTY, AND NO STAMPS': South Carolina and the Stamp Act Crisis" (Ph.D. dissertation, Western Reserve University, 1966), pp. 32–122; Eulalia Maria Lahmeyer Lobo, "Rio De Janeiro e Charleston, S. C. as Comunidades de Mercadores no Século XVIII," *Journal of Inter-American Studies and World Affairs* 12 (October 1970): 565–82; Stuart O. Stumpf, "The Merchants of Colonial Charleston, 1680–1756" (Ph. D. dissertation, Michigan State University, 1971), passim; Waterhouse, "South Carolina's Colonial Elite," passim; Hoyt Paul Canady, Jr., "Gentlemen of the Bar: Lawyers in Colonial South Carolina" (Ph.D. dissertation, University of Tennessee, 1979), pp. 302–46.

While the concept of "republicanism" is becoming increasingly problematic, the implications of some of the ideas associated with this intellectual tradition did, in fact, prove troublesome to elites in South Carolina during the revolutionary era. That black slaves and poor "dependent" whites were potentially threatening to the creation of a republic, they knew perfectly well. The existence of both of these groups in large numbers caused considerable anxiety not only in Charleston but throughout the Plantation South in general. See, for example, Weir, " 'LIBERTY AND PROPERTY, AND NO STAMPS,' " pp. 1–122; Robert E. Shalhope, "Toward a Republican Synthesis: The Emergence of an Understanding of Republicanism in American Historiography," *William and Mary Quarterly*, 3d series, 29 (January 1972): 49–80; Freehling, "The Founding Fathers and Slavery," *American Historical Review* 77 (February 1972): 81–93; Weir, "Portrait of a Hero," *American Heritage* 27 (April 1976): 16–19, 86–88; Walter Kirk Wood, "The Union of the States: A Study of Radical Whig-Republican Ideology and Its Influence Upon the Nation and the South, 1776–1861" (Ph.D. dissertation, University of South Carolina, 1978), pp. 2–96; Mark D. Kaplanoff, "Making the South Solid: Politics and the Structure of Society in South Carolina, 1790–1815" (Ph.D. dissertation, University of Cambridge, 1979), pp. 50–75; Shalhope, *John Taylor of Caroline: Pastoral Republican* (Columbia: University of South Carolina Press, 1980), pp. 35–69; Drew R. McCoy, *The Elusive Republic: Political Economy in Jeffersonian America* (Chapel Hill: University of North Carolina Press, 1980), passim; Daniel Walker Howe, "Virtue and Commerce in Jeffersonian America," *Reviews in American History* 9 (September 1981): 347–53; Walter J. Fraser, Jr., "Controlling the Poor in Colonial Charles Town," *The Proceedings of the South Carolina Historical Association, 1980* (Aiken, S.C., 1982): 13–30; Fraser, "The City Elite, 'Disorder,' and the Poor Children of Pre-Revolutionary Charleston," *South Carolina Historical Magazine* 84 (July 1983): 167–79.

For discussions of such problems by contemporaries, see, for example, Henry Laurens to Alexander Hamilton, April 19, 1785, South Carolina & Miscellaneous, pp. 229, 231, Bancroft Collection, New York Public Library; Henry Laurens to Jas. Bourdieu, May 6, 1785, South Carolina & Miscellaneous, p. 233, Bancroft Collection, New York Public Library; Alice Izard to Ralph Izard, November 21, 1794, Ralph Izard Papers, South Car-

oliniana Library; William Read to Jacob Read, April 17, 1798, Read Family Correspondence, South Carolina Historical Society.

One should note that though Charleston later became a center of Federalist power, scholars of republicanism in recent years have come to view Federalism—even its Hamiltonian strain—within the context of this intellectual tradition. See, for example, Gerald Stourzh, *Alexander Hamilton and the Idea of Republican Government* (Stanford: Stanford University Press, 1970); Lance Banning, *The Jeffersonian Persuasion: Evolution of a Party Ideology* (Ithaca: Cornell University Press, 1978); Forrest McDonald, *Alexander Hamilton: A Biography* (New York: W. W. Norton, 1979); McCoy, *The Elusive Republic*.

On Federalism in Charleston and the South Carolina low country, see Ulrich B. Phillips, "The South Carolina Federalists," *American Historical Review* 14 (April 1909): 529–43 and (July 1909): 731–43, 776–90; Rogers, *Evolution of a Federalist: William Loughton Smith of Charleston (1758–1812)* (Columbia: University of South Carolina Press, 1962); Marvin R. Zahniser, *Charles Cotesworth Pinckney: Founding Father* (Chapel Hill: University of North Carolina Press, 1967); Robert K. Ratzlaff, "John Rutledge, Jr., South Carolina Federalist, 1766–1819" (Ph.D. dissertation, University of Kansas, 1974); James H. Broussard, *The Southern Federalists, 1800–1816* (Baton Rouge: Louisiana State University Press, 1978), pp. 235–46 and passim; Kaplanoff, "Making the South Solid," pp. 137–277 especially.

Finally, one should note that South Carolina, according to Lacy K. Ford, developed its own particular brand of republicanism in the nineteenth century, thereby resolving the problems that had so concerned its statesmen in the late eighteenth century. See Ford, "Social Origins of a New South Carolina: The Upcountry in the Nineteenth Century" (Ph.D. dissertation, University of South Carolina, 1983).

28. Louis H. Sullivan, *Kindergarten Chats on Architecture, Education, and Democracy*, ed. Claude F. Bragdon (Lawrence?, Kansas: Scarab Fraternity Press, 1934), p. 168.

29. On Charleston's closed intellectual life in the nineteenth century, see George Rogers's sensitive portrait in *Charleston in the Age of the Pinckneys*, pp. 141–69. I use the terms "closed" and "repressive" advisedly; I do not mean to convey the idea that Charlestonians were averse to modernity, or to intellectual life per se. See Michael O' Brien and David Moltke-Hansen, eds., *Intellectual Life in Antebellum Charleston* (Knoxville: The University of Tennessee Press, 1986).

A number of works on the relationship between social psychology and architecture proved useful in developing the argument above. See, for example, Jane Jacobs, *The Death and Life of Great American Cities* (New York: Random House, 1961); Edward T. Hall, *The Hidden Dimension* (Garden City, N. Y.: Doubleday, 1966); Constantinos A. Doxiadis, *Ekistics: An Introduction to the Science of Settlement Systems* (New York: Oxford University Press, 1968), pp. 322–42 especially; Georges Duby, *Le Temps des cathédrales: L' Art et la société, 980–1420* (Paris: Gallimard, 1976); Peter F. Smith, *The Syntax of Cities* (London: Hutchinson, 1977); Tuan, *Landscapes of Fear*. Two works by Kevin Lynch were also helpful. See *The Image of the City* (Cambridge: M. I. T. Press, 1960) and *A Theory of Good City Form* (Cambridge: M. I. T. Press, 1981).

30. On the concept "periphery," see Immanuel Wallerstein, *The Modern World-System*, 2 vols. thus far (New York: Academic Press, 1974–). Wallerstein's basic concepts are defined and his argument outlined in "The Rise and Future Demise of the World Capitalist System: Concepts for Comparative Analysis," *Comparative Studies in Society and History* 16 (September 1974): 387–415.

31. *South Carolina Gazette and Country Journal*, September 6, 1768; Bowes, *The Culture of Early Charleston*, p. 95; Clare Jervey, comp., *Inscriptions on the Tablets and Gravestones in St. Michael's Church and Churchyard, Charleston, S.C.* (Columbia: The State Company, 1906), p. 73.

Chapter 1. The Carolina Venture in Economic Context

1. Percy Bysshe Shelley, "Ozymandias" (1818).

On the *Carolina*'s 1669–70 voyage to Kiawah, see Langdon Cheves, ed., *The Shaftesbury Papers and Other Records Relating to Carolina and the First Settlement on Ashley River Prior to the Year 1676*, in *Collections of the South Carolina Historical Society*, vol. 5 (Charleston: Published by the South Carolina Historical Society, 1897), pp. 133–74. Hereinafter cited as Cheves, ed., *Shaftesbury Papers*.

2. On the problem of the "transition" from a traditional to a market society, see Immanuel Wallerstein, *The Modern World-System*, 2 vols. thus far (New York: Academic Press, 1974–), 2: 3–9.

On the transition as a twelfth- or thirteenth-century phenomenon, see Henri Pirenne, "The Stages in the Social History of Capitalism," *American Historical Review* 19 (April 1914): 494–515; Pirenne, *Medieval Cities, Their Origins and the Revival of Trade*, trans. Frank D. Halsey (Princeton: Princeton University Press, 1925); B.H. Slicher van Bath, *The Agrarian History of Western Europe A.D. 500–1850*, trans. Olive Ordish (London: Edward Arnold, 1963), Part III; Robert S. Lopez, *The Commercial Revolution of the Middle Ages 950–1350* (Englewood Cliffs, N.J.: Prentice-Hall, 1971); Alan Macfarlane, *The Origins of English Individualism: The Family, Property, and Social Transition* (Oxford: Basil Blackwell, 1978), passim.

Other scholars see the transition occurring in the "long" sixteenth century. See, for example, Wallerstein, *The Modern World-System*, vol. 1 particularly; Wallerstein, "The Rise and Future Demise of the World Capitalist System: Concepts for Comparative Analysis," *Comparative Studies in Society and History* 16 (September 1974): 387–415; Paul Sweezy, "The Transition from Feudalism to Capitalism," *Science and Society* 14 (Spring 1950): 134–57; André Gunder Frank, *World Accumulation 1492–1789* (New York: Monthly Review Press, 1978), pp. 25–64, 238–71 especially; Fernand Braudel, *The Structures of Everyday Life: Civilization and Capitalism 15th-18th Century*, trans. Siân Reynolds (New York: Harper & Row, 1981).

To still others, however, the decisive break came in the seventeenth century. See, for example, Christopher Hill, "The English Civil War Interpreted by Marx and Engels," *Science and Society* 12 (Winter 1948): 130–56; Hill, *The Century of Revolution 1603–1714* (New York: W.W. Norton, 1966; originally published 1961), pp. 145–61; E.J. Hobsbawm, "The General Crisis of the European Economy in the 17th Century," *Past and Present*, no. 5 (May 1954): 33–53 and no. 6 (November 1954): 44–65; Pierre Chaunu, *La Civilisation de l'Europe classique* (Paris: Arthaud, 1966), pp. 20–21 and passim; Joyce Oldham Appleby, *Economic Thought and Ideology in Seventeenth-Century England* (Princeton: Princeton University Press, 1978), passim.

On the break as coterminous with the Industrial Revolution, see, for example, Carlo M. Cipolla, *Before the Industrial Revolution: European Society and Economy, 1000–1700* (New York: W.W. Norton, 1976), pp. 274–78 particularly. Most Marxists see the 1500–1750 period as one of "transition to capitalism." To these writers as well, "capitalism" per se is coterminous with the Industrial Revolution. See, for example, Maurice H. Dobb, *Studies in the Development of Capitalism* (New York: International Publishers, 1946), passim; Etienne Balibar, "On the Basic Concepts of Historical Materialism," in Etienne Balibar and Louis Althusser, *Reading 'Capital'*, trans. Ben Brewster (New York: Pantheon Books, 1970; originally published 1968), pp. 199–308, 302–8 especially; C.H. George, "The Origins of

Capitalism: A Marxist Epitome & A Critique of Immanuel Wallerstein's Modern World-System," *Marxist Perspectives* 3 (Summer 1980): 70–100.

Recently, some American historians, inspired by the work of Dobb, Karl Polanyi, et al., have argued that many nineteenth-century Americans retained traditional (non- or only semimarket-oriented) attitudes toward economic exchange and, as a result, did not respond to market stimuli in an economically rational manner. See, for example, Eugene D. Genovese, *The Political Economy of Slavery: Studies in the Economy and Society of the Slave South* (New York: Pantheon, 1965), pp. 13–39 especially; Morton Rothstein, "The Antebellum South as a Dual Economy: A Tentative Hypothesis," *Agricultural History* 41 (October 1967): 373–82; James O'Connor, review of Douglas F. Dowd, *The Twisted Dream*, in *Monthly Review* 26 (March 1975): 41–54; O'Connor, "A Note on Independent Commodity Production and Petty Capitalism," *Monthly Review* 28 (May 1976): 60–63; Michael Merrill, "Cash is Good to Eat: Self-Sufficiency and Exchange in the Rural Economy of the United States," *Radical History Review* 3 (Winter 1977): 42–71; James A. Henretta, "Families and Farms: *Mentalité* in Pre-Industrial America," *William and Mary Quarterly*, 3d ser., 35 (January 1978): 3–32; Kevin D. Kelly, "The Independent Mode of Production," *The Review of Radical Political Economics* 11 (Spring 1979): 38–48; Christopher Clark, "The Household Economy, Market Exchange and the Rise of Capitalism in the Connecticut Valley, 1800–1860," *Journal of Social History* 13 (Winter 1979): 169–89; John T. Schlotterbeck, "Plantation and Farm: Social and Economic Change in Orange and Green Counties, Virginia, 1716 to 1860" (Ph.D. dissertation, Johns Hopkins University, 1980); Schlotterbeck, "The 'Social Economy' of an Upper South Community: Orange and Greene Counties, Virginia, 1815–1860," in Orville Vernon Burton and Robert C. McMath, Jr., eds., *Class, Conflict, and Consensus: Antebellum Southern Community Studies* (Westport, Conn.: Greenwood Press, 1982), pp. 3–28; David F. Weiman, "Petty Commodity Production in the Cotton South: Upcountry Farmers in the Georgia Cotton Economy, 1840 to 1880" (Ph.D. dissertation, Stanford University, 1983), pp. 13–119 especially; Steven Hahn, *The Roots of Southern Populism: Yeoman Farmers and the Transformation of the Georgia Upcountry, 1850–1890* (New York: Oxford University Press, 1983); Hahn and Jonathan Prude, eds., *The Countryside in the Age of Capitalist Transformation: Essays in the Social History of Rural America* (Chapel Hill: University of North Carolina Press, 1985), passim. For recent challenges to these approaches, see Robert D. Mitchell, *Commercialism and Frontier: Perspectives on the Early Shenandoah Valley* (Charlottesville: University Press of Virginia, 1977); James T. Lemon, "Early Americans and their Social Environment," *Journal of Historical Geography* 6 (April 1980): 115–31; Winifred B. Rothenberg, "The Market and Massachusetts Farmers, 1750–1855," *Journal of Economic History* 41 (June 1981): 283–314; Peter A. Coclanis, "Rice Prices in the 1720s and the Evolution of the South Carolina Economy," *Journal of Southern History* 48 (November 1982): 531–44; Carole Shammas, "How Self-Sufficient Was Early America?," *Journal of Interdisciplinary History* 13 (Autumn 1982): 247–72; Stephen Innes, *Labor in a New Land: Economy and Society in Seventeenth-Century Springfield* (Princeton: Princeton University Press, 1983); Bettye Hobbs Pruitt, "Self-Sufficiency and the Agricultural Economy of Eighteenth-Century Massachusetts," *William and Mary Quarterly*, 3d ser., 41 (July 1984): 333–64.

3. On the "long" sixteenth century, that is, the 1450–1650 period roughly, see Fernand Braudel, "Qu'est-ce que le XVIᵉ siècle?," *Annales: Economies, sociétés, civilisations* 8 (1953): 69–73; Wallerstein, *The Modern World-System*, 1: 67–129 especially.

4. On the extension of the "seventeenth century" until approximately 1750, see, for example, Jan de Vries, *The Economy of Europe in an Age of Crisis: 1600–1750* (Cambridge:

Cambridge University Press, 1976), pp. 1–29 especially; D.C. Coleman, *The Economy of England 1450–1750* (Oxford: Oxford University Press, 1977), pp. 91–93; Wallerstein, *The Modern World-System*, 2: 8–9.

5. On the "general crisis" of the seventeenth century, see Hobsbawm, "The General Crisis of the European Economy in the 17th Century"; Roland Mousnier, *Les XVIe et XVIIe Siècles: Les Progrès de la civilisation européenne et le déclin de l'orient*, Tome IV, *Histoire Générale des Civilisations*, ed., Maurice Crouzet (Paris: Presses Universitaires de France, 1954), pp. 143–350; Pierre and Huguette Chaunu, *Séville et l'Atlantic 1504–1650*, 8 vols. in 11 tomes (Paris: Armand Colin; S.E.V.P.E.N., 1955–1959), vol. 8 especially; Hugh R. Trevor-Roper, "The General Crisis of the 17th Century," *Past and Present*, no. 16 (November 1959): 31–64; Trevor Aston, ed., *Crisis in Europe, 1560–1660* (Garden City, N.Y.: Anchor Books, 1967; originally published 1965).

The concept of a "general crisis" is an ambiguous one indeed. While Hobsbawm originally used the term to denote a turning point in European history—a turning point which led to the transformation of an entire social system—others (and at times Hobsbawm himself) later used "crisis" in a looser sense to describe the difficulties symptomatic of this turning point. Thus, "crisis" is often used synonymously with terms so varied as instability, stagnation, recession, depression, involution, etc. Hence, much of the historiographic confusion attending the so-called *siècle de malheur*.

One should note that the phrase "century of depression" in the text is borrowed from Woodrow Borah, *New Spain's Century of Depression* (Berkeley: University of California Press, 1951).

One should also note that I am using the term "involution" in an economic sense to denote retrograde or degenerative change rather than in an anthropological sense to denote a trend toward internal complexity and elaboration. For an example of "involution" used in the latter sense, see Clifford Geertz, *Agricultural Involution: The Process of Ecological Change in Indonesia* (Berkeley: University of California Press, 1971; originally published 1963), pp. 80–82 especially.

6. Scholars that stress divergence in the economies of seventeenth-century Europe include Ralph Davis, *The Rise of the Atlantic Economies* (Ithaca: Cornell University Press, 1973); De Vries, *The Economy of Europe in an Age of Crisis*; Cipolla, *Before the Industrial Revolution*; Coleman, *The Economy of England 1450–1750*; Wallerstein, *The Modern World-System*, vol. 2; Peter Kriedte, *Peasants, Landlords and Merchant Capitalists: Europe and the World Economy, 1500–1800*, trans. V.R. Berghahn (New York: Cambridge University Press, 1983).

On the economic expansion and growth of England's North American colonies in the seventeenth century, see, for example, Terry L. Anderson, *The Economic Growth of Seventeenth-Century New England: A Measurement of Regional Income* (New York: Arno Press, 1975); Anderson, "Wealth Estimates for the New England Colonies, 1650–1709," *Explorations in Economic History*, 2d ser., 12 (April 1975): 151–76; Anderson, "Economic Growth in Colonial New England: 'Statistical Renaissance'," *Journal of Economic History* 39 (March 1979): 243–57; Anderson and Robert Paul Thomas, "Economic Growth in the Seventeenth-Century Chesapeake," *Explorations in Economic History*, 2d ser., 15 (October 1978): 368–87; Russell R. Menard, "The Tobacco Industry in the Chesapeake Colonies, 1617–1730: An Interpretation," *Research in Economic History* 5 (1980): 109–77; John J. McCusker and Russell R. Menard, *The Economy of British America, 1607–1789* (Chapel Hill: University of North Carolina Press, 1985), pp. 51–70.

7. See the works mentioned in footnote 6. On the eastern European economy specifically in the seventeenth century, see, for example, Wallerstein, *The Modern World-System*, 2:

129–45; Antoni Mączak, "Export of Grain and the Problem of Distribution of National Income in the Years 1550–1650," *Acta Poloniae Historica*, no. 18 (1968): 75–98; Mączak, "Agricultural and Livestock Production in Poland: Internal and Foreign Markets," *Journal of European Economic History* 1 (Winter 1972): 671–80; Slicher van Bath, "Eighteenth-Century Agriculture on the Continent of Europe: Evolution or Revolution?," *Agricultural History* 43 (January 1969): 169–79; Jerzy Topolski, "Economic Decline in Poland from the Sixteenth to the Eighteenth Centuries," in Peter M. Earle, ed., *Essays in European Economic History, 1500–1800* (Oxford: Clarendon Press, 1974), pp. 127–42; V. Doroschenko *et al.*, *Trade and Agrarian Development in the Baltic Provinces*, preprint (Tallinn: Academy of Sciences of the Estonian S.S.R., 1974). For a powerful literary treatment of economic involution in eastern Europe in the early modern period, see Czeslaw Milosz, *Native Realm: A Search for Self-Definition*, trans. Catherine S. Leach (Garden City: N.Y.: Doubleday, 1968), pp. 7–18.

8. The literature on these matters is, of course, vast. See, for example, Phyllis Deane and W.A. Cole, *British Economic Growth 1688–1959: Trends and Structure* (Cambridge: Cambridge University Press, 1962), pp. 1–97; Coleman, *The Economy of England 1450–1750*, pp. 91–172; Elizabeth B. Schumpeter, *English Overseas Trade Statistics 1697–1808* (Oxford: Clarendon Press, 1960), pp. 15–24, 29–30, 35–38, 44–55, 60–69; Ralph Davis, "English Foreign Trade, 1660–1700," *Economic History Review*, 2d ser., 7 (1954): 150–66; Davis, "English Foreign Trade, 1700–1774," *Economic History Review*, 2d ser., 15 (1962): 285–303.

On Simiand's A and B phases of economic history, see François Simiand, *Recherches anciennes et nouvelles sur le mouvement général des prix du 16e au 19e siècle* (Paris: Editions Domat Montchrestien, 1932); Simiand, *Les Fluctuations économiques à longue période et la crise mondiale* (Paris: Felix Alcan, 1932).

9. On the seventeenth-century Polish economy, see the works on eastern Europe in footnote 7.

10. See, for example, Karl Marx, *Capital*, ed. Frederick Engels, trans. Samuel Moore and Edward Aveling, 3 vols. (New York: International Publishers, 1967; originally published 1867–94), 1: 713–74; Eric Williams, *Capitalism and Slavery* (Chapel Hill: University of North Carolina Press, 1944); Frank, *World Accumulation 1492–1789*; Wallerstein, *The Modern World-System*.

11. On the minor role of foreign trade in the physiocratic growth schema, see Arthur I. Bloomfield, "The Foreign-Trade Doctrines of the Physiocrats," *American Economic Review* 28 (December 1938): 716–35; Max Beer, *An Inquiry into Physiocracy* (New York: Russell & Russell, 1966; originally published 1939), pp. 115–48; Joseph J. Spengler, "Mercantilist and Physiocratic Growth Theory," in Bert F. Hoselitz, Joseph J. Spengler, *et al.*, *Theories of Economic Growth* (Glencoe, Ill.: The Free Press, 1960), pp. 3–64, 299–334, especially pp. 54–64; Elizabeth Fox-Genovese, *The Origins of Physiocracy: Economic Revolution and Social Order in Eighteenth-Century France* (Ithaca: Cornell University Press, 1976), pp. 271–74.

Many scholars in recent years have downplayed the importance of foreign trade, particularly intercontinental trade, in their explanations of Europe's economic expansion during the early modern period. See, for example, Douglass C. North and Robert Paul Thomas, *The Rise of the Western World: A New Economic History* (Cambridge: Cambridge University Press, 1973), passim; Davis, *The Rise of the Atlantic Economies*, pp. xi–xii and passim; De Vries, *The Economy of Europe in an Age of Crisis*, pp. 113–209 especially; Coleman, *The Economy of England 1450–1750*, pp. 196–201 especially; Robert P. Brenner, "The Origins of Capitalist Development: A Critique of Neo-Smithian Marxism," *New Left Review*

104 (July–August 1977): 25–92; Geoffrey Parker, "Homage to Braudel," *London Review of Books* 2 (4 September to 17 September 1980); 8–9; T.H. Aston and C.H.E. Philpin, eds., *The Brenner Debate: Agrarian Class Structure and Economic Development in Pre-Industrial Europe* (Cambridge: Cambridge University Press, 1985), passim.

12. Thomas Mun, *England's Treasure by Forraign Trade. . .* (London: Printed by J.G. for Thomas Clark, 1664). This important tract and a number of others are conveniently available in J.R. McCulloch, ed., *Early English Tracts on Commerce* (Cambridge: Cambridge University Press, 1970; originally published 1856).

13. On the problematic historiography of mercantilism, see, for example, Charles Wilson, *Mercantilism* (London: Published for The Historical Association by Routledge and Kegan Paul, 1958), pp. 3–10; D.C. Coleman, "Editor's Introduction," in Coleman, ed., *Revisions in Mercantilism* (London: Methuen & Co., 1969), pp. 1–17; Walter E. Minchinton, "Introduction," in Minchinton, ed., *Mercantilism: System or Expediency?*, Problems in European Civilization Series (Lexington, Mass.: D.C. Heath, 1969), pp. vii–xiii.

14. My syntheses of mercantilism and mercantilist growth theory are based upon both contemporary and secondary sources, sources primarily, though not exclusively, of English origin. Contemporary English economic tracts, treatises, and pamphlets were perhaps the most important sources used in the construction of the argument above. The following sources proved especially helpful: Jean Bodin, *Discours sur le rehaussement et diminution des monnoyes. . .* (Paris: Chez Iacques du Puys, 1578); Gerard de Malynes, *The Maintenance of Free Trade* (London: Printed by I.L. for W. Sheffard, 1622); Malynes, *The Centre of the Circle of Commerce* (London: Printed by W. Iones, 1623); Edward Misselden, *Free Trade; or, the Means to Make Trade Flourish* (London: Printed by I. Legatt for S. Waterson, 1622); Misselden, *The Circle of Commerce, or the Balance of Trade* (London: Printed by I. Dawson for N. Bourne, 1623); Lewes Roberts, *The Treasure of Traffike or A Discourse on Forraigne Trade* (London: Printed by E.P. for Nicholas Bourne, 1641); Mun, *England's Treasure by Forraign Trade*; Samuel Fortrey, *Englands Interest and Improvement* (London: Printed for Nathanael Brook, 1673); Rice Vaughan, *A Discourse of Coin and Coinage* (London: Printed by T. Dawks for T. Basset, 1675); Nicholas Barbon, *A Discourse of Trade* (London: Printed by Tho. Milbourn for the author, 1690); Sir William Petty, *Political Arithmetick. . .* (London: Printed for Robert Clavel, 1690); Sir Josiah Child, *A New Discourse of Trade . . .*, 2d ed. (London: Printed and Sold by Sam. Crouch, Tho. Horn, & Jos. Hindmarsh, 1694); John Locke, *Several Papers Relating to Money, Interest and Trade, etcetera* (New York: Augustus M. Kelley, 1968; originally published 1696); Charles Davenant, *Discourses on the Public Revenues, and on the Trade of England . . .*, 2 vols. (London: Printed for James Knapton, 1698); Charles King, ed., *The British Merchant; or Commerce Preserv'd*, 3 vols. (New York: Augustus M. Kelley, 1968; originally published 1721); Joshua Gee, *The Trade and Navigation of Great-Britain Considered. . .*, 4th ed. (London: Printed for A. Bettesworth and C. Hitch, 1738; originally published 1729); Sir Matthew Decker, *An Essay on the Causes of the Decline of Foreign Trade*, 2d ed. (London: Printed for J. Brotherton, 1750; originally published 1744); Josiah Tucker, *The Elements of Commerce*, in Tucker, *A Selection from His Economic and Political Writings*, ed. R. L. Schuyler (New York: Columbia University Press, 1931), pp. 51–220; Malachy Postlethwayt, *Britain's Commercial Interest Explained and Improved. . .*, 2 vols. (New York: Augustus M. Kelley, 1968; originally published 1757); Richard Cantillon, *Essai sur la nature du commerce en général*, ed. and trans. Henry Higgs (London: Macmillan, 1931; originally published 1755).

These writers, of course, were not in complete agreement on all economic matters. Their differences in approach and emphasis—and their more fundamental similarities—are

discussed in Philip W. Buck's *Politics of Mercantilism* (New York: Octagon Books, 1964; originally published 1942). Buck's "Bibliographic Notes," pp. 195–226 are especially relevant.

The particular emphases in mercantilist growth theory, one should note, tended to change over time. The early emphasis on the balance of trade, for example, had by the eighteenth century been superseded by a concern over full employment and more efficient factor utilization. On this point, see Edgar S. Furniss, *The Position of the Laborer in a System of Nationalism; A Study in the Labor Theories of the Later English Mercantilists* (Boston: Houghton Mifflin Co., 1920); Appleby, *Economic Thought and Ideology in Seventeenth-Century England*, pp. 242–79; Salim Rashid; "Economists, Economic Historians, and Mercantilism," *Scandinavian Economic History Review* 28 (1980): 1–14; Robert K. Schaeffer, "The Entelechies of Mercantilism," *Scandinavian Economic History Review* 29 (1981): 81–96.

Several other points made in the discussion of mercantilism in the text above require further elaboration. First, it should be noted that Herbert Heaton, A.V. Judges, and D.C. Coleman are the chief critics of the use of the concept "mercantilism" as an analytical tool. See Heaton, "Heckscher on Mercantilism," *Journal of Political Economy* 45 (June 1937): 370–93; Judges, "The Idea of a Mercantile State," *Transactions of the Royal Historical Society*, 4th ser., 21 (1939): 41–69; Coleman, "Mercantilism Revisited," *The Historical Journal* 23 (1980): 773–91. More recently, W.A. Speck has expressed doubts about the existence of a coherent theory that legitimately can be labeled "mercantilism." See Speck, "The International and Imperial Context," in Jack P. Greene and J.R. Pole, eds., *Colonial British America: Essays in the New History of the Early Modern Era* (Baltimore: Johns Hopkins University Press, 1984), pp. 384–407.

Secondly, the "social welfare" aspect of the mercantilist growth scenario outlined above owes much to the work of William D. Grampp, Charles Wilson, and Joyce Appleby. See Grampp, "The Liberal Elements in English Mercantilism," *Quarterly Journal of Economics* 66 (November 1952): 465–501; Wilson, "The Other Face of Mercantilism," *Transactions of the Royal Historical Society*, 5th ser., 9 (1959): 81–101; Appleby, *Economic Thought and Ideology in Seventeenth-Century England*, pp. 242–79. For an interesting, if incomplete, contemporary discussion of the rationale for social welfare policies in seventeenth-century England, see George Monck, Duke of Albemarle, *Observations upon Military and Political Affairs* (London: H. Mortlocke, 1671), p. 145. The illustrious Monck, one should note, was one of the eight original proprietors of Carolina.

Thirdly, my statement in the text about the decline of "peasant" revolts over time refers rather more to England than, shall we say, to France. Revolts continued in France, for example, through most of the seventeenth century. See Emmanuel Le Roy Ladurie, *Les Paysans de Languedoc*, 2 vols. (Paris: S.E.V.P.E.N., 1966), 1: 607–29 especially; Roland Mousnier, *Peasant Uprisings in Seventeenth-Century France, Russia, and China*, trans. Brian Pearce (New York: Harper & Row, 1970); De Vries, *The Economy of Europe in an Age of Crisis*, pp. 63–69; Charles Tilly, *The Contentious French* (Cambridge: The Belknap Press of Harvard University Press, 1986).

Finally, one cannot discuss mercantilism without at least mentioning Eli F. Heckscher and Jacob Viner, the authors of the two most influential twentieth-century works on the subject. See Heckscher, *Mercantilism*, trans. Mendel Shapiro, 2 vols. (London: Allen & Unwin, 1935; originally published 1931); Viner, *Studies in the Theory of International Trade* (New York: Harper & Brothers, 1937), pp. 1–118 especially. While both of these works have serious flaws, both nonetheless represent tremendous research achievements and are still invaluable today.

15. These phenomena are discussed in a vast number of books and articles. On the acts mentioned above, see, for example, Heckscher, *Mercantilism*, passim; Lawrence A. Harper, *The English Navigation Laws: A Seventeenth-Century Experiment in Social Engineering* (New York: Columbia University Press, 1939).

On the Anglo-Dutch wars, see Charles Wilson, *Profit and Power: A Study of England and the Dutch Wars* (London: Longmans, Green, 1957).

On the founding of Carolina, see Charles M. Andrews, *The Colonial Period of American History*, 4 vols. (New Haven: Yale University Press, 1934–38), 3: 182–227; Jack M. Sosin, *English America and the Restoration Monarchy of Charles II: Transatlantic Politics, Commerce, and Kinship* (Lincoln: University of Nebraska Press, 1980), pp. 125–36; Robert M. Weir, *Colonial South Carolina: A History* (Millwood, N.Y.: KTO Press, 1983), pp. 47–59.

The phenomena mentioned in the text relate to England, of course, rather than, let us say, to France. One could, however, point to numerous French examples as well—Colbert's 1664 tariff and the *Pacte Coloniale* to cite but two.

16. On the increases in agricultural productivity and domestic demand in England, for example, see A.H. John, "Aspects of English Economic Growth in the First Half of the Eighteenth Century," *Economica* 28 (1961): 176–90; John, "Agricultural Productivity and Economic Growth in England, 1700–1760," *Journal of Economic History* 25 (March 1965): 19–34; E.L. Jones, "Agriculture and Economic Growth in England, 1660–1750: Agricultural Change," *Journal of Economic History* 25 (March 1965): 1–18; Eric Kerridge, *The Agricultural Revolution* (London: Allen & Unwin, 1967), passim; E.A. Wrigley, "A Simple Model of London's Importance in Changing English Society and Economy 1650–1750," *Past and Present*, no. 37 (July 1967): 44–70; Slicher van Bath, "Eighteenth-Century Agriculture"; De Vries, *The Economy of Europe in an Age of Crisis*, pp. 35–47, 75–82, 176–209; Coleman, *The Economy of England 1450–1750*, pp. 196–201 especially; W.A. Cole, "Factors in Demand 1700–80," in Roderick Floud and Donald McCloskey, eds., *The Economic History of Britain Since 1700*, 2 vols. (Cambridge: Cambridge University Press, 1981), 1: 36–65; E.L. Jones, "Agriculture, 1700–80," in Floud and McCloskey, eds., *The Economic History of Britain Since 1700*, 1: 66–86.

17. Adam Smith, *An Inquiry into the Nature and Causes of the Wealth of Nations*, ed. Edwin Cannan, The Modern Library (New York: Random House, 1937; originally published 1776), Book IV, pp. 397–652.

The most important early revisionists were Gustav Schmoller, William Cunningham, and William Ashley. See Schmoller, *The Mercantile System . . .* , trans. William Ashley (London: Macmillan, 1896; originally published 1884); Cunningham, *The Growth of English Industry and Commerce*, 3 vols. (Cambridge: Cambridge University Press, 1882–1912), vol. 2. One should note that the German economist Freidrich List questioned certain Smithian notions about mercantilism earlier in the nineteenth century. See List, *The National System of Political Economy*, trans. S.S. Lloyd (London: Longmans, Green, 1885; originally published 1841–44), pp. 119–325, 337–42 especially.

18. Liberal scholars such as W.S. Hewins and George Unwin attacked the revisionist position on mercantilism almost immediately. The neoclassical critique of mercantilist economic thought has proved resilient throughout the twentieth century and can be seen, for example, in the works of such scholars as Heckscher, Viner, W.R. Allen, and Harry G. Johnson. See Minchinton, "Introduction," p. ix–x; Heckscher, *Mercantilism*; Viner, *Studies in the Theory of International Trade*; Allen, "Modern Defenders of Mercantilism," *Journal of Political Economy* 2 (Fall 1970): 381–97; Johnson, "Mercantilism: Past, Present and Future," *The Manchester School of Economic and Social Studies* 42 (March 1974): 1–17.

19. John Maynard Keynes, *The General Theory of Employment, Interest and Money* (New York: Harcourt, Brace, 1936), Chap. 23, pp. 333–51 especially.

20. Many scholars over the years have judged mercantilist economic thought in terms of its alleged similarities or differences with classical and neoclassical notions. Those that have looked favorably upon the similarities between certain aspects of mercantilist thought and these later doctrines include Grampp, "The Liberal Elements in English Mercantilism"; Robert Lekachman, *A History of Economic Ideas* (New York: McGraw-Hill, 1959), pp. 33–68; William Letwin, *The Origins of Scientific Economics: English Economic Thought 1660–1776* (London: Methuen, 1963); Appleby, *Economic Thought and Ideology in Seventeenth-Century England*; Karen Iverson Vaughn, *John Locke: Economist and Social Scientist* (Chicago: University of Chicago Press, 1980).

While it is true that writers like Locke, Gervaise, Cantillon, Steuart, and Hume did, indeed, anticipate liberal concepts such as specie flow and comparative advantage, the mercantilist "export of work" argument was not, as some allege, similar to Bertil Ohlin's "factoral proportion" model. On this point, see Spengler, "Mercantilist and Physiocratic Growth Theory," p. 40, fn. 64.

21. See Johnson, "Mercantilism: Past, Present and Future." Some scholars associated with the United Nations Economic Commission for Latin America (ECLA) in the 1950s and 1960s cited both mercantilists and Friedrich List in their arguments for protectionism and governmental intervention in the economies of Latin America. Moreover, even proponents of the "unequal exchange" thesis today, men such as Arghiri Emmanuel and Samir Amin, partly defend mercantilism, arguing that mercantilists opposed free trade because they foresaw the problems which economic liberalism necessarily entailed. See, for example, Emmanuel, *Unequal Exchange: A Study of the Imperialism of Trade*, trans. Brian Pearce (New York: Monthly Review Press, 1972; originally published 1969), pp. vii–xlii especially.

On the so-called neo-mercantilism, see Joan Robinson, "The New Mercantilism," in Robinson, *Collected Economic Essays*, 5 vols. thus far (Oxford: Basil Blackwell, 1951–), 4: 1–13. Nicholas Kaldor defends protectionism and neo-mercantilism in "The Nemesis of Free Trade," in Kaldor, *Further Essays on Applied Economics* (New York: Holmes & Meier, 1978), pp. 234–41, while Jacob Viner decries the same in Viner, *International Trade and Economic Development: Lectures Delivered at the National University of Brazil* (Glencoe, Ill.: The Free Press, 1952), passim.

22. There has long been a tendency among scholars ostensibly studying a particular historical problem or period to devote most of their time instead to the search for the "roots" or "origins" of later phenomena. On this tendency, see François Simiand, "Méthode historique et science sociale," *Annales: Economies, sociétés, civilisations* 15 (1960): 83–119. Simiand's article originally appeared in *Revue de synthèse historique* 6 (1903): 1–22, 129–57. Marc Bloch has also written on the "idol of origins." See Bloch, *The Historian's Craft*, trans. Peter Putnam (New York: Vintage, 1953; originally published 1949), pp. 29–35.

23. See, for example, B. Suviranta, *The Theory of the Balance of Trade in England: A Study in Mercantilism* (New York: Augustus M. Kelley, 1967; originally published 1923); Charles Wilson, "Treasure and Trade Balances: The Mercantilist Problem," *Economic History Review*, 2d ser., 2 (1949): 152–61; Stuart W. Bruchey, "A General Introduction to the Readings," in Bruchey, ed., *The Colonial Merchant: Sources and Readings* (New York: Harcourt, Brace & World, 1966), pp. 1–10, especially pp. 7–8; Rudolph C. Blitz, "Mercantilist Policies and the Pattern of World Trade, 1500–1750," *Journal of Economic History* 27 (March 1967): 39–55; Alexander Gerschenkron, *Europe in the Russian Mirror: Four Lectures in Economic History* (Cambridge: Cambridge University Press, 1970), Lecture

3, pp. 62–96, 143–50; De Vries, *The Economy of Europe in an Age of Crisis*, pp. 236–43; Lars Magnusson, "Eli Heckscher, Mercantilism, and the Favourable Balance of Trade," *Scandinavian Economic History Review* 26 (1978): 103–27; Wallerstein, *The Modern World-System*, 2, passim; Rashid, "Economists, Economic Historians, and Mercantilism"; Schaeffer, "The Entelechies of Mercantilism"; Robert B. Ekelund, Jr., and Robert D. Tollison, *Mercantilism as a Rent-Seeking Society: Economic Regulation in Historical Perspective* (College Station: Texas A & M University Press, 1981), pp. 147–56 especially.

One should also note that D.C. Coleman, who does not accept the usefulness of the concept "mercantilism," nonetheless treats "mercantilist" policies and programs in proper early modern context. See Coleman, *The Economy of England 1450–1750*, pp. 173–95; Coleman, "Mercantilism Revisited."

24. Indeed, the question of the impact of colonization on both the metropolises and their colonies or former colonies has captured much of the attention of developmental economists since the birth of the discipline after World War II. Moreover, the debates on this question between Marxists and neoclassicists, between *dependencia* theorists and scholars associated with the "Chicago School" have had profound policy implications as well.

25. See Spengler, "Mercantilist and Physiocratic Growth Theory," pp. 13–14 especially.

26. For the mercantilist position on colonies, see Spengler, "Mercantilist and Physiocratic Growth Theory," pp. 40–42.

Many British mercantilists commented on colonies; their positions generally support Spengler's argument. See, for example, Fortrey, *Englands Interest and Improvement*, pp. 33–34; Child, *A New Discourse of Trade*, pp. 178–216; Davenant, *Discourses on the Public Revenues*, ᴘ 193–318; Sir William Keith, "A Short Discourse on the Present State of the Colonies in America with Respect to the Interest of Great Britain," in W. Noel Sainsbury, *et al.*, eds., *Calendar of State Papers, Colonial Series, America and West Indies, 1574–*, 44 vols. thus far (London: 1860–), vol.: *1728–1729*, pp. 263–69; Fayrer Hall, *The Importance of the British Plantations in America to this Kingdom*. . . (London: J. Peele, 1731), pp. 2–26; Gee, *The Trade and Navigation of Great-Britain Considered*, pp. 147–57; Postlethwayt, *Britain's Commercial Interest Explained and Improved*, 1: 143–67, 421–60, 461–80, 481–500.

For scholarly treatments of British colonial policy in the early modern period, see Herman Merivale, *Lectures on Colonization and Colonies*, 2d ed. (New York: Augustus M. Kelley, 1967; originally published 1861), pp. 73–78; George Louis Beer, *The Old Colonial System 1660–1754*, 2 vols. (New York: Macmillan, 1912), 1: 1–127; K.E. Knorr, *British Colonial Theories 1570–1850* (Toronto: University of Toronto Press, 1944), pp. 3–151; Jack P. Greene, "Introduction," in Greene, ed., *Great Britain and the American Colonies, 1606–1763* (Columbia: University of South Carolina Press, 1970), pp. xi–xlvii.

27. On the phrase "extended Caribbean," see Wallerstein, *The Modern World-System*, 2: 103. On the similar concept "Plantation America," see, for example, Charles Wagley, "Plantation-America; A Culture Sphere," in Vera Rubin, ed., *Caribbean Studies—A Symposium* (Seattle: University of Washington Press, 1960), pp. 3–13; George L. Beckford, *Persistent Poverty: Underdevelopment in Plantation Economies of the Third World* (New York: Oxford University Press, 1972); Jay R. Mandle, *The Roots of Black Poverty: The Southern Plantation Economy after the Civil War* (Durham: Duke University Press, 1978), pp. v–vii, 3–15 especially.

On the British mercantilists' disdain for the New England colonies, see Petty, *Political Arithmetick*, pp. 87–95; Child, *A New Discourse of Trade*, p. 180; John Cary, *An Essay on the State of England in Relation to its Trade*. . . (Bristol: Printed by W. Bonny, for the author, 1695), pp. 69–70.

28. On the Spanish Southeast in the sixteenth and seventeenth centuries, see Woodbury Lowery, *The Spanish Settlements within the Present Limits of the United States 1513–1561* (New York: G.P. Putnam's Sons, 1901), pp. 123–71, 213–52, 351–77; Lowery, *The Spanish Settlements within the Present Limits of the United States: Florida, 1562–1574* (New York: G.P. Putnam's Sons, 1905), passim; Wesley Frank Craven, *The Southern Colonies in the Seventeenth Century 1607–1689*, History of the South Series (Baton Rouge: Louisiana State University Press, 1949), pp. 1–26; Paul Quattlebaum, *The Land Called Chicora: The Carolinas under Spanish Rule with French Intrusions 1520–1670* (Gainesville: University of Florida Press, 1956); David B. Quinn, *North America from Earliest Discovery to First Settlements: The Norse Voyages to 1612*, The New American Nation Series (New York: Harper & Row, 1977), pp. 137–51, 206–39, 262–321; J. Leitch Wright, Jr., *The Only Land They Knew: The Tragic Story of the American Indians in the Old South* (New York: The Free Press, 1981), pp. 27–52. On the work of the Spanish missionaries in the area, see John T. Lanning, *The Spanish Missions of Georgia* (Chapel Hill: University of North Carolina Press, 1935); Maynard J. Geiger, *The Franciscan Conquest of Florida (1573–1618)* (Washington: Catholic University of America, 1937); Michael V. Gannon, *The Cross in the Sand: The Early Catholic Church in Florida, 1513–1870* (Gainesville: University of Florida Press, 1965), pp. 1–83.

On the French attempts to settle in the Southeast in the sixteenth century, see Quattlebaum, *The Land Called Chicora*, pp. 42–77; Quinn, *North America from Earliest Discovery to First Settlements*, pp. 240–61.

29. On England's Elizabethan flirtation with the Southeast, see Quinn, *North America from Earliest Discovery to First Settlements*, pp. 322–46, 429–39; Edmund S. Morgan, *American Slavery, American Freedom: The Ordeal of Colonial Virginia* (New York: W.W. Norton, 1975), pp. 3–43; Craven, *The Southern Colonies in the Seventeenth Century*, pp. 27–59; Kenneth R. Andrews, *Trade, Plunder and Settlement: Maritime Enterprise and the Genesis of the British Empire, 1480–1630* (Cambridge: Cambridge University Press, 1984), pp. 304–40; Karen O. Kupperman, *Roanoke: The Abandoned Colony* (Totowa, N.J.: Rowman & Allanheld, 1984); David B. Quinn, *Set Fair for Roanoke: Voyages and Colonies, 1584–1606* (Chapel Hill: University of North Carolina Press, 1985).

30. On the English move into the Chesapeake area under the Stuarts, see Craven, *The Southern Colonies in the Seventeenth Century*, pp. 60–309; Morgan, *American Slavery, American Freedom*; Russell R. Menard, *Economy and Society in Early Colonial Maryland* (New York: Garland Publishing, 1985), pp. 1–39.

On English interest and activity in the area south of Virginia in the period between the founding of Jamestown and the Restoration, see William L. Saunders, ed., *The Colonial Records of North Carolina*, 10 vols. (Raleigh: 1886–90), 1: 1–19; Sainsbury, ed., *Calendar of State Papers, Colonial Series, America and West Indies*, vol.: *1574–1660*, pp. 99, 102, 107–11, 113–15, 120–21, 129, 190–91, 194, 197–99, 207; Edward Bland *et. al.*, *The Discovery of New Brittaine, Began August 27, Anno Dom. 1650. . .* (London: Printed by Thomas Harper for John Stephenson, 1651); Francis Yeardley to John Farrar, May 8, 1654, in Alexander S. Salley, Jr., ed., *Narratives of Early Carolina 1650–1708*, Original Narratives of Early American History Series (New York: Barnes & Noble, 1967; originally published 1911), pp. 25–29. Bland's *Discovery*, one should note, is reprinted on pp. 5–19 in Salley's *Narratives of Early Carolina* as well. For scholarly treatments of English involvement in the area in this period, see Andrews, *The Colonial Period of American History*, 3: 187–91; Herbert R. Paschal, Jr., "Proprietary North Carolina: A Study in Colonial Government" (Ph.D. dissertation, University of North Carolina, 1961), pp. 1–62; Lawrence Lee, *The Lower Cape Fear in Colonial Days* (Chapel Hill: University of

North Carolina Press, 1965), pp. 24–25; Daniel W. Fagg, Jr., "Carolina, 1663–1683: The Founding of a Proprietary" (Ph.D. dissertation, Emory University, 1970), pp. 34–37.

31. See Paschal, "Proprietary North Carolina," pp. 62–96; Lee, *The Lower Cape Fear in Colonial Days*, pp. 28–35; Fagg, "Carolina, 1663–1683," pp. 37–40.

32. On the proprietors, see William S. Powell, *The Proprietors of Carolina* (Raleigh: Published by the Carolina Charter Tercentenary Commission, 1963); Fagg, "Carolina, 1663–1683," pp. 7–29. Biographical sketches of all of the original proprietors except Sir John Colleton also appear in Leslie Stephen and Sidney Lee *et al.*, eds., *Dictionary of National Biography*, 22 vols. plus eight supplements thus far (London: Oxford University Press, 1921–; originally published 1885–1901), 2:361–64, 368–69; 3:1117–19; 4:1036–55; 5:45–49; 10:370–89; 13:594–609.

On Lord Ashley, the proprietor most influential in determining proprietary policy toward Carolina during the crucial 1669–75 period, see Louise F. Brown, *The First Earl of Shaftesbury* (New York: D. Appleton-Century, 1933); George C. Rogers, Jr., "The First Earl of Shaftesbury," *South Carolina Historical Magazine* 68 (April 1967): 74–78; K.H.D. Haley, *The First Earl of Shaftesbury* (Oxford: Clarendon Press, 1968).

33. On the financial involvement of the gentry in English overseas commercial expansion and colonization in the Tudor-Stuart period, see Theodore K. Rabb, *Enterprise and Empire: Merchant and Gentry Investment in the Expansion of England, 1575–1630* (Cambridge: Harvard University Press, 1967).

One should note that the proprietors actually obtained charters to Carolina from Charles II in both 1663 and 1665. By the former, the proprietors secured rights to that part of America between 31° and 36° north latitude; by the latter, their jurisdiction was extended to the area between 29° and 36°30′ north latitude. These charters are reprinted in Mattie Erma Edwards Parker, ed., *North Carolina Charters and Constitutions 1578–1698* (Raleigh: Published by the Carolina Charter Tercentenary Commission, 1963), pp. 76–89, 91–104.

On the proprietors' mercantilist posture, see, for example, E.E. Rich, "The First Earl of Shaftesbury's Colonial Policy," *Transactions of the Royal Historical Society*, 5th ser., 7 (1957): 47–70; Haley, *The First Earl of Shaftesbury*, pp. 227–65; Converse D. Clowse, *Economic Beginnings in Colonial South Carolina 1670–1730* (Columbia: University of South Carolina Press, 1971), pp. 1–22.

On the proprietors' desire that Carolina become a staple–producing colony, see "A Lettr to my Lord Willoby from ye Duke of Albemarle," August 31, 1663, Great Britain, Public Record Office, CO 5/286/9. I used a microfilm copy of this document at the South Carolina Department of Archives and History, Columbia, South Carolina. Also see Copy of Instructions for Mr. West about our Plantation, Lord Ashley (?), c. July 1669, Cheves, ed., *Shaftesbury Papers*, pp. 125–27; Proprietors to the Governor and Council at Ashley River, May 18, 1674, Cheves, ed., *Shaftesbury Papers*, pp. 435–38; Proprietors to Governor and Council at Ashley River, April 10, 1677, Records in the British Public Record Office Relating to South Carolina, 1663–1782, 36 volumes in facsimile, South Carolina Department of Archives and History, 1: 53–59. Note that the first five volumes of this thirty-six volume series have been published as *Records in the British Public Record Office Relating to South Carolina, 1663–1710* (Atlanta and Columbia: Printed for the Historical Commission of South Carolina, 1928–47).

Ashley and his secretary, John Locke, were especially interested in agricultural experimentation, particularly in experimentation involving staple crops. See, for example, Ashley to Andrew Percivall, May 23, 1674, Sainsbury, ed., *Calendar of State Papers, Colonial Series, America and West Indies*, vol.: *1669–1674*, pp. 584–86; Stephen and Lee, eds., *Dictionary of National Biography*, 12: 27–37, especially p. 30; Clowse, *Economic Beginnings*

in *Colonial South Carolina*, pp. 59–60; Daniel W. Fagg, Jr., "St. Giles' Seigniory: The Earl of Shaftesbury's Carolina Plantation," *South Carolina Historical Magazine* 71 (April 1970): 117–23. One should also note that Locke wrote a treatise in 1679 on the cultivation of various staples. The treatise was not, however, published until the next century. See Locke, *Observations upon the Growth and Culture of Vines and Olives: the Production of Silk: the Preservation of Fruits. Written at the Request of the Earl of Shaftesbury: to Whom it is inscribed. . .* (London: Printed for W. Sandby, 1766). Finally, one should note that both Ashley and Locke were members of the Royal Society.

34. On the "sugar revolution" in Barbados and the concomitant out-migration from the island, see Richard S. Dunn, *Sugar and Slaves: The Rise of the Planter Class in the English West Indies, 1624–1713* (Chapel Hill: University of North Carolina Press, 1972), pp. 46–116; Carl and Roberta Bridenbaugh, *No Peace Beyond the Line: The English in the Caribbean 1624–1690* (New York: Oxford University Press, 1972), pp. 165–305 especially; Richard B. Sheridan, *Sugar and Slavery: An Economic History of the British West Indies, 1623–1775* (Baltimore: Johns Hopkins University Press, 1974); Alfred D. Chandler, "The Expansion of Barbados," *Journal of the Barbados Museum and Historical Society* 13 (1946): 106–36; Richard Waterhouse, "England, the Caribbean, and the Settlement of Carolina," *Journal of American Studies* 9 (December 1975): 259–81; Gary A. Puckrein, *Little England: Plantation Society and Anglo-Barbadian Politics, 1627–1700* (New York: New York University Press, 1984), pp. 56–72. For general background on Barbados in the seventeenth century and on sugar cultivation, see Vincent T. Harlow, *A History of Barbados 1625–1685* (Oxford: Clarendon Press, 1926); Noel Deerr, *The History of Sugar*, 2 vols. (London: Chapman and Hall, 1949–50); Sidney W. Mintz, *Sweetness and Power: The Place of Sugar in Modern History* (New York: Viking, 1985), pp. 19–73.

On Barbadian migration to Carolina specifically, see John P. Thomas, Jr., "The Barbadians in Early South Carolina," *South Carolina Historical Magazine* 31 (April 1930): 75–92; Adelaide B. Helwig, "The Early History of Barbados and Her Influence upon the Development of South Carolina" (Ph.D. dissertation, University of California-Berkeley, 1930), pp. 172–318 especially; Dunn, "The English Sugar Islands and the Founding of South Carolina," *South Carolina Historical Magazine* 72 (April 1971): 81–93; Waterhouse, "South Carolina's Colonial Elite: A Study in the Social Structure and the Political Culture of a Southern Colony, 1670–1760" (Ph.D. dissertation, Johns Hopkins University, 1973), pp. 8–50; Waterhouse, "England, the Caribbean, and the Settlement of Carolina"; Jack. P. Greene, "Colonial South Carolina and the Caribbean Connection," *South Carolina Historical Magazine* 88 (October 1987): 192–210. For a contemporary discussion of Barbadian migration to Carolina, see, for example, Lord Willoughby to [Clarendon], March 5, 1664, *Calendar of the Clarendon State Papers Preserved in the Bodleian Library. . . ,* 5 vols. (Oxford: Clarendon Press, 1869–1970), 5: 377–78.

On the Barbadian immigrants' desire that the colony at Carolina specialize in provisions for the Barbados market, see Peter H. Wood, *Black Majority: Negroes in Colonial South Carolina from 1670 through the Stono Rebellion* (New York: Knopf, 1974), pp. 13–34, especially pp. 32–34; Waterhouse, "England, the Caribbean, and the Settlement of Carolina," pp. 277–79. For a suggestive discussion of this matter, see Proprietors to the Governor and Council at Ashley River, May 18, 1674, Cheves, ed., *Shaftesbury Papers*, pp. 435–38.

35. See Wood, *Black Majority*, pp. 32–34; Waterhouse, "England, the Caribbean, and the Settlement of Carolina," pp. 277–79. M. Eugene Sirmans sees the battle between the proprietors and the Barbadians in somewhat broader terms. See Sirmans, *Colonial South Carolina: A Political History, 1663–1763* (Chapel Hill: University of North Carolina Press,

1966), pp. 17–100. Once again, see Proprietors to the Governor and Council at Ashley River, May 18, 1674, Cheves, ed., *Shaftesbury Papers*, pp. 435–38.

36. On Barbadian efforts to settle Carolina in the 1663–67 period, see Cheves, ed., *Shaftesbury Papers*, pp. 10–90; "New Plantation at Cape Florida, Carolina," 1667, Sainsbury, ed., *Calendar of State Papers, Colonial Series, America and West Indies*, vol.: *1675–1676*, pp. 144–45. Also see Lee, *The Lower Cape Fear in Colonial Days*, pp. 41–53; Fagg, "Carolina, 1663–1683," pp. 61–111; Waterhouse, "England, the Caribbean, and the Settlement of Carolina."

37. On Ashley's ascendancy, see Sirmans, *Colonial South Carolina*, pp. 6–10; Haley, *The First Earl of Shaftesbury*, pp. 238–55; Fagg, "Carolina, 1663–1683," pp. 116–27. Ashley had apparently risen to a position of leadership among the proprietors sometime before April 26, 1669, for on that date we see his personal secretary, John Locke, acting as secretary for the Carolina proprietors as well. See Articles of Agreement. . . , April 26, 1669, Cheves, ed., *Shaftesbury Papers*, pp. 91–93.

The constitutional arrangement devised by the proprietors, that is, the Fundamental Constitutions, appears in its various versions in Parker, ed., *North Carolina Charters and Constitutions*, pp. 132–240. This constitution is discussed later in the chapter.

On the new settlement terms offered by the proprietors, see the various 1669 and 1670 versions of the Fundamental Constitutions in Parker, ed., *North Carolina Charters and Constitutions*, pp. 132–85, and Copy of Instructions Annexed to the Commission For the Governor and Council, July 27, 1669, Cheves, ed., *Shaftesbury Papers*, pp. 119–23.

On the increased promotional activity by the proprietors in the late 1660s and early 1670s, see Hope Frances Kane, "Colonial Promotion and Promotion Literature of Carolina, 1660–1700" (Ph.D. dissertation, Brown University, 1930), pp. 31–74 especially.

On the proprietors' capital injections into the Carolina project in the late 1660s, see Articles of Agreement. . . , April 26, 1669, Cheves, ed., *Shaftesbury Papers*, pp. 91–93. For an itemized breakdown of the costs involved in outfitting the 1669–70 expedition to Carolina, see Cheves, ed., *Shaftesbury Papers*, pp. 137–52.

38. For contemporary accounts of the 1669–70 expedition to Carolina, see Cheves, ed., *Shaftesbury Papers*, pp. 133–74. Also see Joseph I. Waring, *The First Voyage and Settlement at Charles Town 1670–1680*, Tricentennial Booklet Number 4 (Columbia: Published for the South Carolina Tricentennial Commission by the University of South Carolina Press, 1970), pp. 22–26.

39. Richard Waterhouse has analyzed immigration to South Carolina during the colony's first decade of settlement (1670–1679) and has found that roughly 683 "settlers" arrived in this period. Of these, Waterhouse has found that 129 came from England, 117 from Barbados, 25 from other Caribbean islands, and 9 from other English colonies on the North American mainland. He was unable to identify the geographic origins of the remaining 403. Using these figures, one finds that of the 280 whose origins can be positively identified, 246 or 87.9 percent came from either England or Barbados. Both Waterhouse and Agnes L. Baldwin—upon whose basic research Waterhouse largely derived his findings—generally use "settler" to denote free white immigrants. Thus, the quotations around the word in the text and in this note. As servants and slaves in Carolina in this period generally came from the same places as the "settlers" who brought them, it is highly likely that the patterns discernible from the Waterhouse-Baldwin data are true ones in any case. Indeed, given the fact that a "settler" often brought several servants or slaves to Carolina, the percentage of total immigration to Carolina during the 1670–79 period that came from Barbados alone and from England and Barbados combined may even be a bit higher than the figures for "settlers" only. See Waterhouse, "England, the Caribbean, and the Settlement of Carolina," p. 271; Agnes L. Baldwin, *First Settlers of South Carolina, 1670–1680*, Tricentennial Booklet Number 1

(Columbia: Published for the South Carolina Tricentennial Commission by the University of South Carolina Press, 1969), passim. Note that Baldwin counts 684 "settlers" rather than 683. See p. iv. Baldwin recently has published a broader compilation of settlers in seventeenth-century South Carolina. See *First Settlers of South Carolina 1670–1700* (Easley, S.C.: Southern Historical Press, 1985).

On sources of servants and slaves in early South Carolina, see Wood, *Black Majority*, pp. 40–47.

40. See Waterhouse, "England, the Caribbean, and the Settlement of Carolina"; Clowse, *Economic Beginnings in Colonial South Carolina*, pp. 51–54. Peter Wood argues that between one-fourth and one-third of South Carolina's population "in the earliest years" was black. See Wood, *Black Majority*, p. 25.

On the late seventeenth-century English social hierarchy, see Gregory King's "Scheme of the Income & Expence of the several Families of England Calculated for the Year 1688" in his *Natural and Political Observations and Conclusions upon the State and Condition of England* (1696). This tract is reprinted in George E. Barnett, ed., *Two Tracts by Gregory King* (Baltimore: Johns Hopkins University Press, 1936), pp. 11–55. The "Scheme" mentioned above appears on p. 31. Also see Coleman, *The Economy of England 1450–1750*, pp. 5–11.

41. See, for example, Sirmans, *Colonial South Carolina*, p. 31; Waterhouse, "England, the Caribbean, and the Settlement of Carolina"; Robert K. Ackerman, *South Carolina Colonial Land Policies* (Columbia: University of South Carolina Press, 1977), p. 3.

None of these scholars, however, offers specific evidence for his contentions about the motivations of Carolina's early settlers. While such evidence is, indeed, difficult to locate, one can find certain sources that suggest that the desire for greater economic opportunity, the quest for material gain, was to Carolina's early immigrants the most important factor by far in their decisions to settle in the colony. The tone and emphasis in the early promotional tracts describing Carolina, for example, bear out this point. See Robert Horne (?), *A Brief Description of the Province of Carolina. . .* (London: Printed for Robert Horne, 1666); T.A., *Carolina; or a Description of the Present State of that Country, and the Natural Excellencies thereof. . .* (London: Printed for W.C., 1682); Samuel Wilson, *An Account of the Province of Carolina. . .* (London: Printed by G. Larkin, for Francis Smith, 1682). These tracts are reprinted in Salley, ed., *Narratives of Early Carolina*, pp. 66–73, 138–59, 164–76. Also see John Norris, *Profitable Advice for Rich and Poor. . .* (London: Printed by J. How, 1712).

A number of letters from early settlers in South Carolina are also useful. Some reveal that their writers came to the colony hoping either to make enough money to pay back Old World debts or to escape them altogether. See Albert J. Schmidt, "Applying Old World Habits to the New: Life in South Carolina at the Turn of the Eighteenth Century," *Huntington Library Quarterly* 25 (November 1961): 51–59; Schmidt, "Hyrne Family Letters," *South Carolina Historical Magazine* 63 (July 1962): 150–57; "Hyrne Family Letters, 1701–1710," in H. Roy Merrens, ed., *The Colonial South Carolina Scene: Contemporary Views, 1697–1774* (Columbia: University of South Carolina Press, 1977), pp. 16–27; St. Julien R. Childs, contrib., "A Letter Written in 1711 by Mary Stafford to her Kinswoman in England," *South Carolina Historical Magazine* 81 (January 1980): 1–7. Note that the early governments of South Carolina encouraged debtors to immigrate to the colony by passing laws suspending for a certain number of years all prosecutions of newcomers for any debts contracted before their arrival in the colony. See Thomas Cooper and David J. McCord, eds., *The Statutes at Large of South Carolina*, 10 vols. (Columbia: A.S. Johnston, 1836–41), 2: v, 124. Also see Proprietors to Governor Kirle, June 3, 1684 and June 9, 1684, Records in the British Public Record Office Relating to South Carolina, 1: 287–94, 298–303.

Other letters reveal their writers' concerns over the economic opportunities available in South Carolina. See Maurice Mathews, "A Contemporary View of South Carolina in 1680," *South Carolina Historical Magazine* 55 (July 1954): 153–59; "Letters of Thomas Newe, 1682," in Salley, ed., *Narratives of Early Carolina*, pp. 181–87; Louis Thibou Letter, September 20, 1683, South Caroliniana Library, University of South Carolina, Columbia, S.C.

Even in those few ostensibly religiously motivated attempts at group settlement in South Carolina, such as the one from Essex, Massachusetts, in 1697, the concern for economic gain was not absent. Indeed, in their instructions to prospective settlers, the organizers of the Essex group wrote ". . .we pray you will remember you are in this voiage concerned not only for a worldly interest, but (tho remoatly yet really) for the translating Christs ordinances, and worship into that countrie. . ." See "Instructions for Emigrants, 1694," in Merrens, ed., *The Colonial South Carolina Scene*, pp. 12–16, especially p. 13.

That the grip of "worldly affairs" on the inhabitants of South Carolina was a tight one was apparent to an Anglican minister several years later. In a letter written in 1703, Edward Marston thanked Dr. Thomas Bray for sending over some religious books from England to South Carolina but lamented the fact that ". . .the generality of people here are more mindful of getting money and other worldly affairs than they are of Books and Learning. . ." See Edward Marston to Rev. Thomas Bray, February 2, 1703, Records of the Society for the Propagation of the Gospel, Letter Books, Series A, 1702–1737, 26 ms. vols., Archives of the Society for the Propagation of the Gospel, London, England, 1: LX. I used the microfilm version of the S.P.G. records issued by Micro Methods, Ltd., of East Ardsley, Wakefield, Yorkshire, England, in 1964.

Finally, it is interesting to note that Daniel Defoe, no stranger to South Carolina's early history, sent his intensely materialistic heroine in *Moll Flanders* to America (Virginia actually) to make her fortune. Once in America, supposedly in the early 1680s, Moll Flanders quickly became quite prosperous. See Defoe, *Moll Flanders* (New York: New American Library, 1964; originally published 1722), pp. 269–301 especially.

42. See, for example, Alexander Hewatt, *An Historical Account of the Rise and Progress of the Colonies of South Carolina and Georgia*, 2 vols. (London: Printed for Alexander Donaldson, 1779), vol. 1, passim; David Ramsay, *The History of South-Carolina from Its First Settlement in 1670 to the Year 1808*, 2 vols. (Charleston: Published by David Longworth for the author, 1809), 1: 27–94; William J. Rivers, *A Sketch of the History of South Carolina to the Close of the Proprietary Government by the Revolution of 1719* (Charleston: McCarter & Co., 1856), passim; Edward McCrady, *The History of South Carolina under the Proprietary Government 1670–1719* (New York: Macmillan, 1897), passim; Lewis C. Gray, *History of Agriculture in the Southern United States to 1860*, 2 vols. (Gloucester, Mass.: Peter Smith, 1958; originally published 1933), 1: 50–51, 375–77; Andrews, *The Colonial Period of American History*, 3: 182–246; David D. Wallace, *South Carolina: A Short History 1520–1948* (Chapel Hill: University of North Carolina Press, 1951), pp. 23–105.

43. On the high levels of violence and, indeed, villainy in early modern England, see, for example, J.P. Kenyon, *Stuart England*, The Pelican History of England (Harmondsworth, Middlesex, England: Penguin Books, 1978), pp. 44–47; Lawrence Stone, *The Crisis of the Aristocracy 1558–1641* (Oxford: Clarendon Press, 1965), pp. 223–34 especially; A.L. Rowse, *The Elizabethan Age*, 2 vols. (New York: Macmillan: St. Martin's Press, 1951–55), 1: 344–45; F.G. Emmison, *Elizabethan Life: Disorder* (Chelmsford: Essex County Council, 1970), p. 148; J.M. Beattie, "The Pattern of Crime in England 1660–1800," *Past and Present*, no. 62 (February 1974): 47–95; J.S. Cockburn, "The Nature and Incidence of

Crime in England 1559–1625," in Cockburn, ed., *Crime in England 1550–1800* (Princeton: Princeton University Press, 1977), pp. 49–71, 309–14; Beattie, *Crime and the Courts in England, 1660–1800* (Princeton: Princeton University Press, 1986).

Violence and villainy accompanied English overseas expansion in this period as well. See Nicholas P. Canny, "The Ideology of English Colonization: From Ireland to America," *William and Mary Quarterly*, 3d ser., 30 (October 1973): 575–98; Francis Jennings, *The Invasion of America: Indians, Colonialism, and the Cant of Conquest* (Chapel Hill: University of North Carolina Press, 1975). Early proprietary policy toward the American Indians, one should note, was somewhat less rapacious than policies adopted in other English colonies. See John T. Juricek, "Indian Policy in Proprietary South Carolina, 1670–1693" (M.A. thesis, University of Chicago, 1962), passim; David K. Eliades, "The Indian Policy of Colonial South Carolina, 1670–1763" (Ph.D. dissertation, University of South Carolina, 1981), pp. 47–73.

On the proprietors' recognition of the necessity to slowly nurture their colony, see Articles of Agreement. . . , April 26, 1669, Cheves, ed., *Shaftesbury Papers*, pp. 91–93; Sir Peter Colleton to John Locke, May 28, 1673, in E.S. de Beer, ed., *The Correspondence of John Locke*, 4 vols. thus far (Oxford: Clarendon Press, 1976–), 1: 379–80; Articles Between the Lords Proprietors, May 6, 1674, Cheves, ed., *Shaftesbury Papers*, pp. 431–35; Lord Shaftesbury to Joseph West, May 23, 1674, Cheves, ed., *Shaftesbury Papers*, pp. 446–47; Lords Proprietors to Lord Shaftesbury, November 20, 1674, Cheves, ed., *Shaftesbury Papers*, pp. 454–55; Shaftesbury to the Governor and Council at Charles Town, Carolina, June 10, 1675, Cheves, ed., *Shaftesbury Papers*, pp. 466–68. Note the similarities between the proprietors' policy of slowly nurturing Carolina and the ideas expressed by Francis Bacon in his famous essay "Of Plantations," first published in the third edition of Bacon's *Essays* in 1625. See Bacon, *Essays and New Atlantis*, ed. Gordon S. Haight (New York: Van Nostrand, 1942), pp. 142–45.

Finally, one should note that the specific policies devised by Ashley and Locke will be discussed in the remainder of this chapter.

44. See, for example, Brown, *The First Earl of Shaftesbury*; Craven, *The Southern Colonies in the Seventeenth Century*, pp. 322–59; Rich, "The First Earl of Shaftesbury's Colonial Policy"; Sirmans, *Colonial South Carolina*, pp. 6–16 especially; Rogers, "The First Earl of Shaftesbury"; Haley, *The First Earl of Shaftesbury*, pp. 238–55; Fagg, "Carolina, 1663–1683," passim; Clowse, *Economic Beginnings in Colonial South Carolina*, pp. 14–22; Ackerman, *South Carolina Colonial Land Policies*, pp. 12–37; George D. Terry, " 'Champaign Country': A Social History of an Eighteenth-Century Lowcountry Parish in South Carolina, St. Johns Berkeley County" (Ph.D. dissertation, University of South Carolina, 1981), pp. 41–45 especially. One should note that while these writers are all revisionists, their revisionism varies in both scope and degree. One should also note that the arguments of the revisionists have not convinced everyone. As recently as 1981, for example, a scholar wrote that the proprietors tried in the Fundamental Constitutions ". . .to establish feudalism in the colony. . . ." See Eliades, "The Indian Policy of Colonial South Carolina," p. 46.

45. On these points, see, for example, Fagg, "Carolina, 1663–1683, " pp. 112–84, 330–43 especially. Fagg's excellent dissertation, one should note, is the most complete and far-reaching revisionist study on the proprietors yet written. The limitations of language pose certain technical problems for the argument presented above. The Fundamental Constitutions, that is to say, is not only *progressive* and *liberal* but, in a sense, *restorative* as well, since some of its provisions were modeled after constitutional features associated with Classical and Renaissance commonwealths.

The quote in the text is from the preamble of the Fundamental Constitutions. See Parker, ed., *North Carolina Charters and Constitutions*, p. 165. Note that I am utilizing the March 1, 1670, version of the Fundamental Constitutions, the one which the proprietors considered, according to Parker, the "official" version. See Parker, ed., *North Carolina Charters and Constitutions*, p. 131. The March 1, 1670, version of the Fundamental Constitutions appears on pages 165–85 in Parker's work.

On Ashley's fear of democracy, see Shaftesbury to the Governor and Council at Charles Town, Carolina, June 10, 1675, Cheves, ed., *Shaftesbury Papers*, pp. 466–68.

46. That Ashley and Locke controlled proprietary policy between 1669 and 1675 there is general agreement. See, for example, Sirmans, *Colonial South Carolina*, pp. 6–34 especially; Clowse, *Economic Beginnings in Colonial South Carolina*, pp. 14–22.

On Locke as a mercantilist, see, for example, Heckscher, *Mercantilism*, 2: 22–23 and passim; Peter Laslett, "John Locke, the Great Recoinage, and the Origins of the Board of Trade: 1695–1698," *William and Mary Quarterly*, 3d ser., 14 (July 1957): 370–402, especially p. 397; Lekachman, *A History of Economic Ideas*, pp. 59–62; Letwin, *The Origins of Scientific Economics*, pp. 147–81, especially pp. 180–81; Joyce D. Appleby, "Ideology and Theory: The Tension Between Political and Economic Liberalism in Seventeenth-Century England," *American Historical Review* 81 (June 1976): 499–515; Appleby, *Economic Thought and Ideology in Seventeenth-Century England*, passim. Karen Vaughn, on the other hand, argues that Locke was not truly a mercantilist. See Vaughn, *John Locke: Economist and Social Scientist*.

On Ashley's mercantilism, see, for example, Heckscher, *Mercantilism*, 2: 19, 118–19; Rich, "The First Earl of Shaftesbury's Colonial Policy"; Haley, *The First Earl of Shaftesbury*, pp. 227–65.

47. My position on seventeenth-century political liberalism owes much to the works of Leo Strauss, C.B. Macpherson, Immanuel Wallerstein, Joyce Appleby, Neil Wood, John P. Diggins, and Andrzej Rapaczynski. See Strauss, *Natural Right and History* (Chicago: University of Chicago Press, 1953), pp. 202–51; Macpherson, *The Political Theory of Possessive Individualism: Hobbes to Locke* (Oxford: Oxford University Press, 1962); Wallerstein, *The Modern World-System*, 2: 112–25 especially; Appleby, "Ideology and Theory"; Appleby, *Economic Thought and Ideology in Seventeenth-Century England*; Wood, *John Locke and Agrarian Capitalism* (Berkeley: University of California Press, 1984); Diggins, *The Lost Soul of American Politics: Virtue, Self-Interest, and the Foundations of Liberalism* (New York: Basic Books, 1984), pp. 18–47 especially; Rapaczynski, *Nature and Politics: Liberalism in the Philosophies of Hobbes, Locke, and Rousseau* (Ithaca: Cornell University Press, 1987), pp. 177-217 especially. My thoughts on the subject have, however, been tempered by works of several other scholars as well, scholars with points of view considerably different from, though not necessarily completely antithetical to, those of the writers mentioned above. See especially: Peter Laslett, "Introduction," in John Locke, *Two Treatises of Government*, rev. ed., edited by Laslett (New York: New American Library, 1965; originally published in 1960), pp. 15–135; Martin Seliger, *The Liberal Politics of John Locke* (London: Allen & Unwin, 1968), passim; J.W. Gough, *John Locke's Political Philosophy: Eight Studies*, 2d ed. (Oxford: Clarendon Press, 1973; originally published 1950), pp. 80–103 especially; Geraint Parry, *John Locke*, Political Thinkers Series (London: Allen & Unwin, 1978); Richard Ashcraft, *Revolutionary Politics & Locke's Two Treatises of Government* (Princeton: Princeton University Press, 1986); H.F. Russell-Smith, *Harrington and His Oceana: A Study of a 17th Century Utopia and Its Influence in America* (Cambridge: Cambridge University Press, 1914); J.G.A. Pocock, "Machiavelli, Harrington, and English Political Ideologies in the Eighteenth Century," *William and*

Mary Quarterly, 3d ser., 22 (October 1965): 549–83; Pocock, *The Machiavellian Moment: Florentine Political Thought and the Atlantic Republican Tradition* (Princeton: Princeton University Press, 1975), pp. 383–400 and passim; Michael Downs, *James Harrington*, Twayne's English Authors Series (Boston: Twayne Publishers, 1977); For the sake of brevity I have limited my citations here to works on Locke and Harrington, the seventeenth-century liberals most important to the historian of early Carolina.

On the uneasy, but nonetheless real intellectual alliance between Locke and other Whig liberals of the seventeenth century, see David Resnick's fine essay, "Locke and the Rejection of the Ancient Constitution," *Political Theory* 12 (February 1984): 97–114.

48. There is little disagreement among scholars on these points; see, for example, the works on Locke mentioned in footnote 47 above. This is not to say that everyone interprets these points in precisely the same way.

49. See the works by Macpherson, Wallerstein, Appleby, and Wood mentioned in footnote 47 above.

Note that there were some "liberal mercantilists"—or "economic liberals" as Appleby labels them—who did at times advocate that the market mechanism rather than political and legal sanctions govern economic relationships for all groups in society, including the poor. Moreover, some of these men, prefiguring Mandeville and Hume, recognized the positive role of demand in the process of economic growth and argued for greater consumption by all groups, including the poor. See Appleby, "Ideology and Theory"; Appleby, *Economic Thought and Ideology in Seventeenth-Century England*. While Appleby's work has deeply influenced my thinking on seventeenth-century English economic thought, I feel that she may have overestimated the consistency, representativeness, and importance of her "economic liberals" in particular and perhaps even of pamphleteers in general. On these points of criticism, see D.C. Coleman, review of *Economic Thought and Ideology in Seventeenth-Century England*, in *Journal of Modern History* 53 (March 1981): 105–6; Coleman, "Mercantilism Revisited." Furthermore, I feel that her "economic liberals" are more properly considered within a mercantilist framework, a framework which, as many have pointed out, was not static, but rather evolved over time. On this point, see Kenneth G. Dennis, *"Competition" in the History of Economic Thought*, Dissertations in European Economic History (New York: Arno Press, 1977), pp. iv–xx, 1–87. Also see my discussion in footnote 14. Finally, one should remember in any case that few would argue that seventeenth-century *political liberals* such as Locke, Harrington, Sidney, and Tyrrell opposed the political and legal sanctions that informed economic life in Europe in that period.

50. On the more complete implementation of mercantilist policies in England, see, for example, Ralph Davis, "The Rise of Protection in England, 1689–1786," *Economic History Review*, 2d ser., 19 (1966): 306–17; Appleby, *Economic Thought and Ideology in Seventeenth-Century England*, pp. 242–79.

On the rationalization of the state and, hence, of elite control in England, see Wallerstein, *The Modern World-System*, 2: 112–25, 245–89 especially; P.G.M. Dickson, *The Financial Revolution in England: A Study in the Development of Public Credit 1688–1756* (London: Macmillan, 1967), pp. 3–14.

51. See Strauss, *Natural Right and History*, pp. 248–49 especially; Macpherson, *The Political Theory of Possessive Individualism*; Appleby, "Ideology and Theory"; Wood, *John Locke and Agrarian Capitalism*.

52. See Chapter V entitled "Of Property" in Locke's *Second Treatise of Government*. In the Laslett edition of *Two Treatises* cited earlier, see pp. 327–44. The quote is from page 328.

53. On the labor shortage characteristic of most colonies in the early modern period, see

E.E. Rich, "Colonial Settlement and Its Labour Problems," in E.E. Rich and C.H. Wilson, eds., *The Cambridge Economic History of Europe*, vol. IV: *The Economy of Expanding Europe in the Sixteenth and Seventeenth Centuries* (Cambridge: Cambridge University Press, 1967), pp. 302–73; Evsey D. Domar, "The Causes of Slavery or Serfdom: A Hypothesis," *Journal of Economic History* 30 (March 1970): 18–32. On the problem in the seventeenth-century Southeast specifically, see Morgan, *American Slavery, American Freedom*, passim; Wood, *Black Majority*, pp. 37–55 especially.

54. On Ashley's leadership role in the passage of the 1679 Habeas Corpus Act (31 Car. II, c.2), see Stephen and Lee, eds., *Dictionary of National Biography*, 4: 1050; Powell, *The Proprietors of Carolina*, p. 37; Haley, *The First Earl of Shaftesbury*, pp. 526–28.

55. On the cheap land offered by the proprietors, see Sirmans, *Colonial South Carolina*, pp. 62–64; Clowse, *Economic Beginnings in Colonial South Carolina*, pp. 46–47, 77–78, 97–98. Robert Ackerman contends that land prices in South Carolina in the seventeenth century were much cheaper than prices in colonies farther north. See Ackerman, *South Carolina Colonial Land Policies*, p. 27. Note that land sales apparently did not begin in South Carolina until the 1680s. At first the proprietors generally sold land at £50 sterling per thousand acres; in 1696, however, the proprietors lowered the basic price to £20 sterling per thousand acres and that price became fixed in law in the colony. On the proprietors' land prices, see Proprietors to Governor Kirle (?), June 3, 1684, Records in the British Public Record Office Relating to South Carolina, 1: 287–94; Proprietors to Governor James Colleton, October 10, 1687, Records in the British Public Record Office Relating to South Carolina, 2: 221–28; Proprietors to Governor Colleton and the Rest of the Trustees for Granting Land in Carolina, October 18, 1690, Records in the British Public Record Office Relating to South Carolina, 2: 296; Cooper and McCord, eds., *Statutes*, 2: 96–102.

On the generous headrights offered by the proprietors, see Copy of Instructions Annexed to the Commission for the Governor and Council, July 27, 1669, Cheves, ed., *Shaftesbury Papers*, pp. 119–23. On the later changes in these provisions, see Clowse, *Economic Beginnings in Colonial South Carolina*, pp. 45–46, 76–77, 156.

On the waiver of quitrents for twenty years, see Fundamental Constitutions, March 1, 1670, Parker, ed., *North Carolina Charters and Constitutions*, Article 113, pp. 183–84.

On the proprietors' provisions for representative government in Carolina, see Concessions and Agreement between the Lords Proprietors and Major William Yeamans and Others, January 7, 1665, Parker, ed., *North Carolina Charters and Constitutions*, pp. 109–27, especially 115–18; Fundamental Constitutions, March 1, 1670, Parker, ed., *North Carolina Charters and Constitutions*, Articles 71–79, 92, pp. 177–79, 180; Copy of Instructions Annexed to the Commission for the Governor and Council, July 27, 1669, Cheves, ed., *Shaftesbury Papers*, pp. 119–23.

On the proprietors' advanced position on religious toleration, see Fundamental Constitutions, March 1, 1670, Parker, ed., *North Carolina Charters and Constitutions*, Articles 95–110, pp. 181–83.

On provisions for land registration by the proprietors, see Fundamental Constitutions, March 1, 1670, Parker, ed., *North Carolina Charters and Constitutions*, Article 81, p. 179.

On ease of naturalization, see Fundamental Constitutions, March 1, 1670, Parker, ed., *North Carolina Charters and Constitutions*, Articles 117–18, p. 184.

On the proprietors' waiver of customs duties on a wide range of imports and exports for a number of years, see Concessions and Agreement between the Lords Proprietors and Major William Yeamans and Others, January 7, 1665, Parker, ed., *North Carolina Charters and Constitutions*, pp. 109–27, especially p. 120; Barbados Proclamation, November 4, 1670, Cheves, ed., *Shaftesbury Papers*, pp. 210–13. Carolina tobacco was, however, apparently

excluded from the waiver. See Lords Proprietors to Lord Shaftesbury, November 20, 1674, Cheves, ed., *Shaftesbury Papers*, pp. 454–55. Note that the proprietors obtained the right to grant waivers on customs from Charles II in the Carolina charters of 1663 and 1665. On this right, see Parker, ed., *North Carolina Charters and Constitutions*, pp. 82–83, 97–98.

On the proprietors' expenditures on Carolina as of 1675, see Shaftesbury to the Governor and Council at Charles Town, Carolina, June 10, 1675, Cheves, ed., *Shaftesbury Papers*, pp. 466–68. According to an agreement signed in 1674, the proprietors were to continue plowing funds into Carolina for seven more years. In a letter to the Committee of Trade and Plantations in 1679, the proprietors stated that they had spent a total of £17,000 or £18,000 on Carolina up to that time. See Articles Between the Lords Proprietors, May 6, 1674, Cheves, ed., *Shaftesbury Papers*, pp. 431–35; Carolina Proprietors to the Committee of Trade and Plantations, March 6, 1679, Records in the British Public Record Office Relating to South Carolina, 1: 71–72.

By granting large headrights for each slave brought into Carolina and by making it clear from the start that a Negro slave's conversion to Christianity would in no way alter his or her servile status, the proprietors gave powerful encouragement to the development of a labor system based on Negro slavery in Carolina. See Concessions and Agreement between the Lords Proprietors and Major William Yeamans and Others, January 7, 1665, Parker, ed., *North Carolina Charters and Constitutions*, pp. 109–27, especially pp. 120–25; Fundamental Constitutions, March 1, 1670, Parker, ed., *North Carolina Charters and Constitutions*, Articles 107, 110, p. 183; Copy of Instructions Annexed to the Commission of the Governor and Council, July 27, 1669, Cheves, ed., *Shaftesbury Papers*, pp. 119–23; Lord Ashley *et al.* to Sir John Yeamans, May 1670 (?), Cheves, ed., *Shaftesbury Papers*, pp. 164–65.

One should note that many of the above proprietary policies and provisions were similar to practices associated at the time with the Dutch, the most advanced people, economically speaking, in the world. On Dutch economic practices and the widespread interest in seventeenth-century England in emulating such practices, see, for example, Appleby, *Economic Thought and Ideology in Seventeenth-Century England*, pp. 73–98. Many of Locke's ideas on economic matters, ideas that found expression in the Fundamental Constitutions, were clearly laid out in a set of his notes entitled "Trade 1674." In these notes, which were never published, Locke lists a number of "Promoters of Traders" including among them easy naturalization, freedom of religion, land registration, small customs, and cheap labor! See Mss. Locke, C. 30, folio 18, Bodleian Library, Oxford University, Oxford, England. I used a microfilm copy of this set of notes available at the South Carolina Historical Society, Charleston, S.C. in the collection "John Locke, Correspondence, 1673–1704."

Finally, Ashley's use of the term "Darling" to refer to Carolina is from Shaftesbury to Sir Peter Colleton, November 27, 1672, Cheves, ed., *Shaftesbury Papers*, pp. 416–18.

56. On the contours of South Carolina's economic expansion and growth in the colonial period, see Marc Egnal, "The Economic Development of the Thirteen Continental Colonies, 1720–1775," *William and Mary Quarterly*, 3d ser., 32 (April 1975): 191–222. Also see Chapter 3 of this study. One should note that South Carolina's economic expansion and growth in the colonial period allowed the white population of the low country to become by far the richest single group in British North America. See Alice Hanson Jones, *Wealth of a Nation To Be: The American Colonies on the Eve of the Revolution* (New York: Columbia University Press, 1980), pp. 258–341, 343–74 especially.

On South Carolina's relative political harmony in the late colonial period, see Robert M. Weir, " 'The Harmony We Were Famous For': An Interpretation of Pre-Revolutionary South Carolina Politics," *William and Mary Quarterly*, 3d ser., 26 (October 1969): 473–501.

South Carolina's potential value to England, commented upon by Edward Randolph in 1699 and restated by men such as Fayrer Hall and Joshua Gee in the 1720s and 1730s, was realized by the late colonial period. On the eve of the American Revolution, South Carolina was, as a number of scholars have pointed out, a good mercantilist colony; it not only produced large quantities of valuable staples for export but was also closely tied economically to England, her largest trading partner by a wide margin. On South Carolina's potential, see Edward Randolph to Council of Trade and Plantations, March 16, 1699, *Calendar of State Papers, Colonial Series, America and West Indies*, vol.: *1699*, pp. 104–8; Hall, *The Importance of the British Plantations in America to this Kingdom*, pp. 62–70; Gee, *The Trade and Navigation of Great-Britain Considered*, pp. 31–34.

On the mercantilist nature of South Carolina's economy in the late colonial period, its production of staples for export, and its close ties to the English economy, see, for example, C. Robert Haywood, "Mercantilism and South Carolina Agriculture, 1700–1763," *South Carolina Historical Magazine* 60 (January 1959): 15–27; James F. Shepherd and Gary M. Walton, "Trade, Distribution, and Economic Growth in Colonial America," *Journal of Economic History* 32 (March 1972): 128–45; Shepherd, "Commodity Exports from the British North American Colonies to Overseas Areas, 1768–1772: Ma   tudes and Patterns of Trade," *Explorations in Economic History*, 2d ser., 8 (Fall 1970): 5–76; Shepherd and Samuel H. Williamson, "The Coastal Trade of the British North American Colonies, 1768–1772," *Journal of Economic History* 32 (December 1972): 783–810.

57. On the harshness of South Carolina's laws concerning slavery and the relationship between these laws and actual practices, see Winthrop D. Jordan, *White Over Black: American Attitudes Toward the Negro, 1550–1812* (Chapel Hill: University of North Carolina Press, 1968), pp. 84–85, 587–88 especially; M. Eugene Sirmans, "The Legal Status of the Slave in South Carolina, 1670–1740," *Journal of Southern History* 28 (November 1962): 462–73; Wood, *Black Majority*, passim; John Donald Duncan, "Servitude and Slavery in Colonial South Carolina 1670–1776" (Ph.D. dissertation, Emory University, 1972), pp. 107–13 and passim; A. Leon Higginbotham, Jr., *In the Matter of Color: Race & the American Legal Process: The Colonial Period* (New York: Oxford University Press, 1978), pp. 151–215.

Colonial South Carolina's most important statutes on slavery appear in Cooper and McCord, eds., *Statutes*, 7: 343–429, and in Governor Archdale's Lawes, March 1695–6, leaves 60–66, South Carolina Department of Archives and History.

Finally, one should note that even in recent times the South Carolina low country continues to be one of the poorest sections of one of the poorest states. While not underdeveloped in the se   ? that countries such as Chad or Afghanistan are, data on such variables as per capita mean and median income, per capita commercial bank deposits, infant mortality, median education, urbanization, and percentage of population on food stamps and in substandard housing, reveal that the low country ranks far below levels typical of "developed" areas on these indices. When one allows for the military presence and for the recent development of upper-class enclaves in Beaufort County, both of which distort to a degree the statistical profile of the low country, the area's relative underdevelopment is even more pronounced—particularly for the low country's large black minority. For statistical data illustrating the low country's relative underdevelopment, see South Carolina State Development Board, *South Carolina Statistics, 1975* (Columbia: Planning and Research Division, n.d.), pp. 29–30, 32; Lowcountry Council of Governments, *Lowcountry Policy Framework for Regional Development* (Yemassee, S.C.: Lowcountry Council of Governments, June 1977), pp. 19–37; South Carolina Budget and Control Board, *South Carolina Statistical Abstract 1979* (Columbia: South Carolina Division of Research and Statistical Services, 1980), pp. 14, 22,

34, 54, 58, 60, 66, 87, 93, 141. Also see "Poverty and Disease in Carolina Low Country Belie the New South Boom," *New York Times*, April 1, 1977, A1, A11.

Economic and social conditions in the low country, it is true, have improved somewhat in the 1980s, but the area still remains far behind the more developed parts of the West. The most up-to-date data on economic and social conditions in the low country are available in State of South Carolina Budget and Control Board, *South Carolina Statistical Abstract 1985* (Columbia: South Carolina Division of Research and Statistical Services, 1986), pp. 55, 63, 70, 200–202, 227–28, 236, 244, 248–63, 271, 278–79, 321, 373–74.

Chapter 2. Mise en Scène

1. See, for example, Buck Guignard, *The Treasure of Peyre Gaillard*, arranged by John Bennett (New York: The Century Company, 1906); Dubose Heyward and Hervey Allen, *Carolina Chansons: Legends of the Low Country* (New York: Macmillan, 1922); Federal Writers' Project, *South Carolina Folk Tales: Stories of Animals and Supernatural Beings*, Bulletin of University of South Carolina (Columbia: 1941), pp. 43–103; John Bennett, *The Doctor to the Dead: Grotesque Legends & Folk Tales of Old Charleston* (New York: Rinehart, 1946); Julian S. Bolick, *The Return of the Gray Man and Georgetown Ghosts* (Clinton, S.C.: Jacobs Brothers, c. 1961); Lee R. Gandee, "Haunted Houses in South Carolina. . . ," *Fate* 14 (April 1961): 32–39; Nancy Roberts, *Ghosts of the Carolinas* (Charlotte: McNally and Loftin, 1962); Margaret Rhett Martin, *Charleston Ghosts* (Columbia: University of South Carolina Press, 1963); Bolick, *Ghosts from the Coast: A Collection of Twelve Stories from Georgetown County, South Carolina* (Clinton, S.C.: Jacobs Brothers, c. 1966); Nell S. Graydon, comp., *South Carolina Ghost Tales* (Beaufort, S.C.: Beaufort Book Shop, 1969); Bruce Roberts and Nancy Roberts, *This Haunted Land* (Charlotte: McNally and Loftin, c. 1970); Nancy Rhyne, *Tales of the South Carolina Low Country* (Winston-Salem: John F. Blair, 1982); Elliot J. Gorn, "Black Spirits: The Ghostlore of Afro-American Slaves," *American Quarterly* 36 (Fall 1984): 549–65; Georgia Writers' Project, Savannah Unit, Works Projects Administration, *Drums and Shadows: Survival Studies Among the Georgia Coastal Negroes* (Athens: University of Georgia Press, 1986; originally published 1940), passim.

Descriptions of the supernatural beings mentioned in the text can be found in Federal Writers' Project, *South Carolina Folk Tales*, pp. 46–49.

Note that Edgar Allan Poe lived in the low country for a time and the melancholic landscape of the area is often evoked in his works. Indeed, *The Gold-Bug* is set in the low country. His poem "Fairy-Land," which was written while Poe was living in the Charleston area, opens with a passage that captures the lugubrious quality of the South Carolina low country: "Dim vales—and shadowy floods— / And cloudy-looking woods, / Whose forms we can't discover / For the tears that drip all over / ." See *The Poems of Edgar Allan Poe*, ed. Killis Campbell (New York: Russell & Russell, 1962), pp. 53–56. The poem originally appeared in 1829 in Poe's *Al Aaraaf, Tamerlane, and Minor Poems*. On Poe and the South Carolina low country, see Heyward and Allen, *Carolina Chansons*, pp. 128–29; Arthur Hobson Quinn, *Edgar Allan Poe: A Critical Biography* (New York: Cooper Square Publishers, 1969; originally published 1941), pp. 129–32.

2. On "folklore" and its social functions, see, for example, William Bascom, "Folklore," in *The International Encyclopedia of the Social Sciences*, ed. David L. Sills, 18 vols. (New York: The Free Press, 1968–79), 5: 496–500. More precise discussions of the subject matter and social functions of folklore can be found in the *Journal of American Folklore*

84 (January–March 1971), passim; Richard M. Dorson, "Concepts of Folklore and Folklife Studies," in Dorson, ed., *Folklore and Folklife: An Introduction* (Chicago: University of Chicago Press, 1972), pp. 1–50. Good discussions of these matters can also be found in two recent texts: John H. Brunvand, *The Study of American Folklore: An Introduction*, 2d ed. (New York: W.W. Norton, 1978); Barre Toelken, *The Dynamics of Folklore* (Boston: Houghton Mifflin, 1979).

3. My views on the importance of a culture's beliefs and traditions concerning ghosts and the dead have been deeply influenced by the work of Robert Blauner and Keith Thomas. See Blauner, "Death and Social Structure," *Psychiatry* 29 (November 1966): 378–94; Thomas, *Religion and the Decline of Magic* (New York: Charles Scribner's Sons, 1971), pp. 587–606 especially.

One should note that the development of the "dance of death" motif in the Western artistic tradition arose in the fourteenth century—in the wake of and, indeed, partly the result of a similar demographic crisis, that is to say, the so-called Black Death. See, for example, Johan Huizinga, *The Waning of the Middle Ages: A Study of the Forms of Life, Thought and Art in France and the Netherlands in the XIVth and XVth Centuries*, trans. F. Hopman (Garden City, N.Y.: Anchor Books, 1954; originally published 1924), pp. 138–51; James M. Clark, *The Dance of Death in the Middle Ages and the Renaissance*, Glasgow University Publications LXXXVI (Glasgow: Jackson, Son & Company, 1950), passim; Kathi Meyer-Baer, *Music of the Spheres and the Dance of Death: Studies in Musical Iconology* (Princeton: Princeton University Press, 1970), pp. 291–312 especially; Ivan Illich, *Medical Nemesis: The Expropriation of Health* (New York: Pantheon, 1976), pp. 171–204.

4. Joseph Conrad, *Heart of Darkness and The Secret Sharer* (New York: The New American Library, 1950), p. 77. *Heart of Darkness* was first published in 1902.

5. On the geographical misconceptions attending the European "discovery" of the Southeast and the gradual elimination of such misconceptions, see William P. Cumming, "Geographical Misconceptions of the Southeast in the Cartography of the Seventeenth and Eighteenth Centuries," *Journal of Southern History* 4 (November 1938): 476–92; Cumming, *The Southeast in Early Maps* (Princeton: Princeton University Press, 1958), pp. 1–92; Peter H. Wood, "La Salle: Discovery of a Lost Explorer," *American Historical Review* 89 (April 1984): 294–323.

On the image of early South Carolina in particular, see H. Roy Merrens, "The Physical Environment of Early America: Images and Image Makers in Colonial South Carolina," *Geographical Review* 59 (October 1969): 530–56; Charles F. Kovacik and Lawrence S. Rowland, "Images of Colonial Port Royal, South Carolina," *Annals of the Association of American Geographers* 63 (September 1973): 331–40; Merrens and George D. Terry, "Dying in Paradise: Malaria, Mortality and the Perceptual Environment in Colonial South Carolina," *Journal of Southern History* 50 (November 1984): 533–50.

My own perception of the South Carolina low country in the early modern period has been heavily influenced by V.S. Naipaul's *The Loss of El Dorado: A History* (Harmondsworth, Middlesex, England: Penguin Books, 1973; originally published 1969) and by Werner Herzog's 1973 film *Aguirre der Zorn Gottes*.

6. John Lederer, *The Discoveries of John Lederer, In three several Marches from Virginia To the West of Carolina, And other parts of the Continent. . .* , trans. Sir William Talbot (London: Printed by J.C. for Samuel Heyrick, 1672), p. 1. Also note the map at the front of this volume.

7. Though most writers use this tripartite scheme, other classification schemes also exist. John M. Barry, for example, recognizes the sandhill area as a distinct zone and, thus, divides South Carolina into four provinces, while David D. Wallace divides the state into no less

than seven distinct provinces. See Barry, *Natural Vegetation of South Carolina* (Columbia: University of South Carolina Press, 1980), pp. 3–16; Wallace, *South Carolina: A Short History 1520–1948* (Chapel Hill: University of North Carolina Press, 1951), pp. 1–4.

8. The area beyond the mountains also figured prominently in South Carolina's early history, for many of the most powerful Southeastern Indian peoples lived there. On the physical characteristics of the Mississippi Valley and the Gulf Plain, see Charles B. Hunt, *Natural Regions of the United States and Canada* (San Francisco: W.H. Freeman, 1974), pp. 209–51.

9. Barry, *Natural Vegetation of South Carolina*, pp. 3–53; Henry S. Johnson, *Geology in South Carolina*, Miscellaneous Report 3, Division of Geology, State Development Board, revised ed. (Columbia, S.C.: 1971), pp. 1–11; South Carolina State Planning Board, *The Natural Resources of South Carolina*, Bulletin No. 3, revised (Columbia, S.C.: 1944), pp. 15–25. For a more comprehensive treatment of the Appalachians, see Hunt, *Natural Regions of the United States and Canada*, pp. 253–303.

10. Barry, *Natural Vegetation of South Carolina*, pp. 3–16, 55–94; Johnson, *Geology in South Carolina*, pp. 1–11; South Carolina State Planning Board, *The Natural Resources of South Carolina*, pp. 15–25.

11. Barry, *Natural Vegetation of South Carolina*, pp. 15–16, 120–91; Donald J. Colquhoun, *Geomorphology of the Lower Coastal Plain of South Carolina*, MS-15, Division of Geology, State Development Board (Columbia, S.C.: 1969), passim. On the major shifts of the shoreline, see Colquhoun, pp. 7–8.

12. C. Wythe Cooke, *Geology of the Coastal Plain of South Carolina*, United States Department of the Interior, Geological Survey, Bulletin 867 (Washington, D.C.: United States Government Printing Office, 1936), pp. 1–15. Some divide the coastal plain differently. See, for example, Barry, *Natural Vegetation of South Carolina*, pp. 95–119, 123–35.

Note that the fall line is much more important to geologists than to geographers. Indeed, geographers today tend to downplay the significance of the line, arguing that the change in topography as one moves inland is gradual rather than abrupt. This is, of course, true. The change in stratigraphy is, however, more abrupt. The term "fall line" is used advisedly by this writer for purposes of classification to denote, somewhat arbitrarily to be sure, the geographically-hazy but geologically-distinct boundary between the piedmont and the upper coastal plain. On these points, see Arch C. Gerlach, ed., *The National Atlas of the United States* (Washington, D.C.: United States Department of the Interior, Geological Survey, 1970), p. 61.

13. On the upper coastal plain, see Cooke, *Geology of the Coastal Plain of South Carolina*, pp. 1–4, 9–11; Barry, *Natural Vegetation of South Carolina*, pp. 15–16, 126–35.

14. Cooke, *Geology of the Coastal Plain of South Carolina*, passim; Colquhoun, *Geomorphology of the Lower Coastal Plain of South Carolina*, passim; Barry, *Natural Vegetation of South Carolina*, pp. 15–16, 120–91.

The quote in the text above is from "An Old Letter," c. March 1671 (?), Langdon Cheves, ed., *The Shaftesbury Papers and Other Records Relating to Carolina and the First Settlement on Ashley River Prior to the Year 1676*, in *Collections of the South Carolina Historical Society*, vol. 5 (Charleston: Published by the South Carolina Historical Society, 1897), pp. 307–9, especially p. 308. Hereinafter cited as Cheves, ed., *Shaftesbury Papers*. Mark Catesby, one should also note, commented on the imperceptible slope of the land in the low country. See Catesby, *The Natural History of Carolina, Florida, and the Bahama Islands. . .*, 2d English ed., 2 vols. (London: Printed for C. Marsh, T. Wilcox, B. Stichall, 1754; originally published 1731–43), 2: iv.

15. Barry, *Natural Vegetation of South Carolina*, p. 135. On the plant genera and species present in the low country today, see Richard G. Zingmark, ed., *An Annotated Checklist of the Biota of the Coastal Zone of South Carolina* (Columbia: Published for the Belle W. Baruch Institute for Marine Biology and Coastal Research by the University of South Carolina Press, 1978), pp. 2–84 especially; William D. Webster, James F. Parnell, Walter C. Biggs, Jr., *Mammals of the Carolinas, Virginia, and Maryland* (Chapel Hill: University of North Carolina Press, 1985), passim.

16. On South Carolina's mineral resources and the locations of such resources, see Cooke, *Geology of the Coastal Plain of South Carolina*, pp. 159–88, especially pp. 159–61; South Carolina State Planning Board, *The Natural Resources of South Carolina*, pp. 67–77.

The European search for precious metals in the Southeast, begun by the Spanish in the sixteenth century, continued sporadically through the early modern period. Though some gold was ultimately mined in the Appalachian region, neither gold nor silver was ever found in the South Carolina low country. On early mining schemes and expeditions arising from South Carolina, see Henry Woodward to Sir John Yeamans, September 10, 1670, Cheves, ed., *Shaftesbury Papers*, pp. 186–88; Sir John Yeamans to Lord Ashley, November 15, 1670, Cheves, ed., *Shaftesbury Papers*, pp. 220–21; Lord Ashley to Henry Woodward, April 10, 1671, Cheves, ed., *Shaftesbury Papers*, pp. 315–17; Lord Ashley to William Sayle, May 13, 1671, Cheves, ed., *Shaftesbury Papers*, pp. 327–28; William, Earl of Craven, Palatine of Carolina, to Henry Woodward, May 18, 1682, Records in the British Public Record Office Relating to South Carolina, 1663–1782, 36 vols. in facsimile, 1: 159–60, South Carolina Department of Archives and History, Columbia, S.C.; Records in the British Public Record Office Relating to South Carolina, 4 (1698–1700): 81–83, 84–85, 86–87, 110, 187, 191–93, 194–96; 5 (1701–1710): 9–10, South Carolina Department of Archives and History; W. Noel Sainsbury *et al.*, eds., *Calendar of State Papers, Colonial Series, America and West Indies, 1574–*, 44 vols. thus far (London: 1860–), vol.: *1699*, p. 451; vol.: *1700*, pp. 428–29, 445–46.

Note that the Carolina proprietors, having been granted mineral rights in the colony by the charters of 1663 and 1665, attempted to secure such rights in the Fundamental Constitutions. These charters and the March 1, 1670 version of the Fundamental Constitutions are reprinted on pages 76–89, 91–104, and 165–85 in Mattie Erma Edwards Parker, ed., *North Carolina Charters and Constitutions 1578–1698* (Raleigh: Published by the Carolina Charter Tercentenary Commission, 1963). Provisions pertaining to mineral rights appear on pages 77, 92, and 184.

17. On the river systems of the South Carolina low country, see Cooke, *Geology of the Coastal Plain of South Carolina*, pp. 11–14; South Carolina State Planning Board, *The Natural Resources of South Carolina*, pp. 27–45; Colquhoun, *Geomorphology of the Lower Coastal Plain of South Carolina*, pp. 4–5.

Monographs have been written on two of these systems. See Thomas L. Stokes, *The Savannah*, Rivers of America Series (New York: Rinehart, 1951); Henry Savage, Jr., *River of the Carolinas: The Santee*, Rivers of America Series (New York: Rinehart, 1956). On the Pee Dee system, see Bruce G. Thom, *Coastal and Fluvial Landforms: Horry and Marion Counties, South Carolina*, Coastal Studies Series No. 19 (Baton Rouge: Louisiana State University Press, 1967), pp. 54–59.

To ascertain the economic and social importance of any river one must know something of its discharge, depth, width, grade, direction of flow, turbidity, and circuitry of stream. Though data on some of these matters are scanty for the early modern period, such information has been compiled for the modern period and is useful to the colonial historian despite

the changes in the low country's river systems over time. On these matters, see United States Department of the Interior, Geological Survey, *Water Resources Data for South Carolina. Part 1: Surface Water Records 1969* (Washington, D.C.: 1971); United States Department of the Interior, Geological Survey, *Water Resources Data for South Carolina. Part 2: Water Quality Records 1968* (Washington, D.C.: 1968). Also see Kenneth E. Prince, "Surface Waters of South Carolina" (M.S. thesis, University of South Carolina, 1941).

Good discussions of these river systems at the turn of the eighteenth century can be found in John Drayton, *A View of South-Carolina, As Respects Her Natural and Civil Concerns* (Charleston: W.P. Young, 1802), pp. 30–38; David Ramsay, *The History of South-Carolina from its First Settlement in 1670, to the Year 1808*, 2 vols. (Charleston: David Longworth, 1809), 2: 291–98.

Finally, one should note that the low country possesses abundant, if increasingly threatened, supplies of ground water. See Cooke, *Geology of the Coastal Plain of South Carolina*, pp. 161–88.

18. On "climate" and its alleged relationship to both violence and laziness in South Carolina, see, for example, Ramsay, *The History of South-Carolina*, 2: 387–89, 401–2. Ramsay's arguments have been repeated, albeit in modified forms, ever since. On the alleged relationship between climate and laziness in the South as a whole, see, for example, David Bertelson, *The Lazy South* (New York: Oxford University Press, 1967); C. Vann Woodward, "The Southern Ethic in a Puritan World," *William and Mary Quarterly*, 3d ser., 25 (July 1968): 343–70; Karen O. Kupperman, "Fear of Hot Climates in the Anglo–American Colonial Experience," *William and Mary Quarterly*, 3d ser., 41 (April 1984): 213–40. On climate and southern speech patterns, see Daniel P. Jengst, "Magnitude of Complexity, Least Effort, and the Southern Drawl: George Kingsley Zipf reconsidered on the Midland-Southern Dialect Border," paper delivered at the Fourth Annual Symposium on Language and Culture in South Carolina, University of South Carolina, Columbia, S.C., March 14, 1980.

19. On the distinction between weather and climate, see H.H. Lamb, *Climate: Present, Past and Future*, 2 vols. (London: Methuen, 1972–77), 1: 4–5; Arthur N. Strahler, *Introduction to Physical Geography* (New York: Wiley, 1965), pp. 42–43.

The phrase "deep like the rivers" is from Langston Hughes's 1921 poem "The Negro Speaks of Rivers." See Hughes, *Selected Poems* (New York: Vintage Books, 1974), p. 4.

20. See, for example, Lamb, *Climate: Present, Past and Future*, 2: passim; Emmanuel Le Roy Ladurie, *Histoire du climat depuis l'an mil* (Paris: Flammarion, 1967); Reid A. Bryson and Christine Padoch, "On the Climates of History," *Journal of Interdisciplinary History* 10 (Spring 1980): 583–97. The entire Spring 1980 issue of the *Journal of Interdisciplinary History*, one should note, is devoted to climate and history.

On dendroclimatology, phenology, and palynology specifically, see, for example, Le Roy Ladurie, "Histoire et Climat," *Annales: économies, sociétés, civilisations* 14 (1959): 3–34; Lamb, *Climate: Present, Past and Future*, 2: 213–29 especially; Thompson Webb III, "The Reconstruction of Climatic Sequences from Botanical Data," *Journal of Interdisciplinary History* 10 (Spring 1980): 749–72; Harold C. Fritts, G. Robert Lofgren, and Geoffrey A. Gordon, "Past Climate Reconstructed from Tree Rings," *Journal of Interdisciplinary History* 10 (Spring 1980): 773–93; Le Roy Ladurie and Micheline Baulant, "Grape Harvests from the Fifteenth through the Nineteenth Centuries," *Journal of Interdisciplinary History* 10 (Spring 1980): 839–49.

21. On the so-called little ice age, see Lamb, *Climate: Present, Past and Future*, 2: 449–73; Le Roy Ladurie, *Histoire du climat depuis l'an mil*, passim; Bryson and Padoch, "On the Climates of History"; Jan de Vries, "Measuring the Impact of Climate on History: The Search

for Appropriate Methodologies," *Journal of Interdisciplinary History* 10 (Spring 1980): 599–630; Karen O. Kupperman, "The Puzzle of the American Climate in the Early Colonial Period," *American Historical Review* 87 (December 1982): 1262–89. Gustav Utterström has taken perhaps the most extreme position concerning the role of climatic change in the early modern period. See Utterström, "Climatic Fluctuations and Population Problems in Early Modern History," *Scandinavian Economic History Review* 3 (1955): 3–47.

22. Extant meteorological data pertaining to eighteenth–century South Carolina are, for example, quite similar to present-day data. See James Glen, *A Description of South Carolina*. . . (London: Printed for R. and J. Dodsley, 1761), pp. 11–29; George Milligen-Johnston, *A Short Description of the Province of South-Carolina*. . . (London: John Hinton, 1770), pp. 14–23; Chapman J. Milling, ed., *Colonial South Carolina: Two Contemporary Descriptions* (Columbia: University of South Carolina Press, 1951), pp. 105–9; Lionel Chalmers, *An Account of the Weather and Diseases of South Carolina*, 2 vols. (London: E. and C. Dilly, 1776), 1: 1–28, 42–48; 2: 55–56, 83–84, 200–201, table between pp. 216 and 217; Alexander Hewatt, *An Historical Account of the Rise and Progress of the Colonies of South Carolina and Georgia*, 2 vols. (London: Printed for Alexander Donaldson, 1779), 2: 134–36; Weather Observations by Gabriel Manigault, 1776–1804, Manigault Family Papers, 11–276, South Carolina Historical Society, Charleston, S.C.; Weather Observations in Camden in 1785 by Richard Champion, Manigault Family Papers, 11–276, South Carolina Historical Society; Drayton, *A View of South-Carolina*, pp. 16–27; Ramsay, *The History of South-Carolina*, 2: 49–69; Robert Mills, *Statistics of South Carolina*. . . (Charleston: Hurlbut and Lloyd, 1826), pp. 133–39.

For the seventeenth century one must rely on descriptive accounts of the weather and climate of the South Carolina low country. Though such accounts were often promotional in nature, the discussions of weather and climate therein are, when read critically, essentially consistent with the more precise eighteenth-century data mentioned above. See, for example, Maurice Mathews, "A Contemporary View of Carolina in 1680," *South Carolina Historical Magazine* 55 (July 1954): 153–59, especially p. 157; Thomas Ashe, *Carolina; or a Description of the Present State of that Country and the Natural Excellencies thereof*. . . (London: Printed for W.C., 1682), passim; Louis Thibou Letter, September 20, 1683, South Caroliniana Library, University of South Carolina, Columbia, S.C. On meteorological conditions in the seventeenth-century South, also see David M. Ludlum, *Early American Winters 1604–1820*, The History of American Weather Series (Boston: American Meteorological Society, 1966), pp. 32–37. Finally, one should also take note of Robert C. Aldredge's "Weather Observers and Observations at Charleston, South Carolina, 1670–1871," *Year Book, City of Charleston, S.C., 1940* (Charleston: Published for the City of Charleston by Walker, Evans & Cogswell, 1942), pp. 189–257.

23. Sir Walter Raleigh, *The Marrow of Historie*. . . (London: Printed by W. Du-gard for J. Stephenson, 1650), p. 42. Also see Edward Bland, *The Discovery of New Brittaine, Began August 27, Anno. Dom. 1650*. . . (London: Printed by Thomas Harper for John Stephenson, 1651) in A.S. Salley, Jr., ed., *Narratives of Early Carolina 1650–1708*, Original Narratives of Early American History (New York: Barnes & Noble, 1967; originally published 1911), pp. 5–19, especially pp. 7–8.

24. On the Köppen system, see Lamb, *Climate: Present, Past and Future*, 1: 509–14; Jules Janick *et al.*, *Plant Science: An Introduction to World Crops*, 2d ed. (San Francisco: Freeman, 1974), pp. 257–65. For a modified version of the Köppen framework, see Glenn T. Trewartha, *An Introduction to Climate*, 3d ed. (New York: McGraw-Hill, 1954), passim.

25. Lamb, *Climate: Present, Past and Future*, 1: 509–14; Strahler, *Introduction to Physical Geography*, pp. 102–16, 141–42; Janick *et al.*, *Plant Science*, pp. 257–65; John

F. Lounsbury and Lawrence Ogden, *Earth Science*, 2d ed. (New York: Harper & Row, 1973), pp. 135–63, especially pp. 148–50.

26. Strahler, *Introduction to Physical Geography*, pp. 141–42 and Plate 2; Janick *et al.*, *Plant Science*, pp. 260–61; Lounsbury and Ogden, *Earth Science*, pp. 148–50; D.H. Grist, *Rice*, 3d ed. (London: Longmans, Green, 1959), pp. 8–27; M.Y. Nuttonson, *Global Agroclimatic Analogues for the Rice Regions of the Continental United States* (Washington, D.C.: American Institute of Crop Ecology, 1965), pp. 2–9; Nuttonson, *Rice Culture and Rice–Climate Relationships with Special Reference to the United States Rice Areas and Their Latitudinal and Thermal Analogues in Other Countries* (Washington, D.C.: American Institute of Crop Ecology, 1965), passim.

27. *Histoire structurale* is, of course, associated with the *Annales* group of historians, particularly with Fernand Braudel. On the possibility that biological factors informed the history of the early modern world and brought coherence and unity to the same, see Braudel, *The Structures of Everyday Life: Civilization & Capitalism 15th-18th Century*, trans. Siân Reynolds (New York: Harper & Row, 1981; originally published 1979), pp. 31–103, especially p. 49. On the *Annales* tradition, see Traian Stoianovich, *French Historical Method: The Annales Paradigm* (Ithaca: Cornell University Press, 1976). On the relevance of this tradition to the historian of early South Carolina, see Peter A. Coclanis, "The *Annales* and Early American History: The Charleston Paradigm," paper delivered at the Third Annual Symposium on Language and Culture in South Carolina, University of South Carolina, Columbia, S.C., March 17, 1979.

28. Barry, *Natural Vegetation of South Carolina*, pp. 3–12; Holbrook Landers, *Climate of South Carolina* (Washington, D.C.: United States Government Printing Office, 1970), passim; South Carolina State Planning Board, *The Natural Resources of South Carolina*, pp. 18–25.

For comparative data on meteorological conditions in the South Carolina low country and on the island of Barbados, see Helmut E. Landsberg, editor in chief, *World Survey of Climatology*, 15 vols. (Amsterdam: Elsevier Publishing Co., 1969–), 11: 323; 12: 462; W.G. Kendrew, *The Climates of the Continents*, 5th ed. (Oxford: Clarendon Press, 1961), pp. 459, 462, 524, 527; United States Department of Agriculture, *Soil Survey, Charleston County, South Carolina* (Washington, D.C.: United States Government Printing Office, 1971), pp. 72–74; United States Department of Agriculture, *Soil Survey of Berkeley County, South Carolina* (Washington, D.C.: United States Government Printing Office, 1980), pp. 46, 93–94; United States Department of Agriculture, *Soil Survey of Beaufort and Jasper Counties, South Carolina* (Washington, D.C.: United States Government Printing Office, 1980), pp. 1–2, 104–5; United States Department of Agriculture, Soil Conservation Service, *Soil Survey of Georgetown County, South Carolina* (Washington, D.C.: United States Government Printing Office, 1982), pp. 2, 72–73; United States Department of Agriculture, Soil Conservation Service, *Soil Survey of Colleton County, South Carolina* (Washington, D.C.: United States Government Printing Office, 1982), pp. 2, 108–10. Modern soil surveys exist for these six low-country counties only. Surveys for the remaining low-country counties, however, are under way.

29. See, for example, William Cronon's pioneering *Changes in the Land: Indians, Colonists and the Ecology of New England* (New York: Hill and Wang, 1983), pp. 3–15 and passim. This view, speaking broadly, can be traced back to Marx and Engels. See *The German Ideology Parts I & III*, ed. R. Pascal (New York: International Publishers, 1947), p. 7 and passim.

30. On ecological change in New England, see Cronon, *Changes in the Land*. On ecological accommodation in the low country, see, for example, Sam B. Hilliard, "The

Tidewater Rice Plantation: An Ingenious Adaptation to Nature," *Geoscience and Man* 12 (1975): 57–66; D.W. Meinig, *The Shaping of America: A Geographical Perspective on 500 Years of History*, vol. 1: *Atlantic America, 1492–1800* (New Haven: Yale University Press, 1986), pp. 182–83.

31. See, for example, Harry O. Buckman and Nyle C. Brady, *The Nature and Properties of Soils*, 7th ed. (New York: Macmillan, 1969), pp. 1–17; Janick *et al.*, *Plant Science*, pp. 218–30; Strahler, *Introduction to Physical Geography*, pp. 166–75.

32. On the difference between inorganic and organic soils, see Buckman and Brady, *The Nature and Properties of Soils*, pp. 7–17; Janick *et al.*, *Plant Science*, pp. 223–24.

That the soils of the low country are generally inorganic in nature, see Buckman and Brady, *The Nature and Properties of Soils*, pp. 293–354, especially p. 312 and Figure 12–5; *General Soil Map, South Carolina*, Soil Map 48 (Clemson, S.C.: South Carolina Agricultural Experiment Station, 1979); United States Department of Agriculture, *Soil Survey, Charleston County, South Carolina*; United States Department of Agriculture, *Soil Survey of Berkeley County, South Carolina*; United States Department of Agriculture, *Soil Survey of Beaufort and Jasper Counties, South Carolina*.

33. On the colors of the soils of the low country, see the *Soil Surveys* mentioned in footnote 32 above.

On the relationship between the color of a particular soil and its nature and properties, see Strahler, *Introduction to Physical Geography*, pp. 167–68. Note that the presence of source rocks such as sandstone or red shale can also account for the color red in a particular soil.

34. See William Hilton, *A Relation of a Discovery...* (London: Printed by J.C. for Simon Miller, 1664); Robert Horne (?), *A Brief Description of the Province of Carolina...* (London: Printed for Robert Horne, 1666); Samuel Wilson, *An Account of the Province of Carolina, in America...* (London: Printed by G. Larkin for Francis Smith, 1682); John Archdale, *A New Description of that Fertile and Pleasant Province of Carolina...* (London: Printed for John Wyat, 1707). All four of these accounts are reprinted in Salley, ed., *Narratives of Early Carolina 1650–1708*. For discussions of soil color, cover vegetation, and agricultural potential by these writers, see Salley, pp. 44, 68, 169–70, 290. Perhaps the best discussions of these matters appear, however, in Catesby, *The Natural History of Carolina, Florida, and the Bahama Islands...*, 2: iii–vi, and in Hewatt, *An Historical Account*, 1: 81. Also see Converse D. Clowse, *Economic Beginnings in Colonial South Carolina 1670–1730* (Columbia: University of South Carolina Press, 1971), p. 30.

35. On soil texture and structure, see, for example, Buckman and Brady, *The Nature and Properties of Soils*, pp. 41–66; Janick *et al.*, *Plant Science*, pp. 218–27.

36. On the textural classes, see Strahler, *Introduction to Physical Geography*, pp. 167–69; Buckman and Brady, *The Nature and Properties of Soils*, pp. 42–57; S.R. Eyre, *Vegetation and Soils: A World Picture* (Chicago: Aldine Publishing Company, 1963), pp. 26–29.

37. *General Soil Map, South Carolina*; United States Department of Agriculture, *Soil Survey, Charleston County, South Carolina*, pp. 1–32; United States Department of Agriculture, *Soil Survey of Berkeley County, South Carolina*, pp. 2–32; United States Department of Agriculture, *Soil Survey of Beaufort and Jasper Counties, South Carolina*, pp. 4–45.

38. On soil classification systems, see S.W. Buol, F.D. Hole, R.J. McCracken, *Soil Genesis and Classification*, 2d ed. (Ames: Iowa State University Press, 1980), pp. 180–224; United States Department of Agriculture, *Soil Taxonomy: A Basic System of Soil Classification for Making and Interpreting Soil Surveys*, United States Department of Agriculture Handbook 436 (Washington, D.C.: United States Government Printing Office, 1975), pas-

sim; Buckman and Brady, *The Nature and Properties of Soils*, pp. 293–377; Janick *et al.*, *Plant Science*, pp. 227–36; Strahler, *Introduction to Physical Geography*, pp. 177–91.

39. *General Soil Map, South Carolina*; United States Department of Agriculture, *Soil Survey, Charleston County, South Carolina*, pp. 70–72; United States Department of Agriculture, *Soil Survey of Berkeley County, South Carolina*, p. 92; United States Department of Agriculture, *Soil Survey of Beaufort and Jasper Counties, South Carolina*, p. 179; Buckman and Brady, *The Nature and Properties of Soils*, pp. 312, 318, and Figure 12–5; Strahler, *Introduction to Physical Geography*, pp. 180–85; Janick *et al.*, *Plant Science*, pp. 234.

Though it is true that in the classification system based upon soil morphology the low country is considered to be an area of Ultisols for the most part, other soils occur there as well. In Charleston County alone, for example, soils from six other orders occur, namely, Alfisols, Entisols, Histosols, Inceptisols, Mollisols, and Spodosols. See United States Department of Agriculture, *Soil Survey, Charleston County, South Carolina*, p. 71.

40. Buckman and Brady, *The Nature and Properties of Soils*, pp. 312, 318, and Figure 12–5; Janick *et al.*, *Plant Science*, pp. 234–35; Strahler, *Introduction to Physical Geography*, pp. 180–85 and Plates 2 and 3.

Note that the correlation above refers specifically to humid subtropical areas without distinct dry and rainy seasons, that is, only to those areas classified as "Caf" in the modified Köppen system.

41. See, for example, Harry Robinson, *Biogeography*, "Aspect" Geographies Series (London: Macdonald & Evans, 1972), pp. 205–26; Henry A. Gleason and Arthur Cronquist, *The Natural Geography of Plants* (New York: Columbia University Press, 1964), pp. 239–61; Pierre Dansereau, *Biogeography: An Ecological Perspective* (New York: The Ronald Press, 1957), pp. 81–101.

42. Robinson, *Biogeography*, pp. 236–37, 246–47; Eyre, *Vegetation and Soils*, pp. 62–64; Nicholas Polunin, *Introduction to Plant Geography and Some Related Sciences* (New York: McGraw-Hill, 1960), pp. 350–54; Strahler, *Introduction to Physical Geography*, pp. 213–14.

43. Note that the word "natural" is used cautiously. Today many cultural ecologists and ecological historians argue that habitat analyses should proceed under the following assumptions: (1) man is an integral part of nature rather than an alien intruder/despoiler; (2) ecological change is a perpetual rather than finite process. Obviously, under such assumptions many venerable functionalist concepts in biology—the notion of climax communities, for example—are called into question. See Cronon, *Changes in the Land*, pp. 3–15.

44. On the distribution of warm temperate rain forests on the earth, see Robinson, *Biogeography*, pp. 246–50; Polunin, *Introduction to Plant Geography*, pp. 350–54; Strahler, *Introduction to Physical Geography*, Plate 4.

45. On the low country's forests and other vegetation, see Robinson, *Biogeography*, pp. 236–37, 246–47; Barry, *Natural Vegetation of South Carolina*, pp. 120–91; Zingmark, ed., *An Annotated Checklist of the Biota of the Coastal Zone of South Carolina*, pp. 39–84 especially. On the resistance of pines to fire, see, for example, Charles F. Cooper, "The Ecology of Fire," *Scientific American* 204 (April 1961): 150–60; Barry, *Natural Vegetation of South Carolina*, p. 161.

On the low country's vegetation in the early modern period, see Ashe, *Carolina; or a Description of the Present State of that Country.* . . , passim; John Lawson, *History of North Carolina.* . . (Richmond, Va.: Garrett and Massie, 1937; originally published 1709), pp. 90–118; John Norris, *Profitable Advice for Rich and Poor.* . . (London: Printed by J. How, 1712), pp. 23, 44–45; Catesby, *The Natural History of Carolina, Florida, and the Bahama Islands.* . . , 2: xix–xxiii; Drayton, *A View of South-Carolina*, pp. 60–87; Ramsay,

The History of South-Carolina, 2: 302–5, 336–51; Mills, *Statistics of South Carolina*, pp. 66–100.

46. On the importance of the naval–stores industry in early South Carolina, see Clarence L. Ver Steeg, *Origins of a Southern Mosaic: Studies of Early Carolina and Georgia*, Mercer University Lamar Memorial Lectures, No. 17 (Athens: University of Georgia Press, 1975), pp. 103–32; Clowse, *Economic Beginnings*, passim; Lewis C. Gray, *History of Agriculture in the Southern United States to 1860*, 2 vols. (Gloucester, Mass.: Peter Smith, 1958; originally published 1933), 1: 151–57.

On the importance of Georgia-Pacific and Westvaco to the economy of the low country today, see South Carolina State Development Board, *Industrial Directory of South Carolina 1986* (Columbia, S.C.: South Carolina State Development Board, 1986), pp. G-19, G-20, G-25, G-27, G-35, G-37, G-44, G-81, G-82, G-111. According to the *Directory*, Georgia-Pacific employed 1,263 men and women in 1985 in that part of South Carolina between the coast and the city of Sumter, while Westvaco employed 1,998.

47. E.C. Pielou, *Biogeography* (New York: Wiley, 1979), pp. 4–14; Robinson, *Biogeography*, pp. 364–70.

48. Robinson, *Biogeography*, pp. 365–66; Wilma B. George, *Animal Geography* (London: Heinemann, 1962), p. 13.

49. Robinson, *Biogeography*, pp. 360–63, 364–410. On the evolution and radiation of mammals in particular, see John F. Eisenberg, *The Mammalian Radiations: An Analysis of Trends in Evolution, Adaptation, and Behavior* (Chicago: University of Chicago Press, 1981).

50. On the birds, fish, and invertebrates of the low country, see, for example, Zingmark, ed., *An Annotated Checklist of the Biota of the Coastal Zone of South Carolina*, pp. 85–235, 236–59, 277–95; William D. Anderson, Jr., "The Fishes of Some South Carolina Coastal Plain Streams" (Ph.D. dissertation, University of South Carolina, 1960); Robert G. Lutz, Jr., *Special Study of the Marine Fishery Resources of South Carolina*, South Carolina State Planning Board, Bulletin No. 14 (Columbia, S.C.: 1944), passim; Alexander Sprunt, Jr. and E. Burnham Chamberlain, *South Carolina Bird Life*, Contributions from the Charleston Museum, No. 11 (Columbia: University of South Carolina Press, 1949); Eloise F. Potter, James F. Parnell, and Robert P. Teulings, *Birds of the Carolinas* (Chapel Hill: University of North Carolina Press, 1980).

51. See Robinson, *Biogeography*, pp. 371–76; George Gaylord Simpson, *The Geography of Evolution* (Philadelphia: Chilton Books, 1965), pp. 105–15; Marion I. Newbigin, *Plant and Animal Geography* (London: Methuen & Company, 1936), pp. 248–52.

52. See Zingmark, ed., *An Annotated Checklist of the Biota of the Coastal Zone of South Carolina*, pp. 296–308. In addition to the thirty-nine native species of land mammals in the low country today, there are six non-native species which have been introduced. There are, one should note, about fifty-six species of land mammals in the entire state. See Zingmark, ed., p. 296; Eisenberg, *The Mammalian Radiations*, p. 219. Domestic animals have, of course, been excluded from consideration in the above discussion.

For listings and discussions of South Carolina's fauna in earlier periods, see, for example, Ashe, *Carolina; or a Description of the Present State of the Country...*; Wilson, *An Account of the Province of Carolina*; Lawson, *History of North Carolina*, pp. 90–172; Catesby, *The Natural History of Carolina, Florida, and the Bahama Islands...*, 2: xxiv–xxvii; Glen, *A Description of South Carolina*, pp. 68–69; Hewatt, *An Historical Account*, 1: 83–89; Drayton, *A View of South-Carolina*, pp. 87–91; Ramsay, *The History of South-Carolina*, 2: 332–36; Mills, *Statistics of South Carolina*, pp. 100–103. Also see Michael Tuomey, *Report on the Geology of South Carolina* (Columbia: A.S. Johnston for the State of South Carolina, 1848), pp. i–xxiv of Appendix; Harry Hammond, comp., *South*

Carolina: Resources and Population, Institutions and Industries (Charleston: Walker, Evans & Cogswell for the State Board of Agriculture of South Carolina, 1883), pp. 209–311.

53. Robinson, *Biogeography*, pp. 371–76; Newbigin, *Plant and Animal Geography*, pp. 243–46, 248–52; Zingmark, ed., *An Annotated Checklist of the Biota of the Coastal Zone of South Carolina*, pp. 260–76, 296–308. One should note, however, that some biologists deny that marsupials are less advanced than placental mammals. See, for example, Stephen Jay Gould, "Sticking up for Marsupials," in Gould, *The Panda's Thumb: More Reflections in Natural History* (New York: W.W. Norton & Company, 1982), pp. 289–95.

54. See, for example, Newbigin, *Plant and Animal Geography*, pp. 243–46, 248–52.

55. Robinson, *Biogeography*, pp. 371–76. To most biogeographers, one should note, South Carolina is classified within the Nearctic subregion of the Holarctic region of the Arctogean realm.

56. The belief that a causal relationship existed between climate and disease was, at least in part, an outgrowth of the classical theory of the Qualities, the Elements, and the Humours. On this theory, see, for example, Charles Singer and E. Ashworth Underwood, *A Short History of Medicine*, 2d ed. (New York: Oxford University Press, 1962), pp. 46–47. On other pre–modern etiological theories, see, for example, W. Harding Le Riche and Jean Milner, *Epidemiology as Medical Ecology* (Edinburgh: Churchill Livingstone, 1971), pp. 1–12. On the gradual decline of such theories in the United States, see Charles E. Rosenberg, "The Therapeutic Revolution: Medicine, Meaning, and Social Change in Nineteenth Century America," in Morris J. Vogel and Charles E. Rosenberg, eds., *The Therapeutic Revolution: Essays on the Social History of American Medicine* (Philadelphia: University of Pennsylvania Press, 1979), pp. 3–25.

On the "discovery" of the germ theory in the nineteenth century, see Singer and Underwood, *A Short History of Medicine*, pp. 326–41; Arturo Castiglioni, *A History of Medicine*, trans. and ed. E.B. Krumbhaar (New York: Jason Aronson, 1975; originally published 1940), pp. 803–18.

In recent years medical historians, epidemiologists, anthropologists, and sociologists have broadened our concept of disease pathology by stressing the interaction among agent, environment, and host rather than infectious agents alone. See, for example, Milton J. Rosenau and Kenneth F. Maxcy, *Preventive Medicine and Public Health*, ed. Philip E. Sartwell, 9th ed. (New York: Appleton-Century-Crofts, 1965), pp. 1–4 (hereinafter cited as Maxcy-Rosenau, *Preventive Medicine and Public Health*); Hugh Rodman Leavell and E. Gurney Clark, *Preventive Medicine for the Doctor in his Community: An Epidemiologic Approach*, 3d ed. (New York: McGraw-Hill Book Company, 1965), pp. 39–62; David Mechanic, *Medical Sociology: A Selective View* (New York: The Free Press, 1968), pp. 49–89; Andrew C. Twaddle and Richard M. Hessler, *A Sociology of Health* (St. Louis: Mosby, 1977), pp. 7–27.

On the social and cultural determinants of medicine and disease and changes in such determinants over time, see Illich, *Medical Nemesis*, pp. 110–18 especially; George Rosen, "Medicine as a Function of Society," in Lester S. King, ed., *Mainstreams of Medicine: Essays on the Social and Intellectual Context of Medical Practice* (Austin: Published for the University of Texas Medical School at San Antonio by the University of Texas Press, 1971), pp. 26–38; Walther Riese, *The Conception of Disease: its History, its Versions, and its Nature* (New York: The Philosophical Library, 1953).

The quote in the text above is from the English translation of the 1686 pamphlet *Remarques sur la "Nouvelle Relation de la Caroline," par un Gentilhomme François—MDCLXXXVI*, which appeared in *The Magnolia; or Southern Apalachian*, new series, 1 (October 1842): 226–30, especially p. 228. The original pamphlet is apparently no longer extant.

57. On the epidemiological devastation which resulted from the Old World's expansion into the New, see, for example, Philip D. Curtin, "Epidemiology and the Slave Trade," *Political Science Quarterly* 83 (June 1968): 190–216; Alfred W. Crosby, Jr., *The Columbian Exchange: Biological and Cultural Consequences of 1492* (Westport, Conn.: Greenwood Press, 1972), pp. 35–63; Peter H. Wood, *Black Majority: Negroes in Colonial South Carolina From 1670 through the Stono Rebellion* (New York: Knopf, 1974), pp. 63–91; William H. McNeill, *Plagues and Peoples* (Garden City, N.Y.: Anchor Press/Doubleday, 1976), pp. 199–234; Albert E. Cowdrey, *This Land, This South: An Environmental History* (Lexington: University Press of Kentucky, 1983), pp. 36–43; Crosby, *Ecological Imperialism: The Biological Expansion of Europe, 900–1900* (New York: Cambridge University Press, 1986), pp. 132–44, 195–216.

58. See the works mentioned in footnote 57 above. The classic reference work on historical epidemiology is August Hirsch, *Handbook of Geographical and Historical Pathology*, trans. from the 2d German ed. by Charles Creighton, 3 vols. (London: The New Sydenham Society, 1883–86). Also see Frank Macfarlane Burnet and David O. White, *Natural History of Infectious Disease*, 4th ed. (Cambridge: Cambridge University Press, 1972).

59. For a convenient summary of epidemiological regionalism, see Curtin, "Epidemiology and the Slave Trade." On this and related matters, see Le Riche and Milner, *Epidemiology as Medical Ecology*, passim; C.S. Elton, *The Ecology of Invasions by Animals and Plants* (London: Methuen, 1958).

60. McNeill, *Plagues and Peoples*, passim; Curtin, "Epidemiology and the Slave Trade"; Crosby, *The Columbian Exchange*, pp. 35–63; Crosby, "Virgin Soil Epidemics as a Factor in the Aboriginal Depopulation in America," *William and Mary Quarterly*, 3d series, 33 (April 1976): 289–99.

61. See, for example, Curtin, "Epidemiology and the Slave Trade"; McNeill, *Plagues and Peoples*, pp. 199–234.

62. Curtin, "Epidemiology and the Slave Trade." For an excellent discussion of these points with especial reference to malarial diseases, see Darrett B. Rutman and Anita H. Rutman, "Of Agues and Fevers: Malaria in the Early Chesapeake," *William and Mary Quarterly*, 3d series, 33 (January 1976): 31–60.

63. Curtin, "Epidemiology and the Slave Trade"; McNeill, *Plagues and Peoples*, pp. 77–198. On the degree of immunity possible to each of the diseases mentioned in the text above, see the relevant section on each of these diseases in Maxcy-Rosenau, *Preventive Medicine and Public Health*. That the effects of *Plasmodium vivax* infection were not always mild, see Mary Dobson, " 'Marsh Fever'—The Geography of Malaria in England," *Journal of Historical Geography* 6 (October 1980): 357–89.

64. Curtin, "Epidemiology and the Slave Trade"; Wood, *Black Majority*, pp. 76–91. On the characteristics of the tropical diseases mentioned in the text above, see the relevant sections in Oscar Felsenfeld, *The Epidemiology of Tropical Diseases* (Springfield, Ill.: Charles C. Thomas, 1966); A.R.D. Adams and B.G. Maegraith, *Clinical Tropical Diseases*, 4th ed. (Oxford: Blackwell Scientific Publications, 1966); Maxcy-Rosenau, *Preventive Medicine and Public Health*.

65. Crosby, *The Columbian Exchange*; Crosby, "Virgin Soil Epidemics"; McNeill, *Plagues and Peoples*, pp. 199–234.

One should note that Curtin explains the relative freedom of pre-Columbian populations from infectious diseases by pointing to the infrequency of human communication, while McNeill emphasizes the unimportance of animal domestication in Indian societies. See Curtin, "Epidemiology and the Slave Trade," pp. 200–201; McNeill, *Plagues and Peoples*, pp. 201–2.

The controversy surrounding the origins of venereal syphilis is summarized in Crosby, *The Columbian Exchange*, pp. 122–64. It is interesting to note that the English adventurer John Lawson was quite certain that syphilis originated in America whence it spread to the Old World. See Lawson, *History of North Carolina*, pp. 14–15.

66. Francisco Guerra, "The Influence of Disease on Race, Logistics and Colonization in the Antilles," *Journal of Tropical Medicine and Hygiene* 69 (February 1966): 23–35; Curtin, "Epidemiology and the Slave Trade"; Crosby, *The Columbian Exchange*, pp. 35–63; McNeill, *Plagues and Peoples*, pp. 199–234.

The hellish nature of life in one part of America in the sixteenth century—Guatemala—is poignantly rendered in the chronicles of the Cakchiquel Mayas, chronicles which still survive today. The following quotation, from a section on a devastating sixteenth-century epidemic, requires no further comment.

> Great was the stench of the dead. After our fathers and grandfathers succumbed, half of the people fled to the fields. The dogs and vultures devoured the bodies. The mortality was terrible. Your grandfathers died, and with them died the son of the king and his brothers and kinsmen. So it was that we became orphans, oh, my sons! So we became when we were young. All of us were thus. We were born to die!

See *The Annals of the Cakchiquels and Title of the Lords of Totonicapan*, trans. Adrian Recinos, Dioniscio Jose Chonay, and Delia Goetz (Norman: University of Oklahoma Press, 1953), p. 116.

67. Curtin, "Epidemiology and the Slave Trade"; McNeill, *Plagues and Peoples*, pp. 199–234.

68. See, for example, Herbert S. Klein, *The Middle Passage: Comparative Studies in the Atlantic Slave Trade* (Princeton: Princeton University Press, 1978), pp. 3–22, especially pp. 5–6; McNeill, *Plagues and Peoples*, pp. 199–234; Crosby, *The Columbian Exchange*, pp. 35–63; Curtin, "Epidemiology and the Slave Trade."

On the epidemiological devastation wreaked upon the Carib and Arawak groups of the Greater Antilles and lowlands of the Spanish Main, see J. Leitch Wright, Jr., *The Only Land They Knew: The Tragic Story of the American Indians in the Old South* (New York: The Free Press, 1981), pp. 31–32 especially; Wilbur R. Jacobs, "The Tip of an Iceberg: Pre-Columbian Indian Demography and Some Implications for Revisionism," *William and Mary Quarterly*, 3d series, 31 (January 1974): 123–32; Crosby, *The Columbian Exchange*, pp. 35–63; Sherburne F. Cook and Woodrow W. Borah, *Essays in Population History: Mexico and the Caribbean*, 3 vols. (Berkeley: University of California Press, 1971–79), 1: 376–410; Curtin, "Epidemiology and the Slave Trade," pp. 200–201 especially; Carl O. Sauer, *The Early Spanish Main* (Berkeley: University of California Press, 1966), passim.

On the devastation suffered by the Tupinambas in northeast Brazil, see, for example, John Hemming, *Red Gold: The Conquest of the Brazilian Indians* (London: Macmillan, 1978), pp. 139–46 especially; Alexander Marchant, *From Barter to Slavery: The Economic Relations of Portuguese and Indians in the Settlement of Brazil*, The Johns Hopkins University Studies in Historical and Political Science, Series 60, No. 1 (Baltimore: Johns Hopkins University Press, 1942), pp. 114–19.

On the devastation suffered by the Indians of the South Carolina low country, see Wright, *The Only Land They Knew*, pp. 27–52; Gene Waddell, *Indians of the South Carolina Lowcountry 1562–1751* (Spartanburg, S.C.: Published for the Southern Studies Program of the University of South Carolina by the Reprint Company, 1980), pp. 7–15.

On the meanings of the terms "Sudanese" and "Bantu," see, for example, Daniel C. Littlefield, *Rice and Slaves: Ethnicity and the Slave Trade in Colonial South Carolina* (Baton Rouge: Louisiana State University Press, 1981), pp. 24–25.

69. On smallpox reaching the Incas before Pizarro, see Henry F. Dobyns, "An Outline of Andean Epidemic History to 1720," *Bulletin of the History of Medicine* 37 (November–December 1963): 493–515; Crosby, *The Columbian Exchange*, pp. 47–63.

On the sickness and the slave revolt at San Miguel de Gualdape, see Paul Quattlebaum, *The Land Called Chicora: The Carolinas under Spanish Rule with French Intrusions 1520–1670* (Gainesville: University of Florida Press, 1956), pp. 26–27; Wood, *Black Majority*, pp. 3–4. That this sickness was probably malaria, see Gonzalo Fernandez de Oviedo y Valdés, *Historia general y natural de las Indias, isles, y tierra-firma del mar océano*, 4 vols. (Madrid: La Real Academia de la Historia, 1851–55), 3: 628–29; St. Julien Ravenel Childs, *Malaria and Colonization in the Carolina Low Country 1526–1696*, The Johns Hopkins University Studies in Historical and Political Science, Series 58, No. 1 (Baltimore: Johns Hopkins University Press, 1940), pp. 34–36.

70. Joseph I. Waring has compiled "a list of epidemics in South Carolina" for the period between 1670 and 1825. See Waring, *A History of Medicine in South Carolina 1670–1825* (Columbia: South Carolina Medical Association, 1964), pp. 371–72. Details on a number of these epidemics can be found in John Duffy, *Epidemics in Colonial America* (Baton Rouge: Louisiana State University Press, 1953), passim; Diane M. Sydenham, "Practitioner and Patient: The Practice of Medicine in Eighteenth-Century South Carolina" (Ph.D. dissertation, Johns Hopkins University, 1978), pp. 1–39.

A number of works by earlier writers also contain material on diseases and epidemics in South Carolina. See, for example, Milligen-Johnston, *A Short Description of the Province of South-Carolina*, pp. 43–71; Chalmers, *An Account of the Weather and Diseases of South Carolina*, passim; Drayton, *A View of South-Carolina*, pp. 27–30; Ramsay, *The History of South-Carolina*, 2: 76–105; Mills, *Statistics of South Carolina*, pp. 139–49.

71. See Waring, *A History of Medicine in South Carolina 1670–1825*, pp. 1–91; Wood, *Black Majority*, pp. 63–91; Duffy, *Epidemics in Colonial America*, passim.

On malaria in colonial South Carolina, see Childs, *Malaria and Colonization in the Carolina Low Country 1526–1696*, passim; Wood, *Black Majority*, pp. 63–91; Merrens and Terry, "Dying in Paradise: Malaria, Mortality and the Perceptual Environment in Colonial South Carolina."

On filariasis, see Todd L. Savitt, "Filariasis in the United States," *Journal of the History of Medicine and Allied Sciences* 32 (April 1977): 140–50, especially p. 142; Wood, *Black Majority*, p. 78; Waring, *A History of Medicine in South Carolina 1670–1825*, p. 19. On the disease itself, see Maxcy-Rosenau, *Preventive Medicine and Public Health*, pp. 350–55.

On yellow fever in colonial South Carolina, particularly in Charleston, see M. Foster Farley, *An Account of the History of Stranger's Fever in Charleston, 1699–1876* (Washington, D.C.: University Press of America, 1978), pp. 10–14, 34–58; Farley, "The Mighty Monarch of the South: Yellow Fever in Charleston and Savannah," *Georgia Review* 27 (Spring 1973): 56–70; Wood, *Black Majority*, pp. 63–91; John Duffy, "Yellow Fever in Colonial Charleston," *South Carolina Historical Magazine* 52 (October 1951): 189–97.

Two of the earliest medical studies ever published on yellow fever were in large part clinical descriptions of the epidemics of 1745 and 1748 in Charleston. See John Moultrie, Jr.'s Edinburgh dissertation *De Febre Maligna Biliosa Americae* (Edinburgh: 1749) and John Lining's *Description of the American Yellow Fever, Which Prevailed at Charleston...in...1748* (Philadelphia: Thomas Dobson, 1799).

Outbreaks of dengue fever occurred in the low country even in the nineteenth century. See, for example, Daniel Webb Plantation Book, July 1828; August 7, 1828, South Carolina Historical Society; John Ewing Bonneau to John C. Calhoun, August 8, 1828, in Robert L. Meriwether *et al.*, eds. *The Papers of John C. Calhoun*, 16 vols. thus far (Columbia: University of South Carolina Press, 1959–), 10: 410–11.

On dysentery, typhus, and typhoid fever in South Carolina, see Duffy, *Epidemics in Colonial America*, pp. 214–33. On these diseases in another part of the colonial South, see Carville V. Earle, "Environment, Disease, and Mortality in Early Virginia," in Thad W. Tate and David L. Ammerman, eds., *The Chesapeake in the Seventeenth Century: Essays on Anglo-American Society & Politics* (Chapel Hill: University of North Carolina Press, 1979), pp. 96–125.

72. The quote is from Robert Maule to the Secretary, February 18, 1715/6, Records of the Society for the Propagation of the Gospel, Letter Books, Series A, 1702–1737, 26 ms. vols., 11: 127–30, especially p. 128, Archives of the Society for the Propagation of the Gospel, London, England. I used the microfilm version of these records issued by Micro Methods, Ltd., of East Ardsley, Wakefield, Yorkshire, England in 1964.

73. On seasonal mortality for the white population, see George D. Terry, " 'Champaign Country': A Social History of an Eighteenth Century Lowcountry Parish in South Carolina, St. Johns Berkeley County" (Ph.D. dissertation, University of South Carolina, 1981), p. 93; Merrens and Terry, "Dying in Paradise: Malaria, Mortality and the Perceptual Environment in Colonial South Carolina." For data on the white population in Charleston specifically, see Appendix 1-A below.

Similar seasonal mortality patterns existed for the white population of the colonial Chesapeake. See Carville V. Earle, *The Evolution of a Tidewater Settlement System: All Hallow's Parish, Maryland, 1650–1783*, The University of Chicago, Department of Geography, Research Paper No. 170 (Chicago: University of Chicago, Department of Geography, 1975), p. 161; Darrett B. Rutman, Charles Wetherell, and Anita H. Rutman, "Rhythms of Life: Black and White Seasonality in the Early Chesapeake," *Journal of Interdisciplinary History* 11 (Summer 1980): 29–53.

On seasonal mortality for the black and Indian populations of the New World, see Barry W. Higman, *Slave Population and Economy in Jamaica, 1807–1834* (Cambridge: Cambridge University Press, 1976), pp. 129–33; Higman, *Slave Populations of the British Caribbean 1807–1834* (Baltimore: Johns Hopkins University Press, 1984), pp. 298–302, 336–39; Rutman, Wetherell, and Rutman, "Rhythms of Life." For data on white, black, and Indian seasonal mortality patterns in eighteenth–century Boston, see Appendix 1-A below. Note that many of the great Indian-killers of the early modern period, particularly smallpox and measles, were not associated with a specific time of year.

74. That the white population of the low country had difficulty sustaining itself naturally until the 1770s, see Terry, " 'Champaign Country,' " pp. 90–142; Merrens and Terry, "Dying in Paradise: Malaria, Mortality and the Perceptual Environment in Colonial South Carolina." My own data and those of Scott Wilds also support these findings.

Sustained natural increase among the white population of the low country was made even more difficult during the colonial period because of white emigration from the area. On this point, see Terry, " 'Champaign Country,' " pp. 105–18 especially; David R. Chesnutt, "South Carolina's Expansion into Colonial Georgia 1720–1765" (Ph.D. dissertation, University of Georgia, 1973), passim.

The three low-country parishes referred to in the text above are those of Christ Church, St. John's Berkeley, and St. Philip's Charleston. Terry has collected and analyzed the data for Christ Church and St. John's parishes, while Wilds and I have done the same for St. Philip's Charleston. Wilds, one should note, is working on an important dissertation at the University of Pennsylvania on the demographic history of early South Carolina.

75. Terry, " 'Champáign Country,' " pp. 92–93; Merrens and Terry, "Dying in Paradise: Malaria, Mortality and the Perceptual Environment in Colonial South Carolina."

Available data indicate that mortality levels in colonial South Carolina were higher than those in New England and England, indeed, higher even than in the Chesapeake and in

North Carolina. See, for example, Kenneth A. Lockridge, "The Population of Dedham, Massachusetts,1636–1736," *Economic History Review*, 2d series, 19 (1966): 318–44; Philip J. Greven, Jr., *Four Generations: Population, Land, and Family in Colonial Andover, Massachusetts* (Ithaca: Cornell University Press, 1970), passim; Susan L. Norton, "Population Growth in Colonial America: A Study of Ipswich, Massachusetts," *Population Studies* 25 (November 1971): 433–52; Maris A. Vinovskis, "Mortality Rates and Trends in Massachusetts Before 1860," *Journal of Economic History* 32 (March 1972): 184–213; Michael Drake, "An Elementary Exercise in Parish Register Demography," *Economic History Review*, 2d series, 14 (1962): 427–45; Peter Laslett and John Harrison, "Clayworth and Cogenhoe," in H.E. Bell and R.L. Ollard, eds., *Historical Essays 1600–1750 Presented to David Ogg* (London: Adam & Charles Black, 1963), pp. 157–84; E.A. Wrigley, "Mortality in Pre-Industrial England: The Example of Colyton, Devon, Over Three Centuries," *Daedalus* 97 (Spring 1968): 546–80; E.A. Wrigley and R.S. Schofield, *The Population History of England 1541–1871: A Reconstruction* (Cambridge: Harvard University Press, 1981), pp. 311–20; Lorena S. Walsh and Russell R. Menard, "Death in the Chesapeake: Two Life Tables for Men in Early Colonial Maryland," *Maryland Historical Magazine* 69 (Summer 1974): 211–27; Allan Lee Kulikoff, "Tobacco and Slaves: Population, Economy and Society in Eighteenth–Century Prince George's County, Maryland" (Ph.D. dissertation, Brandeis University, 1976), pp. 436–53 especially; Rutman and Rutman, "Of Agues and Fevers"; Daniel Blake Smith, "Mortality and Family in the Colonial Chesapeake," *Journal of Interdisciplinary History* 8 (Winter 1978): 403–27; James M. Gallman, "Mortality Among White Males: Colonial North Carolina," *Social Science History* 4 (Summer 1980): 295–316; Kulikoff, *Tobacco and Slaves: The Development of Southern Cultures in the Chesapeake, 1680–1800* (Chapel Hill: University of North Carolina Press, 1986), pp. 59–63.

One can, for example, compare the proportion of children dying before the age of twenty in New England, the Chesapeake, and South Carolina to get some idea of the differential mortality levels in these areas. The proportion is much higher in South Carolina than in either of the other areas. See Greven, *Four Generations*, pp. 188–90; Daniel Scott Smith, "The Demographic History of Colonial New England," *Journal of Economic History* 32 (March 1972): 165–83, especially p. 171; Kulikoff, "Tobacco and Slaves," p. 448; Smith, "Mortality and Family in the Colonial Chesapeake," pp. 411–14; Terry, " 'Champaign Country,' " pp. 92–93; Merrens and Terry, "Dying in Paradise: Malaria, Mortality and the Perceptual Environment in Colonial South Carolina." One should note that the data on Christ Church Parish compiled by Terry and Merrens may overstate mortality somewhat because measurements based upon known ages at death tend to inflate real mortality levels. On this problem, see Wrigley, "Mortality in Pre-Industrial England," pp. 561–62; Greven, *Four Generations*, p. 190, fn. 12. Greven's own mortality figures may, however, be inflated as well. See Vinovskis, "Mortality Rates and Trends in Massachusetts Before 1860," pp. 196–98.

Finally, one should note that in making the argument above I do not wish to imply that behavioral patterns played no role in shaping demographic experiences within each area: obviously, behavior affected morbidity and mortality levels to a degree, sometimes positively, sometimes negatively. On the differential demographic effects of human behavior in Georgia and the West Indies respectively, see, for example, Gerald L. Cates, " 'The Seasoning': Disease and Death Among the First Colonists of Georgia," *Georgia Historical Quarterly* 64 (Summer 1980): 146–58; Michael Craton, "Hobbesian or Panglossian? The Two Extremes of Slave Conditions in the British Caribbean, 1783 to 1834," *William and Mary Quarterly*, 3d ser., 35 (April 1978): 324–56.

76. See Terry, " 'Champaign Country,' " pp. 93–98; Merrens and Terry, "Dying in

Paradise: Malaria, Mortality and the Perceptual Environment in Colonial South Carolina." Note that the "one-third" figure in the text was calculated from data pertaining to the 1680–1720 and 1720–60 birth cohorts in the studies by Terry and Merrens cited above.

For comparative data from other areas, see the works cited in footnote 75.

77. See Appendix 1-D.

78. The figures cited in the text were compiled from data in A.S. Salley, Jr., ed., *Register of St. Philip's Parish, Charles Town, South Carolina, 1720–1758* (Charleston: Walker, Evans & Cogswell, 1904). I have slightly adjusted the raw data therein because of isolated instances of double-counting. For the yearly totals of baptisms, births, and burials in the St. Philip's Parish Register between 1720 and 1750, see Appendix 1-B. Note that my yearly totals differ from those of Frederick Dalcho. See Dalcho, *An Historical Account of the Protestant Episcopal Church in South Carolina*. . . (Charleston: E. Thayer, 1820), p. 242.

The problem of under-registration and related problems as well are discussed in Appendix 1-D, wherein I attempt a rough estimation of the crude death rate in St. Philip's Charleston between 1722 and 1732. One should note here, however, that the data *in* the register appear relatively reliable. Demographers frequently test the reliability of a set of vital records today by comparing the sex ratio of the births listed in the records with the known sex ratio of human populations at birth—102 to 108 males to 100 females. The sex ratio for the population listed in the birth section of the St. Philip's Register for the years between 1720 and 1750 is 98.56 to 100, a ratio which is quite close to the predicted ratio for a theoretical population under perfect reporting conditions. See George W. Barclay, *Techniques of Population Analysis* (New York: Wiley, 1958), p. 83; Smith, "Mortality and Family in the Colonial Chesapeake," pp. 406–7; Salley, ed., *Register of St. Philip's Parish*. . .*1720–1758.*

Finally, it should be noted that I have employed the technique of aggregative analysis rather than family reconstitution in this essay because I believe that the former technique is more suitable for early modern urban populations, populations composed largely of singles, transients, and broken families. On the problems associated with reconstitution, particularly in urban settings, see, for example, D.E.C. Eversley, "Exploitation of Anglican Parish Registers by Aggregative Analysis," in E. A. Wrigley, ed., *An Introduction to English Historical Demography: From the Sixteenth to the Nineteenth Century* (New York: Basic Books, 1966), pp. 44–95, especially pp. 44–45; Jacques Dupaquier, "Problèmes de représentativité dans les études fondées sur la reconstitution des familles," *Annales de Démographie Historique* (1972): 83–91; R.S. Schofield, "Representativeness and Family Reconstitution," *Annales de Démographie Historique* (1972): 121–25; Maris A. Vinovskis, "Recent Trends in American Historical Demography: Some Methodological and Conceptual Considerations," *Annual Review of Sociology* 4 (1978): 603–27.

79. Allan Sharlin, "Natural Decrease in Early Modern Cities: A Reconsideration," *Past and Present* 79 (May 1978): 126–38.

80. A comparison of the sex ratios of given populations is generally considered a good way to gauge the overall comparability of such populations, for the ratio is a crucial determinant of broader demographic patterns. Data on white sex ratios in early modern Barbados and South Carolina are sketchy. The extant data do indicate, however, that males predominated initially by wide margins in both colonies, with the sex ratio in each gradually evening out over time.

In Barbados the white sex ratio was 150 to 100 in 1676; by 1715 the ratio was virtually even, that is, 100.42 to 100. Available data suggest that the white sex ratio in South Carolina was also about 150 to 100 in the early years, that is, until 1720 or so, before gradually becoming more even. By 1790 the ratio was 109.6 to 100.

Data for Bridgetown and Charleston are generally consistent with these trends. Bridgetown's ratio, roughly 150 to 100 in the 1670s, had evened out by the early eighteenth century. Indeed, by 1715 women actually predominated in the parish of which the town was part. The sex ratio in Charleston was also heavily unbalanced in favor of males at first. The sex ratio of those persons listed in the burial records of the Parish of St. Philip's Charleston between 1720 and 1750 was, for example, 206.59 to 100 (1911 males, 925 females, 47 unspecified). The actual sex ratio in the town was not nearly so high, however, for the St. Philip's Parish Register includes figures for many transient males, particularly visiting sailors. The sex ratios of persons listed in the incomplete burial records of two other Charleston congregations in this period—the Circular Church and the Quaker Meeting—were much more even, 136 to 100 and 100 to 100 respectively. Data for these two churches, particularly those for the Circular Church, more accurately reflect the sex ratio of the permanent white population of Charleston, for neither church was involved in an important way in the burial of transients. It would appear from these data then that the white sex ratio in Charleston between 1720 and 1750 was somewhere between 136 and 207 to 100, with the average for the period as a whole probably around 150 to 100. Thus, it seems, the white sex ratios in Bridgetown in the seventeenth century and Charleston in the first half of the eighteenth century were roughly comparable. Other demographic data attest to the comparability of the population structures of these towns as well. For a further comparison of the white population structures of Bridgetown and Charleston—and a comparison of each with Bristol, Plymouth—see Appendix 1-C. The data used in the construction of the above sex ratios are from the following sources: Richard S. Dunn, *Sugar and Slaves: The Rise of the Planter Class in the English West Indies, 1624–1713* (Chapel Hill: University of North Carolina Press, 1972), pp. 325–34, especially p. 327; Patricia A. Molen, "Population and Social Patterns in Barbados in the Early Eighteenth Century," *William and Mary Quarterly*, 3d series, 28 (April 1971): 287–300, especially p. 293; Evarts B. Greene and Virginia D. Harrington, *American Population Before the Federal Census of 1790* (New York: Columbia University Press, 1932), pp. 172–79; Herbert Moller, "Sex Composition and Correlated Culture Patterns of Colonial America," *William and Mary Quarterly*, 3d series, 2 (April 1945): 113–53; Wood, *Black Majority*, pp. 164–65; Robert V. Wells, *The Population of the British Colonies in America before 1776: A Survey of Census Data* (Princeton: Princeton University Press, 1975), pp. 168–69, 243–45; Terry, " 'Champaign Country,' " p. 102; Salley, ed., *Register of St. Philip's Parish. . .1720–1758*; Mabel L. Webber, ed., "Register of the Independent or Congregational (Circular) Church, 1732–1738," *South Carolina Historical Magazine* 12 (1911): 27–37, 53–59, 135–40; Transactions of the Society of Friends in Charleston, South Carolina, 1719–1769, Society of Friends Collection, South Carolina Historical Society; United States Department of Commerce and Labor, Bureau of the Census, *Heads of Families at the First Census of the United States Taken in the Year 1790. South Carolina* (Washington, D.C.: U.S. Government Printing Office, 1908), p. 9.

81. Salley, ed., *Register of St. Philip's Parish. . .1720–1758*; Dunn, *Sugar and Slaves*, p. 328. Dunn's four to one ratio for Bridgetown was derived from a fifteen-year sample from the St. Michael's Parish Register. The following years were included in Dunn's sample: 1648–50, 1657–58, 1661–62, 1670, 1674, 1678–79, 1682, 1686, 1690, 1694. See *Sugar and Slaves*, p. 328, fn. 39.

Bridgetown's total population in 1680 was nearly 3000, with blacks comprising almost half of the total population. Charleston's population and the racial composition thereof around 1730 was amazingly similar. See Dunn, *Sugar and Slaves*, pp. 106–7; Governor James Moore, Jr., to Board of Trade, March 21, 1720/1, Records in the British Public Record Office Relating to South Carolina, 9: 22–23; Governor Robert Johnson to Board of Trade,

September 28, 1732, Records in the British Public Record Office Relating to South Carolina, 15: 229–34, especially p. 229, South Carolina Department of Archives and History. Also see Appendix 1-D.

On seventeenth-century Bridgetown, its size and its enlargement after the 1666 fire there, see Richard Ligon, *A True & Exact History of the Island of Barbadoes. . .* (London: Peter Parker, 1673), p. 25; Robert H. Schomburgk, *The History of Barbados* (London: Longman, Brown, Green, and Longmans, 1848), p. 241.

᾽ 82. The ratio for Boston was computed from data in G.B. Warden, *Boston 1689–1776* (Boston: Little, Brown, 1970), p. 347. The data on Charleston are, once again, derived from Salley, ed., *Register of St. Philip's Parish. . .1720–1758*. There are 965 births listed in this register for the years 1720 to 1750 and 2883 burials. See Appendix 1-B.

One should also note that the ratio of burials to births or baptisms was considerably higher in Charleston than in London in the early modern period. Compare, for example, the data for Charleston in the text above with those of D.V. Glass, "Notes on the Demography of London at the End of the Seventeenth Century," *Daedalus* 97 (Spring 1968): 581–92, especially p. 589; Thomas R. Forbes, "Births and Deaths in a London Parish: The Record from the Registers, 1654–1693 and 1729–1743," *Bulletin of the History of Medicine* 55 (Fall 1981): 371–91: Wrigley and Schofield, *The Population History of England*, p. 167.

Finally, to get some idea of the drastic demographic difference between a "sickly" southern port and a "healthy" New England village, compare the burial/birth ratio for St. Philip's Charleston with that computed for Andover, Massachusetts, by Greven. Births *always* outnumbered burials by a very wide margin in Andover. See Greven, *Four Generations*, p. 180.

83. On the sex ratio in Massachusetts in general and Boston in particular during the colonial period, see Moller, "Sex Composition and Correlated Culture Patterns of Colonial America,"; Wells, *The Population of the British Colonies in America Before 1776*, pp. 85–86; Allan Kulikoff, "The Progress of Inequality in Revolutionary Boston," *William and Mary Quarterly*, 3d series, 28 (July 1971): 375–412, especially p. 378, fn. 7.

On differential regional mortality patterns in English America, see, for example, Walsh and Menard, "Death in the Chesapeake," pp. 223–24 especially; Smith, "Mortality and Family in the Colonial Chesapeake," pp. 416–18 especially; Robert W. Fogel, Stanley Engerman, *et al.*, "The Economics of Mortality in North America, 1650–1910: A Description of a Research Project," *Historical Methods* 11 (Spring 1978): 75–108; Gallman, "Mortality Among White Males," p. 306 especially; Jim Potter, "Demographic Development and Family Structure," in Jack P. Greene and J.R. Pole, eds., *Colonial British America: Essays in the New History of the Early Modern Era* (Baltimore: Johns Hopkins University Press, 1984), pp. 123–56.

84. On the tremendous mortality levels for whites in the West Indies during the early modern period, see Curtin, "Epidemiology and the Slave Trade"; Guerra, "The Influence of Disease on Race, Logistics and Colonization in the Antilles"; Dunn, *Sugar and Slaves*, pp. 300–334.

It is interesting to note that despite the Indies' well-earned reputation for high mortality for whites, the burial/baptism ratio for whites on the island of Barbados between 1710 and 1780 was almost equal, that is, 1.03 to 1. Presumably, such a ratio was due largely to the sex and age-structures of the white population on the island during this period. Moreover, it is also interesting to note, given the prominence of malaria in South Carolina's early history, that this disease did not visit Barbados until 1927. The burial/baptism ratio referred to here was computed from data in Frank Wesley Pitman, *The Development of the British West Indies 1700–1763* (New Haven: Yale University Press, 1917), p. 385. On the sex and

age-structures of the white population of Barbados in the eighteenth century, see Molen, "Population and Social Patterns in Barbados." That malaria did not strike until 1927, see L. Schuyler Fonaroff, "Did Barbados Import its Malaria Epidemic?," *Journal of the Barbados Museum and Historical Society* 34 (March 1973): 122–30. Note that Gary M. Puckrein recently has challenged the argument that white mortality levels were high in Barbados in the early modern period. See Puckrein, *Little England: Plantation Society and Anglo-Barbadian Politics, 1627–1700* (New York: New York University Press, 1984), pp. 181–94, 220–22.

On Anglican missionaries in South Carolina requesting transfers to the West Indies for reasons of health, see, for example, Francis Le Jau to David Humphreys, January 3, 1716/7, in Frank J. Klingberg, ed., *The Carolina Chronicle of Dr. Francis Le Jau 1706–1717*, University of California Publications in History, vol. 53 (Berkeley: University of California Press, 1956), pp. 191–94, especially pp. 193–94; William Guy to the Secretary, March 20, 1730/1, Records of the Society for the Propagation of the Gospel, Letter Books, Series A, 23: 232–34; Brian Hunt to the Secretary, November 24, 1726, Records of the Society for the Propagation of the Gospel, Letter Books, Series B, 4: no. 215, Archives of the Society for the Propagation of the Gospel. Note that Hunt wanted the transfer for reasons of wealth as much as health.

Finally, one should note that though mortality rates declined in the low country in the late eighteenth and early nineteenth centuries, the area remained highly mortal to the white population. See Ramsay, *The History of South-Carolina*, 2: 546, 593; Samuel Blodgett, *Economica: A Statistical Manual for the United States of America* (Washington, D.C.: Printed for the Author, 1806), p. 76; Mark D. Kaplanoff, "Making the South Solid: Politics and the Structure of Society in South Carolina, 1790–1815" (Ph.D. dissertation, University of Cambridge, 1979), pp. 29–31, 299–304.

85. That few black slaves in the South Carolina low country were Christianized during the colonial period, see Wood, *Black Majority*, pp. 133–42, especially pp. 141–42; Philip D. Morgan, "The Development of Slave Culture in Eighteenth Century Plantation America" (Ph.D. dissertation, University College London, 1977), pp. 374–426, especially p. 408; John Scott Strickland, "Across Space and Time: Conversion, Community, and Cultural Change Among South Carolina Slaves" (Ph.D. dissertation, University of North Carolina at Chapel Hill, 1985), pp. 56–71, 163. The letters of Anglican missionaries in eighteenth-century South Carolina testify amply to this failure to convert blacks to Christianity. See, for example, Thomas Hasell to the Secretary, August 1, 1719, Records of the Society for the Propagation of the Gospel, Letter Books, Series A, 13: 239–41; Benjamin Pownall to the Secretary, October 24, 1723, Records of the Society for the Propagation of the Gospel, Letter Books, Series A, 17: 108; Richard Ludlam to the Secretary, December 12, 1727, Records of the Society for the Propagation of the Gospel, Letter Books, Series A, 20: 98–104, especially p. 101; William Guy to the Secretary, January 22, 1727–8, Records of the Society for the Propagation of the Gospel, Letter Books, Series A, 20: 110–15, especially p. 114; Brian Hunt to the Secretary, May 6, 1728, Records of the Society for the Propagation of the Gospel, Letter Books, Series A, 21: 97–104, especially p. 102, Archives of the Society for the Propagation of the Gospel.

86. On the failure of South Carolina's black slave population to increase naturally from about 1730 until the 1760s, see Morgan, "The Development of Slave Culture," pp. 282–328, especially pp. 284–88. Peter Wood implies the same. See *Black Majority*, pp. 159–66.

On the demographic patterns of the black slave populations in the colonial Chesapeake and the rates of natural increase of such populations in the eighteenth century, see Russell R. Menard, "The Maryland Slave Population, 1658 to 1730: A Demographic Profile of Blacks in

Four Counties," *William and Mary Quarterly*, 3d series, 32 (January 1975): 29–54; Morgan, "The Development of Slave Culture," pp. 282–328; Allan Kulikoff, "A 'Prolifick' People: Black Population Growth in the Chesapeake Colonies, 1700–1790," *Southern Studies* 16 (Winter 1977): 391–428; Kulikoff, *Tobacco and Slaves*, pp. 64–76.

That the distinguishing feature of North American slavery was natural increase among the enslaved, see Philip D. Curtin, *The Atlantic Slave Trade: A Census* (Madison: University of Wisconsin Press, 1969), pp. 72–75, 86–93; Robert William Fogel and Stanley L. Engerman, *Time on the Cross*, 2 vols. (Boston: Little, Brown, 1974), 1: 20–29.

87. These factors were, of course, interrelated, and most scholars obviously emphasize some sort of combination of factors in their explanations of natural decrease in particular slave populations in the New World. See, for example, Menard, "The Maryland Slave Population, 1658 to 1730"; Wood, *Black Majority*, pp. 159–66 especially; Higman, *Slave Population and Economy in Jamaica, 1807–1834*, pp. 45–138; Stanley L. Engerman, "Some Economic and Demographic Comparisons of Slavery in the United States and the British West Indies," *Economic History Review*, 2d series, 29 (1976): 258–75; Morgan, "The Development of Slave Culture," pp. 282–328; Kulikoff, "A 'Prolifick' People"; Jeffrey P. Koplan, "Slave Mortality in Nineteenth-Century Grenada," *Social Science History* 7 (Summer 1983): 311–20; Higman, *Slave Populations of the British Caribbean 1807–1834*, pp. 303–78; Richard B. Sheridan, *Doctors and Slaves: A Medical and Demographic History of Slavery in the British West Indies, 1680–1834* (Cambridge: Cambridge University Press, 1985), pp. 127–248; Kulikoff, *Tobacco and Slaves*, pp. 64–76. Also see the entire Winter 1986 issue of *Social Science History*, which is entitled "The Biological Past of the Black."

Certain causative factors are, however, generally associated with particular scholars and such associations should be pointed out. On lactation practices and their possible implications, see Herbert S. Klein and Stanley L. Engerman, "Fertility Differentials between Slaves in the United States and the British West Indies: A Note on Lactation Practices and Their Possible Implications," *William and Mary Quarterly*, 3d series, 35 (April 1978): 357–74. On diet deficiencies and diet deficiencies in relation to amenorrhea, sterility, and abortion, see H. Orlando Patterson, *The Sociology of Slavery: An Analysis of the Origins, Development and Structure of Negro Slave Society in Jamaica* (Rutherford, N.J.: Fairleigh Dickinson University Press, 1969; originally published 1967), pp. 100–112; Richard S. Dunn, "A Tale of Two Plantations: Slave Life at Mesopotamia in Jamaica and Mount Airy in Virginia, 1799 to 1828," *William and Mary Quarterly*, 3d series, 34 (January 1977): 32–65, especially p. 62; Kenneth F. Kiple and Virginia H. Kiple, "Deficiency Diseases in the Caribbean," *Journal of Interdisciplinary History* 11 (Autumn 1980): 197–215; Kenneth F. Kiple and Virginia H. King, *Another Dimension to the Black Diaspora: Diet, Disease, and Racism* (New York: Cambridge University Press, 1981), passim; Kenneth F. Kiple, *The Caribbean Slave: A Biological History* (New York: Cambridge University Press, 1984).

88. See Peter A. Coclanis, "Rice Prices in the 1720s and the Evolution of the South Carolina Economy," *Journal of Southern History* 48 (November 1982): 531–44.

89. That roughly two-thirds of the African slaves imported into the New World were male is generally accepted. That this ratio prevailed in South Carolina specifically, see Robert Pringle to Edward Pare, May 5, 1744, in Walter B. Edgar, ed., *The Letterbook of Robert Pringle*, 2 vols. (Columbia: University of South Carolina Press, 1972), 2: 683–85, especially p. 684; Henry Laurens to Smith & Clifton, July 17, 1755, in Philip M. Hamer, George C. Rogers, Jr., *et al.*, eds., *The Papers of Henry Laurens*, 10 vols. thus far (Columbia: University of South Carolina Press, 1968–), 1: 294–95; Henry Laurens to Valentine Powell, November 9, 1756, in Hamer, Rogers, *et al.*, eds., *The Papers of Henry*

Laurens, 2: 347–48; Henry Laurens to Gidney Clarke, November 20, 1756, in Hamer, Rogers, *et al.*, eds., *The Papers of Henry Laurens*, 2: 356–57. For additional corroboration, see Wood, *Black Majority*, pp. 154–55; Littlefield, *Rice and Slaves*, pp. 58–59.

On the strong possibility that fertility was lower for African-born women than for creoles because of differences in lactation practices, see Klein and Engerman, "Fertility Differentials between Slaves in the United States and the British West Indies." That differences in the age-structures of the African-born and creole populations also helped explain differences in aggregate fertility between these groups, see Menard, "The Maryland Slave Population, 1658 to 1730," pp. 47–48 especially; Kulikoff, "Tobacco and Slaves," pp. 61–94. It should be pointed out, however, that Jack Eblen has argued that the generally accepted belief that fertility rates for African immigrants were lower than the rates for creoles is partially incorrect. See Jack B. Eblen, "On the Natural Increase of Slave Populations: The Example of the Cuban Black Population, 1775–1900," in Stanley L. Engerman and Eugene D. Genovese, eds., *Race and Slavery in the Western Hemisphere: Quantitative Studies* (Princeton: Princeton University Press, 1975), pp. 211–47.

Note that the decline in aggregate fertility mentioned in the text above occurred despite the fact that fertility among creole slaves was apparently high. See Terry, " 'Champaign Country,' " pp. 147–50; Cheryll Ann Cody, "A Note on Changing Patterns of Slave Fertility in the South Carolina Rice District, 1735–1865," *Southern Studies* 16 (Winter 1977): 457–63; Cody, "Slave Fertility and Family Formation and Ball Family Slaves, 1710–1865," unpublished paper, 1978.

90. On the relationship among immunities, disease environments, and mortality levels, see Curtin, "Epidemiology and the Slave Trade."

That one-third of all African immigrants would die within three years in the New World, see J. Harry Bennett, Jr., *Bondsmen and Bishops: Slavery and Apprenticeship on the Codrington Plantations of Barbados, 1710–1838*, University of California Publications in History, vol. 62 (Berkeley: University of California Press, 1958), pp. 54, 58–61; Michael Craton, "Jamaican Slave Mortality: Fresh Light from Worthy Park, Longville and the Tharp Estates," *Journal of Caribbean History* 3 (November 1971): 1–27; Craton, *Sinews of Empire: A Short History of British Slavery* (Garden City, N.Y.: Anchor Press/Doubleday, 1974), pp. 194–95; Kulikoff, "A 'Prolifick' People," pp. 396–98 especially; Kulikoff, *Tobacco and Slaves*, pp. 67–69.

91. That death rates were higher for African-born slaves than for creoles even after the "seasoning" process allegedly ended, see Curtin, "Epidemiology and the Slave Trade"; Craton, *Sinews of Empire*, pp. 194–95; Higman, *Slave Population and Economy in Jamaica, 1807–1834*, pp. 105–15; Kulikoff, "A 'Prolifick' People"; Higman, *Slave Populations of the British Caribbean 1807–1834*, pp. 322–24. One should also note that Fogel and Engerman assume that the death rate for African-born slaves was considerably higher than that for creoles during the Africans' first decade in America. See *Time on the Cross*, 2:32. Philip Morgan utilizes the same assumption in his work on slavery in the eighteenth-century South. See "The Development of Slave Culture," pp. 301–2 especially.

92. On the transition to rice in eighteenth-century South Carolina, see Ver Steeg, *Origins of a Southern Mosaic*, pp. 103–32; Coclanis, "Rice Prices in the 1720s and the Evolution of the South Carolina Economy"; Lawrence S. Rowland, "Eighteenth Century Beaufort: A Study of South Carolina's Southern Parishes to 1800" (Ph.D. dissertation, University of South Carolina, 1978), pp. 81–102, 123–30.

On differential occupational mortality rates for slaves in the West Indies, see Higman, *Slave Population and Economy in Jamaica, 1807–1834*, pp. 121–25 especially; Craton, "Hobbesian or Panglossian?"; Higman, *Slave Populations of the British Caribbean 1807–1834*, pp. 324–31.

That natural decrease among the black slave population in South Carolina occurred precisely during the decades when the African-born percentage of the total slave population was greatest and during the period in which rice was cultivated primarily in inland swamps, see Morgan, "The Development of Slave Culture," pp. 284–86, 301–2; Gray, *History of Agriculture*, 1: 279–80; Clowse, *Economic Beginnings*, pp. 125–27; David L. Coon, "The Development of Market Agriculture in South Carolina, 1670–1785" (Ph.D. dissertation, University of Illinois, 1972), pp. 178–84 especially.

Note that while a number of subgenera, species, and subspecies of the mosquito genus *Anopheles* occur in the United States, the mosquito which apparently was most responsible for malaria (both *P. vivax* and *P. falciparum*) in colonial South Carolina—*Anopheles quadrimaculatus*—breeds in fresh water and has a very limited flight range. The cultivation of rice in inland swamps, that is, in fresh-water swamps, would thus expose those who worked and lived nearby to a most dangerous vector indeed. See Wood, *Black Majority*, pp. 70–91; Martin D. Young, Newton F. Hardman, *et al.*, "The Infectivity of Native Malarias in South Carolina to *Anopheles quadrimaculatus*," *American Journal of Tropical Medicine* 28 (March 1948): 303–11; Rutman and Rutman, "Of Agues and Fevers"; Maxcy-Rosenau, *Preventive Medicine and Public Health*, pp. 332–41. One should note, however, that in the 1760s South Carolinians began to make certain changes in their behavioral patterns and living arrangements that in time rendered them less susceptible to the attacks of mosquitos. See Merrens and Terry, "Dying in Paradise: Malaria, Mortality and the Perceptual Environment in Colonial South Carolina"; Wood, *Black Majority*, pp. 74–76.

93. On natural decrease in Brazil and the Greater Antilles, see, for example, Curtin, "Epidemiology and the Slave Trade"; Dunn, *Sugar and Slaves*, pp. 313–25; Franklin W. Knight, *The African Dimension in Latin American Societies* (New York: Macmillan, 1974), pp. 46–48 especially.

On natural decrease in the black slave population in the seventeenth-century Chesapeake, see Menard, "The Maryland Slave Population, 1658–1730"; Kulikoff, "A 'Prolifick' People."

94. For corroboration of this point, see United States Department of Commerce, Bureau of the Census, *Historical Statistics of the United States: Colonial Times to 1970*, 2 vols. (Washington, D.C.: United States Government Printing Office, 1975), 2: 1168; United States Department of Commerce and Labor, Bureau of the Census, *Heads of Families at the First Census of the United States Taken in the Year 1790. South Carolina*, p. 9. In the former source, one should note, only figures up to 1750 should be used, for the population of the "backcountry" began to assume significant proportions after that date. In the latter source, figures for Beaufort District, Charleston District, and Georgetown District only should be used, for these three districts essentially comprised the entire low country. Also see Chapter 3 of this study.

95. Some idea of this desolation, however, can be gained from the Mayan *Book of Chilam Balam of Chumayel*. Commenting on his people in the period before the Conquest, an Indian from Yucatan wrote:

> There was then no sickness; they had no aching bones; they had then no high fever; they had then no smallpox; they had then no burning chest; they had then no abdominal pain; they had then no consumption; they had then no headache. At that time the course of humanity was orderly. The foreigners made it otherwise when they arrived here.

See *The Book of Chilam Balam of Chumayel*, trans. and ed. Ralph L. Roys (Washington, D.C.: Carnegie Institution of Washington, 1933), p. 83. Also see Alfred Crosby's comments on this quotation in *The Columbian Exchange*, pp. 36–37 ff.

96. The controversy surrounding the question of the Indian population of pre–Columbian

America is outlined and summarized in a number of works. See, for example, Henry F. Dobyns, "Estimating Aboriginal American Population: An Appraisal of Techniques with a New Hemispheric Estimate," *Current Anthropology* 7 (October 1966): 395–416; Jacobs, "The Tip of an Iceberg"; Francis Jennings, *The Invasion of America: Indians, Colonialism, and the Cant of Conquest* (Chapel Hill: University of North Carolina Press, 1975), pp. 15–31; Douglas H. Ubelaker, "Prehistoric New World Population Size: Historical Review and Current Appraisal of North American Estimates," *American Journal of Physical Anthropology* 45 (November 1976): 661–65; Wright, *The Only Land They Knew*, pp. 22–26; Dobyns, *Their Number Become Thinned: Native American Population Dynamics in Eastern North America* (Knoxville: University of Tennessee Press, 1983); Daniel K. Richter, review of Dobyns, *Their Number Become Thinned*, in the *William and Mary Quarterly*, 3d ser., 41 (October 1984): 649–53. On this and other questions in Indian demographic history, see Henry F. Dobyns, *Native American Historical Demography: A Critical Bibliography*, The Newberry Library Center for the History of the American Indian Bibliographical Series (Bloomington: Indiana University Press, 1976).

97. The 8 million figure is from Alfred L. Kroeber, the 113 million figure from Henry F. Dobyns. Similarly, the 900,000 figure is from Kroeber, the 18 million figure from Dobyns. See Kroeber, *Cultural and Natural Areas of Native North America*, University of California Publications in American Archaeology and Ethnology, vol. 38 (Berkeley: University of California Press, 1939), pp. 131–81, especially p. 166; Dobyns, "Estimating Aboriginal American Population," pp. 414–15; Dobyns, *Their Number Become Thinned*, p. 42.

98. The 2.2 million figure—actually 2,171,125—is from Ubelaker, "Prehistoric New World Population Size," p. 664. Ubelaker's figures come from data in the articles submitted by the various scholars involved in the Smithsonian Institution's ongoing *Handbook of North American Indians* project. The volume on the Southeastern Indians, one should note, is not due to appear for several years.

On the various approaches employed in estimating the size of prehistoric populations, see, for example Robert M. Schact, "Estimating Past Population Trends," *Annual Review of Anthropology* 10 (1981): 119–40.

On the virtual disappearance by 1770 of the chiefdoms and tribes of the low country, see Chapman J. Milling, *Red Carolinians* (Chapel Hill: University of North Carolina Press, 1940), pp. 35–64, 203–30; Waddell, *Indians of the South Carolina Lowcountry*, pp. 7–15. The nineteen indigenous chiefdoms and tribes of the low country were: the Hoya, Witcheaugh, Escamacu, Wimbee, Touppa, Mayon, Stalame, Combahee, Kussah, Ashepoo, Edisto, Bohicket, Stono, Kiawah, Kussoe, Etiwan, Wando, Sampa, and Sewee. On these groups, their characteristics, and their locations, see Waddell, *Indians of the South Carolina Lowcountry*, passim. Note that Waddell, unlike earlier writers like John R. Swanton, argues that these chiefdoms and tribes were each autonomous rather than allied in any permanent confederation such as that labeled the "Cusabo." See Waddell, pp. 16–22, 368–69; John R. Swanton, *The Indians of the Southeastern United States*, Smithsonian Institution Bureau of American Ethnology, Bulletin 137 (Washington, D.C.: United States Government Printing Office, 1946), pp. 128–29.

99. William Bull to the Earl of Hillsborough, November 30, 1770, Records in the British Public Record Office Relating to South Carolina, 32: 365–406, especially p. 403, South Carolina Department of Archives and History.

100. See, for example, Wright, *The Only Land They Knew*, pp. 27–52, 102–50; Waddell, *Indians of the South Carolina Lowcountry*, pp. 8–15; Charles Hudson, *The Southeastern Indians* (Knoxville: University of Tennessee Press, 1976), pp. 427–43; Milling, *Red Carolinians*, pp. 51–64, 203–30.

101. On the drastic reduction in Indian population in the Greater Antilles, the central highlands of Mexico, and the highlands of Peru in the first half of the sixteenth century, see, for example, Crosby, *The Columbian Exchange*, pp. 35–63; McNeill, *Plagues and Peoples*, pp. 199–234; Sherburne F. Cook and Woodrow Borah, *The Indian Population of Central Mexico 1531–1610*, Ibero-Americana: 44 (Berkeley: University of California Press, 1960), passim; Alfred Métraux, *The History of the Incas*, trans. George Ordish (New York: Random House, 1969; originally published 1961), pp. 164–66 especially. One should note that Métraux attributes the population decline rather more to Spanish abuses than to epidemic diseases. See p. 166.

On the drop in Indian population in the Southeast in the first half of the sixteenth century, see, for example, Wright, *The Only Land They Knew*, pp. 27–52.

102. The figures for the Indian population of the low country cited in the text above are from Waddell, *Indians of the South Carolina Lowcountry*, pp. 8–15.

On the Indian population of the low country today, see State of South Carolina Budget and Control Board, *South Carolina Statistical Abstract 1985* (Columbia: South Carolina Division of Research and Statistical Services, 1986), p. 349.

103. Historians have only recently begun to appreciate the importance of the Indians' role in the development of early American society. Similarly, they have only recently begun to understand that the destinies of red, white, and black alike were interconnected, indeed, hopelessly intertwined. For an excellent discussion of recent trends in the literature on intercultural relations in early America, see James Axtell, "The Ethnohistory of Early America: A Review Essay," *William and Mary Quarterly*, 3d series, 35 (January 1978): 110–44. For a pioneering attempt to place such relations in a comparative context, see the essays in Howard Lamar and Leonard Thompson, eds., *The Frontier in History: North America and South Africa Compared* (New Haven: Yale University Press, 1981).

104. On the Mississippian tradition in the Southeast and the extent to which the Indians of the low country partook of this tradition, see James B. Griffin, "Eastern North American Archaeology: A Summary," *Science* 156 (April 14, 1967): 175–91; Leland G. Ferguson, "South Appalachian Mississippian" (Ph.D. dissertation, University of North Carolina, 1971), pp. 1–12, 242–65 especially; Hudson, *The Southeastern Indians*, pp. 14–20, 77–97; Wright, *The Only Land They Knew*, pp. 1–26.

Chapter 3. The Economic Rise of the South Carolina Low Country

1. See Mons. Chateaufort, Memoire sur la Caroline et le Commerce de la France, avec le Sud de Treize Etats unie, Premier Aoust 1786, p. 9, South Caroliniana Library, University of South Carolina, Columbia S.C.

In order to establish the location of Peyre's home in French Santee and to plot out the route from there to Charleston, I used the following sources: Will, Samuel Peyre, August 18, 1758, Records of the Secretary of the Province, Will Book 1757–1760, p. 121, South Carolina Department of Archives and History, Columbia, S.C.; Samuel Dubose and Frederick A. Porcher, *History of the Huguenots of South Carolina* (New York: The Knickerbocker Press for T. Gaillard Thomas, 1887; reprint ed., Columbia, S.C.: The R.L. Bryan Co., 1972), pp. 55–57; Arthur H. Hirsch, *The Huguenots of Colonial South Carolina* (Durham: Duke University Press, 1928), pp. 26–27; Henry Mouzon, Jr., *A Map of the Parish of St. Stephen, in Craven County* . . . (London: John Lodge, c. 1773); James Cook, *A Map of the Province of South Carolina* . . . (Cornhill, England: H. Parker, 1773); Robert Mills, *Atlas of the State of South Carolina* (Baltimore: F. Lucas, Jr., 1825; reprint ed., Easley, S.C.: Southern Historical Press, 1980), map of Charleston District; George

D. Terry, "'Champaign Country': A Social History of an Eighteenth Century Lowcountry Parish in South Carolina, St. Johns Berkeley County" (Ph.D. dissertation, University of South Carolina, 1981), pp. 18, 176–242.

2. Daybook, Samuel Peyre, Peyre-Porcher Papers, South Carolina Historical Society, Charleston, S.C.

3. See, for example, Converse D. Clowse, *Economic Beginnings in Colonial South Carolina 1670–1730* (Columbia: University of South Carolina Press, 1971); Peter H. Wood, *Black Majority: Negroes in Colonial South Carolina from 1670 through the Stono Rebellion* (New York: Knopf, 1974); Clarence L. Ver Steeg, *Origins of a Southern Mosaic: Studies of Early Carolina and Georgia,* Mercer University Lamar Memorial Lectures, No. 17 (Athens: University of Georgia Press, 1975), pp. 103–32, 145–48.

4. On early arguments for capitalism, particularly those stressing the "innocence" related thereto, see Albert O. Hirschman, *The Passions and the Interests: Political Arguments for Capitalism before Its Triumph* (Princeton: Princeton University Press, 1977), pp. 56–66 and passim.

5. V. I. Lenin, *Imperialism, The Highest Stage of Capitalism: A Popular Outline* (New York: International Publishers, 1939; originally published in 1917), p. 9. Note that this quotation does not appear in the 1917 Russian edition of *Imperialism*. It first appeared in 1921 in the "Preface" to the German and French editions of this work.

6. Gabriel García Márquez, *The Autumn of the Patriarch,* trans. Gregory Rabassa (New York: Harper & Row, 1976; originally published 1975), p. 159. Similar sentiments can be found in the work of the great Paraguayan novelist Augusto Roa Bastos. See, for example, *I, the Supreme,* trans. Helen Lane (New York: Knopf, 1986; originally published 1974), pp. 31–32.

7. The term *mentalité* refers to the particular set of mind, the consciousness, as it were, that informed the thought and behavior of a given group of people at a specific time. The term is generally associated with the *Annales* school of French historians, but recently has been used with reference to early America by James A. Henretta. See Henretta, "Families and Farms: *Mentalité* in Pre-Industrial America," *William and Mary Quarterly,* 3d series, 35 (January 1978): 3–32.

Note that in this study I use the term "hegemonists" to denote those that possessed and exercised preponderant influence, power, and authority in or over the low country. I do not wish to imply that the world view of these individuals—or this class of individuals, if you will—was accepted and deemed legitimate by every white inhabitant of the low country, much less by the area's blacks.

8. Countless scholars have accepted the traditional/modern dichotomy. For theoretical formulations of the dichotomy, see Ferdinand Tönnies, *Community and Society,* ed. and trans. Charles P. Loomis (East Lansing: Michigan State University Press, 1957; originally published 1887); Max Weber, *Economy and Society: An Outline of Interpretive Sociology,* 2 vols., eds. Guenther Roth and Claus Wittich, trans. Ephraim Fishoff, *et al.* (Berkeley: University of California Press, 1978); Robert Redfield, "The Folk Society," *American Journal of Sociology* 52 (January 1947): 292–308; Redfield and Milton Singer, "The Cultural Role of Cities," *Economic Development and Cultural Change* 3 (October 1954): 53–73; Talcott Parsons, *The Social System* (Glencoe, Ill: The Free Press, 1951); Bert F. Hoselitz, *Sociological Aspects of Economic Growth* (Glencoe, Ill.: The Free Press, 1960); C.E. Black, *The Dynamics of Modernization: A Study in Comparative History* (New York: Harper & Row, 1966); S.N. Eisenstadt, *Modernization: Protest and Change* (Englewood Cliffs, N.J.: Prentice-Hall, 1966); pp. 1–19 especially; Eisenstadt, "Studies on Modernization and Development," *History and Theory* 13 (1974): 225–52. One should note that Richard D.

Brown recently has used modernization theory to inform his synthesis of American social history from 1600 to 1865. See Brown, *Modernization: The Transformation of American Life 1600–1865,* American Century Series (New York: Hill and Wang, 1976).

9. Numerous scholarly attacks have been launched during the last two decades on the theory of modernization and on the concepts "traditional" and "modern." See, for example, Joseph Gusfield, "Tradition and Modernity: Misplaced Polarities in the Study of Social Change," *American Journal of Sociology* 72 (January 1967): 351–62; Dean C. Tipps, "Modernization Theory and the Comparative Study of Societies: A Critical Perspective," *Comparative Studies in Society and History* 15 (March 1973): 199–226; Immanuel Wallerstein, "Modernization: Requiescat in Pace," in Lewis A. Coser and Otto N. Larsen, eds., *The Uses of Controversy in Sociology* (New York: The Free Press, 1976), pp. 131–35; Joyce Appleby, "Modernization Theory and the Formation of Modern Social Theories in England and America," *Comparative Studies in Society and History* 20 (April 1978): 259–85. For three recent reappraisals of modernization theory and the critiques of such theory, see Raymond Grew, "More on Modernization," *Journal of Social History* 14 (Winter 1980): 179–87; Peter N. Stearns, "Modernization and Social History: Some Suggestions, and a Muted Cheer," *Journal of Social History* 14 (Winter 1980): 189–209; Leonard Binder,"The Natural History of Development Theory," *Comparative Studies in Society and History* 28 (January 1986): 3–33.

10. Thomas Nairne, *A Letter from South Carolina . . . ,* 2d ed. (London: Printed for R. Smith, 1718; originally published 1710), pp. 39–40.

11. On the political harmony and unity obtaining in the low country by the middle of the eighteenth century, see M. Eugene Sirmans, *Colonial South Carolina: A Political History 1663–1763* (Chapel Hill: University of North Carolina Press, 1966), pp. 223–357; Robert M. Weir, " 'The Harmony We Were Famous For': An Interpretation of Pre-Revolutionary South Carolina Politics," *William and Mary Quarterly,* 3d series, 26 (October 1969): 473–501. One should note that Walter J. Fraser, Jr., has recently argued that whites in pre-Revolutionary Charleston were not unified politically or socially. See Fraser, "Controlling the Poor in Colonial Charles Town," *The Proceedings of the South Carolina Historical Association, 1980* (Aiken, S.C.: 1982): 13–30.

12. Note that Tench Coxe was expressing much the same idea about the effect of "Interest" upon society when he wrote that property "may almost be called *the palladium of communities.*" See Coxe, *Reflexions on the State of the Union* (Philadelphia: Mathew Carey, 1792), p. 30.

For a recent restatement of the view that low-country society—indeed, the Plantation South in general—was based largely upon traditional, "paternalist" assumptions rather than upon modern, "market" assumptions in the colonial period, see James Oakes, *The Ruling Race: A History of American Slaveholders* (New York: Knopf, 1982), pp. ix–xix, 3–34.

On the precise manner in which "Interest" was to countervail the "Passions," see Hirschman, *The Passions and the Interests,* passim.

On the recrudescence of the "Passions" later in South Carolina history, see Robert M. Weir, "The South Carolinian as Extremist," *South Atlantic Quarterly* 74 (Winter 1975): 86–103; Lacy K. Ford, Jr., "Social Origins of a New South Carolina—The Upcountry in the Nineteenth Century" (Ph.D. dissertation, University of South Carolina, 1983), chapters 3, 7, 8.

13. On the backward-bending labor supply curve in early modern Europe, see Sir William Petty, *Political Arithmetick . . .* (London: Printed for Robert Clavel, 1690), p. 45. Also see D.C. Coleman, "Labour in the English Economy of the Seventeenth Century," *Economic History Review,* 2d series, 8 (1956): 280–95; Jan de Vries, *The Economy*

of Europe in an Age of Crisis 1600–1750 (Cambridge: Cambridge University Press, 1976), pp. 178–80.

For evidence of a backward-bending labor supply curve among some whites in the low country in the eighteenth century, see Henry Laurens to Martin & Stevens, March 2, 1763, in Philip M. Hamer, George C. Rogers, Jr., *et al.*, eds., *The Papers of Henry Laurens* 10 vols. thus far (Columbia: University of South Carolina Press, 1968–), 3: 273; Henry Laurens to Reynolds, Getly & Co., February 7, 1769, in Hamer, Rogers, *et al.*, eds., *The Papers of Henry Laurens*, 6: 266–67, especially p. 266.

Despite the existence of such backward bends, neither northwestern Europeans nor white South Carolinians in the early modern period shared much with "traditional" or "peasant" laborers of the twentieth century, as is often alleged. Compare, for example, the discussions by Henry Laurens cited above with that of another conservative, Evelyn Waugh, writing on laborers in Abyssinia in 1930. See Waugh, *They Were Still Dancing* (New York: Farrar & Rinehart, 1932), pp. 36–37.

Finally, one should note that I do not wish to imply in the text that every agriculturalist in the low country planted rice—only a minority did even in 1860—nor that everyone was as committed to the market as the great planters of rice, indigo, and, later, cotton. Indeed, it is clear that smaller planters, yeomen, and "piney woods" people each participated in the market in a distinctive way. Generally speaking, however, patterns of market participation in the low country owed more to differential ability to participate and to differential market strategies than to alleged differences in ideology. We shall know more about some of these matters upon the completion of Stephanie McCurry's important dissertation, currently in progress at SUNY-Binghamton, on the low country yeomanry. On the total number of agricultural units in the low country in 1860 and the number of rice-producing units in the same area at this time, see Dale Evans Swan, *The Structure and Profitability of the Antebellum Rice Industry 1859* (New York: Arno Press, 1975), p. 15.

14. That whites in certain parts of eighteenth-century America allegedly were relatively indifferent to market exchange, see the works cited in Chapter 1, fn. 2.

On violent resistance to the market by "alienated" groups in the South Carolina backcountry in the eighteenth century, see Rachel Klein, "The Rise of the Planters in the South Carolina Backcountry, 1767–1808" (Ph.D. dissertation, Yale University, 1979), pp. 52–79; Klein, "Ordering the Backcountry: The South Carolina Regulation," *William and Mary Quarterly*, 3d series, 38 (October 1981): 661–80.

15. See Klein, "Ordering the Backcountry," pp. 674, 676 and passim. On the filing of lawsuits against so-called Regulators, see, for example, Govr. Bull to Lord Hillsborough, September 10, 1768, Carolina Papers, Chalmers Collection, 1: 169, 171, New York Public Library, New York.

16. On the rapid expansion of trade and market exchange in the backcountry, see Leila Sellers, *Charleston Business on the Eve of the American Revolution* (Chapel Hill: University of North Carolina Press, 1934), pp. 33–36; David L. Coon, "The Development of Market Agriculture in South Carolina, 1670–1785" (Ph.D. dissertation, University of Illinois, 1972), pp. 290–99; Joseph A. Ernst and H. Roy Merrens, " 'Camden's turrets pierce the skies!': The Urban Process in the Southern Colonies during the Eighteenth Century," *William and Mary Quarterly*, 3d series, 30 (October 1973): 549–74; Klein, "Ordering the Backcountry," pp. 663–68. For contemporary evidence of such expansion, see, for example, Charleston *South Carolina Gazette*, November 10, 1766; July 6, 1769; January 15, 1770; March 1, 1773; Charleston *South Carolina Gazette & Country Journal*, December 5, 1769; Josiah Smith, Jr., to George Austin, January 31, 1774, p. 230, Josiah Smith, Jr., Lettercopy Book, Southern Historical Collection, University of North Carolina, Chapel Hill; Coxe,

Reflexions, p. 9. By the late eighteenth century, South Carolinians from the backcountry were becoming involved in the commercial development of the Mississippi Valley. See Joseph Brevard to Alexander Brevard, October 16, 1796, Alexander Brevard Papers, North Carolina State Archives, Raleigh.

17. See Chapter 1 of this study. For a detailed examination of the economic divergence that occurred within early modern Europe, see De Vries, *The Economy of Europe in an Age of Crisis, 1600–1750.*

18. De Vries, *The Economy of Europe in an Age of Crisis, 1600–1750,* pp. 176–209; D.C. Coleman, *The Economy of England, 1450–1750* (Oxford: Oxford University Press, 1977), pp. 91–201; Peter Kriedte, *Peasants, Landlords and Merchant Capitalists: Europe and the World Economy, 1500–1800,* trans. V.R. Berghahn (New York: Cambridge University Press, 1983).

19. On income elasticity of demand, see, for example, H.H. Liebhafsky, *The Nature of Price Theory,* rev. ed. (Homewood, Ill.: The Dorsey Press, 1968), pp. 129–35; Donald S. Watson, *Price Theory and Its Uses,* 3d ed. (Boston: Houghton Mifflin, 1972), pp. 102, 123–25; Edwin Mansfield, *Microeconomics: Theory/Applications,* 5th ed. (New York: W.W. Norton, 1985), pp. 124–26.

20. On inferior goods, see Liebhafsky, *The Nature of Price Theory,* pp. 133–34; Watson, *Price Theory and Its Uses,* pp. 101–2, 107–8; Mansfield, *Microeconomics,* pp. 97–98.

21. On income elasticities for various agricultural commodities and food groups, see Theodore W. Schultz, *The Economic Organization of Agriculture* (New York: McGraw-Hill Book Company, 1953), pp. 44–82, especially pp. 68–74; John W. Mellor, *The Economics of Agricultural Development* (Ithaca: Cornell University Press, 1966), pp. 57–80. Note that Mellor on page 66 presents data on relative income elasticities for populations throughout the world.

Engel's law posits, of course, that expenditures on food form a decreasing proportion of income as income rises.

22. See, for example, De Vries, *The Economy of Europe in an Age of Crisis, 1600–1750,* pp. 84–86, 176–209; Coleman, *The Economy of England, 1450–1750,* pp. 91–103.

For a contemporary estimate of per capita income in England in the late seventeenth century, see Gregory King's "Scheme of the Income & Expence of the several Families of England Calculated for the Year 1688," in his *Natural and Political Observations and Conclusions upon the State and Condition of England* (1696). This tract, which was not published until 1804, is reprinted in George E. Barnett, ed., *Two Tracts by Gregory King* (Baltimore: Johns Hopkins University Press, 1936), pp. 11–55. The "Scheme" mentioned above appears on p. 31. Also see Petty, *Political Arithmetick . . . ,* pp. 101–2.

Note that some of the rise in real income in this period occurred as a result of an income effect: the secular decline in food prices, particularly cereal prices, in relation to wages, that is to say, contributed to the income gains accrued by many Europeans. On income effects, see Liebhafsky, *The Nature of Price Theory,* pp. 183–212.

Note, too, that complexities can arise when one applies this microeconomic argument to entire societies. As per capita income rises in a given society and that society begins to develop, for example, demand for even basic, income-inelastic foodstuffs at times can grow rapidly as well, as a result of increased public and private welfare activities. In such cases, basic foodstuffs are acquired by the state or private charities for redistribution to individuals who formerly either starved or lived marginal existences. A rising tide, that is to say, lifts all ships (more or less). This point is especially important for us to note because some of northern Europe's demand for rice—South Carolina's principal export—went for such purposes. For further discussion of South Carolina's rice markets, See Chapter 4.

23. On the increase in agricultural productivity in northwest Europe during the 1650–1750 period, see De Vries, *The Economy of Europe in an Age of Crisis, 1600–1750, pp. 30–48, 69–83*; Coleman, *The Economy of England, 1450–1750*, pp. 111–30; De Vries, *The Dutch Rural Economy in the Golden Age*, 1500–1700 (New Haven: Yale University Press, 1974), pp. 119–243; A.H. John, "Agricultural Productivity and Economic Growth in England, 1700–1760," *Journal of Economic History* 25 (March 1965): 19–34; E.L. Jones, "Agriculture and Economic Growth in England, 1660–1750: Agricultural Change," *Journal of Economic History* 25 (March 1965): 1–18: E.L Jones, "Agriculture, 1700–80," in Roderick Floud and Donald McCloskey, eds., *The Economic History of Britain Since 1700*, 2 vols. (Cambridge: Cambridge University Press, 1981), 1: 66–86.

24. For different, but related interpretive treatments of this reallocation of resources, see Immanuel Wallerstein, *The Modern World-System*, 2 vols. thus far (New York: Academic Press, 1974–); Ralph Davis, *The Rise of the Atlantic Economies* (Ithaca: Cornell University Press, 1973); De Vries, *The Economy of Europe in an Age of Crisis, 1600–1750*.

25. See Chapter 1 of this study for a detailed discussion of the development of this institutional framework.

26. In formulating this argument I have assumed, on the one hand, that human societies are systems, the parts of which are interrelated. From this assumption a corollary is derived, that is, that the individual parts of this system should be studied not in isolation but rather in terms of their interrelationships with the whole. I have, in addition, assumed that the basic structure of a given human society is primarily, though not solely, determined by material forces, by which I mean a conjunction of biological and economic forces, rather than economic forces alone. Thus, while all parts of a social system are interrelated, it is the material forces that dominate, the material forces that ultimately rule.

27. Critics of the pattern of institutional development in the low country include Carl Bridenbaugh and Eugene Sirmans. See Bridenbaugh, *Myths and Realities: Societies of the Colonial South* (New York: Atheneum, 1971; originally published 1952), pp. 54–118; Sirmans, *Colonial South Carolina*, pp. 225–55.

28. On kinship patterns in colonial South Carolina, see J.E. Crowley, "Family Relations and Inheritance in Early South Carolina," *Histoire Sociale/Social History* 17 (1984): 35–57; Crowley, "The Importance of Kinship: Testamentary Evidence From South Carolina," *Journal of Interdisciplinary History* 16 (Spring 1986): 559–77; Terry, " 'Champaign Country,' " pp. 119–42. For somewhat similar analyses of kinship patterns in another part of the colonial South, see Darrett B. Rutman and Anita Rutman, " 'Now-Wives and Sons-in-Law': Parental Death in a Seventeenth-Century Virginia County," in Thad W. Tate and David L. Ammerman, eds., *The Chesapeake in the Seventeenth Century: Essays on Anglo-American Society* (Chapel Hill: University of North Carolina Press, 1979), pp. 153–82; Rutman and Rutman, *A Place in Time: Middlesex County, Virginia, 1650–1750*, 2 vols. (New York: W.W. Norton, 1984).

On the narrowness of the educational system in colonial South Carolina, see, for example, Alice E. Mathews, "Pre-College Education in the Southern Colonies" (Ph.D. dissertation, University of California, 1968), pp. 81–93, 104–11, 387–91. This narrowness was much noted by early writers, indeed, even by an early governor of South Carolina. See John Drayton, *A View of South-Carolina, as Respects Her Natural and Civil Concerns* (Charleston: W.P. Young, 1802), pp. 217–20. That rates of illiteracy were greater among whites in the South than among whites in other sections of the United States during the colonial and early national periods, see, for example, Kenneth A. Lockridge, *Literacy in Colonial New England: An Enquiry into the Social Context of Literacy in the Early Modern*

West (New York: W.W. Norton & Company, 1974), pp. 72–101; Lee Soltow, "Socioeconomic Classes in South Carolina and Massachusetts in the 1790s and the Observations of John Drayton," *South Carolina Historical Magazine* 81 (October 1980): 283–305.

On the lack of religious piety in the low country, see, for example, Bridenbaugh, *Myths and Realities*, pp. 54–118; M. Eugene Sirmans, "Charleston Two Hundred Years Ago," *The Emory University Quarterly* 19 (Fall 1963): 129–36; Sirmans, *Colonial South Carolina*, pp. 231–33.

On the "underdeveloped" state of political institutions in colonial South Carolina, see, once again, Bridenbaugh, *Myths and Realities*, pp. 54–118; Sirmans, *Colonial South Carolina*, pp. 225–55. George Terry, one should note, recently has shown that political and governmental institutions in the low country were both better developed and more effective than Bridenbaugh and Sirmans have suggested. See Terry, "' Champaign Country,' " pp. 298–340.

29. See, for example, Duncan C. Heyward, *Seed from Madagascar* (Chapel Hill: University of North Carolina Press, 1937), pp. 3–10; Frederick P. Bowes, *The Culture of Early Charleston* (Chapel Hill: University of North Carolina Press, 1942), p. 88; Nell S. Graydon, *Eliza of Wappoo: A Tale of Indigo* (Columbia: R.L. Bryan Co., 1967). That until fairly recently Pinckney was deemed almost solely responsible for the introduction of indigo into South Carolina, see David L. Coon, " Eliza Lucas Pinckney and the Reintroduction of Indigo Culture in South Carolina," *Journal of Southern History* 42 (February 1976): 61–76.

30. See the works mentioned in footnote 3 above. Wood, for example, argues that "most of those who took up 'plantations' in the early 1700s were actually frontier farmers seeking a stable agricultural existence through the employment of a few black slaves." They were, I believe, seeking far more than that. Moreover, Wood argues that Negro slaves on such 'plantations' were "still sharing a common undertaking as members of an interracial family unit." I have my doubts about this conceptualization as well. See Wood, *Black Majority*, p. 106.

31. On Indian slavery in early South Carolina, see Almon W. Lauber, *Indian Slavery in Colonial Times, within the Present Limits of the United States* (New York: Columbia University Press, 1913), passim; William Robert Snell, "Indian Slavery in Colonial South Carolina, 1671–1795" (Ph.D. dissertation, University of Alabama, 1972); Wood, *Black Majority*, pp. 37–40; Robert M. Weir, *Colonial South Carolina: A History* (Millwood, N.Y.: KTO Press, 1983), pp. 24–32.

32. For a good introduction to modern theories of comparative advantage, see Delbert A. Snider, *Introduction to International Economics*, 7th ed. (Homewood, Ill.: Richard D. Irwin, 1979).

33. See, for example, Arghiri Emmanuel, *Unequal Exchange: A Study of the Imperialism of Trade*, trans. Brian Pearce (New York: Monthly Review Press, 1972; originally published 1969); Samir Amin, *Unequal Development: An Essay on the Social Formations of Peripheral Capitalism*, trans. Brian Pearce (New York: Monthly Review Press, 1976; originally published 1973), pp. 133–97; J.O. Andersson, *Studies in the Theory of Unequal Exchange between Nations* (Abo, Finland: Abo Akedemi, 1976), passim; Anthony Brewer, *Marxist Theories of Imperialism: A Critical Survey* (London: Routledge & Kegan Paul, 1980), pp. 208–32.

Paul A. Samuelson has written a very useful critique of Emmanuel's theory of unequal exchange. See Samuelson, "Illogic of Neo-Marxian Doctrine of Unequal Exchange," in David A. Belsley *et al.*, eds. *Inflation, Trade and Taxes: Essays in Honor of Alice Bourneuf* (Columbus: Ohio State University Press, 1976), pp. 96–107.

34. The most complete statement of the Heckscher-Ohlin model appears in Bertil Ohlin, *Interregional and International Trade* (Cambridge: Harvard University Press, 1933), Parts 1 and 2 and chapters 12, 13, and 14. Paul A. Samuelson's classic analytical reformulations appeared in two articles: "International Trade and Equalisation of Factor Prices," *The Economic Journal* 58 (June 1948): 163–84; "International Factor-Price Equalisation Once Again," *The Economic Journal* 59 (June 1949): 181–97. For a good collection of articles on recent modifications in international trade theory, see Jagdish N. Bhagwati, ed., *International Trade: Selected Readings* (Cambridge: The MIT Press, 1981).

35. See David Ricardo, *On the Principles of Political Economy and Taxation,* 3d ed. (London: John Murray, 1821), Chapter VII, pp. 128–49.

36. On the timing of specific developments, see Clowse, *Economic Beginnings;* Coon, "The Development of Market Agriculture in South Carolina, 1670–1785."

37. On systems of land tenure in early America, see Marshall Harris, *Origin of the Land Tenure System in the United States* (Ames: Iowa State College Press, 1953). On the quitrent system specifically, see Beverley W. Bond, Jr., *The Quit-Rent System in the American Colonies* (New Haven: Yale University Press, 1919).

The land tenure and quitrent systems in early South Carolina are described in Robert K. Ackerman, *South Carolina Colonial Land Policies* (Columbia: University of South Carolina Press, 1977).

On inheritance patterns in the low country during the colonial period, see Terry, " 'Champaign Country,' " pp. 119–42; Crowley, "Family Relations and Inheritance in Early South Carolina."

On restrictions on general access to certain natural resources, see, for example, Fundamental Constitutions, March 1, 1670, in Mattie Erma Edwards Parker, ed., *North Carolina Charters and Constitutions 1578–1698* (Raleigh: Published by the Carolina Charter Tercentenary Commission, 1963), Article 114, p. 184. The proprietors' right to restrict access to certain natural resources—minerals, ambergris, and whales among others—was bestowed to them in the Carolina charters of 1663 and 1665.

38. The Navigation Acts, of course, restricted capital utilization in a number of ways. On these acts, see, for example, Lawrence A. Harper, *The English Navigation Laws: A Seventeenth-Century Experiment in Social Engineering* (New York: Columbia University Press, 1939).

For laws prohibiting usurious lending and—for some—certain types of dress, see, for example, Thomas Cooper and David J. McCord, eds., *The Statutes at Large of South Carolina,* 10 vols. (Columbia: A.S. Johnston, 1836–41), 3: 104–5; 7: 385–97, especially p. 396.

39. Negro slaves were prohibited from participating in many economic activities; moreover, according to Peter Wood, such prohibitions increased as time passed. See Wood, *Black Majority,* pp. 205–11, 229–33, and passim.

For laws prohibiting engrossing, forestalling, and regrating, see, for example, Cooper and McCord, *Statutes,* 2: 73, 122–23, 186–88, 351; 3: 122.

40. See, for example, Ernesto Laclau(h), "Feudalism and Capitalism in Latin America," *New Left Review,* No. 67 (May–June 1971): 19–38; Eugene D. Genovese, *The World the Slaveholders Made: Two Essays in Interpretation* (New York: Random House, 1969), pp. 21–102 especially; Eugene D. Genovese and Elizabeth Fox-Genovese, *Fruits of Merchant Capital: Slavery and Bourgeois Property in the Rise and Expansion of Capitalism* (New York: Oxford University Press, 1983).

41. See Karl Marx, *Capital,* ed. Frederick Engels, trans. Samuel Moore and Edward Aveling, 3 vols. (New York: International Publishers, 1967; originally published 1867–

94), 1: 167–76, especially p. 170. That Marx himself did not believe the American colonies founded by European nation-states to be capitalist in nature during the early modern period, see *Capital*, 1: 713–74; 3: 323–37. One should also note, however, that elsewhere—in the *Grundrisse*, for example—Marx writes of American plantation owners as capitalists, despite their dependence upon servile labor. See Marx, *Grundrisse: Foundations of the Critique of Political Economy*, trans. Martin Nicolaus (New York: Vintage Books, 1973; originally published 1939), p. 513.

42. See Wallerstein, *The Modern World-System*; Robert A. Padgug, "Problems in the Theory of Slavery and Slave Society," *Science & Society* 40 (Spring 1976): 3–27; André Gunder Frank, *World Accumulation 1492–1789* (New York: Monthly Review Press, 1978), pp. 238–71 and passim. On the advent of capitalist agriculture in early-modern England specifically, see, for example, E.P. Thompson, "The Peculiarities of the English," in Thompson, *The Poverty of Theory and Other Essays* (New York: Monthly Review Press, 1978), pp. 245–301.

43. See E.E. Rich, "Colonial Settlement and Its Labour Problems," in E.E. Rich and C.H. Wilson, eds., *The Cambridge Economic History of Europe*, vol. IV: *The Economy of Expanding Europe in the Sixteenth and Seventeenth Centuries* (Cambridge: Cambridge University Press, 1967), pp. 302–73; Evsey D. Domar, "The Causes of Slavery or Serfdom: A Hypothesis," *Journal of Economic History* 30 (March 1970): 18–32. On the origins of bound labor systems in the American South specifically, see Winthrop D. Jordan, *White Over Black: American Attitudes Toward the Negro 1550–1812* (Chapel Hill: University of North Carolina Press, 1968), pp. 71–83; Wood, *Black Majority*, pp. 37–55; Edmund S. Morgan, *American Slavery, American Freedom: The Ordeal of Colonial Virginia* (New York: W.W. Norton, 1975), passim.

44. On the relationship between market forces and the evolution of the labor systems in Plantation America, see Wallerstein, *The Modern World-System*, 2; 167–75; Ralph Gray and Betty Wood, "The Transition from Indentured to Involuntary Servitude in Colonial Georgia," *Explorations in Economic History*, 2d series, 13 (October 1976): 353–70; Richard N. Bean and Robert P. Thomas, "The Adoption of Slave Labor in British America," in Henry A. Gemery and Jan S. Hogendorn, eds., *The Uncommon Market: Essays in the Economic History of the Atlantic Slave Trade* (New York: Academic Press, 1979), pp. 377–98; David W. Galenson, "White Servitude and the Growth of Black Slavery in Colonial America," *Journal of Economic History* 41 (March 1981): 39–49; Galenson, *White Servitude in Colonial America: An Economic Analysis* (New York: Cambridge University Press, 1982), passim; Galenson, *Traders, Planters, and Slaves: Market Behavior in Early English America* (New York: Cambridge University Press, 1986).

On the link between racism and racial slavery in the New World, see Carl N. Degler, "Slavery and the Genesis of American Race Prejudice," *Comparative Studies in Society and History* 2 (October 1959): 49–66; Jordan, *White Over Black*, passim.

On epidemiology and its relationship to the evolution of racial slavery in Plantation America, see, for example, Philip D. Curtin, "Epidemiology and the Slave Trade," *Political Science Quarterly* 83 (June 1968): 190–216; Wood, *Black Majority*, pp. 63–91.

That human capital considerations—prior experience in rice production in particular—were often of some importance in determining the precise character of the labor force in the South Carolina low country, see Wood, *Black Majority*; Daniel C. Littlefield, *Rice and Slaves: Ethnicity and the Slave Trade in Colonial South Carolina* (Baton Rouge: Louisiana State University Press, 1981), pp. 74–114. By the late colonial period, for example, notices placed in South Carolina newspapers pertaining to the arrival of slave cargoes often mentioned that those arriving were from "a Rice Country." See *South Carolina Gazette*,

September 5, 1771; May 7, 1772; November 12, 1772, Supplement; May 3, 1773; June 13, 1774; Charleston *South Carolina & American General Gazette,* May 1, 1769; May 23, 1770; September 2, 1771; *South Carolina Gazette & Country Journal,* March 21, 1769; July 2, 1771; June 1, 1773.

Finally, on white indentured servants in colonial South Carolina, see Warren B. Smith, *White Servitude in Colonial South Carolina* (Columbia: University of South Carolina Press, 1961); Aaron M. Shatzman, "Servants into Planters, The Origin of an American Image: Land Acquisition and Status Mobility in Seventeenth Century South Carolina" (Ph.D. dissertation, Stanford University, 1981), passim.

45. The best studies of the labor force in the South Carolina low country during the colonial period are those of Peter Wood and Philip D. Morgan. See Wood, *Black Majority;* Morgan, "The Development of Slave Culture in Eighteenth Century Plantation America" (Ph.D. dissertation, University College London, 1977).

46. Sir Dudley North, *Discourses Upon Trade . . .* (Baltimore: Johns Hopkins University Press, 1907; originally published 1691), p. 16.

47. See, for example, Clowse, *Economic Beginnings,* pp. 56–58. The reference in the text to the peas is from: Joseph West to Lord Ashley, May 28, 1670, in Langdon Cheves, ed., *The Shaftesbury Papers and Other Records Relating to Carolina and the First Settlement on Ashley River Prior to the year 1676* in *Collections of the South Carolina Historical Society,* vol. 5 (Charleston: Published by the South Carolina Historical Society, 1897), pp. 173–74. Hereinafter cited as Cheves, ed., *Shaftesbury Papers.*

48. On Braudel's use of the term "material life," see Fernand Braudel, *The Structures of Everyday Life: Civilization & Capitalism 15th–18th Century,* trans. Siân Reynolds (New York: Harper & Row, 1981; originally published 1979), pp. 23–29 and passim.

49. See, for example, Florence O'Sullivan to Lord Ashley, September 10, 1670, Cheves, ed., *Shaftesbury Papers,* pp. 188–90; Joseph West to Sir Peter Colleton, March 2, 1670/1, Cheves, ed., *Shaftesbury Papers,* pp. 271–73; "An old Letter," March 1671?, Cheves, ed., *Shaftesbury Papers,* pp. 307–9; Maurice Mathews to Lord Ashley, August 30, 1671, Cheves, ed., *Shaftesbury Papers,* pp. 332–36; Joseph Dalton to Lord Ashley, January 20, 1671/2, Cheves, ed., *Shaftesbury Papers,* pp. 376–83, especially pp. 377–78; Lords Proprietors to Lord Shaftesbury, November 20, 1674, Cheves, ed., *Shaftesbury Papers,* pp. 454–55.

50. See Mark Catesby, *The Natural History of Carolina, Florida, and the Bahama Islands . . . ,* 2d English ed., 2 vols. (London: Printed for C. Marsh, T. Wilcox, B. Stichall, 1754; originally published 1731–43), 2: xvi–xviii; Drayton, *A View of South-Carolina,* pp. 112–14, 136–39; David Ramsay, *The History of South-Carolina from Its First Settlement in 1670 to the Year 1808,* 2 vols. (Charleston: David Longworth, 1809), 2: 199–200, 216–18. On the cultivation of small grains and Indian corn in the early South and on the greater relative importance of Indian corn for a considerable period of time, see Lewis C. Gray, *History of Agriculture in the Southern United States to 1860,* 2 vols. (Washington, D.C.: Carnegie Institution, 1933; reprint ed., Gloucester, Mass.: Peter Smith, 1958), 1: 161–76. On the low country specifically, see Coon, "The Development of Market Agriculture in South Carolina, 1670–1785," pp. 132–33.

51. See Chapter 1 of this study. Also see Wood, *Black Majority,* pp. 32–34; Richard Waterhouse, "England, the Caribbean, and the Settlement of Carolina," *Journal of American Studies* 9 (December 1975): 259–81.

52. On the early South Carolina economy, see Clowse, *Economic Beginnings,* pp. 42–138; Coon, "The Development of Market Agriculture in South Carolina, 1670–1785," pp. 73–163; Gary S. Dunbar, "Colonial Carolina Cowpens," *Agricultural History* 35 (July 1961): 125–31; John S. Otto, "The Origins of Cattle-Ranching in Colonial South

Carolina, 1670–1715," *South Carolina Historical Magazine* 87 (April 1986): 117–24; Otto, "Livestock-Raising in Early South Carolina—Prelude to the Rice Plantation Economy," *Agricultural History* 61 (Fall 1987): 13-24.

On early trade relations between South Carolinians and pirates, see Clowse, *Economic Beginnings,* pp. 87–90; Shirley C. Hughson, *The Carolina Pirates and Colonial Commerce, 1670–1740,* The Johns Hopkins University Studies in Historical and Political Science, 12th series (Baltimore: Johns Hopkins University Press, 1894), pp. 237–370.

On the early days of the Indian trade, see Verner W. Crane, *The Southern Frontier 1670–1732* (Ann Arbor: University of Michigan Press, 1956; originally published 1929), pp. 3–46; Anne King Gregorie, "Indian Trade of Carolina in the Seventeenth Century" (M.A. thesis, University of South Carolina, 1926), pp. 1–25; John T. Juricek, "Indian Policy in Proprietary South Carolina, 1670–1693" (M.A. thesis, University of Chicago, 1962); Philip M. Brown, "Early Indian Trade in the Development of South Carolina: Politics, Economics, and Social Mobility during the Proprietary Period, 1670–1719," *South Carolina Historical Magazine* 76 (July 1975): 118–28.

53. See, for example, Clowse, *Economic Beginnings,* pp. 95–138.

54. See Clowse, *Economic Beginnings,* passim; Gray, *History of Agriculture,* 1: 409-33; Victor S. Clark, *History of Manufactures in the United States,* 3 vols. (Washington, D.C.: Carnegie Institution, 1916–29), 1: 31–214; Stuart O. Stumpf, "The Merchants of Colonial Charleston, 1680–1756" (Ph.D. dissertation, Michigan State University, 1971), pp. 1–155.

55. On rice cultivation in colonial South Carolina, see Gray, *History of Agriculture,* 1: 277–90; Clowse, *Economic Beginnings,* pp. 122–32 and passim; Coon, "The Development of Market Agriculture in South Carolina, 1670–1785," pp. 164–214; Wood, *Black Majority,* pp. 55–62; Littlefield, *Rice and Slaves,* pp. 56–114; Morgan, "The Development of Slave Culture in Eighteenth Century Plantation America," pp. 67–85; James M. Clifton, "The Rice Industry in Colonial America," *Agricultural History* 55 (July 1981): 266–83; Philip D. Morgan, "Work and Culture: The Task System and the World of Lowcountry Blacks, 1700 to 1880," *William and Mary Quarterly,* 3d series, 39 (October 1982): 563–99; Peter A. Coclanis, "Rice Prices in the 1720s and the Evolution of the South Carolina Economy," *Journal of Southern History* 48 (November 1982): 531–44. On rice cultivation in colonial Georgia, see Betty Wood, *Slavery in Colonial Georgia 1730–1775* (Athens: University of Georgia Press, 1984), pp. 88–109 especially; Julia Floyd Smith, *Slavery and Rice Culture in Low Country Georgia, 1750–1860* (Knoxville: University of Tennessee Press, 1985), pp. 15–29.

On indigo cultivation in colonial South Carolina, see Gray, *History of Agriculture,* 1: 290–97; G. Terry Sharrer, "Indigo in Carolina, 1671–1796," *South Carolina Historical Magazine* 72 (April 1971): 94–103; Coon, "The Development of Market Agriculture in South Carolina, 1670–1785," pp. 215–68; John J. Winberry, "Reputation of Carolina Indigo," *South Carolina Historical Magazine* 80 (July 1979): 242–50; David H. Rembert, Jr., "The Indigo of Commerce in Colonial North America," *Economic Botany* 33 (April–June 1979): 128–34; Weir, *Colonial South Carolina,* pp. 149–53.

56. For a more detailed explanation of the relative shift toward staple agriculture in eighteenth-century South Carolina, see Coclanis, "Rice Prices in the 1720s and the Evolution of the South Carolina Economy."

57. Ramsay, *The History of South-Carolina,* 1: 123.

58. On the so-called population trap, see for example, Robert E. Baldwin, *Economic Development and Growth,* 2d ed. (New York: Wiley, 1972), pp. 52–54; Michael P. Todaro, *Economic Development in the Third World,* 3d ed. (New York: Longman, 1985), pp. 204–8.

59. Thomas Robert Malthus, *An Essay on the Principle of Population . . . ,* ed. Anthony

Flew (Harmondsworth, Middlesex, England: Penguin Books, 1970; originally published 1798), pp. 104–8, especially p. 105; Benjamin Franklin, *Observations Concerning the Increase of Mankind* (1751) in [William Clark], *Observations On the late and present Conduct of the French . . . . To which is added, wrote by another Hand; Observations Concerning the Increase of Mankind* (Boston: S. Kneeland, 1755); Edward Wigglesworth, *Calculations on American Population . . .* (Boston: John Boyle, 1775). Also see J. Potter, "The Growth of Population in America, 1700–1860," in D.V. Glass and D.E.C. Eversley, eds., *Population in History: Essays in Historical Demography* (Chicago: Aldine, 1965), pp. 631–88, especially pp. 631–33; James H. Cassedy, *Demography in Early America: Beginnings of the Statistical Mind, 1600–1800* (Cambridge: Harvard University Press, 1969), pp. 157–79, 189–92; Jim Potter, "Demographic Development and Family Structure," in Jack P. Greene and J.R. Pole, eds., *Colonial British America: Essays in the New History of the Early Modern Era* (Baltimore: Johns Hopkins University Press, 1984), pp. 123–56.

60. See *Historical Statistics of the United States: Colonial Times to 1970,* Department of Commerce, Bureau of the Census, 2 vols. (Washington, D.C.: U.S. Government Printing Office, 1975), 2: 1168; Potter, "The Growth of Population in America."

61. See *Historical Statistics of the United States,* 2: 1168; Potter, "The Growth of Population in America." Also see Julian J. Petty, *The Growth and Distribution of Population in South Carolina,* South Carolina State Planning Board, Bulletin No. 11 (Columbia: South Carolina State Council for Defense, Industrial Development Committee, 1943), pp. 15–58, 220–25.

62. Compound rates here and elsewhere in this chapter were calculated by using the standard compound interest formula, that is:

$$r = \left(\sqrt[m]{\left(\frac{x_n}{x_t} \right)} - 1 \right) 100$$

In this formula, r is the growth or interest rate, x_n is the value for the last date or period, x_t is the value for the first date or period, and m is the difference between the first and last dates or periods. See Roderick Floud, *An Introduction to Quantitative Methods for Historians,* 2d ed. (London: Methuen, 1979), 93–97.

63. On the settlement of the backcountry, see Robert L. Meriwether's classic work, *The Expansion of South Carolina 1729–1765* (Kingsport, Tenn.: Southern Publishers, 1940).

64. On the population of the backcountry c. 1770, see Richard M. Brown, *The South Carolina Regulators* (Cambridge: The Belknap Press of Harvard University, 1963), p. 182; Klein, "The Rise of the Planters in the South Carolina Backcountry, 1767–1808," pp. 5, 22–23; Klein, "Ordering the Backcountry," p. 665, fn. 10. The estimate in the text above is based on data from these sources.

65. The white population of the low country did grow, however, between 1770 and 1790. According to the 1790 Census of the United States, the white population of the South Carolina low country—Georgetown District, Charleston District, and Beauford District— was 28,644. See United States Department of Commerce and Labor, Bureau of the Census, *Heads of Families at the First Census of the United States Taken in the Year 1790. South Carolina.* (Washington, D.C.: United States Government Printing Office, 1908), p. 9.

66. On white immigration, see Potter, "The Growth of Population in America."

On black immigration, see W. Robert Higgins, "The South Carolina Negro Duty Law" (M.A. thesis, University of South Carolina, 1967), pp. 138–88; Wood, *Black Majority,* pp. 150–55, 333–41; Morgan, "The Development of Slave Culture in Eighteenth Century Plantation America," pp. 282–328; Littlefield, *Rice and Slaves,* pp. 109–73 especially.

67. That the white population of the low country probably began to increase naturally during the second half of the eighteenth century, see Terry, " 'Champaign Country,' " pp. 90–142. For contemporary suggestions of this, see Lionel Chalmers, *An Account of the Weather and Diseases of South-Carolina*, 2 vols. (London: E. and C. Dilly, 1776), 1: 36–37; Alexander Hewatt, *An Historical Account of the Rise and Progress of the Colonies of South Carolina and Georgia*, 2 vols. (London: Printed for Alexander Donaldson, 1779), 2: 292. Also see Chapter 2 of this study.

On white emigration from the low country during the eighteenth century, see Terry, " 'Champaign Country,' " pp. 105–18; David R. Chesnutt, "South Carolina's Expansion into Colonial Georgia 1720–1765" (Ph.D. dissertation, University of Georgia, 1973), passim.

68. That the black population of the low country probably began to increase slightly by natural means in the 1760s, see Morgan, "The Development of Slave Culture in Eighteenth Century Plantation America," pp. 284–86.

69. On the so-called land scarcity hypothesis, see Kenneth A. Lockridge, "Land, Population and the Evolution of New England Society, 1630–1790," *Past and Present*, no. 39 (April 1968): 62–80. The data on Suffolk County in the text above appear on page 68. For a critique of this hypothesis, see John J. McCusker and Russell R. Menard, *The Economy of British America, 1607–1789* (Chapel Hill: University of North Carolina Press, 1985), pp. 104–6.

70. See Terry, " 'Champaign Country,' " p. 248; Mark D. Kaplanoff, "Making the South Solid: Politics and the Structure of Society in South Carolina, 1790–1815" (Ph.D. dissertation, University of Cambridge, 1979), pp. 34, 305.

71. On headrights in colonial South Carolina, see Ackerman, *South Carolina Colonial Land Policies*, passim.

On the so-called Township scheme, see Meriwether, *The Expansion of South Carolina*, pp. 17–30; Sirmans, *Colonial South Carolina*, pp. 161–82.

On landholding patterns in the backcountry at the turn of the eighteenth century, see Kaplanoff, "Making the South Solid," pp. 34, 305.

72. In formulating growth models, economists have disagreed about whether the relationship between capital and output is fixed or variable. In the Rostovian and Harrod-Domar models, for example, the relationship is fixed; in neoclassical models, however, the relationship is variable. See William R. Hosek, *Macroeconomic Theory* (Homewood, Ill: Richard D. Irwin, 1975), pp. 240–62; Robert E. Gallman, "Economic Growth," in Glenn Porter, ed., *Encyclopedia of American Economic History: Studies of the Principal Movements and Ideas*, 3 vols. (New York: Charles Scribner's Sons, 1980), 1: 133–50, especially pp. 144–45.

73. These scattered trade data are from the following sources: Maurice Mathews, "A Contemporary View of Carolina in 1680," *South Carolina Historical Magazine* 55 (July 1954): 153–59, especially p. 157; William Craven to Lordships of Trade, July 1687, *Records in the British Public Record Office Relating to South Carolina, 1663–1782*, 36 vols. in facsimile, South Carolina Department of Archives and History, 2: 199–201; J.G. Dunlop, contrib., "Letters from John Stewart to William Dunlop," *South Carolina Historical Magazine* 32 (1931): 1–33, 81–114, 170–74, especially p. 90.

74. On economic growth in other parts of British America in the seventeenth century, see Terry L. Anderson, *The Economic Growth of Seventeenth-Century New England: A Measurement of Regional Income* (New York: Arno Press, 1975); Anderson, "Wealth Estimates for the New England Colonies, 1650–1709," *Explorations in Economic History*, 2d series, 12 (April 1975): 151–76; Anderson, "Economic Growth in Colonial New England: 'Statistical Renaissance,' " *Journal of Economic History* 39 (March 1979): 243–57; Anderson

and Robert Paul Thomas, "Economic Growth in the Seventeenth-Century Chesapeake," *Explorations in Economic History*, 2d series, 15 (October 1978): 368–87; Richard S. Dunn, *Sugar and Slaves: The Rise of the Planter Class in the English West Indies, 1624–1713* (Chapel Hill: University of North Carolina Press, 1972), pp. 263–99, especially pp. 264–72; McCusker and Menard, *The Economy of British America*, pp. 51–70, 258–76 especially.

75. There are fifty extant South Carolina inventories from the seventeenth century. Data in these inventories indicate—so far as a mere fifty inventories can—that personal wealth in South Carolina was increasing during the late seventeenth century. This can be seen in the figures on mean personal wealth presented below.

Period	Number of Inventories	Mean Personal Wealth (£ sterling)
1670s	5	61.40
1680s	16	187.56
1690s	29	312.48

It should be pointed out, of course, that we do not know for sure how much of the wealth that shows up in the early inventories was brought into South Carolina and how much was actually accumulated in the colony.

Note that values for "land" were included on a few of these inventories. See Records of the Secretary of the Province, 1675–1695; Records of the Secretary of the Province, 1692–1700. These manuscript volumes are part of the series: Records of the Secretary of State, Miscellaneous Records, Main Series, 1671–1973, 153 vols., South Carolina Department of Archives and History.

On the Crown's increasing scrutiny of South Carolina, see Michael G. Hall, *Edward Randolph and the American Colonies, 1676–1703* (Chapel Hill: University of North Carolina Press, 1960); Clowse, *Economic Beginnings*, pp. 69–138.

76. On eighteenth-century British trade statistics and problems relating to the same, see G.N. Clark, *Guide to English Commercial Statistics 1696–1782* (London: Royal Historical Society, 1938); John J. McCusker, "The Current Value of English Exports, 1697 to 1800," *William and Mary Quarterly*, 3d series, 28 (October 1971): 607–28.

77. On South Carolina's close trading ties with the metropolis, see James F. Shepherd, "Commodity Exports from the British North American Colonies to Overseas Areas, 1768–1772: Magnitudes and Patterns of Trade," *Explorations in Economic History*, 2d series, 8 (Fall 1970): 5–76; Shepherd and Samuel H. Williamson, "The Coastal Trade of the British North American Colonies, 1768–1772," *Journal of Economic History* 32 (December 1972): 783–810; Shepherd and Gary M. Walton, *Shipping, Maritime Trade, and the Economic Development of Colonial North America* (Cambridge: Cambridge University Press, 1972), pp. 91–113; Converse D. Clowse, *Measuring Charleston's Overseas Commerce, 1717–1767: Statistics from the Port's Naval Lists* (Washington, D.C.: University Press of America, 1981), pp. 49–140.

78. On "official" and current values, see McCusker, "The Current Value of English Exports, 1697 to 1800"; Shepherd and Walton, *Shipping, Maritime Trade, and the Economic Development of Colonial North America*, pp. 176–87.

79. For most of the colonial period North Carolina and South Carolina were grouped together without individual breakdown in British trade statistics under the heading "Carolina." Thus, the relative shares of North Carolina and South Carolina respectively in "Carolina's" total export and import trades and in "Carolina's" export and import trades with England alone largely are matters of guesswork for most years. Though no one doubts that South Carolina accounted for the vast majority of "Carolina's" overseas trade, the precise percentage at any given time is difficult to ascertain. We do have, however, a few snippets of information

from which we can make some rough approximations. We know, for example, that in the mid-1730s South Carolina accounted for 93.55 percent of the value of "Carolina's" export trade to England. Moreover, we know that at the end of the colonial period, that is to say, between 1768 and 1772, South Carolina accounted for 85.9 percent of the recorded value of the two Carolinas' total overseas commodity export trade. *Faute de mieux*, we shall use these data—to be sure, with certain qualifications—to estimate South Carolina's relative share of "Carolina's" export and import trades with England during the eighteenth century. In using these data we must keep in mind that:

 a. South Carolina's trading ties with England, according to all accounts, were closer than North Carolina's trading ties to England. Thus, between 1768 and 1772, when South Carolina's recorded share of the two Carolinas' total overseas commodity export trade was 85.9 percent, its share of the export trade with England alone—if recorded— would probably have been closer to 90 percent.

 b. some small part of the trade attributed to South Carolina at any given time actually should be attributed to North Carolina, for South Carolina ports served certain parts of North Carolina as well. As A. Roger Ekirch has shown, however, much more of North Carolina's trade was "lost," statistically-speaking, to Virginia than to South Carolina.

With these points in mind, I therefore have assumed in the tables above that South Carolina accounted for roughly 90 percent of the value of "Carolina's" export and import trades with England between 1698 and 1762. Given the rapid expansion of the North Carolina economy in the 1760s, I have assumed that South Carolina's share of these trades fell to 85 percent between 1768 and 1772. See *Historical Statistics of the United States,* 2: 1176–77; (H. McCulloh) to Board of Trade, September 17, 1736, in William L. Saunders, Walter Clark, and Stephen B. Weeks, eds., *The Colonial and State Records of North Carolina,* 30 vols. (Raleigh, Winston, Goldsboro, and Charlotte, N.C.: 1886–1914), 4: 257–59, especially p. 258; Charles C. Crittenden, *The Commerce of North Carolina, 1763–1789* (New Haven: Yale University Press, 1936); Shepherd, "Commodity Exports from the British North American Colonies to Overseas Areas, 1768–1772: Magnitudes and Patterns of Trade"; Shepherd and Walton, *Shipping, Maritime Trade, and the Economic Development of Colonial North America,* pp. 47, 91–113, 204–36; A. Roger Ekirch, *"Poor Carolina": Politics and Society in Colonial North Carolina, 1729–1776* (Chapel Hill: University of North Carolina Press, 1981), pp. 3–18, especially pp. 14–18; Harry Roy Merrens, *Colonial North Carolina in the Eighteenth Century: A Study in Historical Geography* (Chapel Hill: University of North Carolina Press, 1964), pp. 85–141 especially.

 80. James F. Shepherd and Gary M. Walton as well as Alice Hanson Jones, one should note, are exceptional in that they generally use several definitions of "per capita" in their work. See, for example, Shepherd and Walton, *Shipping, Maritime Trade, and the Economic Development of Colonial North America,* p. 47; Jones, *Wealth of a Nation To Be,* passim.

 81. On South Carolina's leading exports to England, see, for example, Clowse, *Measuring Charleston's Overseas Commerce, 1717–1767,* pp. 49–87. Note that leading exports from the backcountry such as corn, peas, and flour were generally sent to areas other than England. See Clowse, pp. 74–77, 86–87.

 82. See Shepherd and Walton, *Shipping, Maritime Trade, and the Economic Development of Colonial North America,* p. 47; Walton, "The Colonial Economy," in Porter, ed., *Encyclopedia of American Economic History,* 1: 34–50, especially p. 40.

 83. One should also note that as time passed the American colonial trade constituted an increasingly important part of England's total foreign trade. See Ralph Davis, "English Foreign Trade, 1660–1700," *Economic History Review,* 2d series, 7 (1954): 150–66; Ralph

Davis, "English Foreign Trade, 1700–1774," *Economic History Review*, 2d series, 15 (1962): 285–303; Coleman, *The Economy of England 1450–1750*, pp. 131–50.

84. In Table 3–7 above, we estimated the "official" value of South Carolina's export trade to England at £343,461.71 sterling annually between 1768 and 1772. James F. Shepherd and Gary M. Walton have put the "official" value of South Carolina's total overseas commodity exports at £463,000 sterling annually during this five-year period. Combining these data, we find that South Carolina's exports to England constituted 74.18 percent of the value of the colony's total overseas exports. See *Historical Statistics of the United States*, 2: 1176–77; Shepherd and Walton, *Shipping, Maritime Trade, and the Economic Development of Colonial North America*, p. 47. Also, see Table 3–7 and footnotes 78 and 79 of this chapter.

85. Indeed, James F. Shepherd and Samuel H. Williamson have argued that the value of exports from the lower South—North Carolina, South Carolina, and Georgia—to other North American colonies was equal to at least 17 percent of the value of *overseas* exports from the lower South between 1768 and 1772. See Shepherd and Williamson, "The Coastal Trade of the British North American Colonies, 1768–1772," pp. 799–800 especially. For an estimate of the relative importance of the coastal trade in South Carolina's total export trade in the early nineteenth century, see *Niles' Weekly Register* 12 (April 19, 1817): 128.

86. Even assuming (as we have) that the value of South Carolina's exports to other parts of North America did not equal 17 percent of the value of the colony's overseas exports—the percentage found by Shepherd and Williamson for the lower South as a whole—but, let us say, 8 to 10 percent of South Carolina's overseas exports, the colony's total exports would have exceeded £500,000 sterling in "official" value annually between 1768 and 1772. See Shepherd and Williamson, "The Coastal Trade of the British North American Colonies, 1768–1772," pp. 799–800 especially; Shepherd and Walton, *Shipping, Maritime Trade, and the Economic Development of Colonial North America*, p. 47. Also see footnotes 84 and 85 above.

87. On white per capita income in other parts of British North America, see, for example, Jones, *Wealth of a Nation To Be*, pp. 50–85 especially; Edwin J. Perkins, *The Economy of Colonial America* (New York: Columbia University Press, 1980), pp. 145–67, especially p. 154; Walton, "The Colonial Economy, " 1: 48–49; McCusker and Menard, *The Economy of British America*, pp. 51–70, 258–76, especially p. 61.

88. On export/output ratios in British North America during the colonial period, see, for example, Robert E. Lipsey, "Foreign Trade," in Lance E. Davis *et al.*, *American Economic Growth: An Economist's History of the United States* (New York: Harper & Row, 1972), pp. 548–81, especially p. 554; Jones, *Wealth of a Nation To Be*, pp. 64–66, 414 fn. 11; Walton, "The Colonial Economy," 1: 40; Diane Lindstrom, "Domestic Trade and Regional Specialization," in Porter, ed., *Encyclopedia of American Economic History*, 1: 264–80, especially p. 266.

89. See, for example, Gray, *History of Agriculture*, 2: 1019–24, 1030; Charles J. Gayle, "The Nature and Volume of Exports from Charleston, 1724–1774," *The Proceedings of the South Carolina Historical Association, 1937* (Columbia: 1937): 25–33; Converse D. Clowse, "The Charleston Export Trade, 1717–1737" (Ph.D. dissertation, Northwestern University, 1963), passim; Clowse, *Economic Beginnings*, pp. 256–58; Clowse, *Measuring Charleston's Overseas Commerce 1717–1767*, pp. 49–87; Coon, "The Development of Market Agriculture in South Carolina, 1670–1785," pp. 349–59; James A. Bernard, Jr., "An Analysis of British Mercantilism As It Related to Patterns of South Carolina Trade from 1717 to 1767" (Ph.D. dissertation, University of Notre Dame, 1973), pp. 144–60 especially; Max M. Schreiber, "The Nature of the Trade between South Carolina and the West Indies: 1717–1737: A Statistical Approach" (M.A. thesis, University of South Carolina, 1975), pp. 45–72, 121–25.

90. James Glen, *A Description of South Carolina* . . . (London: R. and J. Dodsley, 1761), pp. 50–55.

91. One should note especially the eighteenth-century trends and patterns discernible in tables 3–2, 3–9, 3–14, and 3–15; similarities in the growth rates of black population, rice exports, and total exports in the 1740s are particularly striking.

92. See the "Introduction" of this study, for example.

93. See Terry, " 'Champaign Country,' " pp. 284–97. On archeological differences between the so-called Frontier Artifact Pattern and the so-called Carolina Artifact Pattern, see Stanley South, *Method and Theory in Historical Archeology* (New York: Academic Press, 1977), pp. 83–164, especially pp. 107, 145.

A number of scholars in recent years have utilized data on height to help reconstruct patterns of nutritional well-being and, more broadly, material well-being for given populations. The results of several studies on the final height of the native-born white male population of British North America in the eighteenth century reveal that this population was *very tall* by historical standards, having achieved modern stature by the time of the American Revolution. After disaggregation into discrete regional groupings, these data indicate that the tallest native-born white males in British North America lived in the southern colonies. This finding, of course, is generally consistent with the other data presented in this chapter. No scholar has yet focused his or her attention on South Carolina alone, though John Komlos of the University of Pittsburgh and I currently are engaged in such a study. See Robert W. Fogel, Stanley L. Engerman, and James Trussell, "Exploring the Uses of Data on Height," *Social Science History* 6 (Fall 1982): 401–21; Kenneth L. Sokoloff and Georgia C. Villaflor, "The Early Achievement of Modern Stature in America," *Social Science History* 6 (Fall 1982): 453–81; Fogel *et al.*, "Secular Changes in American and British Stature and Nutrition," in Robert I. Rotberg and Theodore K. Rabb, eds., *Hunger and History: The Impact of Changing Food Production and Consumption Patterns on Society* (New York: Cambridge University Press, 1983), pp. 247–83.

94. With only a few exceptions, all extant South Carolina inventories of estates from the colonial period are located at the South Carolina Department of Archives and History in the following series: Records of the Secretary of State, Miscellaneous Records, Main Series, 1671–1973, 153 vols.; Records of the Secretary of State, Inventories of Estates, 1736–1776, 16 vols.

95. All but one of these inventories are from the following sources: Records of the Secretary of the Province, 1675–1695; Records of the Secretary of the Province, 1692–1700; Records of the Secretary of the Province, 1700–1710; Records of the Secretary of the Province, 1711-1717; Records of the Secretary of the Province, 1711–1719; Records of the Secretary of the Province, 1714–1717; Records of the Secretary of the Province, A, 1721–1722. All seven of these manuscript volumes are part of the following series: Records of the Secretary of State, Miscellaneous Records, Main Series, 1671–1973, 153 vols., South Carolina Department of Archives and History. One other inventory—indeed, a partial one at that—is from Elizabeth Sindrey Papers, Estate Account Book, 1705–1721, leaves 2, 4, 5, 6, 77, 78, South Carolina Historical Society.

In making conversions to sterling, I generally followed John J. McCusker's lead. See McCusker, *Money and Exchange in Europe and America, 1600–1775: A Handbook* (Chapel Hill: University of North Carolina Press, 1978), p. 222. Note that I used my own estimates of the currency/sterling ratio for the years 1706 and 1716 because McCusker lacked data for these two years. I estimated the ratio to be 1.5 to 1.0 in 1706 and 4.0 to 1.0 in 1716.

96. According to Rachel N. Klein, there are, for example, only 143 surviving back-country-inventories for the 1760s. There are, one should note, well over 5000 surviving

inventories from South Carolina for the colonial period as a whole. See Klein, "Ordering the Backcountry," p. 665 fn. 10.

97. On biases in probate records and on possible ways to deal with such biases, see, for example, Gloria L. Main, "The Correction of Biases in Colonial American Probate Records," *Historical Methods Newsletter* 8 (December 1974): 10–28; Main, "Probate Records as a Source for Early American History," *William and Mary Quarterly,* 3d series, 32 (January 1975): 89–99; Daniel Scott Smith, "Underregistration and Bias in Probate Records: An Analysis of Data from Eighteenth-Century Hingham, Massachusetts," *William and Mary Quarterly,* 3d series, 32 (January 1975): 100–10; Carole Shammas, "Constructing a Wealth Distribution from Probate Records," *Journal of Interdisciplinary History* 9 (Autumn 1978): 297–307; Jones, *Wealth of a Nation To Be,* pp. xxi–xxxvi, 343–74, 381–88; Peter H. Lindert, "An Algorithm for Probate Sampling," *Journal of Interdisciplinary History* 11 (Spring 1981): 649–68; Jones, "Estimating Wealth of the Living from a Probate Sample," *Journal of Interdisciplinary History* 13 (Autumn 1982): 273–300; Gloria L. Main, *Tobacco Colony: Life in Early Maryland, 1650–1720* (Princeton: Princeton University Press, 1982); Jackson Turner Main, *Society and Economy in Colonial Connecticut* (Princeton: Princeton University Press, 1985), passim.

Note that Jones's 0.76 conversion factor, cited in the text above, appears in *Wealth of a Nation To Be,* p. 350.

In employing weights and conversion factors, however, one would do well to keep in mind what Whitehead called "the fallacy of misplaced concreteness."

98. See Jackson Turner Main, *The Social Structure of Revolutionary America* (Princeton: Princeton University Press, 1965); Jones, *Wealth of a Nation To Be;* Richard Waterhouse, "South Carolina's Colonial Elite: A Study in the Social Structure and the Political Culture of a Southern Colony, 1670–1760" (Ph.D. dissertation, Johns Hopkins University, 1973), pp. 161–86; William George Bentley, "Wealth Distribution in Colonial South Carolina" (Ph.D. dissertation, Georgia State University, 1977), passim; Terry, " 'Champaign Country,' " passim; Shatzman, "Servants into Planters," pp. 174–76.

99. See Bentley, "Wealth Distribution in Colonial South Carolina," pp. 34, 40, 48, 53, 59, 64, 69, 74; McCusker, *Money and Exchange,* pp. 222–24.

100. Note that due to the nature of the data compiled by Bentley I chose to use the thirty-six-year period from 1726 to 1762 to calculate these growth rates.

101. See George Rogers Taylor, "Wholesale Commodity Prices at Charleston, South Carolina, 1732–1791," *Journal of Economic and Business History* 4 (February 1932): 356–77; Arthur H. Cole, *Wholesale Commodity Prices in the United States 1700–1861,* 2 vols. (Cambridge: Harvard University Press, 1938), 2: 7–49; Phyllis Deane and W.A. Cole, *British Economic Growth 1688–1959: Trends and Structure* (Cambridge: Cambridge University Press, 1962), pp. 12–14, 90–92, and Figure 7; McCusker, "The Current Value of English Exports, 1697 to 1800," p. 619.

102. John Stuart Mill, *Principles of Political Economy . . . ,* ed. W.J. Ashley, 7th ed. (London: Longmans, Green, 1909; originally published 1848), p. 8. For a good discussion of the problem of human property, see Jones, *Wealth of a Nation To Be,* pp. 14–27.

103. Note that my term "total wealth" is analogous to Jones's term "net worth." See Jones, *Wealth of a Nation To Be,* p. 27.

104. Jones, *Wealth of a Nation To Be,* p. 380. This figure was derived by dividing the value of "land" by that of "net worth." Note that in the South as a whole, Jones found that "land" comprised 48.7 percent of "net worth" per wealth-holder. See Jones, p. 129.

105. Bentley, "Wealth Distribution in Colonial South Carolina," pp. 17–19.

106. See Jones, *Wealth of a Nation To Be,* p. 10. Note that I have used 1978 dollars

in my conversions so that my data more readily can be compared with the data compiled by Jones in *Wealth of a Nation To Be*—the standard work on American wealth-holding patterns in the colonial period.

107. Jones, *Wealth of a Nation To Be*, p. 42.

108. James Glen, An Attempt towards an Estimate of the Value of South Carolina, for the Right Honourable the Lords Commissioners for Trade and Plantations, March 1750/1, Records in the British Public Record Office Relating to South Carolina, 24: 303–30, especially pp. 318–19, South Carolina Department of Archives and History.

109. I have found 126 inventories for Charlestonians dated between 1722 and 1732 inclusive. According to these records, the poorest 26 wealth-holders combined possessed £293 sterling in personalty or an average of £11.27 sterling each. See Books A–I and Charleston County Inventories 1732–1736, Records of the Secretary of State, Miscellaneous Records, Main Series, 1671–1973, South Carolina Department of Archives and History.

The data on St. John's Berkeley Parish are from Terry, " 'Champaign Country,' " p. 283. The data on the colony of South Carolina as a whole between 1736 and 1775 are from Waterhouse, "South Carolina's Colonial Elite," pp. 170–73.

110. On wealth in other parts of British North America in the late colonial period and in other parts of the world in both earlier and later periods, see, for example, Jones, *Wealth of a Nation To Be*, pp. 50–85; Perkins, *The Economy of Colonial America*, pp. 145–67; McCusker and Menard, *The Economy of British America*, pp. 51–70, 258–76, especially p. 61.

The figures on wealth in the Charleston District and in Anne Arundel County, Maryland, are from Jones, *Wealth of a Nation To Be*, p. 357.

For historical rates of economic growth in a number of nations in various parts of the world, see Simon Kuznets, *Economic Growth of Nations: Total Output and Production Structure* (Cambridge: The Belknap Press of Harvard University, 1971), pp. 1–50; Lloyd G. Reynolds, *Economic Growth in the Third World, 1850–1980* (New Haven: Yale University Press, 1985), passim.

111. See Perkins, *The Economy of Colonial America*, p. 154. Also see Jones, *Wealth of a Nation To Be*, Table 3.7, p. 58. Note that Perkins uses total physical wealth in his conversions from wealth to income, while Jones uses nonhuman physical wealth.

112. Note that even today national economic policies designed to encourage agricultural self–sufficiency have been found to impede economic performance, at least as measured by GNP. See, for example, M.D. Bale and E. Lutz, "Price Distortions in Agriculture and Their Effects: An International Comparison," *American Journal of Agricultural Economics* 63 (February 1981): 8–22; Michael V. Martin and John A. McDonald, "Food Grain Policy in the Republic of Korea: The Economic Costs of Self-Sufficiency," *Economic Development and Cultural Change* 34 (January 1986): 315–31.

113. For theoretical formulations of the so-called staples thesis and for historical applications of such formulations, see, for example, Melville H. Watkins, "A Staple Theory of Economic Growth," *Canadian Journal of Economics and Political Science* 29 (May 1963): 141–58; Douglass C. North, "Location Theory and Regional Economic Growth," *Journal of Political Economy* 63 (June 1955): 243–58; North, "Agriculture in Regional Economic Growth," *Journal of Farm Economics* 41 (December 1959): 943-51; Richard E. Caves, " 'Vent for Surplus' Models of Trade and Growth," in Robert E. Baldwin *et al., Trade, Growth and the Balance of Payments: Essays in Honor of Gottfried Haberler* (Amsterdam: North-Holland Publishing Co., 1965), pp. 95-115; Caves, "Export-Led Growth and the New Economic History," in Jagdish N. Bhagwati *et al., Trade, Balance of Payments and Growth: Papers in International Economics in Honor of Charles P. Kindleberger* (Amsterdam: North-

Holland Publishing Co., 1971), pp. 403–42; Albert O. Hirschman, "A Generalized Linkage Approach to Development, with Special Reference to Staples," *Economic Development and Cultural Change*, 25 Supplement (1977): 67–98; North, *The Economic Growth of the United States 1790–1860* (Englewood Cliffs, N.J.: Prentice-Hall, 1961); Shepherd and Walton, *Shipping, Maritime Trade and the Economic Development of Colonial North America*, pp. 6–26 especially; David W. Galenson and Russell R. Menard, "Approaches to the Analysis of Economic Growth in Colonial British America," *Historical Methods* 13 (Winter 1980): 3–18; Menard and McCusker, *The Economy of British America*, pp. 17–32 and passim.

114. My conception of "theory" draws heavily from the work of William Letwin, *The Origins of Scientific Economics: English Economic Thought 1660–1776* (London: Methuen, 1963), pp. vii–ix especially.

115. That the role of the export sector in the American economy in the antebellum period, for example, has been overstated by scholars employing staples theory, see Stuart W. Bruchey, "Douglass C. North on American Economic Growth," *Explorations in Entrepreneurial History*, 2d series, 1 (Winter 1964): 145–58; Paul A. David, "The Growth of Real Product in the United States Before 1840: New Evidence, Controlled Conjectures," *Journal of Economic History* 27 (June 1967): 151–97; Diane Lindstrom, *Economic Development in the Philadelphia Region, 1810–1850* (New York: Columbia University Press, 1978), pp. 1–21 and passim; Lindstrom, "Domestic Trade and Regional Specialization."

Scholars have registered other complaints against this theory as well. See Jacob M. Price, "The Transatlantic Economy," in Greene and Pole, eds., *Colonial British America*, pp. 18–42; Richard B. Sheridan, "The Domestic Economy," in Greene and Pole, eds., *Colonial British America*, pp. 43–85. While Price and Sheridan are "friendly" critics of the theory and are willing to accept it in large part, another recent critic, Joseph A. Ernst, views the theory—as articulated by U.S. scholars at least—much more negatively. See Ernst, "Caught in a 'Seamless Web': Economic History as 'Getting and Spending,' " *Reviews in American History* 14 (June 1986): 190–94.

116. See, for example, Carville Earle and Ronald Hoffman, "Staple Crops and Urban Development in the Eighteenth-Century South," *Perspectives in American History* 10 (1976): 7–78; Galenson and Menard, "Approaches to the Analysis of Economic Growth in Colonial British America"; Earle, "A Staple Interpretation of Slavery and Free Labor," *Geographical Review* 68 (January 1978): 51–65; Anderson and Thomas, "Economic Growth in the Seventeenth-Century Chesapeake"; Earle and Hoffman, "The Foundation of the Modern Economy: Agriculture and the Costs of Labor in the United States and England, 1800–60," *American Historical Review* 85 (December 1980): 1055–94; Menard and McCusker, *The Economy of British America*, pp. 17–32 and passim.

For the standard theoretical formulation of this thesis, see Robert E. Baldwin, "Patterns of Development in Newly Settled Areas," *Manchester School of Economic and Social Studies* 24 (May 1956): 161–79.

117. See Earle and Hoffman, "Staple Crops and Urban Development in the Eighteenth-Century South"; Galenson and Menard, "Approaches to the Analysis of Economic Growth in Colonial British America." On the type of economic development ostensibly ensuing from the production of wheat in antebellum America, see Morton Rothstein, "Antebellum Wheat and Cotton Exports: A Contrast in Marketing Organization and Economic Development," *Agricultural History* 40 (April 1966): 91–100.

118. Despite their interpretive differences, both François Chevalier and Eric Van Young have found that such characteristics were associated with wheat haciendas in north Mexico and the Guadalajara region respectively. See Chevalier, *Land and Society in Colonial*

Mexico: The Great Hacienda, trans. Alvin Eustis (Berkeley: University of California Press, 1963), pp. 59–71 and passim; Van Young, *Hacienda and Market in Eighteenth-Century Mexico: The Rural Economy of the Guadalajara Region, 1675–1820* (Berkeley: University of California Press, 1981), passim.

While "Mexico" had a much larger pre-Columbian population than any part of "British" North America, numbers dropped cataclysmically in the century after the Conquest. One of the assumptions in Baldwin's hypothetical model—sparse settlement—was thus met in sixteenth- and seventeenth-century Mexico. For background on this depopulation, see Chapter 2 of this study.

One should also note that in the United States in the 1870s and 1880s the production function for wheat proved conducive to the development on the Great Plains of both small "family" farms and huge "bonanza" farms. On the latter, see, for example, Fred A. Shannon, *The Farmer's Last Frontier: Agriculture, 1860–1897,* The Economic History of the United States Series (New York: Harper & Row, 1968; originally published 1945), pp. 154–61 especially.

Even rice historically has been cultivated in far different ways by people sharing the same general culture. In twentieth-century Spain, for example, the contrast between cultivation systems in the Seville and Valencia regions is great. See Raymond E. Crist, "Rice Culture in Spain," *Scientific Monthly* 84 (February 1957): 66–74.

Finally, let me stress again that I believe the production function to be a very powerful explanatory variable in any society. In the discussion above, I tried only to show that arguments based upon it sometimes have been put forth with too much zeal.

119. James F. Shepherd and Gary M. Walton, for example, emphasize productivity gains in shipping and the maritime trade, while Edmund Morgan emphasizes the exploitation and profits possible under the system of slavery. One should note, however, that Marc Egnal takes a broader approach, emphasizing three sets of factors: productivity gains in agriculture and industry, a rise in the real value of colonial exports, and increased amounts of capital available to the white population. See Shepherd and Walton, *Shipping, Maritime Trade and the Economic Development of Colonial North America*; Morgan, *American Slavery, American Freedom,* pp. 295–387 especially; Egnal, "The Economic Development of the Thirteen Continental Colonies, 1720 to 1775," *William and Mary Quarterly,* 3d series, 32 (April 1975): 191–222, especially p. 199.

120. Petty, *Political Arithmetick* . . . , Preface (n.p.).

121. Terry, " 'Champaign Country,' " p. 248.

122. A simple exercise will bear out this point. South Carolina exported an average of 66,327,975 pounds of clean rice annually between 1768 and 1772. In addition, a considerable amount of the annual rice crop was consumed within the colony, with estimates of local consumption generally running between 10 percent and 33.3 percent of the total crop. Thus, South Carolina in all likelihood produced somewhere between 73,000,000 and 100,000,000 pounds of clean rice annually between 1768 and 1772. At 1500 pounds of clean rice per acre—a common estimate of yield on the eve of the Revolution—South Carolina's rice crop could be produced on somewhere between about 49,000 and 67,000 acres of land. Even at 1000 pounds of clean rice per acre, only 73,000 to 100,000 acres would be needed to produce a crop of the size mentioned above. The South Carolina low country encompasses an area of about 13,400 square miles—about 8.6 million acres.

Later estimates put the number of acres devoted to rice production in the low country at about 70,000 in 1842 and about 77,000 in 1885. See Report, Committee on Agriculture, December 14, 1842, *Journal of the Senate of the State of South-Carolina . . . 1842*

(Columbia: Pemberton, 1842) pp. 89–90; *Charleston News and Courier,* September 1, 1885.

On rice exports, see Table 3–13. Though Francis Yonge implied that only about 3.1 percent of the rice crop in 1722 was consumed locally, most other writers place local consumption between the levels mentioned above. See, for example, Francis Yonge to Board of Trade, December 10, 1722, in W. Noel Sainsbury *et al.,* eds. *Great Britain, Calendar of State Papers, Colonial Series, America and West Indies, 1574–,* 44 vols. thus far (London: 1860–), vol.: *1722–1723,* p. 184; John Norris, *Profitable Advice for Rich and Poor . . .* (London: J. How, 1712), p. 26; Meeting, Board of Trade, July 15, 1715, in Great Britain, Public Record Office, *Journal of the Commissioners for Trade and Plantations,* 14 vols. (London: H.M. Stationery Office, 1920–38), 3: 56.

Lewis Gray estimates that one-third of total rice output was consumed locally. David Coon cites Gray but makes no estimate himself, saying only that the total consumed locally and/or destroyed in the threshing process was "not inconsiderable." Converse Clowse puts local consumption at "as much as 10 per cent of the total crop."

I personally feel Clowse's estimate is better than that of Gray. See Gray, *History of Agriculture* 1: 287; Coon, "The Development of Market Agriculture in South Carolina, 1670-1785," pp. 177, 206–7; Clowse, *Economic Beginnings,* p. 168.

On the approximate size of the low country, see South Carolina State Planning Board, *The Natural Resources of South Carolina,* Bulletin No. 3, revised (Columbia: 1944), p. 17.

123. According to South Carolina tax records from the 1760s, for example, the free black population in the colony was as follows:

Year	Number
1761	53
1762	71
1764	92
1765	118
1766	96
1767	67
1768	77
1769	159

See Public Treasurer of South Carolina, General Tax Receipts and Payments, 1761–1769 (1771), 1 ms. vol., South Carolina Department of Archives and History.

124. On the labor involved in the production of rice and indigo in colonial South Carolina, see Gray, *History of Agriculture,* 1: 280–84, 295–97; Coon, "The Development of Market Agriculture in South Carolina, 1670–1785," pp. 183–88, 235–44; Clowse, *Economic Beginnings,* pp. 125–30.

That labor intensity in plantation agriculture, particularly in rice cultivation, was greater than that in earlier "pioneer" activities is a commonplace. See, for example, Wood, *Black Majority,* passim.

125. Forrest McDonald, *E Pluribus Unum: The Formation of the American Republic 1776–1790* (Boston: Houghton Mifflin, 1965), p. 65. For those that prefer Marxian categories, the evidence indicates that the extraction of both absolute and relative surplus value rose with the establishment of the plantation regime in the low country.

126. On the utility—and the obvious limitations—of the concept "aggregate production function," see, for example, Moses Abramovitz and Paul A. David, "Reinterpreting Eco-

nomic Growth: Parables and Realities," *American Economic Review* 63 (May 1973): 428–39; Gallman, "Economic Growth," pp. 137–40.

127. Bentley, "Wealth Distribution in Colonial South Carolina," pp. 93–94. The quote cited in the text appears on page 93.

128. Bentley, "Wealth Distribution in Colonial South Carolina," pp. 95–96.

129. Bentley, "Wealth Distribution in Colonial South Carolina," p. 97.

130. To derive the 11 percent figure cited in the text above I utilized Jones's data on mean private wealth in the Charleston District in 1774. These data appear on p. 380 in *Wealth of a Nation To Be*. I first subtracted the value of "land" per wealth-holder (£558.3 sterling) from Jones's figure for mean net worth per wealth-holder (£1776.7 sterling). I then divided the remainder (£1218.4 sterling) into the value of "producers' capital" per wealth-holder (£131.5 sterling) and got the figure .1079. Producers' capital, in other words, constituted almost 11 percent of mean non-land wealth.

I derived the £1211 current money figure cited in the text by first using the method suggested by Jones *(Wealth of a Nation To Be*, pp. 350–51) to convert her figure on mean "producers' capital" per wealth-holder to mean "producers' capital" per *probate-type wealth-holder* and then converting the figure obtained from sterling to South Carolina currency. In the latter conversion, I utilized John J. McCusker's currency/sterling ratio for 1774 (7.0 to 1.0). See McCusker, *Money and Exchange*, p. 224.

131. For a good discussion of capital—circulating and fixed—and capital accumulation in the early modern period, see De Vries, *The Economy of Europe in an Age of Crisis, 1600–1750*, pp. 192–235.

On financial capital in its various eighteenth-century forms, see Jones, *Wealth of a Nation To Be*, pp. 14–27, 127–54.

On the economic importance of human capital, see, for example, Theodore W. Schultz, *Investing in People: The Economics of Population Quality* (Berkeley: University of California Press, 1981).

132. My conception of technology owes much to the work of Nathan Rosenberg. See Rosenberg, *Technology and American Economic Growth* (New York: Harper & Row, 1972). Also see Edward F. Denison, *The Sources of Economic Growth in the United States and the Alternatives Before Us* (New York: Committee for Economic Development, 1962).

133. A number of South Carolinians in the seventeenth and eighteenth centuries were interested, indeed, actively—if only tangentially—engaged in the development of "modern" science, particularly in such fields as natural history, meteorology, "scientific" agriculture, metallurgy, and mechanics. The reason or reasons for such active interest and engagement remain open to question even today. The debate over the relationship between science and technology—the latter of which entails the economic application of scientific knowledge—during the early modern period is one of the most perdurable in twentieth-century social science. The debate, of course, is between those who see a close link between science and technology—scholars such as Boris Hessen, Robert K. Merton and, more recently, Paolo Rossi—and those who deny that a close relationship existed between the same—most notably George Clark and A.R. Hall. For a recent contribution to the debate written by a scholar sympathetic to the latter position, see Michael Hunter, *Science and Society in Restoration England* (Cambridge: Cambridge University Press, 1981). For an attempt to cast this debate in different—and somewhat broader—terms, see Barbara J. Shapiro's fine study, *Probability and Certainty in Seventeenth-Century England: A Study of the Relationships between Natural Science, Religion, History, Law and Literature* (Princeton: Princeton University Press, 1983), pp. 15–118 and passim.

134. On the geographic shift of the South Carolina rice industry, see, for example, Gray, *History of Agriculture*, 1: 279–80; Coon, "The Development of Market Agriculture in South Carolina, 1670–1785," pp. 178–86; Clifton, "The Rice Industry in Colonial America," pp. 274–76.

On the productivity gains ensuing from irrigated rice cultivation, particularly in tidal swamps, see Gray, *History of Agriculture*, 1: 279; Clifton, "The Rice Industry in Colonial America," pp. 274–75.

On the African contribution to the origination and development of cultivation practices in the South Carolina rice industry, see Wood, *Black Majority*, pp. 59–62 especially; Littlefield, *Rice and Slaves*, pp. 74–114. One should, however, also see Philip D. Morgan's review of *Rice and Slaves* in the *William and Mary Quarterly*, 3d series, 39 (October 1982): 709–12.

135. On yield per acre in the early eighteenth century, see, for example, Nairne, *A Letter from South Carolina . . .* , p. 9; Norris, *Profitable Advice for Rich and Poor . . .* , pp. 40–41.

On yield per acre during the era of the American Revolution, see, for example, Klaus G. Loewald, Beverly Starika, and Paul S. Taylor, trans. and eds., "Johann Martin Bolzius Answers a Questionnaire on Carolina and Georgia," *William and Mary Quarterly*, 3d series, 14 (April 1957): 218–61, especially p. 260; *South Carolina Gazette*, March 2, 1747; Easterby *et al.*, eds., *The Colonial Records of South Carolina*, 1st series: *The Journal of the Commons House of Assembly*, 9:98; *South Carolina Gazette*, July 11, 1761; John Bartram, "Diary of a Journey through the Carolinas, Georgia, and Florida, from July 1, 1765, to April 10, 1766," annotated by Francis Harper, in *Transactions of the American Philosophical Society*, new series, 33 (1942–44): 1–120, especially pp. 15, 53; Henry Laurens to James Grant, December 22, 1768, in Hamer, Rogers, *et al.*, eds., *The Papers of Henry Laurens*, 6: 231–34, especially p. 233; *South Carolina Gazette & Country Journal*, January 5, 1773; Chalmers, *An Account of the Weather and Diseases of South-Carolina*, 1: 4; John Ball Account Book, 1780–1784, pp. 9, 21, Ball Family Account Books, Manuscript Department, William R. Perkins Library, Duke University, Durham, N.C.; J.F.D. Smyth, *Tour in the United States of America . . .* , 2 vols. (Dublin: T. Henshall, 1784), 2: 43; Ralph Izard to Gabriel Manigault, June 9, 1789, Ralph Izard Papers, South Caroliniana Library; J.C. Fitzpatrick, ed., *The Diaries of George Washington, 1748–1799*, 4 vols. (Boston and New York: Houghton Mifflin, 1925), 4: 172; Drayton, *A View of South-Carolina*, p. 120.

136. See Glen, *A Description of South-Carolina . . .* , p. 8; Easterby *et al.*, eds., *The Colonial Records of South Carolina*, 1st series: *The Journal of the Commons House of Assembly*, 9:98; Fitzpatrick, ed., *The Diaries of George Washington*, 4: 172; Littlefield, *Rice and Slaves*, pp. 68–69. Note that the size of the rice barrels involved is not mentioned in the source cited by Littlefield. I therefore used the estimate of barrel size for the appropriate year—1757—made by Lawrence Harper in the *Historical Statistics of the United States*. See volume 2, pp. 1163–64.

137. See, for example, Coon, "The Development of Market Agriculture in South Carolina, 1670–1785," pp. 186–88; Morgan, "Work and Culture: The Task System and the World of Lowcountry Blacks, 1700 to 1880," p. 577 fn. 53.

For contemporary evidence on innovations and improvements in the cultivation and processing of rice, see, for example, Easterby *et al.*, eds., *The Colonial Records of South Carolina*, 1st series: *The Journal of the Commons House of Assembly*, 3:511; *South Carolina Gazette*, April 23, 1744; *South Carolina Gazette & Country Journal*, October 9, 1770, Supplement; Cooper and McCord, *Statutes*, 4: 755–56; 5: 69–70; 6: 618, 620–22; Undated Manuscript, John Lucas, Lucas Family Papers, South Carolina Historical Society; Plowden

Weston to Jonathan Lucas, March 22, 1793, Lucas Family Papers, South Carolina Historical Society; John Hume to Paul Mazyck, October 28, 1793, Thomas Porcher Ravenel Papers, South Carolina Historical Society; Robert Grant to Pierce Butler, March 8, 1796, Butler Family Papers, Historical Society of Pennsylvania, Philadelphia, Pennsylvania.

138. Morgan,"Work and Culture: The Task System and the World of Lowcountry Blacks, 1700 to 1880." While I much admire this article, I believe that Morgan overestimates the role of blacks in the introduction and diffusion of the task system in the low country and, in so doing, necessarily understates the role of management in the same.

On southern planters as self-conscious, rational managers, see, for example, Kenneth M. Stampp, *The Peculiar Institution: Slavery in the Ante-Bellum South* (New York: Knopf, 1956); William K. Scarborough, *The Overseer: Plantation Management in the Old South* (Baton Rouge: Louisiana State University Press, 1966); Keith Aufhauser, "Slavery and Scientific Management," *Journal of Economic History* 33 (December 1973): 811–24; Robert William Fogel and Stanley L. Engerman, *Time on the Cross: The Economics of American Negro Slavery*, 2 vols. (Boston: Little, Brown, 1974); Jacob Metzer, "Rational Management, Modern Business Practices, and Economies of Scale in the Ante-Bellum Southern Plantations," *Explorations in Economic History*, 2d ser., 12 (April 1975): 123–50; Peter A. Coclanis, "Entrepreneurship and the Economic History of the American South: The Case of Charleston and the South Carolina Low Country," in Stanley C. Hollander and Terence Nevett, eds. *Marketing in the Long Run* (East Lansing: Department of Marketing and Transportation Administration, Michigan State University, 1985), pp. 210–19. Note that Scarborough views the overseers of rice plantations in the South Carolina—Georgia low country as the most able plantation managers in the South. See Scarborough, *The Overseer*, pp. 56–58, 199–200. One can readily understand why Scarborough arrived at this conclusion by going through the plantation correspondence of overseers Roswell King, Sr., and Roswell King, Jr., in the Butler Family Papers at the Historical Society of Pennsylvania.

139. The principal parties in the historiographical debate on economies of scale in the Cotton South are, of course, Robert W. Fogel and Stanley L. Engerman on one side arguing that such economies did indeed exist, and Gavin Wright on the other denying their existence. See Fogel and Engerman, *Time on the Cross;* Wright, *The Political Economy of the Cotton South: Households, Markets, and Wealth in the Nineteenth Century* (New York: W.W. Norton, 1978). The debate has continued intermittently since 1978, primarily in the *American Economic Review*. For an excellent, recent contribution to this debate, see Elizabeth B. Field, "Elasticities of Complementarity and Returns to Scale in Antebellum Cotton Agriculture" (Ph.D. dissertation, Duke University, 1985).

140. Swan, *The Structure and Profitability of the Antebellum Rice Industry 1859*, pp. 96–104 especially. Note that James Glen in 1748 wrote that thirty slaves were considered "proper" for a rice plantation. See Glen, *A Description of South Carolina . . .* , p. 8.

141. Terry, " 'Champaign Country,' " p. 249.

142. Morgan, "The Development of Slave Culture in Eighteenth Century Plantation America," p. 2.

143. See Egnal, "The Economic Development of the Thirteen Continental Colonies, 1720 to 1775," pp. 205–14 especially. Also see Egnal, "The Pennsylvania Economy, 1748–1762; An Analysis of Short-Run Fluctuations in the Context of Long-Run Changes in the Atlantic Trading Community" (Ph.D. dissertation, University of Wisconsin, 1974) Appendix G.

144. See, for example, Shepherd and Walton, *Shipping, Maritime Trade, and the Economic Development of Colonial North America*, pp. 6–26, 49–90, 188–203; Walton, "The Colonial Economy," pp. 43–46. Shepherd and Walton's approach and emphases, one

should note, owes much to the earlier work of Douglass C. North. See North, "Ocean Freight Rates and Economic Development 1750–1913," *Journal of Economic History* 18 (December 1958): 537–55; North, "Sources of Productivity Change in Ocean Shipping, 1600–1850," *Journal of Political Economy* 76 (September–October 1968): 953–70; North and Robert Paul Thomas, "An Economic Theory of the Growth of the Western World," *Economic History Review*, 2d series, 23 (1970): 1–17. One should also take note of Christopher J. French's recent study on productivity change in the shipping industry. See French, "Productivity in the Atlantic Shipping Industry: A Quantitative Survey," *Journal of Interdisciplinary History* 17 (Winter 1987): 613–38. For a broader, cultural view of such changes, see Ian K. Steele, *The English Atlantic, 1675–1740: An Exploration of Communication and Community* (New York: Oxford University Press, 1986).

145. See the works cited in footnote 144 above.

146. Note that in compiling data for Table 3–26, each vessel clearing Charleston in a given year was counted only once, regardless of how many times it actually cleared in that year. See Clowse, *Measuring Charleston's Overseas Commerce, 1717–1767*, pp. 89, 112–14.

147. See, for example, Stuart O. Stumpf, "Implications of King George's War for the Charleston Mercantile Community," *South Carolina Historical Magazine* 77 (July 1976): 161–88. Also see Shepherd and Walton, *Shipping, Maritime Trade, and the Economic Development of Colonial North America*, pp. 76–77, 88–89.

148. See Shepherd and Walton, *Shipping, Maritime Trade, and the Economic Development of Colonial North America*, pp. 62–69, 121, 124–25, 188–94.

Mean port-times apparently declined significantly in Charleston between the 1720s and the 1760s. This decline can be seen in the data presented below.

Mean Port-Times by Vessel, Charleston, S.C.

| | 1722 | | 1763 | |
| | Mean Port- | | Mean Port- | |
Type of Vessel	Time (Days)	Observations	Time (Days)	Observations
Ships	51.50	22	38.48	23
Snows	– –	– –	46.45	11
Brigs	38.78	9	34.20	30
Schooners	99.00	1	32.70	10
Sloops	39.94	16	23.96	26
Totals	46.25	48	33.72	100

Source: Great Britain, Public Record Office, Colonial Office, America & West Indies, Naval Office Shipping Lists for South Carolina, 1716–67, CO 5/508–511 (microfilm). The data presented above are for the first quarters of 1722 and 1763 respectively. Note that 102 vessels actually entered Charleston harbor during the first quarter of 1763, but the date of clearance could only be established for one hundred of these vessels.

Mean port-times seem to have declined over time in Philadelphia as well. The average for all vessels—ships, snows, brigs, schooners, and sloops—at Philadelphia in 1732–1733 was 41.6 days. By 1749–1750 the mean figure at that port had fallen to 36.3 days. See Shepherd and Walton, *Shipping, Maritime, Trade, and the Economic Development of Colonial North America*, p. 198

149. The ports of Georgetown and Beaufort and the fall-line town of Camden, for example, became moderately important auxiliary trade and distribution centers by the end of the colonial era. See Ronald E. Bridwell, *". . . That We Should have a Port . . . ": A History of the Port of Georgetown, South Carolina, 1732–1865* (Georgetown: The

Georgetown Times, 1982), pp. 1–23; Lawrence S. Rowland, "Eighteenth Century Beaufort: A Study of South Carolina's Southern Parishes to 1800" (Ph.D. dissertation, University of South Carolina, 1978), passim; Merrens, " 'Camden's turrets pierce the skies!' "

Port facilities in Charleston, of course, improved over time as well. The number of wharves or bridges serving the town, for example, grew in the following manner: 2 by 1704, 8 by 1739, 12 by 1751, 23 by 1788. Moreover, the number of pilots serving Charleston harbor increased from 4 in 1755 to 9 in 1763 and to 11 by 1774. On the number of wharves in Charleston at various points in the eighteenth century, see *A Plan of Charles Town from a Survey by Edward Crisp in 1704*, Map Collection, South Caroliniana Library; George Hunter, *The Ichnography of Charles-Town at High Water* (London: Published by B. Roberts and W.H. Toms, 1739); Glen, An Attempt towards an Estimate of the Value of South Carolina for the Right Honourable the Lords Commissioners of Trade and Plantations, March 1750/51, Records in the British Public Record Office Relating to South Carolina, 24: 303–30, especially p. 330, South Carolina Department of Archives and History; E. Petrie, *Plan of the City of Charleston, South Carolina, from a Survey Taken by E. Petrie, 1788*, in Jacob C. Milligan, *Charleston Directory and Revenue System, 1790* (Charleston: T.R. Bowen, 1790). On the number of pilots in 1755, 1763, and 1774 respectively, see Pilots of Charles-Town Bar, Petition to Speaker Benjamin Smith, Esq., and the Members of the South Carolina Commons House of Assembly, 1755, Charleston Library Society, Charleston; George Andrews, *The South-Carolina Almanack and Register for the Year of our Lord, 1763* (Charleston: Robert Wells, 1763); *Wells's Register: Together With an Almanack . . . By George Andrews, Esq. For the Year of our Lord 1774*, Twelfth ed. (Charleston: Robert Wells, 1774), p. 72.

For evidence of other improvements to port and harbor facilities in Charleston during the eighteenth century, see *South Carolina & American General Gazette*, November 28, 1766; *South Carolina Gazette*, February 9, 1767, Supplement; October 31, 1768; November 5, 1772.

Such improvements, of course, continued in the nineteenth century as well. See Ordinance, September 2, 1840, *A Digest of the Ordinances of the City Council of Charleston, from the Year 1783 to Oct. 1844 . . .*, Prepared under Resolution of the City Council by George B. Eckhard (Charleston: Walker & Burke, 1844), pp. 104–10; *De Bow's Review* 24 (January 1858): 62–63; F.L. Childs to Samuel A. Ashe, January 26, 1879, Samuel A' Court Ashe Papers, North Carolina State Archives. One should also note that the number of pilots and pilot boats serving Charleston harbor rose substantially in the nineteenth century: there were nineteen pilots and seven boats by 1851 and forty-two pilots working eleven boats by 1856. See *Charleston Courier*, January 13, 1851; *Miller's Planters' & Merchants' Almanac . . .* (Charleston: A.E. Miller, 1856?).

On the increasing size of rice barrels over time, see *Historical Statistics of the United States*, 2: 1163–64.

150. For details on the various transportation improvements made in colonial South Carolina, see Cooper and McCord, *Statutes*, 7: 475–519; 9: 1–246. One should note that control over most improvements devolved to the parish level with the establishment of local highway commissions in 1721. The statutes in Cooper and McCord, thus, cover only a small proportion of the transportation improvements authorized after that date.

Note that many transportation improvements in eighteenth-century South Carolina represented forms of "mixed" public-private enterprise. See, for example, Richard Hutson to William Gibbes, March 14, 1776, Charles Woodward Hutson Papers, Southern Historical Collection; Ledger, 1777–1779, Lancelot Smith Collection, South Carolina Historical Society.

151. On the transportation sequence in "newly settled" staple-producing areas and in

"underdeveloped" countries today, see, for example, James E. Vance, Jr., *The Merchant's World: The Geography of Wholesaling,* Foundations of Economic Geography Series (Englewood Cliffs, N.J.: Prentice-Hall, 1970), pp. 80–128, 138–67; Edward J. Taafe, Richard L. Morrill, and Peter R. Gould, "Transport Expansion in Underdeveloped Countries: A Comparative Analysis," *Geographical Review* 53 (October 1963): 503–29.

South Carolina, particularly the low country, was to remain at a "low" stage of transport development—as schematized by Vance or Taafe *et al.*—well beyond the colonial era. This was so, as we shall see, because of the asymmetrical pattern of economic growth and development in this area. For detailed studies of the origins and effects of "conveyor belt" transportation systems in three other colonial areas, see Caio Prado, Jr., *The Colonial Background of Modern Brazil,* trans. Suzette Macedo (Berkeley: University of California Press, 1971), pp. 276–309; Peter W. Rees, "Origins of Colonial Transportation in Mexico," *Geographical Review* 65 (July 1975): 323–34; Stephen G. Britton, "The Evolution of a Colonial Space-Economy: The Case of Fiji," *Journal of Historical Geography* 6 (July 1980): 251–74. That such systems were characteristic of all export-oriented economies based on dependent labor, see Eugene D. Genovese and Elizabeth Fox-Genovese, "The Slave Economies in Political Perspective," *Journal of American History* 66 (June 1979): 7–23, especially p. 16.

152. For road dimensions up to 1720, see, for example, Cooper and McCord, *Statutes,* 9: 3–6, 8–11, 11–12, 13–14, 14–17, 17–21, 26–28, 36, 41–43, 46–48, 49.

For road dimensions after 1720, see, for example, Cooper and McCord, *Statutes,* 9: 49–57, 57–59, 65–66, 67, 68–69.

153. Peter Colleton to Sir, July 22, 1674, Mss. Locke, C.6., Bodleian Library, Oxford University, Oxford, England. I used a microfilm copy of this letter available at the South Carolina Historical Society in the collection "John Locke, Correspondence, 1673–1704."

154. See Francis Le Jau to the Secretary of the Society for the Propagation of the Gospel, November 15, 1708, in Frank J. Klingberg, ed., *The Carolina Chronicle of Dr. Francis Le Jau 1706–1717,* University of California Publications in History, vol. 53 (Berkeley: University of California Press, 1956), pp. 46–48, especially p. 46; Richard Hill to Wm. Jefferis, June 17, 1743, Richard Hill Letter Book, Manuscript Department, William R. Perkins Library; William Vernon to Messrs. Simond, September 3, 1746, William Vernon Manuscripts, 1745–1749, South Caroliniana Library; Henry Laurens to James Crokatt, October 7, 1747, in Hamer, Rogers, *et al.,* eds., *The Papers of Henry Laurens,* 1: 60–64; Josiah Smith, Jr., to Joseph Clay, November 26, 1772, p. 131, Josiah Smith, Jr., Lettercopy Book, Southern Historical Collection.

155. On London coffee houses in general and on the Carolina Coffee House specifically, see Bryant Lillywhite, *London Coffee Houses: A Reference Book of Coffee Houses of the Seventeenth, Eighteenth, and Nineteenth Centuries* (London: Allen and Unwin, 1963), pp. 17–27, 147–49. Note that although Lillywhite says the first contemporary mention of the Carolina Coffee House dates from 1748, the coffee house is in fact mentioned in Samuel Wilson's 1682 pamphlet *An Account of the Province of Carolina . . .* (London: Printed by G. Larkin for Francis Smith, 1682). This pamphlet is reprinted in A.S. Salley, ed., *Narratives of Early Carolina 1650–1708* (New York: Barnes & Noble, 1967; originally published 1911), pp. 164–76. See p. 176 especially. Another London coffee house—the "New Carolina, Georgia, Florida, and Pennsylvania Coffee-House"—also may have served as a communications node for those engaged in commerce with South Carolina. See *South Carolina Gazette & Country Journal,* November 3, 1772.

On the opening of commercial coffee houses in Charleston in the eighteenth century, see, for example, *South Carolina Gazette,* April 4, 1743; November 26, 1753; June 6, 1761.

On the gradual extension and elaboration of postal and packet service between South Carolina and England, between South Carolina and other North American colonies, and within South Carolina itself, see *Boston News-Letter,* February 4, 1711/12; Henry Laurens to Meyler & Hall, October 2, 1756, in Hamer, Rogers, *et al.,* eds., *The Papers of Henry Laurens, 2:* 325-27, especially p. 326; Hamer, Rogers, *et al.,* eds., *The Papers of Henry Laurens* 4: 393 fn. 1; Henry Laurens to Hugh Porter, February 5, 1766, in Hamer, Rogers, *et al.,* eds., *The Papers of Henry Laurens,* 5: 68–69; *South Carolina Gazette,* September 17, 1737; May 3, 1739; July 12, 1740; December 5, 1754; February 13, 1762; October 13, 1766; February 15, 1770; August 30, 1773, Supplement; September 19, 1774, Supplement; *South Carolina Gazette & Country Journal,* July 15, 1766, Supplement; November 22, 1768; September 4, 1770; *South Carolina & American General Gazette,* June 2, 1775.

156. South Carolina's three established newspapers during the colonial period were the *South Carolina Gazette* (founded 1732), the *South-Carolina and American General Gazette* (founded 1758), and the *South-Carolina Gazette and Country Journal* (founded 1765). All three were published in Charleston. See, for example, Bowes, *The Culture of Early Charleston,* pp. 67–71. On the role of the press in the southern colonies in general, see Robert M. Weir, "The Role of the Newspaper Press in the Southern Colonies on the Eve of the Revolution: An Interpretation," in Bernard Bailyn and John B. Hench, eds., *The Press & the American Revolution* (Worcester, Mass.: American Antiquarian Society, 1980), pp. 99–150.

157. *South-Carolina Gazette,* August 25, 1764.

158. Cooper and McCord, *Statutes,* 3: 289–304.

159. See Records of the Register of Mesne Conveyance, Charleston County, Deeds, 1719–1763, Books A through A–3, 50 vols., South Carolina Department of Archives and History; Records of the Secretary of State, Miscellaneous Records, Main Series, 153 vols., vols. 2B (1732–1735), AB (1735–1736), South Carolina Department of Archives and History; Records of the Secretary of State, Mortgages, Charleston Series, 1736–1867, 53 vols., vols. 2K (1736–1738), 2M (1738), 2N (1736–1739), 2O (1739–1740), 2P (1740–1742), 2Q (1742–1744, 2 parts), 2R (1744–1746), 2S (1746–1748), 2T (1748–1750), 2V (1750–1753), 2W (1753–1756, 2 parts), 2X (1756–1759), 2Y (1759–1761), 2Z (1761–1766, 2 parts), 3A (1766–1769, 2 parts), 3B (1766–1771), 3C (1765–1774), South Carolina Department of Archives and History.

Of 832 mortgages recorded in the Deed Books (which actually cover the period 1709–64), for example, 160 were for the period up to 1730 and 672 for the 1731–64 period.

160. On the importance of mortgage debt in the early modern West, see, for example, De Vries, *The Economy of Europe in an Age of Crisis 1600–1750,* p. 222.

On Ashley and Locke's attempt to establish a system of governmental land registration in Carolina, see Fundamental Constitutions, March 1, 1670, Parker, ed., *North Carolina Charters and Constitutions,* Article 81, p. 179.

Ashley's use of the term "Darling" in reference to Carolina is from Shaftesbury to Peter Colleton, November 27, 1672, Cheves, ed., *Shaftesbury Papers,* pp. 416–18.

161. On the paper money question in colonial South Carolina, see Richard M. Jellison, "Paper Currency in Colonial South Carolina, 1703–1764" (Ph.D. dissertation, Indiana University, 1953), passim; Jellison, "Paper Currency in Colonial South Carolina: A Reappraisal," *South Carolina Historical Magazine* 62 (July 1961): 134–47; Jellison, "Antecedents of the South Carolina Currency Acts of 1736 and 1746," *William and Mary Quarterly,* 3d series, 16 (October 1959): 556–67; Clowse, *Economic Beginnings,* passim; Leslie V. Brock, *The Currency of the American Colonies 1700–1764: A Study in Colonial Finance and Imperial Relations* (New York: Arno Press, 1975), pp. 114–29, 446–62; Maurice A. Crouse,

The Public Treasury of Colonial South Carolina (Columbia: University of South Carolina Press, 1977), pp. 25–42. Two essential contemporary tracts should also be consulted. See _____, *An Essay on Currency, Written in August 1732* (Charlestown: Lewis Timothy, 1734); William Bull, Sr. [?], *An Account of the Rise and Progress of the Paper Bills of Credit in South Carolina* . . . (c. 1739), reprinted in Cooper and McCord, *Statutes,* 9: 766–80. For an excellent discussion of the role of paper currency in the economic development of colonial America in general, see Perkins, *The Economy of Colonial America,* pp. 101–22.

On the rigidities associated with international specie flow mechanisms during the early modern period, see, for example, Rudolph C. Blitz, "Mercantilist Policies and the Pattern of World Trade, 1500–1750," *Journal of Economic History* 27 (March 1967): 39–55.

162. Robert Craig West, "Money in the Colonial American Economy," *Economic Inquiry* 16 (January 1978): 1–15.

163. That taxes in colonial America were very low, see, for example, Perkins, *The Economy of Colonial America,* pp. 123–44; R.R. Palmer, *The Age of the Democratic Revolution: A Political History of Europe and America, 1760–1800,* 2 vols. (Princeton: Princeton University Press, 1959), 1: 154–56.

That taxes in South Carolina in particular were generally low, see Crouse, *The Public Treasury of Colonial South Carolina,* pp. 66–87.

Though the structure of taxation in colonial South Carolina would be considered regressive by modern standards, this structure was considerably more equitable than the structures in many other colonies, particularly other southern colonies. See Robert A. Becker, "Revolution and Reform: An Interpretation of Southern Taxation, 1763 to 1783," *William and Mary Quarterly,* 3d series, 32 (July 1975): 417–42; Becker, *Revolution, Reform, and the Politics of American Taxation, 1763–1783* (Baton Rouge: Louisiana State University Press, 1980), pp. 76–112, 189–218; Perkins, *The Economy of Colonial America,* pp. 124–28. One can analyze in detail the tax structure of South Carolina during the 1760s. See Public Treasurer of South Carolina, General Tax Receipts & Payments, 1761–1769 (1771), 1 ms. vol., South Carolina Department of Archives and History. We shall take a closer look at this structure in the next chapter.

On governmental expenditures, see Sirmans, *Colonial South Carolina,* pp. 243–44; Crouse, *The Public Treasury of Colonial South Carolina,* pp. 43–87.

Obviously, the interpretation offered above owes something to Schumpeter. See *The Theory of Economic Development: An Inquiry into Profits, Capital, Credit, Interest, and the Business Cycle,* trans. Redvers Opie (Cambridge: Harvard University Press, 1934; originally published 1911), pp. 115–23 and passim.

164. On the increasing degree of mercantile specialization, see, for example, Sellers, *Charleston Business on the Eve of the American Revolution,* pp. 49–96; Stumpf, "The Merchants of Colonial Charleston, 1680–1756," passim; Jeanne A. Calhoun, Martha A. Zierden, and Elizabeth A. Paysinger, "The Geographic Spread of Charleston's Mercantile Community," *South Carolina Historical Magazine* 86 (July 1985): 182–220; Peter A. Coclanis, "Retailing in Early South Carolina," in Robert L. King, ed., *Retailing: Theory and Practice for the 21st Century* (Charleston, S.C.: Academy of Marketing Science, 1986), pp. 1–5. Note that Thomas M. Doerflinger recently has found even greater levels of mercantile specialization in Philadelphia during the 1750–1800 period. See Doerflinger, "Commercial Specialization in Philadelphia's Merchant Community, 1750–1791," *Business History Review* 57 (Spring 1983): 20–49; Doerflinger, *A Vigorous Spirit of Enterprise: Merchants and Economic Development in Revolutionary Philadelphia* (Chapel Hill: University of North Carolina Press, 1986), pp. 70–134 especially.

165. For examples of the rudimentary "double-entry" accounting practices common in eighteenth-century South Carolina, see Office of the Public Treasurers, Ledgers, 1725–1776, 3 vols., South Carolina Department of Archives and History; Account Book, Ball Plantation Journal 1720–1778, Elias Ball XIV, Family Papers, 1631–1920, South Carolina Historical Society. Such practices, however, were not universal. See, for example, Charleston Account Book, 1745–1747, 1 ms. vol., South Caroliniana Library; Henry Laurens, Ledger, 1766–1773, 1 ms. vol., Special Collections, Robert Scott Small Library, College of Charleston, Charleston. For a good discussion of accounting practices in the South Carolina-Georgia low country on the eve of the American Revolution, see Joseph Clay to William Gibbons, August 17, 1770, William Gibbons, Jr., Papers, Manuscript Department, William R. Perkins Library.

The standard work on accounting practices in colonial America is still W.T. Baxter, "Accounting in Colonial America," in A.C. Littleton and B.S. Yamey, eds. *Studies in the History of Accounting* (Homewood, Ill.: Richard D. Irwin, 1956), pp. 272–87. Note, however, that Stuart Bruchey has argued that the accounting practices of many American merchants were more sophisticated than Baxter suggests. See Bruchey, "Success and Failure Factors: American Merchants in Foreign Trade in the Eighteenth and Early Nineteenth Centuries," *Business History Review* 32 (Autumn 1958): 272–92, especially pp. 276–79; Bruchey, *The Roots of American Economic Growth, 1607–1861: An Essay in Social Causation* (New York: Harper & Row, 1968; originally published 1965), pp. 52–53.

Note that newspaper advertisements placed by teachers of accounting indicate that "Italian" or double-entry practices were being taught in eighteenth-century South Carolina. See *South-Carolina Gazette,* May 19, 1733; February 19, 1737; September 3, 1744; November 27, 1762; November 5, 1764; September 22, 1766; January 11, 1770; October 22, 1772; *South Carolina Gazette & Country Journal,* September 9, 1766; October 11, 1768; *South Carolina & American General Gazette,* October 3, 1766; March 26, 1771.

On the discounting of bills of exchange, see, for example, Henry Laurens to Reynolds, Getly & Co., March 12, 1770, in Hamer, Rogers, *et al.,* eds., *The Papers of Henry Laurens,* 7: 249–50; *South Carolina & American General Gazette,* November 25, 1774. On the economic importance of discounting, see Doerflinger, *A Vigorous Spirit of Enterprise,* pp. 303-10.

On the creation of brokerages in Charleston in the late colonial period, see, for example, *South Carolina Gazette,* July 4, 1768; June 11, 1772; *South Carolina & American General Gazette,* October 14, 1774; Josiah Smith, Jr. to Alexander Taylor, October 11, 1774, p. 275, Josiah Smith, Jr., Lettercopy Book, Southern Historical Collection.

On the presence of professional bill-collectors or "dunners" and advertising specialists or "Stirring Men" in Charleston, see Henry Laurens to William Fisher, October 3, 1767, in Hamer, Rogers, *et al.,* eds., *The Papers of Henry Laurens,* 7: 249–50; *South Carolina & American General Gazette,* September 20, 1774.

166. On the tempo of mercantile life in colonial America generally, see especially Bruchey, "Success and Failure Factors"; Arthur H. Cole, "The Tempo of Mercantile Life in Colonial America," *Business History Review* 33 (Autumn 1959): 277–99; Bruchey, ed., *The Colonial Merchant: Sources and Readings,* The Forces in American Economic Growth Series (New York: Harcourt, Brace & World, 1966), passim; Bruchey, *The Roots of American Economic Growth,* pp. 48–54; Perkins, *The Economy of Colonial America,* pp. 87–96.

The figures on business correspondence cited in the text above were calculated from material in two collections: Walter B. Edgar, ed., *The Letterbook of Robert Pringle,* 2 vols. (Columbia: University of South Carolina Press, 1972); and Hamer, Rogers, *et al.,* eds., *The Papers of Henry Laurens.* In the five full years from 1739 through 1744,

Pringle wrote 629 business letters—an average of 125.8 yearly. In the two-year period from May 12, 1755 to May 12, 1757, Henry Laurens, on the other hand, wrote 620 letters, an average of 310 yearly. See *The Papers of Henry Laurens,* vol. 2. Note that I used this particular period between 1755 and 1757 because there are gaps in earlier correspondence from the 1750s and because in the 1760s Laurens increasingly disengaged himself from full-time involvement in mercantile life.

167. According to Jerome J. Nadelhaft, South Carolina's pre-war debt to British creditors was £412,000 sterling. See Nadelhaft, *The Disorders of War: The Revolution in South Carolina* (Orono, Maine: University of Maine at Orono Press, 1981), p. 89. For estimates of other colonies' pre-war debt to British creditors, see Jacob M. Price, *Capital and Credit in British Overseas Trade: The View from the Chesapeake, 1700–1776* (Cambridge: Harvard University Press, 1980), pp. 7, 9. By dividing the estimated debt for each colony by figures for each colony's white population—one can use population estimates for either 1770 or 1780—one finds that South Carolina had the highest white per capita debt. For estimates of white population, see *Historical Statistics of the United States,* 2: 1168.

168. Records of the South Carolina Court of Common Pleas, Judgment Rolls, 1703–1790, South Carolina Department of Archives and History. Cases from the 1703–1737 period are located in boxes 1–22.

169. That loans were often carried beyond due dates so long as interest payments were made, see, for example, the advertisements of Thomas Lamboll in the *South-Carolina Gazette,* April 17, 1736, and April 2, 1737.

According to extant South Carolina tax records from the 1760s, small taxes on *annuities* were levied in 1761, 1762, 1764, 1766, 1767, 1768, and 1769. See Public Treasurer of South Carolina, General Tax Receipts & Payments, 1761–1769 (1771), 1 ms. vol., South Carolina Department of Archives and History.

170. See, for example, *South Carolina Gazette,* January 1, 1752, Supplement; August 10, 1752; November 20, 1755; April 28, 1757, Supplement; November 17, 1758; March 21, 1761; October 3, 1768; July 18, 1771; *South Carolina & American General Gazette,* November 11, 1771; *South Carolina Gazette & Country Journal,* April 28, 1772.

171. On legal interest rates in South Carolina, see Cooper and McCord, *Statutes,* 3: 709–12; 4: 363–65. Rates, of course, varied a bit in practice and individuals were sometimes accused of charging higher rates than the law allowed. See Records of the South Carolina Court of Common Pleas, Judgment Rolls, Box 18, A, 117A, Fitch v. Flood (1722); Box 20, A, 181A, Wallace v. Harleston (1723); Box 20, A, 209A, Wallace v. Harleston (1723); Box 20, A, 213A, Wallace v. Amory (1723), South Carolina Department of Archives and History.

On interest rates in seventeenth- and eighteenth-century Europe and America, see Sidney Homer, *A History of Interest Rates* (New Brunswick: Rutgers University Press, 1963), pp. 122–32, 147–80, 274–79; De Vries, *The Economy of Europe in an Age of Crisis, 1600–1750,* pp. 211–12.

172. The question of the profitability of staple agriculture in the South Carolina low country will be addressed in the next chapter. Suffice it to say here that profits generally were high in the eighteenth century—well above interest rates prevailing in South Carolina or northwest Europe.

As mercantile life became more advanced in eighteenth-century South Carolina, merchants and others—particularly goldsmiths and silversmiths—increasingly involved themselves in economic activities which we today associate with banks and other financial intermediaries. As early as the 1720s, for example, we find that a number of Charlestonians were deeply involved in money-lending and allied financial activities. See Inventory,

Charles Franchomme, May 1, 1725, Records of the Secretary of the Province, D, 1724–1725, p. 157; Inventory, John LaRoche, September 23, 1724, Records of the Secretary of the Province, D, 1724–1725, pp. 206–14; Inventory, Capt. Albert Muller, January 26–27, 1726/27, and April 6–7, 1727, Records of the Secretary of the Province, E, 1726–1727, pp. 423–30; Inventory, Timothy Bellamy, July 18, 1726, Records of the Secretary of the Province, E, 1726–1727, pp. 431–37; Inventory, Elizabeth Buretel, 1728, Records of the Secretary of the Province, F, 1727–1729, pp. 94–95. These manuscript records are part of the series, Records of the Secretary of State, Miscellaneous Records, Main Series, 1671–1973, South Carolina Department of Archives and History. On goldsmiths and silversmiths in colonial South Carolina, their activities, and their increasing numbers over time, see E. Milby Burton, *South Carolina Silversmiths 1690–1860,* Contributions from the Charleston Museum, no. 10 (Richmond: The Dietz Press for the Charleston Museum, 1942).

Several private "banks" operated for short periods of time in colonial South Carolina. See Extract of a Letter to Sir A. Cuming, May 23, 1730, Sainsbury, ed., *Calendar of State Papers, Colonial Series, America and West Indies,* vol.: *1730,* pp. 189–90; Governor Robert Johnson to the Board of Trade, November 14, 1731, Records in the British Public Record Office Relating to South Carolina, 15: 33-40, especially p. 36, South Carolina Department of Archives and History; *Boston News-Letter,* July 30, 1730; *Boston Gazette,* July 27, 1730; Entry, September 20, 1741, in Elise Pinckney, ed., *The Letterbook of Eliza Lucas Pinckney 1739–1762* (Chapel Hill: University of North Carolina Press, 1972), p. 22. Also see Jellison, "Antecedents of the South Carolina Currency Acts of 1736 and 1746."

173. On the prices of South Carolina's exports, see Taylor, "Wholesale Commodity Prices at Charleston, South Carolina, 1732–1791"; Cole, *Wholesale Commodity Prices in the United States 1700–1861,* vol. 2; Coclanis, "Rice Prices in the 1720s and the Evolution of the South Carolina Economy." For an extension of the argument above to the American colonies in general, see Egnal, "The Economic Development of the Thirteen Continental Colonies, 1720 to 1775."

174. On this point, see Clowse, *Measuring Charleston's Overseas Commerce, 1717–1767,* p. 25. On the import trade with other areas, see Stuart Stumpf and Jennings B. Marshall, "Trends in Charleston's Inter-Regional Import Trade, 1735–1764," *Southern Studies* 23 (Fall 1984): 243–65.

175. See, for example, Robert Pringle to Richard Thompson, September 2, 1738, in Edgar, ed., *The Letterbook of Robert Pringle,* 1: 29–32, especially pp. 31–32; George Nelson to Messrs. Lamberts, February 26, 1784, p. 2; George Nelson to Messrs. Lamberts, March 20, 1784, p. 2 (back); Account of Stock . . . , December 25, 1785, n.p., George Nelson Lettercopy Book, Southern Historical Collection.

176. Deane and Cole, *British Economic Growth 1688–1959: Trends and Structure,* p. 84 and Figure 7; McCusker, "The Current Value of English Exports, 1697 to 1800," p. 619.

177. McCusker, "The Current Value of English Exports, 1697 to 1800," p. 619.

178. This usage, of course, owes something to Marx, but also see Joan Robinson, *The Economics of Imperfect Competition,* 2d ed. (London: Macmillan, 1969; originally published 1933), pp. 281–91, especially pp. 281–83.

For a summary of Marxist views on "exploitation," see, for example, Brewer, *Marxist Theories of Imperialism,* passim.

179. The 10 percent figure is that of Robert W. Fogel and Stanley L. Engerman, while the 50 percent figure is that of Edwin J. Perkins. See Fogel and Engerman, *Time on the Cross,* 1: 107–57, especially pp. 156–57; 2: 87–125; Perkins, *The Economy of Colonial America,* p. 151.

180. See Gray and Wood, "The Transition from Indentured to Involuntary Servitude in Colonial Georgia," pp. 358–59. Note that the above figures refer to costs of food and clothing.

181. *South-Carolina Gazette,* January 25, 1734/5.

Chapter 4. "Lay dis body down"

1. *South-Carolina Gazette*, January 22, 1736/7.

2. *De Bow's Review* 17 (July 1854): 82–84. Alfred Glaze Smith, Jr., William W. Freehling, and George C. Rogers, Jr., all argue, for example, that the low country was still highly prosperous in 1820. See Smith, *Economic Readjustment of an Old Cotton State: South Carolina, 1820–1860* (Columbia: University of South Carolina Press, 1958), pp. 1–18; Freehling, *Prelude to Civil War: The Nullification Controversy in South Carolina, 1816–1836* (New York: Harper & Row, 1965), pp. 7–48; Rogers, *Charleston in the Age of the Pinckneys* (Norman: University of Oklahoma Press, 1969), pp. 3–25.

3. Though there are, of course, many scholars associated with each of these positions on the southern economy, Stanley L. Engerman is perhaps the most prominent proponent of the "impact of the Civil War" position, while Eugene D. Genovese is probably the most prominent "structuralist." For excellent statements of each position, see Engerman, "Some Economic Factors in Southern Backwardness in the Nineteenth Century," in John F. Kain and John R. Meyer, eds., *Essays in Regional Economics* (Cambridge: Harvard University Press, 1971), pp. 279–306; Genovese, *The Political Economy of Slavery: Studies in the Economy and Society of the Slave South* (New York: Pantheon, 1965). Also see Peter Temin, "The Post-Bellum Recovery of the South and the Cost of the Civil War," *Journal of Economic History* 36 (December 1976): 898–907.

4. See, for example, *Charleston Courier*, March 13, 1828; Entry, October 19, 1832, p. 5, Samuel Cram Jackson Diary, Southern Historical Collection, University of North Carolina, Chapel Hill, N.C.; Frances Anne Kemble, *Journal of a Residence on a Georgian Plantation in 1838–1839*, ed. John A. Scott (New York: Meridian Books, 1975; originally published 1863), pp. 36–37.

Note that other observers viewed the Charleston economy more favorably. See, for example, Robert I. Gage to James M. Gage, April 3, 1836, James M. Gage Papers, Southern Historical Collection.

5. In this chapter I basically define the low country as that part of South Carolina included in Georgetown, Charleston, and Beaufort districts during the late eighteenth century. In the antebellum period this area encompassed seven districts: Horry, Marion, Williamsburg, Georgetown, Charleston, Colleton, and Beaufort.

6. On the elaboration of urban networks in nineteenth-century America, see, for example, David Ward, *Cities and Immigrants: A Geography of Change in Nineteenth-Century America* (New York: Oxford University Press, 1971), pp. 3–49; Allan R. Pred, *The Spatial Dynamics of U.S. Urban-Industrial Growth, 1800–1914: Interpretive and Theoretical Essays* (Cambridge: The MIT Press, 1966); Pred, *Urban Growth and the Circulation of Information: The United States System of Cities, 1790–1840* (Cambridge: Harvard University Press, 1973); Pred, *Urban Growth and City Systems in the United States, 1840–1860* (Cambridge: Harvard University Press, 1980).

Numerous attempts were made in the antebellum period to explain Charleston's relative decline. See *De Bow's Review* 1 (January 1846): 44–51; *Hunt's Merchants' Magazine* 34 (January 1856): 137.

7. See, for example, J. L. Dawson and H. W. DeSaussure, *Census of the City of Charleston, South Carolina, for the Year 1848* . . . (Charleston: J. B. Nixon, 1849), pp. 90–103, 112–22; United States Department of Agriculture, Bureau of Statistics, *Rice Crop of the United States, 1712–1911*, by George K. Holmes, Circular 34 (Washington, D. C.: United States Government Printing Office, 1912), pp. 5–11; Lewis C. Gray, *History of Agriculture in the Southern United States to 1860*, 2 vols. (Gloucester, Mass.: Peter Smith, 1958; originally published 1933), 2: 1030.

8. See George Rogers Taylor, "Wholesale Commodity Prices at Charleston, South Carolina, 1732–1791," *Journal of Economic and Business History* 4 (February 1932): 356–77; Taylor, "Wholesale Commodity Prices at Charleston, South Carolina, 1796–1861," *Journal of Economic and Business History* 4, Supplement (August 1932): 848–76; Gray, *History of Agriculture*, 2: 1030; Smith, *Economic Readjustment of an Old Cotton State*, pp. 224–27.

9. On the collapse of the indigo industry late in the eighteenth century, see G. Terry Sharrer, "Indigo in Carolina, 1671–1796," *South Carolina Historical Magazine* 72 (April 1971): 94–103; John J. Winberry, "Reputation of Carolina Indigo," *South Carolina Historical Magazine* 80 (July 1979): 242–50. On the relationship between the decline of indigo in the New World and the rise of indigo exports from India, see Dauril Alden, "The Growth and Decline of Indigo Production in Colonial Brazil: A Study in Comparative Economic History," *Journal of Economic History* 25 (March 1965): 35–60.

On Sea Island cotton production and short-staple cotton production in the low country, see, for example, Charles F. Kovacik and Robert E. Mason, "Changes in the South Carolina Sea Island Cotton Industry," *Southeastern Geographer* 25 (November 1985): 77–104; Smith, *Economic Readjustment of an Old Cotton State*, pp. 45–111.

Low-country cotton production figures for 1839, 1849, and 1859 were as follows:

	Pounds of Ginned Cotton		
District	*1839*	*1849*	*1859*
Beaufort	1,544,850	5,068,800	7,648,400
Charleston	2,130,224	1,688,400	2,552,400
Colleton	420,910	2,636,800	3,892,400
Georgetown	14,174	32,400	42,400
Horry	40,780	6,000	,178,800
Marion	603,496	3,472,000	5,476,800
Williamsburg	515,038	1,719,200	2,628,400
Low Country	5,269,472	14,623,600	22,419,600

See *Sixth Census of the United States, 1840* (Washington, D.C.: Thomas Allen, 1841), p. 192; *Seventh Census of the United States, 1850* (Washington, D.C.: Robert Armstrong, 1853), p. 346; *Eighth Census of the United States, 1860: Agriculture* (Washington, D.C.: United States Government Printing Office, 1864), pp. 128-29.

For good, contemporary descriptions and analyses of the cotton industry in the low country during the antebellum period, see, for example, *The Southern Agriculturalist* 2 (August 1829): 347–51 and (September 1829): 392–95; 3 (March 1830): 141–48; 4 (July 1831): 337–46; 8 (January 1835): 35–46 and (February 1835): 81–87; 8 (August 1835): 401–15; 10 (April 1837): 173–78; *The Southern Agriculturalist*, new series, 2 (January 1842): 1–17 and (February 1842): 57–67; *De Bow's Review* 16 (June 1854): 589–615.

10. On the lumber and naval-stores industries in the low country in the antebellum period, see John A. Eisterhold, "Charleston: Lumber and Trade in a Declining Southern

Port," *South Carolina Historical Magazine* 74 (April 1973): 61–72; Percival Perry, "The Naval Stores Industry in the Ante-Bellum South, 1789–1861" (Ph.D. dissertation, Duke University, 1947), passim; Perry, "The Naval Stores Industry in the Old South, 1790–1860," *Journal of Southern History* 34 (November 1968): 509–26; Virginia Steele Wood, *Live Oaking: Southern Timber for Tall Ships* (Boston: Northeastern University Press, 1981); David L. Carlton, "The Piedmont and Waccamaw Regions: An Economic Comparison," *South Carolina Historical Magazine* 88 (April 1987): 83–100.

11. The dominance in the low country's manufacturing sector of agricultural and raw-material processing activities is evident in the structure of employment in this sector. Data on the structure of employment in the low country's manufacturing sector in 1860 follow below.

Manufacturing Employment in the Low Country, 1860

Type of Establishment	No. of Establishments	Total Number of Employees
Agricultural implements	3	6
Blacksmithing	10	30
Boots and Shoes	3	10
Bread	2	4
Brick	5	100
Carriages	5	75
Cars	4	155
Cooperage	5	63
Flour and Meal	7	13
Lime	1	32
Lumber, planed	1	10
Lumber, sawed	23	236
Machinery, Steam Engines, etc.	5	295
Oil, neat's foot	1	1
Rice cleaning	11	380
Saddlery and Harness	2	27
Sash, Doors and Blinds	2	45
Ships and boatbuilding	2	36
Soap and Candles	1	3
Timber-cutting	2	28
Turpentine, distilled	60	1015
Wagons, Carts, etc.	4	11
	159	2575

See *Eighth Census of the United States, 1860: Manufactures* (Washington, D.C.: United States Government Printing Office, 1865), pp. 552-59. Note that returns from the Colleton District are missing from the 1860 census (both published and manuscript). Note, too, that many of the employees listed under "Turpentine, distilled" were actually extracting turpentine from so-called turpentine orchards.

12. Ernest M. Lander, Jr., "Charleston: Manufacturing Center of the Old South," *Journal of Southern History* 26 (August 1960): 330–51; Lander, "Manufacturing in Antebellum South Carolina" (Ph. D. dissertation, University of North Carolina, 1950), p. 266 and passim; Fred Bateman and Thomas Weiss, *A Deplorable Scarcity: The Failure of Industrialization in the Slave Economy* (Chapel Hill: University of North Carolina Press, 1981), p. 13.

13. On the question of the feasibility of manufacturing activity in the low country, and throughout the South, see Bateman and Weiss, *A Deplorable Scarcity*, passim. On the structure of southern manufacturing in the antebellum period, also see Albert W. Niemi, Jr., "Structural Shifts in Southern Manufacturing, 1849–1899," *Business History Review* 45 (Spring 1971): 79–84.

14. See, for example, Smith, *Economic Readjustment of an Old Cotton State*, pp. 135–92. On specific internal improvement projects in antebellum South Carolina, see Thomas Cooper and David J. McCord, eds., *The Statutes at Large of South Carolina*, 10 vols. (Columbia: A. S. Johnston, 1836–41), 7: 475–588; 8: 106–484; 9: passim; *The Statutes at Large of South Carolina. Volume XI* . . . [1838–1849] (Columbia: Republican Printing Company, 1873), passim; *The Statutes at Large of South Carolina. Volume XII* . . . [1850–1861] (Columbia: Republican Printing Company, 1874), passim. On the towns and "trading places" in South Carolina in the late antebellum period, see *The Southern Business Directory and General Commercial Advertiser* . . . , Vol. I (Charleston: Walker & James, 1854).

15. On the rise of towns and the elaboration of internal markets in the Midwest, see Stanley Elkins and Eric McKitrick, "A Meaning for Turner's Frontier," *Political Science Quarterly* 69 (September 1954): 321–53 and (December 1954): 565–602, especially pp. 341–49; Albert Fishlow, *American Railroads and the Transformation of the Ante-Bellum Economy* (Cambridge: Harvard University Press, 1965), passim; William N. Parker, "Slavery and Southern Economic Development: An Hypothesis and Some Evidence," *Agricultural History* 44 (January 1970): 115–25. On the paucity of commercial establishments in the South Carolina low country (outside of Charleston) in the late antebellum period, see *The Southern Business Directory*, pp. 305–22.

On the importance of small and medium-sized towns in the process of economic growth, see, for example, Dennis A. Rondinelli, "Towns and Small Cities in Developing Countries," *The Geographical Review* 73 (October 1983): 379–95; Rondinelli and Kenneth Ruddle, *Urbanization and Rural Development: A Spatial Policy for Equitable Growth* (New York: Praeger, 1978); E. A. J. Johnson, *The Organization of Space in Developing Countries* (Cambridge: Harvard University Press, 1970). For a related, if somewhat overstated argument, see Jane Jacobs, *Cities and the Wealth of Nations: Principles of Economic Life* (New York: Random House, 1984).

16. On cotton and rice prices in the 1850s, see Taylor, "Wholesale Commodity Prices at Charleston, South Carolina, 1796–1861"; Gray, *History of Agriculture*, 2: 1027–31; Smith, *Economic Readjustment of an Old Cotton State*, pp. 220–27.

On total cotton production in South Carolina in 1849 and 1859, see *Seventh Census of the United States, 1850*, p. 346; *Eighth Census of the United States, 1860: Agriculture*, pp. 128–29. Total production in 1849 was 300,901 bales; in 1859, 353,412 bales.

On rice exports, see United States Department of Agriculture, Bureau of Statistics, *Rice Crop of the United States, 1712–1911*, pp. 7–9.

17. That much of the expansion of South Carolina's export trade in the 1850s was the result of improved transport links with the West, see Smith, *Economic Readjustment of an Old Cotton State*, pp. 191–92. On the development of these—rail—links, see Ulrich B. Phillips, *A History of Transportation in the Eastern Cotton Belt to 1860* (New York: Columbia University Press, 1908), pp. 168–396 especially; Samuel M. Derrick, *Centennial History of South Carolina Railroad* (Columbia, S.C.: The State Company, 1930), pp. 128–219; Smith, *Economic Readjustment of an Old Cotton State*, pp. 156–92; Frederick B. Collins, Jr., "Charleston and the Railroads: A Geographic Study of a South Atlantic Port and Its Strategies for Developing a Railroad System, 1820–1860" (M.S. thesis, University of South Carolina, 1977), pp. 31–114. Contemporary observers were not unaware that much of the cotton exported from South Carolina during the antebellum period originated further

west. See Speech, John C. Calhoun, March 16, 1842, in Robert L. Meriwether *et al.*, eds., *The Papers of John C. Calhoun*, 16 vols. thus far (Columbia: University of South Carolina Press, 1959–), 16: 169–98, especially pp. 189–90, 198; *De Bow's Review* 1 (January 1846): 44–51, especially pp. 46–47.

On the overall importance of the railroad to American farmers during the antebellum period, see *De Bow's Review* 24 (May 1858): 386–96. On the impact of the railroad on the South Carolina upcountry, see Lacy K. Ford, "Social Origins of a New South Carolina: The Upcountry in the Nineteenth Century" (Ph.D. dissertation, University of South Carolina, 1983).

18. See Robert G. Albion, "New York Port and Its Disappointed Rivals, 1815–1860," *Journal of Economic and Business History* 3 (1931): 602–29; Albion, *The Rise of New York Port, 1815–1860* (Newton Abbot, Devon, England: David & Charles, 1970; originally published 1939), pp. 95–121; Smith *Economic Readjustment of an Old Cotton State*, pp. 162–63, 198–99; Gregory A. Greb, "Charleston, South Carolina, Merchants, 1815–1860: Urban Leadership in the Antebellum South" (Ph. D. dissertation, University of California, San Diego, 1978), pp. 79–228.

Spokesmen for the Southeast often seemed preoccupied with the "direct trade" question during the antebellum period. See, for example, Report, presented June 14, 1838, in Meriwether *et al.*, eds., *The Papers of John C. Calhoun*, 14: 321–43; *The Southern Agriculturalist* 12 (May 1839): 237–48 and (June 1839): 299–304 and (July 1839): 337–49.

Charleston's commercial rivalry with nearby Savannah was particularly intense during the late antebellum period, as the Georgia port began to approach its older neighbor in importance. On this rivalry, see *De Bow's Review* 7 (December 1849): 558–59; 10 (April 1851): 462–63. The cities, one should note, are still keen commercial rivals today. See *New York Times*, October 19, 1986, p. 6.

19. Stanley L. Engerman and Robert E. Gallman have recently published by far the best analytical discussion of economic growth and development in the United States from the end of the American Revolution to the eve of the Civil War. See "U. S. Economic Growth, 1783–1860," *Research in Economic History* 8 (1983): 1–46.

20. See Chapter 3. Also see Alice Hanson Jones, *Wealth of a Nation To Be: The American Colonies on the Eve of the Revolution* (New York: Columbia University Press, 1980), pp. 50–85, 294–380 especially.

21. In order to estimate the population of the Charleston District in 1774, I relied upon: (a) estimates of the population of the low country as a whole in 1770, and (b) 1790 census figures on population in each of the low country's three districts. In Chapter 3, we estimated that the total population of the low country in about 1770 was 88,244. We estimated white population at 19,066 and black population at 69,178. By 1790, the low country's total population had grown to 107,860. If we disaggregate this total, we find that in 1790 there were 28,644 whites in the area, 78,000 Negro slaves, and 1216 free blacks. Furthermore, we find that most of the population lived in the Charleston District. Figures on the Charleston District's share of the population of the low country in 1790 appear below.

	Charleston District Pop.	Low-Country Population	Charleston District's Share of Total
White	15,402	28,644	53.77%
Free black	950	1,216	78.12
Total Free	16,352	29,860	54.76
Negro slave	50,633	78,000	64.91
Total	66,985	107,860	62.10%

Because the Georgetown and Beaufort districts developed more rapidly than the older Charleston District between 1770 and 1790, I assumed that the Charleston District's share of the population of the low country was somewhat greater in 1770. *Faute de mieux*, I assumed that the Charleston District had about 60 percent of the low country's free population in 1770 and 70 percent of the area's total slave population. Using these percentages, we find that the Charleston District had a free population (almost entirely white) of about 11,440 in 1770 and a Negro slave population of about 48,425. With the 1790 figures and the dislocations of the American Revolution in mind, I have placed the population of the Charleston District in 1774 at about 62,500—12,500 free, and 50,000 slaves.

We can use the above estimates to calculate mean per capita wealth in the Charleston District in 1774. If the free population of the Charleston District in 1774 was 12,500, we can divide this figure by 4.26—the divisor used by Alice Hanson Jones for the South in 1774—to get the number of wealth-holders in the area. We can then multiply Jones's estimates of private physical wealth per wealth-holder in the Charleston District (£1772.3 sterling for total private physical wealth and £765.1 sterling for nonhuman physical wealth) by the number of wealth-holders in the area (2934.27) to get estimates of private physical wealth in the Charleston District in 1774. These estimates appear below:

Private physical wealth	£5,200,406.7 sterling
Private nonhuman physical wealth	£2,245,009.9 sterling

If we then divide these totals by 62,500—the total population of the Charleston District in 1774—we can get estimates of mean private physical wealth per capita and mean private nonhuman physical wealth per capita. These estimates follow.

Mean private physical wealth per capita:	£83.21 sterling
Mean private nonhuman physical wealth per capita:	£35.92 sterling

See Chapter 3; Jones, *Wealth of a Nation To Be*, pp. 42, 380; U. S. Department of Commerce and Labor, Bureau of the Census, *Heads of Families at the First Census of the United States Taken in the Year 1790. South Carolina* (Washington D.C.: United States Government Printing Office, 1908), p. 9.

22. Note that some slaves in the low country apparently were able to accumulate personal property, i.e. wealth, as well. At present, however, data are still too limited to estimate the aggregate value of such wealth. On wealth-holding by slaves in the low country, see Philip D. Morgan, "Work and Culture: The Task System and the World of Lowcountry Blacks, 1700 to 1880," *William and Mary Quarterly*, 3d ser., 39 (October 1982): 563–99; Morgan, "The Ownership of Property by Slaves in the Mid-Nineteenth-Century Low Country," *Journal of Southern History* 49 (August 1983): 399–420.

23. See, for example, Alfred H. Conrad and John R. Meyer, "The Economics of Slavery in the Antebellum South," in Conrad and Meyer, *The Economics of Slavery and other Studies in Econometric History* (Chicago: Aldine, 1964), pp. 43–114, especially pp. 50–53, 76, 85–92; Robert William Fogel and Stanley L. Engerman, *Time on the Cross: The Economics of American Negro Slavery*, 2 vols. (Boston: Little, Brown, 1974), 1: 48, 79; Lee Soltow, *Men and Wealth in the United States, 1850–1870* (New Haven: Yale University Press, 1975), pp. 137–40.

24. On the prices of prime hands and "average" slaves in the low country in 1860, see Ulrich B. Phillips, "The Slave Labor Problem in the Charleston District," *Political Science Quarterly* 22 (September 1907): 416–39; Phillips, "The Economic Cost of Slaveholding in the Cotton Belt," in Phillips, *The Slave Economy of the Old South: Selected Essays in Economic and Social History*, ed. Eugene D. Genovese (Baton Rouge: Louisiana State

University Press, 1968), pp. 117–35, especially p. 125; Phillips, *American Negro Slavery* . . . (Baton Rouge: Louisiana State University Press, 1966; originally published 1918), p. 371. The essay "The Economic Cost of Slaveholding in the Cotton Belt," one should note, was originally published in the *Political Science Quarterly* 20 (June 1905): 257–75.

Contemporary plantation records from the low country support the conclusions reached by Phillips. See, for example, Joseph Blyth Allston to Robert F. W. Allston, January 18, 1859, pp. 152–53, in J. H. Easterby, ed., *The South Carolina Rice Plantation as Revealed in the Papers of Robert F. W. Allston* (Chicago: University of Chicago Press, 1945); John Berkley Grimball, Tax Return, January 30, 1862, John Berkley Grimball Diary, 13: 9, Southern Historical Collection.

25. The value of personal property in the low country was put at $111,425,936 in the 1860 census. There were 142,805 slaves in the low country at that time. At $900 per slave, the value of slave property alone in the low country would come to $128,524,500. See *Eighth Census of the United States, 1860: Statistics* (Washington D.C.: United States Government Printing Office, 1866), p. 312; *Eighth Census of the United States, 1860: Population* (Washington, D.C.: United States Government Printing Office, 1864), p. 452.

One can only speculate about the reasons why slaves from the low country commanded lower prices than slaves in other parts of the South. Some contemporary observers believed that low-country slaves were overly specialized for rice production, for example, while others pointed out that because the use of the plow was limited in the low country, slaves from the area often lacked skills deemed important in the booming short-staple cotton industry of the interior. The relative "independence" offered to low-country slaves by the task system and the deleterious effects of rigorous "mudwork" in a harsh environment may also have influenced price levels.

26. Obviously, the above estimates are imperfect. At even $600 per slave, the value of slaves in both the Georgetown and Horry districts is greater than the values given in the 1860 census for all personalty in these districts. Nonetheless, the estimates work fairly well for the other five districts in the low country and for the area as a whole. See *Eighth Census of the United States, 1860: Statistics*, p. 312; *Eighth Census of the United States, 1860: Population*, p. 452.

27. See Jeffrey G. Williamson and Peter H. Lindert, *American Inequality: A Macroeconomic History* (New York: Academic Press, 1980), pp. 323–25. For contemporary support of this point, see, for example, W. L. Poole to Colonel Bomford, June 29, 1837, United States Army, Ordnance Department, Charleston Arsenal, Letter Book, 1836–1838, New York Public Library, New York. One should note, of course, that the cost-of-living affects wealth in an indirect rather than direct way. One should also note that wage levels in South Carolina apparently were lower in most economic activities—particularly unskilled activities—than levels prevailing in the U. S. as a whole. See Stanley Lebergott, *Manpower in Economic Growth: The American Record Since 1800* (New York: McGraw-Hill, 1964), pp. 74–87, 539, 541–45. Carville Earle and Ronald Hoffman have recently argued, however, that labor costs in the South as a whole were higher than labor costs in parts of the North at least. See Earle and Hoffman, "The Foundation of the Modern Economy: Agriculture and the Costs of Labor in the United States and England, 1800–60," *American Historical Review* 85 (December 1980): 1055–94.

One should also note that there were no significant differences in the age-structures of the free adult populations in ·Massachusetts, New York, Pennsylvania, and the South Carolina low country in 1860. Thus, the differences among these areas in wealth levels in 1860 apparently were not due to age biases. Figures on the age-structures of the free adult populations in these areas in 1860 appear below.

Age Structures of Free Adult Populations in Massachusetts, New York,
Pennsylvania, and the South Carolina Low Country, 1860

	Age		
Area	Between 20–39	Over 40	Total
Massachusetts	428,224	287,878	716,102
—Percentage	59.80%	40.20%	100.00%
New York	1,288,672	806,177	2,094,849
—Percentage	61.52%	38.48%	100.00%
Pennsylvania	878,529	551,895	1,430,424
—Percentage	61.42%	38.58%	100.00%
SC Low Country	23,371	14,627	37,998
—Percentage	61.51%	38.49%	100.00%

See *Eighth Census of the United States, 1860: Population,* pp. 218–19, 326–27, 410–11, 448–49.

28. See Richard A. Easterlin, "Regional Income Trends, 1840–1950," in Robert W. Fogel and Stanley L. Engerman, eds., *The Reinterpretation of American Economic History* (New York: Harper & Row, 1971), pp. 38–49, especially p. 40; Easterlin, "Interregional Differences in Per Capita Income, Population, and Total Income, 1840–1950," in *Trends in the American Economy in the Nineteenth Century,* ed. William N. Parker, Conference on Research in Income and Wealth, Studies in Income and Wealth, vol. 24 (Princeton: Princeton University Press, 1960), pp. 73–140. Note that the first essay cited above appeared originally in Seymour Harris, ed., *American Economic History* (New York: McGraw-Hill, 1961), pp. 525–47.

29. Aggregate wealth in the low country was valued at $74,172,460. The total population in the low country in 1870 was 213,163. Thus, mean per capita wealth was $347.96. See United States Census, Agriculture, Industry, Social Statistics, and Mortality Schedules for South Carolina, 1850–1880, Ninth Census, Social Statistics, 1870, Abbeville-York, South Carolina Department of Archives and History, Columbia, S. C.; *Ninth Census of the United States, 1870: Statistics of Population* (Washington, D.C.: United States Government Printing Office, 1872), pp. 60–61.

30. See Table 4–19. Moreover, one should also note that according to the Pearson-Warren wholesale price index, prices in the U. S. were higher in 1869 and 1870 than in 1859 and 1860. See United States Department of Commerce, Bureau of the Census, *Historical Statistics of the United States: Colonial Times to 1970,* 2 vols. (Washington, D.C.: United States Government Printing Office, 1975), 1: 201–2.

31. See footnote 28 above. Also see Roger L. Ransom and Richard Sutch, "Growth and Welfare in the American South in the Nineteenth Century," in Gary M. Walton and James F. Shepherd, eds., *Market Institutions and Economic Progress in the New South, 1865–1900* (New York: Academic Press, 1981), pp. 127–53; Gavin Wright, *Old South, New South: Revolutions in the Southern Economy Since the Civil War* (New York: Basic Books, 1986), pp. 17–123 especially. On capital/output ratios in the 1850–70 period—adjusted for slaves, see Soltow, *Men and Wealth in the United States, 1850–1870,* pp. 66–69, 88–90. That the ratios found by Soltow were similar to those obtaining in the American colonies in 1774, see Jones, *Wealth of a Nation To Be,* pp. 61–64, 369–74.

32. On the stagnation and decline of the rice and Sea Island cotton industries, see Table 4–25 in this chapter; Kovacik and Mason, "Changes in the South Carolina Sea Island Cotton Industry"; John Scott Strickland, "Traditional Culture and Moral Economy: Social and Economic Change in the South Carolina Low Country, 1865–1910," in Steven Hahn

and Jonathan Prude, eds., *The Countryside in the Age of Capitalist Transformation: Essays in the Social History of Rural America* (Chapel Hill: University of North Carolina Press, 1985), pp. 141–78, especially p. 167. Note that Strickland's figures on rice production (p. 166) are wrong, as he often has confused government figures on clean and rough rice. Correct figures appear in Table 4–25 of this chapter. On the rise and fall of the low-country phosphate industry, see Tom W. Shick and Don H. Doyle, "The South Carolina Phosphate Boom and the Stillbirth of the New South, 1867–1920," *South Carolina Historical Magazine* 86 (January 1985): 1–31; Francis B. Simkins and Robert H. Woody, *South Carolina During Reconstruction* (Chapel Hill: University of North Carolina Press, 1932), pp. 305–11. As these activities were declining, the manufacturing sector in the low country rose in significance. Whereas the per capita value of manufacturing production in the low country was (at least) $21.48 in 1859, it had risen to $40.90 by 1899. Whether the rise of the manufacturing sector in the late nineteenth century offset the declines manifest in other economic sectors in the low country is still unknown. See tables 4–1 and 4–8; *Twelfth Census of the United States, 1900*, vol. 1, *Population*, pt. 1 (Washington, D.C.: United States Census Office, 1901), pp. 300–305; *Twelfth Census of the United States, 1900*, vol. viii, *Manufactures*, pt. II, States and Territories (Washington, D.C.: United States Census Office, 1902), pp. 832–33.

Figures on cotton production in the low country in 1869, 1879, 1889, and 1899 were as follows:

Bales of Cotton

County	1869	1879	1889	1899[1] Upland	Sea-Island
Beaufort	7,486	2,740	4,344	2,879	2,030
Berkeley			12,557	9,982	216
Charleston	5,512	9,303	1,135	188	5,658
Colleton	2,335	4,869	9,087	8,057	277
Dorchester				6,301	51
Georgetown	61	160	315	689	—
Hampton		7,711	10,303	13,207	47
Horry	74	809	2,808	5,679	11
Marion	6,910	21,748	25,993	31,488	—
Williamsburg	1,791	5,627	9,335	18,631	28
Low Country	24,169	52,967	75,877	97,101	8,318

[1] 1899 figures are for commercial bales reported by farmers.

See *Ninth Census of the United States, 1870: Wealth and Industry* (Washington, D.C.: United States Government Printing Office, 1872), p. 240; *Tenth Census of the United States, 1880: Productions of Agriculture* (Washington, D.C.: United States Government Printing Office, 1883), p. 240; *Eleventh Census of the United States, 1890: Statistics of Agriculture* (Washington, D.C.: United States Government Printing Office, 1895), p. 396; *Twelfth Census of the United States*, Vol. VI, *Agriculture*, pt. II, Crops and Irrigation (Washington, D.C.: United States Government Printing Office, 1902), pp. 433, 436, To compare these figures with antebellum production figures, see footnote 9 of this chapter. Note that the size of commercial bales of short-staple cotton in the low country rose gradually in the late nineteenth century, from about 450 pounds in 1869 to about 500 pounds by 1899. Commercial bales of Sea Island cotton were smaller, generally weighing about 340-350 pounds throughout the late nineteenth century. On market conditions in the cotton industry in the late nineteenth century, see Gavin Wright, *The Political Economy of the Cotton South: Households, Markets, and Wealth in the Nineteenth Century* (New York: W.W. Norton, 1978), pp. 158-84.

33. On the reasons for the rise of population in the low country after the Civil War, see, for example, Joel Williamson, *After Slavery: The Negro in South Carolina During Reconstruction, 1861–1877* (Chapel Hill: University of North Carolina Press, 1965), pp. 61–63, 107–8. Immigration and the continuance of high levels of fertility among whites and blacks alike contributed to population increase as well. Boserup's famous thesis is put forth in *The Conditions of Agricultural Growth: The Economics of Agrarian Change under Population Pressure* (Chicago: Aldine, 1965).

34. Albert O. Hirschman, *The Strategy of Economic Development* (New Haven: Yale University Press, 1958), pp. 50–75 and passim.

35. For superb discussions of the broad cultural changes attending the evolution of the market economy in the West in the nineteenth century, see E. J. Hobsbawm, *The Age of Revolution 1789–1848* (London: Weidenfeld and Nicolson, 1962) and especially Hobsbawm, *The Age of Capital 1848–1875* (New York: Charles Scribner's Sons, 1975).

36. On the intellectual power of pro-slavery political rhetoric in antebellum South Carolina, see Lacy K. Ford's forthcoming book *The Origins of Southern Radicalism* (New York: Oxford University Press).

37. On the transformation in the low country specifically, see especially Strickland, "Traditional Culture and Moral Economy: Social and Economic Change in the South Carolina Low Country, 1865–1910." Also see Willie Lee Rose, *Rehearsal for Reconstruction: The Port Royal Experiment* (Indianapolis: Bobbs-Merrill, 1964); Williamson, *After Slavery*, pp. 64–179 especially; Mary J. McGuire, "Getting Their Hands on the Land: The Revolution in St. Helena Parish, 1861–1900" (Ph.D. dissertation, University of South Carolina, 1985).

38. For estimates of the percentage of low-country rice consumed locally, see Chapter 3, footnote 122. Also see *De Bow's Review* 1 (April 1846): 320–57, especially p. 356. On the grades of rice and types of rice byproducts consumed locally, see *South Carolina Gazette*, March 20, 1742; February 13, 1744; Henry Laurens to Stephenson, Holford & Co., May 21, 1756, in Philip M. Hamer, George C. Rogers, Jr., *et al.*, eds., *The Papers of Henry Laurens*, 10 vols. thus far (Columbia: University of South Carolina Press, 1968–), 2: 198; Henry Laurens to John Tarleton, February 20, 1770, in Hamer, Rogers, *et al.*, eds., *The Papers of Henry Laurens*, 7: 235–36, especially p. 236; Orders from D. Robertson to Mr. Acord, n.d. [1792 or 1793], David Robertson Papers, Manuscript Department, William R. Perkins Library, Duke University, Durham, N.C.; Charles Manigault to Louis Manigault, November 28, 1855, in James M. Clifton, ed., *Life and Labor on Argyle Island: Letters and Documents of a Savannah River Rice Plantation, 1833–1867* (Savannah: The Beehive Press, 1978), pp. 198–99, especially p. 199.

39. For the sources of the adjectives used above, see John Oldmixon, *The British Empire in America . . .*, 2 vols. (London: John Nicholson, 1708), 1: 17; Speech, James Henry Hammond, March 4, 1858, printed in *Congressional Globe*, 35th Congress, 1st session, Appendix, p. 70; G. Cabrera Infante, *Holy Smoke* (New York: Harper & Row, 1985).

40. On the uses of rice in Europe and the Americas in the eighteenth and nineteenth centuries, see, for example, James Glen, *A Description of South Carolina . . .* (London: R. and J. Dodsley, 1761), p. 91; Henry Laurens to James Habersham, April 10, 1770, in Hamer, Rogers, *et al.*, eds., *The Papers of Henry Laurens*, 7: 272–75, especially p. 275; Henry Laurens to Thomas Franklin, December 26, 1771, in Hamer, Rogers, *et al.*, eds., *The Papers of Henry Laurens*, 8: 118–22, especially p. 119; Josiah Smith, Jr., to George Austin, February 25, 1772, pp. 63–74, especially p. 67, Josiah Smith, Jr., Lettercopy Book, Southern Historical Collection; Nicolas Baudeau, . . .*Commerce . . .*, 3 vols. (Paris:

Panckouke, 1783–84), 3: 588–89; Thomas Slater to John Ball, March 30, 1812, John Ball, Sr., and John Ball, Jr., Papers, Manuscript Department, William R. Perkins Library; Thomas Slater to John Ball, November 16, 1815, John Ball, Sr., and John Ball, Jr., Papers, Manuscript Department, William R. Perkins Library; John McMish to Thomas Butler, November 25, 1825, Butler Family Papers, Historical Society of Pennsylvania, Philadelphia, Pennsylvania; United States Congress, House of Representatives, Ways and Means Committee, *Statements to the Committee of Ways and Means on the Morrison Tariff Bill* . . . (Washington, D.C.: United States Government Printing Office, 1886), pp. 210–11; N.W. Posthumus, *Inquiry into the History of Prices in Holland*, 2 vols. (Leiden: E.J. Brill, (1946–1964), 2: 459–66, 773–95, 806–21. Also see the sources cited in footnote 38 above. Note that in the United States at least, patterns of rice consumption have changed substantially in the last generation. See James R. Shortridge and Barbara G. Shortridge, "Patterns of American Rice Consumption 1955 and 1980," *The Geographical Review* 73 (October 1983): 417–29.

    41. On rice consumption in the U.S. brewing industry, see United States Congress, House of Representatives, Ways and Means Committee, *Statements to the Committee of Ways and Means on the Morrison Tariff Bill*, pp. 228–31; Morris Weeks, Jr., *Beer and Brewing in America* (New York: United States Brewers' Foundation, 1949), pp. 12, 80. Note that most of the rice consumed in the brewing industry was either small or broken rice, granulated rice or rice flour. Moreover, much of this rice was imported. Indeed, an interesting, but little-known battle over the rice tariff was waged in the late nineteenth century between domestic producers, seeking protection, and U.S. brewing interests, seeking cheap imported rice and rice byproducts. On this battle, see United States Congress, House of Representatives, Ways and Means Committee, *Statements to the Committee of Ways and Means on the Morrison Tariff Bill*, pp. 228–31; Edward Hake Phillips, "The Historical Significance of the Tariff on Rice," *Agricultural History* 26 (July 1952): 89–92.

    42. See, for example, Glen, *A Description of South Carolina*, pp. 90–93; *South Carolina Gazette*, January 10, 1761; Marie Scholz-Babisch, *Quellen zur Geschichte des Klevischen Rheinzollwesens vom 11. bis 18. Jahrhundert*, 2 vols. (Weisbaden: Franz Steiner Verlag, 1971), 2: 870, 912, 997, 999; Nina E. Bang and Knud Korst, *Tabeller Over Skibsfart Og Varetransport Gennem Øresund, 1661–1783, Og Gennem Storebaelt 1701–1748* . . . , 4 vols. (Kobenhavn: Gyldendalske Boghandel . . . , 1930), 2, pt. II: 275, 293, 310, 330, 374, 393, 410, 428, 503, 524, 593; Ralph Izard to Thomas Jefferson, June 10, 1785, in Julian P. Boyd *et al.*, eds., *The Papers of Thomas Jefferson*, 22 vols. thus far (Princeton: Princeton University Press, 1950–), 8: 195–204, especially p. 198; H. P. H. Nusteling, *De Rijnvaart in Het Tijdperk Van Stoom en Steenkool 1831–1914* (Amsterdam: Holland Universiteits Pers, 1974), pp. 123–79, especially pp. 132, 153–55, 464; *Hunt's Merchants' Magazine* 21 (July 1849): 104; *De Bow's Review* 25 (September 1858): 350–51. As the works by Scholz-Babisch and Nusteling suggest, much of the rice imported into Germany and the Netherlands was sent up the Rhine. On the logistics of the Rhine trade, see Jürgen Heinz Schawacht, *Schiffahrt und Güterverkehr Zwischen den Häfen des Deutschen Niederrheins (Insbesondere Köln) und Rotterdam Vom Ende des 18. bis zur Mitte des 19. Jahrhunderts (1794–1850/51)* (Köln: 1973).

    43. See the works cited in footnote 42 above. In Bang and Korst, however, see Volume 2, part II, pp. 85, 117, 172, 206, 258, 259, 276, 292, 293, 310, 330, 374, 393, 410–11, 428, 463–64, 503, 524–25, 549, 593, 616. Also see Peter Buss to Robert Pringle, February 14, 1784, Pringle Family Papers, South Carolina Historical Society; *Hunt's Merchants' Magazine* 11 (August 1844): 179–80; 16 (February 1847): 138–51, especially pp. 148–49;

23 (August 1850): 177–88; 31 (November 1854): 558–65; J. Thomas Lindblad, *Sweden's Trade with the Dutch Republic 1738–1795: A Quantitative Analysis of the Relationship Between Economic Growth and International Trade in the Eighteenth Century* (Assen, The Netherlands: Van Gorcum & Co., 1982), pp. 151–60. especially p. 152.

44. See, for example, *Hunt's Merchants' Magazine* 13 (August 1845): 193–96; 18 (April 1848): 413–15; 43 (July 1860): 91–94, especially p. 93. That the British generally consumed little of the rice they imported prior to the nineteenth century, see Gray, *History of Agriculture*, 1: 286; Peter A. Coclanis, "Bitter Harvest: The South Carolina Low Country in Historical Perspective," *Journal of Economic History* 45 (June 1985): 251–59. For figures on British consumption of East Indian rice in the early nineteenth century, see Robert Montgomery Martin, *History of the Colonies of the British Empire* . . . (London: Dawsons, 1967; originally published 1843), pp. 352–54.

45. See *Hunt's Merchants' Magazine* 27 (September 1852): 289–309; 28 (January 1853): 81–86.

46. See, for example, Baudeau, *Commerce*, p. 588; Edward Rutledge to Thomas Jefferson, October 14, 1786, in Boyd *et al.*, eds., *The Papers of Thomas Jefferson*, 10: 463–65; Augusta *Georgia State Gazette and Independent Register*, March 10, 1787; Ralph Izard to Thomas Jefferson, November 10, 1787, in Boyd *et al.*, eds., *The Papers of Thomas Jefferson*, 12: 338–40. On the rice industry and rice trade of northern Italy, see Luigi Faccini, *L'economia risicola lombarda dagli inizi del XVIII secolo all'Unità* (Milan: SugarCo., 1976).

47. On rice exports from Georgia during the colonial period, see U.S. Department of Commerce, Bureau of the Census, *Historical Statistics of the United States: Colonial Times to 1970*, 2: 1192. On Brazil's penetration of the Portuguese rice market, see, for example, Ralph Izard to Thomas Jefferson, April 14, 1787, in Boyd *et al.*, eds., *The Papers of Thomas Jefferson*, 11: 262–66, especially p. 264; Ralph Izard to Thomas Jefferson, April 13, 1789, in Boyd *et al.*, eds., *The Papers of Thomas Jefferson*, 15: 21–23. Data on U.S. rice exports for the 1790s support Izard's contention that Brazil had hurt U.S. producers severely in the Portuguese market. During the decade of the 1790s, the U.S. exported only 5319.9 tons of rice to Portugal, which figure constituted but 1.64 percent of total rice exports during the decade. See *American State Papers* . . . , Class IV: Commerce and Navigation, Vol. VII (Washington, D.C.: Gales and Seaton, 1832). On European imports of Indian and/or "Levant" rice in the eighteenth century, see Memo concerning the Carolina rice trade, n.d. [probably 1720s], W.R. Coe Collection, North Carolina State Archives, Raleigh; Glen, *A Description of South Carolina*, p. 90; Baudeau, *Commerce*, 3: 589; Tench Coxe, *A View of the United States of America* . . . (Philadelphia: William Hall, 1794), pp. 84–85; Cheng Siok-Hwa, *The Rice Industry of Burma 1852–1940* (Kuala Lumpur and Singapore: University of Malaya Press, 1968), pp. 8–9.

48. For figures on rice production in Georgia between 1839 and 1919, see Peter A. Coclanis, "Economy and Society in the Early Modern South: Charleston and the Evolution of the South Carolina Low Country" (Ph. D. dissertation, Columbia University, 1984), pp. 387–97.

49. On rice exports from Bengal to Europe in the early nineteenth century, see, for example, John Phipps, *A Guide to the Commerce of Bengal* . . . (Calcutta: 1823), pp. 211, 223–24. According to Phipps, Bengali rice exports to Europe averaged 18.5 million pounds annually between 1813 and 1821, most of which went to northern Europe. This figure, one should note, was equal to about 36 percent of *total* U.S. rice exports during this period. On U.S. exports, see U.S. Department of Agriculture, Bureau of Statistics, *Rice Crop of the United States, 1712–1911*, p. 7. Looking at the British market alone, one

finds that by the mid-1830s imports of Bengali rice exceeded imports of U.S. rice by a wide margin. On British imports of Bengali rice, see H.J.S. Cotton, "The Rice Trade of the World," *The Calcutta Review* 58 (1874): 267–302, especially p. 297; Martin, *History of the Colonies of the British Empire*, pp. 352–54. Note that Cotton's figures on British imports of U.S. rice are too low. For the correct figures, see those reported in *U.S. Senate Executive Documents, 2d Session, 23d Congress, Vol. IV, 1834–35, No. 269; U.S. House of Representatives, Executive Documents, 1st Session, 24th Congress, No. 291; U.S. House of Representatives, Executive Documents, 2d Session, 24th Congress, 1836–1837, No. 304; U.S. Senate Executive Documents, 2d Session, 25th Congress, 1837–1838, No. 318; U.S. Senate Executive Documents, 3d Session, 25th Congress, 1838–1839, No. 342.*

50. See J.S. Furnivall, *Netherlands India: A Study of Plural Economy* (New York: Macmillan, 1944), pp. 1–173 especially; Clifford Geertz, *Agricultural Involution: The Process of Ecological Change in Indonesia* (Berkeley: University of California Press, 1971; originally published 1963), pp. 47–82. Also see R. Reinsma, *Het Verval van het Cultuurstelsel* (s' Gravenhage: van Veulen, 1955); C. Fasseur, "The Cultivation System and Its Impact on the Dutch Colonial Economy and the Indigenous Society in Nineteenth-Century Java," in C.A. Bayly and D.H.A. Kolff, eds., *Two Colonial Empires: Comparative Essays on the History of India and Indonesia in the Nineteenth Century* (Dordrecht, The Netherlands: Martinus Nijhoff, 1986), pp. 137–54.

51. See the works cited in footnote 50 above. Data compiled by G.F. de Bruijn Kops reveal that Javanese rice exports to northern Europe averaged 293,442 pikols annually between 1837 and 1839. Though a pikol generally is considered to weigh 133.5 pounds, a Batavian pikol at the time was calculated at 136 pounds. Thus, Java exported, on average, over 39.9 million pounds of (partially milled, cargo) rice annually to this area between 1837 and 1839. The U.S., on the other hand, exported, on average, about 25.7 million pounds of clean rice equivalents to northern Europe in 1837 and 1838, with another 1 million pounds annually going to southern Europe. Under the conservative assumption that one pound of cargo rice at the time equaled 0.8 pounds of U.S. clean rice, we find that Java was already exporting more rice to northern Europe than the U.S. was sending to Europe as a whole. Moreover, Javanese exports to northern Europe increased in the 1840s and 1850s. On Javanese rice exports, see G. F. de Bruijn Kops, *Statistiek van Den Handel en de Scheepvaart op Java en Madura Sedert 1825*, 2 vols. (Batavia: Lange & Co., 1857–59), 2: 176–80. On U.S. rice exports in 1837 and 1838, see *U.S. Senate Executive Documents, 2d Session, 25th Congress, 1837–1838, No. 318; U.S. Senate Executive Documents, 3d Session, 25th Congress, 1838–1839, No. 342.* On the weight of pikols in Batavia in this period, see *Hunt's Merchants' Magazine* 15 (September 1846): 328–29.

52. On the rise of the rice industry in Lower Burma in this period, see especially Cheng, *The Rice Industry of Burma*; Cotton, "The Rice Trade of the World"; J.S. Furnivall, *An Introduction to the Political Economy of Burma*, 3d ed. (Rangoon: Peoples' Literature Committee and House, 1957); U. Tun Wai, *Economic Development of Burma from 1800 till 1940* (Rangoon: Department of Economics, University of Rangoon, 1961); Michael Adas, *The Burma Delta: Economic Development and Social Change on an Asian Rice Frontier, 1852–1941* (Madison: University of Wisconsin Press, 1974).

53. For aggregate figures on U.S. rice exports during this period, see U.S. Department of Agriculture, Bureau of Statistics, *Rice Crop of the United States, 1712–1911*, pp. 7–9; Gray, *History of Agriculture*, 2: 1030.

54. See the works cited in footnotes 50 and 52 above. On the cost advantages of East Indian rice *vis à vis* U.S. rice in the nineteenth century, see, for example, *The Southern Agriculturalist* 11 (March 1838): 127–29; *Hunt's Merchants' Magazine* 1 (August 1839):

142–47, especially 142–43; *Hunt's Merchants' Magazine* 5 (September 1841): 220–29; C. Edwards Lester, *The Glory and the Shame of England*, 2 vols. (New York: Harper & Brothers, 1850), 2: 27–52; London *Times*, February 6, 1874, p. 7; U.S. Congress, House of Representatives, Ways and Means Committee, *Statements to the Committee of Ways and Means on the Morrison Tariff Bill*, pp. 205–32, especially p. 215.

55. John Komlos and I have compared total factor productivity of rice production in South Carolina–Georgia in 1859 and Lower Burma in the early 1880s. After assembling data on inputs and output and estimating factor shares, we utilized the standard Cobb-Douglas geometric index as the basis of comparison. We found that Burmese productivity levels in the early 1880s were only about 10 percent lower than levels attained in the "modern," capital-intensive rice industry of South Carolina-Georgia in 1859. See Komlos and Coclanis, "Time in the Paddies: A Comparison of Rice Production in the Southeastern United States and Lower Burma in the Nineteentn Century," *Social Science History* 11 (Fall 1987): 343–54.

On the projection of Western power in the areas mentioned above, see the works cited in footnotes 50 and 52. Also see Eric R. Wolf, *Europe and the People Without History* (Berkeley: University of California Press, 1982), pp. 32–383.

56. On technological and organizational changes in transoceanic shipping, see Douglass C. North, "Ocean Freight Rates and Economic Development 1750–1913," *Journal of Economic History* 18 (December 1958): 537–55; North, "Sources of Productivity Change in Ocean Shipping, 1600–1850," *Journal of Political Economy* 76 (September–October 1968): 953–70.

On the importance of the development of Australia and California for the East Indian rice trade with the Western world, see *Hunt's Merchants' Magazine* 41 (October 1859): 445–48; 42 (January 1860): 62–66.

57. On British tariff preferences in favor of imperial rice, for example, see the schedules reprinted in *The Southern Agriculturalist* 1 (October 1828): 459–61; *Hunt's Merchants' Magazine* 7 (October 1842): 367–88, especially p. 379; *Ibid.*, 16 (April 1847): 405–8.

U.S. rice generally was considered by Westerners to be of higher quality than East Indian rice, though some Bengali and Javanese varieties were valued relatively highly in the West. See Cotton, "The Rice Trade of the World," pp. 271, 301 especially; Gray, *History of Agriculture*, 2: 725.

Throughout the nineteenth century dismayed or, conversely, enthusiastic observers commented on the fact that East Indian rice could out-compete U.S. rice in the leading Western markets. See, for example, *The Southern Agriculturalist* 11 (March 1838): 127–29; *Hunt's Merchants' Magazine* 1 (August 1839): 142–47; *Hunt's Merchants' Magazine* 5 (September 1841): 220–29; Lester, *The Glory and the Shame of England*, 2: 27–52; *De Bow's Review* [After the War series] 1 (February 1866): 199; Thurston and Holmes to Benjamin Allston, December 22, 1866, in Easterby, ed., *The South Carolina Rice Plantation as Revealed in the Papers of Robert F.W. Allston*, p. 437; Thurston and Holmes to S.D. Doar, March 2, 1868; May 12, 1868; June 7, 1869; December 12, 1870, Stephen Duvall Doar Papers, South Caroliniana Library; U.S. Congress, House of Representatives, Ways and Means Committee, *Statements to the Committee of Ways and Means on the Morrison Tariff Bill*, pp. 205–32.

58. *The Southern Agriculturalist* 11 (March 1838): 127–29.

59. On U.S. rice tariffs through 1870, see United States Bureau of Statistics, *Report of the Chief of the Bureau of Statistics on Customs-Tariff Legislation. Appendix A. Comparative Statement of the Rates of Duties and Imposts under the Several Tariff Acts from 1789 to 1870, Both Inclusive*, prepared by A.W. Angerer (Washington, D.C.: United States Government

Printing Office, 1872), pp. 72–73, 76–77, 82–83. Despite tariff barriers, one should note, small quantities of foreign rice continued to enter the U.S. during the late antebellum period. See, for example, *Hunt's Merchants' Magazine* 36 (June 1857): 731–32; 42 (June 1860): 725–27.

60. See Minutes, September 15, 1829, South Carolina Agricultural Society, 1: 63, South Caroliniana Library. On the increase in domestic rice consumption in the U.S. in the antebellum period, see U.S. Department of Agriculture, Bureau of Statistics, *Rice Crop of the United States, 1712–1911*, pp. 7–9.

On the rise of markets for U.S. rice in other parts of the Americas, see Table 4–22. As this table indicates, the U.S. exported over 324,000 tons of rice in the 1790s and a little less—about 312,000 tons—in the 1850s. In the 1790s, 26.3 percent of total U.S. exports went to other parts of the Americas, whereas 49.5 percent went to other parts of the Americas in the 1850s. Moreover, while only about 2.6 percent of U.S. rice exports went to Florida and the Spanish West Indies in the 1790s, 26.9 percent of U.S. exports went to Cuba *alone* in the 1850s. The figures for Spanish Florida, the Spanish West Indies, and Cuba were derived from the same sources used for Table 4–22.

61. See Cheng, *The Rice Industry of Burma, 1852–1940*, pp. 9–15, 237–39, 257–259; Peter A. Coclanis, "The Rise and Fall of the South Carolina Low Country: An Essay in Economic Interpretation," *Southern Studies* 24 (Summer 1985): 143–66. The figures for Burmese rice exports to Europe in the 1880s are from Cheng, p. 239. For U.S. production figures in the nineteenth century, see U.S. Department of Agriculture, Bureau of Statistics, *Rice Crop of the United States, 1712–1911*, pp. 7–10.

62. See A.J.H. Latham and Larry Neal, "The International Market in Rice and Wheat, 1868–1914," *Economic History Review* 36 (May 1983): 260–80; Morton Rothstein, "The New South and the International Economy," *Agricultural History* 57 (October 1983): 385–402; Loren Brandt, "Chinese Agriculture and the International Economy, 1870–1930s: A Reassessment," *Explorations in Economic History*, 2d ser., 22 (April 1985): 168–93. Also see Cotton, "The Rice Trade of the World."

63. On exports of East Indian rice to areas other than Europe and the U.S. in the late nineteenth century, see Cotton, "The Rice Trade of the World"; Cotton, "The Rice Trade in Bengal," *The Calcutta Review* 58 (1874): 171–88; Cheng, *The Rice Industry of Burma, 1852–1940*, pp. 198–219.

Note that in the late nineteenth century domestic rice interests opposed—albeit often unsuccessfully—attempts to lower the U.S. tariffs on imported rice. See, for example, Thurston and Holmes to Benjamin Allston, December 22, 1866, in Easterby, ed., *The South Carolina Rice Plantation as revealed in the Papers of Robert F.W. Allston*, p. 437; Thurston and Holmes to S.D. Doar, December 12, 1870, Stephen Duvall Doar Papers, South Caroliniana Library; *The Southern Cultivator* 41 (January 1883): 13; *Charleston News and Courier*, December 1, 1881; September 19, 1882; October 2, 1885; U.S. Congress, House of Representatives, Ways and Means Committee, *Statements to the Committee of Ways and Means on the Morrison Tariff Bill*, pp. 205–32.

64. On the shift of U.S. rice production to the Southwest and on cultivation techniques in this region, see United States Department of Agriculture, Office of Experiment Stations, Bulletin No. 113, *Irrigation of Rice in the United States*, by Frank Bond and George H. Keeney (Washington, D.C.: United States Government Printing Office, 1902), pp. 11–77, especially pp. 11–57; Arthur H. Cole, "The American Rice-Growing Industry: A Study of Comparative Advantage," *Quarterly Journal of Economics* 41 (August 1927): 595–643; Edward Hake Phillips, "The Gulf Coast Rice Industry," *Agricultural History* 25 (April 1951): 91–96; Chan Lee, "A Culture History of Rice with Special Reference to Louisiana"

(Ph.D. dissertation, Louisiana State University, 1960), pp. 92–200; David O. Whitten, "American Rice Cultivation, 1680–1980: A Tercentenary Critique," *Southern Studies* 21 (Spring 1982): 5–26; Pete Daniel, *Breaking the Land: The Transformation of Cotton, Tobacco, and Rice Cultures Since 1880* (Urbana: University of Illinois Press, 1985), pp. 39–61, 215–36 especially.

65. On rice cultivation techniques in the South Carolina low country in the nineteenth century, see, for example, N. Heyward, "Water Culture of Rice," 1800, Butler Family Papers, Historical Society of Pennsylvania; *The Southern Agriculturalist* 1 (April 1828): 166–70; 1 (May 1828): 216-23; 1 (June 1828): 268–70; 1 (August 1828): 352–57; 1 (September 1828): 409–13; 1 (October 1828): 456–58; 1 (November 1828): 498–502; 2 (May 1829): 193–97; 2 (June 1829): 247–54; 2 (August 1829): 370–71; 4 (May 1831): 288–92; *The Southern Agriculturalist*, new series, 3 (July 1843): 241–46; 4 (January 1844): 6–25; *De Bow's Review* 9 (October 1850): 421–26; 16 (June 1854): 589–615, especially pp. 606–15; Charles Manigault, "RICE CULTURE, BY OPEN-PLANTING, on Savannah River," July 1852, in Clifton, ed., *Life and Labor on Argyle Island*, pp. 101–8; *The Southern Cultivator* 20 (January 1862): 16–17 and (February 1862): 42–43; 24 (April 1866): 75–77; 24 (December 1866): 278–79; 25 (January 1867): 2–3 and (February 1867): 31–33; Albert Kenrick Fisher Journal, April 30, 1886; May 4, 1886, Manuscript Department, William R. Perkins Library; U.S. Department of Agriculture, Division of Statistics, Miscellaneous Series, Report No.6, *Rice: Its Cultivation, Production, and Distribution in the United States and Foreign Countries*, by Amory Austin . . .(Washington, D.C.: U.S. Government Printing Office, 1893), pp. 16–24 especially.

On the decline of the low-country rice industry and the reasons for the decline, see, for example, Arthur Middleton to Pa [Nathaniel R. Middleton], April 11, 1870; April 15, 1870, Nathaniel R. Middleton Papers, Southern Historical Collection; U.S. Department of Agriculture, Division of Statistics, Miscellaneous Series, Report No.6, *Rice*, pp. 77–79; U.S. Congress, House of Representatives, Ways and Means Committee, *Statements to the Committee of Ways and Means on the Morrison Tariff Bill*, pp. 205–32; D.E. Huger Smith, *A Charlestonian's Recollections 1846–1913* (Charleston: Carolina Art Association, 1950), pp. 129–36.

On labor problems and the decline of labor productivity in particular, see James R. Sparkman to Benjamin Allston, November 23, 1866, in Easterby, ed., *The South Carolina Rice Plantation as Revealed in the Papers of Robert F.W. Allston*, pp. 224–26; W.G. Westbury to Madam [Mrs. Allston], June 8, 1866, Robert F.W. Allston Papers, South Carolina Historical Society; Rice Crop, 1869, 1870, John and Keating S. Ball Books, 5, n.p., Southern Historical Collection; John Edwin Fripp Papers and Books, 3, c. 1866–68, pp. 120–21 (typescript), Southern Historical Collection; F.W. Johnstone to Sir [James Ritchie Sparkman?], February 7, 1869, James Ritchie Sparkman Papers, South Caroliniana Library; John M. Hucks to Major A. [Arnoldus] Vander Horst, February 4, 1867; April 8, 1867; July 4, 1867; J.B. Larisy to Elias Vander Horst, March 7, 1868, Arnoldus Vander Horst V, Family Papers, South Carolina Historical Society; ___ [Arthur Grimball] to Berkley [Grimball], January 24, 1885, Grimball Papers, Southern Historical Collection.

On problems due to the scarcity of capital in particular, see R.H. Colcock to James Gregorie, October 8, 1865; John Colcock to James Gregorie, July 15, 1867; December 19, 1867, Gregorie-Elliott Papers, Southern Historical Collection; Entry, June 8, 1865, John Berkley Grimball Diary, 15, p. 9, Southern Historical Collection; London *Times*, February 6, 1874, p. 7; U.S. Department of Agriculture, Division of Statistics, Miscellaneous Series, Report No. 6, *Rice*, pp. 77–78.

On the long-term decline of soil fertility on rice lands in much of the low country, see Roswell King, Jr., to Thomas Butler, July 6, 1834, Butler Family Papers, Historical Society of Pennsylvania; *The Southern Agriculturalist*, new series, 3 (July 1843): 241–46; *De Bow's Review* 9 (October 1850): 421–26; Charles Manigault, "RICE CULTURE," in Clifton, ed., *Life and Labor on Argyle Island*, p. 103; J.B. Heyward to Louis Manigault, May 14, 1878, Louis Manigault Papers, Manuscript Department, William R. Perkins Library.

Note that declining soil fertility explains part of the decline in rice yields in the low country–a decline which began in the antebellum period and not after the Civil War. On antebellum rice yields in South Carolina, see Coclanis, "Economy and Society in the Early Modern South," pp. 436–37. On the decline in yields since the late eighteenth century, see, for example, *The Southern Agriculturalist*, new series, 3 (July 1843): 241–46. Also see Whitten, "American Rice Cultivation," p. 16.

Finally, on the relative shift of production toward the Southwest, see Table 4–25.

66. See the works cited in footnotes 64 and 65 above.

67. Among the scholars arguing that low-country planters and merchants were lacking in entrepreneurial initiative, particularly in comparison with similar groups in the North, are Don H. Doyle, Frederic C. Jaher, John P. Radford, Michael P. Johnson, Tom W. Shick, and Jane H. Pease and William H. Pease. See, for example, Doyle, "Leadership and Decline in Postwar Charleston, 1865–1910," in Walter J. Fraser, Jr. and Winfred B. Moore, Jr., eds., *From the Old South to the New: Essays on the Transitional South* (Westport, Conn.: Greenwood Press, 1981), pp. 93–106; Doyle and Shick, "The South Carolina Phosphate Boom and the Stillbirth of the New South"; Jaher, "Antebellum Charleston: Anatomy of an Economic Failure," in Orville V. Burton and Robert C. McMath, Jr., eds., *Class, Conflict, and Consensus: Antebellum Southern Community Studies* (Westport, Conn.: Greenwood Press, 1982), pp. 207–31; Jaher, *The Urban Establishment: Upper Strata in Boston, New York, Charleston, Chicago, and Los Angeles* (Urbana: University of Illinois Press, 1982), passim; John P. Radford, "Culture, Economy, and Urban Structure in Charleston, South Carolina, 1860–1880" (Ph.D. dissertation, Clark University, 1974), passim; Radford, "Testing the Model of the Pre-Industrial City: The Case of Charleston, South Carolina," *Transactions of the Institute of British Geographers*, New Series, 4 (1979): 392–410; Radford, "Social Structure and Urban Form: Charleston, 1860–1880," in Fraser and Moore, eds., *From the Old South to the New*, pp. 81–91; Johnson, "Planters and Patriarchy: Charleston, 1800–1860," *Journal of Southern History* 46 (February 1980): 45–72; Pease and Pease, "Social Structure and the Potential for Urban Change: Boston and Charleston in the 1830s," *Journal of Urban History* 8 (February 1982): 171–95; Pease and Pease, *The Web of Progress: Private Values and Public Styles in Boston and Charleston, 1828–1843* (New York: Oxford University Press, 1985), passim.

68. I am not alone in arguing that low-country planters and merchants tried hard to improve the area's economic position in the nineteenth century. See, for example, Marjorie S. Mendenhall, "A History of Agriculture in South Carolina, 1790 to 1860: An Economic and Social Study" (Ph.D. dissertation, University of North Carolina, 1940), pp. 338–42; Smith, *Economic Readjustment of an Old Cotton State*; Ralph V. Anderson, "Labor Utilization and Productivity, Diversification and Self Sufficiency, Southern Plantations, 1800–1840" (Ph.D. dissertation, University of North Carolina, 1974), pp. 191–95 and passim; Greb, "Charleston, South Carolina, Merchants, 1815–1860," pp. 79–240 especially; Carlton, "The Piedmont and Waccamaw Regions: An Economic Comparison."

69. The particular phraseology used in the text above is, of course, that of Marx and Engels in *The Communist Manifesto*. See *The Communist Manifesto*, ed. Joseph Katz, trans. Samuel Moore (New York: Washington Square Press, 1964; originally published 1848),

p. 61. Only recently have scholars begun to appreciate the degree to which the external environment can condition, if not determine levels of entrepreneurial success. See Donald N. McCloskey and Lars G. Sandberg, "From Damnation to Redemption: Judgments on the Late Victorian Entrepreneur," in McCloskey, *Enterprise and Trade in Victorian Britain* (London: Allen & Unwin, 1981), pp. 55–72; Peter A. Coclanis, "Entrepreneurship and the Economic History of the American South: The Case of Charleston and the South Carolina Low Country," in Stanley C. Hollander and Terence Nevett, eds., *Marketing in the Long Run* (East Lansing: Department of Marketing and Transportation Administration, Michigan State University, 1985), pp. 210–19.

70. According to the 1860 census, the aggregate wealth of the inhabitants of the low country was put at $169,492,927. There were, as we have seen, 142,805 slaves in the area. At $600–$625 per slave, the value of slaves comes to between $85,683,000 and $89,253,125 — or between about 51 and 53 percent of the aggregate wealth of the inhabitants of the area. See *Eighth Census of the United States, 1860: Statistics*, p. 312; *Eighth Census of the United States, 1860: Population*, p. 452. Also see footnote 24 above.

On capital flows from South Carolina to the West, see, for example, Smith, *Economic Readjustment of an Old Cotton State*, pp. 19–44.

On the lack of readily accessible motive power on the coastal plain and the relationship between the shortage of such power and the laggard pace of industrialization in the area, see Carlton, "The Piedmont and Waccamaw Regions: An Economic Comparison"; Stephen J. Goldfarb, "A Note on Limits to the Growth of the Cotton-Textile Industry in the Old South," *Journal of Southern History* 48 (November 1982): 545–58.

71. See Stanley L. Engerman, "Agriculture as Business: The Southern Context," in Fred Bateman, ed., *Business in the New South: A Historical Perspective* (Sewanee, Tenn.: The University Press, The University of the South, 1981), pp. 17–26; Dale E. Swan, *The Structure and Profitability of the Antebellum Rice Industry 1859* (New York: Arno Press, 1975), pp. 12–34 and passim.

72. See Stuart Bruchey, "The Business Economy of Marketing Change, 1790–1840: A Study of Sources of Efficiency," *Agricultural History* 46 (January 1972): 211–26; Coclanis, "Entrepreneurship and the Economic History of the American South."

73. Reavis Cox, Charles S. Goodman, and Thomas C. Fichandler, *Distribution in a High-Level Economy* (Englewood Cliffs, N.J.: Prentice-Hall, 1965), p. 13; Harold D. Woodman, *King Cotton & His Retainers: Financing & Marketing the Cotton Crop of the South, 1800–1925* (Lexington: University of Kentucky Press, 1968), p. 186 and passim.

74. On the efficiency of the factorage system, see Woodman, *King Cotton & His Retainers*; Coclanis, "Entrepreneurship and the Economic History of the American South."

On the low country's transportation system, see, for example, Smith, *Economic Readjustment of an Old Cotton State*, pp. 135–92. Also see the works cited in footnote 98 below. To be sure, this system was not without problems; it did, however, allow for the efficient transportation of staple crops to markets.

On the size, soundness, and reputation of the low country's banks, see Smith, *Economic Readjustment of an Old Cotton State*, pp. 193–217; J. Mauldin Lesesne, *The Bank of the State of South Carolina: A General and Political History* (Columbia: University of South Carolina Press, 1970), passim. One can also establish these points by looking directly at antebellum data. See Albert Gallatin, *Considerations on the Currency and Banking System of the United States* (New York: Greenwood Press, 1968; originally published 1831), pp. 103–05; *De Bow's Review* 19 (July 1855): 78–79; 26 (March 1859): 326–27.

On the "business climate" created by the state, see Ford, *Origins of Southern Radicalism*;

Smith, *Readjustment of an Old Cotton State*, p. 151 and passim; Morton J. Horwitz, *The Transformation of American Law, 1780–1860* (Cambridge: Harvard University Press, 1977); Donald J. Senese, "Legal Thought in South Carolina, 1800–1860" (Ph.D. dissertation, University of South Carolina, 1970); Stephen Goldfarb, "Laws Governing the Incorporation of Manufacturing Companies Passed by Southern Legislatures Before the Civil War," *Southern Studies* 24 (Winter 1985): 407–16. Together, these works reveal the extent to which the state had created in South Carolina a business environment conducive both to the protection of property *and* economic expansion. On the general importance of the state in this regard, see Peter Evans, Dietrich Rueschemeyer, and Theda Skocpol, eds., *Bringing the State Back In* (New York: Cambridge University Press, 1985).

75. Fernand Braudel, *The Structures of Everyday Life: Civilization & Capitalism 15th-18th Century*, trans. Siân Reynolds (New York: Harper & Row, 1981; originally published 1979), pp. 104–82, expecially pp. 145–58. On the rigors of rice cultivation in northern Italy, also see Raimondo Luraghi, "Wage Labor in the 'Rice Belt' of Northern Italy and Slave Labor in the American South—A First Approach," *Southern Studies* 16 (Summer 1977): 109-27.

76. Swan, *The Structure and Profitability of the Antebellum Rice Industry 1859*, Preface, pp. 75–84 especially.

77. That the mean size of agricultural units in the low country fell substantially in the late nineteenth century, see Strickland, "Traditional Culture and Moral Economy: Social and Economic Change in the South Carolina Low Country, 1865–1910," pp. 163–64, 177 especially; Simkins and Woody, *South Carolina During Reconstruction*, pp. 224–38, especially pp. 236–38. Compare Strickland's findings, for example, with those of Swan. See *The Structure and Profitability of the Antebellum Rice Industry 1859*, pp. 25–34.

That the real costs of labor and capital rose in the low country and most other parts of the South after the Civil War is well known. For evidence on the rise of such costs in the low country, see the works cited in footnote 65.

On the decline in rice yields in the low country, compare census estimates for 1879, 1889, and 1899 with that for 1842 by the Committee of Agriculture of the South Carolina House of Representatives. See *Tenth Census of the United States, 1880: Productions of Agriculture*, pp. 262–66, 308; *Eleventh Census of the United States, 1890: Statistics of Agriculture*, pp. 71, 449; *Twelfth Census of the United States*, Vol VI, *Agriculture*, pt. II, Crops and Irrigation, pp. 94–95, 192–193; *Journal of the Senate of the State of South-Carolina . . .1842* (Columbia: Pemberton, 1842), pp. 89–90. Also see Komlos and Coclanis, "Time in the Paddies."

On the decline of rice prices in the late nineteenth century, see United States Department of Agriculture, Bureau of Agricultural Economics, *Gross Farm Income and Indices of Farm Production and Prices in the United States, 1869–1937*, by Frederick Strauss and Louis H. Bean, Technical Bulletin No. 703 (Washington, D.C.: United States Government Printing Office, 1940), pp. 69–71.

78. John Scott Strickland, " 'No More Mud Work': The Struggle for the Control of Labor and Production in Low Country South Carolina, 1863–1880," in Walter J. Fraser, Jr., and Winfred B. Moore, Jr., eds., *The Southern Enigma: Essays on Race, Class, and Folk Culture* (Westport, Conn: Greenwood Press, 1983), pp. 43–62; Strickland, "Traditional Culture and Moral Economy: Social and Economic Change in the South Carolina Low Country, 1865–1910." While we differ fundamentally in our approaches toward and interpretations of the low country's economic history, I regard Strickland's work very highly.

On the black "attachment" to rice, see, for example, *Charleston News and Courier*, September 19, 1882; U.S. Congress, House of Representatives, Ways and Means Committee, *Statements to the Committee of Ways and Means on the Morrison Tariff Bill*, p. 221.

79. See Karl A. Wittfogel, *Oriental Despotism: A Comparative Study of Total Power* (New Haven: Yale University Press, 1957); Braudel, *The Structures of Everyday Life*, pp. 145–58; Donald Worster, "Hydraulic Society in California: An Ecological Interpretation," *Agricultural History* 56 (July 1982): 503–15; Worster, *Rivers of Empire: Water, Aridity, and the Growth of the American West* (New York: Pantheon, 1985), pp. 17–60 and passim. Note that the coercive tendencies inherent in hydraulic rice cultivation may have been accentuated in the low country by the type of institutional coercion described by Roger L. Ransom and Richard Sutch in *One Kind of Freedom: The Economic Consequences of Emancipation* (New York: Cambridge University Press, 1977), pp. 106–99 especially. *In re* Ransom and Sutch, one can get an idea of the small number of stores in the low country (particularly outside of Charleston) in the early 1880s from State Board of Agriculture of South Carolina, *South Carolina: Resources and Population, Institutions and Industries*, comp. Harry Hammond (Charleston: Walker, Evans & Cogswell, 1883), pp. 659–91, 696; R.G. Dun and Company, *The Mercantile Agency Reference Book, 1890*; R.G. Dun and Company, *The Mercantile Agency Reference Book, 1892*. One should note that the generalizations in the text about hydraulic agricultural regimes do not hold true for the hydraulic agricultural regime of the Dutch Republic, a regime with completely different characteristics. On the historic development of the agricultural system of the Dutch, see, for example, Jan de Vries, *The Dutch Rural Economy in the Golden Age, 1500–1700* (New Haven: Yale University Press, 1974).

80. See Geertz, *Agricultural Involution*, pp. 28–37, 70–82, especially pp. 75–82; Albert O. Hirschman, "A Generalized Linkage Approach to Development, with Special Reference to Staples," *Economic Development and Cultural Change* 25, Supplement (1977): 67–98, especially pp. 81–84.

81. See Komlos and Coclanis, "Time in the Paddies." Lacking more precise analyses of the production functions for rice in these areas, for proof of the relative productive efficiency of Burma and the Southwest in comparison to South Carolina we must perforce also rely upon information conveyed by the market—Burmese and southwestern rice were pushing South Carolina rice out of markets—descriptive accounts of the comparative advantage of Burmese and southwestern rice production, and on data on rice yields per acre in these areas. Some data on yields are presented below.

Rice Yield Per Acre

Year	Louisiana	SC Low Country
	(Clean Rice—Pounds)	
1889	896.52	756.33
1899	856.45	694.14
	(Rough Rice—Bushels)	
1909	34.14	28.51
1919	35.04	19.53

See *Eleventh Census of the United States, 1890: Statistics of Agriculture*, pp. 71, 449; *Twelfth Census of the United States*, Vol. VI, *Agriculture*, pt. II, Crops and Irrigation, pp. 94–95, 192–193; *Thirteenth Census of the United States, 1910: Abstract of the Census . . . with Supplement for South Carolina* (Washington, D.C.: United States Government Printing Office, 1913), pp. 391, 516–519; *Fourteenth Census of the United States, 1920*, vol. V, *Agriculture: General Report and Analytical Tables* (Washington, D.C.: United States Government Printing Office, 1922), p. 772; *Fourteenth Census of the United States, 1920*, vol. VI, *Agriculture*, pt. II, Reports for States, The Southern States (Washington, D.C.: United States Government Printing Office, 1922), pp. 286–290.

According to Cheng, rice yields in Lower Burma averaged about 1600 pounds of paddy per acre in the early 1880s, with this figure falling to just under 1500 per acre by the early 1930s. Both figures, one should note, are much higher than levels achieved in South Carolina at any time between the Civil War and World War I. See Cheng, *The Rice Industry of Burma, 1852–1940*, pp. 28–29. To convert figures on Burmese paddy to clean rice, see the note on page 239 of Cheng.

82. On the variable "risk" in agriculture in a microeconomic context, see especially Wright, *The Political Economy of the Cotton South*, pp. 43–88, 158–84. Wright's use of this approach has not gone unchallenged; see, for example, Robert Higgs and Robert McGuire, "Cotton, Corn and Risk: Another View," *Explorations in Economic History*, 2d ser., 14 (April 1977): 167–82.

On "risk" in a macroeconomic context, see, for example, Cathy L. Jabara and Robert L. Thompson, "Agricultural Comparative Advantage under International Price Uncertainty: The Case of Senegal," *American Journal of Agricultural Economics* 62 (May 1980): 188–98.

83. That demand for rice, at least in a Western context, is more price-elastic than demand for wheat or tobacco, see Theodore W. Schultz, *The Economic Organization of Agriculture* (New York: McGraw-Hill, 1953), p. 190; U.S. Department of Agriculture, *A Study of Various Two-Price Systems of Price Support and Marketing Which Could be Made Applicable to Rice* (Washington, D.C.: U.S. Government Printing Office, 1955), p. 12; Parley M. Pratt, *Rice: Domestic Consumption in the United States* (Austin: Bureau of Business Research of the University of Texas, 1960), p. 39. Note, however, that the price elasticity of demand is less than unity for each of these staples.

Note, too, that David Ormrod has argued that even in the eighteenth century demand in Europe for "groceries"—a category that included rice—was marked by relatively high price-elasticity. See Ormrod, "English Re-Exports and the Dutch Staplemarket in the Eighteenth Century," in D.C. Coleman and Peter Mathias, eds., *Enterprise and History: Essays in Honor of Charles Wilson* (Cambridge: Cambridge University Press, 1984), pp. 89–115, especially p. 109.

84. For a good general discussion of some of these problems, see K.K.S. Dadzie, "Economic Development," *Scientific American* 243 (September 1980): 58–65. Much of the work of scholars associated with the various "critical" traditions in developmental studies is, of course, relevant as well. See, for example, Alain de Janvry, *The Agrarian Question and Reformism in Latin America* (Baltimore: Johns Hopkins University Press, 1981), pp. 7–60.

85. Mean per capita wealth in the low country at its nadir, let us say, in 1870 was $347.96. Given a capital/output or wealth/income ratio of 3.0 or 3.5 to 1.0, mean per capita income in the low country was higher by far than income in most of the world at about that time. Upon converting 1870 dollars to 1987 dollars, mean per capita income in the low country in 1870 would still exceed levels in much of the developing world today. See Fogel and Engerman, *Time on the Cross*, 1: 247–57, for some data on income levels in various parts of the world in about 1860. For contemporary data on income levels and living standards in the lesser-developed countries, see, for example, Michael P. Todaro, *Economic Development in the Third World*, 3d ed. (New York: Longman, 1985), pp. 33, 47–59; The World Bank, *World Development Report 1985* (New York: Oxford University Press, 1985), passim.

86. See, for example, Ciao Prado, Jr., *The Colonial Background of Modern Brazil*, trans. Suzette Macedo (Berkeley: University of California Press, 1971); George L. Beckford, *Persistent Poverty: Underdevelopment in Plantation Economies of the Third World* (New York: Oxford University Press, 1972); Jay R. Mandle, *The Roots of Black Poverty: The Southern Plantation Economy after the Civil War* (Durham: Duke University Press, 1978).

87. On linear, "conveyor belt" transport systems, systems characteristic of both "newly settled" staple-producing areas and "underdeveloped" countries today, see James E. Vance, Jr., *The Merchant's World: The Geography of Wholesaling*, Foundations of Economic Geography Series (Englewood Cliffs, N.J.: Prentice-Hall, 1971), pp. 80–128, 138–67; Edward J. Taafe, Richard L. Morrill, and Peter R. Gould, "Transport Expansion in Under-developed Countries: A Comparative Analysis," *Geographical Review* 53 (October 1963): 503–29; Prado, *The Colonial Background of Modern Brazil*, pp. 276–309; Johnson, *The Organization of Space in Developing Countries*, pp. 153–57 and passim; Peter W. Rees, "Origins of Colonial Transportation in Mexico," *Geographical Review* 65 (July 1975): 323–34; Eugene D. Genovese and Elizabeth Fox-Genovese, "The Slave Economies in Political Perspective," *Journal of American History* 66 (June 1979): 7–23, especially p. 16. Note that John H. Coatsworth has argued that under certain conditions, such as those prevailing in Porfirian Mexico, even fairly well-integrated transport networks can inhibit development. See Coatsworth, *Growth Against Development: The Economic Impact of Railroads in Porfirian Mexico* (Dekalb: Northern Illinois University Press, 1981), pp. 121–47, 175–91 especially.

That urban systems tending toward primate form are characteristically found in simple, open, export-oriented areas, particularly those with colonial histories, see, for example, Brian J.L. Berry, "City Size Distributions and Economic Development," *Economic Development and Cultural Change* 9 (July 1961): 573–88; Cesar A. Vapnarsky, "On Rank-Size Distribution of Cities: An Ecological Approach," *Economic Development and Cultural Change* 17 (July 1969): 584–95; Surinder K. Mehta, "Some Demographic and Economic Correlates of Primate Cities: A Case for Revaluation," in Gerald Breese, ed., *The City in Newly Developing Countries: Readings in Urbanism and Urbanization* (Englewood Cliffs, N.J.: Prentice-Hall, 1969): 295–308; William Paul McGreevey, "A Statistical Analysis of Primacy and Lognormality in the Size Distribution of Latin American Cities, 1750–1960," in Richard M. Morse, ed., *The Urban Development of Latin America, 1750–1920* (Stanford: Center for Latin American Studies, Stanford University, 1971), pp. 116–29. Using categories recently developed by Carol A. Smith, we find that the type of urban system in the low country is characteristic of both "premodern" systems and "underdeveloped" economic systems in the contemporary world. See Smith, "Modern and Premodern Urban Primacy," *Comparative Urban Research* 11 (1982): 79–96. For a pathbreaking analysis of urbanization and the formation and meaning of urban systems in early modern Europe, see Jan de Vries, *European Urbanization, 1500–1800* (Cambridge: Harvard University Press, 1984).

On the *comprador* in underdeveloped countries, see, for example, Paul A. Baran, *The Political Economy of Growth* (New York: Monthly Review Press, 1957), pp. 194–98 especially. For a more charitable view of the *comprador* in the South Carolina low country, see Greb, "Charleston, South Carolina, Merchants, 1815–1860," passim. Note that Greb hints at, but never actually uses the term "*comprador.*" See pp. 235–38 especially. One should also note that David Ramsay, writing early in the nineteenth century, already observed that South Carolina merchants "[did] not seem fond of exploring new channels of commerce." See Ramsay, *The History of South-Carolina from Its First Settlement in 1670, to the Year 1808*, 2 vols. (Charleston: Published by David Longworth for the author, 1809), 2: 239.

88. In 1900, according to Jay R. Mandle, 73.4 percent of the labor force in South Carolina was still employed in agriculture. See Mandle, *The Roots of Black Poverty*, p. 59.

89. See, for example, Stanley L. Engerman, "The Effects of Slavery Upon the Southern Economy: A Review of the Recent Debate," *Explorations in Entrepreneurial History*, 2d ser., 4 (Winter 1967): 71–97; Engerman, "Some Economic Factors in Southern Back-

wardness in the Nineteenth Century"; Engerman "A Reconsideration of Southern Economic Growth, 1770–1860," *Agricultural History* 49 (April 1975): 343–61.

90. Of the 1243 vessels entering Charleston, for example, in the quarters for which data exist during the 1721–35 period, 128 or 10.3 percent were carrying ballast only. Of the 128 vessels carrying ballast only, 73 entered from European or African ports, 30 from Caribbean ports or Bermuda, and 25 from North American ports. See Great Britain, Public Record Office, Colonial Office, America and West Indies, CO 5/509, South Carolina, Shipping Returns, December 1721 to December 1735. I used these records in microfilm form (British Manuscripts Project, PRO Reel #52/3 & 4) at the South Carolina Department of Archives and History. Moreover, cargoes consisting largely of stones and/or coals were still common among vessels entering Charleston in the late colonial period. See *South Carolina Gazette*, February 4, 1764; December 3, 1764; December 10, 1764; November 30, 1767; December 21, 1767; April 9, 1772.

One should note, of course, that ballast was common on vessels during the early modern period, particularly on those making westward passages across the Atlantic. It was the relative importance of ballast *vis-à-vis* articles of trade that distinguished vessels bound for staple-producing areas served by dependent labor.

91. See, for example, Henry Laurens to Richard Grubb, June 23, 1747, in Hamer, Rogers, *et al.*, eds., *The Papers of Henry Laurens*, 1: 7–8, especially p. 8; Henry Laurens to Richard Grubb, November 5, 1747, *ibid.*, 1: 68–70; Henry Laurens to Charles Willing & Son, May 16, 1755, *ibid.*, 1: 249–50; Henry Laurens to Rawlinson & Davison, June 28, 1755, *ibid.*, 1: 277–28; Henry Laurens to John Hardman, December 15, 1755, *ibid.*, 2: 38–39; Henry Laurens to James Cowles, July 12, 1756, *ibid.*, 2: 248–49; Henry Laurens to John Thomas, December 13, 1756, *ibid.*, 2: 371–72; Henry Laurens to Joseph Bower, January 13, 1763, *ibid.*, 3: 215–16; Henry Laurens to Coxe & Furman & Co., February 9, 1763, *ibid.*, 3: 242–44, especially p. 243; Henry Laurens to Shepherd, Langton & Birley, December 20, 1763, *ibid.*, 4: 89–90; Henry Laurens to William Fisher, September 12, 1768, *ibid.*, 6: 92–95, especially p. 95; Henry Laurens to John Hopton, January 29, 1771, *ibid.*, 7: 428–34, especially pp. 429–30; Robert Pringle to James Hunter & Co., April 2, 1737, in Walter B. Edgar, ed., *The Letterbook of Robert Pringle*, 2 vols. (Columbia: University of South Carolina Press, 1972), 1: 9–10; Robert Pringle to John Richards, December 27, 1738, *ibid.*, 1: 50–51; Robert Pringle to John Erving, September 9, 1740, *ibid.*, 1: 243–44; Robert Pringle to Andrew Pringle, July 5, 1743, *ibid.*, 2: 576–79, especially p. 578; John Guerard to Tho. Rock, March 17, 1752, John Guerard Letter Book, pp. 4–5, South Carolina Historical Society; John Guerard to Thos. Rock, March 19, 1753, John Guerard Letter Book, pp. 134–35, South Carolina Historical Society; John Guerard to William Jolliff, May 6, 1754, John Guerard Letter Book, pp. 257–60, especially p. 259, South Carolina Historical Society; William Vernon to Samuel Vernon, March 11, 1745, William Vernon Manuscripts, South Caroliniana Library; Richard Hill to William Jefferies, June 6 [?], 1743, Richard Hill Letter Book, Manuscript Department, William R. Perkins Library; Hogg and Clayton to Messrs. Smith, Strachan & Co., July 26, 1764; Hogg and Clayton to Capt. James Rae, January 12, 1765; Hogg and Clayton to Henry Smith, January 18, 1765, Hogg and Clayton Letter Book and Accounts, Manuscript Department, William R. Perkins Library; Josiah Smith, Jr., to James Poyas, January 25, 1774, Josiah Smith, Jr., Lettercopy Book, Southern Historical Collection; George Nelson to Mr. Bellamy, July 9, 1791, George Nelson Lettercopy Book, p. 107 (back), Southern Historical Collection.

Nor did the problem of domestic demand disappear in the antebellum period. See, for example, Thomas Aiton & Co. to Cameron, Stayley & Co., February 20, 1802; Thomas

Aiton & Co. to William Stayley & Co., March 26, 1802, Thomas Aiton and Company Letterbook, South Caroliniana Library; Isaac Child to Joshua Child, March 12, 1816; Greenleaf & Goodivis to J. and I. Child, November 5, 1816; Ebenezer Cheney, Jr., to J. and I. Child, December 5, 1816, Joshua and Isaac Child Papers, New York Public Library; James Adger to Edward Quin & Co., September 27, 1817; James Adger to James Fraser, February 11, 1818, James Adger Letterbook, South Caroliniana Library; Sylvanus Keith to R.H. Treadway, January 14, 1828, Sylvanus Keith and Cary Keith Papers, Manuscript Department, William R. Perkins Library; Charles Edmundston and James Chapman to John A. Sutton, May 10, 1837, Mebane and Sutton Papers, North Carolina State Archives; A.L. Taveau to Wife, March 6, 1863, Augustin Louis Taveau Papers, Manuscript Department, William R. Perkins Library.

92. On the seasonality of trade in the low country, see, for example, Leila Sellers, *Charleston Business on the Eve of the American Revolution* (Chapel Hill: University of North Carolina Press, 1934), pp. 154–55; Robert Pringle to Andrew Pringle, April 14, 1743, in Edgar, ed., *The Letterbook of Robert Pringle*, 1: 537–38; Williamson & Stoney to Manuel Eyre, Jr., June 14, 1802, Williamson & Stoney Letters, Claude W. Unger Collection, Historical Society of Pennsylvania; James Adger to Wilson Hunt, September 25, 1817, James Adger Letterbook, South Caroliniana Library; *Charleston Courier*, September 18, 1821. On also can get a good idea of the seasonality of trade from data on monthly and quarterly shipping entries and clearances at Charleston. See Appendix 1–D, footnote 6; Converse D. Clowse, *Measuring Charleston's Overseas Commerce, 1717–1767: Statistics from the Port's Naval Lists* (Washington, D.C.: University Press of America, 1981), pp. 107–11; Dawson and DeSaussure, *Census of the City of Charleston, South Carolina, for the Year 1848*, pp. 60–71.

93. *Seventh Census of the United States, 1850*, p. 339; *Eighth Census of the United States, 1860: Population*, p. 452. Charleston, Georgetown, Beaufort, Camden, Columbia, and Greenville each had over 1000 inhabitants by 1860; Hamburg and Spartanburg may have as well. On the rise of the town in the South Carolina piedmont, see David L. Carlton, *Mill and Town in South Carolina, 1880–1920* (Baton Rouge: Louisiana State University Press, 1982), pp. 13–39 especially.

94. See the works cited in footnote 15 above.

95. See Robert E. Gallman and Ralph V. Anderson, "Slaves as Fixed Capital: Slave Labor and Southern Economic Development," *Journal of American History* 64 (June 1977): 24–46; Gallman, "Slavery and Southern Economic Growth," *Southern Economic Journal* 45 (April 1979): 1007–22. Note that Gallman and Anderson's argument dovetails in many ways with that of Heywood Fleisig in "Slavery, the Supply of Agricultural Labor, and the Industrialization of the South," *Journal of Economic History* 36 (September 1976): 572–97. One should also note that contemporaries were well aware that the transformation of labor into a variable cost after the Civil War severely hurt the low-country rice industry. Essential off-season "mudwork," for example, became a major expense for planters for the first time in the postbellum period. See U.S. Department of Agriculture, Division of Statistics, Miscellaneous Series, Report No. 6, *Rice*, pp. 78–79.

On the relative degree of self-sufficiency of low-country plantations, see Philip D. Morgan, "The Development of Slave Culture in Eighteenth Century Plantation America" (Ph.D. dissertation, University College London, 1977), pp. 20–47; Swan, *The Structure and Profitability of the Antebellum Rice Industry 1859*, pp. 12–34, 104–78 especially.

96. See Morgan, "The Development of Slave Culture," pp. 20–46; Swan, *The Structure and Profitability of the Antebellum Rice Industry 1859*, pp. 104–78 especially. Note that other

data exist that suggest that the low country was somewhat less self-sufficient in foodstuffs than other parts of the South. See Glen, *A Description of South Carolina*, pp. 36–37; David Klingaman, "Food Surpluses and Deficits in the American Colonies, 1768–1772," *Journal of Economic History* 31 (September 1971): 553–69, especially pp. 558, 562; Diane Lindstrom, "Southern Dependence Upon Interregional Grain Supplies: A Review of the Trade Flows, 1840–1860," *Agricultural History* 44 (January 1970): 101–13.

97. Gallman and Anderson, "Slaves as Fixed Capital"; Gallman, "Slavery and Southern Economic Growth," pp. 1016–20 especially. Also see footnotes 15 and 79.

98. On the linearity of South Carolina's transport system, see James Cook, *A Map of the Province of South Carolina* . . . (Cornhill, England: H. Parker, 1773); George D. Terry, " 'Champaign Country': A Social History of an Eighteenth Century Lowcountry Parish in South Carolina, St. Johns Berkeley County" (Ph.D. dissertation, University of South Carolina, 1981), pp. 176–242; John Drayton, *A View of South-Carolina* . . . (Charleston: Printed by W.P. Young, 1802), map opposite title page; Phillips, *A History of Transportation in the Eastern Cotton Belt to 1860*, map between pp. 338–39, map at back of book; Collins, "Charleston and the Railroads," pp. 15, 19, 39, 49, 65, 77, 113, and passim. On the purposes of South Carolina's internal improvements program, see, for example, Smith, *Economic Readjustment of an Old Cotton State*, pp. 135–92. On the reorientation of rail lines after the Civil War, see State Board of Agriculture of South Carolina, *South Carolina: Resources and Population, Institutions and Industries*, p. 617; John F. Stover, *The Railroads of the South, 1865–1900: A Study in Finance and Control* (Chapel Hill: University of North Carolina Press, 1955), passim; Carlton, *Mill and Town in South Carolina*, pp. 21–23, 44, 73.

99. The mean annual valuation for all urban lots in South Carolina during this period was £2,464,251 current money. The mean annual valuation for Charleston lots alone during this period was £2,365,554 current money. See Public Treasurer of South Carolina, General Tax Receipts & Payments, 1761–1769 (1771), 1 ms. vol., South Carolina Department of Archives and History.

100. Because of certain unexplainable gaps in the 1860 census, I have based the statement in the text above not just on data in the 1860 census but on data from the 1850 and 1870 censuses as well. See *Seventh Census of the United States, 1850*, p. 339; *Eighth Census of the United States, 1860: Population*, p. 452; *Ninth Census of the United States, 1870: Statistics of Population*, pp. 258–60.

101. For an excellent analysis of an area whose growth and development during the period studied was based rather on local, intraregional, and regional trade, see Diane Lindstrom, *Economic Development in the Philadelphia Region, 1810–1850* (New York: Columbia University Press, 1978).

102. On forward and backward linkages, see, for example, Hirschman, *The Strategy of Economic Development*, pp. 98–119 especially. On fiscal and consumption linkages, see Hirschman, "A Generalized Linkage Approach to Development, with Special Reference to Staples."

There were, for example, few full-time merchants or factors in antebellum Georgetown, the "urban center" of the greatest rice-producing district in the United States. Moreover, the Georgetown branch of the Bank of the State of South Carolina was closed down in 1833, largely for lack of business. See J.H. Easterby, "The South Carolina Rice Factor as Revealed in the Papers of Robert F.W. Allston," *Journal of Southern History* 7 (May 1941): 160–72, especially pp. 161–63; Lesesne, *The Bank of the State of South Carolina*, pp. 124–26. For two excellent local studies of the Georgetown area, see George C. Rogers, Jr., *The History of Georgetown County, South Carolina* (Columbia: University of South Carolina Press, 1970)

and Charles Joyner, *Down by the Riverside: A South Carolina Slave Community* (Urbana: University of Illinois Press, 1984).

On the reasons why Charleston never became a true entrepôt, see Jacob M. Price, "Economic Function and the Growth of American Port Towns in the Eighteenth Century," *Perspectives in American History* 8 (1974): 123–86; Carville Earle and Ronald Hoffman, "Staple Crops and Urban Development in the Eighteenth-Century South," *Perspectives in American History* 10 (1976): 7–78; Earle and Hoffman, "The Urban South: The First Two Centuries," in Blaine A. Brownell and David R. Goldfield, eds., *The City in Southern History: The Growth of Urban Civilization in the South* (Port Washington, N.Y: Kennikat Press, 1977), pp. 23–51.

For an early–and outstanding–analysis of the difference between Charleston and more successful port towns, see *Hunt's Merchants' Magazine* 34 (January 1856): 137.

103. See Werner Sombart, *Luxury and Capitalism*, trans., W.R. Dittmar (Ann Arbor: University of Michigan Press, 1967; originally published 1913), pp. 21–38.

104. See the works cited in footnote 87 above. Although Berry, Vapnarsky, Mehta, and McGreevey do not find a statistically significant relationship between low income and wealth levels per se and primate urban form, others do. See, for example, Arnold S. Linsky, "Some Generalizations Concerning Primate Cities," *Annals of the Association of American Geographers* 55 (September 1965): 506–13; William C. Wheaton and Hisanobu Shishido, "Urban Concentration, Agglomeration Economies, and the Level of Economic Development," *Economic Development and Cultural Change* 30 (October 1981): 17–30.

105. The mean annual amount of money-at-interest reported for tax purposes in South Carolina during this period was £2,916,367 current money. The mean annual amount of money-at-interest reported by Charlestonians alone in this period was £2,271,675 current money. See Public Treasurer of South Carolina, General Tax Receipts & Payments, 1761–1769 (1771), South Carolina Department of Archives and History.

106. See Smith, *Economic Readjustment of an Old Cotton State*, p. 194.

107. See, for example, Alice E. Mathews, "Pre-College Education in the Southern Colonies" (Ph.D. dissertation, University of California, 1968), pp. 81–93, 104–11, 387–91; Drayton, *A View of South-Carolina*, pp. 217–20; Kenneth A. Lockridge, *Literacy in Colonial New England: An Enquiry into the Social Context of Literacy in the Early Modern West* (New York: W.W. Norton, 1974), pp. 72–101; Lee Soltow, "Socioeconomic Classes in South Carolina and Massachusetts in the 1790s and the Observations of John Drayton," *South Carolina Historical Magazine* 81 (October 1980): 283–305; George Tucker, *Progress of the United States in Population and Wealth in Fifty Years* . . . (New York: Press of Hunt's Merchants' Magazine, 1855), pp. 144–47; J.D.B. De Bow, *Statistical View of the United States* . . . (Washington, D.C.: Beverley Tucker, 1854), pp. 140–54. For a mildly revisionist look at education in the North and South during the antebellum period, see Albert Fishlow, "The American Common School Revival: Fact or Fancy?," in Henry Rosovsky, ed., *Industrialization in Two Systems: Essays in Honor of Alexander Gerschenkron* (New York: Wiley, 1966), pp. 40–67.

108. See *Seventh Census of the United States, 1850*, pp. 48–49, 56, 334–36, 343, 694–95, 697–99, 724–25.

109. See *Seventh Census of the United States, 1850*, pp. 48–49, 56, 334–36, 343, 694–95, 697–99, 724–25.

110. See Tucker, *Progress of the United States in Population and Wealth in Fifty Years*, pp. 144–47; De Bow, *Statistical View of the United States*, pp. 140–54. One should note that census data from the late nineteenth century reveal that the low country continued to lag in both literacy rates and school attendance figures. On the complex, often convoluted

relationship between education and economic growth at lower levels of development, see Gary S. Fields, "The Private Demand for Education in Relation to Labor Market Conditions in Less Developed Countries," Yale University, Economic Growth Center, Discussion Paper No. 160, Revised Version, June 1973; Fields, *Poverty, Inequality, and Development* (New York: Cambridge University Press, 1980), passim.

111. William G. Bentley, "The Navigation Acts and Income Distribution," unpublished paper, 1971. Bentley reports the results of this study in "Wealth Distribution in Colonial South Carolina" (Ph.D. dissertation, Georgia State University, 1977), pp. 6–7, 110.

112. See Terry, " 'Champaign Country,' " p. 280, Table 36; Jackson Turner Main, *The Social Structure of Revolutionary America* (Princeton: Princeton University Press, 1965), pp. 59–60. Whereas the top 10 percent of wealth-holders among white inventoried decedents in Charleston between 1722 and 1732 controlled 51.37 percent of the personal wealth of all white inventoried decedents during that period, the share controlled by the top 10 percent of wealth-holders among white inventoried decedents in Charleston during the revolutionary era had risen to 62.50 percent. Note that calculation of the correlation ratio, *Eta* (E_{yx}) between wealth and occupation among white inventoried decedents in Charleston during the 1722–32 period indicates that occupation is to some degree associated with wealth: $E_{yx} = .46$, $E_{yx}^2 = .21$. This finding, one should note, is significant at the .01 level.

113. Simon Kuznets, "Economic Growth and Income Inequality," *American Economic Review* 45 (March 1955): 1–28. For more recent demonstrations of this point, see, for example, Felix Paukert, "Income Distribution at Different Levels of Development: A Survey of Evidence," *International Labour Review* 108 (August-September 1973): 97–125, especially pp. 120–22; Williamson and Lindert, *American Inequality: A Macroeconomic History*, pp. 33–63 especially; Fields, *Poverty, Inequality, and Development*, p. 122 and passim: Rolf H. Dumke, "Income Inequality and Industrialization in Germany, 1850–1913: The Kuznets Hypothesis Re-examined," unpublished paper, 1986. Note that numerous studies have shown that income levels and wealth levels vary monotonically.

114. See Joseph A. Schumpeter, *The Theory of Economic Development: An Inquiry into Profits, Capital, Credit, Interest, and the Business Cycle*, trans. Redvers Opie (Cambridge: Harvard University Press, 1934; originally published 1911), pp. 115–23 and passim. On mean and median wealth levels in the eighteenth-century low country, see Bentley, "Wealth Distribution in Colonial South Carolina," pp. 34, 40, 48, 53, 59, 64, 69, 74. Also see Chapter 3 of this study.

115. See, for example, Jones, *Wealth of a Nation To Be*, pp. 258–93; Lee Soltow, "Distribution of Income and Wealth," in Glenn Porter, ed., *Encyclopedia of American Economic History: Studies of the Principal Movements and Ideas*, 3 vols, (New York: Charles Scribner's Sons, 1980), 3: 1087–1119.

116. The Gini coefficient of concentration, named after the man who devised it—Corrado Gini—is a statistical measure of the inequality of a distribution. More precisely, it is a measure of the degree to which a given distribution deviates from perfect equality. The coefficient can range, theoretically at least, from 0, which would indicate perfect equality, to 1.0, which would indicate perfect inequality, or, put another way, complete concentration. A similar, but more precise statistical measure of concentration—the Schutz coefficient—also is employed in this study. On this measure, see Robert R. Schutz, "On the Measurement of Income Inequality," *American Economic Review* 41 (March 1951): 107–22. Also see A.B. Atkinson, "On the Measurement of Inequality," *Journal of Economic Theory* 2 (1970): 244–63.

117. The findings for 1824 are based on the tax returns of 3,828 individuals, representing 17 of the 21 parishes and districts of the low country. In that year, taxes were based upon

assessments on land, slaves, and other forms of personalty. While returns exist for several hundred other inhabitants of the low country, these returns are too scattered geographically to allow for meaningful generalization from them about spatial patterns of wealth concentration in the remaining parts of the region. Note that in a recent and important article, J.P. Ochenkowski has utilized the 1824 tax returns to calculate Schutz coefficients, but not Gini coefficients for the low country. My Schutz coefficients differ slightly from his because I have corrected for computational errors in the returns. Moreover, I was able to locate the place of residence of enough individuals from Williamsburg to include figures for that district. One should also note that Ochenkowski found his results to be statistically significant. See 1824 Lower Division Tax Returns, South Carolina Department of Archives and History; J.P. Ochenkowski, "The Origins of Nullification in South Carolina," *South Carolina Historical Magazine* 83 (April 1982): 121–53.

The figures for 1860 are derived from census data on *every* household in Georgetown, Colleton, and Beaufort districts and every household in Charleston District outside of the city of Charleston itself. Note that regression analyses suggest little correlation in this region between age of head of household and the level of wealth. In All Saints Parish, for example, such analysis resulted in an r^2 of .14, while in St. Stephen's Parish, similar analysis yielded an r^2 of only .07.

118. See Soltow, "Distribution of Income and Wealth"; Soltow, *Men and Wealth in the United States, 1850–1870*, passim; Williamson and Lindert, *American Inequality: A Macroeconomic History*, pp. 3–46. Note that I am not saying that urbanization in and of itself is a primary cause of inequality. Rather, I am pointing out that empirical studies have shown that inequality generally was greater in urban areas that in rural parts of the U.S. in the eighteenth and nineteenth centuries.

119. Jones, *Wealth of a Nation To Be*, p. 164; Soltow, *Men and Wealth in the United States, 1850–1870*, p. 103.

It is, of course, possible—as J.R. Kearl and Clayne L. Pope have pointed out in several important articles—for a society to be highly concentrated *and* fluid, with considerable upward and downward mobility possible for individuals within the context of inequality. It is most unlikely, however, that the South Carolina low country conformed to this pattern during the antebellum period. See Kearl and Pope, "Wealth Mobility: The Missing Element," *Journal of Interdisciplinary History* 13 (Winter 1983): 461–88.

120. See Bentley, "Wealth Distribution in Colonial South Carolina," p. 82; *Eighth Census of the United States, 1860: Statistics*, p. 312; *Eighth Census of the United States, 1860: Population*, p. 452. The value of personal property in the low country, as we have seen, was put at $111,425,936 in the 1860 census. There were, we have also seen, 142,805 slaves in the low country at that time. At $600 to $625 per slave, the value of low-country slaves was between $85,683,000 and $89,253,125.

121. On the role of capital formation in general and producers' durables in particular in the economic growth of the United States, see, for example, Lance E. Davis, "Capital and Growth," in Lance E. Davis *et al.*, *American Economic Growth: An Economist's History of the United States* (New York: Harper & Row, 1972), pp. 280–310. Capital formation in the form of producers' durables at once underpinned and reflected the Northeast's antebellum manufacturing advance. For a comparison of the manufacturing sector of the Northeast with that of the South in the antebellum period, see Bateman and Weiss, *A Deplorable Scarcity*, pp. 14–23 especially.

122. After 1797, for example, British tariff policies were designed to "encourage" the shipment of paddy rather than milled rice into the country. Through this policy, the British government hoped in part to spur the development of the milling industry at home. By

1841, the British import duty on "foreign" milled rice was 15 shillings per bushel, while the duty on paddy was 2s.-6d. per bushel. While duties were lowered after that time—and the differential between duties on imperial and foreign rice narrowed—the differential between duties on milled rice and paddy remained significant. British policies, not suprisingly, had an inhibiting effect on the American rice-cleaning industry, greatly limiting its potential market. Whereas most rice was milled before being exported in the colonial and early national periods, by 1850 most of the rice exported from the United States was paddy. It is both interesting and ironic to note that South Carolina rice producers seemed to welcome the rise of the European rice-milling industry, apparently in the hope that this development would increase competitive pressure on domestic millers. See Gray, *History of Agriculture*, 2: 724–25, 729–30; *The Southern Agriculturalist* 1 (October 1828): 459–61; *Hunt's Merchants' Magazine* 7 (October 1842): 367–88, especially p. 379; *The Southern Agriculturalist*, new series, 4 (January 1844): 6–25, especially pp. 24–25; *Hunt's Merchants' Magazine* 16 (April 1847): 405–08; Minutes, South Carolina Agricultural Society, October 16, 1827; October 21, 1827, 1: 42–49, 56, South Caroliniana Library.

On diplomatic efforts by the U.S. government to secure reductions in British and German duties on rice, see Bingham Duncan, "Diplomatic Support of the American Rice Trade, 1835–1845," *Agricultural History* 23 (April 1949): 92–96.

Note that much valuable information about the South Carolina rice-milling industry during the postbellum period can be found in the records of Breslauer, Lachicotte and Company—operators of Waverly Mills—at the South Caroliniana Library. Finally, information on various South Carolina rice mills can be found in the R.G. Dun and Company Collection at the Baker Library of the Harvard University Graduate School of Business in Boston, Massachusetts. See, for example, R.G. Dun and Company Collection, South Carolina, 6: 84, 224; 7: 365, 411, 582; 8:12, 218, 230; 9–b:136.

123. That planters and merchants in the low country generally attempted to behave in an economically rational manner we have already seen. Their market-oriented behavior and values were made manifest, however, in other ways as well: in their widespread support for modernization, development and even industrialization; in planters' attempts to practice scientific agriculture; and, more surprisingly, in planters' often substantial holdings of—and trading in—stocks and bonds.

On support in the low country for modernization, development, and industrialization, see, for example, William Elliott to Mrs. William Elliott, April 5, 1823; William Elliott to Annie Elliott, July 6, 1836; William Elliott to Mrs. William Elliott, August 25, 1836; William Elliott to Mrs. William Elliott, September 11, 1844, Elliott-Gonzales Papers, Southern Historical Collection: Entry, May 6, 1846, Thomas B. Chaplin Plantation Journal, South Carolina Historical Society; Public Announcement, Winyah and All Saints Agricultural Society, May 27, 1851, Paul Weston Papers, South Carolina Historical Society; Entry, December 15, 1862, David Gavin Diary, Southern Historical Collection; Isaac E. Holmes to Robert F.W. Allston, November 11, 1837, in Easterby, ed., *The South Carolina Rice Plantation as Revealed in the Papers of Robert F.W. Allston*, pp. 75–76; *Charleston Courier*, May 2, 1829; June 27, 1835; July 11, 1843; June 29, 1847; January 18, 1851; February 3, 1851; May 17, 1851; *Charleston Mercury*, January 24, 1849; December 20, 1858; *De Bow's Review* 3 (April 1847): 347; 10 (February 1851): 215; 17 (July 1854): 82–84; 18 (May 1855): 654.

On "scientific" agricultural practices in the low country, see, for example, South Carolina Society for Promoting and Improving Agriculture, *Letters and Observations on Agriculture* . . . (Charleston: Bowen & Co., 1788), pp. 6–32; *The Southern Agriculturalist* 2

(August 1829): 370–71; 3 (December 1830): 629–31; 4 (August 1831): 414–16; 6 (January 1833): 9–14; 6 (March 1833): 128–30; 10 (April 1837): 169–73; *The Southern Agriculturalist*, new series, 3 (July 1843): 241–46; Robert Grant to Pierce Butler, March 8, 1796; Roswell King to Pierce Butler, January 12, 1817, Butler Family Papers, Historical Society of Pennsylvania; Entry, April 24, 1824, Daniel Webb Plantation Book, South Carolina Historical Society; Entries, May 20–24, 1828; May 16, 1829, Rockingham Plantation Journal, Manuscript Department, William R. Perkins Library; Entries, March 22, 1835, p. 30; March 27, 1835, p. 30; —1844, p. 233; —1845, pp. 242–46; —1849, p. 342; —1850, p. 350, Walter Peyre Plantation Journal, South Carolina Historical Society; Entries, January 23, 25–28, 1847; February 1, 5–6, 10–12, 1847; December 6–10, 1847, Plantation Book, 1845–1854, Thomas P. Ravenel Papers, South Carolina Historical Society; Entry, May 29, 1848, Thomas B. Chaplin Plantation Journal, South Carolina Historical Society; Experiments 1841–1845, 1859–1860, Sandford William Barker Plantation Records, South Carolina Historical Society; Entry, 1859, Greenwood Plantation Journal, Library of Congress, Washington, D.C. Note that the noted agricultural reformer Edmund Ruffin acknowledged the quality and sophistication of rice cultivation in the low country. See Entry, February 1, 1843, Diary, Edmund Ruffin Papers, Southern Historical Collection. Note, too, that as early as 1841, there existed seventeen agricultural societies in South Carolina. Though the overall impact of such societies is unclear, they certainly attempted to encourage scientific practices. See *The Farmers' Register* 9 (September 30, 1841): 559.

That planters' "portfolios" often included stocks and bonds, see, for example, John Rutledge, Jr., to Bishop Smith, April 1, 1798, John Rutledge Papers, Southern Historical Collection; Entries, June 15, 1835, p. 18; September 1, 1835, p. 20; October 21, 1836, p. 32; November 27, 1839, p. 62, and passim, Francis Withers Account Book, Southern Historical Collection; Entries, February 9, 1838; October 5, 1839; May 16, 1843; June 13, 1845; August 20, 1847; August 3, 1848, John Berkley Grimball Diary, Southern Historical Collection; Daybook, 1835–1855, passim, Heyward Family Papers, South Caroliniana Library; Entry, January 14, 1859, David Gavin Diary, Southern Historical Collection; Entries, March 3, 1856; July 6, 1857; November 8, 1860, Stephen Doar Account Books, 1:16, 20, 34, Library of Congress.

Nor were low-country planters and merchants unique in their behavior and values. Scholars have found evidence of similar characteristics among planters and merchants in other areas in which the use of dependent labor was widespread—both in the U.S. and in other parts of the Americas. See, for example, Warren Dean, "The Planter as Entrepreneur: The Case of São Paulo," *Hispanic American Historical Review* 46 (May 1966): 138–52; Jacob Metzer, "Rational Management, Modern Business Practices, and Economics of Scale in the Ante-Bellum Southern Plantations," *Explorations in Economic History*, 2d series, 12 (April 1975): 123–50; Engerman, "Agriculture as Business: The Southern Context"; Elizabeth Anne Kuznesof, "The Role of the Merchants in the Economic Development of São Paulo, 1765–1850," *Hispanic American Historical Review* 60 (November 1980): 571–92; John E. Kicza, *Colonial Entrepreneurs: Families and Business in Bourbon Mexico City* (Albuquerque: University of New Mexico Press, 1983).

124. Note that there were a number of stillborn attempts to stave off the decline of the low-country rice industry by creating huge, capital-intensive rice complexes in the region. See, for example, Contract Form, c. 1866; J.W. Cameron to Major A. Vander Horst, November 5, 1866, Arnoldus Vander Horst V Family Papers, South Carolina Historical Society; A. Pearson Longbottom to John Chadwick, November 1, 1872; A. Pearson Longbottom to John Chadwick, October 2, 1873; Secretary, Council of Foreign Bondholders,

to Arthur Middleton, April 13, 1874, Middleton Family Papers, South Carolina Historical Society; Box 1, Lettercopy Books, Volume 1, April–July 1899, pp. 129, 170, 198, 200–201, 272, 318–20, 344, 349, 359, 360–67, 400–415, George Johnson Baldwin Papers, Southern Historical Collection. I am indebted to Walter E. Campbell for the references in the Baldwin Papers.

125. See, for example, the letters from Hugh MacRae to David R. Coker scattered throughout the David R. Coker Collection at the South Caroliniana Library. Also see Minutes, South Carolina Agricultural Society, February 18, 1905; January 24, 1906; June 30, 1927; January 27, 1928, 2: 109, 112, 258–59, 260, 278, South Caroliniana Library; South Carolina Land Settlement Commission, *Report 1923* (Columbia: The State Company, 1923).

On the rise of truck farming in parts of the low country, see Minutes, South Carolina Agricultural Society, January 12, 1899; May 7, 1904; January 24, 1906, 2: 79, 98, 112, South Caroliniana Library; Minute Book, 1872–1935, James Island Agricultural Society, passim, South Caroliniana Library; Entries, c. 1916–1924, John Edwin Fripp Papers and Books, Book 8, pp. 14–27, 38–43, 53–63, 74–77, 84–88, Southern Historical Collection.

126. See, for example, Edward Rutledge to Thomas Jefferson, October 23, 1787; Brailsford & Morris to Thomas Jefferson, October 31, 1787, in Boyd *et al.*, eds., *The Papers of Thomas Jefferson*, 12: 263–64; 298–301; Thomas Aiton & Company to William Stayley & Company, March 26, 1802, Thomas Aiton and Company Letterbook, South Caroliniana Library; James H. Ladson to Frederick Fraser, September 13, 1831, Fraser Family Papers, South Carolina Historical Society. Also see Woodman, *King Cotton & His Retainers*, pp. 5–195.

On the value of South Carolina public and private securities held by foreigners in the late antebellum period, see United States Senate, 33d Congress, 1st Session, Report of the Secretary of the Treasury in Answer to a Resolution of the Senate . . .(1854), reprinted in Mira Wilkins, ed., *Foreign Investments in the United States: Department of Commerce and Department of Treasury Estimates* (New York: Arno Press, 1977), pp. 4, 6, 9, 27, 31, 34–35, 43–44.

127. See Entries, June 8, 1865; August 9, 1865; January 31, 1866, John Berkley Grimball Diary, 15:9, 12, 71, Southern Historical Collection; R.H. Colcock to James Gregorie, October 8, 1865; John Colcock to James Gregorie, January 1866; February 25, 1866; July 15, 1867; July 22, 1867; November 27, 1867, Gregorie-Elliott Papers, Southern Historical Collection; William Gilmore Simms to William Hawkins Ferris, February 1, 1867?, Ferris Manuscripts, Rare Books and Manuscripts, Butler Library, Columbia University; Arthur Middleton to N.R. Middleton, April 11, 1870; April 15, 1870, Nathaniel R. Middleton Papers, Southern Historical Collection; London *Times*, February 6, 1874; Smith, *A Charlestonian's Recollections 1846–1913*, pp. 129–36. Also see William A. Scott, *The Repudiation of State Debts* . . . (New York: Crowell, 1893), pp. 79–93; Reginald C. McGrane, *Foreign Bondholders and American State Debts* (New York: Macmillan, 1935), pp. 344–54 especially; B.U. Ratchford, *American State Debts* (Durham: Duke University Press, 1941), pp. 162–96, especially pp. 185–86; John J. Madden, *British Investment in the United States 1860–1880* (New York: Garland Publishing, 1985), pp. 29–35, 65–72. Other problems also plagued southern capital markets, problems that have been treated at length by Richard Sylla, Roger L. Ransom and Richard Sutch, John A. James, and Harold D. Woodman among others.

128. On the agricultural economy of the low country today, see State of South Carolina Budget and Control Board, *South Carolina Statistical Abstract 1985* (Columbia: South Carolina Division of Research and Statistical Services, 1986), pp. 3–38.

129. On the low-country economy in the twentieth century, see Jamie W. Moore, "The Lowcountry in Economic Transition: Charleston since 1865," *South Carolina Historical Magazine* 80 (April 1979): 156–71. On the defense industry specifically, see August John Marjenhoff, "The Effects of Defense Spending on the Economy of the Charleston, South Carolina, Standard Metropolitan Statistical Area" (Ph.D. dissertation, Indiana University, 1974), passim; Marshall Frady, "The Charleston Cold-Warrior from Hell-Hole Swamp," in Frady, *Southerners: A Journalist's Odyssey* (New York: New American Library, 1980), pp. 77–101; George W. Hopkins, "From Naval Pauper to Naval Power: The Development of Charleston's Metropolitian-Military Complex," in Roger W. Lotchin, ed., *The Martial Metropolis: U.S. Cities in War and Peace* (New York: Praeger, 1984), pp. 1–34; John Hammond Moore, "Charleston in World War I: Seeds of Change," *South Carolina Historical Magazine* 86 (January 1985): 39–49; South Carolina State Development Board, *Industrial Directory of South Carolina 1986* (Columbia: South Carolina State Development Board, 1986), especially pp. G-18, G-19, G-21, G-22, G-23, G-27: Peter A. Coclanis and Lacy K. Ford, "The South Carolina Economy Reconstructed and Reconsidered: Structure, Output, and Performance, 1670–1985," in Winfred B. Moore, Jr., and Joseph F. Tripp, eds., *Developing Dixie: Modernization in a Traditional Society* (Westport, Conn.: Greenwood Press, forthcoming).

That per capita income levels in the low country remained much lower than levels for the United States as a whole in the twentieth century can be seen in the data assembled below.

Mean per Capita Income in Low-Country Counties and in U. S.
1929-1969

County	1929	1940	1950	1959	1969
Beaufort	$306	$784	$1204	$1382	$3992
Berkeley[1]					
Charleston[1]	427	457	1035	1420	2854
Colleton	228	218	747	945	2187
Dillon	192	203	623	882	1733
Dorchester	225	198	553	989	1646
Georgetown	191	219	732	1012	2111
Hampton	174	169	560	986	2292
Horry	223	228	718	1157	2255
Jasper	132	143	439	709	1515
Marion	235	221	666	995	2049
Williamsburg	151	168	456	709	1571
U. S.	$705	$592	$1492	$2161	$3699
—Metropolitan areas	926	760	1736	2437	4054
—Nonmetropolitan counties	400	352	1085	1596	2871

[1] Berkeley and Charleston counties are together considered the Charleston metropolitan area; the other low-country counties are all considered nonmetropolitan.

Source: Robert E. Graham, Jr., *Personal Income in South Carolina by Type, Source, and Geographical Areas, 1929–1969*, Essays in Economics, No. 24 (Columbia: Bureau of Business and Economic Research, College of Business Administration, University of South Carolina, 1971), pp. 37–38.

130. South Carolina State Budget and Control Board, *South Carolina Statistical Abstract 1985*, pp. 55, 63, 70, 200–202, 227–28, 236, 244, 248–63, 271, 278–79, 321, 373–74. Mean per capita income figures from 1983 for low-country counties, South Carolina, the Southeast, and the U.S. appear below.

Low-Country County	Mean per Capita Income (Residence-Adjusted)	County Rank in SC*
Beaufort	$10,676	3
Berkeley	7,957	26
Charleston	9,879	7
Colleton	6,998	38
Dillon	6,355	41
Dorchester	8,880	17
Georgetown	8,382	22
Hampton	7,557	31
Horry	9,139	12
Jasper	7,133	36
Marion	7,130	37
Williamsburg	6,295	43

*There are forty-six counties in South Carolina.

Mean Per Capita Income - 1983

South Carolina	$ 9,168
Southeast	10,215
United States	11,687

See State of South Carolina Budget and Control Board, *South Carolina Statistical Abstract 1985*, p. 248. Data on the extent of poverty—as defined by the U.S. Bureau of the Census—in the low country in 1979 (the most recent figures available) follow.

Low-Country County	Population	Population below Poverty Line	Percentage of County Population below Poverty Line
Beaufort	57,158	9,751	17.1%
Berkeley	93,786	13,533	14.4
Charleston	258,798	46,233	17.9
Colleton	31,600	8,125	25.7
Dillon	30,810	9,239	30.0
Dorchester	58,147	7,739	13.3
Georgetown	42,199	9,173	21.7
Hampton	18,090	5,078	28.1
Horry	99,961	17,949	18.0
Jasper	14,319	4,150	29.0
Marion	33,936	8,913	26.3
Williamsburg	38,076	10,663	28.0
Low Country	776,880	150,546	19.4%
SC	3,013,707	499,574	16.6%

One should note that of the 150,546 inhabitants of the low country living below the poverty line in 1979, 102,537 were black. As the low country's total black population in 1980 was 283,324, this means that about 36 percent of the black population in this twelve-county region was living in poverty. See *South Carolina Statistical Abstract 1985*, pp. 250, 252, 327.

131. See, for example, J. Sampson, Jr., to Captain Dawson, June 5, 1888, Francis Warrington Dawson Correspondence, Charleston Library Society, Charleston, S.C.

132. On the names and locations of the low-country estates owned by members of these families, see Map, Plantations on the South Carolina Coast, Simons and Lapham, Charleston, 1937, South Carolina Historical Society. I am grateful to Charles Kovacik for bringing this map to my attention. Many other estate owners from the Northeast can be identified by using this map in conjunction with *Who's Who in Commerce and Industry, 1936* (New York: Institute for Research in Biography, 1936) and *Who's Who in America* . . . , vol. 19: *1936–1937*, ed. by Albert Nelson Marquis (Chicago: Marquis, 1936).

133. On the early development of Myrtle Beach, see the John T. Woodside Autobiography in the Southern Historical Collection. On Charleston's development into a center of tourism, see the works cited in footnote 3 of the Epilogue.

134. On the economic impact of the tourism/resort industry on the low country today, see State of South Carolina Department of Parks, Recreation, and Tourism, *Travel and Tourism Trends for South Carolina*, Annual Report, November 1985, passim; South Carolina State Budget and Control Board, *South Carolina Statistical Abstract 1985*, pp. 138–43, especially p. 141.

There is, of course, a vast literature on the relationship between the tourism industry and economic development. For a moderate, if somewhat rosy survey of the literature, see Emanuel de Kadt, *Tourism—Passport to Development?: Perspectives on the Social and Cultural Effects of Tourism in Developing Countries* (New York: Oxford University Press for the World Bank, 1979). For more critical assessments, see John M. Bryden, *Tourism and Development: A Case Study of the Caribbean Commonwealth* (Cambridge: Cambridge University Press, 1973), pp. 213–21 and passim; Louis A. Pérez, Jr., "Aspects of Underdevelopment: Tourism in the West Indies," *Science and Society* 37 (Winter 1973– 74): 473–80; R.B. Potter, "Tourism and Development: The Case of Barbados, West Indies," *Geography* 68 (January 1983): 46–50. On the deleterious cultural and psychological effects of tourism on the indigenous population, see V.S. Naipaul, *The Middle Passage: Impressions of Five Societies—British, French & Dutch—in the West Indies & South America* (New York: Random House, 1981; originally published 1962).

135. On the historical development of Kiawah, see Arnoldus Vander Horst V Family Papers, South Carolina Historical Society; Manuscript Census, South Carolina, 1860, Agriculture, Colleton District, South Carolina Department of Archives and History; Kovacik and Mason, "Changes in the South Carolina Sea Island Cotton Industry"; Chalmers G. Davidson, *The Last Foray: The South Carolina Planters of 1860: A Sociological Survey* (Columbia: University of South Carolina Press, 1971), p. 257; Claude Neuffer and Irene Neuffer, *Correct Mispronounciations of Some South Carolina Names* (Columbia: University of South Carolina Press, 1983), p. 168. On the reduction of the Vander Horst plantation to a collection site for palm cuttings, see Box 12-215 of the Arnoldus Vander Horst V Family Papers.

Note that the Kuwaiti group that developed Kiawah recently agreed to sell the entire island to a company headed by a Charleston broadcasting executive named John Rivers, Jr. See *Charlotte Observer*, December 25, 1987, p. 29A.

136. On these formulations, see, for example, Anthony Brewer, *Marxist Theories of Imperialism: A Critical Survey* (London: Routledge & Kegan Paul, 1980), pp. 27–127; Robert E. Baldwin, *Economic Development and Growth*, 2d ed. (New York: Wiley, 1972), pp. 30–34 especially. Also see Albert O. Hirschman, "The Rise and Decline of Development Economics," in Hirschman, *Essays in Trespassing: Economics to Politics and Beyond* (New York: Cambridge University Press, 1981), pp. 1–24.

137. For assessments of *dependencia* and neo-Marxist theories of development and underdevelopment, see Ronald H. Chilcote, "Dependency: A Critical Synthesis of the Literature," *Latin American Perspectives* 1 (Spring 1974): 4–29; Chilcote, "A Question of Dependency," *Latin American Research Review* 13 (1978): 55–68; Steve Jackson, Bruce Russett, *et al.*, "An Assessment of Empirical Research on *Dependencia*," *Latin American Research Review* 14 (1979): 7–28; Chilcote, "Dependency or Mode of Production: Theoretical Issues," in Chilcote and Dale L. Johnson, eds., *Theories of Development: Mode of Production or Dependency?* (Beverly Hills: Sage Publications, 1983), pp. 9–30; Brewer, *Marxist Theories of Imperialism*, pp. 131–294; Paul A. Attewell, *Radical Political Economy Since the Sixties: A Sociology of Knowledge Approach* (New Brunswick, N.J.: Rutgers University Press, 1984), pp. 207–51.

138. Jagdish Bhagwati, "Immiserizing Growth: A Geometric Note," *Review of Economic Studies* 25 (June 1958): 201–05.

139. Hirschman, "A Generalized Linkage Approach to Development, with Special Reference to Staples," pp. 77–80 especially. While his argument differs from mine in some important ways, Norman G. Owen has recently told a story of "once-over" growth in his fine study of the Kabikolan region of the Philippines. See Owen, *Prosperity Without Progress: Manila Hemp and Material Life in the Colonial Philippines* (Berkeley: University of California Press, 1984).

140. Charles W. Joyner, *Folk Song in South Carolina* (Columbia: Published for the South Carolina Tricentennial Commission by the University of South Carolina Press, 1971), p. 89. Also see Thomas Wentworth Higginson, *Army Life in a Black Regiment* (East Lansing: Michigan State University Press, 1960; originally published 1870), pp. 159–60.

Epilogue

1. *Gateway to Historic Charleston* 37 (March 1984): 13. Note that Charles Towne Landing is located west of the Ashley River at Albemarle Point, the first site of the city of Charleston. By the late 1670s, one should note, settlement had begun at Oyster Point on the peninsula between the Ashley and Cooper rivers and, shortly thereafter, the city of Charleston was officially moved to this location.

2. Henry James, *The American Scene* (Bloomington: Indiana University Press, 1968; originally published in 1907), p. 419.

3. The term "Restoration Charleston" is my own; it is meant to refer to that part of Charleston included in the city's 1974 architectural survey and preservation plan. In 1978 this area, which includes many restored eighteenth- and nineteenth-century buildings, won listing in the National Register of Historic Places. See *Historic Preservation Plan, Charleston, S.C.* (Charleston, 1974); 1978 Nomination to the National Register of Historic Places, "Old and Historic District (Extended)," [Charleston], South Carolina Department of Archives and History, Columbia.

On the changing form and face of twentieth-century Charleston, see, for example, John J. Duffy, "Charleston Politics in the Progressive Era" (Ph.D. dissertation, University of South Carolina, 1963); Isabella G. Leland, *Charleston: Crossroads of History* (Woodland Hills, Calif.: Published under the sponsorship of the Charleston Trident Chamber of Commerce by Windsor Publications, 1980), pp. 75–87; Charles B. Hosmer, Jr., *Preservation Comes of Age: From Williamsburg to the National Trust, 1926–1949*, 2 vols. (Charlottesville: Published for the National Trust for Historic Preservation in the United States by the University Press of Virginia, 1981), 1: 231–74; Robert Rosen, *A Short History of Charleston* (San Francisco: LEXICOS, 1982), pp. 123–53; Barbara L. Bellows, "At Peace with the

Past: Charleston, 1900–1950," in Lynn R. Myers, ed., *Mirror of Time: Elizabeth O'Neill Verner's Charleston* (Columbia, S.C.: McKissick Museums of the University of South Carolina, 1983), pp. 1–5; Michael C. Scardaville, "Elizabeth O'Neill Verner: The Artist as Preservationist," in Myers, ed., *Mirror of Time*, pp. 17–25.

For suggestive journalistic accounts of twentieth-century Charleston, see Dubose Heyward, "Charleston: Where Mellow Past and Present Meet," *The National Geographic Magazine* 75 (March 1939): 273–312; Albert Goldman, "Charleston! Charleston!," *Esquire* 87 (June 1977); 110–13, 154–56; Pat Conroy, "Shadows of the Old South," *Geo* 3 (May 1981): 64–80, 82.

4. The phrases in quotations in the text above are derived from titles of books by W.G. MacFarlane and Elizabeth O'Neill Verner. See MacFarlane, *Quaint Old Charleston: America's Most Historic City* (Charleston: Legerton, 1951); Verner, *Mellowed By Time: A Charleston Notebook* (Columbia: Bostick & Thornley, 1941).

5. See James, *The American Scene*, pp. 408–9. On the modern city as a "field" of human interaction, see, for example, William Sharpe and Leonard Wallock, "From 'Great Town' to 'Nonplace Urban Realm': Reading the Modern City," in Sharpe and Wallock, eds., *Visions of the Modern City: Essays in History, Art, and Literature* (New York: Heyman Center for the Humanities, Columbia University, 1983), pp. 7–46.

6. For example, see Hayden White, "The Value of Narrativity in the Representation of Reality," *Critical Inquiry* 7 (Autumn 1980): 5–27.

7. One of these exceptions was W.E.B. Du Bois who noted early in the twentieth century that ". . .in the alleys of Charleston . . .are probably the vilest human habitations in a civilized land . . ." See Du Bois, ed., *The Negro American Family* (Westport, Conn.: Negro Universities Press, 1969; originally published in 1908), p. 60. Also see Idus A. Newby, *Black Carolinians: A History of Blacks in South Carolina from 1895 to 1968* (Columbia: University of South Carolina Press, 1973), passim; Mamie Garvin Fields with Karen Fields, *Lemon Swamp and Other Places: A Carolina Memoir* (New York: The Free Press, 1983), pp. 184–203 especially.

Some information on, and photographs of, the "other Charleston" can also be found in the "year books" issued by the City Council of Charleston earlier in this century. See, for example, *City of Charleston, South Carolina, Year Book 1939* (Charleston: The City Council of Charleston, 1941), photographs between pp. 60–61 and 166–67, pp. 168–70; *City of Charleston, South Carolina, Year Book 1942* (Charleston: The City Council of Charleston, 1942), pp. 178–80; *City of Charleston, South Carolina, Year Book 1943* (Charleston: The City Council of Charleston, 1946), pp. 191–93.

8. Walter Benjamin, "Theses on the Philosophy of History," in Benjamin, *Illuminations*, ed. Hannah Arendt, trans. Harry Zohn (New York: Schocken Books, 1969), pp. 253–64, especially p. 256.

BIBLIOGRAPHY

I. Primary Sources

A. *Manuscripts*

Boston, Massachusetts. Baker Library, Graduate School of Business, Harvard University
  R.G. Dun and Company Collection

Boston, Massachusetts. Massachusetts Historical Society
  Axtell Account Book

Chicago, Illinois. Newberry Library
  Edward E. Ayer Collection

Chapel Hill, North Carolina. Southern Historical Collection, University of North Carolina
  Allston-Pringle-Hill Papers
  George Johnson Baldwin Papers
  John and Keating S. Ball Books
  John Ewing Colhoun Papers
  (Mrs.) Juliana Margaret Conner Diary
  Louis M. DeSaussure Plantation Record
  Elliott-Gonzales Papers
  Joshua Evans Diary
  John Edwin Fripp Papers and Books
  James M. Gage Papers
  Gaillard Plantation Books
  David Gavin Diary
  Gregorie-Elliott Papers
  Grimball Papers
  John Berkley Grimball Diary
  Heyward-Ferguson Papers
  Robert Hogg Account Books
  Charles Woodward Hutson Papers
  Samuel Cram Jackson Diary
  James Lynah Papers
  Manigault Plantation Records
  Nathaniel R. Middleton Papers
  Thomas Middleton Plantation Book
  George Nelson Lettercopy Book
  Palmer and Gaillard Plantation Books
  Ravenel Family Papers
  Robert Barnwell Rhett Papers
  Edmund Ruffin Papers
  John Rutledge Papers
  Josiah Smith, Jr., Lettercopy Book
  Ben Sparkman Plantation Record
  Sparkman Family Papers
  Trenholm Papers
  Francis Withers Account Book
  John T. Woodside Autobiography

Charleston, South Carolina. Charleston Library Society

Jacob Whitman Bailey Letters
Thomas Bee Correspondence
William Bee Letter
Armistead Burt Letters
Dr. Lionel Chalmers Correspondence
Charleston and Savannah Railroad
Company. Minutes of Stockholders'
Meetings
Francis Warrington Dawson
Correspondence
Thomas Elfe Account Book
John Lewis Gervais Letters
James S. Gibbes Letter Books
Thomas Grey Letter
Henry S. Holmes Diary
John Lining Letters
Joseph Hinson Mellichamp
Correspondence
Andrew Pickens Correspondence
Pilots of Charles-Town Bar. Petition
Charles Cotesworth Pinckney
Correspondence
Thomas Pinckney Account Book
Prince Frederick Parish. Register Book
John Rutledge Letters
St. James Santee Parish. Register
Archibald Simpson Diary
George Washington Letterbook and Letters
Joseph R. Wilmer Correspondence
John Wilson Journal
Windsor and Kensington Plantation
Records

Charleston, South Carolina. South Carolina Historical Society

Robert F.W. Allston Papers
Allston-Pringle-Hill Papers
Bacot-Huger Papers
Baker-Grimké Papers
Ball Family Papers
Samuel G. Barker Estate Account Books
Sanford William Barker Plantation
Records
Allard Belin, Sr., Plantation Journals
Bowen-Cooke Papers
Broughton Family Papers
Thomas B. Chaplin Plantation Journal
Charleston, S.C. Chamber of Commerce
Journal
Langdon Cheves III Papers
Thomas Aston Coffin Plantation Book
Commissioners of Fortifications. Journal
Commissioners of Trade and Plantations.
Documents
Courtenay Family Papers
Deas Commonplace Book
William Dunlap Correspondence
Arthur B. Flagg Journal and Commonplace
Book
Fraser Family Papers
Reverend Alexander Glennie Parish Diary
Glover Family Papers
Theodore Gourdin Papers
Gourdin-Gaillard Family Papers
John Guerard-Gaillard Family Papers
John Guerard Letter Book
Dr. Andrew Hasell Medical Account Book
W.E. Holmes & Company Records
John Locke Correspondence
Lucas Family Papers
Peter Manigault Letterbooks
Manigault Family Papers
Map. Plantations on the South Carolina
Coast. 1937
Middleton Family Papers
John B. Milliken Plantation Journals
Miscellaneous Manuscripts
Naval Officer Records
Walter Peyre Plantation Journal
James Poyas Day Book
Pringle Family Papers
Henry Ravenel Papers
Thomas Porcher Ravenel Papers
Read Family Correspondence
"Richmond" Overseer Journal
Benjamin Huger Rutledge Family Papers
John Rutledge Account Book
St. Philip's Church. Records
Mrs. Elizabeth Sindrey Estate Account
Book
M. Eugene Sirmans, Jr., Papers
Sir Hans Sloane Papers
Daniel Elliott Huger Smith Papers
Lancelot Smith. Ledger Book
Society of Friends. Transactions

John Sparkman Plantation Book
Thomas Tobias Papers
Arnoldus Vander Horst V Family Papers
Frances Vanderhorst Papers
John Joshua Ward Plantation Journals
Daniel Webb Plantation Book

Paul Weston Papers
Alonzo White Slave Auction Book
Frances Leigh Williams Papers
Francis Withers Plantation Book
Wragg Family Papers

Charleston, South Carolina. Special Collections, Robert Scott Small Library, College of
Charleston
Bank of Charleston. Records
Charleston, S.C. Chamber of Commerce
Papers
Charleston City Council Papers
Charleston Miscellany

John Cordes Papers
Henry Laurens Ledger
Charles Cotesworth Pinckney Plantation
Diary
Plowden Weston Papers

Columbia, South Carolina. South Carolina Department of Archives and History
Governor Archdale's Lawes. 1695–96
Office of the Public Treasurers: General Tax Receipts & Payments, 1761–1769 (1771).
1 ms. vol.; Ledgers, 1725–1776. 3 vols.
Office of the Surveyor General: Surveys of Charles Town Lots, 1679–1757. 2 ms. vols.
Records in the British Public Record Office Relating to South Carolina, 1663–1782. 36
vols. in facsimile.
Records of the General Assembly. Acts, Bills, and Joint Resolutions, 1691–.
Records of the Register of Mesne Conveyance. Charleston County. Deeds, 1719–
1763. Books A through A-3. 50 vols.
Records of the Secretary of State: Inventories of Estates, 1736–1776. 16 vols.; Miscellaneous
Records. Main Series. 1671–1973. 153 vols.; Mortgages. Charleston Series, 1736–
1867. 53 vols.
Records of the South Carolina Court of Common Pleas: Judgment Rolls, 1703–1790
South Carolina Lower Division Tax Returns, 1824
United States Census. Manuscript Returns, South Carolina. 1850–1880. Abbeville-York.

Columbia, South Carolina. South Caroliniana Library, University of South Carolina
James Adger Letterbook
Thomas Aiton and Company Letterbook
Allston Family Papers
R.F.W. Allston Papers
Ball Family Papers
Belfast Newspaper Collection
Black Oak Agricultural Society Minute
Book
Breslauer, Lachicotte and Company
Records
British Army Manuscripts
Charleston Account Books
Charleston Extracts
Paul Cross Papers
DeSaussure Family Papers
Stephen Duvall Doar Collection
John Evans Manuscript

Thomas Eveleigh Papers
John Lewis Gervais Papers
James Glen Papers
John Berkley Grimball Papers
Oliver Hart Collection
Isaac Peace Hazard Papers
Heyward Family Papers
Hill & Guerard Letter
John Holmes Manuscript
A.M. Huger Letterbook
Pryce Hughes Letters
Solomon Isaacs Letters
Ralph Izard Papers
James Island Agricultural Society
Minute Book
Robert Johnson Manuscripts
William Johnston Collection

Alexander Keith Commonplace Book
George Logan Letter
Manigault Family Papers
Capt. Martin Manuscript
Memoire sur la Caroline . . . 1786
. . . (by Mons. Chateaufort)
Williams Middleton Papers
Thomas Morris Papers
Motte Family Papers
Thomas Napier Papers
Charles Pinckney Manuscripts

Charles Cotesworth Pinckney Papers
Philip Porcher Papers
Thomas Davis Porcher Papers
Sam Sanford Letter
South Carolina Agricultural Society
Records
James Ritchie Sparkman Collection
Louis Thibou Letter
William Vernon Manuscripts
Ephraim Mikell Whaley Papers
Samuel Wragg Manuscript

Durham, North Carolina. Manuscript Department, William R. Perkins Library, Duke
University
Mrs. Eleanor J.W. Baker Papers
John Ball, Sr., and John Ball, Jr.
Papers and Account Books
Keating Simons Ball. Record Book
of Comingtee Plantation
Elizabeth F. Blyth Papers
Eli Whitney Bonney Papers
Francis Porteus Corbin Papers
S.D. Doar Papers
Thomas Rhett Smith Elliott Papers
Albert Kenrick Fisher Journal
Mary (De Saussure) Fraser Papers
James Gairdner Papers
John Gibbons Papers
William Gibbons, Jr., Papers
William Gilliland Papers
Robert Newman Gourdin Papers
Jacob Henry Papers
Richard Hill Letter Book
Hogg and Clayton Letter Book and
Accounts

George Noble Jones Papers
John Jones Papers
Sylvanus Keith and Carey Keith Papers
Charles Livingston Papers
William Henry Lyttelton Letter Book
Louis Manigault Papers
Samuel Arell Marsteller Papers
A. McLoy and J.W. Rice Ledger
Jacob Rhett Motte Papers
Caleb Pratt Daybook
James Reid Pringle Letters
David Robertson Papers
Rockingham Plantation Journal
Robert Rowand Diary
Sanders Family Papers
Charles J. Stroman Papers
Augustin Louis Taveau Letters, Papers,
and Literary Works
Edward Telfair Papers
Joshua Ward Papers
Edward Mitchell Whaley Papers

New York, New York. New-York Historical Society
Barnett Abraham Elzas Collection
Henry A. Frey Correspondence
Miscellaneous Manuscripts. Charleston
Miscellaneous Manuscripts. South
Carolina

Naval History Society Collection
Judge Tallmadge Memorandum Book
John Quincy Adams Ward Papers
Watt-Jones Papers

New York, New York. New York Public Library
John Bowie Papers
Carolina Papers (Chalmers Collection)
Charleston, S.C. Account Book
Joshua & Isaac Child Papers
Edisto Island Tax Assessment. 1732
Peter Horry Collection
Alexander Leslie Letterbook

Map Collection
Francis Marion Papers
Virgil Maxcy Diary
South Carolina & Miscellaneous Letters
South Carolina Papers
U.S. Army. Ordnance Department,
Charleston Arsenal. Letterbook

New York, New York. Rare Book and Manuscript Library. Columbia University
  Ferris Manuscripts

Philadelphia, Pennsylvania. Historical Society of Pennsylvania
  Peter Baynton Ledger and Letterbook   Joseph Oxley Journal
  Butler Family Papers   Claude W. Unger Collection. Williamson
  Hughes Papers   and Stoney Letters
  William Jones Papers

Raleigh, North Carolina. North Carolina State Archives
  James Abercromby Letter Book   W.R. Coe Collection
  Samuel A'Court Ashe Papers   John Hogg & Company. Records
  Kader Biggs Papers   John Huske and Company. Journal
  William Brailsford Paper   Julian S. Mann Collection
  Alexander Brevard Papers   Mebane and Sutton Papers
  Joseph Cathey Papers   William Righton Ledger

Washington, D.C. Library of Congress
  John Archdale Papers
  Duncan Clinch Letterbook
  Stephen Doar Account Books
  Edward Frost Papers
  Greenwood Plantation Journal

Worcester, Massachusetts. American Antiquarian Society
  Oglethorpe Family Papers

British Manuscript Collections Cited (Microfilm)
  Great Britain. Public Record Office: Colonial Office. America & West Indies. CO
    5/286; Colonial Office. America & West Indies. CO 5/358; Colonial Office
    America & West Indies. CO 5/508-511; Customs Office. 3/1-82
  London. Archives of the Society for the Propagation of the Gospel. Letter Books. Series
    A. 1702–1737. 26 ms. vols.
  London. Lambeth Palace Library: The American Papers of the Society for the Propaga-
    tion of the Gospel, 16, Correspondence—South Carolina, 1702–1710; The Fulham
    Papers, American Colonial Section. 40 ms. vols.
  Oxford. Bodleian Library. Oxford University. Mss. Locke

B. Published Primary Sources and Pre-1900 Scholarship

Allston, R.F.W. *A Memoir on the Introduction and Cultivation of Rice in South-Carolina*
  (1835). Printed in *Supplement to the Proceedings of the State Agricultural Society of
  South Carolina*, pp. 31–66. Columbia: Summer & Carroll for the Society, 1847.
American State Papers.
*Analyse des loix commerciales. Avec les tarifs. des états des deux Carolines et de La
  Géorgie.* Fayette-ville: Bowen & Howard, 1788.
Andrews, George. *The South-Carolina Almanack and Register for the Year of our Lord,
  1763.* Charlestown: Robert Wells, 1763.

The Annals of the Cakchiquels and Title of the Lord of Totonicapan. Translated by Adrian Recinos, Dioniscio José Chonay, and Delia Goetz. Norman: University of Oklahoma Press, 1953.

Archdale, John. *A New Description of that Fertile and Pleasant Province of Carolina . . .* London: Printed for John Wyat, 1707.

Ashe, Thomas. *Carolina: or a Description of the Present State of that Country and the Natural Excellencies thereof . . .* London: Printed for W.C., 1682.

Bacon, Francis. "Of Plantations." In *Essays and New Atlantis*, pp. 142–45. Edited by Gordon S. Haight. New York: D. Van Nostrand, 1942. Originally published 1625.

Barbon, Nicholas. *A Discourse of Trade*. London: Printed by Tho. Milbourn for the author, 1690.

Barnwell, Joseph E., ed., "Diary of Timothy Ford 1785–1786." *South Carolina Historical Magazine* 13 (July 1912): 132–47.

Bartram, John. "Diary of a Journey through the Carolinas, Georgia, and Florida, from July 1, 1765, to April 10, 1766." Annotated by Francis Harper. *Transactions of the American Philosophical Society*. New series, 33 (1942–44): 1–120.

Baudeau, Nicolas. . . . *Commerce* . . . 3 vols. Paris: Panckouke, 1783–84.

Bennett, J. Harry, Jr. *Bondsmen and Bishops: Slavery and Apprenticeship on the Codrington Plantations of Barbados, 1710–1838*. University of California Publications in History, vol. 62. Berkeley: University of California Press, 1958.

Bland, Edward, *et al. The Discovery of New Brittaine, Began August 27, Anno Dom. 1650 . . .* London: Printed by Thomas Harper for John Stephenson, 1651.

Blodgett, Samuel. *Economica: A Statistical Manual for the United States of America*. Washington, D.C.: Printed for the Author, 1806.

Bodin, Jean. *Discours sur le rehaussement et diminution des monnoyes . . .* Paris: Chez Iacques du Puys, 1578.

Bonner, John. *The Town of Boston in New England*. Boston: Printed by Fra. Dewing, 1722.

The Book of Chilam Balam of Chumayel. Translated and edited by Ralph L. Roys. Washington, D.C.: Carnegie Institution of Washington, 1933.

Boyd, Julian P., *et al.*, eds. *The Papers of Thomas Jefferson*. 22 vols. thus far. Princeton: Princeton University Press, 1950–.

Bull, William, Sr. (?). *An Account of the Rise and Progress of the Paper Bills of Credit in South Carolina . . .* (c. 1739). Reprinted in *The Statutes at Large of South Carolina*, 9: 766–80. Edited by Thomas Cooper and David J. McCord. 10 vols. Columbia: A.S. Johnston, 1836–41.

Calendar of the Clarendon State Papers Preserved in the Bodleian Library . . . . 5 vols. Oxford: Clarendon Press, 1869–1970.

Cantillon, Richard. *Essai sur la nature du commerce en général*. Edited and translated by Henry Higgs. London: Macmillan, 1931. Originally published 1755.

Cary, John. *An Essay on the State of England in Relation to Its Trade . . .* Bristol: Printed by W. Bonny, for the author, 1695.

Catesby, Mark. *The Natural History of Carolina, Florida, and the Bahama Islands . . .* 2d English edition. 2 vols. London: Printed by C. Marsh, T. Wilcox, B. Stichall, 1754. Originally published 1731–43.

Chalmers, Lionel. *An Account of the Weather and Diseases of South Carolina*. 2 vols. London: E. and C. Dilly, 1776.

"Charleston, S.C., in 1774 as Described by an English Traveller." *Historical Magazine* 9 (November 1865): 341–47.

Cheves, Langdon, ed. *The Shaftesbury Papers and Other Records Relating to Carolina and the First Settlement on Ashley River Prior to the Year 1676*. In *Collections of the South Carolina Historical Society*, vol. 5. Charleston: Published by the South Carolina Historical Society, 1897.

Child, Sir Josiah. *A New Discourse of Trade* . . . 2d edition. London: Printed and Sold by Sam. Crouch, Tho. Horn, & Jos. Hindmarsh, 1694.

Childs, St. Julien R., contrib., "A Letter Written in 1711 by Mary Stafford to Her Kinswoman in England." *South Carolina Historical Magazine* 81 (January 1980): 1–7.

City Council of Charleston, South Carolina. *A Digest of the Ordinances of the City Council of Charleston from the Year 1783 to Oct. 1844* . . . Prepared by George B. Eckhard. Charleston: Walker & Burke, 1844.

City of Charleston, South Carolina. *Year Books*.

Clifton, James M., ed. *Life and Labor on Argyle Island: Letters and Documents of a Savannah River Rice Plantation, 1833–1867*. Savannah: The Beehive Press, 1978.

Congressional Globe.

Cook, James. *A Map of the Province of South Carolina* . . . Cornhill, England: H. Parker, 1773.

Cooper, Thomas, and David J. McCord, eds. *The Statutes at Large of South Carolina*. 10 vols. Columbia: A.S. Johnston, 1836–41.

Cotton, H.J.S. "The Rice Trade in Bengal." *The Calcutta Review* 58 (1874): 171–88.

———. "The Rice Trade of the World." *The Calcutta Review* 58 (1874): 267–302.

Coxe, Tench. *Reflexions on the State of the Union*. Philadelphia: Mathew Carey, 1792.

———. *A View of the United States of America*. . . . Philadelphia: William Hall, 1794.

Cunningham, William. *The Growth of English Industry and Commerce*. 3 vols. Cambridge: Cambridge University Press, 1882–1912.

"A Curious New Description of Charles-Town in South Carolina . . . ," *The Universal Museum* 1 (August 1762): 435–37 and (September 1762): 477–79.

Dalcho, Frederick. *An Historical Account of the Protestant Episcopal Church in South Carolina* . . . Charleston: E. Thayer, 1820.

Davenant, Charles. *Discourses on the Public Revenues, and on the Trade of England* . . . 2 vols. London: Printed for James Knapton, 1698.

Dawson, J.L., and H.W. DeSaussure. *Census of the City of Charleston, South Carolina, for the Year 1848* . . . Charleston: J.B. Nixon, 1849.

de Beer, E.S., ed. *The Correspondence of John Locke*. 4 vols. thus far. Oxford: The Clarendon Press, 1976–.

de Bow, J.D.B. *Statistical View of the United States* . . . *Being a Compendium of the Seventh Census* . . . Washington, D.C.: 1854.

De Bow's Review.

de Brahm, William Gerard. *De Brahm's Report of the General Survey of the Southern District of North America*. Edited by Louis de Vorsey, Jr. Columbia: University of South Carolina Press, 1971.

de Bruijn Kops, G.F. *Statistiek van Den Handel en de Scheepvaart op Java en Madura Sedert 1825*. 2 vols. Batavia: Lange & Co., 1857–59.

Decker, Matthew. *An Essay on the Causes of the Decline of Foreign Trade*. 2d ed. London: Printed for J. Brotherton, 1750. Originally published 1744.

Defoe, Daniel. *Moll Flanders*. New York: New American Library, 1964. Originally published 1722.

Drayton, John. *A View of South-Carolina, as Respects Her Natural and Civil Concerns*. Charleston: W.P. Young, 1802.

Dubose, Samuel, and Frederick A. Porcher. *History of the Huguenots of South Carolina*. New York: Knickerbocker Press for T. Gaillard Thomas, 1887; reprint ed., Columbia: R.L. Bryan Co., 1972.

Dunlop, J.G., contrib. "Letters from John Stewart to William Dunlop." *South Carolina Historical Magazine* 32 (1931): 1–33, 81–114, 170–74.

Easterby, J.H., ed. *The South Carolina Rice Plantation as Revealed in the Papers of Robert F.W. Allston*. Chicago: University of Chicago Press, 1945.

Easterby, James H., *et al.*, eds. *The Colonial Records of South Carolina*. 1st series: *The Journal of the Commons House of Assembly, 1736–*. 13 vols. to date. Columbia: Printed for the South Carolina Department of Archives and History, 1951–.

Edgar, Walter B., ed. *The Letterbook of Robert Pringle*. 2 vols. Columbia: University of South Carolina Press, 1972.

Enright, Brian J., contrib. "An Account of Charles Town in 1725." *South Carolina Historical Magazine* 61 (January 1960): 13–18.

An Essay on Currency, Written in August 1732, Charleston: Lewis Timothy, 1734.

The Farmers' Register.

Fitzpatrick, J.C., ed. *The Diaries of George Washington, 1748–1799*, 4 vols. Boston and New York: Houghton Mifflin, 1925.

Fortrey, Samuel. *Englands Interest and Improvement*. London: Printed for Nathanael Brook, 1673.

Franklin, Benjamin. *Observations Concerning the Increase of Mankind* (1751). In [Clark, William]. *Observations On the late and present Conduct of the French . . . To which is added, wrote by another Hand; Observations concerning the Increase of Mankind . . .* Boston: S. Kneeland, 1755.

Fuller, Thomas. *The Worthies of England*. Edited by John Freeman. London: Allen & Unwin, 1952. Originally published in 1662.

Gallardo, José Miguel, trans. "The Spaniards and the English Settlement in Charles Town." *South Carolina Historical Magazine* 37 (April 1936): 49–64 and (July 1936): 91–99.

Gallatin, Albert. *Considerations on the Currency and Banking System of the United States*. New York: Greenwood Press, 1968. Originally published 1831.

The Gentleman's Magazine.

Gee, Joshua. *The Trade and Navigation of Great-Britain Considered . . .* 4th edition. London: Printed for A. Bettesworth and C. Hitch, 1738. Originally published 1729.

Glen, James. *A Description of South Carolina . . .* London: Printed for R. and J. Dodsley, 1761.

Great Britain. Public Record Office. *Journal of the Commissioners for Trade and Plantations*. 14 vols. London: H.M. Stationery Office, 1920–38.

Hall, Fayrer. *The Importance of the British Plantations in America to this Kingdom . . .* London: J. Peele, 1731.

Hamer, Philip M., and George C. Rogers, Jr., *et al.*, eds. *The Papers of Henry Laurens*. 10 vols. thus far. Columbia: University of South Carolina Press, 1968–.

Harrison, T.P., ed. *Journal of a Voyage to Charleston in So. Carolina by Pelatiah Webster in 1765*. Publications of the South Carolina Historical Society. Charleston: Published by the Society, 1898.

Hewatt, Alexander. *An Historical Account of the Rise and Progress of the Colonies of South Carolina and Georgia*. 2 vols. London: Printed for Alexander Donaldson, 1779.

Higginson, Thomas Wentworth. *Army Life in a Black Regiment*. East Lansing: Michigan State University Press, 1960. Originally published 1870.

Hilton, William. *A Relation of a Discovery* . . . London: Printed by J.C. for Simon Miller, 1664.

Hirsch, August. *Handbook of Geographical and Historical Pathology*. Translated from the 2d German edition by Charles Creighton. 3 vols. London: The New Sydenham Society, 1883–86.

Hoff's Agricultural Almanac, calculated for the States of Georgia and the Carolinas; for the year of our Lord 1818 . . . Columbia: D. and J.J. Faust, 1818.

Hooker, Richard R., ed. *The Carolina Backcountry on the Eve of the Revolution: The Journal and Other Writings of Charles Woodmason, Anglican Itinerant*. Chapel Hill: University of North Carolina Press, 1953.

Horne (?), Robert. *A Brief Description of the Province of Carolina* . . . London: Printed for Robert Horne, 1666.

House, Albert Virgil, ed. *Planter Management and Capitalism in Ante-Bellum Georgia: The Journal of Hugh Fraser Grant, Ricegrower*. New York: Columbia University Press, 1954.

Howe, George. *History of the Presbyterian Church of South Carolina*. Columbia: Duffie & Chapman, 1870.

Hughson, Shirley C. *The Carolina Pirates and Colonial Commerce, 1670–1740*. The Johns Hopkins University Studies in Historical and Political Science, 12th series. Baltimore: Johns Hopkins University Press, 1894.

Hunter, George. *The Ichnography of Charles-Town at High Water*. London: Published by B. Roberts and W.H. Toms, 1739.

Hunt's Merchants' Magazine.

Jervey, Clare, comp. *Inscriptions on the Tablets and Gravestones in St. Michael's Church and Churchyard, Charleston, S.C.* Columbia: The State Company, 1906.

Jones, George Fenwick, trans. "John Martin Boltzius' Trip to Charleston, October 1742." *South Carolina Historical Magazine* 82 (April 1981): 87–110.

Keith, Sir William. "A Short Discourse on the Present State of the Colonies in America with Respect to the Interest of Great Britain." In *Calendar of State Papers, Colonial Series, America and West Indies, 1574–*. Edited by W. Noel Sainsbury *et al.* 44 vols. thus far. Vol.: *1728–1729*. London: 1860–.

Kellar, Herbert A., ed. *Solon Robinson, Pioneer and Agriculturalist: Selected Writings*. 2 vols. Indianapolis: Indiana Historical Bureau, 1936.

Kemble, Frances Anne. *Journal of a Residence on a Georgian Plantation in 1838–1839*. Edited by John A. Scott. New York: Meridian Books, 1975. Originally published 1863.

King, Charles, ed. *The British Merchant; or Commerce Preserv'd*. 3 vols. New York: Augustus M. Kelly, 1968. Originally published 1721.

King, Gregory. *Natural and Political Observations upon the State and Condition of England (1696)*. In *Two Tracts by Gregory King*, pp. 11–55. Edited by George E. Barnett. Baltimore: Johns Hopkins University Press, 1936.

Klingberg, Frank J., ed. *Carolina Chronicle: The Papers of Commissary Gideon Johnston 1707–1716*. University of California Publications in History, vol. 35. Berkeley: University of California Press, 1946.

———. *The Carolina Chronicle of Dr. Francis Le Jau 1706–1717*. University of California Publications in History, vol. 53. Berkeley: University of California Press, 1956.

Lamb, Roger. *An Original and Authentic Journal of Occurrences during the late American War, from its Commencement to the Year 1783* . . . Dublin: Printed by Wilkinson & Courtney, 1809.

Lawson, John. *History of North Carolina* . . . Richmond, Va.: Garrett and Massie, 1937. Originally published 1709.

Lederer, John. *The Discoveries of John Lederer. In three several Marches from Virginia to the West of Carolina, And other parts of the Continent* . . . Translated by Sir William Talbot. London: Printed by J.C. for Samuel Heyrick, 1672.

Lester, C. Edwards. *The Glory and the Shame of England.* 2 vols. New York: Harper & Brothers, 1850.

The Letters of Hon. James Habersham, 1756–1775. In *Collections of the Georgia Historical Society,* vol. 6. Savannah: The Georgia Historical Society, 1904.

Letters of Joseph Clay, Merchant of Savannah 1776–1793 . . . In *Collections of the Georgia Historical Society,* vol. 8. Savannah: The Georgia Historical Society, 1913.

Ligon, Richard. *A True and Exact History of the Island of Barbadoes* . . . London: Peter Parker, 1673.

Lining, John. *Description of the American Yellow Fever, Which Prevailed at Charleston . . . in . . . 1748.* Philadelphia: Thomas Dobson, 1799.

List, Friedrich. *The National System of Political Economy.* Translated by S.S. Lloyd. London: Longmans, Green, 1885. Originally published 1841–44.

Locke, John. *Observations upon the Growth and Culture of Vines and Olives: the Production of Silk: the Preservation of Fruits. Written at the Request of the Earl of Shaftesbury: to Whom it is inscribed* . . . London: Printed for W. Sandby, 1766.

———. *Several Papers Relating to Money, Interest and Trade, etcetera.* New York: Augustus M. Kelley, 1968. Originally published 1696.

———. *Two Treatises of Government.* Rev. ed. Edited by Peter Laslett. New York: New American Library, 1965.

Loewald, Klaus G., Beverly Starika, and Paul S. Taylor, trans. and eds. "Johann Martin Bolzius Answers a Questionnaire on Carolina and Georgia." *William and Mary Quarterly.* 3d series. 14 (April 1957): 218–61.

Malthus, Thomas Robert. *An Essay on the Principle of Population* . . . Edited by Anthony Flew. Harmondsworth, Middlesex, England: Penguin Books, 1970. Originally published 1798.

Malynes, Gerard de. *The Centre of the Circle of Commerce.* London: Printed by W. Iones, 1623.

———. *The Maintenance of Free Trade.* London: Printed by I.L. for W. Sheffard, 1622.

Martin, Robert Montgomery. *History of the Colonies of the British Empire* . . . London: Dawsons, 1967. Originally published 1843.

Marx, Karl. *Capital.* Edited by Frederick Engels. Translated by Samuel Moore and Edward Aveling. 3 vols. New York: International Publishers, 1967. Originally published 1867–94.

———. *Grundrisse: Foundations of the Critique of Political Economy.* Translated by Martin Nicolaus. New York: Vintage Books, 1973. Originally published 1939.

Marx, Karl, and Frederick Engels. *The Communist Manifesto.* Edited by Joseph Katz and translated by Samuel Moore. New York: Washington Square Press, 1964. Originally published 1848.

———. *The German Ideology Parts I and III.* Edited by R. Pascal. New York: International Publishers, 1947.

Mathews, Maurice. "A Contemporary View of Carolina in 1680." *South Carolina Historical Magazine* 55 (July 1954): 153–59.

McCrady, Edward. *The History of South Carolina under the Proprietary Government 1670– 1719.* New York: Macmillan, 1897.

McCulloch, J.R., ed. *Early English Tracts on Commerce.* Cambridge: Cambridge University Press, 1970. Originally published 1856.

McPherson, Robert G., ed. *The Journal of the Earl of Egmont: Abstract of the Trustees Proceedings for Establishing the Colony of Georgia 1732–1738.* Wormsloe Foundation Publications No. 5. Athens: University of Georgia Press, 1962.

Merivale, Herman. *Lectures on Colonization and Colonies.* 2d edition. New York: Augustus M. Kelley, 1967. Originally published 1861.

Meriwether, Robert L., *et al.*, eds. *The Papers of John C. Calhoun.* 16 vols. thus far. Columbia: University of South Carolina Press, 1959–.

Merrens, H. Roy, ed. *The Colonial South Carolina Scene: Contemporary Views 1697–1774.* Columbia: University of South Carolina Press, 1977.

———. "A View of Coastal South Carolina in 1778: The Journal of Ebenezer Hazard." *South Carolina Historical Magazine* 73 (October 1972): 177–93.

Mill, John Stuart. *Principles of Political Economy* . . . . Edited by W.J. Ashley. 7th edition. London: Longmans, Green, 1909. Originally published 1848.

Miller, A.E. *Miller's Planters' & Merchants' Almanac* . . . Charleston: A.E. Miller, 1856?.

Milligen-Johnston, George. *A Short Description of the Province of South Carolina: With an Account of the Air, Weather, and Diseases, at Charlestown, Written in the Year 1763.* London: Printed for John Hilton, 1770.

Milling, Chapman, J., ed. *Colonial South Carolina: Two Contemporary Descriptions.* Columbia: University of South Carolina Press, 1951.

Mills, Robert. *Atlas of the State of South Carolina.* Baltimore: F. Lucas, Jr., 1825; reprint ed., Easley, S.C.: Southern Historical Press, 1980.

———. *Statistics of South Carolina* . . . Charleston: Hurlbut and Lloyd, 1826.

Misselden, Edward. *The Circle of Commerce, or the Balance of Trade.* London: Printed by I. Dawson for N. Bourne, 1623.

———. *Free Trade, or, the Means to Make Trade Flourish.* London: Printed by I. Legatt for S. Waterson, 1622.

Monck, George, Duke of Albemarle. *Observations upon Military and Political Affairs.* London: H. Mortlocke, 1671.

Morgan, Philip D., ed. "Profile of a Mid-eighteenth Century South Carolina Parish: The Tax Return of St. James' Goose Creek." *South Carolina Historical Magazine* 81 (January 1980): 51–65.

Moultrie, John, Jr. *De Febre Maligna Biliosa Americae.* Edinburgh: 1749.

Mouzon, Henry, Jr. *A Map of the Parish of St. Stephen, in Craven County* . . . . London: John Lodge, c. 1773.

Mun, Thomas. *England's Treasure by Forraign Trade* . . . London: Printed by J.G. for Thomas Clark, 1664.

Nairne, Thomas. *A Letter from South Carolina* . . . . 2d ed. London: Printed for R. Smith, 1718. Originally published 1710.

Niles' Weekly Register.

Norris, John. *Profitable Advice for Rich and Poor* . . . London: J. How, 1712.

North, Sir Dudley. *Discourses Upon Trade* . . . Baltimore: Johns Hopkins University Press, 1907. Originally published 1691.

Oldmixon, John. *The British Empire in America* . . . 2 vols. London: John Nicholson, 1708.

Oviedo y Valdés, Gonzalo Fernández de. *Historia general y natural de las Indias, isles, y tierrafirma del mar océano.* 4 vols. Madrid: La Real Academia de la Historia, 1851–55.

Parker, Mattie Erma Edwards, ed. *North Carolina Charters and Constitutions 1578–1698.* Raleigh: Published by the Carolina Charter Tercentenary Commission, 1963.

Petrie, E. *Plan of the City of Charleston, South Carolina, from a Survey Taken by E. Petrie, 1788.* In *Charleston Directory and Revenue System, 1790,* by Jacob C. Milligan. Charleston: T.R. Bowen, 1790.

Petty, Sir William. *Political Arithmetick* . . . London: Printed for Robert Clavel, 1690.

Phipps, John. *A Guide to the Commerce of Bengal* . . . Calcutta: 1823.

Pinckney, Elise, ed. *The Letterbook of Eliza Lucas Pinckney 1739–1762.* Chapel Hill: University of North Carolina Press, 1972.

Pitkin, Timothy. *A Statistical View of the United States of America* . . . . Hartford: Charles Hosmer, 1816.

Poe, Edgar Allan. "Fairy-land." In *The Poems of Edgar Allan Poe* pp. 53–56. Edited by Killis Campbell. New York: Russell & Russell, 1962. Originally published 1829.

Postlethwayt, Malachy. *Britain's Commercial Interest Explained and Improved* . . . . 2 vols. New York: Augustus M. Kelley, 1968. Originally published 1757.

Purry, Jean Pierre. *Proposals* . . . *Drawn Up at Charles-Town. In September, 1731* (1732). Reprinted in *Historical Collections of South Carolina,* 2: 121–40. Compiled by B.R. Carroll. 2 vols. New York: Harper & Brothers, 1836.

Quincy, Josiah. *Memoir of the Life of Josiah Quincy, Junior, of Massachusetts Bay: 1744–1775.* Edited by Eliza Susan Quincy. Boston: Little, Brown, 1875. Originally published in 1825.

Raleigh, Sir Walter. *The Marrow of Historie* . . . . London: Printed by W. Du-gard for J. Stephenson, 1650.

Ramsay, David. *The History of the Independent or Congregational Church in Charleston, South Carolina, From Its Origin till the Year 1814* . . . . Philadelphia: Printed for the Author by J. Maxwell, 1815.

———. *The History of South Carolina from Its First Settlement in 1670, to the Year 1808.* 2 vols. Charleston: Published by David Longworth for the author, 1809.

Reimensperger, Hans Jacob. *Wahrhafftige und Ganz Zuverlasse gute Zeitung von den königlich englischen Provinz Carolina.* St. Gall, Switzerland: Ruprecht Weniger, 1740.

R.G. Dun and Company. *The Mercantile Agency Reference Books.*

Remarques sur la "Nouvelle Relation de la Caroline," par un Gentilhomme François—MDCLXXXVI. In *The Magnolia; or Southern Apalachian,* new series, 1 (October 1842): 226–30.

Ricardo, David. *On the Principles of Political Economy and Taxation.* 3d edition. London: John Murray, 1821.

Rivers, William J. *A Sketch of the History of South Carolina to the Close of the Proprietary Government by the Revolution of 1719.* Charleston: McCarter & Co., 1856.

Roberts, Lewes. *The Treasure of Traffike or A Discourse on Forraigne Trade.* London: Printed by E.P. for Nicholas Bourne, 1641.

Rochefoucauld-Liancourt, Duc de la. *Travels through the United States of North America* . . . . Translated by H. Neuman. London: R. Phillips, 1799.

Sainsbury, W. Noel, *et al.,* eds. *Great Britain, Calendar of State Papers, Colonial Series, America and West Indies, 1574–.* 44 vols. thus far. London: 1860–.

Salley, A.S., ed. "Diary of William Dillwyn During a Visit to Charles Town in 1772." *South Carolina Historical Magazine* 36 (January 1935): 1–6.

————, ed. *Journal of the Commons House of Assembly of South Carolina*. 22 vols. Columbia: Printed for the Historical Commission of South Carolina by The State Company, 1907–47.

————, ed. *Narratives of Early Carolina 1650–1708*. Original Narratives of Early American History Series. New York: Barnes & Noble, 1967. Originally published 1911.

————, ed. *Register of St. Philip's Parish, Charles Town, South Carolina, 1720–1758*. Charleston: Walker, Evans & Cogswell, 1904.

Saunders, William L., Walter Clark, and Stephen B. Weeks, eds. *The Colonial and State Records of North Carolina*. 30 vols. Raleigh, Winston, Goldsboro, and Charlotte: 1886–1914.

Schmidt, Albert J. "Applying Old World Habits to the New: Life in South Carolina at the Turn of the Eighteenth Century." *Huntington Library Quarterly* 25 (November 1961): 51–59.

————. "Hyrne Family Letters." *South Carolina Historical Magazine* 63 (July 1962): 150–57.

Schmoller, Gustav. *The Mercantile System . . .* Translated by William Ashley. London: Macmillan, 1896. Originally published 1884.

Schomburgk, Robert H. *The History of Barbados*. London: Longman, Brown, Green, and Longmans, 1848.

Scott, William A. *The Repudiation of State Debts . . .* New York: T.Y. Crowell, 1893.

Senate of the State of South Carolina. *Journal of the Senate of the State of South-Carolina . . . 1842*. Columbia: Pemberton, 1842.

Shecut, J.L.E.W. *Shecut's Medical and Philosophical Essays*. Charleston: Printed for the author by A.E. Miller, 1819.

Smith, Adam. *An Inquiry into the Nature and Causes of the Wealth of Nations*. Edited by Edwin Cannan, The Modern Library. New York: Random House, 1937. Originally published 1776.

Smyth, J.F.D. *Tour of the United States of America . . .* 2 vols. Dublin: T. Henshall, 1784.

South-Carolina Almanacks. (J. Tobler)

South Carolina Society for Promoting and Improving Agriculture. *Letters and Observations on Agriculture . . . .* Charleston: Bowen & Co., 1788.

The Southern Agriculturalist.

The Southern Business Directory and General Commercial Advertiser . . . Charleston: Walker & James, 1854.

The Southern Cultivator.

State Board of Agriculture of South Carolina. *South Carolina: Resources and Population, Institutions and Industries*. Compiled by Harry Hammond. Charleston: Walker, Evans & Cogswell, 1883.

The Statutes at Large of South Carolina. Volume XI . . . .

Stephen, Leslie, and Sidney Lee, *et al.*, eds. *Dictionary of National Biography*. 22 vols. plus eight supplements thus far. London: Oxford University Press, 1921–. Originally published 1885–1901.

T.A. *Carolina; or a Description of the Present State of that Country and the Natural Excellencies thereof . . .* London: Printed for W.C., 1682.

Tönnies, Ferdinand. *Community and Society*. Edited and translated by Charles P. Loomis. East Lansing: Michigan State University Press, 1957. Originally published 1887.

Tucker, George. *Progress of the United States in Population and Wealth in Fifty Years . . . .* New York: Press of the Hunt's Merchants' Magazine, 1855.

Tucker, Josiah. *A Selection from His Economic and Political Writings*. Edited by R.L. Schuyler. *The Elements of Commerce*, pp. 51–220. New York: Columbia University Press, 1931.

Tuomey, Michael. *Report on the Geology of South Carolina*. Columbia: A.S. Johnston for the State of South Carolina, 1848.

Uhlendorf, Bernhard A., trans. and ed. *The Siege of Charleston with an Account of the Province of South Carolina: Diaries and Letters of Hessian Officers from the von Jungkenn Papers in the William L. Clements Library*. Ann Arbor: University of Michigan Press, 1938.

United States Bureau of Statistics. *Report of the Chief of the Bureau of Statistics on Customs-Tariff Legislation. Appendix A. Comparative Statement of the Rates of Duties and Imposts under the Several Tariff Acts from 1789 to 1870, Both Inclusive*. Prepared by A.W. Angerer. Washington, D.C.: U.S. Government Printing Office, 1872.

United States Congress, House of Representatives, Ways and Means Committee. *Statements to the Committee of Ways and Means on the Morrison Tariff Bill* . . . . Washington, D.C.: U.S. Government Printing Office, 1886.

United States Department of Agriculture. Division of Statistics. *Rice: Its Cultivation, Production, and Distribution in the United States and Foreign Countries*. By Amory Austin. Miscellaneous Series. Report No. 6. Washington, D.C.: U.S. Government Printing Office, 1893.

United States Department of the Treasury. *Statistical Abstracts of the United States*. For 1881, 1891, 1901, 1911.

United States House of Representatives Executive Documents.

United States Senate Executive Documents.

Vaughan, Rice. *A Discourse of Coin and Coinage*. London: Printed by T. Dawks for T. Basset, 1675.

Walsh, Richard, ed. *The Writings of Christopher Gadsden, 1746–1805*. Columbia: University of South Carolina Press, 1966.

Webber, Mabel L., ed. "Register of the Independent or Congregational (Circular) Church, 1732–1738." *South Carolina Historical Magazine* 12 (1911): 27–37, 53–59, 135–40.

Weeks, Stephen B. *Southern Quakers and Slavery: A Study in Institutional History*. Johns Hopkins University Studies in Historical and Political Science. Extra volume, XV. Baltimore: Johns Hopkins University Press, 1896.

Wells's Register: Together with An Almanack . . . By George Andrews. Esq. for the Year of our Lord 1774. Twelfth edition. Charleston: Printed and Sold by Robert Wells, 1774.

Wigglesworth, Edward. *Calculations on American Populations* . . . . Boston: John Boyle, 1775.

Wilkins, Mira, ed. *Foreign Investments in the United States: Department of Commerce and Department of Treasury Estimates*. New York: Arno Press, 1977.

Williams, Harold, ed. *The Poems of Jonathan Swift*. 3 vols. Oxford: Clarendon Press, 1937.

Wilson, Samuel. *An Account of the Province of Carolina* . . . . London: Printed by G. Larkin for Francis Smith, 1682.

Withington, Lothrop, contrib. "South Carolina Gleanings in England." *South Carolina Historical Magazine* 5 (July 1904): 161–67 and 9 (July 1908): 122–26.

C. Newspapers

American Weekly Mercury (Philadelphia)
Boston Gazette
Boston News-Letter
Charleston Courier
Charleston Mercury
Charleston News and Courier
Charlotte Observer
Gazette of the State of South Carolina (Charleston)
Georgetown Enquirer (South Carolina)
Georgia State Gazette and Independent Register (Augusta)
London Times
New York Times
South-Carolina and American General Gazette (Charleston)
South-Carolina Gazette (Charleston)
South Carolina Gazette and Country Journal (Charleston)

D. United States Census–Published

U.S. Department of Commerce. Bureau of the Census:

Historical Statistics of the United States: Colonial Times to 1970. 2 vols. Washington, D.C.: U.S. Government Printing Office, 1975.

Heads of Families at the First Census of the United States Taken in the Year 1790. South Carolina. Washington, D.C.: U.S. Government Printing Office, 1908.

Second Census of the United States, 1800. Washington, D.C.: Duane, 1801.

Third Census of the United States, 1810. Book 1: *Aggregate Amount of Persons Within the United States in the Year 1810*. Washington, D.C., 1811.

Fourth Census of the United States, 1820. Book 1. Washington, D.C.: Gale and Seaton, 1821.

Fifth Census of the United States, 1830. Washington, D.C.: Duff Green, 1832.

Sixth Census of the United States, 1840. Washington, D.C.: Thomas Allen, 1841.

Seventh Census of the United States, 1850. Washington, D.C.: Robert Armstrong, 1853.

Eighth Census of the United States, 1860: Agriculture. Washington, D.C.: U.S. Government Printing Office, 1864.

Eighth Census of the United States, 1860: Manufactures. Washington, D.C.: U.S. Government Printing Office, 1865.

Eighth Census of the United States, 1860: Population. Washington, D.C.: U.S. Government Printing Office, 1864.

Eighth Census of the United States, 1860: Statistics. Washington, D.C.: U.S. Government Printing Office, 1866.

Ninth Census of the United States, 1870: Statistics of Population. Washington, D.C.: U.S. Government Printing Office, 1872.

Ninth Census of the United States, 1870: Industry and Wealth. Washington, D.C.: U.S. Government Printing Office, 1872.

Tenth Census of the United States, 1880: Agriculture. Washington, D.C.: U.S. Government Printing Office, 1883.

Tenth Census of the United States, 1880: Population. Washington, D.C.: U.S. Government Printing Office, 1883.

Eleventh Census of the United States, 1890: Population, Part I. Washington, D.C.: U.S. Government Printing Office, 1895.

Eleventh Census of the United States, 1890: Statistics of Agriculture. Washington, D.C.: U.S. Government Printing Office, 1896.

Twelfth Census of the United States, 1900. Vol. I. *Population*, pt. 1. Washington, D.C.: U.S. Census Office, 1902.

Twelfth Census of the United States, 1900. Vol. VI. *Agriculture*, pt. II, Crops and Irrigation. Washington, D.C.: U.S. Government Printing Office, 1902.

Twelfth Census of the United States, 1900. Vol. VIII. *Manufactures*, pt. II. Washington, D.C.: U.S. Census Office, 1902.

Thirteenth Census of the United States, 1910: Abstract of the Census . . . with Supplement for South Carolina. Washington, D.C.: U.S. Government Printing Office, 1922.

Thirteenth Census of the United States, 1910: Population, Vol. III. Washington, D.C.: U.S. Government Printing Office, 1913.

Fourteenth Census of the United States, 1920. Vol. V: *Agriculture: General Report and Analytical Tables.* Washington, D.C.: U.S. Government Printing Office, 1922.

Fourteenth Census of the United States, 1920. Vol. VI: *Agriculture*, pt. II. Reports for the States. The Southern States. Washington, D.C.: U.S. Government Printing Office, 1922.

Fourteenth Census of the United States, 1920: Population, Vol. III. Washington, D.C.: U.S. Government Printing Office, 1922.

II. Secondary Sources

A. Books and Articles

Abramovitz, Moses, and Paul A. David. "Reinterpreting Economic Growth: Parables and Realities." *American Economic Review* 63 (May 1973): 428–39.

Ackerman, Robert K. *South Carolina Colonial Land Policies.* Columbia: University of South Carolina Press, 1977.

Adams, A.R.D., and B.G. Maegraith. *Clinical Tropical Diseases.* 4th ed. Oxford: Blackwell Scientific Publications, 1966.

Adas, Michael. *The Burma Delta: Economic Development and Social Change on an Asian Rice Frontier, 1852–1941.* Madison: University of Wisconsin Press, 1974.

Albion, Robert G. "New York Port and Its Disappointed Rivals, 1815–1860." *Journal of Economic and Business History* 3 (1931): 602–29.

———. *The Rise of New York Port, 1815–1860.* Newton Abbot, Devon, England: David & Charles, 1970. Originally published 1939.

Alden, Dauril. "The Growth and Decline of Indigo Production in Colonial Brazil: A Study in Comparative Economic History." *Journal of Economic History* 25 (March 1965): 35–60.

Aldredge, Robert C. "Weather Observers and Observations at Charleston, South Carolina, 1670–1871." In *Year Book, City of Charleston, S.C., 1940*, pp. 189–257. Charleston: Published for the City of Charleston by Walker, Evans & Cogswell, 1942.

Allen, W.R. "Modern Defenders of Mercantilism." *Journal of Political Economy* 2 (Fall 1970): 381–97.

Amin, Samir. *Unequal Development: An Essay on the Social Formations of Peripheral Capitalism*. Translated by Brian Pearce. New York: Monthly Review Press, 1976. Originally published 1973.

Anderson, Terry L. "Economic Growth in Colonial New England: 'Statistical Renaissance.'" *Journal of Economic History* 39 (March 1979): 243–57.

———. *The Economic Growth of Seventeenth-Century New England: A Measurement of Regional Income*. New York: Arno Press, 1975.

———. "Wealth Estimates for the New England Colonies, 1650–1709." *Explorations in Economic History*. 2d series, 12 (April 1975): 151–76.

Anderson, Terry L., and Robert Paul Thomas. "Economic Growth in the Seventeenth-Century Chesapeake." *Explorations in Economic History*. 2d series, 15 (October 1978): 368–87.

Andersson, J.O. *Studies in the Theory of Unequal Exchange between Nations*. Abo, Finland: Abo Akedemi, 1976.

Andrews, Charles M. *The Colonial Period of American History*. 4 vols. New Haven: Yale University Press, 1934–38.

Andrews, Kenneth R. *Trade, Plunder and Settlement: Maritime Enterprise and the Genesis of the British Empire, 1480–1630*. Cambridge: Cambridge University Press, 1984.

Appleby, Joyce Oldham. *Economic Thought and Ideology in Seventeenth-Century England*. Princeton: Princeton University Press, 1978.

———. "Ideology and Theory: The Tension Between Political and Economic Liberalism in Seventeenth-Century England." *American Historical Review* 81 (June 1976): 499–515.

———. "Modernization Theory and the Formation of Modern Social Theories in England and America." *Comparative Studies in Society and History* 20 (April 1978): 259–85.

Argan, Giulio C. *The Renaissance City*. New York: George Braziller, 1969.

Ashcraft, Richard. *Revolutionary Politics & Locke's Two Treatises of Government*. Princeton: Princeton University Press, 1986.

Aston, Trevor, ed. *Crisis in Europe, 1560–1660*. Garden City, N.Y.: Anchor Books, 1967. Originally published 1965.

Aston, T.H., and C.H.E. Philpin, eds. *The Brenner Debate: Agrarian Class Structure and Economic Development in Pre-Industrial Europe*. Cambridge: Cambridge University Press, 1985.

Atkinson, A.B. "On the Measurement of Inequality." *Journal of Economic Theory* 2 (1970): 244–63.

Attewell, Paul A. *Radical Political Economy Since the Sixties: A Sociology of Knowledge Approach*. New Brunswick, N.J.: Rutgers University Press, 1984.

Aufhauser, Keith. "Slavery and Scientific Management." *Journal of Economic History* 33 (December 1973): 811–24.

Axtell, James. "The Ethnohistory of Early America: A Review Essay." *William and Mary Quarterly*. 3d series, 35 (January 1978): 110–44.

Bacon, Edmund N. *Design of Cities*, revised edition. New York: Penguin Books, 1976.

Baldwin, Agnes L. *First Settlers of South Carolina, 1670–1680*. Tricentennial Booklet Number 1. Columbia: Published for the South Carolina Tricentennial Commission by the University of South Carolina Press, 1969.

———. *First Settlers of South Carolina 1670–1700*. Easley, S.C.: Southern Historical Press, 1985.

Baldwin, Robert E. *Economic Development and Growth*. 2d ed. New York: Wiley, 1972.
———. "Patterns of Development in Newly Settled Areas." *Manchester School of Economic and Social Studies* 24 (May 1956): 161–79.
Bale, M.D., and E. Lutz. "Price Distortions in Agriculture and Their Effects: An International Comparison." *American Journal of Agricultural Economics* 63 (February 1981): 8–22.
Balibar, Etienne. "On the Basic Concepts of Historical Materialism." In Etienne Balibar and Louis Althusser, *Reading "Capital."* Translated by Ben Brewster. New York: Pantheon, 1970. Originally published in 1968.
Bang, Nina E. and Knud Korst. *Tabeller Over Skibsfart Og Varetransport Gennem Øresund, 1661–1783, Og Gennem Storebaelt 1701–1748*. 4 vols. Copenhagen: Gyldendalske Boghandel . . . , 1930.
Banning, Lance. *The Jeffersonian Persuasion: Evolution of a Party Ideology*. Ithaca: Cornell University Press, 1978.
Baran, Paul A. *The Political Economy of Growth*. New York: Monthly Review Press, 1957.
Barclay, George W. *Techniques of Population Analysis*. New York: Wiley, 1958.
Barley, M.W. *The English Farmhouse and Cottage*. London: Routledge and Kegan Paul, 1961.
———. *The House and Home: A Review of 900 Years of House Planning and Furnishing in Britain*. Greenwich, Conn.: New York Graphic Society, 1963.
Barry, John M. *Natural Vegetation of South Carolina*. Columbia: University of South Carolina Press, 1980.
Bascom, William. "Folklore." In *The International Encyclopedia of the Social Sciences*, vol. 5: 496–500. Edited by David L. Sills. 18 vols. New York: The Free Press, 1968–79.
Bateman, Fred, and Thomas Weiss. *A Deplorable Scarcity: The Failure of Industrialization in the Slave Economy*. Chapel Hill: University of North Carolina Press, 1981.
Baxter, W.T. "Accounting in Colonial America." In *Studies in the History of Accounting*, pp. 272–87. Edited by A.C. Littleton and B.S. Yamey. Homewood, Ill.: Richard D. Irwin, 1956.
Bean, Richard N., and Robert P. Thomas. "The Adoption of Slave Labor in British America." In *The Uncommon Market: Essays in the Economic History of the Atlantic Slave Trade*, pp. 377–98. Edited by Henry A. Gemery and Jan S. Hogendorn. New York: Academic Press, 1979.
Beattie, J.M. *Crime and the Courts in England, 1660–1800*. Princeton: Princeton University Press, 1986.
———. "The Pattern of Crime in England 1660–1800." *Past and Present* 62 (February 1974): 47–95.
Becker, Robert A. "Revolution and Reform: An Interpretation of Southern Taxation, 1763 to 1783." *William and Mary Quarterly*. 3d series, 32 (July 1975): 417–42.
———. *Revolution, Reform, and the Politics of American Taxation, 1763–1783*. Baton Rouge: Louisiana State University Press, 1980.
Beckford, George L. *Persistent Poverty: Underdevelopment in Plantation Economies of the Third World*. New York: Oxford University Press, 1972.
Beer, George Louis. *The Old Colonial System 1660–1754*. 2 vols. New York: Macmillan, 1912.
Beer, Max. *An Inquiry into Physiocracy*. New York: Russell & Russell, 1966. Originally published 1939.

Bell, Malcom, Jr. *Major Butler's Legacy: Five Generations of a Slaveholding Family*. Athens: University of Georgia Press, 1987.

Bellows, Barbara L. "At Peace with the Past: Charleston 1900–1950." In *Mirror of Time: Elizabeth O'Neill Verner's Charleston*, pp. 1–5. Edited by Lynn R. Myers. Columbia: McKissick Museums of the University of South Carolina, 1983.

Benjamin, Walter. "Theses on the Philosophy of History." In Benjamin, *Illuminations*, pp. 253–64. Edited by Hannah Arendt. Translated by Harry Zohn. New York: Schocken Books, 1969.

Bennett, John. *The Doctor to the Dead: Grotesque Legends & Folk Tales of Old Charleston*. New York: Rinehart, 1946.

Berry, Brian J.L. "City Size Distributions and Economic Development." *Economic Development and Cultural Change* 9 (July 1961): 573–88.

Bertelson, David. *The Lazy South*. New York: Oxford University Press, 1967.

Bhagwati, Jagdish. "Immiserizing Growth: A Geometric Note." *Review of Economic Studies* 25 (June 1958): 201–05.

———., ed. *International Trade: Selected Readings*. Cambridge: MIT Press, 1981.

Binder, Leonard. "The Natural History of Development Theory." *Comparative Studies in Society and History* 28 (January 1986): 3–33.

Black, C.E. *The Dynamics of Modernization: A Study in Comparative History*. New York: Harper & Row, 1966.

Blauner, Robert. "Death and Social Structure." *Psychiatry* 29 (November 1966): 378–94.

Blitz, Rudolph C. "Mercantilist Policies and the Pattern of World Trade, 1500–1750." *Journal of Economic History* 27 (March 1967): 39–55.

Bloch, Marc. *The Historian's Craft*. Translated by Peter Putnam. New York: Vintage, 1952. Originally published 1949.

Bloomfield, Arthur I. "The Foreign-Trade Doctrines of the Physiocrats." *American Economic Review* 28 (December 1938): 716–35.

Bolick, Julian S. *Ghosts from the Coast: A Collection of Twelve Stories from Georgetown County, South Carolina*. Clinton, S.C.: Jacobs Brothers, c. 1966.

———. *The Return of the Gray Man and Georgetown Ghosts*. Clinton, S.C.: Jacobs Brothers, c. 1961.

Bond, Beverley W., Jr. *The Quit-Rent System in the American Colonies*. New Haven: Yale University Press, 1919.

Borah, Woodrow. *New Spain's Century of Depression*. Berkeley: University of California Press, 1951.

Boserup, Ester. *The Conditions of Agricultural Growth: The Economics of Agrarian Change under Population Pressure*. Chicago: Aldine, 1965.

Bowes, Frederick P. *The Culture of Early Charleston*. Chapel Hill: University of North Carolina Press, 1942.

Brandt, Loren. "Chinese Agriculture and the International Economy, 1870–1930s: A Reassessment." *Explorations in Economic History*. 2d series, 22 (April 1985): 168–93.

Braudel, Fernand. "Qu'est-ce que le XVIe siècle?" *Annales: Economies, sociétés, civilisations* 8 (1953): 69–73.

———. *The Structures of Everyday Life: Civilization & Capitalism 15th–18th Century*. Translated by Siân Reynolds. New York: Harper & Row, 1981. Originally published 1979.

Brenner, Robert P. "The Origins of Capitalist Development: A Critique of Neo-Smithian Marxism." *New Left Review* 104 (July–August 1977): 25–92.

Brewer, Anthony. *Marxist Theories of Imperialism: A Critical Survey*. London: Routledge & Kegan Paul, 1980.

Bridenbaugh, Carl. *Cities in Revolt: Urban Life in America 1743–1776*. New York: Capricorn Books, 1964. Originally published 1955.

———. *Cities in the Wilderness: The First Century of Urban Life in America 1625–1742*. New York: Oxford University Press, 1971. Originally published 1938.

———. *Myths and Realities: Societies of the Colonial South*. New York: Atheneum, 1971. Originally published 1952.

Bridenbaugh, Carl, and Roberta Bridenbaugh. *No Peace Beyond the Line: The English in the Caribbean 1624–1690*. New York: Oxford University Press, 1972.

Bridwell, Ronald E. *". . . That We Should have a Port . . .": A History of the Port of Georgetown, South Carolina, 1732–1865*. Georgetown: The Georgetown Times, 1982.

Briggs, Loutrel W. *Charleston Gardens*. Columbia: University of South Carolina Press, 1951.

Britton, Stephen G. "The Evolution of a Colonial Space Economy: The Case of Fiji." *Journal of Historical Geography* 6 (July 1980): 251–74.

Brock, Leslie V. *The Currency of the American Colonies 1700–1764: A Study in Colonial Finance and Imperial Relations*. New York: Arno Press, 1975.

Broussard, James H. *The Southern Federalists, 1800–1816*. Baton Rouge: Louisiana State University Press, 1978.

Brown, Louise F. *The First Earl of Shaftesbury*. New York: D. Appleton-Century, 1933.

Brown, Philip M. "Early Indian Trade in the Development of South Carolina: Politics, Economics, and Social Mobility during the Proprietary Period, 1670–1719." *South Carolina Historical Magazine* 76 (July 1975): 118–28.

Brown, Richard D. *Modernization: The Transformation of American Life 1600–1865*. American Century Series. New York: Hill and Wang, 1976.

Brown, Richard M. *The South Carolina Regulators*. Cambridge: The Belknap Press of Harvard University, 1963.

Bruchey, Stuart W. "The Business Economy of Marketing Change, 1790–1840: A Study of Sources of Efficiency." *Agricultural History* 46 (January 1972): 211–26.

———., ed. *The Colonial Merchant: Sources and Readings*. The Forces in American Economic Growth Series. New York: Harcourt, Brace & World, 1966.

———. "Douglass C. North on American Economic Growth." *Explorations in Entrepreneurial History*. 2d series, 1 (Winter 1964): 145–58.

———. *The Roots of American Economic Growth, 1607–1861: An Essay in Social Causation*. New York: Harper & Row, 1968. Originally published 1965.

———. "Success and Failure Factors: American Merchants in Foreign Trade in the Eighteenth and Early Nineteenth Centuries." *Business History Review* 32 (Autumn 1958): 272–92.

Brunvand, John H. *The Study of American Folklore: An Introduction*. 2d edition. New York: W.W. Norton, 1978.

Bryden, John M. *Tourism and Development: A Case Study of the Caribbean Commonwealth*. Cambridge: Cambridge University Press, 1973.

Bryson, Reid A., and Christine Padoch. "On the Climates of History." *Journal of Interdisciplinary History* 10 (Spring 1980): 583–97.

Buck, Philip W. *Politics of Mercantilism*. New York: Octagon Books, 1964. Originally published 1942.

Buckman, Harry O., and Nyle C. Brady. *The Nature and Properties of Soils*. 7th ed. New York: Macmillan, 1969.

Buol, S.W., F.D. Hole, and R.J. McCracken. *Soil Genesis and Classification*. 2d ed. Ames: Iowa State University Press, 1980.

Burnet, Frank Macfarlane, and David O. White. *Natural History of Infectious Disease*. 4th ed. Cambridge: Cambridge University Press, 1972.

Burton, E. Milby. *South Carolina Silversmiths 1690–1860*. Contributions from the Charleston Museum, no. 10. Richmond: The Dietz Press for the Charleston Museum, 1942.

Calhoun, Jeanne A., Martha A. Zierden, and Elizabeth A. Paysinger. "The Geographic Spread of Charleston's Mercantile Community." *South Carolina Historical Magazine* 86 (July 1985): 182–220.

Camblin, Gilbert. *The Town in Ulster: An Account of the Origin and Building of the Towns of the Province and the Development of Their Rural Setting*. Belfast: W. Mullan, 1951.

Canny, Nicholas P. "The Ideology of English Colonization: From Ireland to America." *William and Mary Quarterly*. 3d series, 30 (October 1973): 575–98.

Carlton, David L. *Mill and Town in South Carolina 1880–1920*. Baton Rouge: Louisiana State University Press, 1982.

———. "The Piedmont and Waccamaw Regions: An Economic Comparison." *South Carolina Historical Magazine* 88 (April 1987): 83–100.

Carr-Saunders, A.M. *World Population: Past Growth and Present Trends*. Oxford: Clarendon Press, 1936.

Carson, Cary. "Segregation in Vernacular Buildings." *Vernacular Architecture* 7 (1976): 24–29.

Carson, Cary, Norman F. Barka, *et al.* "Impermanent Architecture in the Southern American Colonies." *Winterthur Portfolio* 16 (Summer/Autumn 1981): 135–96.

Cassedy, James H. *Demography in Early America: Beginnings of the Statistical Mind, 1600–1800*. Cambridge: Harvard University Press, 1969.

Castiglione, Arturo. *A History of Medicine*. Translated and edited by E.B. Krumbhaar. New York: Jason Aronson, 1975. Originally published 1940.

Cates, Gerald L. "'The Seasoning': Disease and Death Among the First Colonists of Georgia." *Georgia Historical Quarterly* 64 (Summer 1980): 146–58.

Cauthen, Henry F., Jr. *Charleston Interiors*. Charleston: Published by the Preservation Society of Charleston, 1979.

Caves, Richard E. "Export-Led Growth and the New Economic History." In *Trade, Balance of Payments and Growth: Papers in International Economics in Honor of Charles P. Kindleberger*, pp. 403–42. Edited by Jagdish Bhagwati *et al.* Amsterdam: North-Holland Publishing Co., 1971.

———. "'Vent for Surplus' Models of Trade and Growth." In *Trade, Growth and the Balance of Payments: Essays in Honor of Gottfried Haberler*, pp. 95–115. Edited by Robert E. Baldwin *et al.* Amsterdam: North-Holland Publishing Co., 1965.

Chamberlain, Samuel, and Narcissa Chamberlain. *Southern Interiors of Charleston, South Carolina*. New York: Hastings House, 1956.

Chandler, Alfred D. "The Expansion of Barbados." *Journal of the Barbados Museum and Historical Society* 13 (1946): 106–36.

Chaunu, Pierre. *La Civilisation de l'Europe classique*. Paris: Arthaud, 1966.

Chaunu, Pierre, and Huguette Chaunu. *Séville et l'Atlantic 1504–1650*. 8 vols. in 11 tomes. Paris: Armand Colin; S.E.V.P.E.N., 1955–59.

Cheng Siok-Hwa. *The Rice Industry of Burma 1852–1940*. Kuala Lumpur and Singapore: University of Malaya Press, 1968.

Chevalier, François. *Land and Society in Colonial Mexico: The Great Hacienda*. Translated by Alvin Eustis. Berkeley: University of California Press, 1963.

Chilcote, Ronald H. "Dependency: A Critical Synthesis of the Literature." *Latin American Perspectives* 1 (Spring 1974): 4–29.

———. "Dependency or Mode of Production: Theoretical Issues." In *Theories of Development: Mode of Production or Dependency?*, pp. 9–30. Edited by Ronald H. Chilcote and Dale L. Johnson. Beverly Hills: Sage Publications, 1983.

———. "A Question of Dependency." *Latin American Research Review* 13 (1978): 55–68.

Childs, St. Julien Ravenel. *Malaria and Colonization in the Carolina Low Country 1526–1696*. The Johns Hopkins University Studies in Historical and Political Science, Series 58, No. 1. Baltimore: Johns Hopkins University Press, 1940.

Chou, Ya-lun. *Statistical Analysis With Business and Economic Applications*. New York: Holt, Rinehart and Winston, 1969.

Cipolla, Carlo M. *Before the Industrial Revolution: European Society and Economy, 1000–1700*. New York: W.W. Norton, 1976.

Clark, Christopher. "The Household Economy, Market Exchange and the Rise of Capitalism in the Connecticut Valley, 1800–1860." *Journal of Social History* 13 (Winter 1979): 169–89.

Clark, G.N. *Guide to English Commercial Statistics 1696–1782*. London: The Royal Historical Society, 1938.

Clark, James M. *The Dance of Death in the Middle Ages and the Renaissance*. Glasgow University Publications LXXXVI. Glasgow: Jackson, Son & Company, 1950.

Clark, Victor S. *History of Manufactures in the United States*. 3 vols. Washington, D.C.: Carnegie Institution, 1916–29.

Clarke, Colin G. *Kingston, Jamaica: Urban Development and Social Change, 1692–1962*. Berkeley: University of California Press, 1975.

Clifton, James M. "Hopeton, Model Plantation of the Antebellum South." *Georgia Historical Quarterly* 66 (Winter 1982): 429–49.

———. "The Rice Industry in Colonial America." *Agricultural History* 55 (July 1981): 266–83.

Clowse, Converse D. *Economic Beginnings in Colonial South Carolina 1670–1730*. Columbia: University of South Carolina Press, 1971.

———. *Measuring Charleston's Overseas Commerce, 1717–1767: Statistics from the Port's Naval Lists*. Washington, D.C.: University Press of America, 1981.

Coatsworth, John H. *Growth Against Development: The Economic Impact of Railroads in Porfirian Mexico*. Dekalb: Northern Illinois University Press, 1981.

Cockburn, J.S. "The Nature and Incidence of Crime in England 1559–1625." In Cockburn, ed., *Crime in England 1550–1800*, pp., 49–71, 309–14. Princeton: Princeton University Press, 1977.

Coclanis, Peter A. "Bitter Harvest: The South Carolina Low Country in Historical Perspective." *Journal of Economic History* 45 (June 1985): 251–59.

———. "Death in Early Charleston: An Estimate of the Crude Death Rate for the White Population of Charleston, 1722–1732." *South Carolina Historical Magazine* 85 (October 1984): 280–91.

———. "Entrepreneurship and the Economic History of the American South: The Case of Charleston and the South Carolina Low Country." In *Marketing in the Long Run*, pp.

210–19. Edited by Stanley C. Hollander and Terence Nevett. East Lansing: Department of Marketing and Transportation Administration, Michigan State University, 1985.

————. "Retailing in Early South Carolina." In *Retailing: Theory and Practice for the 21st Century*, pp. 1–5. Edited by Robert L. King. Charleston, S.C.: Academy of Marketing Science, 1986.

————. "Rice Prices in the 1720s and the Evolution of the South Carolina Economy." *Journal of Southern History* 48 (November 1982): 531–44.

————. "The Rise and Fall of the South Carolina Low Country: An Essay in Economic Interpretation." *Southern Studies* 24 (Summer 1985): 143–66.

Coclanis, Peter, and Lacy K. Ford. "The South Carolina Economy Reconstructed and Reconsidered: Structure, Output, and Performance 1670–1985." In *Developing Dixie: Modernization in a Traditional Society*. Edited by Winfred B. Moore, Jr., and Joseph F. Tripp. Westport, Conn.: Greenwood Press, forthcoming.

Cody, Cheryll Ann. "A Note on Changing Patterns of Slave Fertility in the South Carolina Rice District, 1735–1865." *Southern Studies* 16 (Winter 1977): 457–63.

Cole, Arthur H. "The American Rice-Growing Industry: A Study of Comparative Advantage." *Quarterly Journal of Economics* 41 (August 1927): 595–643.

————. "The Tempo of Mercantile Life in Colonial America." *Business History Review* 33 (Autumn 1959): 277–99.

————. *Wholesale Commodity Prices in the United States 1700–1861*. 2 vols. Cambridge: Harvard University Press, 1938.

Cole, W.A. "Factors in Demand 1700–80." In *The Economic History of Britain Since 1700*, 1: 36–65. 2 vols. Edited by Roderick Floud and Donald McCloskey. Cambridge: Cambridge University Press, 1981.

Coleman, D.C. *The Economy of England 1450–1750*. Oxford: Oxford University Press, 1977.

————. "Editor's Introduction." In *Revisions in Mercantilism*, pp. 1–17. Edited by D.C. Coleman. London: Methuen, 1969.

————. "Labour in the English Economy of the Seventeenth Century." *Economic History Review*. 2d series, 8 (1956): 280–95.

————. "Mercantilism Revisited." *The Historical Journal* 23 (1980): 773–91.

————. Review of *Economic Thought and Ideology in Seventeenth-Century England*, by Joyce D. Appleby. *Journal of Modern History* 53 (March 1981): 105–6.

Colquhoun, Donald J. *Geomorphology of the Lower Coastal Plain of South Carolina*. MS15, Division of Geology, State Development Board. Columbia, 1969.

Conrad, Alfred H., and John R. Meyer. *The Economics of Slavery and Other Studies in Econometric History*. Chicago: Aldine, 1964.

Conrad, Joseph. *Heart of Darkness and the Secret Sharer*. New York: The New American Library, 1950. *Heart of Darkness* originally published 1902.

Conroy, Pat. "Shadows of the Old South." *Geo* 3 (May 1981): 64–80, 82.

Cook, Sherburne F., and Woodrow W. Borah. *Essays in Population History: Mexico and the Caribbean*. 3 vols. Berkeley: University of California Press, 1971–79.

————. *The Indian Population of Central Mexico 1531–1610*. Ibero-Americana: 44. Berkeley: University of California Press, 1960.

Cooke, C. Wythe. *Geology of the Coastal Plain of South Carolina*. U.S. Department of the Interior, Geological Survey, Bulletin 867. Washington, D.C.: U.S. Government Printing Office, 1936.

Coon, David L. "Eliza Lucas Pinckney and the Reintroduction of Indigo Culture in South Carolina." *Journal of Southern History* 42 (February 1976): 61–76.

Cooper, Charles F. "The Ecology of Fire." *Scientific American* 204 (April 1961): 150–60.

Cowdrey, Albert E. *This Land, This South: An Environmental History*. Lexington: University Press of Kentucky, 1983.

Cox, Reavis, Charles S. Goodman, and Thomas C. Fichandler. *Distribution in a High-Level Economy*. Englewood Cliffs, N.J.: Prentice-Hall, 1965.

Crane, Verner W. *The Southern Frontier 1670–1732*. Ann Arbor: University of Michigan Press, 1956. Originally published 1929.

Craton, Michael. "Hobbesian or Panglossian? The Two Extremes of Slave Conditions in the British Caribbean, 1783 to 1834." *William and Mary Quarterly*. 3d series, 35 (April 1978): 324–56.

———. "Jamaican Slave Mortality: Fresh Light from Worthy Park, Longville and the Tharp Estates." *Journal of Caribbean History* 3 (November 1971): 1–27.

———. *Sinews of Empire: A Short History of British Slavery*. Garden City, N.Y.: Anchor Press/Doubleday, 1974.

Craven, Wesley Frank. *The Southern Colonies in the Seventeenth Century 1607–1689*. History of the South Series. Baton Rouge: Louisiana State University Press, 1949.

Crist, Raymond E. "Rice Culture in Spain." *Scientific Monthly* 84 (February 1957): 66–74.

Crittenden, Charles C. *The Commerce of North Carolina, 1763–1789*. New Haven: Yale University Press, 1936.

Cronon, William. *Changes in the Land: Indians, Colonists and the Ecology of New England*. New York: Hill and Wang, 1983.

Crosby, Alfred W., Jr. *The Columbian Exchange: Biological and Cultural Consequences of 1492*. Westport, Conn.: Greenwood Press, 1972.

———. *Ecological Imperialism: The Biological Expansion of Europe, 900–1900*. New York: Cambridge University Press, 1986.

———. "Virgin Soil Epidemics as a Factor in the Aboriginal Depopulation in America." *William and Mary Quarterly*. 3d series, 33 (April 1976): 289–99.

Crouse, Maurice A. *The Public Treasury of Colonial South Carolina*. Columbia: University of South Carolina Press, 1977.

Crowley, J.E. "Family Relations and Inheritance in Early South Carolina." *Histoire Sociale/-Social History* 17 (1984): 35–57.

———. "The Importance of Kinship: Testamentary Evidence from South Carolina." *Journal of Interdisciplinary History* 16 (Spring 1986): 559–77.

Cumming, William P. "Geographical Misconceptions of the Southeast in the Cartography of the Seventeenth and Eighteenth Centuries." *Journal of Southern History* 4 (November 1938): 476–92.

———. *The Southeast in Early Maps*. Princeton: Princeton University Press, 1958.

Cummings, Abbott Lowell. *The Framed Houses of Massachusetts Bay, 1624–1725*. Cambridge: The Belknap Press of Harvard University, 1979.

Curtin, Philip D. *The Atlantic Slave Trade: A Census*. Madison: University of Wisconsin Press, 1969.

———. "Epidemiology and the Slave Trade." *Political Science Quarterly* 83 (June 1968): 190–216.

Dadzie, K.K.S. "Economic Development." *Scientific American* 243 (September 1980): 58–65.

Daniel, Pete. *Breaking the Land: The Transformation of Cotton, Tobacco, and Rice Cultures*

Since 1880. Urbana: University of Illinois Press, 1985.

David, Paul A. "The Growth of Real Product in the United States Before 1840: New Evidence, Controlled Conjectures." *Journal of Economic History* 27 (June 1967): 151–97.

Davidson, Chalmers G. *The Last Foray: The South Carolina Planters of 1860: A Sociological Survey*. Columbia: University of South Carolina Press, 1971.

Davis, Lance E. "Capital and Growth." In Davis *et al.*, *American Economic Growth: An Economist's History of the United States*, pp. 280–310. New York: Harper & Row, 1972.

Davis, Ralph. "English Foreign Trade, 1660–1700." *Economic History Review*. 2d series, 7 (1954): 150–66.

———. "English Foreign Trade, 1700–1774." *Economic History Review*. 2d series, 15 (1962): 285–303.

———. *The Rise of the Atlantic Economies*. Ithaca: Cornell University Press, 1973.

———. "The Rise of Protection in England, 1689–1786." *Economic History Review*. 2d series, 19 (1966): 306–17.

Dean, Warren. "The Planter as Entrepreneur: The Case of São Paulo." *Hispanic American Historical Review* 46 (May 1966): 138–52.

Deane, Phyllis and W.A. Cole. *British Economic Growth 1688–1959: Trends and Structure*. Cambridge: Cambridge University Press, 1962.

Deas, Alston. *The Early Ironwork of Charleston*. Columbia: Bostick & Thornley, 1941.

Deerr, Noel. *The History of Sugar*. 2 vols. London: Chapman and Hall, 1949–50.

Degler, Carl N. "Slavery and the Genesis of American Race Prejudice." *Comparative Studies in Society and History* 2 (October 1959): 49–66.

de Janvry, Alain. *The Agrarian Question and Reformism in Latin America*. Baltimore: Johns Hopkins University Press, 1981.

de Kadt, Emanuel. *Tourism—Passport to Development?: Perspectives on the Social and Cultural Effects of Tourism in Developing Countries*. New York: Oxford University Press for the World Bank, 1979.

Demos, John. *A Little Commonwealth: Family Life in Plymouth Colony*. New York: Oxford University Press, 1970.

———. "Families in Colonial Bristol, Rhode Island: An Exercise in Historical Demography." *William and Mary Quarterly*. 3d series, 25 (January 1968): 40-57.

Denison, Edward F. *The Sources of Economic Growth in the United States and the Alternatives Before Us*. New York: Committee for Economic Development, 1962.

Dennis, Kenneth G. *"Competition" in the History of Economic Thought*. New York: Arno Press, 1977.

Derrick, Samuel M. *Centennial History of South Carolina Railroad*. Columbia: The State Company, 1930.

de Vries, Jan. *The Dutch Rural Economy in the Golden Age, 1500–1700*. New Haven: Yale University Press, 1974.

———. *The Economy of Europe in an Age of Crisis: 1600–1750*. Cambridge: Cambridge University Press, 1976.

———. *European Urbanization, 1500–1800*. Cambridge: Harvard University Press, 1984.

———. "Measuring the Impact of Climate on History: The Search for Appropriate Methodologies." *Journal of Interdisciplinary History* 10 (Spring 1980): 599–630.

Dickson, P.G.M. *The Financial Revolution in England: A Study in the Development of Public Credit 1688–1756*. London: Macmillan, 1967.

Diggins, John P. *The Lost Soul of American Politics: Virtue, Self-Interest, and the Foundations of Liberalism.* New York: Basic Books, 1984.

Dixon, Caroline Wyche. "The Miles Brewton House: Ezra Waite's Architectural Books and Other Possible Design Sources." *South Carolina Historical Magazine* 82 (April 1981): 118–42.

Doar, David. *Rice and Rice Planting in the South Carolina Low Country.* Contributions from the Charleston Museum, no. 8. Charleston: The Charleston Museum, 1936.

Dobb, Maurice H. *Studies in the Development of Capitalism.* New York: International Publishers, 1946.

Dobson, Mary. "'Marsh Fever'—The Geography of Malaria in England." *Journal of Historical Geography* 6 (October 1980): 357–89.

Dobyns, Henry F. "Estimating Aboriginal American Population: An Appraisal of Techniques with a New Hemispheric Estimate." *Current Anthropology* 7 (October 1966): 395–416.

———. *Native American Historical Demography: A Critical Bibliography.* The Newberry Library. Center for the History of the American Indian Bibliographical Series. Bloomington: Indiana University Press, 1976.

———. "An Outline of Andean Epidemic History to 1720." *Bulletin of the History of Medicine* 37 (November–December 1963): 493–515.

———. *Their Number Become Thinned: Native American Population Dynamics in Eastern North America.* Knoxville: University of Tennessee Press, 1983.

Doerflinger, Thomas M. "Commercial Specialization in Philadelphia's Merchant Community, 1750–1791." *Business History Review* 57 (Spring 1983): 20–49.

———. *A Vigorous Spirit of Enterprise: Merchants and Economic Development in Revolutionary Philadelphia.* Chapel Hill: University of North Carolina Press, 1986.

Domar, Evsey D. "The Causes of Slavery or Serfdom: A Hypothesis." *Journal of Economic History* 30 (March 1970): 18–32.

Doroschenko, V., et al. *Trade and Agrarian Development in the Baltic Provinces.* Preprint. Tallinn: Academy of Sciences of the Estonian S.S.R., 1974.

Dorson, Richard M. "Concepts of Folklore and Folklife Studies." In *Folklore and Folklife: An Introduction*, pp. 1–50. Edited by Dorson. Chicago: University of Chicago Press, 1972.

Downs, Michael. *James Harrington.* Twayne's English Authors Series. Boston: Twayne Publishers, 1977.

Doxiadis, Constantinos A. *Ekistics: An Introduction to the Science of Settlement Systems.* New York: Oxford University Press, 1968.

Doyle, Don H. "Leadership and Decline in Postwar Charleston, 1865–1910." In *From the Old South to the New: Essays on the Transitional South*, pp. 93–106. Edited by Walter J. Fraser, Jr., and Winfred B. Moore, Jr. Westport, Conn.: Greenwood Press, 1981.

Drake, Michael. "An Elementary Exercise in Parish Register Demography." *Economic History Review.* 2d series, 14 (1962): 427–45.

Du Bois, W.E.B., ed. *The Negro American Family.* Westport, Conn.: Negro Universities Press, 1969. Originally published 1908.

Duby, Georges. *Le Temps des cathédrales: L'art et la société, 980–1420.* Paris: Gaillimard, 1976.

Duffy, John. *Epidemics in Colonial America.* Baton Rouge: Louisiana State University Press, 1953.

―――. "Yellow Fever in Colonial Charleston." *South Carolina Historical Magazine* 52 (October 1951): 189–97.

Dunbar, Gary S. "Colonial Carolina Cowpens." *Agricultural History* 35 (July 1961): 125–31.

Duncan, Bingham. "Diplomatic Support of the American Rice Trade, 1835–1845." *Agricultural History* 23 (April 1949): 92–96.

Dunn, Richard S. "The Barbados Census of 1680: Profile of the Richest Colony in English America." *William and Mary Quarterly*. 3d series, 26 (January 1969): 3-30.

―――. "The English Sugar Islands and the Founding of South Carolina." *South Carolina Historical Magazine* 72 (April 1971): 81–93.

―――. *Sugar and Slaves: The Rise of the Planter Class in the English West Indies, 1624–1713*. Chapel Hill: University of North Carolina Press, 1972.

―――. "A Tale of Two Plantations: Slave Life at Mesopotamia in Jamaica and Mount Airy in Virginia, 1799 to 1828." *William and Mary Quarterly*. 3d series, 34 (January 1977): 32–65.

Dupaquier, Jacques. "Problèmes de représentativité dans les études fondées sur la reconstitution des familles." *Annales de Démographie Historique* (1972): 83–91.

Earle, Carville V. "Environment, Disease, and Mortality in Early Virginia." In *The Chesapeake in the Seventeenth Century: Essays on Anglo-American Society and Politics*, pp. 96–125. Edited by Thad W. Tate and David L. Ammerman. Chapel Hill: University of North Carolina Press, 1979.

―――. *The Evolution of a Tidewater Settlement System: All Hallow's Parish, Maryland, 1650–1783*. The University of Chicago Department of Geography, Research Paper No. 170. Chicago: University of Chicago, Department of Geography, 1975.

―――. "A Staple Interpretation of Slavery and Free Labor." *Geographical Review* 68 (January 1978): 51–65.

Earle, Carville, and Ronald Hoffman. "The Foundation of the Modern Economy: Agriculture and the Costs of Labor in the United States and England 1800–60." *American Historical Review* 85 (December 1980): 1055–94.

―――. "Staple Crops and Urban Development in the Eighteenth-Century South." *Perspectives in American History* 10 (1976): 7–78.

―――. "The Urban South: The First Two Centuries." In *The City in Southern History: The Growth of Urban Civilization in the South*, pp. 23–51. Edited by Blaine A. Brownell and David R. Goldfield. Port Washington, N.Y.: Kennikat Press, 1977.

Easterby, J.H. "The South Carolina Rice Factor as Revealed in the Papers of Robert F.W. Allston." *Journal of Southern History* 7 (May 1941): 160–72.

Easterlin, Richard A. "Interregional Differences in Per Capita Income, Population, and Total Income, 1840–1950." In *Trends in the American Economy in the Nineteenth Century*, pp. 73–140. Edited by William N. Parker. Conference on Research in Income and Wealth, vol. 24. Princeton: Princeton University Press, 1960.

―――. "Regional Income Trends, 1840–1950." In *The Reinterpretation of American Economic History*, pp. 38–49. Edited by Robert W. Fogel and Stanley L. Engerman. New York: Harper & Row, 1971.

Eblen, Jack E. "On the Natural Increase of Slave Populations: The Example of the Cuban Black Population, 1775–1900." In *Race and Slavery in the Western Hemisphere: Quantitative Studies*, pp. 211–47. Edited by Stanley L. Engerman and Eugene D. Genovese. Princeton: Princeton University Press, 1975.

Edwards, George N. *A History of the Independent or Congregational Church of Charleston South Carolina*. Boston: The Pilgrim Press, 1947.

Egnal, Marc. "The Economic Development of the Thirteen Continental Colonies, 1720 to 1775." *William and Mary Quarterly.* 3d series, 32 (April 1975): 191–222.

Eisenberg, John F. *The Mammalian Radiations: An Analysis of Trends in Evolution, Adaptation, and Behavior.* Chicago: University of Chicago Press, 1981.

Eisenstadt, S.N. *Modernization: Protest and Change.* Englewood Cliffs, N.J.: Prentice-Hall, 1966.

———. "Studies on Modernization and Development." *History and Theory* 13 (1974): 225–52.

Eisterhold, John A. "Charleston: Lumber and Trade in a Declining Southern Port." *South Carolina Historical Magazine* 74 (April 1973): 61–72.

Ekelund, Robert B., Jr., and Robert D. Tollison. *Mercantilism as a Rent-Seeking Society: Economic Regulation in Historical Perspective.* College Station: Texas A & M University Press, 1981.

Ekirch, A. Roger. *"Poor Carolina": Politics and Society in Colonial North Carolina, 1729–1776.* Chapel Hill: University of North Carolina Press, 1981.

Elkins, Stanley, and Eric McKitrick. "A Meaning for Turner's Frontier." *Political Science Quarterly* 69 (September 1954): 321–49 and (December 1954): 565–602.

Elton, C.S. *The Ecology of Invasions by Animals and Plants.* London: Methuen, 1958.

Emmanuel, Arghiri. *Unequal Exchange: A Study of the Imperialism of Trade.* Translated by Brian Pearce. New York: Monthly Review Press, 1972. Originally published 1969.

Emmison, F.G. *Elizabethan Life: Disorder.* Chelmsford: Essex County Council, 1970.

Engerman, Stanley L. "Agriculture as Business: The Southern Context." In *Business in the New South: A Historical Perspective*, pp. 17–26. Edited by Fred Bateman. Sewanee, Tenn.: The University Press, The University of the South, 1981.

———. "The Effects of Slavery Upon the Southern Economy: A Review of the Recent Debate." *Explorations in Entrepreneurial History.* 2d series, 4 (Winter 1967): 71–97.

———. "A Reconsideration of Southern Economic Growth, 1770–1860." *Agricultural History* 49 (April 1975): 343–61.

———. "Some Economic and Demographic Comparisons of Slavery in the United States and the British West Indies." *Economic History Review.* 2d series, 29 (1976): 258–75.

———. "Some Economic Factors in Southern Backwardness in the Nineteenth Century." In *Essays in Regional Economics*, pp. 279–306. Edited by John F. Kain and John R. Meyer. Cambridge: Harvard University Press, 1971.

Engerman, Stanley L., and Robert E. Gallman. "U.S. Economic Growth, 1783–1860." *Research in Economic History* 8 (1983): 1–46.

Ernst, Joseph A. "Caught in a 'Seamless Web': Economic History as 'Getting and Spending.'" *Reviews in American History* 14 (June 1986): 190–94.

Ernst, Joseph A., and H. Roy Merrens. "'Camden's turrets pierce the skies!': The Urban Process in the Southern Colonies during the Eighteenth Century." *William and Mary Quarterly.* 3d series, 30 (October 1973): 549–74.

Evans, Peter, Deitrich Rueschemeyer, and Theda Skocpol, eds., *Bringing the State Back In.* New York: Cambridge University Press, 1985.

Eversley, D.E.C. "Exploitation of Anglican Parish Registers by Aggregative Analysis." In *An Introduction to English Historical Demography: From the Sixteenth to the Nineteenth Century*, pp. 44–95. Edited by E.A. Wrigley. New York: Basic Books, 1966.

Eyre, S.R. *Vegetation and Soils: A World Picture.* Chicago: Aldine, 1963.

Faccini, Luigi. *L'economia risicola lombarda dagli inizi del XVIII secolo all' Unità*. Milan: SugarCo., 1976.

Fagg, Daniel W., Jr. "St. Giles' Seigniory: The Earl of Shaftesbury's Carolina Plantation." *South Carolina Historical Magazine* 71 (April 1970): 117–23.

Farley, M. Foster. *An Account of the History of Stranger's Fever in Charleston, 1699–1876*. Washington, D.C.: University Press of America, 1978.

———. "The Mighty Monarch of the South: Yellow Fever in Charleston and Savannah." *Georgia Review* 27 (Spring 1973): 56–70.

Fasseur, C. "The Cultivation System and Its Impact on the Dutch Colonial Economy and the Indigenous Society in Nineteenth-Century Java." In *Two Colonial Empires: Comparative Essays on the History of India and Indonesia in the Nineteenth Century*, pp. 137–54. Edited by C.A. Bayly and D.H.A. Kolff. Dordrecht, The Netherlands: Martinus Nijhoff, 1986.

Faust, Drew Gilpin. *James Henry Hammond and the Old South: A Design for Mastery*. Baton Rouge: Louisiana State University Press, 1982.

Federal Writers' Project. *South Carolina Folk Tales: Stories of Animals and Supernatural Beings*. Bulletin of University of South Carolina. Columbia, 1941.

Felsenfeld, Oscar. *The Epidemiology of Tropical Diseases*. Springfield, Ill.: Charles C. Thomas, 1966.

Fields, Gary S. *Poverty, Inequality, and Development*. New York: Cambridge University Press, 1980.

Fields, Mamie Garvin with Karen Fields. *Lemon Swamp and Other Places: A Carolina Memoir*. New York: The Free Press, 1983.

Fishlow, Albert. "The American Common School Revival: Fact or Fancy?" In *Industrialization in Two Systems: Essays in Honor of Alexander Gerschenkron*, pp. 40–67. Edited by Henry Rosovsky. New York: Wiley, 1966.

———. *American Railroads and the Transformation of the Ante-Bellum Economy*. Cambridge: Harvard University Press, 1965.

Fleisig, Heywood. "Slavery, the Supply of Agricultural Labor, and the Industrialization of the South." *Journal of Economic History* 36 (September 1976): 572–97.

Floud, Roderick. *An Introduction to Quantitative Methods for Historians*. 2d edition. London: Methuen, 1979.

Fogel, Robert William, and Stanley L. Engerman. *Time on the Cross: The Economics of American Negro Slavery*. 2 vols. Boston: Little, Brown, 1974.

Fogel, Robert W., Stanley L. Engerman, and James Trussell. "Exploring the Uses of Data on Height." *Social Science History* 6 (Fall 1982): 401–21.

Fogel, Robert W., Stanley Engerman, *et al*. "The Economics of Mortality in North America, 1650–1910: A Description of a Research Project." *Historical Methods* 11 (Spring 1978): 75–108.

Fogel, Robert W., *et al*. "Secular Changes in American and British Stature and Nutrition." In *Hunger and History: The Impact of Changing Food Production and Consumption Patterns on Society*, pp. 247–83. Edited by Robert I. Rotberg and Theodore K. Rabb. New York: Cambridge University Press, 1983.

Fonaroff, L. Schuyler. "Did Barbados Import its Malaria Epidemic?" *Journal of the Barbados Museum and Historical Society* 34 (March 1973): 122–30.

Foner, Eric. *Nothing But Freedom: Emancipation and Its Legacy*. Baton Rouge: Louisiana State University Press, 1983.

Forbes, Thomas R. "Births and Deaths in a London Parish: The Record from the Registers,

1654–1693 and 1729–1743." *Bulletin of the History of Medicine* 55 (Fall 1981): 371–91.

Ford, Lacy K. *The Origins of Southern Radicalism*. New York: Oxford University Press, forthcoming.

Forman, Henry Chandlee. *The Architecture of the Old South: The Medieval Style, 1585–1850*. Cambridge: Harvard University Press, 1948.

Fox-Genovese, Elizabeth. *The Origins of Physiocracy: Economic Revolution and Social Order in Eighteenth-Century France*. Ithaca: Cornell University Press, 1976.

Frady, Marshall. "The Charleston Cold-Warrior from Hell-Hole Swamp." In Frady, *Southerners: A Journalist's Odyssey*, pp. 77–101. New York: New American Library, 1980.

Frank, André Gunder. *World Accumulation 1492–1789*. New York: Monthly Review Press, 1978.

Fraser, Walter J., Jr. "The City Elite, 'Disorder,' and the Poor Children of Pre-Revolutionary Charleston." *South Carolina Historical Magazine* 84 (July 1983): 167–79.

———. "Controlling the Poor in Colonial Charles Town." *The Proceedings of the South Carolina Historical Association, 1980* (1982): 13–30.

Freehling, William W. "The Founding Fathers and Slavery." *American Historical Review* 77 (February 1972): 81–93.

———. *Prelude to Civil War: The Nullification Controversy in South Carolina, 1816–1836*. New York: Harper & Row, 1965.

French, Christopher J. "Productivity in the Atlantic Shipping Industry: A Quantitative Survey." *Journal of Interdisciplinary History* 17 (Winter 1987): 613–38.

Friedmann, Karen J. "Victualling Colonial Boston." *Agricultural History* 47 (July 1973): 189–205.

Fritts, Harold C., G. Robert Lofgren, and Geoffrey A. Gordon. "Past Climate Reconstructed from Tree Rings." *Journal of Interdisciplinary History* 10 (Spring 1980): 773–93.

Furniss, Edgar S. *The Position of the Laborer in a System of Nationalism: A Study in the Labor Theories of the Later English Mercantilists*. Boston: Houghton Mifflin, 1920.

Furnivall, J.S. *An Introduction to the Political Economy of Burma*. 3d ed. Rangoon: Peoples' Literature Committee and House, 1957.

———. *Netherlands India: A Study of Plural Economy*. New York: Macmillan, 1944.

Galenson, David W. *Traders, Planters, and Slaves: Market Behavior in Early English America*. New York: Cambridge University Press, 1986.

———. "White Servitude and the Growth of Black Slavery in Colonial America." *Journal of Economic History* 41 (March 1981): 39–49.

———. *White Servitude in Colonial America: An Economic Analysis*. New York: Cambridge University Press, 1982.

Galenson, David W., and Russell R. Menard. "Approaches to the Analysis of Economic Growth in Colonial British America." *Historical Methods* 13 (Winter 1980): 3–18.

Gallion, Arthur B. and Simon Eisner. *The Urban Pattern: City Planning and Design*. 3d ed. New York: Van Nostrand, 1975.

Gallman, James M. "Mortality Among White Males: Colonial North Carolina." *Social Science History* 4 (Summer 1980): 295–316.

Gallman, Robert E. "Economic Growth." In *Encyclopedia of American Economic History: Studies of the Principal Movements and Ideas*, 1: 133–50. Edited by Glenn Porter. 3 vols. New York: Charles Scribner's Sons, 1980.

———. "Slavery and Southern Economic Growth." *Southern Economic Journal* 45 (April 1979): 1007–22.

Gallman, Robert E. and Ralph V. Anderson. "Slaves as Fixed Capital: Slave Labor and Southern Economic Development." *Journal of American History* 64 (June 1977): 24–46.

Gandee, Lee R. "Haunted Houses in South Carolina . . . ." *Fate* 14 (April 1961): 32–39.

Gannon, Michael V. *The Cross in the Sand: The Early Catholic Church in Florida, 1513–1879*. Gainesville: University of Florida Press, 1965.

García Márquez, Gabriel. *The Autumn of the Patriarch*. Translated by Gregory Rabassa. New York: Harper & Row, 1976. Originally published 1975.

Gateway to Historic Charleston.

Gayle, Charles J. "The Nature and Volume of Exports from Charleston, 1724–1774." *The Proceedings of the South Carolina Historical Association, 1937* (1937): 25–33.

Geertz, Clifford. *Agricultural Involution: The Process of Ecological Change in Indonesia*. Berkeley: University of California Press, 1971. Originally published 1963.

Geiger, Maynard J. *The Franciscan Conquest of Florida (1573–1618)*. Washington, D.C.: Catholic University of America, 1937.

General Soil Map, South Carolina. Soil Map 48. Clemson: South Carolina Agricultural Experiment Station, 1979.

Genovese, Eugene D. *The Political Economy of Slavery: Studies in the Economy and Society of the Slave South*. New York: Pantheon, 1965.

———. *The World the Slaveholders Made: Two Essays in Interpretation*. New York: Random House, 1969.

Genovese, Eugene D., and Elizabeth Fox-Genovese. *Fruits of Merchant Capital: Slavery and Bourgeois Property in the Rise and Expansion of Capitalism*. New York: Oxford University Press, 1983.

———. "The Slave Economies in Political Perspective." *Journal of American History* 66 (June 1979): 7–23.

George, C.H. "The Origins of Capitalism: A Marxist Epitome & A Critique of Immanuel Wallerstein's Modern World-System." *Marxist Perspectives* 3 (Summer 1980): 70–100.

George, Wilma B. *Animal Geography*. London: Heinemann, 1962.

Georgia Writers' Project, Savannah Unit, Works Projects Administration. *Drums and Shadows: Survival Studies Among the Georgia Coastal Negroes*. Athens: University of Georgia Press, 1986. Originally published 1940.

Gerschenkron, Alexander. *Europe in the Russian Mirror: Four Lectures in Economic History*. Cambridge: Cambridge University Press, 1970.

Gerlach, Arch C., ed. *The National Atlas of the United States*. Washington, D.C.: U.S. Department of the Interior, Geological Survey, 1970.

Gille, H. "The Demographic History of the Northern European Countries in the Eighteenth Century." *Population Studies* 3 (June 1949): 3–65.

Glass, D.V. "Notes on the Demography of London at the End of the Seventeenth Century." *Daedalus* 97 (Spring 1968): 581–92.

Glassie, Henry. *Pattern in the Material Folk Culture of the Eastern United States*. Philadelphia: University of Pennsylvania Press, 1968.

Gleason, Henry A., and Arthur Cronquist. *The Natural Geography of Plants*. New York: Columbia University Press, 1964.

Goldfarb, Stephen. "Laws Governing the Incorporation of Manufacturing Companies Passed by Southern Legislatures Before the Civil War." *Southern Studies* 24 (Winter 1985): 407–16.

————. "A Note on Limits to the Growth of the Cotton-Textile Industry in the Old South." *Journal of Southern History* 48 (November 1982): 545–58.

Goldman, Albert. "Charleston! Charleston!" *Esquire* 87 (June 1977): 110–13, 154–56.

Gorn, Elliott J. "Black Spirits: The Ghostlore of Afro-American Slaves." *American Quarterly* 36 (Fall 1984): 549–65.

Gough, J.W. *John Locke's Political Philosophy: Eight Studies.* 2d ed. Oxford: Clarendon Press, 1973. Originally published 1950.

Gould, Stephen Jay. "Sticking Up for Marsupials." In Gould, *The Panda's Thumb: More Reflections in Natural History*, pp. 289–95. New York: W.W. Norton, 1982.

Graham, Robert E., Jr. *Personal Income in South Carolina by Type, Source, and Geographical Areas, 1929–1969.* Essays in Economics, No. 24. Columbia: Bureau of Business and Economic Research, College of Business Administration, University of South Carolina, 1971.

Grampp, William D. "The Liberal Elements in English Mercantilism." *Quarterly Journal of Economics* 66 (November 1952): 465–501.

Gray, Lewis C. *History of Agriculture in the Southern United States to 1860.* 2 vols. Gloucester, Mass.: Peter Smith, 1958. Originally published 1933.

Gray, Ralph, and Betty Wood. "The Transition from Indentured to Involuntary Servitude in Colonial Georgia." *Explorations in Economic History.* 2d series, 13 (October 1976): 353–70.

Graydon, Nell S. *Eliza of Wappoo: A Tale of Indigo.* Columbia: The R.L. Bryan Co., 1967.

————. comp. *South Carolina Ghost Tales.* Beaufort: Beaufort Book Shop, 1969.

Greene, Evarts B., and Virginia D. Harrington. *American Population Before the Federal Census of 1790.* New York: Columbia University Press, 1932.

Greene, Jack P. "Colonial South Carolina and the Caribbean Connection." *South Carolina Historical Magazine* 88 (October 1987): 192-210.

————. "Introduction." In Greene, ed., *Great Britain and the American Colonies, 1606–1763*, pp. xi–xlvii. Columbia: University of South Carolina Press, 1970.

Greven, Philip J., Jr. *Four Generations: Population, Land, and Family in Colonial Andover, Massachusetts.* Ithaca: Cornell University Press, 1970.

Grew, Raymond. "More on Modernization." *Journal of Social History* 14 (Winter 1980): 179–87.

Griffin, James B. "Eastern North American Archaeology: A Summary." *Science* 156 (April 14, 1967): 175–91.

Grist, D.H. *Rice.* 3d ed. London: Longmans, Green, 1959.

Guerra, Francisco. "The Influence of Disease on Race, Logistics and Colonization in the Antilles." *Journal of Tropical Medicine and Hygiene* 69 (February 1966): 23–35.

Guignard, Buck. *The Treasure of Peyre Gaillard.* Arranged by John Bennett. New York: The Century Company, 1906.

Gusfield, David. "Tradition and Modernity: Misplaced Polarities in the Study of Social Change." *American Journal of Sociology* 72 (January 1967): 351–62.

Gutkind, E.A. *International History of City Development.* 8 vols. New York: The Free Press, 1964–72.

Hahn, Steven. *The Roots of Southern Populism: Yeoman Farmers and the Transformation of the Georgia Upcountry, 1850–1890.* New York: Oxford University Press, 1983.

Hahn, Steven, and Jonathan Prude, eds. *The Countryside in the Age of Capitalist Transformation: Essays in the Social History of Rural America.* Chapel Hill: University of North Carolina Press, 1985.

Haley, K.H.D. *The First Earl of Shaftesbury*. Oxford: Clarendon Press, 1968.

Hall, Edward T. *The Hidden Dimension*. Garden City, N.Y.: Doubleday, 1966.

Hall, Michael G. *Edward Randolph and the American Colonies, 1676–1703*. Chapel Hill: University of North Carolina Press, 1960.

Harlow, Vincent T. *A History of Barbados 1625–1685*. Oxford: Clarendon Press, 1926.

Harper, Lawrence A. *The English Navigation Laws: A Seventeenth-Century Experiment in Social Engineering*. New York: Columbia University Press, 1939.

Harris, Marshall. *Origin of the Land Tenure System in the United States*. Ames: Iowa State College Press, 1953.

Harris, Seymour, ed. *American Economic History*. New York: McGraw-Hill, 1961.

Haywood, C. Robert. "Mercantilism and South Carolina Agriculture, 1700–1763." *South Carolina Historical Magazine* 60 (January 1959): 15–27.

Heaton, Herbert. "Heckscher on Mercantilism." *Journal of Political Economy* 45 (June 1937): 370–93.

Heckscher, Eli F. *Mercantilism*. Translated by Mendel Shapiro. 2 vols. London: Allen & Unwin, 1935. Originally published 1931.

Hemming, John. *Red Gold: The Conquest of the Brazilian Indians*. London: Macmillan, 1978.

Henretta, James A. "Economic Development and Social Structure in Colonial Boston." *William and Mary Quarterly*. 3d series, 22 (January 1965): 75–92.

———. "Families and Farms: *Mentalité* in Pre-Industrial America." *William and Mary Quarterly*. 3d series, 35 (January 1978): 3–32.

Heyward, Dubose. "Charleston: Where Mellow Past and Present Meet." *The National Geographic Magazine* 75 (March 1939): 273–312.

Heyward, Dubose, and Hervey Allen. *Carolina Chansons: Legends of the Low Country*. New York: Macmillan, 1922.

Heyward, Duncan Clinch. *Seed from Madagascar*. Chapel Hill: University of North Carolina Press, 1937.

Higginbotham, A. Leon. *In the Matter of Color: Race & the American Legal Process: The Colonial Period*. New York: Oxford University Press, 1978.

Higgs, Robert, and Robert McGuire. "Cotton, Corn and Risk: Another View." *Explorations in Economic History*. 2d series, 14 (April 1977): 167–82.

Higman, Barry W. *Slave Population and Economy in Jamaica, 1807–1834*. Cambridge: Cambridge University Press, 1976.

———. *Slave Populations of the British Caribbean 1807–1834*. Baltimore: Johns Hopkins University Press, 1984.

Hill, Christopher. *The Century of Revolution 1603–1714*. New York: Norton, 1966. Originally published 1961.

———. "The English Civil War Interpreted by Marx and Engels." *Science and Society* 12 (Winter 1948): 130–56.

Hilliard, Sam B. "The Tidewater Rice Plantation: An Ingenious Adaptation to Nature." *Geoscience and Man* 12 (1975): 57–66.

Hirsch, Arthur H. *The Huguenots of Colonial South Carolina*. Durham: Duke University Press, 1928.

Hirschman, Albert O. "A Generalized Linkage Approach to Development, with Special Reference to Staples." *Economic Development and Cultural Change*. 25, Supplement (1977): 67–98.

———. *The Passions and the Interests: Political Arguments for Capitalism before Its Triumph*. Princeton: Princeton University Press, 1977.

————. "The Rise and Decline of Development Economics." In Hirschman, *Essays in Trespassing: Economics to Politics and Beyond*, pp. 1–24. New York: Cambridge University Press, 1981.

————. *The Strategy of Economic Development*. New Haven: Yale University Press, 1958.

Historic Preservation Plan, Charleston, S.C. Charleston, 1974.

Hobsbawm, E.J. *The Age of Capital 1848–1875*. New York: Charles Scribner's Sons, 1975.

————. *The Age of Revolution 1789–1848*. London: Weidenfeld and Nicolson, 1962.

————. "The General Crisis of the European Economy in the 17th Century." *Past and Present*. No. 5 (May 1954): 33–53 and No. 6 (November 1954): 44–65.

Homer, Sidney. *A History of Interest Rates*. New Brunswick, N.J.: Rutgers University Press, 1963.

Hopkins, George W. "From Naval Pauper to Naval Power: The Development of Charleston's Metropolitan-Military Complex." In *The Martial Metropolis: U.S. Cities in War and Peace*, pp. 1–34. Edited by Roger W. Lotchin. New York: Praeger, 1984.

Horwitz, Morton J. *The Transformation of American Law, 1780–1860*. Cambridge: Harvard University Press, 1977.

Hosek, William R. *Macroeconomic Theory*. Homewood, Ill.: Richard D. Irwin, 1975.

Hoselitz, Bert F. *Sociological Aspects of Economic Growth*. Glencoe, Ill.: The Free Press, 1960.

Hosmer, Charles B., Jr. *Preservation Comes of Age: From Williamsburg to the National Trust, 1926–1949*. 2 vols. Charlottesville: Published for the National Trust for Historical Preservation in the United States by the University Press of Virginia, 1981.

Howe, Daniel Walker. "Virtue and Commerce in Jeffersonian America." *Reviews in American History* 9 (September 1981): 347–53.

Hudson, Charles. *The Southeastern Indians*. Knoxville: University of Tennessee Press, 1976.

Hughes, Langston. *Selected Poems*. New York: Vintage Books, 1974.

Huizinga, Johan. *The Waning of the Middle Ages: A Study of the Forms of Life, Thought and Art in France and the Netherlands in the XIVth and XVth Centuries*. Translated by F. Hopman. Garden City, N.Y.: Anchor Books, 1954. Originally published 1924.

Hunt, Charles B. *Natural Regions of the United States and Canada*. San Francisco: W.H. Freeman, 1974.

Hunter, Michael. *Science and Society in Restoration England*. Cambridge: Cambridge University Press, 1981.

Illich, Ivan. *Medical Nemesis: The Expropriation of Health*. New York: Pantheon, 1976.

Infante, G. Cabrera. *Holy Smoke*. New York: Harper & Row, 1985.

Innes, Stephen. *Labor in a New Land: Economy and Society in Seventeenth-Century Springfield*. Princeton: Princeton University Press, 1983.

Ivers, Larry E. *Colonial Forts of South Carolina 1670–1775*. Columbia: Published for the South Carolina Tricentennial Commission by the University of South Carolina Press, 1970.

Jabara, Cathy L., and Robert L. Thompson. "Agricultural Comparative Advantage under International Price Uncertainty: The Case of Senegal." *American Journal of Agricultural Economics* 62 (May 1980): 188–98.

Jackson, Steve, Bruce Russett, *et al.* "An Assessment of Empirical Research on Dependencia." *Latin American Research Review* 14 (1979): 7–28.

Jacobs, Jane. *Cities and the Wealth of Nations: Principles of Economic Life*. New York: Random House, 1984.

————. *The Death and Life of Great American Cities*. New York: Random House, 1961.

Jacobs, Wilbur E. "The Tip of an Iceberg: Pre-Columbian Indian Demography and Some Implications for Revisionism." *William and Mary Quarterly*. 3d series, 31 (January 1974): 123–32.

Jaher, Frederic C. "Antebellum Charleston: Anatomy of an Economic Failure." In *Class, Conflict, and Consensus: Antebellum Southern Community Studies*, pp. 207–31. Edited by Orville V. Burton and Robert C. McMath, Jr. Westport, Conn.: Greenwood Press, 1982.

———. *The Urban Establishment: Upper Strata in Boston, New York, Charleston, Chicago, and Los Angeles*. Urbana: University of Illinois Press, 1982.

James, Henry. *The American Scene*. Bloomington: Indiana University Press, 1968. Originally published 1907.

Jellison, Richard M. "Antecedents of the South Carolina Currency Acts of 1736 and 1746." *William and Mary Quarterly*. 3d series, 16 (October 1959): 556–67.

———. "Paper Currency in Colonial South Carolina: A Reappraisal." *South Carolina Historical Magazine* 62 (July 1961): 134–47.

Jennings, Francis. *The Invasion of America: Indians, Colonialism, and the Cant of Conquest*. Chapel Hill: University of North Carolina Press, 1975.

John, A.H. "Agricultural Productivity and Economic Growth in England, 1700–1760." *Journal of Economic History* 25 (March 1965): 19–34.

———. "Aspects of English Economic Growth in the First Half of the Eighteenth Century." *Economica* 28 (1961): 176–90.

Johnson, E.A.J. *The Organization of Space in Developing Countries*. Cambridge: Harvard University Press, 1970.

Johnson, Harry G. "Mercantilism: Past, Present and Future." *The Manchester School of Economic and Social Studies* 42 (March 1974): 1–17.

Johnson, Henry S. *Geology in South Carolina*. Miscellaneous Report 3, Division of Geology, State Development Board. Revised edition. Columbia, 1971.

Johnson, Michael P. "Planters and Patriarchy: Charleston, 1800–1860." *Journal of Southern History* 46 (February 1980): 45–72.

———. "Wealth and Class in Charleston in 1860." In *From the Old South to the New: Essays on the Transitional South*, pp. 65–80. Edited by Walter J. Fraser, Jr., and Winfred B. Moore, Jr. Westport, Conn.: Greenwood Press, 1981.

Jones, Alice Hanson. "Estimating Wealth of the Living from a Probate Sample." *Journal of Interdisciplinary History* 13 (Autumn 1982): 273–300.

———. *Wealth of a Nation To Be: The American Colonies on the Eve of the Revolution*. New York: Columbia University Press, 1980.

Jones, E.L. "Agriculture and Economic Growth in England, 1660–1750: Agricultural Change." *Journal of Economic History* 25 (March 1965): 1–18.

———. "Agriculture, 1700–80." In *The Economic History of Britain Since 1700*, 1: 66–86. 2 vols. Edited by Roderick Floud and Donald McCloskey. Cambridge: Cambridge University Press, 1981.

———. *The European Miracle: Environments, Economies and Geopolitics in the History of Europe and Asia*. 2d ed. New York: Cambridge University Press, 1987.

Jordan, Winthrop D. *White Over Black: American Attitudes Toward the Negro, 1550–1812*. Chapel Hill: University of North Carolina Press, 1968.

Journal of American Folklore 84 (January–March 1971).

Joyner, Charles W. *Down by the Riverside: A South Carolina Slave Community*. Urbana: University of Illinois Press, 1984.

———. *Folk Song in South Carolina*. Columbia: Published for the South Carolina Tricentennial Commission by the University of South Carolina Press, 1971.

Judges, A.V. "The Idea of a Mercantile State." *Transactions of the Royal Historical Society.* 4th series, 21 (1939): 41–69.

Kaldor, Nicholas. *Further Essays on Applied Economics.* New York: Holmes & Meier, 1978.

Kearl, J.R., and Clayne L. Pope. "Wealth Mobility: The Missing Element." *Journal of Interdisciplinary History* 13 (Winter 1983): 461-88.

Kelly, Kevin D. "The Independent Mode of Production." *The Review of Radical Political Economics* 11 (Spring 1979): 38–48.

Kendrew, W.G. *The Climates of the Continents.* 5th ed. Oxford: Clarendon Press, 1961.

Kenyon, J.P. *Stuart England.* The Pelican History of England. Harmondsworth, Middlesex, England: Penguin Books, 1978.

Kerridge, Eric. *The Agricultural Revolution.* London: Allen & Unwin, 1967.

Kershaw, John. *History of the Parish and Church of Saint Michael Charleston.* n.p.: privately printed, 1915.

Keynes, John Maynard. *The General Theory of Employment, Interest and Money.* New York: Harcourt, Brace, 1936.

Kicza, John E. *Colonial Entrepreneurs: Families and Business in Bourbon Mexico City.* Albuquerque: University of New Mexico Press, 1983.

Kimball, Fiske. *American Architecture.* Indianapolis: Bobbs-Merrill, 1928.

Kiple, Kenneth F. *The Caribbean Slave: A Biological History.* New York: Cambridge University Press, 1984.

Kiple, Kenneth F., and Virginia H. King. *Another Dimension to the Black Diaspora: Diet, Disease and Racism.* New York: Cambridge University Press, 1981.

––––––. "Deficiency Diseases in the Caribbean." *Journal of Interdisciplinary History* 11 (Autumn 1980): 197–215.

Kirk, Videau L.B. "Charleston Exchange." In *Three Centuries of Customs Houses,* pp. 161–65. National Society of the Colonial Dames of America publication. Hartford, Conn.: Published by the Colonial Dames of America, 1972.

Klein, Herbert S. *The Middle Passage: Comparative Studies in the Atlantic Slave Trade.* Princeton: Princeton University Press, 1978.

Klein, Herbert S., and Stanley L. Engerman. "Fertility Differentials between Slaves in the United States and the British West Indies: A Note on Lactation Practices and Their Possible Implications." *William and Mary Quarterly.* 3d series, 35 (April 1978): 357–74.

Klein, Rachel. "Ordering the Backcountry: The South Carolina Regulation." *William and Mary Quarterly.* 3d series, 38 (October 1981): 661–80.

Klingaman, David. "Food Surpluses and Deficits in the American Colonies, 1768–1772." *Journal of Economic History* 31 (September 1971): 553–79.

Kniffen, Fred. "Folk Housing: Key to Diffusion." *Annals of the Association of American Geographers* 55 (December 1965): 549–77.

Knight, Franklin W. *The African Dimension in Latin American Societies.* New York: Macmillan, 1974.

Knorr, K.E. *British Colonial Theories 1570–1850.* Toronto: University of Toronto Press, 1944.

Komlos, John, and Peter A. Coclanis. "Time in the Paddies: A Comparison of Rice Production in the Southeastern United States and Lower Burma in the Nineteenth Century." *Social Science History* 11 (Fall 1987): 343–54.

Koplan, Jeffrey P. "Slave Mortality in Nineteenth-Century Grenada." *Social Science History* 7 (Summer 1983): 311–20.

Kovacik, Charles F., and Robert E. Mason. "Changes in the South Carolina Sea Island Cotton Industry." *Southeastern Geographer* 25 (November 1985): 77–104.

Kovacik, Charles F., and Lawrence S. Rowland. "Images of Colonial Port Royal, South Carolina." *Annals of the Association of American Geographers* 63 (September 1973): 331–40.

Kriedte, Peter. *Peasants, Landlords, and Merchant Capitalists: Europe and the World Economy, 1500–1800*. Translated by V.R. Berghahn. New York: Cambridge University Press, 1983.

Kroeber, Alfred L. *Cultural and Natural Areas of Native North America*. University of California Publications in American Archeology and Ethnology, vol. 38. Berkeley: University of California Press, 1939.

Kulikoff, Allan. "The Progress of Inequality in Revolutionary Boston." *William and Mary Quarterly*. 3d series, 28 (July 1971): 375–412.

———. "A 'Prolifick' People: Black Population Growth in the Chesapeake Colonies, 1700–1790." *Southern Studies* 16 (Winter 1977): 391–428.

———. *Tobacco and Slaves: The Development of Southern Cultures in the Chesapeake, 1680–1800*. Chapel Hill: University of North Carolina Press, 1986.

Kupperman, Karen O. "Fear of Hot Climates in the Anglo-American Colonial Experience." *William and Mary Quarterly*. 3d series, 41 (April 1984): 213–40.

———. "The Puzzle of the American Climate in the Early Colonial Period." *American Historical Review* 87 (December 1982): 1262–89.

———. *Roanoke: The Abandoned Colony*. Totowa, N.J.: Rowman & Allanheld, 1984.

Kuznesof, Elizabeth Anne. "The Role of the Merchants in the Economic Development of São Paulo, 1765–1850." *Hispanic American Historical Review* 60 (November 1980): 571–92.

Kuznets, Simon. "Economic Growth and Income Inequality." *American Economic Review* 45 (March 1955): 1–28.

———. *Economic Growth of Nations: Total Output and Production Structure*. Cambridge: The Belknap Press of Harvard University, 1971.

Laclau(h), Ernesto. "Feudalism and Capitalism in Latin America." *New Left Review*. No. 67 (May–June 1971): 19–38.

Lamar, Howard, and Leonard Thompson, eds. *The Frontier in History: North America and South Africa Compared*. New Haven: Yale University Press, 1981.

Lamb, H.H. *Climate: Present, Past and Future*. 2 vols. London: Methuen, 1972–77.

Lander, Ernest M., Jr. "Charleston: Manufacturing Center of the Old South." *Journal of Southern History* 26 (August 1960): 330–51.

Landers, Holbrook. *Climate of South Carolina*. Washington, D.C.: U.S. Government Printing Office, 1970.

Landsberg, Helmut E., editor in chief. *World Survey of Climatology*. 15 vols. Amsterdam: Elsevier, 1969-.

Lane, Mills. *Architecture of the Old South: South Carolina*. Savannah: The Beehive Press, 1984.

Langton, John. "Residential Patterns in Pre-Industrial Cities: Some Case Studies from Seventeenth-Century Britain." *The Transactions of the Institute of British Geographers* 65 (July 1975): 1–27.

Lanning, John T. *The Spanish Missions of Georgia*. Chapel Hill: University of North Carolina Press, 1935.

Lapham, Samuel. *Our Walled City: Charles Town, Province of South Carolina 1677–1718*. n.p.: Published by Society of Colonial Wars in the State of South Carolina, 1970.

Laslett, Peter. "Introduction." In John Locke, *Two Treatises of Government*, pp. 15–135. Rev. ed. Edited by Laslett. New York: New American Library, 1965. Originally published 1960.

———. "John Locke, the Great Recoinage, and the Origins of the Board of Trade: 1695–1698." *William and Mary Quarterly*. 3d series, 14 (July 1957): 370–402.

Laslett, Peter, and John Harrison. "Clayworth and Cogenhoe." In *Historical Essays 1600–1750 Presented to David Ogg*, pp. 157–84. Edited by H.E. Bell and R.L. Ollard. London: Adam and Charles Black, 1963.

Latham, A.J.H., and Larry Neal. "The International Market in Rice and Wheat, 1868–1914." *Economic History Review* 36 (May 1983): 160–80.

Lauber, Almon W. *Indian Slavery in Colonial Times, within the Present Limits of the United States*. New York: Columbia University Press, 1913.

Leavell, Hugh Rodman, and E. Gurney Clark. *Preventive Medicine for the Doctor in his Community: An Epidemiologic Approach*. 3d ed. New York: McGraw-Hill, 1965.

Lebergott, Stanley. *Manpower in Economic Growth: The American Record Since 1800*. New York: McGraw-Hill, 1964.

Lee, Lawrence. *The Lower Cape Fear in Colonial Days*. Chapel Hill: University of North Carolina Press, 1965.

Lekachman, Robert. *A History of Economic Ideas*. New York: McGraw-Hill, 1959.

Leland, Isabella G. *Charleston: Crossroads of History*. Woodland Hills, Calif.: Windsor Publications, 1980.

Lemon, James T. "Early Americans and their Social Environment." *Journal of Historical Geography* 6 (April 1980): 115–31.

Lenin, V.I. *Imperialism, The Highest Stage of Capitalism: A Popular Outline*. New York: International Publishers, 1939. Originally published 1917.

Le Riche, W. Harding, and Jean Milner. *Epidemiology as Medical Ecology*. Edinburgh: Churchill Livingston, 1971.

Le Roy Ladurie, Emmanuel. *Histoire du climat depuis l'an mil*. Paris: Flammarion, 1967.

———. "Histoire et Climat." *Annales: Economies, sociétés, civilizations* 14 (1959): 3–34.

———. *Les Paysans de Languedoc*. 2 vols. Paris: S.E.V.P.E.N., 1966.

Le Roy Ladurie, Emmanuel, and Micheline Baulant. "Grape Harvests from the Fifteenth through the Nineteenth Centuries." *Journal of Interdisciplinary History* 10 (Spring 1980): 839–49.

Lesesne, J. Mauldin. *The Bank of the State of South Carolina: A General and Political History*. Columbia: University of South Carolina Press, 1970.

Letwin, William. *The Origins of Scientific Economics: English Economic Thought 1660–1776*. London: Methuen, 1963.

Lewis, Peirce F. "Common Houses, Cultural Spoor." *Landscape* 19 (January 1975): 1–22.

Liebhafsky, H.H. *The Nature of Price Theory*. Revised edition. Homewood, Ill.: Dorsey Press, 1968.

Lillywhite, Bryant. *London Coffee Houses: A Reference Book of Coffee Houses of the Seventeenth, Eighteenth, and Nineteenth Centuries*. London: Allen and Unwin, 1963.

Lindblad, J. Thomas. *Sweden's Trade with the Dutch Republic 1738–1795: A Quantitative Analysis of the Relationship Between Economic Growth and International Trade in the Eighteenth Century*. Assen, The Netherlands: Van Gorcum, 1982.

Lindert, Peter H. "An Algorithm for Probate Sampling." *Journal of Interdisciplinary History* 11 (Spring 1981): 649–68.

Lindstrom, Diane. "Domestic Trade and Regional Specialization." In *Encyclopedia of American Economic History: Studies of the Principal Movements and Ideas*, 1: 264–80.

Edited by Glenn Porter. 3 vols. New York: Charles Scribner's Sons, 1980.

———. *Economic Development in the Philadelphia Region, 1810–1850*. New York: Columbia University Press, 1978.

———. "Southern Dependence Upon Interregional Grain Supplies: A Review of the Trade Flows, 1840–1860." *Agricultural History* 44 (January 1970): 101–13.

Linsky, Arnold S. "Some Generalizations Concerning Primate Cities." *Annals of the Association of American Geographers* 55 (September 1965): 503–13.

Lipsey, Robert E. "Foreign Trade." In *American Economic Growth: An Economist's History of the United States*, pp. 548–81. Edited by Lance E. Davis *et al*. New York: Harper & Row, 1972.

Littlefield, Daniel C. *Rice and Slaves: Ethnicity and the Slave Trade in Colonial South Carolina*. Baton Rouge: Louisiana State University Press, 1981.

Lobo, Eulalia Maria Lahmeyer. "Rio de Janeiro e Charleston, S.C. as Comunidades de Mercadores no Século XVIII." *Journal of Inter-American Studies and World Affairs* 12 (October 1970): 565–82.

Lockridge, Kenneth A. "Land, Population and the Evolution of New England Society, 1630–1790." *Past and Present* 39 (April 1968): 62–80.

———. *Literacy in Colonial New England: An Enquiry into the Social Context of Literacy in the Early Modern West*. New York: W.W. Norton, 1974.

———. "The Population of Dedham, Massachusetts, 1636–1736." *Economic History Review*. 2d series, 19 (1966): 318–44.

Lopez, Robert S. *The Commercial Revolution of the Middle Ages 950–1350*. Englewood Cliffs, N.J.: Prentice-Hall, 1971.

Lounsbury, John F. and Lawrence Ogden. *Earth Science*. 2d ed. New York: Harper & Row, 1973.

Lowcountry Council of Governments. *Lowcountry Policy Framework For Regional Development*. Yemassee, S.C.: Lowcountry Council of Governments, June 1977.

Lowery, Woodbury. *The Spanish Settlements within the Present Limits of the United States 1513–1561*. New York: G.P. Putnam's Sons, 1901.

———. *The Spanish Settlements within the Present Limits of the United States: Florida, 1562–1574*. New York: G.P. Putnam's Sons, 1905.

Ludlum, David M. *Early American Winters 1604–1820*. The History of American Weather Series. Boston: American Meteorological Society, 1966.

Luraghi, Raimondo. "Wage Labor in the 'Rice Belt' of Northern Italy and Slave Labor in the American South—A First Approach." *Southern Studies* 16 (Summer 1977): 109–27.

Lutz, Robert G., Jr. *Special Study of the Marine Fishery Resources of South Carolina*. South Carolina State Planning Board, Bulletin No. 14. Columbia, 1944.

Lynch, Kevin. *The Image of the City*. Cambridge: MIT Press, 1960.

———. *A Theory of Good City Form*. Cambridge: MIT Press, 1981.

Macfarlane, Alan. *The Origins of English Individualism: The Family, Property, and Social Transition*. Oxford: Basil Blackwell, 1978.

McFarlane, W.G. *Quaint Old Charleston: America's Most Historic City*. Charleston: Legerton, 1951.

Macpherson, C.B. *The Political Theory of Possessive Individualism: Hobbes to Locke*. Oxford: Oxford University Press, 1962.

Maçzak, Antoni. "Agricultural and Livestock Production in Poland: Internal and Foreign Markets." *Journal of European Economic History* 1 (Winter 1972): 671–80.

————. "Export of Grain and the Problem of Distribution of National Income in the Years 1550–1650." *Acta Poloniae Historica*. No. 18 (1968): 75–98.

Madden, John J. *British Investment in the United States, 1860–1880*. New York: Garland Publishing, 1985.

Magnusson, Lars. "Eli Heckscher, Mercantilism, and the Favourable Balance of Trade." *Scandinavian Economic History Review* 26 (1978): 103–27.

Main, Gloria L. "The Correction of Biases in Colonial American Probate Records." *Historical Methods Newsletter* 8 (December 1974): 10–28.

————. "Inequality in Early America: The Evidence from Probate Records of Massachusetts and Maryland." *Journal of Interdisciplinary History* 7 (Spring 1977): 559–81.

————. "Probate Records as a Source for Early American History." *William and Mary Quarterly*. 3d series, 32 (January 1975): 89–99.

————. *Tobacco Colony: Life in Early Maryland, 1650–1720*. Princeton: Princeton University Press, 1982.

Main, Jackson Turner. *The Social Structure of Revolutionary America*. Princeton: Princeton University Press, 1965.

————. *Society and Economy in Colonial Connecticut*. Princeton: Princeton University Press, 1985.

Mandle, Jay R. *The Roots of Black Poverty: The Southern Plantation Economy after the Civil War*. Durham: Duke University Press, 1978.

Mansfield, Edwin. *Microeconomics: Theory/Applications*. 5th ed. New York: W.W. Norton, 1985.

Marchant, Alexander. *From Barter to Slavery: The Economic Relations of Portuguese and Indians in the Settlement of Brazil*. The Johns Hopkins University Studies in Historical and Political Science, Series 60, No. 1. Baltimore: Johns Hopkins University Press, 1942.

Martin, Margaret Rhett. *Charleston Ghosts*. Columbia: University of South Carolina Press, 1963.

Martin, Michael V., and John A. McDonald. "Food Grain Policy in the Republic of Korea: The Economic Costs of Self-Sufficiency." *Economic Development and Cultural Change* 34 (January 1986): 315–31.

McCloskey, Donald N., and Lars G. Sandberg. "From Damnation to Redemption: Judgments on the Late Victorian Entrepreneur." In McCloskey, *Enterprise and Trade in Victorian Britain*, pp. 55–72. London: Allen & Unwin, 1981.

McCoy, Drew R. *The Elusive Republic: Political Economy in Jeffersonian America*. Chapel Hill: University of North Carolina Press, 1980.

McCrady, Edward. *A Sketch of St. Philip's Church, Charleston, S.C.* Charleston: Walker, Evans & Cogswell, 1901.

McCusker, John J. "The Current Value of English Exports, 1697–1800." *William and Mary Quarterly*. 3d series, 28 (October 1971): 607–28.

————. *Money and Exchange in Europe and America, 1600–1775: A Handbook*. Chapel Hill: University of North Carolina Press, 1978.

McCusker, John J., and Russell R. Menard. *The Economy of British America, 1607–1789*. Chapel Hill: University of North Carolina Press, 1985.

McDonald, Forrest. *Alexander Hamilton: A Biography*. New York: W.W. Norton, 1979.

————. *E. Pluribus Unum: The Formation of the American Republic 1776–1790*. Boston: Houghton Mifflin, 1965.

McGrane, Reginald C. *Foreign Bondholders and American State Debts*. New York: Macmillan, 1935.

McGreevy, William Paul. "A Statistical Analysis of Primacy and Lognormality in the Size Distribution of Latin American Cities, 1750–1960." In *The Urban Development of Latin America, 1750–1920*, pp. 116–29. Edited by Richard M. Morse. Stanford: Center for Latin American Studies, Stanford University, 1971.

McNeill, William H. *Plagues and Peoples*. Garden City, N.Y.: Anchor Press/Doubleday, 1976.

Mechanic, David. *Medical Sociology: A Selective View*. New York: The Free Press, 1968.

Mehta, Surinder K. "Some Demographic and Economic Correlates of Primate Cities: A Case for Revaluation." In *The City in Newly Developing Countries: Readings in Urbanism and Urbanization*, pp. 295–308. Edited by Gerald Breese. Englewood Cliffs, N.J.: Prentice-Hall, 1969.

Meinig, D.W. *The Shaping of America: A Geographical Perspective on 500 Years of History*, vol. 1: *Atlantic America, 1492–1800*. New Haven: Yale University Press, 1986.

Mellor, John W. *The Economics of Agricultural Development*. Ithaca: Cornell University Press, 1966.

Menard, Russell R. *Economy and Society in Early Colonial Maryland*. New York: Garland Publishing, 1985.

———. "The Maryland Slave Population, 1658 to 1730: A Demographic Profile of Blacks in Four Counties." *William and Mary Quarterly*. 3d series, 32 (January 1975): 29–54.

———. "The Tobacco Industry in the Chesapeake Colonies, 1617–1730: An Interpretation." *Research in Economic History* 5 (1980): 109–77.

Mercer, Eric. *English Vernacular Houses: A Study of Traditional Farmhouses and Cottages*. London: H.M. Stationery Office, 1975.

Meriwether, Robert L. *The Expansion of South Carolina 1729–1765*. Kingsport, Tenn.: Southern Publishers, 1940.

Merrens, Harry Roy. *Colonial North Carolina in the Eighteenth Century: A Study in Historical Geography*. Chapel Hill: University of North Carolina Press, 1964.

———. "The Physical Environment of Early America: Images and Image Makers in Colonial South Carolina." *Geographical Review* 59 (October 1969): 530–56.

Merrens, Harry Roy, and George D. Terry. "Dying in Paradise: Malaria, Mortality, and the Perceptual Environment in Colonial South Carolina." *Journal of Southern History* 50 (November 1984): 533–50.

Merrill, Michael. "Cash Is Good to Eat: Self-Sufficiency and Exchange in the Rural Economy of the United States." *Radical History Review* 3 (Winter 1977): 42–71.

Métraux, Alfred. *The History of the Incas*. Translated by George Ordish. New York: Random House, 1969. Originally published 1961.

Metzer, Jacob. "Rational Management, Modern Business Practices, and Economies of Scale in the Ante-Bellum Southern Plantations." *Explorations in Economic History*. 2d series, 12 (April 1975): 123–50.

Meyer-Baer, Kathy. *Music of the Spheres and the Dance of Death: Studies in Musical Iconology*. Princeton: Princeton University Press, 1970.

Milling, Chapman J. *Red Carolinians*. Chapel Hill: University of North Carolina Press, 1940.

Milosz, Czeslaw. *Native Realm: A Search for Self-Definition*. Translated by Catherine S. Leach. Garden City, N.Y.: Doubleday, 1968.

Minchinton, Walter E. "Introduction." In *Mercantilism: System or Expediency?*, pp. vii–xiii. Problems in European Civilization Series. Lexington, Mass.: D.C. Heath, 1969.

Mintz, Sidney W. *Sweetness and Power: The Place of Sugar in Modern History*. New York: Viking, 1985.

Mitchell, Robert D. *Commercialism and Frontier: Perspectives on the Early Shenandoah Valley*. Charlottesville: University Press of Virginia, 1977.

Molen, Patricia A. "Population and Social Patterns in Barbados in the Early Eighteenth Century." *William and Mary Quarterly*. 3d series, 28 (April 1971): 287–300.

Moller, Herbert. "Sex Composition and Correlated Culture Patterns of Colonial America." *William and Mary Quarterly*. 3d series, 2 (April 1945): 113–53.

Moore, Jamie W. "The Lowcountry in Economic Transition: Charleston Since 1865." *South Carolina Historical Magazine* 80 (April 1979): 156–71.

Moore, John Hammond. "Charleston in World War I: Seeds of Change." *South Carolina Historical Magazine* 86 (January 1985): 39–49.

Morgan, Edmund S. *American Slavery, American Freedom: The Ordeal of Colonial Virginia*. New York: W.W. Norton, 1975.

Morgan, Philip D. "Black Life in Eighteenth-Century Charleston." *Perspectives in American History*. New series, 1 (1984): 187–232.

———. "The Ownership of Property by Slaves in the Mid-Nineteenth-Century Low Country." *Journal of Southern History* 49 (August 1983): 399–420.

———. Review of *Rice and Slaves*, by Daniel C. Littlefield. *William and Mary Quarterly*. 3d series, 39 (October 1982): 709–12.

———. "Work and Culture: The Task System and the World of Lowcountry Blacks, 1700 to 1880." *William and Mary Quarterly*. 3d series, 39 (October 1982): 563–99.

Morgan, Theodore. *Economic Development: Concept and Strategy*. New York: Harper & Row, 1975.

Mousnier, Roland. *Les XVIᵉ et XVIIᵉ Siècles: Les progrès de la civilisation européenne et le déclin de l'Orient*. Tome IV: *Histoire Générale des Civilisations*. Edited by Maurice Crouzet. Paris: Presses Universitaires de France, 1954.

———. *Peasant Uprisings in Seventeenth-Century France, Russia, and China*. Translated by Brian Pearce. New York: Harper & Row, 1970.

Mumford, Lewis. *The Culture of Cities*. New York: Harcourt, Brace, 1938.

Mutch, Michael E. "Yeoman and Merchant in Pre-Industrial America: Eighteenth Century Massachusetts as a Case Study." *Societas* 7 (Autumn 1977): 279–302.

Nadelhaft. Jerome J. *The Disorders of War: The Revolution in South Carolina*. Orono: University of Maine at Orono Press, 1981.

Naipaul, V.S. *The Loss of El Dorado: A History*. Harmondsworth, Middlesex, England: Penguin Books, 1973. Originally published 1969.

———. *The Middle Passage: Impressions of Five Societies—British, French & Dutch—in the West Indies & South America*. New York: Random House, 1981. Originally published 1962.

Nash, Gary. "Up from the Bottom in Franklin's Philadelphia." *Past and Present* 77 (November 1977): 57–83.

———. *The Urban Crucible: Social Change, Political Consciousness, and the Origins of the American Revolution*. Cambridge: Harvard University Press, 1979.

———. "Urban Wealth and Poverty in Pre-Revolutionary America." *Journal of Interdisciplinary History* 6 (Spring 1976): 545–84.

Nelson, Howard, J. "Walled Cities in the United States." *Annals of the Association of American Geographers* 51 (March 1961): 1–22.

Neuffer, Claude, and Irene Neuffer. *Correct Mispronunciations of Some South Carolina Names*. Columbia: University of South Carolina Press, 1983.

Newbigin, Marion I. *Plant and Animal Geography*. London: Methuen, 1936.

Newby, Idus A. *Black Carolinians: A History of Blacks in South Carolina from 1895 to 1968*. Columbia: University of South Carolina Press, 1973.

Niemi, Albert W., Jr. "Structural Shifts in Southern Manufacturing, 1849–1899." *Business History Review* 45 (Spring 1971): 79–84.

Noble, Allen G. *Wood, Brick, and Stone: The North American Settlement Landscape*. 2 vols. Amherst: University of Massachusetts Press, 1984.

North, Douglass C. "Agriculture and Regional Economic Growth." *Journal of Farm Economics* 41 (December 1959): 943–51.

———. *The Economic Growth of the United States 1790–1860*. Englewood Cliffs, N.J.: Prentice-Hall, 1961.

———. "Location Theory and Regional Economic Growth." *Journal of Political Economy* 63 (June 1955): 243–58.

———. "Ocean Freight Rates and Economic Development 1750–1913." *Journal of Economic History* 18 (December 1958): 537–55.

———. "Sources of Productivity Change in Ocean Shipping, 1600–1850." *Journal of Political Economy* 76 (September–October 1968): 953–70.

North, Douglass C., and Robert Paul Thomas. "An Economic Theory of the Growth of the Western World." *Economic History Review*. 2d series, 23 (1970): 1–17.

———. *The Rise of the Western World: A New Economic History*. Cambridge: Cambridge University Press, 1973.

Norton, Susan L. "Population Growth in Colonial America: A Study of Ipswich, Massachusetts." *Population Studies* 25 (November 1971): 433–52.

Nusteling, H.P.H. *De Rijnvaart in Het Tijdperk Van Stoom en Steenkool 1831–1914*. Amsterdam: Holland Universiteits Pers, 1974.

Nuttonson, M.Y. *Global Agroclimatic Analogues for the Rice Regions of the Continental United States*. Washington, D.C.: American Institute of Crop Ecology, 1965.

———. *Rice Culture and Rice-Climate Relationships with Special Reference to the United States Rice Areas and their Latitudinal and Thermal Analogues in Other Countries*. Washington, D.C.: American Institute of Crop Ecology, 1965.

Oakes, James. *The Ruling Race: A History of American Slaveholders*. New York: Knopf, 1982.

O'Brien, Michael, and David Moltke-Hansen, eds. *Intellectual Life in Antebellum Charleston*. Knoxville: University of Tennessee Press, 1986.

Ochenkowski, J.P. "The Origins of Nullification in South Carolina." *South Carolina Historical Magazine* 83 (April 1982): 121–53.

O'Connor, James. "A Note on Independent Commodity Production and Petty Capitalism." *Monthly Review* 28 (May 1976): 60–63.

———. Review of *The Twisted Dream*, by Douglas F. Dowd. *Monthly Review* 26 (March 1975): 41–54.

Ohlin, Bertil. *Interregional and International Trade*. Cambridge: Harvard University Press, 1933.

Ormrod, David. "English Re-Exports and the Dutch Staplemarket in the Eighteenth Century." In *Enterprise and History: Essays in Honor of Charles Wilson*, pp. 89–115. Edited by D.C. Coleman and Peter Mathias. Cambridge: Cambridge University Press, 1984.

Otto, John S. "Livestock-Raising in Early South Carolina, 1670-1700: Prelude to the Rice Plantation Economy." *Agricultural History* 61 (Fall 1987): 13-24.

————. "The Origins of Cattle-Ranching in Colonial South Carolina, 1670–1715." *South Carolina Historical Magazine* 87 (April 1986): 117–24.

Owen, Norman G. *Prosperity without Progress: Manila Hemp and Material Life in the Colonial Philippines.* Berkeley: University of California Press, 1984.

Padgug, Robert A. "Problems in the Theory of Slavery and Slave Society." *Science and Society* 40 (Spring 1976): 3–27.

Palmer, R.R. *The Age of the Democratic Revolution: A Political History of Europe and America, 1760–1800.* 2 vols. Princeton: Princeton University Press, 1959.

Parker, Geoffrey. "Homage to Braudel." *London Review of Books* 2 (4 September to 17 September 1980): 8–9.

Parker, William N. "Slavery and Southern Economic Development: An Hypothesis and Some Evidence." *Agricultural History* 44 (January 1970): 115–25.

Parry, Geraint. *John Locke.* Political Thinkers Series. London: Allen & Unwin, 1978.

Parsons, Talcott. *The Social System.* Glencoe, Ill.: The Free Press, 1951.

Patterson, H. Orlando. *The Sociology of Slavery: An Analysis of the Origins, Development and Structure of Negro Slave Society in Jamaica.* Rutherford, N.J.: Fairleigh Dickinson University Press, 1969. Originally published 1967.

Paukert, Felix. "Income Distribution at Different Levels of Development: A Survey of Evidence." *International Labour Review* 108 (August–September 1973): 97–125.

Pease, Jane H., and William H. Pease. "Social Structure and the Potential for Urban Change: Boston and Charleston in the 1830s." *Journal of Urban History* 8 (February 1982): 171–95.

————. *The Web of Progress: Private Values and Public Styles in Boston and Charleston, 1828–1843.* New York: Oxford University Press, 1985.

Pérez, Louis A., Jr. "Aspects of Underdevelopment: Tourism in the West Indies." *Science and Society* 37 (Winter 1973–74): 473–80.

Perkins, Edwin J. *The Economy of Colonial America.* New York: Columbia University Press, 1980.

Perry, Percival. "The Naval-Stores Industry in the Old South, 1790–1860." *Journal of Southern History* 34 (November 1968): 509–26.

Petty, Julian J. *The Growth and Distribution of Population in South Carolina.* South Carolina State Planning Board, Bulletin No. 11. Columbia: South Carolina State Council For Defense, Industrial Development Committee, 1943.

Phillips, Edward Hake. "The Gulf Coast Rice Industry." *Agricultural History* 25 (April 1951): 91–96.

————. "The Historical Significance of the Tariff on Rice." *Agricultural History* 26 (July 1952): 89–92.

Phillips, Ulrich B. *American Negro Slavery . . .* Baton Rouge: Louisiana State University Press, 1966. Originally published 1918.

————. "The Economic Cost of Slaveholding in the Cotton Belt." *Political Science Quarterly* 20 (June 1905): 257–75.

————. *A History of Transportation in the Eastern Cotton Belt to 1860.* New York: Columbia University Press, 1908.

————. *The Slave Economy of the Old South: Selected Essays in Economic and Social History.* Edited by Eugene D. Genovese. Baton Rouge: Louisiana State University Press, 1968.

————. "The Slave Labor Problem in the Charleston District." *Political Science Quarterly* 22 (September 1907): 416–39.

————. "The South Carolina Federalists." *American Historical Review* 14 (April 1909): 529–43 and (July 1909): 731–43, 776–90.

Pielou, E.C. *Biogeography*. New York: Wiley, 1979.

Pierson, William H., Jr. *American Buildings and Their Architects*. 2 vols. Garden City, N.Y.: Doubleday, 1970.

Pirenne, Henri. *Medieval Cities, Their Origins and the Revival of Trade*. Translated by Frank D. Halsey. Princeton: Princeton University Press, 1925.

————. "The Stages in the Social History of Capitalism." *American Historical Review* 19 (April 1914): 494–515.

Pitman, Frank Wesley. *The Development of the British West Indies 1700–1763*. New Haven: Yale University Press, 1917.

Pocock, J.G.A. "Machiavelli, Harrington, and English Political Ideologies in the Eighteenth Century." *William and Mary Quarterly*. 3d series, 22 (October 1965): 549–83.

————. *The Machiavellian Moment: Florentine Political Thought and the Atlantic Republican Tradition*. Princeton: Princeton University Press, 1975.

Polunin, Nicholas. *Introduction to Plant Geography and Some Related Sciences*. New York: McGraw-Hill, 1960.

Posthumus, N.W. *Inquiry into the History of Prices in Holland*. 2 vols. Leiden: E.J. Brill, 1946–1964.

Potter, Eloise F., James F. Parnell, and Robert P. Teulings. *Birds of the Carolinas*. Chapel Hill: University of North Carolina Press, 1980.

Potter, J. "Demographic Development and Family Structure." In *Colonial British America: Essays in the New History of the Early Modern Era*, pp. 123–156. Edited by Jack P. Greene and J.R. Pole. Baltimore: Johns Hopkins University Press, 1984.

————. "The Growth of Population in America, 1700–1860." In *Population in History: Essays in Historical Demography*, pp. 631-88. Edited by D. V. Glass and D. E. C. Eversley. Chicago: Aldine, 1965.

Potter, R.B. "Tourism and Development: The Case of Barbados, West Indies." *Geography* 68 (January 1983): 46–50.

"Poverty and Disease in Carolina Low Country Belie the New South Boom." *New York Times*, 1 April 1977, A1, A11.

Powell, William S. *The Proprietors of Carolina*. Raleigh: Published by the Carolina Charter Tercentenary Commission, 1963.

Prado, Caio, Jr. *The Colonial Background of Modern Brazil*. Translated by Suzette Macedo. Berkeley: University of California Press, 1971.

Pratt, Parley M. *Rice: Domestic Consumption in the United States*. Austin: The Bureau of Business Research of the University of Texas, 1960.

Pred, Allan R. *The Spatial Dynamics of U.S. Urban-Industrial Growth, 1800–1914: Interpretive and Theoretical Essays*. Cambridge: MIT Press, 1966.

————. *Urban Growth and City Systems in the United States, 1840–1860*. Cambridge: Harvard University Press, 1980.

————. *Urban Growth and the Circulation of Information: The United States System of Cities, 1790–1840*. Cambridge: Harvard University Press, 1973.

Price, Jacob M. *Capital and Credit in British Overseas Trade: The View from the Chesapeake, 1700–1776*. Cambridge: Harvard University Press, 1980.

————. "Economic Function and the Growth of American Port Towns in the Eighteenth Century." *Perspectives in American History* 8 (1974): 123–86.

————. "The Transatlantic Economy." In *Colonial British America: Essays in the New History of the Early Modern Era*, pp. 18–42. Edited by Jack P. Greene and J.R. Pole. Baltimore: Johns Hopkins University Press, 1984.

Pruitt, Bettye Hobbs. "Self-Sufficiency and the Agricultural Economy of Eighteenth-Century Massachusetts." *William and Mary Quarterly.* 3d series, 41 (July 1984): 333–64.

Puckrein, Gary A. *Little England: Plantation Society and Anglo-Barbadian Politics, 1627–1700.* New York: New York University Press, 1984.

Quattlebaum, Paul. *The Land Called Chicora: The Carolinas under Spanish Rule with French Intrusions 1520–1670.* Gainesville: University of Florida Press, 1956.

Quinn, Arthur Hobson. *Edgar Allan Poe: A Critical Biography.* New York: Cooper Square Publishers, 1969. Originally published 1941.

Quinn, David B. *North America From Earliest Discovery To First Settlements: The Norse Voyages to 1612.* The New American Nation Series. New York: Harper & Row, 1977.

———. *Set Fair for Roanoke: Voyages and Colonies, 1584–1606.* Chapel Hill: University of North Carolina Press, 1985.

Rabb, Theodore K. *Enterprise and Empire: Merchant and Gentry Investment in the Expansion of England, 1575–1630.* Cambridge: Harvard University Press, 1967.

Radford, John P. "Social Structure and Urban Form: Charleston, 1860–1880." In *From the Old South to the New: Essays on the Transitional South,* pp. 81–91. Edited by Walter J. Fraser, Jr., and Winfred B. Moore, Jr. Westport, Conn.: Greenwood Press, 1981.

———. "Testing the Model of the Pre-Industrial City: The Case of Ante-Bellum Charleston, South Carolina." *Transactions of the Institute of British Geographers.* New series, 4 (1979): 392–410.

Ransom, Roger L. and Richard Sutch. "Growth and Welfare in the American South in the Nineteenth Century." In *Market Institutions and Economic Progress in the New South, 1865–1900,* pp. 127–53. Edited by Gary M. Walton and James F. Shepherd. New York: Academic Press, 1981.

———. *One Kind of Freedom: The Economic Consequences of Emancipation.* New York: Cambridge University Press, 1977.

Rapaczynski, Andrzej. *Nature and Politics: Liberalism in the Philosophies of Hobbes, Locke, and Rousseau.* Ithaca: Cornell University Press, 1987.

Rashid, Salim. "Economists, Economic Historians, and Mercantilism." *Scandinavian Economic History Review* 28 (1980): 1–14.

Ratchford, B.U. *American State Debts.* Durham: Duke University Press, 1941.

Ravenel, Beatrice St. Julien. *Architects of Charleston.* Charleston: Carolina Art Association, 1945.

Redfield, Robert. "The Folk Society." *American Journal of Sociology* 52 (January 1947): 292–308.

Redfield, Robert, and Milton Singer. "The Cultural Role of Cities." *Economic Development and Cultural Change* 3 (October 1954): 53–73.

Rees, Peter W. "Origins of Colonial Transportation in Mexico." *Geographical Review* 65 (July 1975): 323–34.

Reinsma, R. *Het Verval van het Cultuurstelsel.* s'Gravenhage: van Veulen, 1955.

Rembert, David H., Jr. "The Indigo of Commerce in Colonial North America." *Economic Botany* 33 (April–June 1979): 128–34.

Reps, John W. "$C^2 + L^2 = S^2$? Another Look at the Origins of Savannah's Town Plan." In *Forty Years of Diversity: Essays on Colonial Georgia,* pp. 101–51. Edited by Harvey H. Jackson and Phinizy Spalding. Athens: University of Georgia Press, 1984.

———. *The Making of Urban America: A History of City Planning in the United States.* Princeton: Princeton University Press, 1965.

Resnick, David. "Locke and the Rejection of the Ancient Constitution." *Political Theory* 12 (February 1984): 97–114.

Reynolds, Lloyd G. *Economic Growth in the Third World, 1850–1980.* New Haven: Yale University Press, 1985.

Rich, E.E. "Colonial Settlement and Its Labour Problems." In *The Cambridge Economic History of Europe*, vol. IV: *The Economy of Expanding Europe in the Sixteenth and Seventeenth Centuries*, pp. 302–73. Edited by E.E. Rich and C.H. Wilson. Cambridge: Cambridge University Press, 1967.

————. "The First Earl of Shaftesbury's Colonial Policy." *Transactions of the Royal Historical Society.* 5th series, 7 (1957): 47–70.

Richter, Daniel K. Review of *Their Number Become Thinned*, by Henry F. Dobyns. *William and Mary Quarterly.* 3d series, 41 (October 1984): 649–53.

Riese, Walter. *The Conception of Disease: its History, its Versions, and its Nature.* New York: The Philosophical Library, 1953.

Roa Bastos, Augusto. *I the Supreme.* Translated by Helen Lane. New York: Knopf, 1986. Originally published 1974.

Roberts, Bruce, and Nancy Roberts. *This Haunted Land.* Charlotte: McNally and Loftin, c. 1970.

Roberts, Nancy. *Ghosts of the Carolinas.* Charlotte: McNally and Loftin, 1962.

Robinson, Harry. *Biogeography.* "Aspect" Geographies series. London: Macdonald & Evans, 1972.

Robinson, Joan. *The Economics of Imperfect Competition.* 2d edition. London: Macmillan, 1969. Originally published 1933.

————. "The New Mercantilism." In Robinson, *Collected Economic Essays*, 4: 1–13. 5 vols. thus far. Oxford: Basil Blackwell, 1951–.

Rogers, George C., Jr. *Charleston in the Age of the Pinckneys.* Norman: University of Oklahoma Press, 1969.

————. *Evolution of a Federalist: William Loughton Smith of Charleston (1758–1812).* Columbia: University of South Carolina Press, 1962.

————. "The First Earl of Shaftesbury." *South Carolina Historical Magazine* 68 (April 1967): 74–78.

————. *The History of Georgetown County, South Carolina.* Columbia: University of South Carolina Press, 1970.

Rondinelli, Dennis A. "Towns and Small Cities in Developing Countries." *The Geographical Review* 73 (October 1983): 379–95.

Rondinelli, Dennis A., and Kenneth Ruddle. *Urbanization and Rural Development: A Spatial Policy For Equitable Growth.* New York: Praeger, 1978.

Rose, Willie Lee. *Rehearsal for Reconstruction: The Port Royal Experiment.* Indianapolis: Bobbs-Merrill, 1964.

Rosen, George. "Medicine as a Function of Society." In *Mainstreams of Medicine: Essays on the Social and Intellectual Context of Medical Practice*, pp. 26–38. Edited by Lester S. King. Austin: Published for the University of Texas Medical School at San Antonio by the University of Texas Press, 1971.

Rosen, Robert. *A Short History of Charleston.* San Francisco: LEXICOS, 1982.

Rosenau, Milton J., and Kenneth F. Maxcy. *Preventive Medicine and Public Health.* Edited by Philip E. Sartwell. 9th ed. New York: Appleton-Century-Crofts, 1965.

Rosenberg, Charles E. "The Therapeutic Revolution: Medicine, Meaning, and Social Change in Nineteenth-Century America." In *The Therapeutic Revolution: Essays on the*

Social History of American Medicine, pp. 3–25. Edited by Morris J. Vogel and Charles E. Rosenberg. Philadelphia: University of Pennsylvania Press, 1979.

Rosenberg, Nathan. *Technology and American Economic Growth*. New York: Harper & Row, 1972.

Rosengarten, Theodore. *Tombee: Portrait of a Cotton Planter*. New York: William Morrow, 1986.

Roth, Leland M. *A Concise History of American Architecture*. New York: Harper & Row, 1979.

Rothenberg, Winifred B. "The Market and Massachusetts Farmers, 1750–1855." *Journal of Economic History* 41 (June 1981): 283–314.

Rothstein, Morton. "The Antebellum South as a Dual Economy: A Tentative Hypothesis." *Agricultural History* 41 (October 1967): 373–82.

———. "Antebellum Wheat and Cotton Exports: A Contrast in Marketing Organization and Economic Development." *Agricultural History* 40 (April 1966): 91–100.

———. "The New South and the International Economy." *Agricultural History* 57 (October 1983): 385–402.

Rowland, Lawrence S. " 'Alone on the River': The Rise and Fall of the Savannah River Rice Plantations of St. Peter's Parish, South Carolina." *South Carolina Historical Magazine* 88 (July 1987): 121-50.

Rowse, A.L. *The Elizabethan Age*. 2 vols. New York: Macmillan/St. Martin's Press, 1951–55.

Russell-Smith, H.F. *Harrington and his Oceana: A Study of the 17th Century Utopia and Its Influence in America*. Cambridge: Cambridge University Press, 1914.

Rutman, Darrett B., and Anita H. Rutman. " 'Now-Wives and Sons-in-Law': Parental Death in a Seventeenth-Century Virginia County." In *The Chesapeake in the Seventeenth Century: Essays on Anglo-American Society*, pp. 153–82. Edited by Thad W. Tate and David L. Ammerman. Chapel Hill: University of North Carolina Press, 1979.

———. "Of Agues and Fevers: Malaria in the Early Chesapeake." *William and Mary Quarterly*. 3d series, 33 (January 1976): 31–60.

———. *A Place in Time: Middlesex County, Virginia, 1650–1750*. 2 vols. New York: W.W. Norton, 1984.

Rutman, Darrett B., Charles Wetherell, and Anita H. Rutman. "Rhythms of Life: Black and White Seasonality in the Early Chesapeake." *Journal of Interdisciplinary History* 11 (Summer 1980): 29–53.

Saalman, Howard. *Medieval Cities*. New York: George Braziller, 1968.

Samuelson, Paul A. "Illogic of Neo-Marxian Doctrine of Unequal Exchange." In *Inflation, Trade and Taxes: Essays in Honor of Alice Bourneauf*, pp. 96–107. Edited by David A. Belsley *et al*. Columbus: Ohio State University Press, 1976.

———. "International Factor-Price Equalisation Once Again." *The Economic Journal* 59 (June 1949): 181–97.

———. "International Trade and Equalisation of Factor Prices." *The Economic Journal* 58 (June 1948): 163–84.

Sauer, Carl O. *The Early Spanish Main*. Berkeley: University of California Press, 1966.

Savage, Henry, Jr. *River of the Carolinas: The Santee*. Rivers of America Series. New York: Rinehart, 1956.

Savitt, Todd L. "Filariasis in the United States." *Journal of the History of Medicine and Allied Sciences* 32 (April 1977): 140–50.

Scarborough, William K. *The Overseer: Plantation Management in the Old South*. Baton Rouge: Louisiana State University Press, 1966.

Scardaville, Michael C. "Elizabeth O'Neill Verner: The Artist as Preservationist." In *Mirror of Time: Elizabeth O'Neill Verner's Charleston*, pp. 17–25. Edited by Lynn R. Myers. Columbia: McKissick Museums of the University of South Carolina, 1983.

Schacht, Robert M. "Estimating Past Population Trends." *Annual Review of Anthropology* 10 (1981): 119–40.

Schaeffer, Robert K. "The Entelechies of Mercantilism." *Scandinavian Economic History Review* 29 (1981): 81–96.

Schafer, R. Murray. *The Tuning of the World*. New York: Knopf, 1977.

Schawacht, Jürgen Heinz. *Schiffahrt und Güterverkehr Zwischen den Häfen des Deutschen Niederrheins (Insbesondere Köln) und Rotterdam Vom Ende des 18. bis zur Mitte des 19. Jahrhunderts (1794–1850/51)*. Köln: 1973.

Schlotterbeck, John T. "The 'Social Economy' of an Upper South Community: Orange and Greene Counties, Virginia, 1815–1860." In *Class, Conflict, and Consensus: Antebellum Southern Community Studies*, pp. 3–28. Edited by Orville Vernon Burton and Robert C. McMath, Jr. Westport, Conn.: Greenwood Press, 1982.

Schofield, R.S. "Representativeness and Family Reconstitution." *Annales de Démographie Historique* (1972): 121–25.

Scholz-Babisch, Marie. *Quellen zur Geschichte des Klevischen Rheinzollwesens vom 11. bis 18. Jahrhundert*. 2 vols. Weisbaden: Franz Steiner Verlag, 1971.

Schultz, Theodore W. *The Economic Organization of Agriculture*. New York: McGraw-Hill, 1953.

———. *Investing in People: The Economics of Population Quality*. Berkeley: University of California Press, 1981.

Schumpeter, Elizabeth B. *English Overseas Trade Statistics 1697–1803*. Oxford: Clarendon Press, 1960.

Schumpeter, Joseph A. *The Theory of Economic Development: An Inquiry into Profits, Capital, Credit, Interest, and the Business Cycle*. Translated by Redvers Opie. Cambridge: Harvard University Press, 1934. Originally published 1911.

Schutz, Robert R. "On the Measurement of Income Inequality." *American Economic Review* 41 (March 1951): 107–22.

Seliger, Martin. *The Liberal Politics of John Locke*. London: Allen & Unwin, 1968.

Sellers, Leila. *Charleston Business on the Eve of the American Revolution*. Chapel Hill: University of North Carolina Press, 1934.

Severens, Kenneth. *Southern Architecture: 350 Years of Distinctive American Buildings*. New York: E.P. Dutton, 1981.

Shaffer, E.T.H. *Carolina Gardens*. Chapel Hill: University of North Carolina Press, 1939.

Shalhope, Robert E. *John Taylor of Caroline: Pastoral Republican*. Columbia: University of South Carolina Press, 1980.

———. "Toward a Republican Synthesis: The Emergence of an Understanding of Republicanism in American Historiography." *William and Mary Quarterly*. 3d series, 29 (January 1972): 49–80.

Shammas, Carole. "Constructing a Wealth Distribution from Probate Records." *Journal of Interdisciplinary History* 9 (Autumn 1978): 297–307.

———. "How Self-Sufficient Was Early America?" *Journal of Interdisciplinary History* 13 (Autumn 1982): 247–72.

Shannon, Fred A. *The Farmer's Last Frontier: Agriculture, 1860–1897*. The Economic History of the United States Series. New York: Harper & Row, 1968. Originally published 1945.

Shapiro, Barbara J. *Probability and Certainty in Seventeenth-Century England: A Study of the Relationships between Natural Science, Religion, History, Law, and Literature*. Princeton: Princeton University Press, 1983.

Sharlin, Allan. "Natural Decrease in Early Modern Cities: A Reconsideration." *Past and Present* 79 (May 1978): 126–38.

Sharpe, William, and Leonard Wallock. "From 'Great Town' to 'Nonplace Urban Realm': Reading the Modern City." In *Visions of the Modern City: Essays in History, Art, and Literature.*, pp. 7–46. Edited by William Sharpe and Leonard Wallock. New York: Heyman Center for the Humanities, Columbia University, 1983.

Sharrer, G. Terry. "Indigo in Carolina, 1671–1796." *South Carolina Historical Magazine* 72 (April 1971): 94–103.

Shepherd, James F. "Commodity Exports from the British North American Colonies to Overseas Areas, 1768–1772: Magnitudes and Patterns of Trade." *Explorations in Economic History*. 2d series, 8 (Fall 1970): 5–76.

Shepherd, James F., and Gary M. Walton. *Shipping, Maritime Trade, and the Economic Development of Colonial North America*. Cambridge: Cambridge University Press, 1972.

———. "Trade, Distribution, and Economic Growth in Colonial America." *Journal of Economic History* 32 (March 1972): 128–45.

Shepherd, James F., and Samuel H. Williamson. "The Coastal Trade of the British North American Colonies, 1768–1772." *Journal of Economic History* 32 (December 1972): 783–810.

Sheridan, Richard B. *Doctors and Slaves: A Medical and Demographic History of Slavery in the British West Indies, 1680–1834*. Cambridge: Cambridge University Press, 1985.

———. "The Domestic Economy." In *Colonial British America: Essays in the New History of the Early Modern Era*, pp. 43–85. Edited by Jack P. Greene and J.R. Pole. Baltimore: Johns Hopkins University Press, 1984.

———. *Sugar and Slavery: An Economic History of the British West Indies, 1623–1775*. Baltimore: Johns Hopkins University Press, 1974.

Shick, Tom W., and Don H. Doyle. "The South Carolina Phosphate Boom and the Stillbirth of the New South, 1867–1920." *South Carolina Historical Magazine* 86 (January 1985): 1–31.

Shortridge, James R., and Barbara G. Shortridge. "Patterns of American Rice Consumption 1955 and 1980." *The Geographical Review* 73 (October 1983): 417–29.

Simiand, François. *Les Fluctuations économique à longue période et la crise mondiale*. Paris: Feliz Alcan, 1932.

———. "Methode historique et science sociale." *Annales: Economies, sociétés, civilisations* 15 (1960): 83–119.

———. *Recherches anciennes et nouvelles sur le mouvement général des prix du 16ᵉ au 19ᵉ siècle*. Paris: Editions Doma Montchrestien, 1932.

Simkins, Francis B., and Robert H. Woody. *South Carolina During Reconstruction*. Chapel Hill: University of North Carolina Press, 1932.

Simons, Albert. "Architectural Trends in Charleston." *Antiques* 97 (April 1970): 545–55.

Simons, Albert, and Samuel Lapham, Jr. *Charleston, South Carolina*. The Octagon Library of Early American Architecture. New York: Press of the American Institute of Architects, 1927.

Simpson, George Gaylord. *The Geography of Evolution*. Philadelphia: Chilton Books, 1965.

Singer, Charles, and E. Ashworth Underwood. *A Short History of Medicine*. 2d ed. New York: Oxford University Press, 1962.

Sirmans, M. Eugene. "Charleston Two Hundred Years Ago." *The Emory University Quarterly* 19 (Fall 1963): 129–36.

————. *Colonial South Carolina: A Political History, 1663–1763*. Chapel Hill: University of North Carolina Press, 1966.

————. "The Legal Status of the Slave in South Carolina, 1670–1740." *Journal of Southern History* 28 (November 1962): 462–73.

Slicher van Bath, B.H. *The Agrarian History of Western Europe A.D. 500–1850*. Translated by Olive Ordish. London: Edward Arnold, 1963.

————. "Eighteenth-Century Agriculture on the Continent of Europe: Evolution or Revolution?" *Agricultural History* 43 (January 1969): 169–79.

Smith, Alfred Glaze. *Economic Readjustment of an Old Cotton State: South Carolina, 1820–1860*. Columbia: University of South Carolina Press, 1958.

Smith, Alice R. Huger, and D.E. Huger Smith. *The Dwelling Houses of Charleston, South Carolina*. Philadelphia: J.B. Lippincott, 1917.

Smith, Billy G. "Death and Life in a Colonial Immigrant City: A Demographic Analysis of Philadelphia." *Journal of Economic History* 37 (December 1977): 863–89.

————. "The Material Lives of Laboring Philadelphians, 1750 to 1800." *William and Mary Quarterly*. 3d series, 38 (April 1981): 163–202.

Smith, Carol A. "Modern and Premodern Urban Primacy." *Comparative Urban Research* 11 (1982): 79–96.

Smith, Daniel Blake. "Mortality and Family in the Colonial Chesapeake." *Journal of Interdisciplinary History* 8 (Winter 1978): 403–27.

Smith, Daniel Scott. "The Demographic History of Colonial New England." *Journal of Economic History* 32 (March 1972): 165–83.

————. "Underregistration and Bias in Probate Records: An Analysis of Data from Eighteenth-Century Hingham, Massachusetts." *William and Mary Quarterly*. 3d series, 32 (January 1975): 100–110.

Smith, D.E. Huger. *A Charlestonian's Recollections 1846–1913*. Charleston: Carolina Art Association, 1950.

Smith, G.E. Kidder. *A Pictorial History of Architecture in America*. 2 vols. New York: American Heritage, 1976.

Smith, Henry A.M. "Charleston—The Original Plan and the Earliest Settlers." *South Carolina Historical Magazine* 9 (January 1908): 12–27.

Smith, J.T. "The Evolution of the English Peasant House to the Late Seventeenth Century: The Evidence of Buildings." *Journal of the British Archaeological Society*. 3d series, 33 (1970): 122–47.

Smith, Julia Floyd. *Slavery and Rice Culture in Low Country Georgia, 1750–1860*. Knoxville: University of Tennessee Press, 1985.

Smith, Peter F. *The Syntax of Cities*. London: Hutchison, 1977.

Smith, Warren B. *White Servitude in Colonial South Carolina*. Columbia: University of South Carolina Press, 1961.

Snider, Delbert A. *Introduction to International Economics*. 7th edition. Homewood, Ill.: Richard D. Irwin, 1979.

Social Science History 10 (Winter 1986).

Sokoloff, Kenneth L. and Georgia C. Villaflor. "The Early Achievement of Modern Stature in America." *Social Science History* 6 (Fall 1982): 453–81.

Soltow, Lee. "Distribution of Income and Wealth." In *Encyclopedia of American Economic History*, 3: 1087–1119. Edited by Glenn Porter. 3 vols. New York: Charles Scribner's Sons, 1980.

————. *Men and Wealth in the United States, 1850–1870*. New Haven: Yale University Press, 1975.

————. "Socioeconomic Classes in South Carolina and Massachusetts in the 1790s and the Observations of John Drayton." *South Carolina Historical Magazine* 81 (October 1980): 282–305.

Sombart, Werner. *Luxury and Capitalism*. Translated by W.R. Dittmar. Ann Arbor: University of Michigan Press, 1967. Originally published 1913.

Sosin, Jack M. *English America and the Restoration Monarchy of Charles II: Transatlantic Politics, Commerce, and Kinship*. Lincoln: University of Nebraska Press, 1980.

South Carolina Land Settlement Commission. *Report, 1923*. Columbia: The State Company, 1923.

South Carolina State Budget and Control Board. *South Carolina Statistical Abstract 1979*. Columbia: South Carolina Division of Research and Statistical Services, n.d.

————. *South Carolina Statistical Abstract 1981*. Columbia: South Carolina Division of Research and Statistical Services, 1981.

————. *South Carolina Statistical Abstract 1982*. Columbia: South Carolina Division of Research and Statistical Services, 1983.

————. *South Carolina Statistical Abstract 1985*. Columbia: South Carolina Division of Research and Statistical Services, 1986.

South Carolina State Department of Parks, Recreation and Tourism. *Travel and Tourism Trends for South Carolina*. Columbia: November 1985.

South Carolina State Development Board. *Industrial Directory of South Carolina 1981*. Columbia: 1980.

————. *Industrial Directory of South Carolina 1986*. Columbia: South Carolina State Development Board, 1986.

South Carolina State Development Board, Planning and Research Division. *South Carolina Statistics, 1975*.

South Carolina State Planning Board. *The Natural Resources of South Carolina*. Bulletin No. 3, revised. Columbia: 1944.

South, Stanley. *Method and Theory in Historical Archeology*. New York: Academic Press, 1977.

Speck, W.A. "The International and Imperial Context." In *Colonial British America: Essays in the New History of the Early Modern Era*, pp. 384–407. Edited by Jack P. Greene and J.R. Pole. Baltimore: Johns Hopkins University Press, 1984.

Spengler, Joseph J. "Mercantilist and Physiocratic Growth Theory." In *Theories of Economic Growth*, pp. 3–64, 299–334. Edited by Bert F. Hoselitz, Joseph J. Spengler, *et al*. Glencoe, Ill.: The Free Press, 1960.

Spreiregen, Paul D. *Urban Design: The Architecture of Towns and Cities*. New York: McGraw-Hill, 1965.

Sprunt, Alexander, Jr., and E. Burnham Chamberlain. *South Carolina Bird Life*. Contributions from the Charleston Museum, No. 11. Columbia: University of South Carolina Press, 1949.

Stampp, Kenneth M. *The Peculiar Institution: Slavery in the Ante-Bellum South*. New York: Knopf, 1956.

Stearns, Peter N. "Modernization and Social History: Some Suggestions, and a Muted Cheer." *Journal of Social History* 14 (Winter 1980): 189–209.

Steele, Ian K. *The English Atlantic, 1675–1740: An Exploration of Communication and Community*. New York: Oxford University Press, 1986.

Stevenson, Frederick R., and Carl Feiss. "Charleston and Savannah." *Journal of the Society of Architectural Historians* 10 (December 1951): 3–9.

Stoianovich, Traian. *French Historical Method: The Annales Paradigm*. Ithaca, Cornell University Press, 1976.

Stone, Lawrence. *The Crisis of the Aristocracy 1558–1641*. Oxford: Clarendon Press, 1965.

Stoney, Samuel G. *This Is Charleston: A Survey of the Architectural Heritage of a Unique American City*, 3d revised edition. Charleston: The Carolina Art Association, 1976; originally published 1944.

Stourzh, Gerald. *Alexander Hamilton and the Idea of Republican Government*. Stanford: Stanford University Press, 1970.

Stover, John F. *The Railroads of the South, 1865–1900: A Study in Finance and Control*. Chapel Hill: University of North Carolina Press, 1955.

Strahler, Arthur N. *Introduction to Physical Geography*. New York: Wiley, 1965.

Strauss, Leo. *Natural Right and History*. Chicago: University of Chicago Press, 1953.

Strickland, John Scott. "'No More Mud Work': The Struggle for the Control of Labor and Production in Low Country South Carolina, 1863–1880." In *The Southern Enigma: Essays on Race, Class, and Folk Culture*, pp. 43–62. Edited by Walter J. Fraser, Jr., and Winfred B. Moore, Jr. Westport, Conn.: Greenwood Press, 1983.

———. "Traditional Culture and Moral Economy: Social and Economic Change in the South Carolina Low Country, 1865–1910." In *The Countryside in the Age of Capitalist Transformation: Essays in the Social History of Rural America*, pp. 141–78. Edited by Steven Hahn and Jonathan Prude. Chapel Hill: University of North Carolina Press, 1985.

Stumpf, Stuart O. "Implications of King George's War for the Charleston Mercantile Community." *South Carolina Historical Magazine* 77 (July 1976): 161–88.

Stumpf, Stuart, and Jennings B. Marshall. "Trends in Charleston's Inter-Regional Import Trade, 1735–1764." *Southern Studies* 23 (Fall 1984): 243–65.

Sullivan, Louis H. *Kindergarten Chats on Architecture, Education, and Democracy*. Edited by Claude F. Bragdon. Lawrence?, Kansas: Scarab Fraternity Press, 1934.

Suviranta, B. *The Theory of the Balance of Trade in England: A Study in Mercantilism*. New York: Augustus M. Kelley, 1967. Originally published 1923.

Swan, Dale Evans. *The Structure and Profitability of the Antebellum Rice Industry 1859*. New York: Arno Press, 1975.

Swanton, John R. *The Indians of the Southeastern United States*. Smithsonian Institution Bureau of American Ethnology, Bulletin 137. Washington, D.C.: U.S. Government Printing Office, 1946.

Sweezy, Paul. "The Transition from Feudalism to Capitalism." *Science and Society* 14 (Spring 1950): 134–57.

Taafe, Edward J., Richard L. Morrill, and Peter R. Gould. "Transport Expansion in Underdeveloped Countries: A Comparative Analysis." *Geographical Review* 53 (October 1963): 503–29.

Taylor, George Rogers. "Wholesale Commodity Prices at Charleston, South Carolina, 1732–1791." *Journal of Economic and Business History* 4 (February 1932): 356–77.

———. "Wholesale Commodity Prices at Charleston, South Carolina, 1796–1861." *Journal of Economic and Business History* 4, Supplement (August 1932): 848–76.

Temin, Peter. "The Post-Bellum Recovery of the South and the Cost of the Civil War." *Journal of Economic History* 36 (December 1976): 898–907.

Thom, Bruce G. *Coastal and Fluvial Landforms: Horry and Marion Counties, South*

Carolina. Coastal Studies Series No. 19. Baton Rouge: Louisiana State University Press, 1967.

Thomas, John P., Jr. "The Barbadians in Early South Carolina." *South Carolina Historical Magazine* 31 (April 1930): 75–92.

Thomas, Keith. *Religion and the Decline of Magic*. New York: Charles Scribner's Sons, 1971.

Thompson, E.P. "The Peculiarities of the English." In Thompson, *The Poverty of Theory and Other Essays*, pp. 245–301. New York: Monthly Review Press, 1978.

Tilly, Charles. *The Contentious French*. Cambridge: The Belknap Press of Harvard University, 1986.

Tipps, Dean C. "Modernization Theory and the Comparative Study of Societies." *Comparative Studies in Society and History* 15 (March 1973): 199–226.

Todaro, Michael P. *Economic Development in the Third World*. 3d ed. New York: Longman, 1985.

Toelken, Barre. *The Dynamics of Folklore*. Boston: Houghton Mifflin, 1979.

Topolski, Jerzy. "Economic Decline in Poland from the Sixteenth to the Eighteenth Centuries." In *Essays in European Economic History, 1500–1800*, pp. 127–42. Edited by Peter M. Earle. Oxford: Clarendon Press, 1974.

Townsend, Leah. *South Carolina Baptists, 1670–1805*. Florence, S.C.: Florence Printing Co., 1935.

Trevor-Roper, Hugh R. "The General Crisis of the 17th Century." *Past and Present* 16 (November 1959): 31–64.

Trewartha, Glenn T. *An Introduction to Climate*. 3d ed. New York: McGraw-Hill, 1954.

Tuan, Yi-fu. *Landscapes of Fear*. New York: Pantheon, 1979.

Tunnard, Christopher, and Henry Hope Reed. *American Skyline: The Growth and Form of our Cities and Towns*. New York: New American Library, 1956; originally published 1955.

Tun Wai, U. *Economic Development of Burma from 1800 till 1940*. Rangoon: Department of Economics, University of Rangoon, 1961.

Twaddle, Andrew C., and Richard M. Hessler. *A Sociology of Health*. St. Louis: C.V. Mosby, 1977.

Ubelaker, Douglas H. "Prehistoric New World Population Size: Historic Review and Current Appraisal of North American Estimates." *American Journal of Physical Anthropology* 45 (November 1976): 661–65.

United States Department of Agriculture. *Soil Survey of Beaufort and Jasper Counties, South Carolina*. Washington, D.C.: U.S. Government Printing Office, 1980.

———. *Soil Survey of Berkeley County, South Carolina*. Washington, D.C.: U.S. Government Printing Office, 1980.

———. *Soil Survey of Charleston County, South Carolina*. Washington, D.C.: U.S. Government Printing Office, 1971.

———. *Soil Survey of Colleton County, South Carolina*. Washington, D.C.: U.S. Government Printing Office, 1982.

———. *Soil Survey of Georgetown County, South Carolina*. Washington, D.C.: U.S. Government Printing Office, 1982.

———. *Soil Taxonomy: A Basic System of Soil Classification for Making and Interpreting Soil Surveys*. U.S. Department of Agriculture Handbook 436. Washington, D.C.: U.S. Government Printing Office, 1975.

———. *A Study of Various Two-Price Systems of Price Support and Marketing Which*

Could Be Made Applicable to Rice. Washington, D.C.: U.S. Government Printing Office, 1955.

———. Bureau of Agricultural Economics. *Gross Farm Income and Indices of Farm Production and Prices in the United States, 1869–1937*. By Frederick Strauss and Louis H. Bean. Technical Bulletin No. 703. Washington, D.C.: United States Government Printing Office, 1940.

———. Bureau of Statistics. *Irrigation of Rice in the United States*. By Frank Bond and George H. Keeney. Bulletin No. 113. Washington, D.C.: United States Government Printing Office, 1902.

———. Bureau of Statistics. *Rice Crop of the United States, 1712-1911*. By George K. Holmes. Circular 34. Washington, D.C.: United States Government Printing Office, 1912.

United States Department of the Interior, Geological Survey. *Water Resources Data for South Carolina, Part 1: Surface Water Records 1969*. Washington, D.C.: 1971

———. *Water Resources Data for South Carolina. Part 2: Water Quality Records 1968*. Washington, D.C. : 1968.

Upton, Dell. "The Origins of Chesapeake Architecture." In *Three Centuries of Maryland Architecture*, pp. 44-57. Annapolis: Maryland Historical Trust, 1982.

———. "The Power of Things: Recent Studies in American Vernacular Architecture." *American Quarterly* 35 (Bibliography 1983): 262-79.

Utterström, Gustav. "Climatic Fluctuations and Population Problems in Early Modern History." *Scandinavian Economic History Review* 3 (1955): 3–47.

Vance, James E., Jr. "Land Assignment in the Precapitalist, Capitalist, and Postcapitalist City." *Economic Geography* 47 (April 1971): 101–20.

———. *The Merchant's World: The Geography of Wholesaling*. Foundations of Economic Geography Series. Englewood Cliffs, N.J.: Prentice-Hall, 1970.

Vaughn, Karen Iverson. *John Locke: Economist and Social Scientist*. Chicago: University of Chicago Press, 1980.

Van Young, Eric. *Hacienda and Market in Eighteenth-Century Mexico: The Rural Economy of the Guadalajara Region, 1675–1820*. Berkeley: University of California Press, 1981.

Vapnarsky, Cesar A. "On Rank-Size Distribution of Cities: An Ecological Approach." *Economic Development and Cultural Change* 17 (July 1969): 584–95.

Verner, Elizabeth O'Neill. *Mellowed by Time: A Charleston Notebook*. Columbia: Bostick & Thornley, 1941.

Ver Steeg, Clarence L. *Origins of a Southern Mosaic: Studies of Early Carolina and Georgia*. Mercer University Lamar Memorial Lectures, No. 17. Athens: University of Georgia Press, 1975.

Viner, Jacob. *International Trade and Economic Development: Lectures Delivered at the National University of Brazil*. Glencoe, Ill.: The Free Press, 1952.

———. *Studies in the Theory of International Trade*. New York: Harper & Brothers, 1937.

Vinovskis, Maris A. "Mortality Rates and Trends in Massachusetts Before 1860." *Journal of Economic History* 32 (March 1972): 184–213.

———. "Recent Trends in American Historical Demography: Some Methodological and Conceptual Considerations." *Annual Review of Sociology* 4 (1978): 603–27.

Vlach, John Michael. *The Afro-American Tradition in the Decorative Arts*. Cleveland: Cleveland Museum of Art, 1978.

———. *Charleston Blacksmith: The Work of Philip Simmons*. Athens: University of Georgia Press, 1981.

Waddell, Gene. *Indians of the South Carolina Lowcountry 1562–1751*. Spartanburg, S.C.: Published for the Southern Studies Program of the University of South Carolina by the Reprint Company, 1980.

Wagley, Charles. "Plantation-America: A Culture Sphere." In *Caribbean Studies—A Symposium*, pp. 3–13. Edited by Vera Rubin. Seattle: University of Washington Press, 1960.

Wallace, David D. *South Carolina: A Short History 1520–1948*. Chapel Hill: University of North Carolina Press, 1951.

Wallerstein, Immanuel. *The Modern World-System*. 2 vols. thus far. New York: Academic Press, 1974–.

———. "Modernization: Requiescat in Pace." In *The Uses of Controversy in Sociology*, pp. 131–35. Edited by Lewis A. Coser and Otto N. Larsen. New York: The Free Press, 1976.

———. "The Rise and Future Demise of the World Capitalist System: Concepts for Comparative Analysis." *Comparative Studies in Society and History* 16 (September 1974): 387–415.

Walsh, Lorena S., and Russell R. Menard. "Death in the Chesapeake: Two Life Tables for Men in Early Colonial Maryland." *Maryland Historical Magazine* 69 (Summer 1974): 211–27.

Walsh, Richard. *Charleston's Sons of Liberty: A Study of the Artisans 1763–1789*. Columbia: University of South Carolina Press, 1959.

Walton, Gary M. "The Colonial Economy." In *Encyclopedia of American Economic History: Studies of the Principal Movements and Ideas*, 1: 34–50. Edited by Glenn Porter. 3 vols. New York: Charles Scribner's Sons, 1980.

Walton, Gary M., and James. F. Shepherd, eds. *Market Institutions and Economic Progress in the New South, 1865–1900*. New York: Academic Press, 1981.

Warden, G.B. *Boston 1689–1776*. Boston: Little, Brown, 1970.

———. "Inequality and Instability in Eighteenth-Century Boston: A Reappraisal." *Journal of Interdisciplinary History* 6 (Spring 1976): 585–620.

Waring, Joseph I. *The First Voyage and Settlement at Charles Town 1670–1680*. Tricentennial Booklet Number 4. Columbia: Published for the South Carolina Tricentennial Commission by the University of South Carolina Press, 1970.

———. *A History of Medicine in South Carolina 1670–1825*. Columbia: South Carolina Medical Association, 1964.

Waterhouse, Richard. "England, the Caribbean, and the Settlement of Carolina." *Journal of American Studies* 9 (December 1975): 259–81.

Waterman, Thomas T. *The Dwellings of Colonial America*. Chapel Hill: University of North Carolina Press, 1950.

Watkins, Melville H. "A Staple Theory of Economic Growth." *Canadian Journal of Economics and Political Science* 29 (May 1963): 141–58.

Watson, Donald S. *Price Theory and Its Uses*. 3d ed. Boston: Houghton Mifflin, 1972.

Waugh, Evelyn. *They Were Still Dancing*. New York: Farrar & Rinehart, 1932.

Webb, Thompson, III. "The Reconstruction of Climatic Sequences from Botannical Data." *Journal of Interdisciplinary History* 10 (Spring 1980): 749–72.

Weber, Max. *Economy and Society: An Outline of Interpretive Sociology*. 2 vols. Edited by Guenther Roth and Claus Wittich. Translated by Ephraim Fishoff *et al.* Berkeley: University of California Press, 1978.

Webster, William D., James F. Parnell, and Walter C. Biggs, Jr. *Mammals of the Carolinas, Virginia, and Maryland*. Chapel Hill: University of North Carolina Press, 1985.

Weeks, Morris, Jr. *Beer and Brewing in America*. New York: United States Brewers' Foundation, 1949.

Weir, Robert M. *Colonial South Carolina: A History*. Millwood, N.Y.: KTO Press, 1983.

———. "'The Harmony We Were Famous For': An Interpretation of Pre-Revolutionary South Carolina Politics." *William and Mary Quarterly*. 3d series, 26 (October 1969): 473–501.

———. "Portrait of a Hero." *American Heritage* 27 (April 1976): 16–19, 86–88.

———. "The Role of the Newspaper Press in the Southern Colonies on the Eve of the Revolution: An Interpretation." In *The Press and the American Revolution*, pp. 99–150. Edited by Bernard Bailyn and John B. Hench. Worcester, Mass.: American Antiquarian Society, 1980.

———. "The South Carolinian as Extremist." *South Atlantic Quarterly* 74 (Winter 1975): 86–103.

Wells, Robert V. *The Population of the British Colonies in America before 1776: A Survey of Census Data*. Princeton: Princeton University Press, 1975.

West, Robert Craig. "Money in the Colonial American Economy." *Economic Inquiry* 16 (January 1978): 1–15.

Wheaton, William C., and Hisanobu Shishido. "Urban Concentration, Agglomeration Economies, and the Level of Economic Development." *Economic Development and Cultural Change* 30 (October 1981): 17–30.

White, Hayden. "The Value of Narrativity in the Representation of Reality." *Critical Inquiry* 7 (Autumn 1980): 5–27.

Whitehill, Walter M. *Boston: A Topographical History*. Second edition, enlarged. Cambridge: The Belknap Press of Harvard University, 1968.

Whitten, David O. "American Rice Cultivation, 1680–1980: A Tercentenary Critique." *Southern Studies* 21 (Spring 1982): 5–26.

Who's Who in America . . ., Vol. 19: *1936–1937*. Edited by Albert Nelson Marquis. Chicago: Marquis, 1936.

Who's Who in Commerce and Industry, 1936. New York: Institute for Research in Biography, 1936.

Williams, Eric. *Capitalism and Slavery*. Chapel Hill: University of North Carolina Press, 1944.

Williams, George W. *St. Michael's, Charleston, 1751–1951*. Columbia: University of South Carolina Press, 1951.

Williamson, Jeffrey G., and Peter H. Lindert. *American Inequality: A Macroeconomic History*. New York: Academic Press, 1980.

Williamson, Joel. *After Slavery: The Negro in South Carolina During Reconstruction, 1861–1877*. Chapel Hill: University of North Carolina Press, 1965.

Willis, Eola. *The Charleston Stage in the XVIII Century*. Columbia: The State Co., 1924.

Wilson, Charles. *Mercantilism*. London: Published for The Historical Association by Routledge and Kegan Paul, 1958.

———. "The Other Face of Mercantilism." *Transactions of the Royal Historical Society*. 5th series, 9 (1959): 81–101.

———. *Profit and Power: A Study of England and the Dutch Wars*. London: Longmans, Green, 1957.

———. "Treasure and Trade Balances: The Mercantilist Problem." *Economic History Review*. 2d series, 2 (1949): 152–61.

Winberry, John J. "Reputation of Carolina Indigo." *South Carolina Historical Magazine* 80 (July 1979): 242–50.

Wittfogel, Karl A. *Oriental Despotism: A Comparative Study of Total Power*. New Haven: Yale University Press, 1957.

Wolf, Eric R. *Europe and the People Without History*. Berkeley: University of California Press, 1982.

Wood, Betty. *Slavery in Colonial Georgia, 1730–1775*. Athens: University of Georgia Press, 1984.

Wood, Neil. *John Locke and Agrarian Capitalism*. Berkeley: University of California Press, 1984.

Wood, Peter H. *Black Majority: Negroes in Colonial South Carolina from 1670 Through the Stono Rebellion*. New York: Knopf, 1974.

———. "La Salle: Discovery of a Lost Explorer." *American Historical Review* 89 (April 1984): 294–323.

Wood, Virginia Steele. *Live Oaking: Southern Timber for Tall Ships*. Boston: Northeastern University Press, 1981.

Wood-Jones, Raymond B. *Traditional Domestic Architecture in the Banbury Region*. Manchester: Manchester University Press, 1963.

Woodman, Harold D. *King Cotton & His Retainers: Financing & Marketing the Cotton Crop of the South, 1800–1925*. Lexington: University of Kentucky Press, 1968.

Woodward, C. Vann. "The Southern Ethic in a Puritan World." *William and Mary Quarterly*. 3d series, 25 (July 1968): 343–70.

World Bank. *World Development Report 1985*. New York: Oxford University Press, 1985.

Worster, Donald. "Hydraulic Society in California: An Ecological Interpretation." *Agricultural History* 56 (July 1982): 503–15.

———. *Rivers of Empire: Water, Aridity, and the Growth of the American West*. New York: Pantheon, 1985.

Wright, Gavin. *Old South, New South: Revolutions in the Southern Economy Since the Civil War*. New York: Basic Books, 1986.

———. *The Political Economy of the Cotton South: Households, Markets, and Wealth in the Nineteenth Century*. New York: W.W. Norton, 1978.

Wright, J. Leitch, Jr. *The Only Land They Knew: The Tragic Story of the American Indians in the Old South*. New York: The Free Press, 1981.

Wright, Louis B. *The Cultural Life of the American Colonies 1607–1763*. New York: Harper & Row, 1957.

Wrigley, E.A., ed. *An Introduction to English Historical Demography: From the Sixteenth to the Nineteenth Century*. New York: Basic Books, 1966.

———. "Mortality in Pre-Industrial England: The Example of Colyton, Devon, Over Three Centuries." *Daedalus* 97 (Spring 1968): 546–80.

———. *Population and History*. World University Library Series. New York: McGraw-Hill, 1969.

———. "A Simple Model of London's Importance in Changing Society and Economy 1650–1750." *Past and Present*. No. 37 (July 1967): 44–70.

Wrigley, E.A., and R.S. Schofield. *The Population History of England 1541–1871: A Reconstruction*. Cambridge: Harvard University Press, 1981.

Wyatt-Brown, Bertram. *Southern Honor: Ethics and Behavior in the Old South*. New York: Oxford University Press, 1982.

Young, Martin D., Newton F. Hardman, *et al*. "The Infectivity of Native Malarias in South Carolina to *Anopheles quadrimaculatus*." *American Journal of Tropical Medicine* 28 (March 1948): 303–11.

Zahniser, Marvin R. *Charles Cotesworth Pinckney: Founding Father*. Chapel Hill: University of North Carolina Press, 1967.
Zierden, Martha A. "Urban Archaeology in Charleston: A Museum Interpretation." *South Carolina Antiquities* 16 (1984): 29–40.

B. Dissertations, Theses, and Unpublished Papers

Anderson, Ralph V. "Labor Utilization and Productivity, Diversification and Self Sufficiency, Southern Plantations, 1800–1840." Ph.D. dissertation, University of North Carolina, 1974.
Anderson, William D., Jr. "The Fishes of Some South Carolina Coastal Plain Streams." Ph.D. dissertation, University of South Carolina, 1960.
Bentley, William George. "The Navigation Acts and Income Distribution." Unpublished paper, 1971.
———. "Wealth Distribution in Colonial South Carolina." Ph.D. dissertation, Georgia State University, 1977.
Bernard, James A., Jr. "An Analysis of British Mercantilism As It Related to Patterns of South Carolina Trade from 1717 to 1767." Ph.D. dissertation, University of Notre Dame, 1973.
Canady, Hoyt Paul, Jr. "Gentlemen of the Bar: Lawyers in Colonial South Carolina." Ph.D. dissertation, University of Tennessee, 1979.
Carson, Cary. "Homestead Architecture in the Chesapeake Colonies." Unpublished paper, 1981.
Chan Lee. "A Culture History of Rice with Special Reference to Louisiana." Ph.D. dissertation, Louisiana State University, 1960.
Chesnutt, David R. "South Carolina's Expansion into Colonial Georgia, 1720–1765." Ph.D. dissertation, University of Georgia, 1973.
Clowse, Converse D. "The Charleston Export Trade, 1717–1737." Ph.D. dissertation, Northwestern University, 1963.
Coclanis, Peter A. "The *Annales* and Early American History: The Charleston Paradigm." Paper delivered at the Third Annual Symposium on Language and Culture in South Carolina, University of South Carolina, Columbia, March 17, 1979.
———. "Economy and Society in the Early Modern South: Charleston and the Evolution of the South Carolina Low Country." Ph.D. dissertation, Columbia University, 1984.
Cody, Cheryll Ann. "Slave Fertility and Family Formation and Ball Family Slaves, 1710–1865." Unpublished paper, 1978.
Collins, Frederick B., Jr. "Charleston and the Railroads: A Geographic Study of a South Atlantic Port and Its Strategies for Developing a Railroad System, 1820–1860." M.S. thesis, University of South Carolina, 1977.
Coon, David L. "The Development of Market Agriculture in South Carolina, 1670–1785." Ph.D. dissertation, University of Illinois, 1972.
Curtis, Mary Julia. "The Early Charleston Stage: 1703–1798." Ph.D. dissertation, Indiana University, 1968.
Devlin, George A. "South Carolina and Black Migration 1865–1940: In Search of the Promised Land." Ph.D. dissertation, University of South Carolina, 1984.
Duffy, John J. "Charleston Politics in the Progressive Era." Ph.D. dissertation, University of South Carolina, 1963.

Dumke, Rolf H. "Income Inequality and Industrialization in Germany, 1850–1913: The Kuznets Hypothesis Re-examined." Unpublished paper, 1986.

Duncan, John Donald. "Servitude and Slavery in Colonial South Carolina 1670–1776." Ph.D. dissertation, Emory University, 1972.

Egnal, Marc. "The Pennsylvania Economy, 1748–1762: An Analysis of Short-Run Fluctuations in the Context of Long-Run Changes in the Atlantic Trading Community." Ph.D. dissertation, University of Wisconsin, 1974.

Eliades, David K. "The Indian Policy of Colonial South Carolina, 1670–1763." Ph.D. dissertation, University of South Carolina, 1981.

Fagg, Daniel W., Jr. "Carolina, 1663–1683: The Founding of a Proprietary." Ph.D. dissertation, Emory University, 1970.

Ferguson, Leland G. "South Appalachian Mississippian." Ph.D. dissertation, University of North Carolina, 1971.

Field, Elizabeth B. "Elasticities of Complementarity and Returns to Scale in Antebellum Cotton Agriculture." Ph.D. dissertation, Duke University, 1985.

Fields, Gary S. "The Private Demand for Education in Relation to Labor Market Conditions in Less Developed Countries." Yale University, Economic Growth Center, Discussion Paper No. 160. Revised Version. June 1973.

Ford, Lacy K. "Social Origins of a New South Carolina: The Upcountry in the Nineteenth Century." Ph.D. dissertation, University of South Carolina, 1983.

Greb, Gregory A. "Charleston, South Carolina, Merchants, 1815–1860: Urban Leadership in the Antebellum South." Ph.D. dissertation, University of California, San Diego, 1978.

Gregorie, Anne King. "Indian Trade of Carolina in the Seventeenth Century." M.A. thesis, University of South Carolina, 1926.

Heider, Karl G. "The Charleston Single House: Negotiating Good Form between Africa and Britain." Paper delivered at the Fourth Annual Symposium on Language and Culture in South Carolina, University of South Carolina, March 14, 1980.

Helwig, Adelaide B. "The Early History of Barbados and Her Influence upon the Development of South Carolina." Ph.D. dissertation, University of California-Berkeley, 1930.

Hetrick, John R. "Treatise on the Economics of Rice Production in Georgetown County, South Carolina: The Middle Period, 1786–1860." M.A. thesis, University of South Carolina, 1979.

Higgins, W. Robert. "The South Carolina Negro Duty Law." M.A. thesis, University of South Carolina, 1967.

Jellison, Richard M. "Paper Currency in Colonial South Carolina, 1703–1764." Ph.D. dissertation, Indiana University, 1953.

Jengst, Daniel P. "Magnitude of Complexity, Least Effort, and the Southern Drawl: George Kingsley Zipf reconsidered on the Midland-Southern Dialect Border." Paper delivered at the Fourth Annual Symposium on Language and Culture in South Carolina, University of South Carolina, March 14, 1980.

Juricek, John T. "Indian Policy in Proprietary South Carolina, 1670–1693." M.A. thesis, University of Chicago, 1962.

Kane, Hope Frances. "Colonial Promotion and Promotion Literature of Carolina, 1660–1700." Ph.D. dissertation, Brown University, 1930.

Kaplanoff, Mark D. "Making the South Solid: Politics and the Structure of Society in South Carolina, 1790–1815." Ph.D. dissertation, University of Cambridge, 1979.

Klein, Rachel. "The Rise of the Planters in the South Carolina Backcountry, 1767–1808." Ph.D. dissertation, Yale University, 1979.

Lander, Ernest M., Jr. "Manufacturing in Ante-Bellum South Carolina." Ph.D. dissertation, University of North Carolina, 1950.

Marjenhoff, August John. "The Effects of Defense Spending on the Economy of the Charleston, South Carolina, Standard Metropolitan Statistical Area." Ph.D. dissertation, Indiana University, 1974.

Mathews, Alice E. "Pre-College Education in the Southern Colonies." Ph.D. dissertation, University of California, 1968.

McGuire, Mary J. "Getting Their Hands on the Land: The Revolution in St. Helena Parish, 1861–1900." Ph.D. dissertation, University of South Carolina, 1985.

Mendenhall, Marjorie S. "A History of Agriculture in South Carolina, 1790 to 1860: An Economic and Social Study." Ph.D. dissertation, University of North Carolina, 1940.

Morgan, Philip D. "The Development of Slave Culture in Eighteenth Century Plantation America." Ph.D. dissertation, University College London, 1977.

Paschal, Herbert R., Jr. "Proprietary North Carolina: A Study in Colonial Government." Ph.D. dissertation, University of North Carolina, 1961.

Perry, Percival. "The Naval Stores Industry in the Ante-Bellum South, 1789–1861." Ph.D. dissertation, Duke University, 1947.

Prince, Kenneth E. "Surface Waters of South Carolina." M.S. thesis, University of South Carolina, 1941.

Radford, John P. "Culture, Economy, and Urban Structure in Charleston, South Carolina, 1860–1880." Ph.D. dissertation, Clark University, 1974.

Ratzlaff, Robert K. "John Rutledge, Jr., South Carolina Federalist, 1766–1819." Ph.D. dissertation, University of Kansas, 1974.

Rowland, Lawrence S. "Eighteenth Century Beaufort: A Study of South Carolina's Southern Parishes to 1800." Ph.D. dissertation, University of South Carolina, 1978.

Schlotterbeck, John T. "Plantation and Farm: Social and Economic Change in Orange and Greene Counties, Virginia, 1716 to 1860." Ph.D. dissertation, The Johns Hopkins University, 1980.

Schreiber, Max M. "The Nature of the Trade between South Carolina and the West Indies: 1717–1737: A Statistical Approach." M.A. thesis, University of South Carolina, 1975.

Senese, Donald J. "Legal Thought in South Carolina, 1800–1860." Ph.D. dissertation, University of South Carolina, 1970.

Shatzman, Aaron M. "Servants into Planters, The Origin of an American Image: Land Acquisition and Status Mobility in Seventeenth Century South Carolina." Ph.D. dissertation, Stanford University, 1981.

Snell, William Robert. "Indian Slavery in Colonial South Carolina, 1671–1795." Ph.D. dissertation, University of Alabama, 1972.

Stockton, Robert P. "The Evolution of Rainbow Row." M.A. thesis, University of South Carolina, 1979.

Strickland, John Scott. "Across Space and Time: Conversion, Community, and Cultural Change among South Carolina Slaves." Ph.D. dissertation, University of North Carolina at Chapel Hill, 1985.

Stumpf, Stuart O. "The Merchants of Colonial Charleston, 1680–1756." Ph.D. dissertation, Michigan State University, 1971.

Sydenham, Diane M. "Practitioner and Patient: The Practice of Medicine in Eighteenth-Century South Carolina." Ph.D. dissertation, The Johns Hopkins University, 1978.

ibliography 365</cite>

Terry, George D. "'Champaign Country': A Social History of an Eighteenth Century Low-country Parish in South Carolina, St. Johns Berkeley County." Ph.D. dissertation, University of South Carolina, 1981.

Waterhouse, Richard. "South Carolina's Colonial Elite: A Study in the Social Structure and the Political Culture of a Southern Colony, 1670–1760." Ph.D. dissertation, The Johns Hopkins University, 1973.

Weiman, David F. "Petty Commodity Production in the Cotton South: Upcountry Farmers in the Georgia Cotton Economy, 1840 to 1880." Ph.D. dissertation, Stanford University, 1983.

Weir, Robert M. "'LIBERTY AND PROPERTY AND NO STAMPS': South Carolina and the Stamp Act Crisis." Ph.D. dissertation, Western Reserve University, 1966.

Wilkenfeld, Bruce M. "The Social and Economic Structure of the City of New York, 1695–1796." Ph.D. dissertation, Columbia University, 1973.

Wood, Walter Kirk. "The Union of the States: A Study of Radical Whig-Republican Ideology and Its Influence Upon the Nation and the South, 1776–1861." Ph.D. dissertation, University of South Carolina, 1978.

C. Other

Herzog, Werner. *Aguirre der Zorn Gottes*. West Germany. Film, 1973.

Index

Printed in the United States
2534

The Shadow of a Dream